T4-ALC-122

26-22

# The Study of
# ABNORMAL BEHAVIOR

## Selected Readings

# The Study of
# ABNORMAL BEHAVIOR

## Selected Readings
### Second Edition

**Melvin Zax, Ph.D.**
PROFESSOR OF PSYCHOLOGY
UNIVERSITY OF ROCHESTER

**George Stricker, Ph.D.**
ASSOCIATE PROFESSOR OF PSYCHOLOGY
ADELPHI UNIVERSITY

THE MACMILLAN COMPANY
COLLIER-MACMILLAN LIMITED, LONDON

CARNEGIE LIBRARY
LIVINGSTONE COLLEGE
SALISBURY, N. C. 28144

© Copyright, The Macmillan Company, 1969

All rights reserved. No part of this book may be
reproduced or transmitted in any form or by any
means, electronic or mechanical, including photo-
copying, recording or by any information storage
and retrieval system, without permission in writing
from the Publisher.

First Printing

Earlier edition © copyright 1964 by The Macmillan Company.

Library of Congress catalog card number: 69–12172

The Macmillan Company

Collier-Macmillan Canada, Ltd., Toronto, Ontario

Printed in the United States of America

6.804
19

# Preface

The instructive merits of primary source material and its motivating appeal to students are unchallenged. To place a reasonable selection of such material in a convenient format begets a favored teaching aid, the book of readings. Obviously, no single collection of source writing can satisfy all needs, but a book that supplies the kind of close view of empirical literature that is missing from most textbooks can prove at once useful and illuminating.

In selecting from the literature of abnormal behavior, we sought to compile articles that reflect the breadth of research in the area. Simultaneously, we attempted to avoid imbalance among the various theoretical positions. It was our further aim to balance the theoretical and the empirical, and thus our choices range from the very well known to younger, less well-established researchers and pathfinders. The overriding criterion for every choice was that it represent a significant contribution to student understanding of its particular area. Some important but overly sophisticated papers regretfully had to be eliminated.

The book is organized in four major units, each with an introductory section explaining chapter divisions. Each chapter is preceded by a brief commentary and all articles are introduced with material intended to provide both a context for the paper and a basis for understanding any potential obscurities in it. The first unit covers significant theoretical problems of current concern in the study of abnormal behavior. We hope the student will derive from the selections an adequate background of the content of the field, and progress to the second unit with a working appreciation of the many problems involved. The next section offers a variety of approaches to psychopathology, the core of any consideration of abnormal psychology. The third section represents a separate and extensive treatment of psychotherapy, reinforcing its intimate relationship with psychopathology. The final section of the book is devoted to recent issues and trends.

Acknowledgments are more directly appreciated in a book of readings than in any other work, and we wish to express our gratitude to the authors and publishers who were kind enough to allow us to reprint their works. Specific acknowledgments are included in the first page of each article. Special thanks are due Miss Willa Cobert, Mrs. Elsie Hayes, and Mrs. Thelma Levin, who helped assemble the manuscript. As ever, our wives, Joanne Zax and Joan Stricker, must be acknowledged for their support and encouragement.

M. Z.
G. S.

71529

# Contents

# Section I

# General Issues
# in Abnormal Psychology

*As in all fields there are numerous general issues of far-reaching consequence which workers in abnormal psychology have found reason to debate over the years. This section includes a sampling of these. Some have only become prominent in recent years, while others have been the cause of concern over a much longer period. It will be noted further that while in some cases the questions raised seem specifically relevant to the domain of abnormal psychology, in other cases their generality takes them well beyond the subject matter of this area. If the editors have made good choices, the reader should be left with many more questions than answers after a careful and thoughtful reading of the material in this section. Definitive answers are not easily provided in these speculative realms, and there was no intention to provide anything more than a sampling of a variety of representative views.*

# Chapter I

# Models for the Understanding of Abnormal Behavior

Traditionally, the diagnosis and treatment of abnormal behavior have been conceptualized within a framework known as the medical model. Recently a number of different approaches have developed, all of which have criticized the medical model, although each for a different reason. One principal component of the medical model is the disease or illness concept of abnormal behavior. This views such behavior as the result of the presence of some internal, sickness-producing agent, and is similar to the germ theory of physical disorder. This conception leads to the widely used term "mental illness," as though such behavior were an illness produced in a manner similar to other physical illnesses. This section includes a number of papers critical of the illness formulation, although from different points of view, and a reformulation and defense of the illness model. Another component of the medical model views the therapist as a removed, passive individual to whom patients come for treatment. This aspect also has been critically questioned, and questions of this nature will be explored later in the book in a section concerned with developments in community psychology.

Thomas S. Szasz

## The Myth of Mental Illness

It has been traditional to view "abnormal" behavior as an indication of mental illness. In this paper, T. S. Szasz examines the implications of the term "mental illness," and rejects it as no longer useful or appropriate. He allows that behavior occasionally displays peculiarities that make it appear abnormal, but does not feel that it is appropriate to label this behavior "mental illness." To do so implies that the behavior is caused by some damage to the brain, can be diagnosed without any value judgments, and can be treated medically by the physician. Dr. Szasz prefers to see these behaviors as deviations from social, ethical, and legal codes which result in problems of living for the troubled individual. They are not the direct result of neural malfunctioning, can only be diagnosed by the application of value judgments, and must be treated in a social rather than a medical context. The implications of this point of view

Reprinted from the American Psychologist, 15(1960), 113–118 with the permission of the American Psychological Association and Dr. Szasz. Copyright 1960 by the American Psychological Association.

are far-reaching and enormous. It follows, from this argument, that the individual cannot be called a "patient," should not be treated in a hospital, and need not be treated by a physician. In fact, he should not be "treated" at all, since his problems are not medical, but are problems of adjustment in society. The legal implications of this approach are that "mental illness" cannot be used as a defense in a court of law, since the defendant is not actually "ill," and that individuals are committed to institutions for the convenience of society rather than because of their inherent illness. A strict adherence to the implications of Dr. Szasz' views would necessitate a drastic reorganization of our approach to phenomena currently referred to as "mental illness."

My aim in this essay is to raise the question "Is there such a thing as mental illness?" and to argue that there is not. Since the notion of mental illness is extremely widely used nowadays, inquiry into the ways in which this term is employed would seem to be especially indicated. Mental illness, of course, is not literally a "thing"—or physical object—and hence it can "exist" only in the same sort of way in which other theoretical concepts exist. Yet, familiar theories are in the habit of posing, sooner or later—at least to those who come to believe in them—as "objective truths" (or "facts"). During certain historical periods, explanatory conceptions such as deities, witches, and microorganisms appeared not only as theories but as self-evident causes of a vast number of events. I submit that today mental illness is widely regarded in a somewhat similar fashion, that is, as the cause of innumerable diverse happenings. As an antidote to the complacent use of the notion of mental illness—whether as a self-evident phenomenon, theory, or cause—let us ask this question: What is meant when it is asserted that someone is mentally ill?

In what follows I shall describe briefly the main uses to which the concept of mental illness has been put. I shall argue that this notion has outlived whatever usefulness it might have had and that it now functions merely as a convenient myth.

## MENTAL ILLNESS AS A SIGN OF BRAIN DISEASE

The notion of mental illness derives its main support from such phenomena as syphilis of the brain or delirious conditions—intoxications, for instance—in which persons are known to manifest various peculiarities or disorders of thinking and behavior. Correctly speaking, however, these are diseases of the brain, not of the mind. According to one school of thought, all so-called mental illness is of this type. The assumption is made that some neurological defect, perhaps a very subtle one, will ultimately be found for all the disorders of thinking and behavior. Many contemporary psychiatrists, physicians, and other scientists hold this view. This position implies that people cannot have troubles—expressed in what are now called "mental illnesses"—because of differences in personal needs, opinions, social aspirations, values, and so on. All problems in living are attributed to physicochemical processes which in due time will be discovered by medical research.

"Mental illnesses" are thus regarded as basically no different than all other diseases (that is, of the body). The only difference, in this view, between mental and bodily diseases is that the former, affecting the brain, manifest themselves by means of mental symptoms; whereas the latter, affecting other organ systems (for example, the skin, liver, etc.), manifest themselves by means of symptoms referable to those parts of the body. This view rests on and expresses what are, in my opinion, two fundamental errors.

In the first place, what central nervous system symptoms would correspond to a skin eruption or a fracture? It would *not* be some emotion or complex bit of behavior. Rather, it would be blindness or a paralysis of some part of the body. The crux of the matter is that a disease of the brain, analogous to a disease of the skin or bone, is a neurological defect, and not a problem in living. For example, a *defect* in a person's visual field may be satisfactorily explained by correlating it with certain definite lesions in the nervous system. On the other hand, a person's *belief*— whether this be a belief in Christianity, in Communism, or in the idea that his internal organs are "rotting" and that his body is, in fact, already "dead"— cannot be explained by a defect or disease of the nervous system. Explanations of this sort of occurrence—assuming that one is interested in the belief itself and does not regard it simply as a "symptom" or expression of something else that is *more interesting*—must be sought along different lines.

The second error in regarding complex psychosocial behavior, consisting of communications about ourselves and the world about us, as mere symptoms of neurological functioning is *epistemological*. In other words, it is an error pertaining not to any mistakes in observation or reasoning, as such, but rather to the way in which we organize and express our knowledge. In the present case, the error lies in making a symmetrical dualism between mental and physical (or bodily) symptoms, a dualism which is merely a habit of speech and to which no known observa-

tions can be found to correspond. Let us see if this is so. In medical practice, when we speak of physical disturbances, we mean either signs (for example, a fever) or symptoms (for example, pain). We speak of mental symptoms, on the other hand, when we refer to a patient's *communications about himself, others, and the world about him.* He might state that he is Napoleon or that he is being persecuted by the Communists. These would be considered mental symptoms *only* if the observer believed that the patient was *not* Napoleon or that he was *not* being persecuted by the Communists. This makes it apparent that the statement that "X is a mental symptom" involves rendering a judgment. The judgment entails, moreover, a covert comparison or matching of the patient's ideas, concepts, or beliefs with those of the observer and the society in which they live. The notion of mental symptom is therefore inextricably tied to the *social* (including *ethical*) *context* in which it is made in much the same way as the notion of bodily symptom is tied to an *anatomical* and *genetic context* (Szasz, 1957a, 1957b).

To sum up what has been said thus far: I have tried to show that for those who regard mental symptoms as signs of brain disease, the concept of mental illness is unnecessary and misleading. For what they mean is that people so labeled suffer from diseases of the brain; and, if that is what they mean, it would seem better for the sake of clarity to say that and not something else.

## MENTAL ILLNESS AS A NAME FOR PROBLEMS IN LIVING

The term "mental illness" is widely used to describe something which is very different than a disease of the brain. Many people today take it for granted that living is an arduous process. Its hardship for modern man, moreover, derives not so much from a struggle for biological survival as from the stresses and strains inherent in the social intercourse of complex human personalities. In this context, the notion of mental illness is used to identify or describe some feature of an individual's so-called personality. Mental illness—as a deformity of the personality, so to speak—is then regarded as the *cause* of the human disharmony. It is implicit in this view that social intercourse between people is regarded as something *inherently harmonious*, its disturbance being due solely to the presence of "mental illness" in many people. This is obviously fallacious reasoning, for it makes the abstraction "mental illness" into a *cause*, even though this abstraction was created in the first place to serve only as a shorthand expression for certain types of human behavior. It now becomes necessary to ask: "What kinds of behavior are regarded as indicative of mental illness, and by whom?"

The concept of illness, whether bodily or mental, implies *deviation from some clearly defined norm*. In the case of physical illness, the norm is the structural and functional integrity of the human body. Thus, although the desirability of physical health, as such, is an ethical value, what health *is* can be stated in anatomical and physiological terms. What is the norm, deviation from which is regarded as mental illness? This question cannot be easily answered. But whatever this norm might be, we can be certain of only one thing: namely, that it is a norm that must be stated in terms of *psychosocial, ethical,* and *legal* concepts. For example, notions such as "excessive repression" or "acting out an unconscious impulse" illustrate the use of psychological concepts for judging (so-called)

mental health and illness. The idea that chronic hostility, vengefulness, or divorce are indicative of mental illness would be illustrations of the use of ethical norms (that is, the desirability of love, kindness, and a stable marriage relationship). Finally, the widespread psychiatric opinion that only a mentally ill person would commit homicide illustrates the use of a legal concept as a norm of mental health. The norm from which deviation is measured whenever one speaks of a mental illness is a *psychosocial and ethical one*. Yet, the remedy is sought in terms of *medical* measures which—it is hoped and assumed—are free from wide differences of ethical value. The definition of the disorder and the terms in which its remedy are sought are therefore at serious odds with one another. The practical significance of this covert conflict between the alleged nature of the defect and the remedy can hardly be exaggerated.

Having identified the norms used to measure deviations in cases of mental illness, we will now turn to the question: "Who defines the norms and hence the deviation?" Two basic answers may be offered: (*a*) It may be the person himself (that is, the patient) who decides that he deviates from a norm. For example, an artist may believe that he suffers from a work inhibition; and he may implement this conclusion by seeking help *for* himself from a psychotherapist. (*b*) It may be someone other than the patient who decides that the latter is deviant (for example, relatives, physicians, legal authorities, society generally, etc.). In such a case a psychiatrist may be hired by others to do something *to* the patient in order to correct the deviation.

These considerations underscore the importance of asking the question "Whose agent is the psychiatrist?" and of giving a candid answer to it (Szasz,

1956, 1958). The psychiatrist (psychologist or nonmedical psychotherapist), it now develops, may be the agent of the patient, of the relatives, of the school, of the military services, of a business organization, of a court of law, and so forth. In speaking of the psychiatrist as the agent of these persons or organizations, it is not implied that his values concerning norms, or his ideas and aims concerning the proper nature of remedial action, need to coincide exactly with those of his employer. For example, a patient in individual psychotherapy may believe that his salvation lies in a new marriage; his psychotherapist need not share this hypothesis. As the patient's agent, however, he must abstain from bringing social or legal force to bear on the patient which would prevent him from putting his beliefs into action. If his *contract* is with the patient, the psychiatrist (psychotherapist) may disagree with him or stop his treatment; but he cannot engage others to obstruct the patient's aspirations. Similarly, if a psychiatrist is engaged by a court to determine the sanity of a criminal, he need not fully share the legal authorities' values and intentions in regard to the criminal and the means available for dealing with him. But the psychiatrist is expressly barred from stating, for example, that it is not the criminal who is "insane" but the men who wrote the law on the basis of which the very actions that are being judged are regarded as "criminal." Such an opinion could be voiced, of course, but not in a courtroom, and not by a psychiatrist who makes it his practice to assist the court in performing its daily work.

To recapitulate: In actual contemporary social usage, the finding of a mental illness is made by establishing a deviance in behavior from certain psychosocial, ethical, or legal norms. The judgment may be made, as in

medicine, by the patient, the physician (psychiatrist), or others. Remedial action, finally, tends to be sought in a therapeutic—or covertly medical—framework, thus creating a situation in which *psychosocial, ethical,* and/or *legal deviations* are claimed to be correctible by (so-called) *medical action.* Since medical action is designed to correct only medical deviations, it seems logically absurd to expect that it will help solve problems whose very existence had been defined and established on nonmedical grounds. I think that these considerations may be fruitfully applied to the present use of tranquilizers and, more generally, to what might be expected of drugs of whatever type in regard to the amelioration or solution of problems in human living.

## THE ROLE OF ETHICS IN PSYCHIATRY

Anything that people *do*—in contrast to things that *happen* to them (Peters, 1958)—takes place in a context of value. In this broad sense, no human activity is devoid of ethical implications. When the values underlying certain activities are widely shared, those who participate in their pursuit may lose sight of them altogether. The discipline of medicine, both as a pure science (for example, research) and as a technology (for example, therapy), contains many ethical considerations and judgments. Unfortunately, these are often denied, minimized, or merely kept out of focus; for the ideal of the medical profession as well as of the people whom it serves seems to be having a system of medicine (allegedly) free of ethical value. This sentimental notion is expressed by such things as the doctor's willingness to treat and help patients irrespective of their religious or political beliefs, whether they are rich or poor, etc. While there may be some grounds for this belief—albeit it is a view that is not impressively true even in these regards—the fact remains that ethical considerations encompass a vast range of human affairs. By making the practice of medicine neutral in regard to some specific issues of value need not, and cannot, mean that it can be kept free from all such values. The practice of medicine is intimately tied to ethics; and the first thing that we must do, it seems to me, is to try to make this clear and explicit. I shall let this matter rest here, for it does not concern us specifically in this essay. Lest there be any vagueness, however, about how or where ethics and medicine meet, let me remind the reader of such issues as birth control, abortion, suicide, and euthanasia as only a few of the major areas of current ethicomedical controversy.

Psychiatry, I submit, is very much more intimately tied to problems of ethics than is medicine. I use the word "psychiatry" here to refer to that contemporary discipline which is concerned with *problems in living* (and not with diseases of the brain, which are problems for neurology). Problems in human relations can be analyzed, interpreted, and given meaning only within given social and ethical contexts. Accordingly, it *does* make a difference—arguments to the contrary notwithstanding—what the psychiatrist's socioethical orientations happen to be; for these will influence his ideas on what is wrong with the patient, what deserves comment or interpretation, in what possible directions change might be desirable, and so forth. Even in medicine proper, these factors play a role, as for instance, in the divergent orientations which physicians, depending on their religious affiliations, have toward such things as birth control and therapeutic abortion. Can anyone really believe that a psychotherapist's ideas concerning religious belief, slavery, or other similar issues play no role in his practical work? If they do make a difference, what are we to infer from it? Does it not seem reasonable that we ought to have different psychiatric therapies—each expressly recognized for the ethical positions which they embody—for, say, Catholics and Jews, religious persons and agnostics, democrats and communists, white supremacists and Negroes, and so on? Indeed, if we look at how psychiatry is actually practiced today (especially in the United States), we find that people do seek psychiatric help in accordance with their social status and ethical beliefs (Hollingshead & Redlich, 1958). This should really not surprise us more than being told that practicing Catholics rarely frequent birth control clinics.

The foregoing position which holds that contemporary psychotherapists deal with problems in living, rather than with mental illnesses and their cures, stands in opposition to a currently prevalent claim, according to which mental illness is just as "real" and "objective" as bodily illness. This is a confusing claim since it is never known exactly what is meant by such words as "real" and "objective." I suspect, however, that what is intended by the proponents of this view is to create the idea in the popular mind that mental illness is some sort of disease entity, like an infection or a malignancy. If this were true, one could *catch* or *get* a "mental illness," one might *have* or *harbor* it, one might *transmit* it to others, and finally one could get *rid* of it. In my opinion, there is not a shred of evidence to support this idea. To the contrary, all the evidence is the other way and supports the view that what people now call mental illnesses are for the most part *communications* expressing unacceptable ideas, often framed, moreover, in an unusual idiom. The scope of this essay allows me to do no more than mention this alternative theoretical approach to this problem (Szasz, 1957c).

This is not the place to consider in detail the similarities and differences between bodily and mental illnesses. It shall suffice for us here to emphasize only one important difference between them: namely, that whereas bodily disease refers to public, physicochemical occurrences, the notion of mental illness is used to codify relatively more private, sociopsychological happenings of which the observer (diagnostician) forms a part. In other words, the psychiatrist does not stand *apart* from what he observes, but is, in Harry Stack Sullivan's apt words, a "participant observer." This means that he is *committed* to some picture of what he considers reality—and to what he thinks society considers reality—and he observes and judges the patient's behavior in the light of these considerations. This touches on our earlier observation that the notion of mental symptom itself implies a comparison between observer and observed, psychiatrist and patient. This is so obvious that I may be charged with belaboring trivialities. Let me therefore say once more that my aim in presenting this argument was expressly to criticize and counter a prevailing contemporary tendency to deny the moral aspects of psychiatry (and psychotherapy) and to substitute for them allegedly value-free medical considerations. Psychotherapy, for example, is being widely practiced as though it entailed nothing other than restoring the patient from a state of mental sickness to one of mental health. While it is generally accepted that mental illness has something to do with man's social (or interpersonal) relations, it is paradoxically maintained that problems of values (that is, of ethics) do not arise in this process.[1] Yet, in one sense, much of psychotherapy may revolve around nothing other than the elucidation and weighing of goals and values —many of which may be mutually contradictory—and the means whereby they might best be harmonized, realized, or relinquished.

The diversity of human values and the methods by means of which they may be realized is so vast, and many of them remain so unacknowledged, that they cannot fail but lead to conflicts in human relations. Indeed, to say that human relations at all levels—from mother to child, through husband and wife, to nation and nation—are fraught with stress, strain, and disharmony is, once again, making the obvious explicit. Yet, what may be obvious may be also poorly understood. This I think is the case here. For it seems to me that—at least in our scientific theories of behavior—we have failed to *accept* the simple fact that human relations are inherently fraught with difficulties and that to make them even relatively harmonious requires much patience and hard work. I submit that the idea of mental illness is now being put to work to obscure certain difficulties which at present may be inherent—not that they need be unmodifiable—in the social intercourse of persons. If this is true, the concept functions as a disguise;

[1] Freud went so far as to say that: "I consider ethics to be taken for granted. Actually I have never done a mean thing" (Jones, 1957, p. 247). This surely is a strange thing to say for someone who has studied man as a social being as closely as did Freud. I mention it here to show how the notion of "illness" (in the case of psychoanalysis, "psychopathology," or "mental illness") was used by Freud—and by most of his followers—as a means for classifying certain forms of human behavior as falling within the scope of medicine, and hence (by *fiat*) outside that of ethics!

for instead of calling attention to conflicting human needs, aspirations, and values, the notion of mental illness provides an amoral and impersonal "thing" (an "illness") as an explanation for *problems in living* (Szasz, 1959). We may recall in this connection that not so long ago it was devils and witches who were held responsible for men's problems in social living. The belief in mental illness, as something other than man's trouble in getting along with his fellow man, is the proper heir to the belief in demonology and witchcraft. Mental illness exists or is "real" in exactly the same sense in which witches existed or were "real."

## CHOICE, RESPONSIBILITY, AND PSYCHIATRY

While I have argued that mental illnesses do not exist, I obviously did not imply that the social and psychological occurrences to which this label is currently being attached also do not exist. Like the personal and social troubles which people had in the Middle Ages, they are real enough. It is the labels we give them that concerns us and, having labelled them, what we do about them. While I cannot go into the ramified implications of this problem here, it is worth noting that a demonologic conception of problems in living gave rise to therapy along theological lines. Today, a belief in mental illness implies—nay, requires—therapy along medical or psychotherapeutic lines.

What is implied in the line of thought set forth here is something quite different. I do not intend to offer a new conception of "psychiatric illness" nor a new form of "therapy." My aim is more modest and yet also more ambitious. It is to suggest that the phenomena now called mental illnesses be looked at afresh and more simply, that they be removed from the category of illnesses, and that they be regarded as the expressions of man's struggle with the problem of *how* he should live. The last mentioned problem is obviously a vast one, its enormity reflecting not only man's inability to cope with his environment, but even more his increasing self-reflectiveness.

By problems in living, then, I refer to that truly explosive chain reaction which began with man's fall from divine grace by partaking of the fruit of the tree of knowledge. Man's awareness of himself and of the world about him seems to be a steadily expanding one, bringing in its wake an ever larger *burden of understanding* (an expression borrowed from Susanne Langer, 1953). *This burden, then, is to be expected and must not be misinterpreted.* Our only *rational* means for lightening it is *more understanding*, and appropriate *action* based on such understanding. The main alternative lies in acting as though the burden were not what in fact we perceive it to be and taking refuge in an outmoded theological view of man. In the latter view, man does not fashion his life and much of his world about him, but merely lives out his fate in a world created by superior beings. This may logically lead to pleading nonresponsibility in the face of seemingly unfathomable problems and difficulties. Yet, if man fails to take increasing responsibility for his actions, individually as well as collectively, it seems unlikely that some higher power or being would assume this task and carry this burden for him. Moreover, this seems hardly the proper time in human history for obscuring the issue of man's responsibility for his actions by hiding it behind the skirt of an all-explaining conception of mental illness.

## CONCLUSIONS

I have tried to show that the notion of mental illness has outlived whatever usefulness it might have had and that it now functions merely as a convenient myth. As such, it is a true heir to religious myths in general, and to the belief in witchcraft in particular; the role of all these belief-systems was to act as *social tranquilizers*, thus encouraging the hope that mastery of certain specific problems may be achieved by means of substitutive (symbolic-magical) operations. The notion of mental illness thus serves mainly to obscure the everyday fact that life for most people is a continuous struggle, not for biological survival, but for a "place in the sun," "peace of mind," or some other human value. For man aware of himself and of the world about him, once the needs for preserving the body (and perhaps the race) are more or less satisfied, the problem arises as to what he should do with himself. Sustained adherence to the myth of mental illness allows people to avoid facing this problem, believing that mental health, conceived as the absence of mental illness, automatically insures the making of right and safe choices in one's conduct of life. But the facts are all the other way. It is the making of good choices in life that others regard, retrospectively, as good mental health!

The myth of mental illness encourages us, moreover, to believe in its logical corollary: that social intercourse would be harmonious, satisfying, and the secure basis of a "good life" were it not for the disrupting influences of mental illness or "psychopathology." The potentiality for universal human happiness, in this form at least, seems to me but another example of the I-wish-it-were-true type of fantasy. I do believe that human happiness or well-being on a hitherto unimaginably large scale, and not just for a select few, is possible. This goal could be achieved, however, only at the cost of many men, and not just a few being willing and able to tackle their personal, social, and ethical conflicts. This means having the courage and integrity to forego waging battles on false fronts, finding solutions for substitute problems—for instance, fighting the battle of stomach acid and chronic fatigue instead of facing up to a marital conflict.

Our adversaries are not demons, witches, fate, or mental illness. We have no enemy whom we can fight, exorcise, or dispel by "cure." What we do have are *problems in living*—whether these be biologic, economic, political, or sociopsychological. In this essay I was concerned only with problems belonging in the last mentioned category, and within this group mainly with those pertaining to moral values. The field to which modern psychiatry addresses itself is vast, and I made no effort to encompass it all. My argument was limited to the proposition that mental illness is a myth, whose function it is to disguise and thus render more palatable the bitter pill of moral conflicts in human relations.

## REFERENCES

HOLLINGSHEAD, A. B., & REDLICH, F. C. *Social class and mental illness.* New York: Wiley, 1958.

JONES, E. *The life and work of Sigmund Freud.* Vol. III. New York: Basic Books, 1957.

LANGER, S. K. *Philosophy in a new key.* New York: Mentor Books, 1953.

PETERS, R. S. *The concept of motivation.* London: Routledge & Kegan Paul, 1958.

SZASZ, T. S. Malingering: "Diagnosis" or social condemnation? *AMA Arch Neurol. Psychiat.*, 1956, **76**, 432–443.

SZASZ, T. S. *Pain and pleasure: A study of bodily feelings.* New York: Basic Books, 1957. (a)

SZASZ, T. S. The problem of psychiatric nosology: A contribution to a situational analysis of psychiatric operations. *Amer. J. Psychiat.*, 1957, **114**, 405–413. (b)

SZASZ, T. S. On the theory of psychoanalytic treatment. *Int. J. Psycho-Anal.*, 1957, **38**, 166–182. (c)

SZASZ, T. S. Psychiatry, ethics and the criminal law. *Columbia law Rev.*, 1958, **58**, 183–198.

SZASZ, T. S. Moral conflict and psychiatry, *Yale Rev.*, 1959, in press.

O. Hobart Mowrer

# "Sin," the Lesser of Two Evils

*In this paper, Mowrer objects to the conception of abnormal behavior as a product of mental illness. His major objection is that this formulation allows no moral dimensions to such behavior. To consider an individual as sick removes any responsibility for his behavior from him, and makes any moral judgment of his actions inappropriate. In searching for an alternative to the illness model, Dr. Mowrer leans heavily on theology and arrives at sin as an alternative to illness in understanding abnormal behavior. If an individual's behavior is seen as sinful, it places responsibility for that behavior on the individual himself, instead of excusing him by saying that it was the product of illness and thus beyond his control. Mowrer's attempt to restore responsibility for his behavior to the individual is very much in keeping with an emphasis on existentialist thought that is prevalent currently in some areas of psychology, although his emphasis on sin and moral values is somewhat atypical. The implications of this approach for psychotherapy are drastic. Rather than have the individual learn to accept his behavior, he must reject it as sinful, and the therapist's job is not to promote understanding in a nonevaluative atmosphere, but to blame the patient in a guilt-arousing atmosphere. It is only through the experience of guilt and the rejection of sinful behavior that an individual can find personal peace.*

Following the presentation of a paper on "Constructive Aspects of the Concept of Sin in Psychotherapy" at the 1959 APA convention in Cincinnati, I have repeatedly been asked by psychologists and psychiatrists: "But *why* must you use that awful word 'sin,' instead of some more neutral term such as 'wrongdoing,' 'irresponsibility,' or 'immorality'?" And even a religious layman has reproached me on the grounds that "Sin is such a *strong*

*Reprinted from the* American Psychologist, *15(1960), 301–304 with the permission of the American Psychological Association and Dr. Mowrer. Copyright 1960 by the American Psychological Association.*

word." Its *strength*, surely, is an asset, not a liability; for in the face of failure which has resulted from our erstwhile use of feebler concepts, we have very heavy work for it to do. Besides, sin (in contrast to its more neutral equivalents) is such a handy *little* word that it would be a pity to let it entirely disappear from usage. With Humpty-Dumpty, we ought to expect words to be "well-behaved" and to mean what *we* want them to!

A few years ago I was invited to teach in the summer session at one of our great Pacific Coast universities; and toward the end of the term, a student in my class on Personality Theory said to me one day: "Did you know that near the beginning of this course you created a kind of scandal on this campus?" Then he explained that I had once used the word "sin" without saying "so-called" or making a joke about it. This, the student said, was virtually unheard-of in a psychology professor and had occasioned considerable dismay and perplexity. I did not even recall the incident; but the more I have thought about the reaction it produced, the more frequently I have found myself using the term—with, I hope, something more than mere perversity.

Traditionally, sin has been thought of as whatever causes one to go to Hell; and since Hell, as a place of otherworldly retribution and torment, has conveniently dropped out of most religious as well as secular thought, the concept of sin might indeed seem antiquated and absurd. But, as I observed in the Cincinnati paper, Hell is still very much with us in those states of mind and being which we call neurosis and psychosis; and I have come increasingly, at least in my own mind, to identify anything that carries us toward these forms of perdition as *sin*. Irresponsibility, wrongdoing, immorality, sin: what do the terms matter if we

can thus understand more accurately the nature of psychopathology and gain greater practical control over its ramified forms and manifestations?

But now the fat is in the fire! Have we not been taught on high authority that personality disorder is not one's own "fault," that the neurotic is *not* "responsible" for his suffering, that he has done nothing wrong, committed no "sin"? "Mental illness," according to a poster which was widely circulated a few years ago, "is no disgrace. It might happen to anyone." And behind all this, of course, was the Freudian hypothesis that neurosis stems from a "too severe superego," which is the product of a too strenuous socialization of the individual at the hands of harsh, unloving parents and an irrational society. The trouble lay, supposedly, not in anything wrong or "sinful" which the individual has himself *done*, but in things he merely *wants* to do but cannot, because of *repression*.

The neurotic was thus not sinful but *sick*, the helpless, innocent victim of "the sins of the fathers," and could be rescued only by a specialized, esoteric form of *treatment*. Anna Russell catches the spirit of this doctrine well when she sings, in "Psychiatric Folksong,"

At three I had a feeling of
  Ambivalence toward my brothers,
And so it follows naturally
  I poisoned all my lovers.
But now I'm happy; I have learned
  The lesson this has taught;
That everything I do that's wrong
  Is someone else's fault.

Freud saw all this not only as a great scientific discovery but also as a strategic gain for the profession which had thus far treated him so indifferently. It was, one may conjecture, a sort of gift, an offering or service which would place medicine in such debt to him that it could no longer ignore or reject him.

In his *Autobiography* Freud (1935) puts it thus:

My medical conscience felt pleased at my having arrived at this conclusion [that neurosis has a sexual basis]. I hoped that I had filled up a gap in medical science, which, in dealing with a function of such great biological importance, had failed to take into account any injuries beyond those caused by infection or by gross anatomical lesions. The medical aspect of the matter was, moreover, supported by the fact that sexuality was not something purely mental. It had a somatic side as well . . . (p. 45).

In his book on *The Problem of Lay Analysis*, Freud (1927) later took a somewhat different position (see also Chapter 9 of the third volume of Jones' biography of Freud, 1957); but by this time his Big Idea had been let loose in the world and was no longer entirely under his control.

Psychologists were, as we know, among the first of the outlying professional groups to "take up" psychoanalysis. By being analyzed, we not only learned—in an intimate, personal way —about this new and revolutionary science; we also (or so we imagined) were qualifying ourselves for the practice of analysis as a form of therapy. Now we are beginning to see how illusory this all was. We accepted psychoanalytic theory long before it had been adequately tested and thus embraced as "science" a set of presuppositions which we are now painfully having to repudiate. But, more than this, in accepting the premise that the neurotically disturbed person is basically *sick*, we surrendered our professional independence and authenticity. Now, to the extent that we have subscribed to the doctrine of mental *illness* (and tried to take part in its "treatment"), we have laid ourselves open to some really very embarrassing charges from our friends in psychiatry.

In 1954 the American Psychiatric Association, with the approval of the American Medical Association and the American Psychoanalytic Association, published a resolution on "relations between medicine and psychology," which it reissued (during the supposed "moratorium") in 1957. This document needs no extensive review in these pages; but a few sentences may be quoted to indicate what a powerful fulcrum the sickness conception of neurosis provides for the aggrandizement of medicine.

For centuries the Western world has placed on the medical profession responsibility for the diagnosis and treatment of illness. Medical practice acts have been designed to protect the public from unqualified practitioners and to define the special responsibilities assumed by those who practice the healing art. . . . Psychiatry is the medical specialty concerned with illness that has chiefly mental symptoms. . . . Psychotherapy is a form of medical treatment and does not form the basis for a separate profession. . . . When members of these [other] professions contribute to the diagnosis and treatment of illness, their professional contributions must be coordinated under medical responsibility (pp. 1–2).

So long as we subscribe to the view that neurosis is a bona fide "illness," without moral implications or dimensions, our position will, of necessity, continue to be an awkward one. And it is here I suggest that, as between the concept of sin (however unsatisfactory it may in some ways be) and that of sickness, sin is indeed the lesser of two evils. We have tried the sickness horn of this dilemma and impaled ourselves upon it. Perhaps, despite our erstwhile protestations, we shall yet find sin more congenial.

We psychologists do not, I believe, object *in principle* to the type of authority which psychiatrists wish to exercise, or to our being subject to other medical controls, if they were truly functional. But authority and power ought to go with demonstrated competence, which medicine clearly has in the physical realm but, equally clearly, does not have in "psychiatry." Despite some pretentious affirmations to the contrary, the fact is that psychoanalysis, on which modern "dynamic" psychiatry is largely based, is in a state of virtual collapse and imminent demise. And the tranquilizers and other forms of so-called chemotherapy are admittedly only ameliorative, not basically curative. So now, to the extent that we have accepted the "illness" postulate and thus been lured under the penumbra of medicine, we are in the ungraceful maneuver of "getting out." [1]

But the question remains: Where do we *go*, what do we *do*, now? Some believe that our best policy is to become frankly agnostic for the time being, to admit that we know next to nothing about either the cause or correction of psychopathology and therefore ought to concentrate on *research*. This is certainly a safe policy, and it may also be the wisest one. But since this matter of man's total adjustment and psychosocial survival does not quickly yield up its innermost secrets to conventional types of scientific inquiry, I believe it will do no harm for us at the same time to be thinking about some frankly ideological matters.

For several decades we psychologists looked upon the whole matter of sin and moral accountability as a great incubus and acclaimed our liberation

from it as epoch-making. But at length we have discovered that to be "free" in this sense, i.e., to have the excuse of being "sick" rather than *sinful*, is to court the danger of also becoming *lost*. This danger is, I believe, betokened by the widespread interest in Existentialism which we are presently witnessing. In becoming amoral, ethically neutral, and "free," we have cut the very roots of our being; lost our deepest sense of self-hood and identity; and, with neurotics themselves, find ourselves asking: Who *am* I? What is my *destiny*? What does living (existence) *mean*?

In reaction to the state of near-limbo into which we have drifted, we have become suddenly aware, once again, of the problem of *values* and of their centrality in the human enterprise. This trend is clearly apparent in the programs at our recent professional meetings, in journal articles, and, to some extent already, in our elementary textbooks. Something very basic is obviously happening to psychologists and their "self-image."

In this process of moving away from our erstwhile medical "entanglements," it would be a very natural thing for us to form a closer and friendlier relationship than we have previously had with religion and theology. And something of this sort is unquestionably occurring. At the APA Annual Convention in 1956 there was, for the first time in our history I believe, a symposium on religion and mental health; and each ensuing year has seen other clear indications of a developing rapprochement.

However, here too there is a difficulty

---

[1] Thoughtful psychiatrists are also beginning to question the legitimacy of the disease concept in this area. In an article entitled "The Myth of Mental Illness" which appeared after this paper went to press, Thomas S. Szasz (1960) is particularly outspoken on this score. He says: ". . . the notion of mental illness has outlived whatever usefulness it might have had and . . . now functions merely as a convenient myth. . . . mental illness is a myth, whose function it is to disguise and thus render more palatable the bitter pill of moral conflicts in human relations" (p. 118). Szasz' entire article deserves careful attention.

—of a most surprising kind. At the very time that psychologists are becoming distrustful of the sickness approach to personality disturbance and are beginning to look with more benign interest and respect toward certain moral and religious precepts, religionists themselves are being caught up in and bedazzled by the same preposterous system of thought as that from which we psychologists are just recovering. It would be possible to document this development at length; but reference to such recent "theological" works as Richard V. McCann's *Delinquency— Sickness or Sin?* (1957) and Carl Michalson's *Faith for Personal Crises* (1958, see especially Chapter 3) will suffice.

We have already alluded to Anna Russell's "Psychiatric Folksong" and, in addition, should call attention to Katie Lee's 12-inch LP recording "Songs of Couch and Consultation." That entertainment and literary people are broadly rejecting psychoanalytic froth for the more solid substance of moral accountability is indicated by many current novels and plays. It is not without significance that Arthur Miller's *Death of a Salesman*, written in the philosophical vein of Hawthorne's great novel *The Scarlet Letter*, has, for example, been received so well.

How very strange and inverted our present situation therefore is! Traditionally clergymen have worried about the world's entertainments and entertainers and, for a time at least, about psychology and psychologists. Now, ironically, the entertainers and psychologists are *worrying about the clergymen*. Eventually, of course, clergymen will return to a sounder, less fantastic position; but in the meantime, we psychologists can perhaps play a socially useful and, also, scientifically productive role if we pursue, with all serious-ness and candor, our discovery of the essentially moral nature of human existence and of that "living death" which we call psychopathology. This, of course, is not the place to go deeply into the substantive aspects of the problem; but one illustration of the fruitfulness of such exploration may be cited.

In reconsidering the possibility that sin must, after all, be taken seriously, many psychologists seem perplexed as to what attitude one should take *toward the sinner*. "Nonjudgmental," "nonpunitive," "nondirective," "warm," "accepting," "ethically neutral": these words have been so very generally used to form the supposedly proper therapeutic imago that reintroduction of the concept of sin throws us badly off balance. *Our* attitudes, as would-be therapists or helping persons, toward the neurotic (sinner) are apparently less important than his attitude *toward himself*; and, as we know, it is usually —in the most general sense—a rejecting one. Therefore, we have reasoned, the way to get the neurotic to accept and love himself is for us to love and accept *him*, an inference which flows equally from the Freudian assumption that the patient is not really guilty or sinful but only fancies himself so and from the view of Rogers that we are all inherently good and are corrupted by our experiences with the external, everyday world.

But what is here generally overlooked, it seems, is that recovery (constructive change, redemption) is most assuredly attained, not by helping a person reject and rise above his sins, but by helping him *accept them*. This is the paradox which we have not at all understood and which is the very crux of the problem. Just so long as a person lives under the shadow of real, unacknowledged, and unexpiated guilt, he *cannot* (if he has any character at all) "accept himself"; and all *our* efforts to reassure and accept him will avail nothing. He will continue to hate himself and to suffer the inevitable consequences of self-hatred. But the moment he (with or without "assistance") begins to accept his guilt and his sinfulness, the possibility of radical reformation opens up; and with this, the individual may legitimately, though not without pain and effort, pass from deep, pervasive self-rejection and self-torture to a new freedom, of self-respect and peace.

Thus we arrive, not only at a new (really very old) conception of the nature of "neurosis" which may change our entire approach to this problem, but also at an understanding of one of the most fundamental fallacies of Freudian psychoanalysis and many kindred efforts at psychotherapy. Freud observed, quite accurately, that the neurotic tortures himself; and he conjectured that this type of suffering arose from the irrationality and overseverity of the superego. But at once there was an empirical as well as logical difficulty which Freud (unlike some of his followers) faithfully acknowledged. In the *New Introductory Lectures on Psychoanalysis* (1933), he said:

The superego [paradoxically] seems to have made a one-sided selection [as between the loving and the punitive attitudes of the parents], and to have chosen only the harshness and severity of the parents, their preventive and punitive functions, while their loving care is not taken up and continued by it. If the parents have really ruled with a rod of iron, we easily understand the child developing a severe superego, but, contrary to our expectations, experience shows that the superego may reflect the same relentless harshness even when the up-bringing has been gentle and kind (p. 90).

And then Freud adds, candidly: "We ourselves do not feel that we have fully understood it." In this we can fully agree. For the only way to resolve the paradox of self-hatred and self-punishment is to assume, not that it represents merely an "introjection" of the attitudes of others, but that the self-hatred is realistically justified and will persist until the individual, by radically altered attitude *and action*, honestly and realistically comes to feel that he now deserves something better. As long as one remains, in old-fashioned religious phraseology, hard-of-heart and unrepentant, just so long will one's conscience hold him in the vise-like grip of "neurotic" rigidity and suffering. But if, at length, an individual confesses his past stupidities and errors and makes what poor attempts he can at restitution, then the superego (like the parents of an earlier day—and society in general) forgives and relaxes its stern hold; and the individual once again is free, "well" (Mowrer, 1959).

But here we too, like Freud, encounter a difficulty. There is some evidence that human beings do not change radically unless they first acknowledge their sins; but we also know how hard it is for one to make such an acknowledgment unless he has *already changed*. In other words, the full realization of deep worthlessness is a severe ego "insult"; and one must have some new source of strength, it seems, to endure it. This is a mystery (or is it only a mistaken observation?) which traditional theology has tried to resolve in various ways —without complete success. Can we psychologists do better?

## REFERENCES

AMERICAN PSYCHIATRIC ASSOCIATION, Committee on Relations between Psychiatry and Psychology. Resolution on relations of medicine and psychology. *Amer. Psychiat. Ass. Mail Pouch*, 1954, October.

FREUD, S. *The problem of lay analysis*. New York: Brentano, 1927.

FREUD, S. *New introductory lectures on psychoanalysis*. New York: Norton, 1933.

FREUD, S. *Autobiography*. New York: Norton, 1935.

JONES, E. *The life and work of Sigmund*

*Freud*. Vol. 3. New York: Basic Books, 1957.

McCANN, R. V. *Delinquency: Sickness or sin?* New York: Harper, 1957.

MICHALSON, C. *Faith for personal crises*. London: Epworth, 1958.

MOWRER, O. H. Changing conceptions of the unconscious. *J. nerv. ment. Dis.*, 1959, 129, 222–234.

SZASZ, T. S. The myth of mental illness. *Amer. Psychologist*, 1960, 15, 113–118.

David P. Ausubel

# Personality Disorder Is Disease

Dr. Ausubel prepared this paper as a rejoinder to the views expressed by Drs. Szasz and Mowrer, and as a defense of the term "disease" in viewing abnormal behavior. He systematically reviews the arguments in the first two papers and attempts to refute them. He does express agreement with two of the principal positions taken by Szasz and Mowrer. He agrees that it is not necessary for the handling of behavior disorders to be restricted to physicians, or to be controlled by the medical profession, and he also objects to a distant, nonjudgmental approach to the treatment of these problems. However, Dr. Ausubel maintains that these two approaches can be rejected without discarding the concept of disease. He views disease as a marked deviation of any sort from usual standards, and sees merit in viewing disordered behavior in this manner. By doing so, it should be clear that disease is used as a description rather than an explanation of abnormal behavior.

In two recent articles in the *American Psychologist*, Szasz (1960) and Mowrer (1960) have argued the case for discarding the concept of mental illness. The essence of Mowrer's position is that since medical science lacks "demonstrated competence . . . in psychiatry," psychology would be wise to "get out" from "under the penumbra of medicine," and to regard the behavior disorders as manifestations of sin rather than of disease (p. 302). Szasz' position, as we shall see shortly, is somewhat more complex than Mowrer's, but agrees with the latter in emphasizing the moral as opposed to the psychopathological basis of abnormal behavior.

For a long time now, clinical psychology has both repudiated the rele-

*Reprinted from the* American Psychologist, 16(1961), 69–74 *with the permission of the American Psychological Association and Dr. Ausubel. Copyright 1961 by the American Psychological Association.*

vance of moral judgment and accountability for assessing behavioral acts and
choices, and has chafed under medical
(psychiatric) control and authority in
diagnosing and treating the personality
disorders. One can readily appreciate,
therefore, Mowrer's eagerness to sever
the historical and professional ties that
bind clinical psychology to medicine,
even if this means denying that psychological disturbances constitute a form
of illness, and even if psychology's close
working relationship with psychiatry
must be replaced by a new rapprochement with sin and theology, as "the
lesser of two evils" (pp. 302–303).
One can also sympathize with Mowrer's
and Szasz' dissatisfaction with prevailing amoral and nonjudgmental trends
in clinical psychology and with their
entirely commendable efforts to restore
moral judgment and accountability to
a respectable place among the criteria
used in evaluating human behavior,
both normal and abnormal.

Opposition to these two trends in
the handling of the behavior disorders
(i.e., to medical control and to nonjudgmental therapeutic attitudes),
however, does not necessarily imply
abandonment of the concept of mental
illness. There is no inconsistency whatsoever in maintaining, on the one hand,
that most purposeful human activity
has a moral aspect the reality of which
psychologists cannot afford to ignore
(Ausubel, 1952, p. 462), that man is
morally accountable for the majority of
his misdeeds (Ausubel, 1952, p. 469),
and that psychological rather than
medical training and sophistication are
basic to competence in the personality
disorders (Ausubel, 1956, p. 101), and
affirming, on the other hand, that the
latter disorders are genuine manifestations of illness. In recent years psychology has been steadily moving away from
the formerly fashionable stance of ethical neutrality in the behavioral sciences;

and in spite of strident medical claims
regarding superior professional qualifications and preclusive legal responsibility for treating psychiatric patients,
and notwithstanding the nominally restrictive provisions of medical practice
acts, clinical psychologists have been
assuming an increasingly more important, independent, and responsible role
in treating the mentally ill population
of the United States.

It would be instructive at this point
to examine the tactics of certain other
medically allied professions in freeing
themselves from medical control and
in acquiring independent, legally recognized professional status. In no instance
have they resorted to the devious strat-
agem of denying that they were treating
diseases, in the hope of mollifying medical opposition and legitimizing their
own professional activities. They took
the position instead that simply because
a given condition is defined as a disease,
its treatment need not necessarily be
turned over to doctors of medicine if
other equally competent professional
specialists were available. That this position is legally and politically tenable
is demonstrated by the fact that an
impressively large number of recognized
diseases are legally treated today by
both medical *and* nonmedical specialists (e.g., diseases of the mouth, face,
jaws, teeth, eyes, and feet). And there
are few convincing reasons for believing
that psychiatrists wield that much more
political power than physicians, maxil-
lofacial surgeons, ophthalmologists, and
orthopedic surgeons, that they could be
successful where these latter specialists
have failed, in legally restricting practice in their particular area of competence to holders of the medical degree.
Hence, even if psychologists were not
currently managing to hold their own
vis-à-vis psychiatrists, it would be far
less dangerous and much more forth-
right to press for the necessary amelio-

rative legislation than to seek cover behind an outmoded and thoroughly discredited conception of the behavior disorders.

## THE SZASZ-MOWRER POSITION

Szasz' (1960) contention that the concept of mental illness "now functions merely as a convenient myth" (p. 118) is grounded on four unsubstantiated and logically untenable propositions, which can be fairly summarized as follows:

1. Only symptoms resulting from demonstrable physical lesions qualify as legitimate manifestations of disease. Brain pathology is a type of physical lesion, but its symptoms properly speaking, are neurological rather than psychological in nature. Under no circumstances, therefore, can mental symptoms be considered a form of illness.

2. A basic dichotomy exists between *mental* symptoms, on the one hand, which are subjective in nature, dependent on subjective judgment and personal involvement of the observer, and referable to cultural-ethical norms, and *physical* symptoms, on the other hand, which are allegedly objective in nature, ascertainable without personal involvement of the observer, and independent of cultural norms and ethical standards. Only symptoms possessing the latter set of characteristics are genuinely reflective of illness and amenable to medical treatment.

3. Mental symptoms are merely expressions of problems of living and, hence, cannot be regarded as manifestations of a pathological condition. The concept of mental illness is misleading and demonological because it seeks to explain psychological disturbance in particular and human disharmony in

general in terms of a metaphorical but nonexistent disease entity, instead of attributing them to inherent difficulties in coming to grips with elusive problems of choice and responsibility.

4. Personality disorders, therefore, can be most fruitfully conceptualized as products of moral conflict, confusion, and aberration. Mowrer (1960) extends this latter proposition to include the dictum that psychiatric symptoms are primarily reflective of unacknowledged sin, and that individuals manifesting these symptoms are responsible for and deserve their suffering, both because of their original transgressions and because they refuse to avow and expiate their guilt (pp. 301, 304).

Widespread adoption of the Szasz-Mowrer view of the personality disorders would, in my opinion, turn back the psychiatric clock twenty-five hundred years. The most significant and perhaps the only real advance registered by mankind in evolving a rational and humane method of handling behavioral aberrations has been in substituting a concept of disease for the demonological and retributional doctrines regarding their nature and etiology that flourished until comparatively recent times. Conceptualized as illness, the symptoms of personality disorders can be interpreted in the light of underlying stresses and resistances, both genic and environmental, and can be evaluated in relation to *specifiable* quantitative and qualitative norms of appropriately adaptive behavior, both cross-culturally and within a particular cultural context. It would behoove us, therefore, before we abandon the concept of mental illness and return to the medieval doctrine of unexpiated sin or adopt Szasz' ambiguous criterion of difficulty in ethical choice and responsibility, to subject the foregoing propositions to careful and detailed study.

## Mental Symptoms and
## Brain Pathology

Although I agree with Szasz in rejecting the doctrine that ultimately some neuroanatomic or neurophysiologic defect will be discovered in *all* cases of personality disorder, I disagree with his reasons for not accepting this proposition. Notwithstanding Szasz' straw man presentation of their position, the proponents of the extreme somatic view do not really assert that the *particular nature* of a patient's disordered beliefs can be correlated with "certain definite lesions in the nervous system" (Szasz, 1960, p. 113). They hold rather that normal cognitive and behavioral functioning depends on the anatomic and physiologic integrity of certain key areas of the brain, and that impairment of this substrate integrity, therefore, provides a physical basis for disturbed ideation and behavior, but does not explain, except in a very gross way, the particular kinds of symptoms involved. In fact, they are generally inclined to attribute the *specific* character of the patient's symptoms to the nature of his pre-illness personality structure, the substrate integrity of which is impaired by the lesion or metabolic defect in question.

Nevertheless, even though this type of reasoning plausibly accounts for the psychological symptoms found in general paresis, various toxic deleria, and other comparable conditions, it is an extremely improbable explanation of *all* instances of personality disorder. Unlike the tissues of any other organ, brain tissue possesses the unique property of making possible awareness of and adjustment to the world of sensory, social, and symbolic stimulation. Hence by virtue of this unique relationship of the nervous system to the environment, diseases of behavior and personality may reflect abnormalities in personal and social adjustment, quite apart from any structural or metabolic disturbance in the underlying neural substrate. I would conclude, therefore, that although brain pathology is probably not the most important cause of behavior disorder, it is undoubtedly responsible for the incidence of *some* psychological abnormalities *as well as* for various neurological signs and symptoms.

But even if we completely accepted Szasz' view that brain pathology does not account for any symptoms of personality disorder, it would still be unnecessary to accept his assertion that to qualify as a genuine manifestation of disease a given symptom must be caused by a physical lesion. Adoption of such a criterion would be arbitrary and inconsistent both with medical and lay connotations of the term "disease," which in current usage is generally regarded as including any marked deviation, physical, mental, or behavioral, from normally desirable standards of structural and functional integrity.

## Mental Versus Physical Symptoms

Szasz contends that since the analogy between physical and mental symptoms is patently fallacious, the postulated parallelism between physical and mental disease is logically untenable. This line of reasoning is based on the assumption that the two categories of symptoms can be sharply dichotomized with respect to such basic dimensions as objectivity-subjectivity, the relevance of cultural norms, and the need for personal involvement of the observer. In my opinion, the existence of such a dichotomy cannot be empirically demonstrated in convincing fashion.

Practically all symptoms of bodily disease involve some elements of subjective judgment—both on the part of the patient and of the physician. Pain is perhaps the most important and commonly used criterion of physical illness. Yet, any evaluation of its reported locus, intensity, character, and duration is dependent upon the patient's subjective appraisal of his own sensations and on the physician's assessment of the latter's pain threshold, intelligence, and personality structure. It is also a medical commonplace that the severity of pain in most instances of bodily illness may be mitigated by the administration of a placebo. Furthermore, in taking a meaningful history the physician must not only serve as a participant observer but also as a skilled interpreter of human behavior. It is the rare patient who does not react psychologically to the signs of physical illness; and hence physicians are constantly called upon to decide, for example, to what extent precordial pain and reported tightness in the chest are manifestations of coronary insufficiency, of fear of cardiac disease and impending death, or of combinations of both conditions. Even such allegedly objective signs as pulse rate, BMR, blood pressure, and blood cholesterol have their subjective and relativistic aspects. Pulse rate and blood pressure are notoriously susceptible to emotional influences, and BMR and blood cholesterol fluctuate widely from one cultural environment to another (Dreyfuss & Czaczkes, 1959). And anyone who believes that ethical norms have no relevance for physical illness has obviously failed to consider the problems confronting Catholic patients and/or physicians when issues of contraception, abortion, and preferential saving of the mother's as against the fetus' life must be faced in the context of various obstetrical emergencies and medical contraindications to pregnancy.

It should now be clear, therefore, that symptoms not only do not need a physical basis to qualify as manifestations of illness, but also that the

evaluation of *all* symptoms, physical as well as mental, is dependent in large measure on subjective judgment, emotional factors, cultural-ethical norms, and personal involvement on the part of the observer. These considerations alone render no longer tenable Szasz' contention (1960, p. 114) that there is an inherent contradiction between using cultural and ethical norms as criteria of mental disease, on the one hand, and of employing medical measures of treatment on the other. But even if the postulated dichotomy between mental and physical symptoms were valid, the use of physical measures in treating subjective and relativistic psychological symptoms would still be warranted. Once we accept the proposition that impairment of the neutral substrate of personality can result in behavior disorder, it is logically consistent to accept the corollary proposition that other kinds of manipulation of the same neural substrate can conceivably have therapeutic effects, irrespective of whether the underlying cause of the mental symptoms is physical or psychological.

## Mental Illness and Problems of Living

"The phenomena now called mental illness," argues Szasz (1960), can be regarded more forthrightly and simply as "expressions of man's struggle with the problem of how he should live" (p. 117). This statement undoubtedly oversimplifies the nature of personality disorders; but even if it were adequately inclusive it would not be inconsistent with the position that these disorders are a manifestation of illness. There is no valid reason why a particular symptom cannot both reflect a problem in living *and* constitute a manifestation of disease. The notion of mental illness, conceived in this way, would not "obscure the everyday fact that life for most people is a continuous struggle . . . for a 'place in the sun,' 'peace of mind,' or some other human value" (p. 118). It is quite true, as Szasz points out, that "human relations are inherently fraught with difficulties" (p. 117), and that most people manage to cope with such difficulties without becoming mentally ill. But conceding this fact hardly precludes the possibility that some individuals, either because of the magnitude of the stress involved, or because of genically or environmentally induced susceptibility to ordinary degrees of stress, respond to the problems of living with behavior that is either seriously distorted or sufficiently unadaptive to prevent normal interpersonal relations and vocational functioning. The latter outcome—gross deviation from a designated range of desirable behavioral variability—conforms to the generally understood meaning of mental illness.

The plausibility of subsuming abnormal behavioral reactions to stress under the general rubric of disease is further enhanced by the fact that these reactions include the same three principal categories of symptoms found in physical illness. Depression and catastrophic impairment of self-esteem, for example, are manifestations of personality disorder which are symptomologically comparable to edema in cardiac failure or to heart murmurs in valvular disease. They are indicative of underlying pathology but are neither adaptive nor adjustive. Symptoms such as hypomanic overactivity and compulsive striving toward unrealistically high achievement goals, on the other hand, are both adaptive and adjustive, and constitute a type of compensatory response to basic feelings of inadequacy, which is not unlike cardiac hypertrophy in hypertensive heart disease or ele-

vated white blood cell count in acute infections. And finally, distortive psychological defenses that have some adjustive value but are generally maladaptive (e.g., phobias, delusions, autistic fantasies) are analogous to the pathological situation found in conditions like pneumonia, in which the excessive outpouring of serum and phagocytes in defensive response to pathogenic bacteria literally causes the patient to drown in his own fluids.

Within the context of this same general proposition, Szasz repudiates the concept of mental illness as demonological in nature, i.e., as the "true heir to religious myths in general and to the belief in witchcraft in particular" (p. 118) because it allegedly employs a reified abstraction ("a deformity of personality") to account in causal terms both for "human disharmony" and for symptoms of behavior disorder (p. 114). But again he appears to be demolishing a straw man. Modern students of personality disorder do not regard mental illness as a cause of human disharmony, but as a co-manifestation with it of inherent difficulties in personal adjustment and interpersonal relations; and in so far as I can accurately interpret the literature, psychopathologists do not conceive of mental illness as a cause of particular behavioral symptoms but as a generic term under which these symptoms can be subsumed.

## Mental Illness and Moral Responsibility

Szasz' final reason for regarding mental illness as a myth is really a corollary of his previously considered more general proposition that mental symptoms are essentially reflective of problems of living and hence do not legitimately qualify as manifestations of disease. It focuses on difficulties of ethical choice and responsibility as the particular life problems most likely to be productive of personality disorder. Mowrer (1960) further extends this corollary by asserting that neurotic and psychotic individuals are responsible for their suffering (p. 301), and that unacknowledged and unexpiated sin, in turn, is the basic cause of this suffering (p. 304). As previously suggested, however, one can plausibly accept the proposition that psychiatrists and clinical psychologists have erred in trying to divorce behavioral evaluation from ethical considerations, in conducting psychotherapy in an amoral setting, and in confusing the psychological explanation of unethical behavior with absolution from accountability for same, *without* necessarily endorsing the view that personality disorders are basically a reflection of sin, and that victims of these disorders are less ill than responsible for their symptoms (Ausubel, 1952, pp. 392–397, 465–471).

In the first place, it is possible in most instances (although admittedly difficult in some) to distinguish quite unambiguously between mental illness and ordinary cases of immorality. The vast majority of persons who are guilty of moral lapses knowingly violate their own ethical precepts for expediential reasons—despite being volitionally capable at the time, both of choosing the more moral alternative and of exercising the necessary inhibitory control (Ausubel, 1952, pp. 465–471). Such persons, also, usually do not exhibit any signs of behavior disorder. At crucial choice points in facing the problems of living they simply choose the opportunistic instead of the moral alternative. They are not mentally ill, but they are clearly accountable for their misconduct. Hence, since personality disorder and immorality are neither coextensive nor

mutually exclusive conditions, the concept of mental illness need not necessarily obscure the issue of moral accountability.

Second, guilt may be a contributory factor in behavior disorder, but is by no means the only or principal cause thereof. Feelings of guilt may give rise to anxiety and depression; but in the absence of catastrophic impairment of self-esteem induced by *other* factors, these symptoms tend to be transitory and peripheral in nature (Ausubel, 1952, pp. 362–363). Repression of guilt, is more a consequence than a cause of anxiety. Guilt is repressed in order to avoid the anxiety producing trauma to self-esteem that would otherwise result if it were acknowledged. Repression per se enters the causal picture in anxiety only secondarily—by obviating "the possibility of punishment, confession, expiation, and other guilt reduction mechanisms" (Ausubel, 1952, p. 456). Furthermore, in most types of personality disorder other than anxiety, depression, and various complications of anxiety such as phobias, obsessions, and compulsion, guilt feelings are either not particularly prominent (schizophrenic reactions), or are conspicuously absent (e.g., classical cases of inadequate or aggressive, antisocial psychopathy).

Third, it is just as unreasonable to hold an individual responsible for symptoms of behavior disorder as to deem him accountable for symptoms of physical illness. He is no more culpable for his inability to cope with sociopsychological stress than he would be for his inability to resist the spread of infectious organisms. In those instances where warranted guilt feelings *do* contribute to personality disorder, the patient is accountable for the misdeeds underlying his guilt, but is hardly responsible for the symptoms brought on by the guilt feelings or for unlawful acts committed during his illness. Acknowledgment of guilt may be therapeutically beneficial under these circumstances, but punishment for the original misconduct should obviously be deferred until after recovery.

Lastly, even if it were true that all personality disorder is a reflection of sin and that people are accountable for their behavioral symptoms, it would still be unnecessary to deny that these symptoms are manifestations of disease. Illness is no less real because the victim happens to be culpable for his illness. A glutton with hypertensive heart disease undoubtedly aggravates his condition by overeating, and is culpable in part for the often fatal symptoms of his disease, but what reasonable person would claim that for this reason he is not really ill?

## CONCLUSIONS

Four propositions in support of the argument for discarding the concept of mental illness were carefully examined, and the following conclusions were reached:

First, although brain pathology is probably not the major cause of personality disorder, it does account for *some* psychological symptoms by impairing the neural substrate of personality. In any case, however, a symptom need not reflect a physical lesion in order to qualify as a genuine manifestation of disease.

Second, Szasz' postulated dichotomy between mental and physical symptoms is untenable because the assessment of *all* symptoms is dependent to some extent on subjective judgment, emotional factors, cultural-ethical norms, and personal involvement of the observer. Furthermore, the use of medical measures in treating behavior disorders— irrespective of whether the underlying

causes are neural or psychological—is defensible on the grounds that if inadvertent impairment of the neural substrate of personality can have distortive effects on behavior, directed manipulation of the same substrate may have therapeutic effects.

Third, there is no inherent contradiction in regarding mental symptoms both as expressions of problems in living *and* as manifestations of illness. The latter situation results when individuals are for various reasons unable to cope with such problems, and react with seriously distorted or maladaptive behavior. The three principal categories of behavioral symptoms—manifestations of impaired functioning, adaptive compensation, and defensive overreaction—are also found in bodily disease. The concept of mental illness has never been advanced as a demonological cause of human disharmony, but only as a co-manifestation with it of certain inescapable difficulties and hazards in personal and social adjustment. The same concept is also generally accepted as a generic term for all behavioral symptoms rather than as a reified cause of these symptoms.

Fourth, the view that personality disorder is less a manifestation of illness than of sin, i.e., of culpable inadequacy in meeting problems of ethical choice and responsibility, and that victims of behavior disorder are therefore morally accountable for their symptoms, is neither logically nor empirically tenable. In most instances immoral behavior and mental illness are clearly distinguishable conditions. Guilt is only a secondary etiological factor in anxiety and depression, and in other personality disorders is either not prominent or conspicuously absent. The issue of culpability for symptoms is largely irrelevant in handling the behavior disorders, and in any case does not detract from the reality of the illness.

In general, it is both unnecessary and potentially dangerous to discard the concept of mental illness on the grounds that only in this way can clinical psychology escape from the professional domination of medicine. Dentists, podiatrists, optometrists, and osteopaths have managed to acquire an independent professional status without rejecting the concept of disease. It is equally unnecessary and dangerous to substitute the doctrine of sin for illness in order to counteract prevailing amoral and nonjudgmental trends in psycho-therapy. The hypothesis of repressed guilt does not adequately explain most kinds and instances of personality disorder, and the concept of mental illness does not preclude judgments of moral accountability where warranted. Definition of behavior disorder in terms of sin or of difficulties associated with ethical choice and responsibility would substitute theological disputation and philosophical wrangling about values for specifiable quantitative and qualitative criteria of disease.

## REFERENCES

AUSUBEL, D. P. *Ego development and the personality disorders.* New York: Grune & Stratton, 1952.

AUSUBEL, D. P. Relationships between psychology and psychiatry: The hidden issues. *Amer. Psychologist*, 1956, **11**, 99–105.

DREYFUSS, F., & CZACZKES, J. W. Blood cholesterol and uric acid of healthy medical students under the stress of an examination. *AMA Arch. intern. Med.,* 1959, **103**, 708.

MOWRER, O. H. "Sin," the lesser of two evils. *Amer. Psychologist*, 1960, **15**, 301–304.

SZASZ, T. S. The myth of mental illness. *Amer. Psychologist*, 1960, **15**, 113–118.

Henry B. Adams

# "Mental Illness" or Interpersonal Behavior?

Dr. Adams also joins in the growing trend among contemporary psychologists to reject the illness model of abnormal behavior. He agrees that so-called mental illnesses have different causes, and are responsive to different approaches to treatment, than the more clearly determined physical illnesses and, for this reason, he feels that it is inappropriate to conceptualize these behaviors as illness. He injects an interesting historical note in his paper by discussing moral therapy, a method of treatment that was used with success in the nineteenth century and which was replaced by medically inspired approaches that have not proven to be more effective. Moral therapy did not focus on sin and guilt, as Dr. Mowrer's approach might suggest, but on the social and psychological context in which disordered behavior might arise. Dr. Adams applauds this orientation,

Reprinted from the American Psychologist, 19(1964), 191–197 with the permission of the American Psychological Association and Dr. Adams. Copyright 1964 by the American Psychological Association.

*and sees the phenomena traditionally referred to as mental illness as being better conceptualized as maladaptive interpersonal behavior. He rejects the numerous medical and physical analogies that have been offered to explain behavior in favor of purely human terms to explain human behavior.*

There is no such thing as a "mental illness" in any significantly meaningful sense. In medicine the term "illness" is used in a literal, nonfigurative way to denote an undesirable alteration or change away from optimal levels of organic bodily functioning. But the term "mental illness" is applied to various patterns of behavior considered maladaptive or inappropriate by implicit psychological and social standards (Szasz, 1960, 1961).

The concept of a functional mental illness is a *verbal analogy*. While it is appropriate to speak of neurological disorders as true organic illnesses of the nervous system, comparable to organic illnesses involving the circulatory or digestive system, it seems questionable to apply the term "illness" to arbitrarily defined patterns of behavior, particularly when there may be no evidence of any physiological malfunctioning. The plain fact is that the term "mental illness" is applied in an indiscriminate way to a motley collection of interpersonal behavior patterns. Often there is no positive evidence whatever of any physiological or organic malfunctioning, as in the so-called "functional disorders." Actually, organic physical illnesses and the functional types of mental illnesses are defined by *different kinds of criteria*, and they are modified or ameliorated ("treated" or "cured") by *fundamentally different procedures*.

Failure to clarify these distinctions has had unfortunate consequences. Efforts toward understanding and effective alleviation have long been hampered by the semantic confusion which results when the word "illness" is used to denote both physical disease entities and

maladaptive patterns of interpersonal behavior. This ambiguous usage has perpetuated the glib fallacy that mental and physical illnesses are the same thing. It has interfered with the understanding of fundamental psychological phenomena and made for an ineffectual and often harmful approach to some of the most serious recurring problems in human relationships.

This semantic confusion is an important fact in the history of psychiatry since 1800. A number of studies have been published in recent years on the "moral therapy" of the early nineteenth century (Bockoven, 1956, 1957; Brown, 1960; Joint Commission on Mental Illness and Health, 1961; Rees, 1957). These studies all agree that the results of moral therapy (at a time when physical medicine was in a relatively primitive stage of development) compare favorably with the very best mental-hospital programs of today. "Moral therapy" was essentially a program of planned psychological retraining within a positive, sympathetic social milieu.

Moral therapy had its inception near the end of the eighteenth century under the leadership of Pinel, Tuke, Chiarugi, and others. The word "moral" was used at that time in a sense comparable to the contemporary usage of the words "psychological" or "interpersonal." During that era more attention began to be given to

social and environmental factors in the causation of mental illness, and it was found that organic changes in the brain were rather rare at post mortem examinations. The insane came to be regarded as normal people who had lost their reason as a result of having been exposed to severe psychological and social stresses. These stresses were called the moral causes of insanity, and moral treatment aimed at relieving the patient by friendly association, discussion of his difficulties, and the daily pursuit of purposeful activity; in other words, social therapy, individual therapy, and occupational therapy. Moral treatment reached its zenith in the years between 1820 and 1860. The results of treatment during that period were outstandingly good and bear comparison with some of the figures obtainable today. For example, in all patients admitted to the York Retreat [in England] within three months of the onset of illness—between the years 1796 and 1861 the discharge rate was 71% . . . . These are truly remarkable figures, especially when one takes into consideration that a substantial portion of the patients must have been general paralytics, for which there was at that time no effective treatment [Rees, 1957, pp. 306–307].

Cope and Packard (1841) reported on the results of moral treatment in state institutions in the United States. They mentioned institutions in nine states and observed that with moral treatment "ninety per cent of the recent cases can be restored so as to be able to maintain themselves and family." Bockoven (1956) found comparable figures from private institutions utilizing moral treatment. Beginning in the 1820s, the Hartford Retreat reported recoveries in over 90% of all patients admitted with mental illnesses of less than a year's duration. Bockoven also supplied statistics extending from 1833 to 1950 on discharges from the Worcester State Hospital in Massachusetts. During the 1833–1852 period, when moral therapy was being practiced, 71% of all patients ill less than 1 year when admitted were discharged as recovered or improved. Patients discharged during the years 1833–1846 were later followed up until 1893, and it was found that half suffered no recurrences.

Despite ample evidence of its effectiveness, moral therapy was quietly abandoned in American and British mental institutions after 1860 and later almost completely forgotten. The consequences are illustrated by Bockoven's (1956) data from the Worcester State Hospital, showing that recovery rates declined over 90% after 1860, reaching their lowest point between 1923 and 1950 (pp. 292–293). Certainly, one may raise legitimate questions about these old statistics and the validity of conclusions drawn from them. Nevertheless, every recent study on the subject of moral therapy agreed that the results have not been surpassed during the contemporary period, despite all the advances made by physical medicine since 1860.

One important reason for its abandonment was that moral therapy was supposed to be a form of treatment for mental illnesses. But as physical medicine developed during the late nineteenth century, it was thought that the types of procedures found effective with physical illnesses could be carried over unaltered into the treatment of mental illnesses. Since both kinds of phenomena were defined as illnesses this notion sounded reasonable, so long as no one inquired seriously into the possibility that there might be an error in semantics.

An additional factor in the abandonment of moral therapy was that it was regarded as "unscientific" according to the scientific and medical doctrines which developed in the intellectual climate of the last half of the nineteenth century. These doctrines held that true science is impersonal and concerned solely with material things, that feeling, beauty, and moral values are mere illusions in a world of fact, that the human will is powerless against the laws of nature and society, and that every observable phenomenon is reducible to the motions of material particles.[2] Since psychiatric patients were regarded as suffering from a medical condition defined as mental illness, it was held that treatment procedures had to rest on a scientific physical basis, as conceptualized by a mechanistic, materialistic view which held that things rather than persons were the only reality. In keeping with this tough-minded impersonal dogma, the psychological sensitivity and insight which were major factors in the success of moral therapy were dismissed from serious consideration as mystical, sentimental, and unscientific. The treatment of hospitalized psychiatric patients became cold, distant, and unfeeling, consistent with a Zeitgeist of impersonal scientism. Discharge and recovery rates, which had been high wherever moral therapy programs were in effect, declined steadily after 1860. In time, falling discharge rates led to the piling up of chronic patients in hospitals, attitudes of hopelessness, and a growing belief in the "incurability" of insanity. This pessimistic belief had become widespread by 1900, despite the fact that 70% to 90% recovery rates had been commonplace in 1840 during the moral therapy era.

As recovery rates fell and the treatment of hospitalized patients became more detached and impersonal, leaders in psychiatry turned to the laboratory hoping to find a scientific cure for mental illness. They were persuaded that the answers lay in the discovery and identification of physical disease entities. Physicalistic and mechanistic concepts of mental illness were adopted by analogy with physical medicine, while efforts to understand psychiatric pa-

tients as individual persons were largely discontinued (Zilboorg, 1941). Patients were no longer thought of as human beings with problems in human relationships, but as "cases." This impersonal approach led one of the leading American psychiatrists of the 1880s to state in all sincerity that the insane do not suffer unhappiness, and that depressed patients go through the motions of acting sad in a machinelike fashion without feeling genuine sadness (Bockoven, 1956). As Brown's (1960) data indicate, changing attitudes of the medical profession at different historical periods have played a great part in changing rates of discharge and chronicity among hospitalized patients.

The great irony is that after 100 years these laboratory-centered physically oriented research efforts have failed to produce techniques for the "treatment" and "cure" of functional personality disorders significantly more effective than the best techniques of 1840. Actually, the most progressive contemporary mental-hospital programs are those which have revived practices much like those generally prevalent during the moral-therapy era (Greenblatt, York, & Brown, 1955; Rees, 1957).

## THE IMPERSONAL APPROACH TO PERSONALITY

The theoretical concepts most widely used in the mental-health professions today consist largely of misleading analogies, metaphors, and figures of speech. These sonorous but inappropriate terms have made for confusion, trained incapacities, and intellectual stagnation. The Joint Commission on Mental Ill-

---

[2] The doctrines of nineteenth-century impersonal scientism have been more fully described elsewhere by Barzun (1958). He analyzes the modes of thought inherited from that era and shows how strongly they still influence contemporary thinking. Bockoven (1956) notes that the widespread acceptance of these doctrines in both popular and scientific circles contributed to the abandonment of moral therapy after 1860.

ness and Health (1961) has commented on this stagnation with the observation that "twentieth-century psychiatry can add little" to Pinel's principles for the moral treatment of psychotics, which were first published in 1801,

except to convert them into modern terminological dress, contribute more systematic thought to the significance of various symptoms, intensify the doctor-patient relationship through scientific knowledge of psychological mechanisms, treat the patient as a member of a social group which expects him to behave in accepted ways, and specify that moral treatment has been subject to an incredible amount of distortion and misinterpretation . . . [pp. 29–30].

Similarly, psychotherapy in essentially its present-day form was described by Reil in a book published in the year 1803 (Harms, 1957c). Almost every important issue in contemporary clinical psychology was discussed at length by leaders of the moral-therapy movement between 1790 and 1860 (Harms, 1957a, 1957b, 1957c; Roback, 1961).

Much of the terminology now used in contemporary psychology developed in an intellectual climate of impersonal scientism quite different in its basic outlook from the humanitarianism of the moral-therapy era. Psychology first arose as a separate independent science during the 1870s and 1880s. Reflecting the predominant spirit of their times, the early founders of experimental psychology were not concerned with the systematic understanding of human problems and personal relationships. Instead, they imitated the outward appearances and procedures of the physical and biological sciences, hoping that they too might thus be regarded as true scientists. They felt that in order to be scientifically respectable they had to study man impersonally, using techniques, assumptions, and conceptual approaches much like those of the physical and biological sciences. For example, the doctrine of determinism was carried over from the physical sciences without any empirical evidence to show that it was appropriate in explaining human conduct.

The impersonal approach adopted in the late nineteenth century is reflected in the conceptual language of psychology today. These concepts center around words borrowed from nonpsychological fields such as medicine, physics, mechanical engineering, biology, and electronics. This point is best illustrated by listing some verbal analogies commonly used in psychology. All the examples listed below appeared in psychological or psychiatric journals, or in books written for professional readers:

1. *Pseudomedical analogies:* mental illness, mental health, mental hygiene, prophylaxis, diagnosis, pathology, prognosis, etiology, therapy, treatment, cure, trauma, nosology, catharsis, syndrome, neurosis, psychosis, psychopathy, sick

2. *Pseudophysical and pseudoengineering analogies:* motor apparatus, dynamics, reaction potential, valences, field forces, psychic energy, power system, energy transformation, tension, stress, drive, mechanism, dynamogenesis, adjustment, reinforcing machine

3. *Pseudobiological analogies:* organism, homeostasis, phenotypic, genotypic, polymorphous, ontogenetic

4. *Pseudoelectronic analogies:* input, output, amplitude, radar, circuit, feedback, scanning, encoding, signals, charge, discharge, servomechanism

5. *Pseudogenitourinary and pseudogastrointestinal (i.e., psychoanalytic) analogies:* urethral character, phallic character, castration, oral optimism, anal submission, vaginal libido organization, anal-expulsive expression

Such analogies implicitly suggest that human behavior is *just like* the events observed in the nonpsychological sciences from which these words were borrowed. In using such terminology a false assumption is unwittingly made (but rarely recognized) that the *psychological phenomena* to which these terms are applied are therefore just like the *nonpsychological phenomena* where the terms originated. It is taken as *having already been decided* that these words are suitable for labeling and describing human behavior. The actions of living persons are thus conceptualized in the language of impersonal things and processes. Having accepted this glib semantic juggling, it is then quite easy to coin confusing, misleading slogans such as "mental illness is just like any other illness."

## WHAT IS "MENTAL ILLNESS"?

What is the phenomenon to which the label "mental illness" is applied? It is applied to arbitrarily designated types of maladaptive interpersonal behavior, often accompanied by reports of subjective discomfort, unsatisfying human relationships, and social rejection.

Explicit distinctions must be made between these behavioral phenomena and illnesses of the body. Physical illnesses (including neurological disorders) are not in themselves patterns of interaction with other persons. They are disturbances in the organic functions of the body. So far as immediate experience is concerned, a bodily illness such as a cold, fever, or pneumonia is an abnormal, usually unpleasant, subjective condition which *happens to* the individual person. It is not a direct overt manifestation of his characteristic patterns of interacting with others.

But, in cases where the term "mental illness" is used and no organic pathol-

ogy is in evidence, the term refers to some arbitrarily defined pattern of conduct, with "symptoms" of a psychosocial rather than a medical nature. Any effective program directed toward "cure" must consequently provide opportunities for learning new, more adaptive patterns. It should be remembered that the learning process is a normal function of the nervous system, regardless of the nature of the material being learned, be it the subject of medicine, playing a musical instrument, or new social skills.

## A COMPREHENSIVE APPROACH TO INTERPERSONAL BEHAVIOR

Mental illness is a phenomenon involving interpersonal behavior, not a health or medical problem. Programs of alleviation and prevention must therefore rest upon a systematic understanding of interpersonal conduct. A considerable body of recent research in this area suggests that the basic dimensions are surprisingly simple. The supposed complexity of personality and interaction between persons has been shown to be a purely semantic, verbal complexity, rather than a real complexity in actual fact.

These empirical studies have three distinguishing features: (a) The basic observations involve interpersonal actions. To be more explicit, the observations are focused on the acts of *persons* interacting with other *persons*, rather than organisms, psychobiological units, dynamic systems, or other impersonal abstractions. (b) The observers are concerned not with superficial stylistic features, but with the *content* of the interpersonal acts themselves. Content variables are to be contrasted with formalistic or stylistic variables, such as percentage of adjectives, manner of speaking, speed of tapping, etc.

"Content" refers to *what* the individual person is doing or communicating to others by word and deed. (*c*) The investigators aim for *comprehensiveness*, classifying every act systematically in relation to every other.

Most of these studies have dispensed with terminology not meaningfully related to observable conduct. If behavior can be systematically described in *behavioral* terms, there is no need for the confusing nonpsychological analogies and metaphors which have long plagued the mental-health professions. It becomes unnecessary to borrow words from medicine, engineering, or electronics to describe human relationships. This approach makes it possible to clarify fundamental principles which have long been concealed by inappropriate, misleading jargon.

The results of these studies indicate that all interpersonal behavior, both adaptive ("healthy" or "normal") and maladaptive ("sick" or "abnormal"), can be meaningfully categorized within one systematic frame of reference. In a review of these studies, Foa (1961) was impressed by the "strong convergence" of thinking and results obtained in research on interpersonal interaction, since the investigators "proceeded from different research traditions, studied different types of groups . . . and, apparently, followed independent lines of design and analysis. The convergence is toward a simple ordered structure for the organization of interpersonal behavior." Foa suggested that the observations can be ordered into a simple comprehensive framework "that accounts for the empirical interrelations in a parsimonious and meaningful manner." The findings "suggest a circumplex structure around the two orthogonal axes of Dominance-Submission and Affection-Hostility."

Let us examine these two axes or dimensions in more detail. One pole of the Dominance-Submission axis is defined by acts of self-confident, assertive leadership and achievement in the face of obstacles. At the opposite pole are acts of passivity, submissiveness, and acquiescence. This dimension is of course a continuum, with most acts falling midway between extremes. The Affection-Hostility dimension reflects variations in the degree of positive or negative affect manifested toward others. The positive extreme describes warm, friendly, kind, affiliative acts, while the negative extreme describes hostile, critical, angry, disaffiliative acts.

Foa suggests that "an interpersonal act is an attempt to establish the emotional relationship of the actor toward himself and toward the other person," and that "the same act states the position of the actor toward the self and toward the other. . . ." Each type of behavior is thus meaningful toward the self and the other person. The Dominance-Submission axis defines the degree of acceptance or rejection of self, while the Affection-Hostility axis defines the degree of acceptance or rejection of the other. An interpersonal act may be regarded as the Cartesian product of these two sets of values.

The basic framework systematized by this two-dimensional structure has been described repeatedly ever since the time of Hippocrates. If there are only two dimensions of variation in the content of interpersonal acts, and the individual's personality is identified by the relative frequency, intensity, and nature of his acts, we have a simple but comprehensive basis for categorizing all personality types. Classification above and below the mean of these two axes would give four categories which correspond roughly to the traditional four temperaments, as they have been delineated by Hippocrates, Galen, Kant, Wundt, Höffding, Herbart, Külpe, Ebbinghaus, Klages, and Pavlov (Allport, 1961). Thus, persons with the "sanguine" temperament would show behavior which falls above the mean on both dimensions. Such persons typically show active leadership, optimism, and assertiveness, coupled with friendly acceptance of others. Likewise, the other three groups correspond to the traditional choleric, melancholic, and phlegmatic temperaments.

Freud has alluded to these dimensions in his writings (Leary, 1957, pp. 71–72). He has delineated a love-hate, sex-aggression, libido-mortido, or Eros-Thanatos polarity, which is comparable to the Affection-Hostility dimension. He also refers to power or domination in social interaction, analogous to Foa's Dominance-Submission dimension. This two-dimensional structure has appeared in the theories of Parsons, Merton, and Stagner (Leary, 1957, pp. 73–74). It has been used with impressive results in the coaction-compass analysis of the Rorschach (Gottlieb & Parsons, 1960; Lodge & Gibson, 1953) and in scoring and interpreting the TAT (Leary, 1956, 1957).

These dimensions recur in factor-analytic studies of the MMPI. Welsh (1956) reviewed the results of 11 analyses of the MMPI and found consistent agreement as to the first two factors but little agreement as to any additional factors. He developed two special scales, A and R, as measures of these factors. For example, subjects scoring high on A tend to agree with items expressing obsessional thinking, negative emotional tone, pessimism, personal sensitivity, and malignant mentation. Such items express attitudes typical of the "melancholic temperament" as depicted for many centuries. High A scores would fall below the mean on both dimensions. In their overt behavior they show passivity and negative affect toward themselves and others (Dahlstrom & Welsh, 1960).

Jackson and Messick (1961) investigated response style on the MMPI and found that most of the variance was due to two response-set factors. One was an acquiescence factor like Foa's Dominance-Submission dimension. The other was a factor of social desirability, which is essentially the same as the Affection-Hostility dimension, a similarity which may not be recognized immediately. But it has been found that individuals who respond to personality questionnaires in socially desirable directions typically behave in bland, friendly, conventional ways, while those responding in the opposite fashion tend to be blunt, outspoken, critical of conventional standards, and uninhibited in the presence of others. Jackson and Messick noted that the test vectors emerging from their analysis of the MMPI tended toward a circular arrangement, like the circumplex structure described by Foa.

If the response to each item on the MMPI is viewed as a separate interpersonal communication, the convergences between MMPI studies and direct behavioral observations are not surprising. These convergences are all the more significant since the MMPI was developed to facilitate psychiatric diagnosis. The clinical scales of the MMPI were initially validated against Kraepelinian disease-entity diagnostic criteria. The results of these MMPI factor-analytic studies imply that the Kraepelinian labels presently employed in psychiatric diagnosis are nonexistent verbal abstractions.

A factor analysis of rating scales and questionnaires by Goldman-Eisler (1953) tested certain hypotheses drawn from psychoanalytic theory. Two orthogonal factors emerged, the first being a factor of "oral" optimism versus "oral" pessimism. Oral optimists show the same traits of active, friendly, assertiveness as the sanguine temperament, while oral pessimists show the contrasting patterns of the melancholic temperament. The second factor was interpreted as Impatience-Aggression-Autonomy versus Deliberation-Conservatism-Dependence. The traits of impatience, aggression, and autonomy are analogous to the hostile dominance of the choleric temperament, while deliberation, conservatism, and dependence describe the affectionate submissiveness ascribed to the phlegmatic temperament. The factor loadings emerging from this analysis were interrelated in a circular order, much like the circumplex structure of interpersonal behavior described by Foa and the circular array of MMPI test vectors suggested by Jackson and Messick. Although Goldman-Eisler considered her findings as a confirmation of psychoanalytic theory, her results are much like those of other investigators whose theoretical orientation was quite different. The convergences between her results and other studies imply that the elaborate verbal complexities of psychoanalytic theory are needlessly involved. The empirical data can be much more parsimoniously explained.

It is clear that the same fundamental patterns have been repeatedly observed by many contemporary and historical writers, even though the words used may seem very different. These similarities and convergences would not have been so consistently noted unless there were certain universal features in all human conduct. Apparently these universal features were perceived, understood, and implicitly acted upon during the moral therapy era, overlooked by later generations enamoured of impersonal scientism, and spelled out once again in recent empirical investigations. It seems obvious that a sound understanding of human behavior must begin with these universal features rather than the vague jargon that has dominated psychological and psychiatric theorizing to date.

How do these universal features relate to mental health and mental illness? Within the two-dimensional circular structure outlined above an elaborate system has been developed for classifying the interpersonal behavior of both psychiatric patients and "normals" (Leary, 1956, 1957). The major differences between mental illness and mental health are to be found in the characteristic frequency, intensity, and nature of interpersonal acts.

For example, schizophrenics manifest intense degrees of passivity and hostility by unconventional, bizarre, negativistic, and distrustful acts. In contrast, hysterics prefer bland, pleasant, friendly, conventional types of interaction. Hostile, rebellious, and distrustful acts are infrequent and extremely mild in intensity among hysterics. These two contrasting types of interpersonal behavior have long been considered mental illnesses. Both are differentiated from normality, adjustment, or mental health, i.e., versatile, appropriate, effective, adaptive behavior patterns. In this semantic usage the words "illness" and "health" are applied to observable patterns of conduct, not to states of the mind or body. The most effective programs of "therapy," "treatment," or "cure" for these illnesses are those which succeed best in altering the characteristic nature, frequency, and intensity of maladaptive acts in the direction of greater moderation, versatility, appropriateness, and effectiveness.

The more we question the terminology of the mental-health professions today, the more obvious its inadequacies become. It is doubtful that any major advances can be expected so long as understanding is obscured by unsuitable, misleading terms. Every concept in our professional vocabulary needs to be carefully and critically reassessed by asking the question: *Is it appropriate?* Many fundamental problems need to be com-

pletely restated in words that communicate rather than obfuscate. Suitable
*psychological* terminology is badly
needed to clarify numerous vaguely
worded, inappropriately phrased, and

poorly understood questions in psychology today. Only in this way can psychologists create a basis for genuine
understanding of human behavior.

# REFERENCES

ALLPORT, G. W. *Pattern and growth in
personality*. New York: Holt, Rinehart
& Winston, 1961.

BARZUN, J. *Darwin, Marx, Wagner: Critique of a heritage*. (2nd ed.) Garden
City, N. Y.: Doubleday Anchor, 1958.

BOCKOVEN, J. S. Moral treatment in American psychiatry. *J. nerv. ment. Dis.*, 1956,
124, 167–194, 292–321. (Reprinted in
book form: New York: Springer, 1963.)

BOCKOVEN, J. S. Some relationships between cultural attitudes toward individuality and care of the mentally ill: An
historical study. In M. Greenblatt, D. J.
Levinson, & R. H. Williams (Eds.), *The
patient and the mental hospital*. Glencoe,
Ill.: Free Press, 1957. Pp. 517–526.

BROWN, G. W. Length of hospital stay and
schizophrenia: A review of statistical studies. *Acta psychiat. neurol. Scand.*, Copenhagen, 1960, 35, 414–430.

COPE, T. P., & PACKARD, F. A. *A second
appeal to the people of Pennsylvania on
the subject of an asylum for the insane
poor of the commonwealth*. Philadelphia:
Waldie, 1841.

DAHLSTROM, W. G., & WELSH, G. S. *An
MMPI handbook: A guide to use in
clinical practice and research*. Minneapolis: Univer. Minnesota Press, 1960.

FOA, U. G. Convergences in the analysis of
the structure of interpersonal behavior.
*Psychol. Rev.*, 1961, 68, 341–353.

GOLDMAN-EISLER, FRIEDA. Breastfeeding
and character formation. In C. Kluck-
hohn & H. A. Murray (Eds.), *Personality
in nature, society, and culture*. (2nd ed.)
New York: Knopf, 1953. Pp. 146–184.

GOTTLIEB, ANN L., & PARSONS, O. A. A.
coaction compass evaluation of Rorschach
determinants in brain damaged individuals. *J. consult. Psychol.*, 1960, 24, 54–
60.

GREENBLATT, M., YORK, R. H., & BROWN,
ESTHER L. *From custodial to therapeutic*

care in mental hospitals. New York: Russell Sage Foundation, 1955.

HARMS, E. The early historians of psychiatry. *Amer. J. Psychiat.*, 1957, 113, 749–
752. (a)

HARMS, E. Historical considerations in the
science of psychiatry. *Dis. nerv. Sys.*,
1957, 18, 397–400. (b)

HARMS, E. Modern psychotherapy—150
years ago. *J. ment. Sci.*, 1957, 103, 804–
809. (c)

JACKSON, D. N., & MESSICK, S. Acquiescence
and desirability as response determinants
on the MMPI. *Educ. psychol. Measmt.*,
1961, 21, 771–790.

JOINT COMMISSION ON MENTAL ILLNESS
AND HEALTH. *Action for mental health*.
New York: Basic Books, 1961.

LEARY, T. *Multilevel measurement of interpersonal behavior*. Berkeley, Calif.:
Psychological Consultation Service, 1956.

LEARY, T. *Interpersonal diagnosis of personality*. New York: Ronald Press, 1957.

LODGE, G. T., & GIBSON, R. L. A coaction
map of the personalities described by
H. Rorschach and S. J. Beck. *J. proj.
Tech.*, 1953, 17, 482–488.

REES, T. P. Back to moral treatment and
community care. *J. ment. Sci.*, 1957, 103,
303–313.

ROBACK, A. A. *History of psychology and
psychiatry*. New York: Citadel Press,
1961.

SZASZ, T. S. The myth of mental illness.
*Amer. Psychologist*, 1960, 15, 113–118.

SZASZ, T. S. *The myth of mental illness*.
New York: Hoeber-Harper, 1961.

WELSH, G. S. Factor dimensions A and R.
In G. S. Welsh & W. G. Dahlstrom
(Eds.), *Basic readings on the MMPI in
psychology and medicine*. Minneapolis:
Univer. Minnesota Press, 1956. Pp. 264–
281.

ZILBOORG, G. *A history of medical psychology*. New York: Norton, 1941.

# Chapter 2

# Problems in the Diagnosis
# of Abnormal Behavior

*Although some highly humanistic psychologists completely eschew the need for diagnosis, most clinicians agree that the diagnostic procedure is a critical first step in the understanding and treatment of abnormal behavior. However, a number of issues have been raised, both about the diagnostic categories that have been employed and about the system by which we arrive at diagnoses. The papers in this section deal with one or both of these issues. In some cases the standard approaches are subjected to critical scrutiny, and in other cases alternative approaches are suggested.*

**Edward Zigler**
**and Leslie Phillips**

## Psychiatric Diagnosis: A Critique

*Psychiatric diagnosis is an attempt to classify individuals into categories, based on similarities in their problems. The similarities can be of symptoms or of causes, but the aim of the system of categorization is to impose some order on a highly complicated mass of data. For a number of reasons indicated in this paper, some psychologists have begun to question the utility of diagnosis. Zigler and Phillips begin by defending the process of diagnosis as a scientific enterprise of value in describing basic phenomena. They weigh a number of arguments against psychiatric diagnosis, accepting some as valid and rejecting others as inappropriate, and conclude that diagnosis, if it is based on descriptive principles, can be of great merit. They emphasize the need to find reliable behavioral correlates of each of the categories employed, and reject diagnosis based on causation in favor of a system based on description.*

The inadequacies of conventional psychiatric diagnosis have frequently been noted (4, 10, 13, 18, 21, 23, 30, 34, 36, 42, 43, 45, 49, 52, 54, 55, 58, 62, 71, 72). The responses to this rather imposing body of criticism have ranged from the position that the present classificatory system is in need of further refinement (11, 18), through steps towards major revisions (10, 13, 36, 49, 62, 72), to a plea for the abolishment of all "labeling" (43, 45,

*Reprinted from the* Journal of Abnormal & Social Psychology, *63(1961), 607–618, with the permission of the American Psychological Association and Dr. Zigler. Copyright 1961 by the American Psychological Association.*

54). As other investigators have noted (11, 30), this last position suggests that the classificatory enterprise is value-less. This reaction against classification has gained considerable popularity in clinical circles. The alacrity with which many clinicians have accepted this view seems to represent more than a disillu-sionment with the specific current form of psychiatric diagnosis. These negative attitudes appear to reflect a belief that diagnostic classification is inherently antithetical to such clinically favored concepts as "dynamic," "idiographic," etc. Thus, a question is raised as to whether any diagnostic schema can be of value. Let us initially direct our attention to this question.

## ON CLASSIFICATION

The growth among clinicians of sen-timent against categorization has coin-cided with a period of critical reap-praisal within the behavioral sciences generally (5, 8, 12, 19, 20, 35, 37, 39, 50, 51, 57, 63, 64). This parallel de-velopment is more than coincidental. The reaction against "labeling" can be viewed as an extreme outgrowth of this critical self-evaluation, i.e., that psy-chology's conceptual schemata are arti-ficial in their construction, sterile in terms of their practical predictions, and lead only to greater and greater pre-cision about matters which are more and more irrelevant. It is little wonder that in this atmosphere, conceptualiza-tion has itself become suspect nor that Maslow's (41) exposition of the pos-sible dangers of labeling or naming has been extended (55) as a blanket in-dictment of the categorizing process.

The error in this extension is the fail-ure to realize that what has been criti-cized is not the conceptual process but only certain of its products. The criti-cisms mentioned above have not been in favor of the abolishment of con-ceptualization, but have rather been directed at the prematurity and rari-fications of many of our conceptual schemata and our slavish adherence to them. Indeed, many of these criticisms have been accompanied by pleas for lower-order conceptualization based more firmly on observational data (35, 37, 63).

In the clinical area, the sentiment against classification has become suffi-ciently serious that several investigators (10, 11, 13, 30) have felt the need to champion the merits of psychiatric cate-gorization. They have pointed out that diagnosis is a basic scientific classifica-tory enterprise to be viewed as essen-tially the practice of taxonomy, which is characteristic of all science. Eysenck (13) puts the matter quite succinctly in his statement, "Measurement is es-sential to science, but before we can measure, we must know what it is we want to measure. Qualitative or taxo-nomic discovery must precede quanti-tative measurement" (p. 34).

Reduced to its essentials, diagnostic classification involves the establishment of categories to which phenomena can be ordered. The number of class systems that potentially may be constructed is limited only by man's ability to abstract from his experience. The principles em-ployed to construct such classes may be inductive, deductive, or a combination of both, and may vary on a continuum from the closely descriptive to the highly abstract.

Related to the nature of the classifi-catory principle are the implications to be derived from class membership. Class membership may involve nothing more than descriptive compartmentalization, its only utility being greater ease in the handling of data. Obversely, the attri-butes or correlates of class membership may be widespread and far-reaching in their consequences. The originators of a classificatory schema may assert that specified behavioral correlates accompany class membership. This assertion is open to test. If the hypothesized correlates represent the full heuristic value of the diagnostic schema and class membership is found not to be related to these correlates, then revision or discard is in order. A somewhat different type of problem may also arise. With the passage of time, correlates not originally related to the schema may erroneously be attributed to class membership. Nevertheless, the original taxonomy may still possess a degree of relevance to current objectives in a discipline. In these circumstances, its maintenance may be the rational choice, although a clarification and purification of categories is called for. The relationship of the two problems outlined here to the criticism of contemporary psychiatric diagnosis will be discussed later. What should be noted at this point is that the solution to neither problem implies the abolishment of the attempt at classification.

Another aspect of taxonomy is in need of clarification. When a phenomenon is assigned to a class, certain individual characteristics of that phenomenon are forever lost. No two class members are completely identical. Indeed, a single class member may be viewed as continuously differing from itself over time. It is this loss of uniqueness and an implied unconcern with process that have led many clinicians to reject classification in principle. While classificatory schemata inevitably involve losses of this type, it must be noted that they potentially offer a more than compensatory gain. This gain is represented in the significance of the class attributes and correlates. Class membership conveys information ranging from the descriptive similarity of two phenomena to a knowledge of the common operative processes underlying the phenomena.

A conceptual system minimizes the aforementioned loss to the extent that only irrelevant aspects of a phenomenon are deleted in the classificatory process. The implicit assumption is made that what is not class relevant is inconsequential. The dilemma, of course, lies in our lacking divine revelation as to what constitutes inconsequentiality. It is this issue which lies at the heart of the idiographic versus nomothetic controversy (1, 2, 6, 15, 16, 25, 26, 60, 61). The supporters of the idiographic position (1, 6) have criticized certain conceptual schemata for treating idiosyncratic aspects of behavior as inconsequential when they are in fact pertinent data which must be utilized if a comprehensive and adequate view of human behavior is to emerge. However, the idiographic position is not a movement toward the abolishment of classification, a fact emphasized by Allport (1) and Falk (16). Rather, it represents a plea for broader and more meaningful classificatory schemata.

A conceptually different type of argument against the use of any diagnostic classification has been made by the adherents of nondirective psychotherapy (46, 53, 54). This position has advanced the specific contention that differential diagnosis is unnecessary for, and perhaps detrimental to, successful psychotherapy. This attitude of the nondirectivists has been interpreted (62) as an attack on the entire classificatory enterprise. To argue against diagnosis on the grounds that it affects therapeutic outcome is to confuse diagnosis as an act of scientific classification with the present clinical practice of diagnosis with its use of interviewing, psychological testing, etc. The error here lies in turning one's attention away from diagnosis as an act of classification, a basic scientific enterprise, and attending instead to the immediate and prognostic consequences of some specific diagnostic technique in a specific therapeutic situation, i.e., an applied aspect. To reject the former on the basis of the latter would appear to be an unsound decision.

Although the nondirectivists' opposition to diagnosis seems to be based on a confusion between the basic and applied aspects of classification, implicitly contained within their position is a more fundamental argument against the classificatory effort. Undoubtedly, diagnosis both articulates and restricts the range of assumptions which may be entertained about a client. However, the philosophy of the nondirectivist forces him to reject any theoretical position which violates a belief in the unlimited psychological growth of the client. It would appear that this position represents the rejection, in principle, of the view that any individual can be like another in his essential characteristics, or that any predictable relationship can be established between a client's current level of functioning and the ends which may be achieved. In the setting of this assumption, a transindividual classificatory schema is inappropriate. There is no appeal from such a judgment, but one should be cognizant that it rejects the essence of a scientific discipline. If one insists on operating within the context of a predictive psychology, one argues for the necessity of a classificatory system, even though particular diagnostic schemata may be rejected as irrelevant, futile, or obscure.

Let us now direct our discussion toward some of the specific criticisms of conventional psychiatric diagnosis— that the categories employed lack homogeneity, reliability, and validity.

## HOMOGENEITY

A criticism often leveled against the contemporary diagnostic system is that its categories encompass heterogeneous groups of individuals, i.e., individuals varying in respect to symptomatology,

test scores, prognosis, etc. (34, 55, 67, 68, 71). Contrary to the view of one investigator (55), a lack of homogeneity does not necessarily imply a lack of reliability. King (34) has clearly noted the distinction between these two concepts. Reliability refers to the agreement in assigning individuals to different diagnostic categories, whereas homogeneity refers to the diversity of behavior subsumed within categories. While the two concepts may be related, it is not difficult to conceptualize categories which, though quite reliable, subsume diverse phenomena.

King (34) has argued in favor of constructing a new diagnostic classification having more restrictive and homogeneous categories. He supports his argument by noting his own findings and those of Kantor, Wallner, and Winder (31), which have indicated that within the schizophrenic group subcategories may be formed which differ in test performance. King found further support for the construction of new and more homogeneous diagnostic categories in a study by Windle and Hamwi (65). This study indicated that two subgroups could be constructed within a psychotic population which was composed of patients with diverse psychiatric diagnoses. Though matched on the distribution of these diagnostic types, the subgroups differed in the relationship obtained between test performance and prognosis. On the basis of these studies, King suggests that the type of homogeneous categories he would favor involves such classificatory dichotomies as reactive versus process schizophrenics and chronic versus nonchronic psychotics.

An analysis of King's (34) criticism of the present diagnostic system discloses certain difficulties. The first is that King's heterogeneity criticism does not fully take into consideration certain basic aspects of classification. A common feature of classificatory systems is that they utilize classes which contain subclasses. An example drawn from biology would be a genus embracing a number of species. If schizophrenia is conceptualized as a genus, it cannot be criticized on the grounds that all its members do not share a particular attribute. Such a criticism would involve a confusion between the more specific attributes of the species and the more general attributes of the genus. This is not to assert that schizophrenia does in fact possess the characteristics of a genus. It is, of course, possible that a careful analysis will reveal that it does not, and the class schizophrenia will have to be replaced by an aggregate of entities which does constitute a legitimate genus. However, when a genus is formulated, it cannot be attacked because of its heterogeneous nature since genera are characterized by such heterogeneity.

A more serious difficulty with King's (34) heterogeneity criticism lies in the inherent ambiguity of a homogeneity-heterogeneity parameter. To criticize a classificatory system because its categories subsume heterogeneous phenomena is to make the error of assuming that homogeneity is a quality which inheres in phenomena when in actuality it is a construction of the observer or classifier. In order to make this point clear, let us return to King's argument. What does it mean to assert that chronic psychosis is an example of an homogeneous class, while schizophrenia is an example of an heterogeneous one? In terms of the descriptively diverse phenomena encompassed, the latter would appear to have the greater homogeneity. The statement only has meaning insofar as a particular correlate—for instance, the relationship of test score to prognosis—is shared by all members of one class but not so shared by the members of the other class. Thus, the meaningfulness of the ho-

mogeneity concept is ultimately dependent on the correlates or attributes of class membership or to the classificatory principle related to these correlates or attributes. The intimacy of the relationship between the attributes of classes and the classificatory principle can best be exemplified by the extreme case in which a class has but a single attribute, and that attribute is defined by the classificatory principle, e.g., the classification of plants on the basis of the number of stamens they possess. Therefore, the heterogeneity criticism of a classificatory system is nothing more than a plea for the utilization of a new classificatory principle so that attention may be focused on particular class correlates or attributes not considered in the original schema. While this plea may be a justifiable one, depending on the significance of the new attributes, it has little to do with the homogeneity, in an absolute sense, of phenomena. Indeed, following the formulation of a new classificatory schema, the heterogeneity criticism could well be leveled against it by the adherents of the old system, since the phenomena encompassed by the new categories would probably not be considered homogeneous when evaluated by the older classificatory principle.

Although differing in its formulation, the heterogeneity criticism of present psychiatric classification made by Wittenborn and his colleagues (67, 68, 71) suffers from the same difficulties as does King's (34) criticism. Wittenborn's findings indicated that individuals given a common diagnosis showed differences in their symptom cluster score profiles based on nine symptom clusters isolated earlier by means of factor analytic techniques (66, 69). It is upon the existence of these different profiles within a diagnostic category that Wittenborn bases his heterogeneity criticism. Here again the homogeneity-heterogeneity distinction is only meaningful in terms of an independent criterion, a particular symptom cluster score profile. Had it been discovered that all individuals placed into a particular diagnostic category shared a common symptom cluster score profile, then this category would be described as subsuming homogeneous phenomena. But the phenomena—the symptoms mirrored by the symptom profile—are not homogeneous in any absolute sense because the pattern of symptoms may involve the symptoms in descriptively diverse symptom clusters. Thus, the homogeneity ascribed to the category would refer only to the fact that individuals within the category homogeneously exhibited a particular pattern of descriptively diverse behaviors. However, the organization of symptoms mirrored by the symptom cluster profiles is not in any fundamental sense different from that observed in conventional diagnostic syndromes. Both methods of categorization systematize diverse behaviors because of an observed regularity in their concurrent appearance.

The difference between these two approaches, then, lies only in the pattern of deviant behaviors that define the categories. Indeed, Eysenck (14) has noted that both the clinician and the factor analyst derive syndromes in essentially the same manner, i.e., in terms of the observed intercorrelations of various symptoms. It is the difference in method, purely observational versus statistical, that explains why the final symptom structure may differ. The assumption must not be made that the advantage lies entirely with the factor analytic method. The merit accruing through the greater rigor of factor analysis may be outweighed by the limitations imposed in employing a restricted group of symptoms and a particular sample of patients. Thus, the factor analyst cannot claim that the class-de-

fining symptom pattern he has derived is a standard of homogeneity against which classes within another schema can be evaluated. The plea that symptom cluster scores, derived from factor analytic techniques, substitute for the present method of psychiatric classification has little relevance to the heterogeneity issue.

In the light of this discussion we may conclude that the concept of homogeneity has little utility in evaluating classificatory schemata. Since the heterogeneity criticism invariably involves an implicit preference for one classificatory principle over another, it would perhaps be more fruitful to dispense entirely with the homogeneity-heterogeneity distinction, thus, allowing us to direct our attention to the underlying problem of the relative merits of different classificatory principles.

## RELIABILITY AND VALIDITY

A matter of continuing concern has been the degree of reliability of the present diagnostic system. Considerable energy has been expended by both those who criticize the present system for its lack of reliability (4, 7, 13, 42, 52, 55, 58) and those who defend it against this criticism (18, 29, 56, 59). Certain investigators (18, 56) who have offered evidence that the present system is reliable have also pointed out that the earlier studies emphasizing the unreliability of psychiatric diagnosis have suffered from serious conceptual and methodological difficulties.

In evaluating the body of studies concerned with the reliability of psychiatric diagnosis, one must conclude that so long as diagnosis is confined to broad diagnostic categories, it is reasonably reliable, but the reliability diminishes as one proceeds from broad, inclusive class categories to narrower, more specific ones. As finer discriminations are called for, accuracy in diagnosis becomes increasingly difficult. Since this latter characteristic appears to be common to the classificatory efforts in many areas of knowledge, it would appear to be inappropriate to criticize psychiatric diagnosis on the grounds that it is less than perfectly reliable. This should not lead to an underestimation of the importance of reliability. While certain extraclassificatory factors, e.g., proficiency of the clinicians, biases of the particular clinical settings, etc., may influence it, reliability is primarily related to the precision with which classes of a schema are defined. Since the defining characteristic of most classes in psychiatric diagnosis is the occurrence of symptoms in particular combinations, the reliability of the system mirrors the specificity with which the various combinations of symptoms (syndromes) have been spelled out. It is mandatory for a classificatory schema to be reliable since reliability refers to the definiteness with which phenomena can be ordered to classes. If a system does not allow for such a division of phenomena, it can make no pretense of being a classificatory schema.

While reliability is a prerequisite if the diagnostic system is to have any value, it must not be assumed that if human effort were to make the present system perfectly reliable, it could escape all the difficulties attributed to it. This perfect reliability would only mean that individuals within each class shared a particular commonality in relation to the classificatory principle of symptom manifestation. If one were interested in attributes unrelated or minimally related to the classificatory principle employed, the perfect reliability of the system would offer little cause for rejoicing. Perfect reliability of the present system can only be the goal of those who are interested in nothing more than the present classificatory principle and the particular attributes of the classes constructed on the basis of this principle.

When attention is shifted from characteristics which define a class to the correlates of class membership, this implies a shift in concern from the reliability of a system to its validity. The distinction between the reliability and validity of a classificatory system would appear to involve certain conceptual difficulties. It is perhaps this conceptual difficulty which explains why the rather imposing body of literature concerned with diagnosis has been virtually silent on the question of the validity of the present system of psychiatric diagnosis. Only one group of investigators (25, 27, 28, 29, 73) has specifically been concerned with the predictive efficacy of diagnoses and, thus, to the validity of psychiatric classifications; and even in this work, the distinction between validity and reliability is not clearly drawn.

In order to grasp the distinction between the reliability and the validity of a classificatory schema, one must differentiate the defining characteristics of the classes from the correlates of the classes. In the former case, we are interested in the principles upon which classes are formed; in the latter, in the predictions or valid statements that can be made about phenomena once they are classified. The difficulty lies in the overlap between the classifying principles and the class correlates. If a classificatory system is reliable, it is also valid to the extent that we can predict that the individuals within a class will exhibit certain characteristics, namely, those behaviors or attributes which serve to define the class.

It is the rare class, however, that does not connote correlates beyond its defining characteristics. The predictions associated with class membership may vary from simple extensions of the clas-

sificatory principles to correlates which
would appear to have little connection
with these principles. Let us examine
a simple illustration and see what follows from categorizing an individual.
Once an individual has been classified
as manifesting a manic-depressive reaction, depressed type, on the basis of the
symptoms of depression of mood, motor
retardation, and stupor (3), the prediction may be made that the individual
will spend a great deal of time in bed,
which represents an obvious extension
of the symptom pattern. One may also
hypothesize that the patient will show
improvement if electroshock therapy is
employed. This is a correlate which has
little direct connection with the symptoms themselves. These predictions are
open to test, and evidence may or may
not be found to support them. Thus,
measures of validity may be obtained
which are independent of the reliability
of the system of classification.

The problem of validity lies at the
heart of the confusion which surrounds
psychiatric diagnosis. When the present
diagnostic schema is assailed, the common complaint is that class membership
conveys little information beyond the
gross symptomatology of the patient
and contributes little to the solution of
the pressing problems of etiology, treatment procedures, prognosis, etc. The
criticism that class membership does not
predict these important aspects of a
disorder appears to be a legitimate one.
This does not mean the present system
has no validity. It simply indicates that
the system may be valid in respect to
certain correlates but invalid in respect
to others. Much confusion would be
dispelled if as much care were taken
in noting the existing correlates of
classes as is taken in noting the classificatory principles. A great deal of effort
has gone into the formalization of the
defining characteristics of classes (3),
but one looks in vain for a formal de-

lineation of the extraclassificatory attributes and correlates of class membership. As a result, the various diagnostic
categories have been burdened with
correlates not systematically derived
from a classificatory principle but which
were attributed to the classes because
they were the focal points of clinical
interest. A major question is just what
correlates can justifiably be attributed to
the class categories. To answer this
question we must turn our attention to
the purposes and philosophy underlying contemporary psychiatric diagnosis.

## PHILOSOPHY AND
## PURPOSE OF
## CONVENTIONAL DIAGNOSIS

The validity of the conventional diagnostic system is least ambiguous and
most free from potential criticism as
a descriptive schema, a taxonomy of
mental disorders analogous to the work
of Ray and Linnaeus in biology. In this
sense, class membership confirms that
the inclusion of an individual within a
class guarantees only that he exhibit
the defining characteristics of that class.
Only a modest extension of this system,
in terms of a very limited number of
well established correlates, makes for a
system of impressive heuristic value,
even though it falls considerably short
of what would now be considered an
optimal classificatory schema. As has
been noted (11, 29), the present diagnostic system is quite useful when
evaluated in terms of its administrative and, to a lesser extent, its preventive implications. Caveny et al. (11)
and Wittenborn, Holzberg, and Simon
(70) should be consulted for a comprehensive list of such uses, but examples would include legal determination
of insanity, declaration of incompetence, type of ward required for custodial care, census figures and statistical
data upon which considerable planning

is based, screening devices for the military services or other agencies, etc. In view of the extensive criticism of contemporary diagnosis, the surprising fact is not that so few valid predictions can be derived from class membership, but that so many can.

The value of the present psychiatric classification system would be further enhanced by its explicit divorcement from its Kraepelinian heritage by an emphasis on its descriptive aspect and, through careful empirical investigation, the cataloging of the reliable correlates of its categories. That this catalog of correlates would be an impressive one is expressed in Hoch's (22) view that the present system is superior to any system which has been evolved to replace it. It is an open question whether the system merits this amount of praise. In general, however, the defense of the present system—or, for that matter, diagnosis in general (11, 13, 29, 30) —tends to rest on the merits of its descriptive, empirical, and nondynamic aspects.

The present classificatory system, even as a purely descriptive device, is still open to a certain degree of criticism. Its classificatory principle is organized primarily about symptom manifestation. This would be adequate for a descriptive system if this principle were consistently applied to all classes of the schema and if the symptoms associated with each diagnostic category were clearly specified. There is some question, however, whether the system meets these requirements (49, 55). The criticism has been advanced that the present system is based on a number of diverse principles of classification. Most classes are indeed defined by symptom manifestation, but the organic disorders, for example, tend to be identified by etiology, while such other factors as prognosis, social conformity, etc. are also employed as classificatory prin-

ciples. This does not appear, however, to be an insurmountable problem, for the system could be made a completely consistent one by explicitly defining each category by the symptoms encompassed. The system would appear to be eminently amenable to the unitary application of this descriptive classificatory principle, for there are actually few cases where classes are not so defined. Where reliable relations between the present categories and etiology and prognosis have been established, these also could be incorporated explicitly within the system. Etiology and prognosis would be treated not as inherent attributes of the various classifications, but rather as correlates of the particular classes to which their relationship is known. They would, thus, not be confounded with the classificatory principle of the system.

This course of action would satisfy the requirement of consistency in the application of the classificatory principle. A remaining area of ambiguity would be the lack of agreement in what constitutes a symptom. In physical medicine, a clear distinction has been made between a symptom, which is defined as a subjectively experienced abnormality, and a sign, which is considered an objective indication of abnormality (24). This differentiation has not, however, been extended to the sphere of mental disorders. A source of difficulty may lie in the definition of what is psychologically abnormal. In psychiatric terminology, symptoms include a wide range of phenomena from the grossest type of behavior deviation, through the complaints of the patient, to events almost completely inferential in nature. One suggestion (74) has been to eliminate the term "symptom" and direct attention to the manifest responses of the individual. This suggestion appears to be embodied in the work of Wittenborn and his colleagues

(66, 67, 68, 69, 70, 71). Wittenborn's diagnostic system, in which symptoms are defined as currently discernible behaviors, represents a standard of clarity for purely descriptive systems of psychiatric classification. This clarity was achieved by clearly noting and limiting the group of behaviors which would be employed in the system. But even here a certain amount of ambiguity remains. The number of responses or discernible behaviors which may be considered for inclusion within a diagnostic schema borders on the infinite. The question arises, then, as to how one goes about the selection of those behaviors to be incorporated in the classificatory system. Parsimony demands that only "meaningful" items of behavior be chosen for inclusion, and this selective principle has certainly been at work in the construction of all systems of diagnosis. In this sense, the present method of psychiatric classification is not a purely descriptive one, nor can any classification schema truly meet this criterion of purity. Meaning and utility inevitably appear among the determinants of classificatory systems.

Several investigators (9, 30, 38) have stressed the inappropriateness of discussing diagnosis in the abstract, pointing out that such a discussion should center around the question of "diagnosis for what?" Indeed, a diagnostic system cannot be described as "true" or "false," but only as being useful or not useful in attaining prescribed goals. Therefore, when a system is devised, its purposes should be explicitly stated so that the system can be evaluated in terms of its success or failure in attaining these objectives. Furthermore, these goals should be kept explicit throughout the period during which the system is being employed. The present diagnostic schema has not met this requirement. Instead, its goals have been carried along in

an implicit manner and have been allowed to become vague. The result has been that some see the purpose of the schema as being an adequate description of mental disorders (29), others view it as being concerned with prognosis (22), and still others view the schemata goal as the discovery of etiology (9).

Typically, the present schema has been conceptualized as descriptive in nature, but a brief glance at its history indicates that the original purposes and goals in the construction of this schema went far beyond the desire for a descriptive taxonomy. As Zilboorg and Henry (76) clearly note, Kraepelin not only studied the individual while hospitalized, but also the patient's premorbid history and post-hospital course. His hope was to make our understanding of all mental disorders as precise as our knowledge of the course of general paresis. He insisted on the classification of mental disorders according to regularities in symptoms and course of illness, believing this would lead to a clearer discrimination among the different disease entities. He hoped for the subsequent discovery of a specific somatic malfunction responsible for each disease. For Kraepelin, then, classification was related to etiology, treatment, and prognosis. Had the system worked as envisaged, these variables would have become the extra-classificatory attributes of the schema. When matched against this aspiration, the present system must be considered a failure since the common complaint against it is that a diagnostic label tells us very little about etiology, treatment, or prognosis (44). However, it would be erroneous to conclude that the present system is valueless because its classes are only minimally related to etiology and prognosis.

What should be noted is that etiology and prognosis, though important, are but two of a multitude of variables of interest. The importance of these variables should not obscure the fact that their relationship to a classificatory system is exactly the same as that of any other variables. This relationship may take one of two forms. Etiology and prognosis may be the correlates of the classes of a diagnostic system which employs an independent classificatory principle like symptom manifestation. Optimally, we should prefer a classificatory schema in which the indices of etiology and preferred modes of treatment would be incorporated (29, 47). In essence, this was Kraepelin's approach, and it continues to underlie some promising work in the area of psychopathology. Although Kraepelin's disease concept is in disrepute (23, 40, 55), it is the opinion of several investigators (14, 49, 70) that further work employing the descriptive symptomatic approach could well lead to a greater understanding of the etiology underlying abnormal "processes."

Another manner in which etiology, treatment, or prognosis could be related to a classificatory schema is by utilizing each of these variables as the classificatory principle for a new diagnostic system. For instance, we might organize patients into groups which respond differentially to particular forms of treatment like electroshock, drugs, psychotherapy, etc. The new schemata which might be proposed could be of considerable value in respect to certain goals but useless in regard to others: Since we do not possess a diagnostic system based on all the variables of clinical interest, we might have to be satisfied with the construction of a variety of diagnostic systems, each based on a different principle of classification. These classificatory techniques would exist side by side, their use being determined by the specific objectives of the diagnostician.

## ETIOLOGY VERSUS DESCRIPTION IN DIAGNOSIS

The classical Kraepelinian classification schema shows two major characteristics: a commitment to a detailed description of the manifest symptomatic behaviors of the individual and an underlying assumption that such a descriptive classification would be transitory, eventually leading to and being replaced by a system whose classificatory principle was the etiology of the various mental disorders. Major criticism of this classificatory effort has been directed at the first of these. The reservations are that, in practice, such a descriptive effort allows no place for a process interpretation of psychopathology and that it has not encouraged the development of prevention and treatment programs in the mental disorders.

The authors do not feel that the failure of the Kraepelinian system has demonstrated the futility of employing symptoms as the basis for classification. It does suggest that if one approaches the problem of description with an assumption as to the necessary correlates of such descriptions, then the diagnostic system may well be in error. Kraepelin's empiricism is contaminated in just this way. For example, he refused to accept as cases of dementia praecox those individuals who recovered from the disorder, since he assumed irreversibility as a necessary concomitant of its hypothesized neurophysiological base. Bleuler, on the other hand, who was much less committed to any particular form of causality in this illness, readily recognized the possibility of its favorable outcome. It is not, then, the descriptive approach itself which is open to criticism, but description contaminated by preconception. An unfettered description of those schizophrenics with good prognosis in contrast to those with poor prognosis reveals clear differences in the symptom configuration between these kinds of patients (17, 48).

Kraepelin's basic concern with the problem of etiology has remained a focus of efforts in the clinical area. Although his postulate of central nervous system disease as the basis of mental disorder is in disrepute, and his systematic classificatory efforts are assailed, one nevertheless finds a striking congruence between Kraepelin's preconceptions and certain current attempts at the solution of the problem of psychopathology. There is an unwavering belief that some simple categorical system will quickly solve the mysteries of etiology. The exponents of these newer classificatory schemata have merely replaced symptoms by other phenomena like test scores (34), particular patterns of interpersonal relations (36), etc. It is the authors' conviction that these new efforts to find short-cut solutions to the question of etiology will similarly remain unsuccessful. The amount of descriptive effort required before etiological factors are likely to be discovered has been underestimated (32, 33), and the pursuit of etiology should represent an end point rather than a beginning for classificatory systems. The process of moving from an empirical orientation to an etiological one is, of necessity, inferential and therefore susceptible to the myriad dangers of premature inference. We propose that the greatest safeguard against such prematurity is not to be found in the scrapping of an empirical descriptive approach, but in an accelerated program of empirical research. What is needed at this time is a systematic, empirical attack on the problem of mental disorders. Inherent in this program is the employment of symptoms, broadly defined as meaningful and discernible behaviors, as the basis of a classificatory

system. Rather than an abstract search for etiologies, it would appear more currently fruitful to investigate such empirical correlates of symptomatology as reactions to specific forms of treatment, outcome in the disorders, case history phenomena, etc.

The pervasive concern with etiology may derive from a belief that if this were known, prevention would shortly be forthcoming, thus, making the present complex problems of treatment and prognosis inconsequential. Unfortunately, efforts to short-circuit the drudgery involved in establishing an empirically founded psychiatry has not resulted in any major breakthroughs. Etiology is typically the last characteristic of a disorder to be discovered. Consequently, we would suggest the search for etiology be put aside and attempted only when a greater number of the correlates of symptomatic behaviors have been established.

The authors are impressed by the amount of energy that has been expended in both attacking and defending various contemporary systems of classification. We believe that a classificatory system should include any behavior or phenomenon that appears promising in terms of its significant correlates. At this stage of our investigations, the system employed should be an open and expanding one, not one which is closed and defended on conceptual grounds. Systems of classification must be treated as tools for further discovery, not as bases for polemic disputation.

As stated above, it is possible that a number of systems of classification may be needed to encompass the behaviors presently of clinical interest. It may appear that the espousal of this position, in conjunction with a plea for empirical exploration of the correlates of these behaviors, runs headlong into a desire for conceptual neatness and parsimony. It may be feared that the use of a number of classificatory systems concurrently, each with its own correlates, may lead to the creation of a gigantic actuarial table of unrelated elements. However, the authors do not feel that such a fear is well founded because it assumes that the correlates of these systems have no eventual relation one to the other.

We believe that this latter view is unnecessarily pessimistic. While in principle a multiplicity of classificatory systems might be called for, results from the authors' own research program suggests that a single, relatively restricted and coherent classification system can be derived from an empirical study of the correlates of symptomatic behaviors (49, 75). Such a system might serve a number of psychiatrically significant functions, including the optimum selection of patients for specific treatment programs and the prediction of treatment outcomes. In conclusion, a descriptive classificatory system appears far from dead, and if properly employed, it can lead to a fuller as well as a more conceptually based understanding of the psychopathologies.

## REFERENCES

1. ALLPORT, G. *Personality: A psychological interpretation.* New York: Holt, 1937.

2. ——— Personalistic psychology as science: A reply. *Psychol. Rev.*, 53(1946), 132–135.

3. AMERICAN PSYCHIATRIC ASSOCIATION, Mental Hospital Service, Committee on Nomenclature and Statistics of the American Psychiatric Association. *Diagnostic and statistical manual: Mental disorders.* Washington, D.C.: APA, 1952.

4. ASH, P. The reliability of psychiatric diagnosis. *J. Abnorm. Soc. Psychol.*, 44(1949), 272–277.

5. BEACH, F. The snark was a boojum. *Amer. Psychologist*, 5(1950), 115–124.

6. BECK, S. The science of personality: Nomothetic or idiographic? *Psychol. Rev.*, 60(1953), 353–359.

7. BOISEN, A. Types of dementia praecox: A study in psychiatric classification. *Psychiatry*, 1(1938), 233–236.

8. BROWER, D. The problem of quantification in psychological science. *Psychol. Rev.*, 56(1949), 325–333.

9. CAMERON, D. A theory of diagnosis. *In* P. Hoch & J. Zubin, eds. *Current problems in psychiatric diagnosis.* New York: Grune & Stratton, 1953. Pages 33–45.

10. CATTELL, R. *Personality and motivation structure and measurement.* New York: World Book, 1957.

11. CAVENY, E., WITTSON, C., HUNT, W., and HERMAN, R. Psychiatric diagnosis, its nature and function. *J. Nerv. Ment. Dis.*, 121(1955), 367–380.

12. CRONBACH, L. The two disciplines of scientific psychology. *Amer. Psychologist*, 12(1957), 671–684.

13. EYSENCK, H. *The scientific study of personality.* London: Routledge & Kegan Paul, 1952.

14. ——— The logical basis of factor analysis. *Amer. Psychologist*, 8(1953), 105–113.

15. ——— The science of personality: Nomothetic. *Psychol. Rev.*, 61(1954), 339–341.

16. FALK, J. Issues distinguishing idiographic from nomothetic approaches to personality theory. *Psychol. Rev.*, 63 (1956), 53–62.

17. FARINA, A., and WEBB, W. Premorbid adjustment and subsequent discharge. *J. Nerv. Ment. Dis.*, 124(1956), 612–613.

18. FOULDS, G. The reliability of psychiatric, and the validity of psychological diagnosis. *J. Ment. Sci.*, 101(1955), 851–862.

19. GUTHRIE, E. The status of systematic psychology. *Amer. Psychologist*, 5 (1950), 97–101.

20. HARLOW, H. Mice, monkeys, men, and motives. *Psychol. Rev.*, 60(1953), 23–32.

21. HARROWER, MOLLY, ed. *Diagnostic psy-*

*chological testing.* Springfield, Ill.: Charles C. Thomas, 1950.

22. HOCH, P. Discussion. *In* P. Hoch & J. Zubin, eds. *Current problems in psychiatric diagnosis.* New York: Grune & Stratton, 1953. Pages 46–50.

23. ———, and ZUBIN, J., eds. *Current problems in psychiatric diagnosis.* New York: Grune & Stratton, 1953.

24. HOLMES, G. *Introduction to clinical neurology.* Edinburgh: Livingstone, 1946.

25. HUNT, W. Clinical psychology—science or superstitution. *Amer. Psychologist,* 6(1951), 683–687. (a)

26. ——— An investigation of naval neuropsychiatric screening procedures. *In* H. Gruetskaw, ed. *Groups, leadership, and men.* Pittsburgh, Pa.: Carnegie Press, 1951. Pages 245–256. (b)

27. ———, WITTSON, C., and BARTON, H. A further validation of naval neuropsychiatric screening. *J. Consult. Psychol.,* 14(1950), 485–488. (a)

28. ——— A validation study of naval neuropsychiatric screening. *J. Consult. Psychol.,* 14(1950), 35–39. (b)

29. ———, WITTSON, C., and HUNT, E. A theoretical and practical analysis of the diagnostic process. *In* P. Hoch & J. Zubin, eds. *Current problems in psychiatric diagnosis.* New York: Grune & Stratton, 1953. Pages 53–65.

30. JELLINEK, E. Some principles of psychiatric classification. *Psychiatry,* 2 (1939), 161–165.

31. KANTOR, R., WALLNER, J., and WINDER, C. Process and reactive schizophrenia. *J. Consult. Psychol.,* 17 (1953), 157–162.

32. KETY, S. Biochemical theories of schizophrenia. Part I. *Science,* 129(1959), 1528–1532. (a)

33. ——— Biochemical theories of schizophrenia. Part II. *Science,* 129(1959), 1590–1596. (b)

34. KING, G. Research with neuropsychiatric samples. *J. Psychol.,* 38(1954), 383–387.

35. KOCH, S. The current status of motivational psychology. *Psychol. Rev.,* 58 (1951), 147–154.

36. LEARY, T., and COFFEY, H. Interpersonal diagnosis: Some problems of methodology and validation. *J. Abnorm. Soc. Psychol.,* 50(1955), 110–126.

37. MACKINNON, D. Fact and fancy in personality research. *Amer. Psychologist,* 8(1953), 138–146.

38. MAGARET, ANN. Clinical methods: Psychodiagnostics. *Annu. Rev. Psychol.,* 3(1952), 283–320.

39. MARQUIS, D. Research planning at the frontiers of science. *Amer. Psychologist,* 3(1948), 430–438.

40. MARZOFF, S. S. The disease concept in psychology. *Psychol. Rev.,* 54(1947), 211–221.

41. MASLOW, A. Cognition of the particular and of the generic. *Psychol. Rev.,* 55(1948), 22–40.

42. MEHLMAN, B. The reliability of psychiatric diagnosis. *J. Abnorm. Soc. Psychol.,* 47(1952), 577–578.

43. MENNINGER, K. The practice of psychiatry. *Dig. Neurol. Psychiat.,* 23 (1955), 101.

44. MILES, H. Discussion. In P. Hoch & J. Zubin, eds. *Current problems in psychiatric diagnosis.* New York: Grune & Stratton, 1953. Pages 107–111.

45. NOYES, A. *Modern clinical psychiatry.* Philadelphia: Saunders, 1953.

46. PATTERSON, C. Is psychotherapy dependent on diagnosis? *Amer. Psychologist,* 3(1948), 155–159.

47. PEPINSKY, H. B. Diagnostic categories in clinical counseling. *Appl. Psychol. Monogr.* (1948), No. 15.

48. PHILLIPS, L. Case history data and prognosis in schizophrenia. *J. Nerv. Ment. Dis.,* 117(1953), 515–525.

49. ———, and RABINOVITCH, M. Social role and patterns of symptomatic behaviors. *J. Abnorm. Soc. Psychol.,* 57 (1958), 181–186.

50. RAPAPORT, D. The future of research in clinical psychology and psychiatry. *Amer. Psychologist,* 2(1947), 167–172.

51. ROBY, T. An opinion on the construction of behavior theory. *Amer. Psychologist,* 14(1959), 129–134.

52. ROE, ANNE. Integration of personality theory and clinical practice. *J. Abnorm. Soc. Psychol.,* 44(1949), 36–41.

53. ROGERS, C. Significant aspects of client-centered therapy. *Amer. Psychologist,* 1(1946), 415–422.

54. ——— *Client-centered therapy.* Boston: Houghton Mifflin, 1951.
55. ROTTER, J. *Social learning and clinical psychology.* New York: Prentice-Hall, 1954.
56. SCHMIDT, H., and FONDA, C. The reliability of psychiatric diagnosis: A new look. *J. Abnorm. Soc. Psychol.,* 52 (1956), 262–267.
57. SCOTT, J. The place of observation in biological and psychological science. *Amer. Psychologist,* 10(1955), 61–63.
58. SCOTT, W. Research definitions of mental health and mental illness. *Psychol. Bull.,* 55(1958), 1–45.
59. SEEMAN, W. Psychiatric diagnosis: An investigation of interperson-reliability after didactic instruction. *J. Nerv. Ment. Dis.,* 118(1953), 541–544.
60. SKAGGS, E. Personalistic psychology as science. *Psychol. Rev.,* 52(1945), 234–238.
61. ——— Ten basic postulates of personalistic psychology. *Psychol. Rev.,* 54 (1947), 255–262.
62. THORNE, F. Back to fundamentals. *J. Clin. Psychol.,* 9(1953), 89–91.
63. TOLMAN, R. Virtue rewarded and vice punished. *Amer. Psychologist,* 8(1953), 721–733.
64. TYLER, LEONA. Toward a workable psychology of individuality. *Amer. Psychologist,* 14(1959), 75–81.
65. WINDLE, C., and HAMWI, V. An exploratory study of the prognostic value of the complex reaction time tests in early and chronic psychotics. *J. Clin. Psychol.,* 9(1953), 156–161.

66. WITTENBORN, J. Symptom patterns in a group of mental hospital patients. *J. Consult. Psychol.,* 15(1951), 290–302.
67. ——— The behavioral symptoms for certain organic psychoses. *J. Consult. Psychol.,* 16(1952), 104–106.
68. ——— and BAILEY, C. The symptoms of involutional psychosis. *J. Consult. Psychol.,* 16(1952), 13–17.
69. ———, and HOLZBERG, J. The generality of psychiatric syndromes. *J. Consult. Psychol.,* 15(1951), 372–380.
70. ———, HOLZBERG, J., and SIMON, B. Symptom correlates for descriptive diagnosis. *Genet. Psychol. Monogr.,* 47 (1953), 237–301.
71. ———, and WEISS, W. Patients diagnosed manic-depressive psychosismanic state. *J. Consult. Psychol.,* 16(1952), 193–198.
72. WHITTMAN, P., and SHELDON, W. A proposed classification of psychotic behavior reactions. *Amer. J. Psychiat.,* 105(1948), 124–128.
73. WITTSON, C., and HUNT, W. The predictive value of the brief psychiatric interview. *Amer. J. Psychiat.,* 107 (1951), 582–585.
74. YATES, A. Symptoms and symptom substitution. *Psychol. Rev.,* 65(1958), 371–374.
75. ZIGLER, E., and PHILLIPS, L. Social effectiveness and symptomatic behaviors. *J. Abnorm. Soc. Psychol.,* 61 (1960), 231–238.
76. ZILBOORG, G., and HENRY, G. W. *History of medical psychology.* New York: Norton, 1941.

Frederick H. Kanfer
and George Saslow

# Behavioral Analysis: An Alternative to Diagnostic Classification

*Kanfer and Saslow agree with Zigler and Phillips in rejecting systems of classification based on the cause or the prognosis of a syndrome. However, they disagree on the basic utility of a broad classification system, and reject a system based on symptoms as having little relationship to therapy and being unreliable. They offer behavioral analysis as an alternative to diagnosis. Behavioral analysis is a technique that grows out of the behavior modification approach to therapy, an approach that emphasizes the applicability of laws of learning to clinical phenomena. It is most strikingly different from traditional diagnosis in that it is an attempt to arrive at a unique diagnostic assessment for each individual, instead of grouping individuals according to common features. It is also remarkably different from traditional approaches in being action oriented instead of descriptive. It is tied in specifically with a treatment plan, and organizes an individual's behavior in such a manner as to clarify antecedent conditions, current behavioral patterns, and areas and techniques of possible therapeutic intervention. On the other hand, this great detail sacrifices the efficiency of a descriptive system, and seems to represent an excellent organizational scheme for a case history instead of a simple act of descriptive classification.*

During the past decade attacks on conventional psychiatric diagnosis have been so widespread that many clinicians now use diagnostic labels sparingly and apologetically. The continued adherence to the nosological terms of the traditional classificatory scheme suggests some utility of the present categorization of behavior disorders, despite its apparently low reliability (1, 21); its limited prognostic value (7, 26); and its multiple feebly related assumption supports. In a recent study of this problem, the symptom patterns of carefully diagnosed paranoid schizophrenics were compared. Katz et al. (12) found considerable divergence among patients with the same diagnosis and concluded that "diagnostic systems which are more circumscribed in their intent, for example, based on manifest behavior alone, rather than systems which attempt to comprehend etiology, symptom patterns and prognosis, may be more directly applicable to current problems in psychiatric research" (p. 202).

We propose here to examine some sources of dissatisfaction with the present approach to diagnosis, to describe a framework for a behavioral analysis of individual patients which implies both suggestions for treatment and outcome criteria for the single case, and to indicate the conditions for collecting the data for such an analysis.

*Reprinted from the* Archives of General Psychiatry, *12(1965), 529–538 with the permission of the American Medical Association and Dr. Kanfer.*

## I. PROBLEMS IN CURRENT DIAGNOSTIC SYSTEMS

Numerous criticisms deal with the internal consistency, the explicitness, the precision, and the reliability of psychiatric classifications. It seems to us that the more important fault lies in our lack of sufficient knowledge to categorize behavior along those pertinent dimensions which permit prediction of responses to social stresses, life crises, or psychiatric treatment. This limitation obviates anything but a crude and tentative approximation to a taxonomy of effective individual behaviors.

Zigler and Phillips (28), in discussing the requirement for an adequate system of classification, suggest that an etiologically-oriented closed system of diagnosis is premature. Instead, they believe that an empirical attack is needed, using "symptoms broadly defined as meaningful and discernible behaviors, as the basis of the classificatory system" (p. 616). But symptoms as a class of responses are defined after all only by their nuisance value to the patient's social environment or to himself as a social being. They are also notoriously unreliable in predicting the patient's particular etiological history or his response to treatment. An alternate approach lies in an attempt to identify classes of dependent variables in human behavior which would allow inferences about the particular controlling factors, the social stimuli, the physiological stimuli, and the reinforcing stimuli, of which they are a function. In the present early stage of the art of psychological prognostication, it appears most reasonable to develop a program of analysis which is closely related to subsequent treatment. A classification scheme which implies a program for behavioral change is one which has not only utility but the potential for experimental validation.

The task of assessment and prognosis can therefore be reduced to efforts which answer the following three questions: (a) which specific behavior patterns require change in their frequency of occurrence, their intensity, their duration or in the conditions under which they occur, (b) what are the best practical means which can produce the desired changes in this individual (manipulation of the environment, of the behavior, or the self-attitudes of the patient), and (c) what factors are currently maintaining it and what are the conditions under which this behavior was acquired. The investigation of the history of the problematic behavior is mainly of academic interest, except as it contributes information about the probable efficacy of a specific treatment method.

### Expectations of Current Diagnostic Systems

In traditional medicine, a diagnostic statement about a patient has often been viewed as an essential prerequisite to treatment because a diagnosis suggests that the physician has some knowledge of the origin and future course of the illness. Further, in medicine diagnosis frequently brings together the accumulated knowledge about the pathological process which leads to the manifestation of the symptoms, and the experiences which others have had in the past in treating patients with such a disease process. Modern medicine recognizes that any particular disease need not have a single cause or even a small number of antecedent conditions. Nevertheless, the diagnostic label attempts to define at least the necessary conditions which are most relevant in considering a treatment pro-

CARNEGIE LIBRARY
LIVINGSTONE COLLEGE
SALISBURY, N. C. 28144

gram. Some diagnostic classification system is also invaluable as a basis for many social decisions involving entire populations. For example, planning for treatment facilities, research efforts and educational programs take into account the distribution frequencies of specified syndromes in the general population.

Ledley and Lusted (14) give an excellent conception of the traditional model in medicine by their analysis of the reasoning underlying it. The authors differentiate between a disease complex and a symptom complex. While the former describes known pathological processes and their correlated signs, the latter represents particular signs present in a particular patient. The bridge between disease and symptom complexes is provided by available medical knowledge and the final diagnosis is tantamount to labeling the disease complex. However, the current gaps in medical knowledge necessitate the use of probability statements when relating disease to symptoms, admitting that there is some possibility for error in the diagnosis. Once the diagnosis is established, decisions about treatment still depend on many other factors including social, moral, and economic conditions. Ledley and Lusted (14) thus separate the clinical diagnosis into a two-step process. A statistical procedure is suggested to facilitate the primary or diagnostic labeling process. However, the choice of treatment depends not only on the diagnosis proper. Treatment decisions are also influenced by the moral, ethical, social, and economic conditions of the individual patient, his family and the society in which he lives. The proper assignment of the weight to be given to each of these values must in the last analysis be left to the physician's judgment (Ledley and Lusted, 14).

The Ledley and Lusted model presumes available methods for the observation of relevant behavior (the symptom complex), and some scientific knowledge relating it to known antecedents or correlates (the disease process). Contemporary theories of behavior pathology do not yet provide adequate guidelines for the observer to suggest what is to be observed. In fact, Szasz (25) has expressed the view that the medical model may be totally inadequate because psychiatry should be concerned with problems of living and not with diseases of the brain or other biological organs. Szasz (25) argues that "mental illness is a myth, whose function it is to disguise and thus render more potable the bitter pill of moral conflict in human relations" (p. 118).

The attack against use of the medical model in psychiatry comes from many quarters. Scheflen (23) describes a model of somatic psychiatry which is very similar to the traditional medical model of disease. A pathological process results in onset of an illness; the symptoms are correlated with a pathological state and represent our evidence of "mental disease." Treatment consists of removal of the pathogen, and the state of health is restored. Scheflen suggests that this traditional medical model is used in psychiatry not on the basis of its adequacy but because of its emotional appeal.

The limitations of the somatic model have been discussed even in some areas of medicine for which the model seems most appropriate. For example, in the nomenclature for diagnosis of disease of the heart and blood vessels, the criteria committee of the New York Heart Association (17) suggests the use of multiple criteria for cardiovascular diseases, including a statement of the patient's functional capacity. The committee suggests that the functional capacity be ". . . estimated by appraising the patient's ability to perform physical activity" (p. 80), and decided largely by inference from his history. Further (17), ". . . (it) should not be influenced by the character of the structural lesion or by an opinion as to treatment or prognosis" (p. 81). This approach makes it clear that a comprehensive assessment of a patient, regardless of the physical disease which he suffers, must also take into account his social effectiveness and the particular ways in which physiological, anatomical, and psychological factors interact to produce a particular behavior pattern in an individual patient.

## Multiple Diagnosis

A widely used practical solution and circumvention of the difficulty inherent in the application of the medical model to psychiatric diagnosis is offered by Noyes and Kolb (18). They suggest that the clinician construct a diagnostic formulation consisting of three parts: (1) A *genetic* diagnosis incorporating the constitutional, somatic, and historical-traumatic factors representing the primary sources or determinants of the mental illness; (2) A *dynamic* diagnosis which describes the mechanisms and techniques unconsciously used by the individual to manage anxiety, enhance self-esteem, i.e., that traces the psychopathological processes; and (3) A *clinical* diagnosis which conveys useful connotations concerning the reaction syndrome, the probable course of the disorder, and the methods of treatment which will most probably prove beneficial. Noyes' and Kolb's multiple criteria (18) can be arranged along three simpler dimensions of diagnosis which may have some practical value to the clinician: (1) etiological, (2) behavioral, and (3) predictive. The kind of information which is conveyed by each type of diagnostic label is somewhat different and specifically adapted to the

purpose for which the diagnosis is used. The triple-label approach attempts to counter the criticism aimed at use of any single classificatory system. Confusion in a single system is due in part to the fact that a diagnostic formulation intended to describe current behavior, for example, may be found useless in an attempt to predict the response to specific treatment, or to postdict the patient's personal history and development, or to permit collection of frequency data on hospital populations.

## Classification by Etiology

The Kraepelinian system and portions of the 1952 APA classification emphasize etiological factors. They share the assumption that common etiological factors lead to similar symptoms and respond to similar treatment. This dimension of diagnosis is considerably more fruitful when dealing with behavior disorders which are mainly under control of some biological condition. When a patient is known to suffer from excessive intake of alcohol his hallucinatory behavior, lack of motor coordination, poor judgment, and other behavioral evidence disorganization can often be related directly to some antecedent condition such as the toxic effect of alcohol on the central nervous system, liver, etc. For these cases, classification by etiology also has some implications for prognosis and treatment. Acute hallucinations and other disorganized behavior due to alcohol usually clear up when the alcohol level in the blood stream falls. Similar examples can be drawn from any class of behavior disorders in which a change in behavior is associated primarily or exclusively with a single, *particular* antecedent factor. Under these conditions this factor can be called a pathogen and the situation closely approximates the condition described by the traditional medical model.

Utilization of this dimension as a basis for psychiatric diagnosis, however, has many problems apart from the rarity with which a specified condition can be shown to have a direct "causal" relationship to a pathogen. Among the current areas of ignorance in the fields of psychology and psychiatry, the etiology of most common disturbances probably takes first place. No specific family environment, no dramatic traumatic experience, or known constitutional abnormality has yet been found which results in the same pattern of disordered behavior. While current research efforts have aimed at investigating family patterns of schizophrenic patients, and several studies suggest a relationship between the mother's behavior and a schizophrenic process in the child (10), it is not at all clear why the presence of these same factors in other families fails to yield a similar incidence of schizophrenia. Further, patients may exhibit behavior diagnosed as schizophrenic when there is no evidence of the postulated mother-child relationship.

In a recent paper Meehl (16) postulates schizophrenia as a neurological disease, with learned content and a dispositional basis. With this array of interactive etiological factors, it is clear that the etiological dimension for classification would at best result in an extremely cumbersome system, at worst in a useless one.

## Classification by Symptoms

A clinical diagnosis often is a summarizing statement about the way in which a person behaves. On the assumption that a variety of behaviors are correlated and consistent in any given individual, it becomes more economical to assign the individual to a class of persons than to list and categorize all of his behaviors. The utility of such a system rests heavily on the availability of empirical evidence concerning correlations among various behaviors (response-response relationships), and the further assumption that the frequency of occurrence of such behaviors is relatively independent of specific stimulus conditions and of specific reinforcement. There are two major limitations to such a system. The first is that diagnosis by symptoms, as we have indicated in an earlier section, is often misleading because it implies common etiological factors. Freedman (7) gives an excellent illustration of the differences both in probable antecedent factors and subsequent treatment response among three cases diagnosed as schizophrenics. Freedman's patients were diagnosed by at least two psychiatrists, and one would expect that the traditional approach should result in whatever treatment of schizophrenia is practiced in the locale where the patients are seen. The first patient eventually gave increasing evidence of an endocrinopathy, and when this was recognized and treated, the psychotic symptoms went into remission. The second case had a definite history of seizures and appropriate anticonvulsant medication was effective in relieving his symptoms. In the third case, treatment directed at an uncovering analysis of the patient's adaptive techniques resulted in considerable improvement in the patient's behavior and subsequent relief from psychotic episodes. Freedman (7) suggests that schizophrenia is not a disease entity in the sense that it has a unique etiology, pathogenesis, etc., but that it represents the evocation of a final common pathway in the same sense as do headache, epilepsy, sore throat, or indeed any other symptom complex. It is further suggested that the term "schizophrenia has outlived its usefulness and should be discarded" (p. 5). Opler (19, 20) has further shown the importance of cultural factors in the divergence of symptoms observed in patients collectively labeled as schizophrenic.

Descriptive classification is not always this deceptive, however. Assessment of intellectual performance sometimes results in a diagnostic statement which has predictive value for the patient's behavior in school or on a job. To date, there seem to be very few general statements about individual characteristics, which have as much predictive utility as the IQ.

A second limitation is that the current approach to diagnosis by symptoms tends to center on a group of behaviors which is often irrelevant with regard to the patient's total life pattern. These behaviors may be of interest only because they are popularly associated with deviancy and disorder. For example, occasional mild delusions interfere little or not at all with the social or occupational effectiveness of many ambulatory patients. Nevertheless, admission of their occurrence is often sufficient for a diagnosis of psychosis. Refinement of such an approach beyond current usage appears possible, as shown for example by Lorr et al. (15) but this does not remove the above limitations.

Utilization of a symptom-descriptive approach frequently focuses attention on by-products of larger behavior patterns, and results in attempted treatment of behaviors (symptoms) which may be simple consequences of other important aspects of the patient's life. Emphasis on the patient's subjective complaints, moods and feelings tends to encourage use of a syndrome-oriented classification. It also results frequently in efforts to change the feelings, anxieties, and moods (or at least the patient's report about them), rather than

to investigate the life conditions, interpersonal reactions, and environmental factors which produce and maintain these habitual response patterns.

## Classification by Prognosis

To date, the least effort has been devoted to construction of a classification system which assigns patients to the same category on the basis of their similar response to specific treatments. The proper question raised for such a classification system consists of the manner in which a patient will react to treatments, regardless of his current behavior, or his past history. The numerous studies attempting to establish prognostic signs from projective personality tests or somatic tests represent efforts to categorize the patients on this dimension.

Windle (26) has called attention to the low degree of predictability afforded by personality (projective) test scores, and has pointed out the difficulties encountered in evaluating research in this area due to the inadequate description of the population sampled and of the improvement criteria. In a later review Fulkerson and Barry (8) came to the similar conclusion that psychological test performance is a poor predictor of outcome in mental illness. They suggest that demographic variables such as severity, duration, acuteness of onset, degree of precipitating stress, etc., appear to have stronger relationships to outcome than test data. The lack of reliable relationships between diagnostic categories, test data, demographic variables, or other measures taken on the patient on the one hand, and duration of illness, response to specific treatment, or degree of recovery, on the other hand, precludes the construction of a simple empiric framework for a diagnostic-prognostic classification system based only on an array of symptoms.

None of the currently used dimensions for diagnosis is directly related to methods of modification of a patient's behavior, attitudes, response patterns, and interpersonal actions. Since the etiological model clearly stresses causative factors, it is much more compatible with a personality theory which strongly emphasizes genetic-developmental factors. The classification by symptoms facilitates social-administrative decisions about patients by providing some basis for judging the degree of deviation from social and ethical norms. Such a classification is compatible with a personality theory founded on the normal curve hypothesis and concerned with characterization by comparison with a fictitious average. The prognostic-predictive approach appears to have the most direct practical applicability. If continued research were to support certain early findings, it would be indeed comforting to be able to predict outcome of mental illness from a patient's premorbid social competence score (28), or from the patient's score on an ego-strength scale (4), or from many of the other signs and single variables which have been shown to have some predictive powers. It is unfortunate that these powers are frequently dissipated in cross validation. As Fulkerson and Barry have indicated (8), single predictors have not yet shown much success.

## II. A FUNCTIONAL (BEHAVIORAL-ANALYTIC) APPROACH

The growing literature on behavior modification procedures derived from learning theory (3, 6, 11, 13, 27) suggests that an effective diagnostic procedure would be one in which the

eventual therapeutic methods can be directly related to the information obtained from a continuing assessment of the patient's current behaviors and their controlling stimuli. Ferster (6) has said ". . . a functional analysis of behavior has the advantage that it specifies the causes of behavior in the form of explicit environmental events which can be objectively identified and which are potentially manipulable" (p. 3). Such a diagnostic undertaking makes the assumption that a description of the problematic behavior, its controlling factors, and the means by which it can be changed are the most appropriate "explanations." It further makes the assumption that a diagnostic evaluation is never complete. It implies that additional information about the circumstances of the patient's life pattern, relationships among his behaviors, and controlling stimuli in his social milieu and his private experience is obtained continuously until it proves sufficient to effect a noticeable change in the patient's behavior, thus resolving "the problem." In a functional approach it is necessary to continue evaluation of the patient's life pattern and its controlling factors, concurrent with attempted manipulation of these variables by reinforcement, direct intervention, or other means until the resultant change in the patient's behavior permits restoration of more efficient life experiences.

The present approach shares with some psychological theories the assumption that psychotherapy is *not* an effort aimed at removal of intrapsychic conflicts, nor at a change in the personality structure by therapeutic interactions of intense nonverbal nature, (e.g., transference, self-actualization, etc.). We adopt the assumption instead that the job of psychological treatment involves the utilization of a variety of methods to devise a program which controls the patient's environment, his behavior, and the consequences of his behavior in such a way that the presenting problem is resolved. We hypothesize that the essential ingredients of a psychotherapeutic endeavor usually involve two separate stages: (1) a change in the perceptual discriminations of a patient, i.e., in his approach to perceiving, classifying, and organizing sensory events, including perception of himself, and (2) changes in the response patterns which he has established in relation to social objects and to himself over the years (11). In addition, the clinician's task may involve direct intervention in the patient's environmental circumstances, modification of the behavior of other people significant in his life, and control of reinforcing stimuli which are available either through self-administration, or by contingency upon the behavior of others. These latter procedures complement the verbal interactions of traditional psychotherapy. They require that the clinician, at the invitation of the patient or his family, participate more fully in planning the total life pattern of the patient outside the clinician's office.

It is necessary to indicate what the theoretical view here presented does *not* espouse in order to understand the differences from other procedures. It does *not* rest upon the assumption that (*a*) insight is a sine qua non of psychotherapy, (*b*) changes in thoughts or ideas inevitably lead to ultimate changes in actions, (*c*) verbal therapeutic sessions serve as replications of and equivalents for actual life situations, and (*d*) a symptom can be removed only by uprooting its cause or origin. In the absence of these assumptions it becomes unnecessary to conceptualize behavior disorder in etiological terms, in psychodynamic terms,

or in terms of a specifiable disease process. While psychotherapy by verbal means may be sufficient in some instances, the combination of behavior modification in life situations as well as in verbal interactions serves to extend the armamentarium of the therapist. Therefore verbal psychotherapy is seen as an *adjunct* in the implementation of therapeutic behavior changes in the patient's total life pattern, not as an end in itself, nor as the sole vehicle for increasing psychological effectiveness.

In embracing this view of behavior modification, there is a further commitment to a constant interplay between assessment and therapeutic strategies. An initial diagnostic formulation seeks to ascertain the major variables which can be directly controlled or modified during treatment. During successive treatment stages additional information is collected about the patient's behavior repertoire, his reinforcement history, the pertinent controlling stimuli in his social and physical environment, and the sociological limitations within which both patient and therapist have to operate. Therefore, the initial formulation will constantly be enlarged or changed, resulting either in confirmation of the previous therapeutic strategy or in its change.

## A Guide to a Functional Analysis of Individual Behavior

In order to help the clinician in the collection and organization of information for a behavioral analysis, we have constructed an outline which aims to provide a working model of the patient's behavior at a relatively low level of abstraction. A series of questions are so organized as to yield immediate implications for treatment. This outline has been found useful both in clinical practice and in teaching. Following is a brief summary of the categories in the outline.

1. Analysis of a Problem Situation: [1] The patient's major complaints are categorized into classes of behavioral excesses and deficits. For each excess or deficit the dimensions of frequency, intensity, duration, appropriateness of form, and stimulus conditions are described. In content, the response classes represent the major targets of the therapeutic intervention. As an additional indispensable feature, the behavioral assets of the patient are listed for utilization in a therapy program.

2. Clarification of the Problem Situation: Here we consider the people and circumstances which tend to maintain the problem behaviors, and the consequences of these behaviors to the patient and to others in his environment. Attention is given also to the consequences of changes in these behaviors which may result from psychiatric intervention.

3. Motivational Analysis: Since reinforcing stimuli are idiosyncratic and depend for their effect on a number of unique parameters for each person, a hierarchy of particular persons, events, and objects which serve as reinforcers is established for each patient. Included in this hierarchy are those reinforcing events which facilitate approach behaviors as well as those which, because of their aversiveness, prompt avoidance responses. This information has as its purpose to lay plans for utilization of various reinforcers in prescription of a specific behavior therapy program for the patient, and to permit utilization of appropriate reinforcing behaviors by the therapist and significant others in the patient's social environment.

4. Developmental Analysis: Questions are asked about the patient's biological equipment, his sociocultural experiences, and his characteristic behavioral development. They are phrased in such a way as (a) to evoke descriptions of his habitual behavior at various chronological stages of his life, (b) to relate specific new stimulus conditions to noticeable changes from his habitual behavior, and (c) to relate such altered behavior and other residuals of biological and sociocultural events to the present problem.

5. Analysis of Self-Control: This section examines both the methods and the degree of self-control exercised by the patient in his daily life. Persons, events, or institutions which have successfully reinforced self-controlling behaviors are considered. The deficits or excesses of self-control are evaluated in relation to their importance as therapeutic targets and to their utilization in a therapeutic program.

6. Analysis of Social Relationships: Examination of the patient's social network is carried out to evaluate the significance of people in the patient's environment who have some influence over the problematic behaviors, or who in turn are influenced by the patient for his own satisfactions. These interpersonal relationships are reviewed in order to plan the potential participation of significant others in a treatment program, based on the principles of behavior modification. The review also helps the therapist to consider the range of actual social relationships in which the patient needs to function.

7. Analysis of the Social-Cultural-Physical Environment: In this section we add to the preceding analysis of the patient's behavior as an individual, consideration of the norms in his natural environment. Agreements and discrepancies between the patient's idiosyncratic life patterns and the

---

[1] For each patient a detailed analysis is required. For example, a list of behavioral excesses may include specific aggressive acts, hallucinatory behaviors, crying, submission to others in social situations, etc. It is recognized that some behaviors can be viewed as excesses or deficits depending on the vantage point from which the imbalance is observed. For instance, excessive withdrawal and deficient social responsiveness, or excessive social autonomy (nonconformity) and deficient self-inhibitory behavior may be complementary. The particular view taken is of consequence because of its impact on a treatment plan. Regarding certain behavior as excessively aggressive, to be reduced by constraints, clearly differs from regarding the same behavior as a deficit in self-control, subject to increase by training and treatment.

norms in his environment are defined so that the importance of these factors can be decided in formulating treatment goals which allow as explicitly for the patient's needs as for the pressures of his social environment.

The preceding outline has its purpose to achieve definition of a patient's problem in a manner which suggests specific treatment operations, or that none are feasible, and specific behaviors as targets for modification. Therefore, the formulation is *action oriented*. It can be used as a guide for the initial collection of information, as a device for organizing available data, or as a design for treatment.

The formulation of a treatment plan follows from this type of analysis because knowledge of the reinforcing conditions suggests the motivational controls at the disposal of the clinician for the modification of the patient's behavior. The analysis of specific problem behaviors also provides a series of goals for psychotherapy or other treatment, and for the evaluation of treatment progress. Knowledge of the patient's biological, social, and cultural conditions should help to determine what resources can be used, and what limitations must be considered in a treatment plan.

The various categories attempt to call attention to important variables affecting the patient's *current* behavior. Therefore, they aim to elicit descriptions of low-level abstraction. Answers to these specific questions are best phrased by describing classes of events reported by the patient, observed by others, or by critical incidents described by an informant. The analysis does not exclude description of the patient's habitual verbal-symbolic behaviors. However, in using verbal behaviors as the basis for this analysis, one should be cautious not to "explain" verbal processes in terms of postulated internal mechanisms without adequate supportive evidence, nor should inference be made about nonobserved processes or events without corroborative evidence. The analysis includes many items which are not known or not applicable for a given patient. Lack of information on some items does not necessarily indicate incompleteness of the analysis. These lacks must be noted nevertheless because they often contribute to the better understanding of what the patient needs to learn to become an autonomous person. Just as important is an inventory of his existing socially effective behavioral repertoire which can be put in the service of any treatment procedure.

This analysis is consistent with our earlier formulations of the principles of comprehensive medicine (9, 22) which emphasized the joint operation of biological, social and psychological factors in psychiatric disorders. The language and orientation of the proposed approach are rooted in contemporary learning theory. The conceptual framework is consonant with the view that the course of psychiatric disorders can be modified by systematic application of scientific principles from the fields of psychology and medicine to the patient's habitual mode of living.

This approach is not a substitute for assignment of the patient to traditional diagnostic categories. Such labeling may be desirable for statistical, administrative, or research purposes. But the current analysis is intended to replace other diagnostic formulations purporting to serve as a basis for making decisions about specific therapeutic interventions.

## III. METHODS OF DATA COLLECTION FOR A FUNCTIONAL ANALYSIS

Traditional diagnostic approaches have utilized as the main sources of information the patient's verbal report, his nonverbal behavior during an interview, and his performance on psychological tests. These observations are sufficient if one regards behavior problems only as a property of the patient's particular pattern of associations or his personality structure. A mental disorder would be expected to reveal itself by stylistic characteristics in the patient's behavior repertoire. However, if one views behavior disorders as sets of response patterns which are learned under particular conditions and maintained by definable environmental and internal stimuli, an assessment of the patient's behavior output is insufficient unless it also describes the conditions under which it occurs. This view requires an expansion of the clinician's sources of observations to include the stimulation fields in which the patient lives, and the variations of patient behavior as a function of exposure to these various stimulational variables. Therefore, the resourceful clinician need not limit himself to test findings, interview observations in the clinician's office, or referral histories alone in the formulation of the specific case. Nor need he regard himself as hopelessly handicapped when the patient has little observational or communicative skill in verbally reconstructing his life experiences for the clinician. Regardless of the patient's communicative skills the data must consist of a description of the patient's behavior *in relationship* to varying environmental conditions.

A behavioral analysis excludes no data relating to a patient's past or present experiences as irrelevant. However, the relative merit of any information (as, e.g., growing up in a broken home or having had homosexual experiences) lies in its relation to the independent variables which can be identified as controlling the current problematic behavior. The observation that a patient has hallucinated on occasions may be important only if it has bearing on his present problem. If looked upon in isolation, a report about hallucinations may be misleading, resulting in emphasis on classification rather than treatment.

In the *psychiatric interview* a behavioral-analytic approach opposes acceptance of the content of the verbal self-report as equivalent to actual events or experiences. However, verbal reports provide information concerning the patient's verbal construction of his environment and of his person, his recall of past experiences, and his fantasies about them. While these self-descriptions do not represent data about events which actually occur internally, they do represent current behaviors of the patient and indicate the verbal chains and repertoires which the patient has built up. Therefore, the verbal behavior may be useful for description of a patient's thinking processes. To make the most of such an approach, variations on traditional interview procedures may be obtained by such techniques as role playing, discussion, and interpretation of current life events, or controlled free association. Since there is little experimental evidence of specific relationships between the patient's verbal statements and his nonverbal behavioral acts, the verbal report alone remains insufficient for a complete analysis and for prediction of his daily behavior. Further, it is well known that a person responds to environmental conditions and to internal cues which he cannot describe adequately. Therefore, any verbal report may miss or mask the most important aspects of a behavioral analysis, i.e., the description of the relationship between antecedent conditions and subsequent behavior.

In addition to the use of the clinician's own person as a controlled stimulus object in interview situations, *observations of interaction with significant others* can be used for the analysis of variations in frequency of various behaviors as a function of the person with whom the patient interacts. For example, use of prescribed standard roles for nurses and attendants, utilization of members of the patient's family or his friends, may be made to obtain data relevant to the patient's habitual interpersonal response pattern. Such observations are especially useful if in a later interview the patient is asked to describe and discuss the observed sessions. Confrontations with tape recordings for comparisons between the patient's report and the actual session as witnessed by the observer may provide information about the patient's perception of himself and others as well as his habitual behavior toward peers, authority figures, and other significant people in his life.

Except in working with children or family units, insufficient use has been made of material obtained from *other informants* in interviews about the patient. These reports can aid the observer to recognize behavioral domains in which the patient's report deviates from or agrees with the descriptions provided by others. Such information is also useful for contrasting the patient's reports about his presumptive effects on another person with the stated effects by that person. If a patient's interpersonal problems extend to areas in which social contacts are not clearly defined, contributions by informants other than the patient are essential.

It must be noted that verbal reports by other informants may be no more congruent with actual events than the patient's own reports and need to be equally related to the informant's own credibility. If such crucial figures as parents, spouses, employers can be so interviewed, they also provide the clinician with some information about those people with whom the patient must interact repeatedly and with whom interpersonal problems may have developed.

Some observation of the patient's daily *work behavior* represents an excellent source of information, if it can be made available. Observation of the patient by the clinician or his staff may be preferable to descriptions by peers or supervisors. Work observations are especially important for patients whose complaints include difficulties in their daily work activity or who describe work situations as contributing factors to their problem. While freer use of this technique may be hampered by cultural attitudes toward psychiatric treatment in the marginally adjusted, such observations may be freely accessible in hospital situations or in sheltered work situations. With use of behavior rating scales or other simple measurement devices, brief samples of patient behaviors in work situations can be obtained by minimally trained observers.

The patient himself may be asked to provide samples of his own behavior by using tape recorders for the recording of segments of interactions in his family, at work, or in other situations during his everyday life. A television monitoring system for the patient's behavior is an excellent technique from a theoretical viewpoint but it is extremely cumbersome and expensive. Use of recordings for diagnostic and therapeutic purposes has been reported by some investigators (2, 5, 24). Playback of the recordings and a recording

of the patient's reactions to the playback can be used further in interviews
to clarify the patient's behavior toward
others and his reaction to himself as
a social stimulus.

*Psychological tests* represent problems to be solved under specified inter-
actional conditions. Between the highly
standardized intelligence tests and the
unstructured and ambiguous projective
tests lies a dimension of structure along
which more and more responsibility for
providing appropriate responses falls on
the patient. By comparison with interview procedures, most psychological
tests provide a relatively greater stan-
dardization of stimulus conditions. But,
in addition to the specific answers given
on intelligence tests or on projective
tests these tests also provide a behavioral sample of the patient's reaction to
a problem situation in a relatively
stressful interpersonal setting. Therefore, psychological tests can provide not
only quantitative scores but they can
also be treated as a miniature life experience, yielding information about the
patient's interpersonal behavior and
variations in his behavior as a function
of the nature of the stimulus conditions.

In this section we have mentioned
only some of the numerous life situations which can be evaluated in order
to provide information about the patient. Criteria for their use lies in
economy, accessibility to the clinician,
and relevance to the patient's problem.
While it is more convenient to gather
data from a patient in an office, it may
be necessary for the clinician to have
first-hand information about the actual
conditions under which the patient lives
and works. Such familiarity may be
obtained either by utilization of informants or by the clinician's entry into
the home, the job situation, or the
social environment in which the patient
lives. Under all these conditions the
clinician is effective only if it is possible

for him to maintain a nonparticipating,
objective, and observational role with
no untoward consequences for the patient or the treatment relationship.

The methods of data collecting for
a functional analysis described here
differ from traditional psychiatric approaches only in that they require inclusion of the physical and social stimulus field in which the patient actually
operates. Only a full appraisal of the
patient's living and working conditions
and his way of life allow a description of
the actual problems which the patient
faces and the specification of steps to
be taken for altering the problematic
situation.

## SUMMARY

Current psychiatric classification falls
short of providing a satisfactory basis
for the understanding and treatment of
maladaptive behavior. Diagnostic sche-
mas now in use are based on etiology,
symptom description, or prognosis.
While each of these approaches has a
limited utility, no unified schema is
available which permits prediction of
response to treatment or future course
of the disorder from the assignment of
the patient to a specific category.

This paper suggests a behavior-ana-
lytic approach which is based on contemporary learning theory, as an alternative to assignment of the patient to a
conventional diagnostic category. It
includes the summary of an outline
which can serve as a guide for the
collection of information and formulation of the problem, including the biological, social, and behavioral conditions
which are determining the patient's
behavior. The outline aims toward integration of information about a patient
for formulation of an action plan which
would modify the patient's problematic
behavior. Emphasis is given to the par-

ticular variables affecting the *individual* patient rather than determination of the similarity of the patient's history or his symptoms to known pathological groups.

The last section of the paper deals with methods useful for collection of information necessary to complete such a behavioral analysis.

This paper was written in conjunction with Research grant MH 06921-03 from the National Institutes of Mental Health, United States Public Health Service.

# REFERENCES

1. Ash, P.: Reliability of Psychiatric Diagnosis, J. Abnorm Soc Psychol 44:272–277, 1949.
2. Bach, G.: In Alexander, S.: Fight Promoter for Battle of Sexes, Life 54:102–108 (May 17) 1963.
3. Bandura, A.: Psychotherapy as Learning Process, Psychol Bull 58:143–159, 1961.
4. Barron, F.: Ego-Strength Scale Which Predicts Response to Psychotherapy, J Consult Psychol 17:235–241, 1953.
5. Cameron, D. E., et al: Automation of Psychotherapy, Compr Psychiat 5:1–14, 1964.
6. Ferster, C. B.: Classification of Behavioral Pathology in Ullman, L. P. and Krasner, L. (eds.): Behavior Modification Research, New York: Holt, Rinehart & Winston, 1965.
7. Freedman, D. A.: Various Etiologies of Schizophrenic Syndrome, Dis Nerv Syst 19:1–6, 1958.
8. Fulkerson, S. E., and Barry, J. R.: Methodology and Research on Prognostic Use of Psychological Tests, Psychol Bull 58:177–204, 1961.
9. Guze, S. B.; Matarazzo, J. D.; and Saslow, G.: Formulation of Principles of Comprehensive Medicine With Special Reference to Learning Theory, J Clin Psychol 9:127–136, 1953.
10. Jackson, D. D. A.: Etiology of Schizophrenia, New York: Basic Books, Inc., 1960.
11. Kanfer, F. H.: Comments on Learning in Psychotherapy, Psychol Rep 9:681–699, 1961.
12. Katz, M. M.; Cole, J. O.; and Lowery, H. A.: Non-specificity of Diagnosis of Paranoid Schizophrenia, Arch Gen Psychiat 11:197–202, 1964.
13. Krasner, L.: "Therapist as Social Reinforcement Machine," in Strupp, H., and Luborsky, L. (eds.); Research in Psychotherapy, Washington, D.C.: American Psychological Association, 1962.
14. Ledley, R. S., and Lusted, L. B.: Reasoning Foundations of Medical Diagnosis, Science 130:9–21, 1959.
15. Lorr, M.; Klett, C. J.; and McNair, D. M.: Syndromes of Psychosis, New York: Macmillan Co., 1963.
16. Meehl, P. E.: Schizotaxia, Schizotypy, Schizophrenia, Amer Psychol 17:827–838, 1962.
17. New York Heart Association: Nomenclature and Criteria for Diagnosis of Disease of the Heart and Blood Vessels, New York: New York Heart Association, 1953.
18. Noyes, A. P., and Kolb, L. C.: Modern Clinical Psychiatry, Philadelphia: W. B. Saunders & Co., 1963.
19. Opler, M. K.: Schizophrenia and Culture, Sci Amer 197:103–112, 1957.
20. Opler, M. K.: Need for New Diagnostic Categories in Psychiatry, J Nat Med Assoc 55:133–137, 1963.
21. Rotter, J. B.: Social Learning and Clinical Psychology, New York: Prentice-Hall, 1954.
22. Saslow, G.: On Concept of Comprehensive Medicine, Bull Menninger Clin 16:57–65, 1952.
23. Scheflen, A. E.: Analysis of Thought Model Which Persists in Psychiatry, Psychosom Med 20:235–241, 1958.
24. Slack, C. W.: Experimenter-Subject Psychotherapy—A New Method of Introducing Intensive Office Treatment for Unreachable Cases, Ment Hyg 44:238–256, 1960.
25. Szasz, T. S.: Myth of Mental Illness, Amer Psychol 15:113–118, 1960.

26. WINDLE, C.: Psychological Tests in Psychopathological Prognosis, Psychol Bull 49:451–482, 1952.
27. WOLPE, J.: Psychotherapy in Reciprocal Inhibition, Stanford, Calif: Stan-

ford University Press, 1958.
28. ZIGLER, E., and PHILLIPS, L.: Psychiatric Diagnosis: Critique, J Abnorm Soc Psychol 63:607–618, 1961.

Paul E. Meehl

# Wanted—A Good Cookbook

*In 1954, Dr. Meehl published an influential and provocative book contrasting the operation of the clinician who uses his artistic or intuitive skills to predict the behavior of patients with what Meehl termed a statistical approach to prediction. In this approach, predictions are made on the basis of probability, or the statistical likelihood that an individual would be appropriately placed in any particular category. Clearly, one advantage of the statistical approach is that it may be carried out by relatively unskilled and inexperienced workers. However, more traditional clinicians would argue that something unique and important is lost by reducing predictions about behavior to statistical formulae. In this paper, Dr. Meehl reports on the efforts of a doctoral student of his to devise a recipe to implement his approach to cookbook prediction, and offers some evidence supporting his actuarial bent. This article has been slightly abridged, and a section explaining the mathematical basis of the approach to cookbook construction has been omitted. The basis of this approach is a set of inequalities used to calculate inverse probability, which is known as a Bayesian approach, and the interested reader might wish to refer to the original article to review this material.*

Once upon a time there was a young fellow who, as we say, was "vocationally maladjusted." He wasn't sure just what the trouble was, but he knew that he wasn't happy in his work. So, being a denizen of an urban, sophisticated, psychologically oriented culture, he concluded that what he needed was some professional guidance. He went to the counseling bureau of a large midwestern university (according to some versions of the tale, it was located on the banks of a great river), and there he was interviewed by a world-famous vocational psychologist. When the psychologist explained that it would first be necessary to take a 14-hour battery of tests, the young man hesitated a little; after all, he was still employed at his job and 14 hours seemed like quite a lot of time. "Oh, well," said the great psychologist reassuringly, "don't worry about *that*. If you're too busy, you can arrange to have my assistant take these tests *for* you. I don't care who takes them, just so long as they come out in quantitative form."

Lest I, a Minnesotan, do too great

Abridged from the American Psychologist, 11(1956), 263–272 with the permission of the American Psychological Association and Dr. Meehl. Copyright 1956 by the American Psychological Association.

violence to your expectations by telling this story on the dustbowl empiricism with which we Minnesotans are traditionally associated, let me now tell you a true story having the opposite animus. Back in the days when we were teaching assistants, my colleague MacCorquodale was grading a young lady's elementary laboratory report on an experiment which involved a correlation problem. At the end of an otherwise flawless report, this particular bobbysoxer had written "The correlation was seventy-five, with a standard error of ten, which is significant. However, I do not think these variables are related." MacCorquodale wrote a large red "FAIL" and added a note: "Dear Miss Fisbee: The correlation coefficient was devised expressly to relieve you of all responsibility for deciding whether these two variables are related."

If you find one of these anecdotes quite funny, and the other one rather stupid (I don't care which), you are probably suffering from a slight case of bias. Although I have not done a factor analysis with these two stories in the matrix, my clinical judgment tells me that a person's spontaneous reactions to them reflect his position in the perennial conflict between the tough-minded and the tender-minded, between those for whom the proper prefix to the word "analysis" is "factor" and those for whom it is "psycho," between the groups that Lord Russell once characterized as the "simple-minded" and the "muddle-headed." In a recent book (10), I have explored one major facet of this conflict, namely the controversy over the relative merits of clinical and statistical methods of *prediction*. Theoretical considerations, together with introspections as to my own mental activities as a psychotherapist, led me to conclude that the clinician has certain unique, practically unduplicable powers by virtue of being himself an

organism like his client; but that the domain of straight *prediction* would not be a favorable locus for displaying these powers. Survey of a score of empirical investigations in which the actual predictive efficiency of the two methods could be compared, gave strong confirmation to this latter theoretical expectation. After reading these studies, it almost looks as if the first rule to follow in trying to predict the subsequent course of a student's or patient's behavior is carefully to avoid talking to him, and that the second rule is to avoid thinking about him!

Statisticians (and rat men) with castrative intent toward clinicians should beware of any temptation to overextend these findings to a generalization that "clinicians don't actually add anything." Apart from the clinician's therapeutic efforts—the power of which is a separate issue and also a matter of current dispute—a glance at a sample of clinical diagnostic documents, such as routine psychological reports submitted in a VA installation, shows that a kind of mixed predictive-descriptive statement predominates which is different from the type of gross prediction considered in the aforementioned survey. (I hesitate to propose a basic distinction here, having learned that proposing a distinction between two classes of concepts is a sure road to infamy.) Nevertheless, I suggest that we distinguish between: (*a*) the clinician's predictions of such gross, outcome-type, "administrative" dimensions as recovery from psychosis, survival in a training program, persistence in therapy, and the like; and (*b*) a rather more detailed and ambitious enterprise roughly characterizable as "describing the person." It might be thought that *a* always presupposes *b*, but a moment's reflection shows this to be false; since there are empirical prediction systems in which the sole property ascribed to the person *is* the disposition to a predicted gross outcome. A very considerable fraction of the typical clinical psychologist's time seems to be spent in giving tests or semitests, the intention being to come out with some kind of characterization of the individual. In part this characterization is "phenotypic," attributing such behavior-dispositions as "hostile," "relates poorly," "loss in efficiency," "manifest anxiety," or "depression"; in part it is "genotypic," inferring as the causes of the phenotype certain inner events, states, or structures, e.g., "latent n Aggression," "oral-dependent attitudes," "severe castration anxiety," and the like. While the phenotypic-genotypic question is itself deserving of careful methodological analysis, in what follows I shall use the term "personality description" to cover both phenotypic and genotypic inferences, i.e., statements of all degrees of internality or theoreticalness. I shall also assume, while recognizing that at least one group of psychologists has made an impressive case to the contrary, that the description of a person is a worthwhile stage in the total clinical process. Granted, then, that we wish to use tests as a means to securing a description of the person, how shall we go about it? Here we sit, with our Rorschach and Multiphasic results spread out before us. From this mess of data we have to emerge with a characterization of the person from whose behavior these profiles are a highly abstracted, much-reduced distillation. How to proceed?

Some of you are no doubt wondering, "What is the fellow talking about? You look at the profiles, you call to mind what the various test dimensions mean for dynamics, you reflect on other patients you have seen with similar patterns, you think of the research literature; then you combine these considerations to make inferences. Where's the problem?" The problem is, *whether or not this is the most efficient way to do it.* We ordinarily do it this way; in fact, the practice is so universal that most clinicians find it shocking, if not somehow sinful, to imagine any other. We feed in the test data and let that rusty digital computer in our heads go to work until a paragraph of personality description emerges. It requires no systematic study, although some quantitative data have begun to appear in the literature (2, 3, 6, 7, 8, 9), to realize that there is a considerable element of vagueness, hit-or-miss, and personal judgment involved in this approach. Because explicit rules are largely lacking, and hence the clinician's personal experience, skill, and creative artistry play so great a role, I shall refer to this time-honored procedure for generating personality descriptions from tests as the *rule-of-thumb* method.

I wish now to contrast this rule-of-thumb method with what I shall call the *cookbook method*. In the cookbook method, any given configuration (holists please note—I said "configuration," not "sum"!) of psychometric data is associated with each facet (or configuration) of a personality description, and the closeness of this association is explicitly indicated by a number. This number need not be a correlation coefficient—its form will depend upon what is most appropriate to the circumstances. It may be a correlation, or merely an ordinary probability of attribution, or (as in the empirical study I shall report upon later) an average Q-sort placement. Whatever its form, the essential point is that the transition from psychometric pattern to personality description is an automatic, mechanical, "clerical" kind of task, proceeding by the use of explicit rules set forth in the cookbook. I am quite aware that the mere prospect of such a method will horrify some of you; in my weaker moments it horrifies me. All I can say is that many clinicians are also horrified by the cookbook method as applied in the crude prediction situation; whereas the studies reported to date indicate this horror to be quite groundless (10, Chap. 8). As Fred Skinner once said, some men are less curious about nature than about the accuracy of their guesses (15, p. 44). Our responsibility to our patients and to the taxpayer obliges us to decide between the rule-of-thumb and the cookbook methods on the basis of their empirically demonstrated efficiency, rather than upon which one is more exciting, more "dynamic," more like what psychiatrists do, or more harmonious with the clinical psychologist's self concept.

Let us sneak up the clinician's avoidance gradient gradually to prevent the negative therapeutic reaction. Consider a particular complex attribute, say, "strong dependency with reaction-formation." Under what conditions should we take time to give a test of moderate validity as a basis for inferring the presence or absence of this complex attribute? Putting it negatively, it appears to me pretty obvious that there are two circumstances under which we should *not* spend much skilled time on testing even with a moderately valid test, because we stand to lose if we let the test finding influence our judgments. First, when the attribute is found in almost all our patients; and second, when it is found in almost none of our patients. (A third situation, which I shall not consider here, is one in which the attribute makes no practical difference anyhow.) A disturbingly large fraction of the assertions made in routine psychometric reports or uttered by psychologists in staff conferences fall in one of these classes.

It is not difficult to show that when a given personality attribute is almost always or almost never present in a specified clinical population, rather

severe demands are made upon the test's validity if it is to contribute in a practical way to our clinical decision-making. . . .

The moral to be drawn from these considerations, which even we clinicians can follow because they involve only high-school algebra, is that a great deal of skilled psychological effort is probably being wasted in going through complex, skill-demanding, time-consuming test procedures of moderate or low validity, in order to arrive at conclusions about the patient which could often be made with high confidence without the test, and which in other cases ought not to be made (because they still tend to be wrong) even with the test indications positive. Probably most surprising is the finding that there are certain quantitative relations between the base rates and test validity parameters such that the use of a "valid" test will produce a net rise in the frequency of clinical mistakes. The first task of a good clinical cookbook would be to make explicit quantitative use of the inverse probability formulas in constructing efficient "rules of attribution" when test data are to be used in describing the personalities of patients found in various clinical populations. For example, I know of an outpatient clinic which has treated, by a variety of psychotherapies, in the course of the past eight years, approximately 5000 patients, not one of whom has committed suicide. If the clinical psychologists in this clinic have been spending much of their time scoring suicide keys on the Multiphasic or counting suicide indicators in Rorschach content, either these test indicators are close to infallible (which is absurd), or else the base rate is so close to zero that the expenditure of skilled time is of doubtful value. Suicide is an extreme case, of course (14); but the point so dramatically reflected there is valid, with suitable quantitative modifications, over a wider range of base rates. To take some examples from the high end of the base-rate continuum, it is not very illuminating to say of a known psychiatric patient that he has difficulty in accepting his drives, experiences some trouble in relating emotionally to others, and may have problems with his sexuality! Many psychometric reports bear a disconcerting resemblance to what my colleague Donald G. Paterson calls "personality description after the manner of P. T. Barnum" (13). I suggest—and I am quite serious—that we adopt the phrase *Barnum effect* to stigmatize those pseudo-successful clinical procedures in which personality descriptions from tests are made to fit the patient largely or wholly by virtue of their triviality; and in which any nontrivial, but perhaps erroneous, inferences are hidden in a context of assertions or denials which carry high confidence simply because of the population base rates, regardless of the test's validity. I think this fallacy is at least as important and frequent as others for which we have familiar labels (halo effect, leniency error, contamination, etc.). One of the best ways to increase the general sensitivity to such fallacies is to give them a name. We ought to make our clinical students as acutely aware of the Barnum effect as they are of the dangers of countertransference or the standard error of *r*.

The preceding mathematical considerations, while they should serve as a check upon some widespread contemporary forms of tea-leaf reading, are unfortunately not very "positive" by way of writing a good cookbook. "Almost anything needs a little salt for flavor" or "It is rarely appropriate to put ketchup on the dessert" would be sound advice but largely negative and not very helpful to an average cook. I wish now to describe briefly a piece of empirical research, reported in a thesis just completed at Minnesota by Charles C. Halbower, which takes the cookbook method 100 per cent seriously; and which seems to show, at least in one clinical context, what can be done in a more constructive way by means of a cookbook of even moderate trustworthiness.[1] By some geographical coincidence, the psychometric device used in this research was a structured test consisting of a set of 550 items, commonly known as MMPI. Let me emphasize that the MMPI is not here being compared with anything else, and that the research does not aim to investigate Multiphasic validity (although the general order of magnitude of the obtained correlations does give some incidental information in that respect). What Dr. Halbower asked was this: given a Multiphasic profile, how does one arrive at a personality description from it? Using the rule-of-thumb method, a clinician familiar with MMPI interpretation looks at the profile, thinks awhile, and proceeds to describe the patient he imagines would have produced such a pattern. Using the cookbook method, we don't need a clinician; instead, a $230-per-month clerk-typist in the outer office simply reads the numbers on the profile, enters the cookbook, locates the page on which is found some kind of "modal description" for patients with such a profile, and this description is then taken as the best available approximation to the patient. We know, of course, that every patient is unique—absolutely, unqualifiedly unique. Therefore, the application of a cookbook description will inevitably make errors, some of them perhaps serious ones. If we

---

[1] I am indebted to Dr. Halbower for permission to present this summary of his thesis data in advance of his own more complete publication.

knew *which* facets of the cookbook sketch needed modification as applied to the present unique patient, we would, of course, depart from the cookbook at these points; but we don't know this. If we start monkeying with the cookbook recipe in the hope of avoiding or reducing these errors, we will in all likelihood improve on the cookbook in some respects but, unfortunately, will worsen our approximation in others. Given a finite body of information, such as the 13 two-digit numbers of a Multiphasic profile, there is obviously *in fact* (whether we have yet succeeded in *finding* it or not) a "most probable" value for any personality facet, and also for any configuration of facets, however complex or "patterned" (10, pp. 131–134). It is easy to prove that a method of characterization which departs from consistant adherence to this "best guess" stands to lose. Keep in mind, then, that the raw data from which a personality description was to be inferred consisted of an MMPI profile. In other words, the Halbower study was essentially a comparison of the rule-of-thumb versus the cookbook method where each method was, however, functioning upon the same information—an MMPI. We are in effect contrasting the validity of two methods of "reading" Multiphasics.

In order to standardize the domain to be covered, and to yield a reasonably sensitive quantification of the goodness of description, Dr. Halbower utilized Q sorts. From a variety of sources he constructed a Q pool of 154 items, the majority being phenotypic or intermediate and a minority being genotypic. Since these items were intended for clinically expert sorters employing an "external" frame of reference, many of them were in technical language. Some sample items from his pool are: "Reacts against his dependency needs with hostility"; "manifests reality distortions";

"takes a dominant, ascendant role in interactions with others"; "is rebellious toward authority figures, rules, and other constraints"; "is counteractive in the face of frustration"; "gets appreciable secondary gain from his symptoms"; "is experiencing pain"; "is naive"; "is impunitive"; "utilizes intellectualization as a defense mechanism"; "shows evidence of latent hostility"; "manifests inappropriate affect." The first step was to construct a cookbook based upon these 154 items as the ingredients; the recipes were to be in the form of directions as to the optimal Q-sort placement of each item.

How many distinguishable recipes will the cookbook contain? If we had infallible criterion Q sorts on millions of cases, there would be as many recipes as there are possible MMPI profiles. Since we don't have this ideal situation, and never will, we have to compromise by introducing coarser grouping. Fortunately, we know that the validity of our test is poor enough so that this coarseness will not result in the sacrifice of much, if any, information. How coarsely we group, i.e., how different two Multiphasic curves have to be before we refuse to call them "similar" enough to be coordinated with the same recipe, is a very complicated matter involving both theoretical and practical considerations. Operating within the limits of a doctoral dissertation, Halbower confined his study to four profile "types." These curve types were specified by the first two digits of the Hathaway code plus certain additional requirements based upon clinical experience. The four MMPI codes used were those beginning 123', 13', 27', and 87' (5). The first three of these codes are the most frequently occurring in the Minneapolis VA Mental Hygiene Clinic population, and the fourth code, which is actually fifth in frequency of occurrence, was chosen in order to have a quasipsychotic type in the study. It is worth noting that these four codes constitute 58 per cent of all MMPI curves seen in the given population; so that Halbower's gross recipe categories already cover the majority of such outpatients. The nature of the further stipulations, refining the curve criteria within each two-digit code class, is illustrated by the following specifications for code 13', the "hysteroid valley" or "conversion V" type:

1. $Hs$ and $Hy \geqq 70$.
2. $D < (Hs$ and $Hy)$ by at least one sigma.
3. $K$ or $L > ?$ and $F$.
4. $F \leqq 65$.
5. Scales 4, 5, 6, 7, 8, 9, 0 all $\leqq 70$.

For each of these MMPI curve types, the names of nine patients were then randomly chosen from the list of those meeting the curve specifications. If the patient was still in therapy, his therapist was asked to do a Q sort (11 steps, normal distribution) on him. The MMPI had been withheld from these therapists. If the patient had been terminated, a clinician (other than Halbower) did a Q sort based upon study of the case folder, including therapist's notes and any available psychometrics (except, of course, the Multiphasic). This yields Q sorts for nine patients of a given curve type. These nine sorts were then pairwise intercorrelated, and by inspection of the resulting 36 coefficients, a subset of five patients was chosen as most representative of the curve type. The Q sorts on these five "representative" patients were then average, and this average Q sort was taken as the cookbook recipe to be used in describing future cases having the given MMPI curve. Thus, this modal, crystallized, "distilled-essence" personality description was obtained by eliminating patients with atypical sortings and pooling sortings on the more typical, hoping

to reduce both errors of patient sampling and of clinical judgment. This rather complicated sequence of procedures may be summarized thus:

Deriving cookbook recipe for a specified curve type, such as the "conversion V" above:

1. Sample of $N =$ nine patients currently or recently in therapy and meeting the MMPI specifications for conversion V curve.
2. 154-item Q sort done on each patient by therapist or from therapist notes and case folder. (These sorts MMPI-uncontaminated.)
3. Pairwise Q correlations of these nine patients yields 36 intercorrelations.
4. Selection of subset $N' =$ five "modal" patients from this matrix by inspectional cluster method.
5. Mean of Q sorts on these five "core" patients is the cookbook recipe for the MMPI curve type in question.

Having constructed one recipe, he started all over again with a random sample of nine patients whose Multiphasics met the second curve-type specifications, and carried out these cluster-and-pooling processes upon them. This was done for each of the four curve types which were to compose the cookbook. If you have reservations about any of the steps in constructing this miniature cookbook, let me remind you that this is all preliminary, i.e., *it is the means of arriving at the cookbook recipe.* The proof of the pudding will be in the eating, and any poor choices of tactics or patients up to this point should merely make the cookbook less trustworthy than it would otherwise be.

Having thus written a miniature cookbook consisting of only four recipes, Halbower then proceeded to cook some dishes to see how they would taste. For cross validation he chose at random four new Mental Hygiene Clinic patients meeting the four curve specifications and who had been seen in therapy for a minimum of ten hours. With an eye to validity generalization to a somewhat different clinical population, with different base rates, he also chose four patients who were being seen as inpatients at the Minneapolis VA Hospital. None of the therapists involved had knowledge of the patients' Multiphasics. For purposes of his study, Halbower took the therapist's Q sort, based upon all of the case folder data (minus MMPI) plus his therapeutic contacts, as the best available criterion; although this "criterion" is acceptable only in the sense of construct validity (1). An estimate of its absolute level of trustworthiness is not important since it is being used as the common reference basis for a comparison of two methods of test reading.

Given the eight criterion therapist Q sorts (2 patients for each MMPI curve type), the task of the cookbook is to predict these descriptions. Thus, for each of the two patients having MMPI code 123', we simply assign the Q-sort recipe found in the cookbook as the best available description. How accurate this description is can be estimated (in the sense of construct validity) by Q correlating it with the criterion therapist's description. These eight "validity" coefficients varied from .36 to .88 with a median of .69. As would be expected, the hospital inpatients yielded the lower correlations. The Mental Hygiene Clinic cases, for whom the cookbook was really intended, gave validities of .68, .69, .84, and .88 (see Table 1).

**TABLE 1. Validation of the Four Cookbook Descriptions on New Cases, and Comparative Validities of the Cookbook MMPI Readings and Rule-of-Thumb Readings by Clinicians**

1. Four patients currently in therapy Q-described by the therapist (10 hours or more therapy plus case folder minus MMPI). This is taken as best available criterion description of each patient.
2. MMPI cookbook recipe Q-correlated with this criterion description.
3. For each patient, 4 or 5 clinicians "read" his MMPI in usual rule-of-thumb way, doing Q-sorts.
4. These rule-of-thumb Q-sorts also Q-correlated with criterion description.
5. Cross-validation results in outpatient sample.

| Validities | MMPI Curve Type | | | |
|---|---|---|---|---|
| | Code 123' | Code 27' | Code 13' | Code 87' |
| Cookbook | .88 | .69 | .84 | .68 |
| Rule-of-thumb (mean) | .75 | .50 | .50 | .58 |

Range (4–5 readers) .55 to .63 .29 to .54 .37 to .52 .34 to .58
Mean of 4 cookbook validities, through $z_r = .78$
Mean of 17 rule-of-thumb validities, through $z_r = .48$
Cookbook's superiority in validly predicted variance = 38%

6. Validity generalization to inpatient (psychiatric hospital) sample with different base rates; hence, an "unfair" test of cookbook.

| Validities | MMPI Curve Type | | | |
|---|---|---|---|---|
| | Code 123' | Code 27' | Code 13' | Code 87' |
| Cookbook | .63 | .64 | .36 | .70 |
| Rule-of-thumb (2 readers) | .37, .49 | .29, 42 | .30, .30 | .50, 50 |

Mean of 4 cookbook validities, through $z_r = .60$
Mean of 8 rule-of-thumb validities, through $z_r = .41$
Cookbook's superiority in validly predicted variance = 19%

How does the rule-of-thumb method show up in competition with the cookbook? Here we run into the problem of differences in clinical skill, so Halbower had each MMPI profile read blind by more than one clinician. The task was to interpret the profile by doing a Q sort. From two to five clinicians thus "read" each of the eight individual profiles, and the resulting 25 sorts were Q correlated with the appropriate therapist criterion sorts. These validity coefficients run from .29 to .63 with a median of .46. The clinicians were all Minnesota trained and varied in their experience with MMPI from less than a year (first-year VA trainees) through all training levels to PhD staff psychologists with six years' experience. The more experienced clinicians had probably seen over two thousand MMPI profiles in relation to varying amounts of other clinical data, including intensive psychotherapy. Yet not one of the 25 rule-of-thumb readings was as valid as the cookbook reading. Of the 25 comparisons which can be made between the validity of a single clinician's rule-of-thumb reading and that of the corresponding cookbook reading of the same patient's profile, 18 are significant in favor of the cookbook at the .01 level of confidence and 4 at the .05 level. The remaining 3 are also in favor of the cookbook but not significantly so.

Confining our attention to the more appropriate outpatient population, for (and upon) which the cookbook was developed, the mean $r$ (estimated through $z$ transformation) is .78 for the cookbook method, as contrasted with a mean (for 17 rule-of-thumb descriptions) of only .48, a difference of 30 points of correlation, which in this region amounts to a difference of 38 per cent in the validly predicted variance! The cookbook seems to be superior to the rule-of-thumb not merely in the sense of statistical significance but by an amount which is of very practical importance. It is also remarkable that even when the cookbook recipes are applied to patients from a quite different kind of population, their validity still excels that of rule-of-thumb MMPI readers who are in daily clinical contact with that other population. The improvement in valid variance in the hospital sample averages 19 per cent (see item 6 in Table 1).

A shrewd critic may be thinking, "Perhaps this is because all kinds of psychiatric patients are more or less alike, and the cookbook has simply taken advantage of this rather trivial fact." In answer to this objection, let me say first that to the extent the cookbook's superiority did arise from its actuarially determined tendency to "follow the base rates," that would be a perfectly sound application of the inverse probability considerations I at first advanced. For example, most psychiatric patients are in some degree depressed. Let us suppose the mean Q-sort placement given by therapists to the item "depressed" is seven. "Hysteroid" patients, who characteristically exhibit the so-called "conversion V" on their MMPI profiles (Halbower's cookbook code 13), are less depressed than most neurotics. The clinician, seeing such a conversion valley on the Multiphasic, takes this relation into account by attributing "lack of depression" to the patient. But maybe he overinterprets, giving undue weight to the psychometric finding and understressing the base rate. So his rule-of-thumb placement is far down at the nondepressed end, say at position three. The cookbook, on the other hand, "knows" (actuarially) that the mean Q placement for the item "depressed" is at five in patients with such profiles—lower than the over-all mean seven but not displaced as much in the conversion subgroup as the clinician thinks. If patients are so homogeneous with respect to a certain characteristic that the psychometrics ought not to influence greatly our attribution or placement in defiance of the over-all actuarial trend, then the clinician's tendency to be unduly influenced is a source of erroneous clinical decisions and a valid argument in favor of the cookbook.

However, if this were the chief explanation of Halbower's findings, the obvious conclusion would be merely that MMPI was not differentiating, since any test-induced departure from a description of the "average patient" would tend to be more wrong than right. Our original question would then be rephrased, "What is the comparative efficiency of the cookbook and the rule-of-thumb method *when each is applied to psychometric information having some degree of intrinsic validity?*" Time permits me only brief mention of the several lines of evidence in Halbower's study which eliminate the Barnum effect as an explanation. First of all, Halbower had selected his 154 items from

items recur in the top quartile of all four recipes; 60 per cent of the items occur in the top quartile of only one recipe). Third, several additional correlational findings combine to show that the cookbook was not succeeding merely by describing an "average patient" four times over. For example, the clinicians' Q description of their conception of the "average patient" gave very low validity for three of the four codes, and a "mean average patient" description constructed by pooling these clinicians' stereotypes was not much better (see Table 2). For Code 123' (interestingly enough, the commonest code among therapy cases in this clinic) the pooled stereotype was actually more valid than rule-of-thumb Multiphasic readings. (This is Bayes' Theorem with a vengence!) Nevertheless, I am happy to report that this "average patient" description was still inferior to the Multiphasic cookbook (significant at the .001 level).

TABLE 2. Validities of Four Clinicians' Description of "Average Patient," of the Mean of These Stereotypes, and of the Cookbook Recipe (Outpatient Cases Only)

| MMPI Curve Type | Validities of "Average Patient" Descriptions by 4 Clinicians | Validity of Mean of These 4 "Average Patient" Stereotypes | Validity of Cookbook Recipe |
|---|---|---|---|
| Code 123' | .63 to .69 | .74 | .88 |
| Code 27' | −.03 to .20 | .09 | .69 |
| Code 13' | .25 to .37 | .32 | .84 |
| Code 87' | .25 to .35 | .31 | .68 |

a much larger initial Q pool by a preliminary study of therapist sortings on a heterogeneous sample of patients in which items were eliminated if they showed low interpatient dispersal. Second, study of the placements given an item over the four cookbook recipes reveals little similarity (e.g., only two

In the little time remaining, let me ruminate about the implications of this study, supposing it should prove to be essentially generalizable to other populations and to other psychometric instruments. From a theoretical point of view, the trend is hardly surprising. It amounts to the obvious fact that the human brain is an inefficient recording and computing device. The cookbook method has an advantage over the rule-of-thumb method because it (a) samples more representatively, (b) records and stores information better, and (c) computes statistical weights which are closer to the optimal. We can perhaps learn more by putting the theoretical question negatively: when should we *expect* the cookbook to be inferior to the brain? The answer to this question presumably lies in the highly technical field of computing machine theory, which I am not competent to discuss. As I understand it, the use of these machines requires that certain rules of data combination be fed initially into the machine, followed by the insertion of suitably selected and coded information. Putting it crudely, the machine can "remember" and can "think routinely," but it cannot "spontaneously notice what is relevant" nor can it "think" in the more high-powered, creative sense (e.g., it cannot invent theories). To be sure, noticing what is relevant must involve the exemplification of some rule, perhaps of a very complex form. But it is a truism of behavior science that organisms can *exemplify* rules without *formulating* them. To take a noncontroversial example outside the clinical field, no one today knows how to state fully the rules of "similarity" or "stimulus equivalence" for patterned visual perception or verbal generalization; but of course we all exemplify daily these undiscovered rules. This suggests that as long as psychology cannot give a complete, explicit, quantitative account of the "dimensions of relevance" in behavior connections, the cookbook will not completely duplicate the clinician (11). The clinician *here* acts as an inefficient computer, but that is better than a computer with certain major rules completely left out (because we can't build

them in until we have learned how to formulate them). The use of the therapist's own unconscious in perceiving verbal and imaginal relations during dream interpretation is, I think, the clearest example of this. But I believe the exemplification of currently unformulable rules is a widespread phenomenon in most clinical inference. However, you will note that these considerations apply chiefly (if not wholly) to matters of *content*, in which a rich, highly varied, hard-to-classify content (such as free associations) is the input information. The problem of "stimulus equivalence" or "noticing the relevant" does not arise when the input data are in the form of preclassified responses, such as a Multiphasic profile or a Rorschach psychogram. I have elsewhere (10, pp. 110–111) suggested that even in the case of such prequantified patterns there arises the possibility of causal-theory-mediated idiographic extrapolations into regions of the profile space in which we lack adequate statistical experience; but I am now inclined to view that suggestion as a mistake. The underlying theory must itself involve some hypothesized function, however crudely quantified; otherwise, how is the alleged "extrapolation" possible? I can think of no reason why the estimation of the parameters in this underlying theoretical function should constitute an exception to the cookbook's superiority. If I am right in this, my "extrapolation" argument applies strictly only when a clinician literally *invents new theoretical relations or variables* in thinking about the individual patient. In spite of some clinicians' claims along this line, I must say I think it very rarely happens in daily clinical practice. Furthermore, even when it does happen, Bayes' Rule still applies. The *joint* probability of the theory's correctness, and of the attribute's presence (granting the theory but remembering nuisance variables) must be high enough to satisfy the inequalities I have presented, otherwise use of the theory will not pay off.

What are the pragmatic implications of the preceding analysis? Putting it bluntly, it suggests that for a rather wide range of clinical problems involving personality description from tests, the clinical interpreter is a costly middleman who might better be eliminated. An initial layout of research time could result in a cookbook whose recipes would encompass the great majority of psychometric configurations seen in daily work. I am fully aware that the prospect of a "clinical clerk" simply looking up Rorschach pattern number 73 J 10–5 or Multiphasic curve "Halbower Verzeichnis 626" seems very odd and even dangerous. I reassure myself by recalling that the number of phenotypic and genotypic attributes is, after all, finite; and that the number which are ordinarily found attributed or denied even in an extensive sample of psychological reports on patients is actually very limited. A best estimate of a Q-sort placement is surely more informative than a crude "Yes-or-No" decision of low objective confidence. I honestly cannot see, in the case of a *determinate trait domain* and a *specified clinical population*, that

there is a serious intellectual problem underlying one's uneasiness. I invite you to consider the possibility that the emotional block we all experience in connection with the cookbook approach could be dissolved simply by trying it out until our daily successes finally get us accustomed to the idea.

Admittedly this would take some of the "fun" out of psychodiagnostic activity. But I suspect that most of the clinicians who put a high value on this kind of fun would have even more fun doing intensive psychotherapy. The great personnel needs today, and for the next generation or more, are for psychotherapists and researchers. (If you don't believe much in the efficacy of therapy, this is the more reason for research.) If all the thousands of clinical hours currently being expended in concocting clever and flowery personality sketches from test data could be devoted instead to scientific investigation (assuming we are still selecting and training clinicians to be scientists), it would probably mean a marked improvement in our net social contribution. If a reasonably good cookbook could help bring about this result, the achievement would repay tenfold the expensive and tedious effort required in its construction.

# REFERENCES

1. Cronbach, L. J., and Meehl, P. E. Construct validity in psychological tests. *Psychol. Bull.*, 52(1955), 281–302.
2. Dailey, C. A. The practical utility of the clinical report. *J. Consult. Psychol.*, 17(1953), 297–302.
3. Davenport, Beverly, F. The semantic validity of TAT interpretations. *J. Consult. Psychol.*, 16(1952), 171–175.
4. Halbower, C. C. A comparison of actuarial versus clinical prediction to classes discriminated by MMPI. Unpublished doctor's dissertation, Univ. of Minn., 1955.
5. Hathaway, S. R. A coding system for MMPI profiles. *J. Consult. Psychol.*, 11 (1947) 334–337.
6. Holsopple, J. Q., and Phelan, J. G. The skills of clinicians in analysis of projective tests. *J. Clin. Psychol.*, 10 (1954), 307–320.
7. Kostlan, A. A method for the empirical study of psychodiagnosis. *J. Consult. Psychol.*, 18(1954), 83–88.
8. Little, K. B., and Shneidman, E. S. The validity of MMPI interpretations. *J. Consult. Psychol.*, 18(1954), 425–428.

9. ——— The validity of thematic projective technique interpretations. *J. Pers.*, 23(1955), 285–294.
10. MEEHL, P. E. *Clinical versus statistical prediction.* Minneapolis: Univ. of Minn. Press, 1954.
11. ——— "Comment" on McArthur, C. Analyzing the clinical process. *J. Counsel. Psychol.*, 1(1954), 203–208.
12. ———, and ROSEN, A. Antecedent probability and the efficiency of psychometric signs, patterns, or cutting scores. *Psychol. Bull.*, 52(1955), 194–216.
13. PATERSON, D. G. Character reading at sight of Mr. X according to the system of Mr. P. T. Barnum. (Mimeographed, unpublished.)
14. ROSEN, A. Detection of suicidal patients: an example of some limitations in the prediction of infrequent events. *J. Counsult. Psychol.*, 18(1954), 397–403.
15. SKINNER, B. F. *The behavior of organisms.* New York: Appleton-Century-Crofts, 1938.

Robert R. Holt

# Clinical and Statistical Prediction:
# A Reformulation and Some New Data

*The immediate reaction in the community of clinical psychologists to Meehl's championing of actuarial prediction was one of resistance and defensiveness. Although, interestingly, many psychologists indicate a preference for psychotherapy instead of psychodiagnostics, they resent the implication that a computer would be a more effective diagnostician. In this paper, Holt represents the views of many clinicians when he suggests a possible alternative to Meehl's argument. Dr. Holt draws a distinction between naive and sophisticated clinical prediction. He claims that it is only proper to compare actuarial prediction, which is a sophisticated technique, with sophisticated clinical prediction, but Meehl, he feels, often compares it with naive clinical prediction. Sophisticated clinical prediction is rooted in data, and involves careful attention to known empirical relationships. After drawing this distinction, Holt goes on to suggest that the proper relationship between clinical and statistical prediction is one of rapprochement rather than competition.*

The controversial discussions started a few years ago by Meehl's tightly packed little book, *Clinical vs. Statistical Prediction* (10), still continue— especially among graduate students in psychology, most of whom have to read it. Clinical students in particular complain of a vague feeling that a fast one has been put over on them, that under a great show of objectivity, or at least bipartisanship, Professor Meehl has actually sold the clinical approach up the river. The specific complaints they lodge against the book are, in my opinion, mostly based on misinterpretations, wishful thinking, or

*Reprinted from the* Journal of Abnormal & Social Psychology, 56(1958), 1–12, *with the permission of the American Psychological Association and Dr. Holt. Copyright 1958 by the American Psychological Association.*

other errors, yet I have felt for some time that there was something valid in the irrational reaction without knowing why.

What I propose to show here is that clinicians do have a kind of justified grievance against Meehl, growing out of his formulation of the issues rather than his arguments, which are sound. Finally, I want to offer a slightly different approach to the underlying problems, illustrated by some data. It may not quite make the lion lie down with the lamb, but I hope that it will help us all get on with our business, which is the making of a good science and profession.

## THE ISSUES RESTATED

Meehl's book contains a review of the controversy, a logical analysis of the nature of clinical judgment, a survey of empirical studies, and some conclusions. I am not going to go into his treatment of the logical issues and his psychological reconstruction of clinical thinking; for the most part, I agree with this part of the book and consider it a useful contribution to methodology. I want to focus rather on his conception of what the issues are in the controversy, on his treatment of the evidence, and on some of his conclusions.

Many issues make better reading when formulated as battles, and the field of the assessment and prediction of human behavior has not lacked for controversy-loving gauntlet-flingers. The sane and thoughtful voices of Horst and his collaborators, urging compromise and collaboration (5), have been shouted down by the war cries of such partisans as Sarbin (14) on the actuarial side and Murray (12) on the clinical or (as he put it) organismic. Meehl approached the problem with a full awareness of the feelings on both

sides, and apparently with the hope that the therapeutic ploy of bringing them all out into the open at the beginning would enable him to discuss the issues objectively.

In a recent discussion of the stir his book has raised, Meehl has expressed surprise and dismay (11) that his effort to take a balanced and qualified position has led so many people to misunderstand him as claiming that clinical prediction has been proved worthless. Yet he is not blameless; by posing the question of clinical *vs.* statistical prediction, he has encouraged two warring camps to form. This in turn makes it appear all the more compellingly that there *are* two clear-cut types of prediction to be compared.

The root difficulty, I believe, lies in Meehl's acceptance of *clinical* and *actuarial* as concepts that can without further analysis be meaningfully applied to a variety of predictive endeavors of an experimental or practical sort. Accepting them as valid types, he can hardly do anything other than pit one against the other and try to decide what is the proper sphere of exercise for each. But the terms in this antithesis mean many things; they are constellations of parts that are not perfectly correlated and can be separated.

The issue cannot therefore be sharply drawn so long as we speak about anything as complex as "clinical prediction" or "the clinical method." Rather, I think the central issue is the *role of clinical judgment in predicting human behavior.* By clinical judgment here, I mean nothing more complicated than the problem-solving or decision-reaching behavior of a person who tries to reach conclusions on the basis of facts and theories already available to him by thinking them over.

Let us make a fresh start, therefore, by examining the logical structure of the predictive process with an eye to locating the points where clinical judgment may enter. The following five-step process is idealized, and in practice some of the steps are more or less elided, but that does not hurt this analysis.

*First,* if we are to predict some kind of behavior, it is presupposed that we acquaint ourselves with what we are trying to predict. This may be called job analysis or the study of the criterion. Perhaps those terms sound a little fancy when their referent is something that seems so obvious to common sense. Nevertheless, it is surprising how often people expend a great deal of time and effort trying to predict a kind of behavior about which they know very little and apparently without even thinking that it might help if they could find out more. Consider the job of predicting outcome of flight training, for example. Many attempts to predict passing or washing out have been made by clinicians without any direct experience in learning to fly, without any study of flight trainees to see what they have to *do* in order to learn how to fly a plane, or of the ways they can fail to make the grade (cf. 4).

There is a hidden trick in predicting something like success in flight training, because that is not itself a form of behavior. It is an outcome, a judgment passed by someone on a great deal of concrete behavior. The same is true for grades in college, success in any type of treatment, and a host of other criteria that are the targets in most predictive studies. Because it is hidden by the label, there is a temptation to forget that the behavior you should be trying to predict exists and must be studied if it is to be rationally forecast. In the highly effective pilot selection work carried out by psychologists during the war, careful job analyses were an important step in the total predictive process and undoubtedly con-

tributed a good deal to the over-all success.

This first stage is hardly a good point at which to try to rely on clinical judgment. The result is most likely to be that guesses, easy and arbitrary assumptions, and speculative extrapolations will attempt to substitute for real information. And no matter how remarkable clinical judgment may sometimes be, it can never create information where there is none.

The *second* logical step is to decide what intervening variables need to be considered if the behavior is to be predicted. As soon as we get away from the simplest kind of prediction—that someone will continue to act the way he has been acting, or that test behavior A will continue to correlate (for an unknown reason) with criterion behavior B—we have to deal with the inner constructs that mediate behavior and the determining situational variables as well. You cannot make a rational choice of the kind of information you will need to have about a person to make predictions without some intervening variables, though they may remain entirely implicit. At this point, judgment enters—always, I think, though it may be assisted by empirical study. The best practice seems to be to give explicit consideration to this step, and to supply judgment with as many relevant facts as possible. This means studying known instances, comparing people who showed the behavior in question with others who in the same situation failed to.

All too often, when the problem of intervening variables is considered at all, it is handled by unaided clinical judgment. For example, in the Michigan project on the selection of clinical psychologists (7), a good many personality variables were rated, but there was no previous work highlighting the ones that might be related to success as a clinical psychologist. It was left up to each judge to form his own conception (from experience, theory, and guess) about what qualities mattered most. Again, this puts a greater burden on clinical judgment than it should reasonably be asked to bear. Yet some clinicians seem to have the mistaken notion that they are being false to their professional ideals if they stir from their armchairs at this point; nothing could be further from the best in clinical tradition, which is unashamedly empirical.

*Third,* it is necessary to find out what types of data afford measures or indications of the intervening variables, and can thus be used to predict the criterion behavior. If a good job has been done of the preceding step, it may be possible to rely entirely on judgment to make the preliminary selection of appropriate means of gathering predictive data. For example, if a job analysis and study of persons who have done well at the performance in question both suggest that verbal intelligence and information of a certain type are the main requisites, it would be easy to make good guesses about appropriate instruments to provide the predictive data. I use the word "guesses" deliberately, however, to emphasize the fact that judgment can do no more than supply hypotheses; it cannot substitute for an empirical trial to see whether in fact and under the conditions of this particular study the likely looking instruments do yield data that predict the criterion.

Notice that almost any actuarial predictive system presupposes carrying through this step. If there is to be an actuarial table, one has to collect great numbers of cases to determine the success frequencies for each cell in the table; if a regression equation is to be used, there must be a preliminary study to fix the beta weights. Unfortunately,

it is possible to work clinically *without* first getting an empirical check on one's hypotheses about likely-seeming instruments. At the risk of boring you, I repeat: there simply is no substitute for empirical study of the actual association between a type of predictive data and the criterion. Just as judgment is indispensable in forming hypotheses, it cannot be used to test them.

Perhaps this caution seems misplaced. Do I seem to be urging that you should first *do* a predictive study before embarking on one? I am. That is exactly what happens in actuarial prediction: the formula or table being pitted against judgmental prediction is typically being *cross*-validated, while in none of the studies Meehl cites were the clinical predictions under test being cross-validated. This alone is a major reason to expect superior performance from the actuarial predictions, and again it is a disadvantage under which the clinician by no means has to labor.

The next step, the *fourth* one, is to gather and process the data to give measures of the intervening variables. Meehl clearly recognizes that at this point clinical judgment either may play a large role or may be minimized. At one extreme, the data-yielding instrument may be a machine, a gadget like a complex coordination tester, which automatically counts errors and successes and makes a cumulative record of them. The resulting numbers may be directly usable in a regression equation without the intervention of anyone more skilled than a clerk. At an intermediate level, scoring most psychological tests requires a modicum of clinical judgment, though a high degree of reliability may be attained. At the other extreme is the interview; a great deal of clinical judgment is needed to convert the raw data into indices of the constructs the interviewer wants to assess.

It is easily overlooked that judgment needs the help of empirical study in this phase of the work too. The clinician's training supplies this empirical base in large part, but when he is using a familiar instrument to measure unusual intervening variables, or when he is working with an unfamiliar instrument, judgment grows fallible, and it is no more than prudent to piece it out by careful study of the same kind of predictive data on known subjects on whom the intervening variables have been well assessed independently.

The *fifth* and final step is the crucial one: at last the processed predictive data are *combined* so as to yield definite predictions in each case. The job can be done by clinical judgment, or it can be done by following a fixed rule (an actuarial table or regression equation) in a mechanical way. That much is clear; indeed, this is the locus of Meehl's main interest. I am taking it as granted that a clinician often integrates data in a different way than a statistician—as Meehl says, by performing a creative act, constructing a model of the person from the given facts put together with his theoretical understanding and thus generating perhaps a new type of prediction from a pattern he has never encountered before. We are all curious to know how well good clinicians can do it, and wonder if actuarial combination of data can do as well or better.

But it now seems plain that Meehl has been *too much* interested in this last stage, and as a result has neglected to pay enough attention to the way the earlier aspects of the predictive process were handled in the studies he has reviewed. Here I want to state my main critical point: *If two attempts to predict the same behavior differ significantly in the role played by clinical judgment as against actual study of the facts in one or more of the four*

*earlier parts of the predictive process, a comparison of the successes of the two attempts can tell us nothing definite about the effectiveness of clinical judgment at the final, crucial stage.* For this reason, in none of the 20 studies Meehl cites were the comparisons pertinent to the point. Particularly at the vital third step, the predicting statisticians have had the advantage of having previously studied the way their predictive data are related to the criterion; the clinicians have not.

If your reaction is, "So much the worse for the clinicians; nobody stopped them," I am afraid you are thinking about a different question from the one Meehl has raised. If the issue were whether some clinicians have made themselves look foolish by claiming too much, then I should agree: these studies show that they have, and unhappily, they have brought discredit on clinical methods generally. But the studies cited by Meehl and more recently by Cronbach in the *Annual Review of Psychology* (2) unfortunately have too many flaws at other points to tell us what clinical judgment can or cannot do as a way of combining data to make predictions. It is as if two riflemen were having a target match, but one took a wrong turn on the way to the shoot, never showed up, and lost by default. He demonstrated himself to be a poor driver, perhaps, but we never found out how well he could shoot, which is what we really wanted to know.

The other point I want to make in connection with the five-step analysis of the predictive process is this: Since there are so many ways in which clinical judgment can enter, for better or for worse, it makes little sense to classify every attempt to predict behavior on one side or the other of a simple dichotomy, clinical vs. statistical. There can be many types of clinical and actuarial combinations, and many are in fact found in Meehl's mixed bag.

For purposes of exposition, I should like to suggest an only slightly extended typology. Extracting from the best actuarial studies those parts of their procedure during the first four steps that are simply the application of common sense and the scientific method, I propose that we make it quite plain that these can be separated from actuarial prediction at the final step by creating a third type. Thus we should have:

Type I. *Pure actuarial*: Only objective data are used to predict a clear-cut criterion by means of statistical processes. The role of judgment is held to a minimum, and maximal use is made of a sequence of steps exemplified in the most successful Air Force studies in selecting air crew personnel (job analysis, item analysis, cross-validation, etc.).

Type II. *Naive clinical*: The data used are primarily qualitative with no attempt at objectification; their processing is entirely a clinical and intuitive matter, and there is no prior study of the criterion or of the possible relation of the predictive data to it. Clinical judgment is at every step relied on not only as a way of integrating data to produce predictions, but also as an alternative to acquaintance with the facts.

Type III. *Sophisticated clinical*: Qualitative data from such sources as interviews, life histories, and projective techniques are used as well as objective facts and scores, but as much as possible of objectivity, organization, and scientific method are introduced into the planning, the gathering of the data, and their analysis. All the refinements of design that the actuarial tradition has furnished are employed, including job analysis, pilot studies, item analysis, and successive cross-validations. Quantification and statistics are used wherever helpful, but the clinician himself is retained as one of the prime instruments, with an effort to make him as reliable and valid a data-proces-

sor as possible; and he makes the final organization of the data to yield a set of predictions tailored to each individual case.

If we now re-examined the studies cited by Meehl and Cronbach, we see that most of them have pitted approximations to Type I actuarial predictive designs against essentially Type II naive clinical approaches. It seems hardly remarkable that Type I has generally given better results than Type II; indeed, the wonder should be that the naive clinical predictions have done as well as they have, in a number of instances approaching the predictive efficiency of actuarial systems.

Other studies cited have come closer to comparing Type II with Type III— naive vs. sophisticated clinical prediction instead of clinical vs. statistical. For example, the prognostic studies by Wittman (16) compared predictions of reaction to shock treatment made in a global way at staff conference with a system she devised. But her system used highly judgmental predictive variables, as Meehl himself points out (ranging from *duration of psychosis* to *anal erotic vs. oral erotic*), and they were combined using a set of weights assigned on judgmental, not statistical grounds.[1] What she showed was that a systematic and comprehensive evaluation of the thirty items in her scale (all based on previous empirical work) made better predictions of the outcome of shock treatment than global clinical judgments not so organized and guided. A study of movement in family case work by Blenkner came to a very similar conclusion with somewhat different subject matter (1). When social workers rated an initial interview according to their general impressions, they were unable to predict the outcome of the case, whereas when their judgments

[1] It is true that the weights were applied in the same way for all cases; in this respect, the system deviates from the ideal Type III.

were organized and guided by means of an outline calling for appraisals of five factors which had been shown in previous studies to be *meaningfully*, not statistically related to the criterion, then these judgmentally derived predictive variables, combined (like Wittman's) in an a priori formula, predicted the criterion quite well. Yet both studies are tallied as proving actuarial predictions superior to clinical.

Meehl's conclusion from his review of this "evidence" is that clinical prediction is an expensive and inefficient substitute for the actuarial method, and one that keeps clinicians from using their talents more constructively in psychotherapy or exploratory research.

The evidence available tells us hardly anything about the relative efficacy of clinical judgment in making predictions. The weight of numbers should not impress us; as long as the studies don't really bear on the issue, no matter how many are marshalled, they still have no weight. Remember the *Literary Digest* poll: many times more straw votes than Gallup used, but a faulty sampling principle, so that piling up numbers made the conclusion less valid as it got more reliable. Moreover, the studies tallied are so different in method, involving varying amounts of clinical judgment at different points (in the "actuarial" instances as well as the "clinical" ones), that they cannot sensibly be added together.

What is fair to conclude, I think, is that many clinicians are wasting their time when they try to fall back on their clinical judgment in place of knowing what they are talking about. They have been guilty of over-extending themselves, trying to predict things they know nothing about, and learning nothing in the process of taking part in what Cronbach calls "horserace experimental designs," in which clinicians and statisticians merely try to outsmart each other. A multiplication of

such studies will not advance clinical psychology.

One kind of comparative study might teach us something even though it would be hard to do properly: simultaneous attempts to predict the same criterion from the same data by clinicians and statisticians *who have gone through the same preliminary steps*. As the statistician studies the original group to determine the critical scores for his multiple cutting point formula (or whatever), the clinician will study the configurations of these scores in individuals of known performance. Then we will see how their respective predictive techniques work.

Does it really make sense, however, for both to use the same data and predict the same criterion? A second possibility would be for two otherwise equally sophisticated methods to predict the same criterion, each using the kind of data most appropriate to it. Or, third, the more clinical and the more statistical methods would not predict the same criterion, but each would undertake to predict the kind of behavior it is best suited to, using the most appropriate kind of data.

Doesn't this third proposal abandon experimental controls necessary for intelligible results? To some extent, yes; but one may have to give up some control to avoid absurdity. As long as clinician and statistician are trying to predict the same criterion, the clinician is likely to be working under a severe, though concealed, handicap. The study will usually have been designed by the statistician; that is his business. He will naturally choose the kind of criterion for which *his* methods seem best adapted; indeed, the nature of his method makes it impossible for him to choose the kind of predictive task that would be most congenial to the clinician, such as drawing a multidimensional diagnostic picture of a total personality, or predicting what a patient will do next in psychotherapy. Thus, the statistician takes advantage of the foolish boast of the clinician, "Anything you can do, I can do better," and plans the contest on his own grounds. The clinician ends up trying to predict grade-point average in the freshman year by a "clinical synthesis" of high school grades and an intelligence test. This is a manifest absurdity; under the circumstances, how could the clinician do other than operate like a second-rate Hollerith machine? If clinical judgment is really to be tested, it must operate on data that are capable of yielding insights. Moreover, it makes hardly any more sense to expect it to grind out numerical averages of course grades than to expect an actuarial table to interpret dreams.

For reasons of this kind, McArthur (9) recently called for studies of the third type just listed, and maintained that there have as yet been no studies in which the clinician has been given a chance to show what he can do on his own terms. I want therefore to present briefly some results from one such attempt: a study in which clinicians tried to predict criteria of their own choosing, using clinical types of data—interviews and psychological tests (mainly projective techniques).[2] Since some preliminary reports of this work have already been quoted as showing the ineffectiveness of clinical predictions (cf. 2), I have a special desire to set the record straight.

## VALIDATING NAIVE AND SOPHISTICATED CLINICAL PREDICTIONS: SOME NEW DATA

The project was an effort to improve the methods by which medical men were selected for specialty training in the Menninger School of Psychiatry. It was begun by Dr. David Rapaport, together with Drs. Karl A. Menninger, Robert P. Knight, and other psychiatrists at the Menninger Foundation at the time the Menninger School of Psychiatry was founded 11 years ago. In the late summer of 1947, Dr. Lester Luborsky and I began work on it, and since then we have jointly carried major responsibility for the project although quite a number of other people have made important contributions.

Our work consisted of two predictive studies. Following the terminology suggested above, one used a naive clinical method, while the other was an attempt at a more sophisticated clinical method. The naive clinical design was simple: Psychiatrists and psychologists used their favorite means of assessing personality to forecast the level of future performance of psychiatric residents at the time when they applied to the School. The applicant came to Topeka after some preliminary correspondence, having survived a rough screening of credentials and application forms. He was seen by three psychiatrists, each of whom interviewed him for about an hour, rated his probable success as a resident on a 10-point scale, and made a recommendation: Take, Reject, or Doubtful. The psychologist made similar ratings and recommendations after analyzing results of a Wechsler-Bellevue, Rorschach, and Word Association test. In addition, both psychologists and psychiatrists submitted brief qualitative reports of their appraisals of the man's positive and negative potentialities. All of the data and predictions were turned over to the Admissions Committee, which made the final decision to accept or reject each man.

During the years of the project, from 1946 through 1952, six successive

[2] This study is presented at length in a book (3).

classes of residents were chosen. The first 456 applicants who went through this procedure formed our experimental population (excluding small numbers of Negroes, women, and persons from Latin-American and non-European cultures, since these minorities offered special problems of assessment). A little over 62 per cent of these applicants were accepted by the Committee, but only 238 actually entered the School; 46 changed their minds and went elsewhere. Nevertheless, we kept in touch with them and the 172 rejectees by a mail follow-up questionnaire for several years, so that we have data on certain aspects of their subsequent careers.

The clinicians making the predictions had in some cases had considerable experience in training psychiatric residents, but there was no explicit job analysis or preliminary study of criterion groups. They simply fell to and made their predictions and their decisions.

To test the validity of these clinical decisions, let us use as a criterion, first, whether or not a man passed the certifying examination of the American Board of Psychiatry and Neurology—the criterion set up by the specialty itself. We have this information on all subjects from the lists published by the Board. The Admissions Committee's decisions had a good deal of validity as predictors of this criterion: 71 per cent of the men they voted to accept had passed the Board examination in psychiatry by the end of 1956, while only 36 per cent of the rejected candidates had done so. This difference is significant at better than the .001 point. The recommendations made by interviewers (taking them all as a group) and the recommendations of the psychological

testers to accept or reject likewise were highly valid predictors of this criterion, significances in both cases also being beyond .001.

It is interesting that the Committee decisions were slightly *better* at predicting both staying in psychiatry and passing the certification examination of the American Board of Psychiatry and Neurology—better than either the psychiatric interviewers or the psychological testers. It is possible, however, that much or all of this apparent superiority is due to the fact that rejection by the committee did discourage a few applicants from seeking training elsewhere.

Data of this kind are encouraging to the people trying to run a school of psychiatry but hard to interpret in a larger context. Who knows but that an actuarial table based on objectively ascertainable facts like grades in medical school, marital status, age, etc. might not have done just as well? We never took such a possibility very seriously, but we did try out a few such objective predictors in our spare time, just out of curiosity. None of them showed any particular promise as a predictor of any criterion taken alone, though it is possible that patterns of them such as an actuarial table uses might have operated a little better than chance.

The criteria on which we spent most time and labor were measures of competence in psychiatric work during the last two years of the three-year residency. Whenever a resident completed a period of time on a particular service, we would interview the staff men, consultants, and others who had directly supervised his clinical work, and get them to rate it quantitatively. The resulting criterion measure had a coefficient of internal consistency above .9 [3]

[3] Correlations in bold type are significant at the one per cent point, those in italics, at the five per cent point. One-tailed tests are used throughout to test the null hypothesis that the predictor does not correlate *positively* with the criterion.

(for the last few classes), and we have every reason to think it has a great deal of intrinsic validity. We also got the residents to rate each other's work. The reliability of their pooled ratings of over-all competence is also .9, and this criterion (which we call "Peers' Evaluations") correlates from .66 to .78 with Supervisors' Evaluations.

These criterion judgments enable us to test the validity of the predictive *ratings*. The validity correlations are not exciting, though for the entire group of residents in the Menninger School of Psychiatry they are all significantly better than zero at the one percent point. Taking the *mean* of the ratings given by the psychiatrists who interviewed an applicant, this predictor correlates .24 with Supervisors' Evaluations. The predictions of the psychological testers were not significantly better: the validity coefficient is .27. There was some fluctuation from class to class, the interviewers' validities varying from exactly .00 to .52, the testers' validities from .12 to .47. Likewise, the validities of ratings made by individual clinicians vary over the same range: psychiatric interviewers from .01 to .27 ($N = 93$) or .47 (significant at only the 5 percent point because the $N$ was only 13), and psychologists from .20 to .41 ($N = 40$). At the same time, those individual clinicians all did much better in making the basic discrimination: recommending acceptance of men who actually became psychiatrists.

These correlations are nothing to get excited about, and nothing to be ashamed of either, particularly in view of the restriction of range in this selected, accepted sample. They show that the naive clinical method depends a good deal on the ability of the particular clinician doing the predicting, and that—at least in this study—a pooling of judgment helped make up for the deficiencies of individuals.

Let us turn now to the second experimental design, which I have called a *sophisticated clinical* type of prediction. I shall have to skip lightly over many complicated details, and make things look a little more orderly than they actually were. The design included a job analysis of the work done by psychiatric residents, which was broken down into a few major functions (such as diagnosis, psychotherapy, administration of wards) and 14 more specific aspects of work. Then we attempted to specify attributes of personality that would facilitate or hinder a man in carrying out such work, first by collecting the opinions of persons who had had long experience in training psychiatrists, psychotherapists, or psychoanalysts. The second way we went about it was to make an intensive study of a dozen excellent residents and a dozen who were rated at the bottom by their supervisors. We went over all the original assessment data on them, interviewed them and tested them extensively, trying out many novel approaches and then seeing what discriminated these known extreme groups. Thus, we learned what personological constructs differentiated good from poor residents, and what tests and test indicators gave evidence of these constructs. Hoping to guide clinical judgment in the use of interviews and projective tests, we used the data from these small samples of extremes to help us write detailed manuals on the use of the interview, TAT, Rorschach, and other techniques in the selection of psychiatric residents. The manuals listed discriminating cues, both positive and negative, which were to be summed algebraically. We then made preliminary cross-validations of these manuals (as many as we could) with encouraging results (cf. 8) and revised them after studying predictive successes and failures.

As a last step, we set up another predictive study to submit our manuals to a final cross-validation on a group of 64 subjects and to accomplish several other purposes at the same time. Four psychologists served as judges; each of them scored tests or interviews according to our manuals and also made free clinical judgments based on increasing amounts of data. Two of the judges made such predictive ratings after going through an entire file of assessment data: credentials, intellectual and projective tests, and a recorded and transcribed interview.

How did we make out? Considering first the manuals, only indifferently well. Of the six, two proved worthless (TAT Content and a special projective test); the other four all showed more or less promise, but there was none that yielded consistently significant validities regardless of who used it. Reliability, in terms of scorer agreement, was on the whole not very good, for a good deal of clinical judgment was still demanded. Consider, for example, one TAT cue that worked well for one judge (validity of .26 against Supervisors' Evaluations of Over-all Competence). This cue called for judgments of the *originality* of each TAT story, obviously a matter on which psychologists might fairly easily disagree: scores by Judges I and II correlated—.04. The validities attained by the manuals for the Interview, Rorschach, Formal Aspects of the TAT, and Self-Interpretation of the TAT were on about the same general level as those from our first, naive clinical design—mostly in the .20's.

Now for the free clinical predictive ratings. When the judge had only one test or an interview to go on he usually added little by going beyond the manual and drawing on his general experience and intuition. Some judges did slightly better with free ratings than with manual scores, some a little worse.

At this point, you may wonder at all this exposition for so small a result: barely significant validity coefficients, about the same size as those from a naive clinical approach, despite the attempt to create a sophisticated clinical predictive system that involved many actuarial elements. I believe that the lesson of our findings up to this point is simple: *With an inadequate sample of information about a person, no matter how sophisticated the technique of prediction, there is a low ceiling on the predictive validity that can be attained.* In our experience, even a battery of two or three tests (if exclusively projective), or an interview and a couple of projective techniques, does not give an adequate informational sample to enable clinicians to make very accurate predictions of complex behavioral outcomes over a period of three years.

Look next at the results when experimental judges made their predictions from as complete a body of information about a man as could be assembled at the time he applied. The hard-headed statistical expectation *should* be that validities would at best remain at the same level, and more likely would decline. The widely read preliminary report of the Michigan project on the selection of clinical psychologists (6) reported declining validities as increasing amounts of information were made available to judges (in a design which, for all its complexity, was essentially a naive clinical one). Not so many people have read the full final report (7), where this issue is not discussed; it is necessary to pore over many tables and tally numbers of significant correlations at various stages to find out for oneself that with the final criteria there was a slight *rising* trend in validities of clinical predictions as the amount of information available to the predicting judge was increased.

The same thing is true of our results,

but in a dramatic and unmistakable way (see Table 1). Considering only the two judges who went through the entire mass of material, their final free clinical ratings of Over-all Competence correlated .57 and .22 with Supervisors' Evaluations and .52 and .48 with the sociometric Peers' Evaluations. In considering these correlations, remember that they are attenuated by a significant restriction of range, since all subjects had successfully passed through an Admissions Committee screening which had considerable validity. They have not been corrected for less than perfect reliabilities, either.

An incidental finding is even more remarkable. The predictive analysis was made approximately a year after the assessment data had been gathered. The judges went right through the entire series of cases, making their ratings in a *blind* analysis; names and other identifying data were concealed, and there was no direct contact with the subjects. Nevertheless, judges formed rather vivid impressions from the material, including a feeling of how well they would like each candidate personally. For control purposes, they were required to rate this feeling of *liking*. When we undertook to correlate

the liking rating with predictors and criteria so as to partial out this possible source of error, we found that it was the best predictor we had! These ratings of liking by Judges I and II correlated highly with their predictive ratings, but even more highly with Supervisors' Evaluations (.58 and .25) and especially with Peers' Evaluations (.64 and .49).[4] A study of these liking ratings suggests to us as the most plausible explanation that they differed from our intentional clinical predictions in being somewhat more irrational, affective—perhaps intuitive—reactions to the same data.

In all of the correlations I have been citing, you will perhaps have noticed that one judge consistently did slightly better than the other. This is certainly to be expected. When clinical judgment is the main technique of processing data, there are bound to be differences due to the skill of clinicians in doing this particular job.

Are we justified in citing these few high validities as evidence of what the sophisticated clinical method can do in a study where it is given a chance to prove itself on grounds of its own choosing? I believe that we are. The psychologists who were our Judges I and II

---

[4] One consequence of the delay between the gathering of the data and their analysis was that some of the Ss who entered the Menninger School of Psychiatry became known to the predictive judges, raising the possibility of contamination of their predictions by criterion-relevant knowledge. Despite the fact that the analysis of the assessment material was done "blind," identifying data having been removed or concealed, Judge I fairly often recognized the identity of Ss at the final stage of analysis. He therefore did not make predictive ratings, which is why his Ns are so low for this stage. There were a few borderline instances of partial or questionable recognition, however, in which Judge I (four cases) or II (two cases) had some information or misinformation about the subject. If these cases are eliminated, Judge II's validities go up more often than they go down, the range being from a decrease of .16 to an increase of .15. Judge I's validities against Supervisors' Evaluations are negligibly affected, the range of effects extending from a loss of .08 to a gain of .20. Most of his validities against Peers' Evaluations were more seriously affected, however, especially at the final (all-data) stage of analysis, where losses of up to 28 correlation points occurred. On the whole, however, even a very conservative handling of the problem of possibly contaminated cases does not change the essential import of the results: It was still possible for Judge I to obtain four validities of .50 or higher, and for Judge II to obtain two validities of .36 or higher. (For a fuller discussion of the problem of contamination in these results, see [3].)

TABLE 1. Some Validities from Systematic Clinical Assessment of Applicants for Residencies in the Menninger School of Psychiatry

| Predictors: | Validities of Predictors Against Criterion Evaluations of: | | | | | | | | | |
| --- | --- | --- | --- | --- | --- | --- | --- | --- | --- | --- |
| | Over-all Competence | | Competence in Psychotherapy | | Competence in Diagnosis | | Competence in Management | | Competence in Administration | |
| | Sup.[a] | Peer[a] | Sup. | Peer | Sup. | Peer | Sup. | Peer | Sup. | Peer |
| Predictive Ratings | | | | | | | | | | |
| Judge I: PRT[b] | .26 | .23 | .12 | .26 | .13 | .21 | .31 | .00 | .20 | .10 |
| Judge II: TAT | −.10 | −.02 | −.16 | −.01 | −.05 | .20 | −.08 | .01 | .04 | .11 |
| Judge I: All data | .57 | .52 | .48 | .55 | .58 | .42 | .52 | .36 | .55 | .42 |
| Judge II: All data | .22 | .48 | .15 | .36 | .24 | .42 | .13 | .24 | .24 | .27 |
| Liking Ratings | | | | | | | | | | |
| Judge I: PRT | .29 | .34 | .16 | .35 | .24 | .36 | .15 | .17 | .19 | .16 |
| Judge II: TAT | −.02 | .13 | −.08 | .15 | .00 | .30 | −.17 | −.02 | −.14 | .10 |
| Judge I: All data | .58 | .64 | .45 | .58 | .51 | .52 | .52 | .52 | .50 | .46 |
| Judge II: All data | .25 | .49 | .20 | .47 | .21 | .56 | .10 | .30 | .18 | .30 |

[a] Sup. = Supervisors' Evaluations; Peer = Peers' (Sociometric) Evaluations.

[b] PRT = Picture Reaction Test, a specially devised projective test similar to TAT.

Numbers of cases: For Judge I—Supervisors' Evaluations, PRT: 63, all data: 37
　　　　　　　　　　　　　　　Peers' Evaluations, PRT: 45, all data: 30
　　　　　　　　　For Judge II—Supervisors' Evaluations, TAT: 63, all data: 64
　　　　　　　　　　　　　　　　Peers' Evaluations, TAT: 45, all data: 46

were considered to be good but not extraordinary clinicians, certainly no better than the best of the psychologists and psychiatrists who made the "naive clinical" predictions. They differed principally in that they had an adequate sample of data and had been through all the preliminary stages of studying the criterion in relation to the predictors in earlier groups of subjects. Moreover, they used systematic methods of analyzing the data, attempting to record all inferences and working with a set of intervening variables—personality constructs which were directly inferred from the test and interview data, and from which in turn the behavioral predictions were made. In a true sense, their clinical ratings were not naively based on unguided and uncontrolled judgment; they constituted a cross-validation of a whole structure of hypotheses about the determinants of psychiatric performance based on intensive prior study. Even so, our study left a great deal to be desired as a model of the sophisticated clinical approach—particularly on the scores of (a) a better job analysis, (b) a more broadly based, configurational approach to the design of manuals, and (c) a better stabilized criterion (see 3).

By way of contrast, a few more data before a final summing up. You remember that the battery of tests used in the first naive clinical predictive design consisted of the Wechsler-Bellevue, Rorschach, and Word Association tests. (The Szondi was also given, but was usually ignored; and the Strong Vocational Interest Blank was also routinely given, but was never scored in time to be used in the actual assessment for the Admissions Committee.) The Rorschachs we gave were of course scored in the conventional way as well as by our special manual, and we thought it might be fun to see how some of the usual Rorschach scores would be related

to the criterion. So we tried 14 scores and simple indices (like A%) with one class, and were surprised to find some rather high correlations. We decided therefore to see how a straight statistical-actuarial method of using the Rorschach would perform. Scrutinizing the table of intercorrelations between the Rorschach scores, we chose five of them that promised the greatest chances of success: DR%, number of good M, new F+%, F% and Stereotype% (scored after Rapaport, 13)—the last two because they looked as if they might be good "suppressor variables." A multiple regression equation was worked out to give the best linear combination of these variables to predict Over-all Competence; R for this Class was .43 ($N = 64$). We noticed, however, that in the regression equation only the first two scores seemed to be playing any appreciable part, and in fact the multiple correlation using only per cent of rare details and number of good M was also .43. The other three were dropped from the formula, which was then tested on the Rorschach scores and criterion ratings of the first three classes. As expected, the correlation dropped out of sight on being cross-validated; with the new group of 116 subjects, it was .04.

The Strong Vocational Interest Blank, which (with an intelligence test) gave the best validities in the Kelly-Fiske study, likewise failed to yield any good predictor of competence in psychiatry. Even the special key ("Psychiatrist A") produced by Strong from a statistical analysis of thousands of blanks filled out by diplomats in psychiatry (15) failed to predict any of our criteria at a statistically significant level: no r's as high as .2. This last finding deserves emphasis, because Strong's key was the product of a highly developed statistical technology, had an adequate numerical base, and had every opportunity to show what a pure actuarial method could achieve.

We made a further attempt to combine the best-predicting scores from the tests used in the standard battery into a regression equation. The R between Verbal IQ (Wechsler-Bellevue), Lawyer key (Strong VIB), DR% and No. Good M (Rorschach), and Over-all Competence was .56 on the original group of 64; cross-validated on 100 cases, it dropped to .13.

## SOME PRACTICAL IMPLICATIONS

If we had concentrated on an actuarial rather than a clinical approach and had come up with a simple, objective procedure that had a high and stable level of validity in predicting psychiatric performance, it could have been misused. It might have tempted many psychiatric training centers to adopt a single mold from which would have been cast a generation of psychiatrists, who would have had to meet the problems of the future with a standard set of resources derived from the past. The more successful we are in finding objective, impersonal, and statistical methods of selecting members of a profession in the image of its past leaders, the more rigid will be the pattern into which it is frozen.

For a concrete example, consider Strong's Psychiatrist A key again for a moment. It expresses the pattern of interests held in common by men who were diplomates in psychiatry at the end of the war, most of whom must have trained fifteen to twenty years ago. It should hardly be surprising that residents whose interests most closely approached this pattern tended to have skills as administrators and diagnosticians rather than as psychotherapists. If they had happened to achieve a high

correlation with our over-all criterion, it might have helped populate American psychiatry of the 1960's and 1970's with near-replicas of the old state hospital superintendent.

It might be argued, however, that a similar result could have been expected if we had succeeded in providing explicit methods of clinically analyzing other types of data to select psychiatric residents. They too would have been based on a study of men who were successful at one time in history, and would have suffered the same danger of getting out of date. The answer is that even sophisticated clinical prediction never gets quite that rigid. Changes creep in; the result may be that validities gradually regress, or the drift may be determined by valid appraisals of newly important variables. Clinical methods are more flexible than their actuarial counterparts; they *can* be more readily modified by new studies based on observations of developing trends in the criterion. Moreover, valid clinical impressions can be obtained from an intensive study of a few known cases, while it takes large samples to set up or revise an actuarial system. There can be no guarantee that clinical methods *will* be kept up to date, of course, nor that the attempt to do so will not spoil their validities. Any predictive system needs constant overhaul and revalidation.

By sticking with the only capriciously accurate, sporadically reliable, and eminently flexible method of clinical judgment in selecting trainees, psychiatry will at least be able to keep in touch with developments in a growing and changing profession. Moreover, it will be able to maintain a healthy diversity within its ranks. There are many jobs to be done in psychiatry, requiring quite different kinds of men. There must be thoughtful men who like to sit in deep chairs and analyze patients all day long. There must be activists to organize new institutions and give inspirational leadership to groups of colleagues. Psychiatry needs many more men than it has whose main interest is in research and teaching, others to work with broad preventive programs in public health, group therapists, specialists in somatic treatments, and many more varieties of the general species. If the pure actuarial approach were to be seriously applied to psychiatry, it would be necessary to develop a formula for each of many different types of practice and to revise it constantly as new developments created needs for new types of practitioners. To do so would be impossibly expensive and laborious. Psychiatry is well off, therefore, sticking with a basically clinical approach to assessment and prediction in selecting its members, but trying constantly to make it more scientific.

The important issue, however, is not what method of selecting its members is best for any particular profession, but the relative inertia of actuarial predictive systems and the maneuverability introduced when the generating of predictions is done by clinical judgment. This freedom is a source of weakness as well as strength; it enables the clinician to fall into errors of many kinds (to which statistical predictions are less subject) and also to adapt himself sensitively to all kinds of changing circumstances. When clinical methods are given a chance—when skilled clinicians use methods with which they are familiar, predicting a performance about which they know something—and especially when the clinician has a rich body of data and has made the fullest use of the systematic procedures developed by actuarial workers, including a prior study of the bearing of the predictive data on the criterion performance, then sophisticated clinical prediction can achieve quite respectable successes. I hope that clinicians will take some heart from our results, but I urge them to refine their procedures by learning as much as possible about statistical prediction and adapting it to their own ends.

To summarize: Meehl failed in his aim to mediate the statistical-clinical quarrel because he defined the issues in a way that perpetuates competition and controversy. The real issue is not to find the proper sphere of activity for clinical predictive methods and for statistical ones, conceived in ideal-type terms as antithetical. Rather, we should try to find the optimal combination of actuarially controlled methods and sensitive clinical judgment for any particular predictive enterprise. To do so, we must strike the right balance between freedom and constraint, a balance which may shift a good deal in one direction or the other depending on the nature of the behavior being predicted. But we can find such balances only if clinically and statistically oriented workers give up contentious, competitive attitudes and seek to learn from each other.

## REFERENCES

1. BLENKNER, M. Predictive factors in the initial interview in family casework. *Soc. Serv. Rev.*, 28(1954), 65–73.
2. CRONBACH, L. J. Assessment of individual differences. In P. Farnsworth and Q. McNemar, eds., *Annual review of psychology*. Stanford, Calif.: Annual Reviews, 1956. Volume VII, pages 173–196.
3. HOLT, R. R., and LUBORSKY, L. *Personality patterns of psychiatrists* (2 vols.). New York: Basic Books, 1958.
4. HOLTZMAN, W. H., and SELLS, S. B. Prediction of flying success by clinical

analysis of test protocols. *J. Abnorm. Soc. Psychol.*, **49**(1954), 485–490.

5. HORST, P. *et al. The prediction of personal adjustment.* New York: Soc. Sci. Res. Council Bull. 48(1941).

6. KELLY, E. L., and FISKE, D. W. The prediction of success in the VA training program in clinical psychology. *Amer. Psychologist*, **5**(1950), 395–406.

7. ———— *The prediction of performance in clinical psychology.* Ann Arbor, Mich.: Univ. of Michigan Press, 1951.

8. LUBORSKY, L. L., HOLT, R. R., and MORROW, W. R. Interim report of the research project on the selection of medical men for psychiatric training. *Bull. Menninger Clinic*, **14**(1950), 92–101.

9. McARTHUR, C. Clinical versus actuarial prediction. In *Proceedings, 1955 invitational conference on testing problems.* Princeton, N.J.: Educational Testing Service, 1956. Pages 99–106.

10. MEEHL, P. E. *Clinical vs. statistical prediction.* Minneapolis: Univ. of Minnesota Press, 1954.

11. ———— Clinical versus actuarial prediction. In *Proceedings, 1955 invitational conference on testing problems.* Princeton, N.J.: Educational Testing Service, 1956. Pages 136–141.

12. OSS Assessment Staff. *Assessment of men.* New York: Rinehart, 1948.

13. RAPAPORT, D., GILL, M. M., and SCHAFER, R. *Diagnostic psychological testing.* (Second edition, revised and condensed by R. R. Holt) New York: International Universities Press, 1968.

14. SARBIN, T. R. A contribution to the study of actuarial and statistical methods of prediction. *Amer. J. Sociol.*, **48** (1943), 593–603.

15. STRONG, E. K., JR., and TUCKER, A. J. The use of vocational interest scores in planning a medical career. *Psychol. Monogr.*, **66**(1952), (9), No. 341.

16. WITTMAN, M. P. A scale for measuring prognosis in schizophrenic patients. *Elgin Papers*, **4**(1941), 20–33.

# Section II

# Psychopathology

*Traditionally, psychopathology has been studied in terms of more or less discrete classes or subdivisions. Long before man had much of an understanding of the causes of behavioral abnormality, he made attempts to classify it. In fact, he often seems to have thought that by classifying abnormality he could understand it better. Certain disorders, like manic-depressive psychosis, were described in the Bible and in the writings of classical Greece. Others, like schizophrenia, were not even beginning to be conceptualized in their present form until the late nineteenth century or even more recently. Despite the many disadvantages and potential pitfalls of the business of creating nosologies, such systems have tended to cut the behavioral pie into certain kinds of slices that then draw specific attention.*

*This section presents examples of research and theories that have been developed about the various major subdivisions of abnormal behavior. The number of pages devoted to each slice of the abnormal behavioral pie bears little relation to the severity of that problem for society. Instead, it reflects the amount of attention devoted to the problem by professionals. Therefore, while there are far fewer people suffering from psychoses than from personality disorders, much more professional attention has been devoted to psychoses, especially schizophrenia.*

# Chapter 3

# Psychoneuroses

*Neurotic problems became a major concern of the mental health professional only after Freud devoted much time and thought to them. His perceived success in understanding and treating such disorders was a potent impetus to the development of a variety of personality theories. It was also the basis for considerable faith that all behavior could be fathomed eventually. Certainly one of the major legacies of the early work on psychoneurosis was a redefinition of the field of abnormal psychology which broadened it out from the narrow involvement with the psychoses which had characterized it earlier. This expansion also laid the groundwork for a still further enlargement of the mental health worker's area of concern that was to come.*

## Sigmund Freud

## My Views on the Part Played by Sexuality in the Aetiology of the Neuroses

*One cornerstone of the psychoanalytic theory of psychoneurosis is the basic role seen to be played by infantile sexuality in personality development. In the following paper, which was written in 1905, Freud attempts to explain the basis for his conclusions concerning the key role of sexuality in the life of the very young child and the way in which inadequacies in sexual development lead to neurotic problems. It is a valuable testament to the way his theoretical approach was shaped by his clinical experience.*

My theory of the aetiological importance of the sexual factor in the neuroses can best be appreciated, in my opinion, by following the history of its development. For I have no desire whatever to deny that it has gone through a process of evolution and been modified in the course of it. My professional colleagues may find a guarantee in this admission that the theory is nothing other than the product of continuous and ever deeper-going experience. What is born of speculation, on the contrary, may easily spring into existence complete, and thereafter remain unchangeable.

*Reprinted with permission from Chapter XIV of Vol. 1 of* The Collected Papers of Sigmund Freud, *edited by Ernest Jones, authorized translation under the supervision of Joan Riviere, Basic Books, Inc., Publishers, New York, 1959. Acknowledgment is also made to* The Hogarth Press Ltd., London, *publishers of* The Complete Psychological Works of Sigmund Freud, Standard Edition.

Originally my theory related only to the clinical pictures comprised under the term 'neurasthenia,' among which I was particularly struck by two, which occasionally appear as pure types and which I described as 'neurasthenia proper' and 'anxiety neurosis.' It had, to be sure, always been a matter of common knowledge that sexual factors *may* play a part in the causation of these forms of illness; but those factors were not regarded as invariably operative, nor was there any idea of giving them precedence over other aetiological influences. I was surprised to begin with at the frequency of gross disturbances in the *vita sexualis* of nervous patients; the more I set about looking for such disturbances—bearing in mind the fact that everyone hides the truth in matters of sex—and the more skilful I became at pursuing my enquiries in the face of a preliminary denial, the more regularly was I able to discover pathogenic factors in sexual life, till little seemed to stand in the way of my assuming their universal occurrence. It was necessary, however, to presuppose from the start that sexual irregularities occurred with similar frequency in our ordinary society under the pressure of social conditions; and a doubt might remain as to the degree of deviation from normal sexual functioning which should be regarded as pathogenic. I was therefore obliged to attach less importance to the invariable evidence of sexual noxae than to a second discovery which seemed to me less ambiguous. It emerged that the form taken by the illness—neurasthenia or anxiety neurosis—bore a constant relation to the nature of the sexual noxa involved. In typical cases of neurasthenia a history of regular masturbation or persistent emissions was found; in anxiety neurosis factors appeared such

as *coitus interruptus*, 'unconsummated excitation,' and other conditions—in all of which there seemed to be the common element of an insufficient discharge of the libido that had been produced. It was only after this discovery, which was easy to make and could be confirmed as often as one liked, that I had the courage to claim a preferential position for sexual influences in the aetiology of the neuroses. Furthermore, in the mixed forms of neurasthenia and anxiety neurosis which are so common it was possible to trace a combination of the aetiologies which I had assumed for the two pure forms. Moreover, this twofold form assumed by the neurosis seemed to tally with the polar (i.e. the masculine and feminine) character of sexuality.

At the time at which I was attributing to sexuality this important part in the production of the *simple* neuroses,[1] I was still faithful to a purely psychological theory in regard to the *psychoneuroses*—a theory in which the sexual factor was regarded as no more significant than any other emotional source of feeling. On the basis of some observations made by Josef Breuer on a hysterical patient more than ten years earlier, I collaborated with him in a study of the mechanism of the generation of hysterical symptoms, using the method of awakening the patient's memories in a state of hypnosis; and we reached conclusions which enabled us to bridge the gap between Charcot's traumatic hysteria and common non-traumatic hysteria (Breuer and Freud, 1895). We were led to the assumption that hysterical symptoms are the permanent results of psychical traumas, the sum of affect attaching to which has, for particular reasons, been prevented from being

[1] In my [first] paper on anxiety neurosis (1895*b*).

worked over consciously and has therefore found an abnormal path into somatic innervation. The terms 'strangulated affect,' 'conversion' and 'abreaction' cover the distinctive features of this hypothesis.

But in view of the close connections between the psychoneuroses and the simple neuroses, which go so far, indeed, that a differential diagnosis is not always easy for inexperienced observers, it could not be long before the knowledge arrived at in the one field was extended to the other. Moreover, apart from this consideration, a deeper investigation of the psychical mechanism of hysterical symptoms led to the same result. For if the psychical traumas from which the hysterical symptoms were derived were pursued further and further by means of the 'cathartic' procedure initiated by Breuer and me, experiences were eventually reached which belonged to the patient's childhood and related to his sexual life. And this was so, even in cases in which the onset of the illness had been brought about by some commonplace emotion of a non-sexual kind. Unless these sexual traumas of childhood were taken into account it was impossible either to elucidate the symptoms (to understand the way in which they were determined) or to prevent their recurrence. In this way the unique significance of sexual experiences in the aetiology of the psychoneuroses seemed to be established beyond a doubt; and this fact remains to this day one of the corner-stones of my theory.

This theory might be expressed by saying that the cause of life-long hysterical neuroses lies in what are in themselves for the most part the trivial sexual experiences of early childhood; and, put in this way, it might no doubt sound strange. But if we take the historical development of the theory into account, and see as its essence the proposition that hysteria is the expression of a particular behaviour of the individual's sexual function and that this behaviour is decisively determined by the first influences and experiences brought to bear in childhood, we shall be a paradox the poorer but the richer by a motive for turning our attention to something of the highest importance (though it has hitherto been grossly neglected)—the after-effects of the impressions of childhood.

I will postpone until later in this paper a more thorough-going discussion of the question whether we are to regard the sexual experiences of childhood as the causes of hysteria (and obsessional neurosis), and I will now return to the form taken by the theory in some of my shorter preliminary publications during the years 1895 and 1896 (Freud, 1896*b* and 1896*c*). By laying stress on the supposed aetiological factors it was possible at that time to draw a contrast between the common neuroses as disorders with a *contemporary* aetiology and psychoneuroses whose aetiology was chiefly to be looked for in the sexual experiences of the remote past. The theory culminated in this thesis: if the *vita sexualis* is normal, there can be no neurosis.

Though even to-day I do not consider these assertions incorrect, it is not to be wondered at that, in the course of ten years of continuous effort at reaching an understanding of these phenomena, I have made a considerable step forward from the views I then held, and now believe that I am in a position, on the basis of deeper experience, to correct the insufficiencies, the displacements and the misunderstandings under which my theory then laboured. At that time my material was still scanty, and it happened by chance to include a disproportionately large number of cases in which sexual seduction by an adult or by older children played the chief part in the history of the patient's childhood. I thus over-estimated the frequency of such events (though in other respects they were not open to doubt). Moreover, I was at that period unable to distinguish with certainty between falsifications made by hysterics in their memories of childhood and traces of real events. Since then I have learned to explain a number of phantasies of seduction as attempts at fending off memories of the subject's *own* sexual activity (infantile masturbation). When this point had been clarified, the 'traumatic' element in the sexual experiences of childhood lost its importance and what was left was the realization that infantile sexual activity (whether spontaneous or provoked) prescribes the direction that will be taken by later sexual life after maturity. The same clarification (which corrected the most important of my early mistakes) also made it necessary to modify my view of the mechanism of hysterical symptoms. They were now no longer to be regarded as direct derivatives of the repressed memories of childhood experiences; but between the symptoms and the childish impressions there were inserted the patient's *phantasies* (or imaginary memories), mostly produced during the years of puberty, which on the one side were built up out of and over the childhood memories and on the other side were transformed directly into the symptoms. It was only after the introduction of this element of

hysterical phantasies that the texture of the neurosis and its relation to the patient's life became intelligible; a surprising analogy came to light, too, between these unconscious phantasies of hysterics and the imaginary creations of paranoics which become conscious as delusions.[2]

After I had made this correction, 'infantile sexual traumas' were in a sense replaced by the 'infantilism of sexuality.' A second modification of the original theory lay not far off. Along with the supposed frequency of seduction in childhood, I ceased also to lay exaggerated stress on the *accidental* influencing of sexuality on to which I had sought to thrust the main responsibility for the causation of the illness, though I had not on that account denied the constitutional and hereditary factors. I had even hoped to solve the problem of choice of neurosis (the decision to which form of psychoneurosis the patient is to fall a victim) by reference to the details of the sexual experiences of childhood. I believed at that time—though with reservations— that a passive attitude in these scenes produced a predisposition to hysteria and, on the other hand, an active one a predisposition to obsessional neurosis. Later on I was obliged to abandon this view entirely, even though some facts demand that in some way or other the supposed correlation between passivity and hysteria and between activity and obsessional neurosis shall be maintained.[3] Accidental influences derived

[2] [This passage was Freud's first explicit published intimation of his change of views on the relative importance of traumatic experiences and unconscious phantasies in childhood, apart from a brief allusion in his *Three Essays* (1905d; this volume, p. 190). In fact, however, he had become aware of his error many years earlier, for he revealed it in a letter to Fliess on September 21, 1897 (Freud, 1950a, Letter 69). The effects on Freud's own mind of the discovery of his mistake are vividly related by him in the first section of his 'History of the Psycho-Analytic Movement' (1914d) and in the third section of his 'Autobiographical Study' (1925d).]

[3] [This particular solution of the problem of 'choice of neurosis' is most clearly expressed in Freud's second paper on the 'Neuropsychoses of Defence' (1896b) and his French

from experience having thus receded into the background, the factors of constitution and heredity necessarily gained the upper hand once more; but there was this difference between my views and those prevailing in other quarters, that on my theory the 'sexual constitution' took the place of a 'general neuropathic disposition.' In my recently published *Three Essays on the Theory of Sexuality* (1905d [this volume p. 125]) I have tried to give a picture of the variegated nature of this sexual constitution as well as of the composite character of the sexual instinct in general and its derivation from contributory sources from different parts of the organism.

As a further corollary to my modified view of 'sexual traumas in childhood,' my theory now developed further in a direction which had already been indicated in my publications between 1894 and 1896. At that time, and even before sexuality had been given its rightful place as an aetiological factor, I had maintained that no experience could have a pathogenic effect unless it appeared intolerable to the subject's ego and gave rise to efforts at defence (Freud, 1894a). It was to this defence that I traced back the split in the psyche (or, as we said in those days, in consciousness) which occurs in hysteria. If the defence was successful, the intolerable experience with its affective consequences was expelled from consciousness and from the ego's memory.

In certain circumstances, however, what had been expelled pursued its activities in what was now an unconscious state, and found its way back into consciousness by means of symptoms and the affects attaching to them, so that the illness corresponded to a failure in defence. This view had the merit of entering into the interplay of the psychical forces and of thus bringing the mental processes in hysteria nearer to normal ones, instead of characterizing the neurosis as nothing more than a mysterious disorder insusceptible to further analysis.

Further information now became available relating to people who had remained normal; and this led to the unexpected finding that the sexual history of *their* childhood did not necessarily differ in essentials from that of neurotics, and, in particular, that the part played by seduction was the same in both cases. As a consequence, accidental influences receded still further into the background as compared with 'repression' (as I now began to say instead of 'defence').[4] Thus it was no longer a question of what sexual experiences a particular individual had had in his childhood, but rather of his reaction to those experiences—of whether he had reacted to them by 'repression' or not. It could be shown how in the course of development a spontaneous infantile sexual activity was often broken off by an act of repression. Thus a mature neurotic in-

---

paper of the same date (1896a). His interest in the general question of choice of neurosis goes back at least to the beginning of the same year (Draft K in Freud, 1950a) and he used the term itself in a letter to Fliess of May 30, 1896 (Letter 46). He was to return to the subject a few years later in special reference to obsessional neurosis (1913i), and indeed the problem never ceased to occupy his mind.]

[4] [Actually the term '*Verdrängung*' ('repression') had made its first published appearance as early as in the Breuer and Freud 'Preliminary Communication' (1893). Many years later, in *Inhibitions, Symptoms and Anxiety* (1926d; see particularly Section X c), Freud once more returned to the term '*Abwehr*' ('defence') as denoting a comprehensive concept, of which 'repression' represented only a single form.]

dividual was invariably pursued by a certain amount of 'sexual repression' from his childhood; this found expression when he was faced by the demands of real life, and the psychoanalyses of hysterics showed that they fell ill as a result of the conflict between their libido and their sexual repression and that their symptoms were in the nature of compromises between the two mental currents.

I could not further elucidate this part of my theory without a detailed discussion of my views on repression. It will be enough here to refer to my *Three Essays* (1905*d*), in which I have attempted to throw some light— if only a feeble one—on the somatic processes in which the essential nature of sexuality is to be looked for. I have there shown that the constitutional sexual disposition of children is incomparably more variegated than might have been expected, that it deserves to be described as 'polymorphously perverse' and that what is spoken of as the normal behaviour of the sexual function emerges from this disposition after certain of its components have been repressed. By pointing out the infantile elements in sexuality I was able to establish a simple correlation between health, perversion and neurosis. I showed that *normality* is a result of the repression of certain component instincts and constituents of the infantile disposition and of the subordination of the remaining constituents under the primacy of the genital zones in the service of the reproductive function. I showed that *perversions* correspond to disturbances of this coalescence owing to the overpowering and compulsive development of certain of the component instincts, while *neuroses* can be traced back to an excessive repression of the libidinal trends. Since almost all the perverse instincts of the infantile disposition

can be recognized as the forces concerned in the formation of symptoms in neuroses, though in a state of repression, I was able to describe neurosis as being the 'negative' of perversion.

I think it is worth emphasizing the fact that, whatever modifications my views on the aetiology of the psychoneuroses have passed through, there are two positions which I have never repudiated or abandoned—the importance of sexuality and of infantilism. Apart from this, accidental influences have been replaced by constitutional factors and 'defence' in the purely psychological sense has been replaced by organic 'sexual repression.' The question may, however, be raised of where convincing evidence is to be found in favour of the alleged aetiological importance of sexual factors in the psychoneuroses, in view of the fact that the onset of these illnesses may be observed in response to the most commonplace emotions or even to somatic precipitating causes, and since I have had to abandon a specific aetiology depending on the particular form of the childhood experiences concerned. To such a question I would reply that the psycho-analytic examination of neurotics is the source from which this disputed conviction of mine is derived. If we make use of that irreplaceable method of research, we discover that *the patient's symptoms constitute his sexual activity* (whether wholly or in part), which arises from the sources of the normal or perverse component instincts of sexuality. Not only is a large part of the symptomatology of hysteria derived directly from expressions of sexual excitement, not only do a number of erotogenic zones attain the significance of genitals during neuroses owing to an intensification of infantile characteristics, but the most complicated symptoms are themselves revealed as representing, by means of 'conversion,' phantasies which have a sexual situation as their subject-matter. Anyone who knows how to interpret the language of hysteria will recognize that the neurosis is concerned only with the patient's repressed sexuality. The sexual function must, however, be understood in its true extent, as it is laid down by disposition in infancy. Wherever some commonplace emotion must be included among the determinants of the onset of the illness, analysis invariably shows that it is the sexual component of the traumatic experience—a component that is never lacking—which has produced the pathogenic result.

We have been led on imperceptibly from the question of the causation of the psychoneuroses to the problem of their essential nature. If we are prepared to take into account what has been learnt from psycho-analysis, we can only say that the essence of these illnesses lies in disturbances of the sexual processes, the processes which determine in the organism the formation and utilization of sexual libido. It is scarcely possible to avoid picturing these processes as being in the last resort of a chemical nature; so that in what are termed the 'actual' neuroses [5] we may recognize the *somatic* effects of disturbances of the sexual metabolism, and in the psychoneuroses the *psychical* effects of those disturbances as well. The similarity of the neuroses to the phenomena of intoxication and abstinence after the use of certain alkaloids, as well as to Graves' disease and Addison's disease, is forced upon our notice clinically. And just as these last two illnesses should no longer be described as 'nervous diseases,' so also the 'neuroses' proper, in spite of their

name, may soon have to be excluded from that category as well.[6]

Accordingly, the aetiology of the neuroses comprises everything which can act in a detrimental manner upon the processes serving the sexual function. In the forefront, then, are to be ranked the noxae which affect the sexual function itself—in so far as these are regarded as injurious by the sexual constitution, varying as it does with different degrees of culture and education. In the next place comes every other kind of noxa and trauma which, by causing general damage to the organism, may lead secondarily to injury to its sexual processes. It should not, however, be forgotten that the aetiological problem in the case of the neuroses is at least as complicated as the causative factors of any other illness. A single pathogenic influence is scarcely ever sufficient; in the large majority of cases a *number* of aetiological factors are required, which support one another and must therefore not be regarded as being in mutual opposition. For this reason a state of neurotic illness cannot be sharply differentiated from health. The onset of the illness is the product of a summation and the necessary total of aetiological determinants can be completed from any direction. To look for the aetiology of the neuroses exclusively in heredity or in the constitution would be just as one-sided as to attribute that aetiology solely to the accidental influences brought to bear upon sexuality in the course of the subject's life—whereas better insight shows that the essence of these illnesses lies solely in a disturbance of the organism's sexual processes.

Vienna, June 1905

---

[5] [I.e. those with a contemporary aetiology (neurasthenia and anxiety neurosis).]
[6] [Cf. *Three Essays*, this volume p. 216 and footnote.]

George C. Rosenwald

# The Assessment of Anxiety in Psychological Experimentation: A Theoretical Reformulation and Test

*Anxiety, either overtly experienced or defended against, is an essential feature of psychoneurosis and is thought by many theorists to be a basic factor in all manner of emotional and behavior disorders. In this paper by Rosenwald, a good review of the psychoanalytic theory of anxiety is presented and a study is reported which differentiates between subjects who are high and low in defensiveness.*

The effects of anxiety on performance have been subjected to fairly intensive experimental study in past years (1). A good deal of this research has shed light on the type of performance that is disrupted by anxiety. For instance, it has been shown that anxiety interferes with the accomplishment of complex tasks but facilitates the performance of simple tasks (3). Considerably less attention has been given to a theoretical analysis of anxiety itself, the conditions of its arousal, and its defining properties. Experimenters do not always agree with each other or with theoreticians and clinicians as to the exact meaning of anxiety as a conceptual term. The first part of the present paper is a review of the psychoanalytic theory of anxiety. This framework is selected because many authors have operated within it. Following the presentation of the theoretical outline, some shortcomings of conventional experimental approaches to anxiety will be pointed out. Finally, an experiment will be reported, the procedures of which approximate the theoretical specifications more closely.

The first of the two conventional procedures to be discussed segregates the subjects with respect to anxiety level on the basis of a questionnaire to which the subject responds with an introspective report of his characteristic anxiety level and stress experiences (7, 15). The second procedure produces a stress in the subject through fictitious reports of his inadequate performance on tasks which are presented as tests of intelligence or as other measures of adequacy (6, 10). Sometimes these two procedures are employed jointly. They are subject to limitations which will become clear after the theoretical outline is presented.

The psychoanalytic theory of anxiety (4) begins with the observation that for some people the intensification of a particular drive constitutes a psychic danger. The nature and origin of this danger are to be sought in the individual histories of such persons. Unconsciously fantasied physical damage, helplessness, or loss of love are frequently encountered examples of such danger. In anticipation of this danger, such people characteristically distort

*Reprinted from the* Journal of Abnormal and Social Psychology, *62(1961), 666–673. Copyright 1961 by the American Psychological Association and reprinted by permission.*

the recognition and expression of the drive in question by means of defense mechanisms. These mechanisms avert the expected danger to the extent that they block or distort the drive successfully. Anxiety is defined as the psychological mechanism whereby the current intensification of a dangerous drive results in the elicitation of defenses. The term "signal anxiety" refers to this function specifically. Anxiety is therefore a theoretical construct which is anchored on the antecedent side to the intensification of a dangerous drive and on the consequent side to the rise of defensive behavior.[1] It should be noted that this strict definition of anxiety makes no phenomenological references to feelings of distress, heart palpitations, etc.

Defenses are therefore a central concept in the definition of anxiety. They are recognized when the individual behaves in ways which interfere with the experience or expression of his needs. For example, when it is observed that a person responds to extreme aggressive provocation with inexhaustible forbearance and forgiveness for the offender, it may be said that he is defending himself against aggression. In clinical practice and experimental studies (2) it has been found that people who are defensive characteristically distort their perception of stimuli which are associated with the arousal of dangerous drives. Moreover, it is found that the greater the danger, the greater is the distortion (11).

It is well known that anxiety is in certain instances further characterized by conscious experiences of distress and by physiological stress symptoms. However, these additional conditions are of secondary importance in the definition of anxiety and may be completely lacking. Thus the term anxiety may be applied regardless of whether subjective experiential factors and physiological stress symptoms play a minimal role or assume spectacular importance, as they do, for instance, in anxiety attacks. Only its traceable origin in past experience, which has rendered the drive dangerous, and the automatic elicitation of defenses are central to the definition of anxiety. In fact, the concomitance of anxiety, whatever its experiential salience, and of defensiveness is so constant that it is difficult to distinguish conceptually or experimentally between the behavioral consequences of the one and the other. Under what conditions do the secondary experiential and physiological factors appear at all? The theory provides an explanation in terms of the effectiveness of the defense. If the defense mechanism does not sufficiently block or distort the dangerous drive, and the drive grows in intensity, then the experiential and physiological aspects of anxiety will gradually become more conspicuous. In other words, in the case of a person with ineffective defenses, these aspects will be added to signal anxiety when the drive is intensified. They subside as soon as the drive is sufficiently distorted.

It is an important part of the theory that anxiety operates automatically in many cases. That is to say, the elicitation of defenses does not depend on the experiential and physiological aspects of anxiety. This is especially char-

---

[1] Anxiety as a mechanism should not be confused with anxiety as a character trait. To say "John is anxious about aggression," does not necessarily mean that John is aggressively stimulated at the present time and is counteracting this stimulation with defenses. Rather, it means that John would become defensive *if* he were aggressively stimulated. This is another way of saying that aggression is a dangerous drive for John or that John has conflicts about aggression.

acteristic of functioning normal adults. In fact, people who are frequently subject to anxiety *experiences* are often in need of treatment. Anxiety is not an ever-present condition or mood in well functioning individuals. Even in patients, the intensity and effects of anxiety and defensiveness vary with the intensity of the drive that gives rise to them. Only an acute intensification of dangerous drives will result in anxiety—experiential or otherwise. For instance, a person for whom aggressive stimulation is dangerous will try not to expose himself to social situations in which he may be aggressively stimulated. Thus anxiety and defense arousing situations may only rarely occur in his life.

The view outlined here reserves the concepts of "anxiety" and "defense" for situations in which the danger has an internal source, specifically a drive, and the term "fear" for those in which the threat originates in the external world. Although borderline instances and cases of overlapping may be cited, the paradigm itself is clear in this respect.

In the light of this theory, both the questionnaire and the stress procedures mentioned initially have serious shortcomings. As for the questionnaire, its outstanding limitation is its reliance on the subject's introspective report of anxiety. By theory, subjects who rate themselves high on anxiety by reporting experiences of psychic distress and physiological stress are not only anxious in the primary sense of the word—they not only become defensive in the presence of the drive—but in addition, they utilize ineffective defenses which do not distort the drive sufficiently. Furthermore, they may not be successful in avoiding situations in which they are likely to be dangerously stimulated. While these individuals represent a challenging clinical problem, it is incorrect to designate others, who do not report experiences of anxiety, as not anxious in the strict sense. The only admissible distinction between subjects who report and subjects who do not report anxiety experiences is on the basis of the effectiveness of their defenses, not on the basis of whether or not defenses are being elicited. Subjects who do not report anxiety experiences are either not anxious about the drive, or they avoid anxiety arousing situations; or, if they do not avoid them, then anxiety never becomes more than a signal because their defenses are effective. It should be noted that people who resolve underlying conflict with relatively flexible defenses are not detectable by means of a questionnaire.

As for the stress procedure, it seems to approximate the specifications of fear arousal more than those of anxiety arousal. True, the prospects of failing an intelligence test or of showing up poorly on a measure of masculinity are dangerous both internally and externally; such failures would involve a compromise in the eyes of others as well as a drop in self-esteem. Yet it seems preferable to investigate these effects separately rather than under confounded conditions. If it were possible to bring about the intensification of a dangerous drive without simultaneously producing an immediate external threat, the conditions of anxiety arousal specified in the theory would seem to be most nearly met.

In view of these considerations, the following method was proposed. Aggression was selected as a drive about which people are anxious to varying degrees.[2]

[2] The choice of aggression is not crucial to the theoretical formulation of this paper. Anxiety about dependency or sexuality could have been utilized as easily. This will be discussed later on.

First, the degree of anxiety about aggression was to be determined for each subject by noting his extremity of defensive distortion in response to an aggressive assessment stimulus. Then, independently of this determination, subjects were to be exposed to an acute aggressive provocation. It was assumed that anxiety and defensiveness would automatically be aroused again, just as they were in response to the assessment stimulus, and that the effects of anxiety and defensiveness on behavior could then be measured. In other words, the subject's own "built-in" predisposition to become anxious as a result of drive arousal was to be utilized rather than a fictitious external threat. Nor was any use to be made of the subjects' awareness of their anxiety.

An anagram solving task was selected as a measure of the effects of anxiety on performance. Findings indicate that the effect of anxiety upon performance varies with the complexity of the task (3). A task is considered complex if the correct response is either weak in the initial response hierarchy or is in competition with other equally strong responses, whereas a simple task, like that in classical conditioning, is one in which the correct response is strong in the hierarchy. In the former tasks, anxiety has been found to have an impairing but in the latter a facilitating effect on performance. Anagram solution is a complex task which is known to be vulnerable to the effects of anxiety as measured by questionnaire (5).

The prediction tested by the present experiment is the following: In the case of subjects who are observed to become defensive in reaction to an aggressive assessment stimulus, an experimental intervention designed to arouse aggression results in impaired performance on a complex problem solving task. Subjects who do not become defensive in response to the assessment stimulus are not so affected by the experimental intervention.

## METHOD

The experimental subjects were 62 high school students who were tested individually during two separate sessions. During the first session, a Story Completion test, an Anagrams test, and an abbreviated Intelligence test were administered (9). Thirty-nine of the subjects constituted the experimental group. At the beginning of their second session, they were subjected to an experimental intervention designed to arouse aggression. For the remaining 23 control subjects, this intervention was omitted. Following this, alternate forms of the three tests were administered to all subjects. Differences between the forms of the tests were controlled for by the use of a counterbalanced design.

The Story Completion test consisted of five incomplete stories which the subject was asked to complete. Each contained an aggressive provocation of the main figure. This thematic test was selected as the assessment stimulus because projective devices are traditional for detecting anxiety and defensiveness in the sense defined, and because responses to such tests are ordinarily less subject to influence by socially conditioned attitudes. Such tests may identify individuals who characteristically respond to increases in drive in a defensive manner but are not necessarily aware of their anxiety or of the entailed defensive drive distortion. Because projective test responses reflect anxiety and defensiveness concerning which the subject has little or no control or awareness, they seem particularly suited to the present experimental paradigm.

The Anagrams test consisted of 10 scrambled four and five-letter words which the subject was asked to convert into meaningful words by rearranging the letters in his mind. Half the anagram solutions were "loaded"—that is, they had aggression related connotations; the other half was neutral. According to the conception of the present study and the findings of past research (5), the anagrams task should be subject to the effects of anxiety regardless of the content of the anagrams. The rationale of this prediction is entirely in terms of task complexity, and in this respect it differs from studies of perceptual defense. "Loaded" stimuli were included out of interest in the effects which content may perhaps have beyond those postulated. Just as incomplete stories with aggressive themes are more likely to point up a subject's anxiety about aggression than stories with other themes, so the aggressive content of the anagrams may add to the anxiety which a subject already experiences as a result of the experimental drive arousal.

The Information subtest of the Wechsler Adult Intelligence Scale was administered as a measure of intelligence (16).

The experimental intervention consisted of two parts. First, the subject was accused of and reprimanded for having discussed the experiment with his friends after having been asked at the end of the first session to refrain from doing so. He was told that this was childish, disobedient, and irresponsible. Second, he was asked to take a mirror tracing test as part of the study. His performance in this was characterized as inadequate, and the experimenter demanded that the subject return after school to continue practicing mirror tracing. The intervention was delivered in a sarcastic, belittling manner, and no replies were tolerated. (Mirror tracing, a measure external to the experiment proper, was chosen for the intervention because of possible changes in task set which might have affected performance on the Anagrams test had it been used for this purpose.) All of the subject's verbalizations at this time were recorded by the experimenter. The demand for after school practice was retracted at the end of the experiment, and the overall purpose of the study was explained.

## RESULTS

The five story completions obtained in the first session were used to obtain an index of defensiveness. Each completion was ranked with respect to defensiveness in relation to all others obtained in response to the same incomplete story. A completion was judged to be defensive in proportion to the extent to which aggression was *not* expressed, the extent to which the main figure of the story was *not* seen as active in bringing about a favorable solution to the presented conflict, the extent to which he was *not* seen as capable of acknowledging the discrepancy of interest between himself and the instigator of the aggressive provocation, and the extent to which he was *not* seen as blaming the instigator but rather as blaming himself. No attempt was made to categorize the completions according to specific defense mechanisms exemplified by them. Rather, the degree of defensiveness was determined by the magnitude of the distortion. By using an objective scoring manual (9), an alternate judge arrived at reliably similar rankings, with rho coefficients ranging from .71 to .92. The ranks obtained for each of the subject's five stories were summed, yielding his defensiveness score. The subjects were then divided at the median into a high defensive and a low defensive group.

In comparing the times required for solution on the first administration of the Anagrams test, it was found that high defensive and low defensive subjects performed comparably.

An analysis of performance changes from the first to the second administration of the Anagrams test is shown in Table 1. The breakdown of the chi square into the components attributable to Defensiveness, Treatment, and their interaction was undertaken, using Wilson's (1956) test. It was concluded that the performance changes of the high defensive and low defensive groups were significantly different, the former showing impairment and the latter improvement of performance when compared to the control subjects. Furthermore, these changes could be attributed

TABLE 1. Extended Median Test (Siegel, 1956) and Wilson's Distribution Test (Wilson, 1956) for the Difference between Solution Times on the First and Second Administration of the Anagrams Test (High scores indicate relative impairment)

|  | Experimental | | Control | |
|---|---|---|---|---|
|  | High-De-fensive | Low-De-fensive | High-De-fensive | Low-De-fensive |
| Above Overall Median | 14 | 4 | 6 | 7 |
| Below | 5 | 16 | 5 | 5 |
| $\chi^2$ Total | 11.90 | $3df$ | $p < .001$ | |
| $\chi^2$ Defensiveness | 6.46 | $1df$ | $p < .02$ | |
| $\chi^2$ Treatment | 0.62 | $1df$ | — | |
| $\chi^2$ Defensiveness × Treatment | 4.82 | $1df$ | $p < .05$ | |

Note.—A nonparametric test was employed to permit the pooling of difference scores obtained from two replications differing in the order of administration of parallel test forms and therefore not comparable in absolute values of solution time.

to the effects of the experimental intervention since the interaction of Defensiveness and Treatment was found to be significant.

In addition, there is suggestive but statistically unreliable evidence that high defensive subjects required longer solution times for "loaded" than for neutral anagrams on the *first* administration of the test and that this was not so for the low defensive subjects. However, the reported effects of the experimental intervention were not limited to the loaded items. If anything, neutral items seemed to be affected somewhat more noticeably by the intervention than were loaded ones.

The high defensive and low defensive subjects did not differ in their performance on the intelligence scale either before or after the intervention.

## DISCUSSION

The above findings may be briefly summarized as follows: High defensive and low defensive subjects do not at the outset differ from each other in regard to their performance on the Anagrams test; they are differentially affected by the experimental intervention, with the high defensive subjects showing impairment and the low defensive subjects improvement as measured by solution times, and the content of the items does not seem to influence their susceptibility to the facilitating or impairing effects of the experimental intervention.

In connection with the first of these three findings, it should be noted that investigators assessing anxiety with questionnaires have found that subjects differ in performance even in the absence of any experimental arousal (3, 15). The failure of the present study to corroborate this observation may be taken as indirect evidence that Defensiveness rankings are not interchangeable with scores on an anxiety questionnaire, as indeed they were not intended to be. The present findings can be accounted for without assuming that any of the subjects ever became consciously distressed or experienced physiological stress symptoms, although such a contingency is certainly not ruled out. Since the effectiveness of defenses is theoretically related to the presence or absence of the experiential aspects of anxiety, it is possible that differences in performance which have been found in past studies between subjects high and low on an anxiety questionnaire are due to the degree of defense effectiveness rather than to the degree to which the subject becomes anxious in the theoretically strict sense. The present study is only a first attempt to elucidate experimentally the differences between the behavioral consequences of overt anxiety, introspectively observed by the subject and reported on a questionnaire, and of the disposition to become defensive, measured by projective devices and not necessarily accompanied by conscious experiences of distress.

An inspection of the items of the Taylor (14) scale suggests that a high score is likely to indicate a more or less permanent drive or affective state. The rationale and findings of the present study, however, explicitly provide for and give positive evidence of an acute rise in anxiety conditional on an acute rise in a dangerous drive. Once again, it appears that the present procedure for controlling anxiety could be applied to people who are not characteristically subject to the experiential accompaniments of anxiety, even though they may be judged anxious and defensive about a particular drive. The method described here might, therefore, facilitate the conceptual disentanglement of the effects of anxiety and defense.

The first and second findings, taken together, suggest strongly that the defensiveness rankings measure what it was hoped they would measure: not the person's usual or typical level of anxiety, but his disposition to become anxious and to defend when dangerously aroused. In accordance with the rationale of this study, it should be possible to replicate the reported findings by raising the level of any other drive in subjects for whom that drive is known to be dangerous.

With regard to the second finding, the question arises as to what psychological mechanisms were responsible for

the observed performance changes. It may be argued that a high defensive subject could so distort the meaning of the experimental intervention and of his reaction to it that he might ignore its provocative implications. After all, the intervention is a stimulus associated with drive arousal just as the incomplete stories were. In that case, should the intervention not fail to affect him? This is certainly possible, but it must be remembered that anxiety always occurs in combination with defensive efforts of varying kinds and degrees of success. At the present state of knowledge, the effects of anxiety and defense on cognitive behavior cannot yet be distinguished either experimentally or even conceptually. In other words, the high defensive subjects' test performance was impaired by anxiety or the defensive distortion of the experimental intervention or both. Parallel with this, it is unclear whether investigators of anxiety who have not been systematically concerned with the effects of defense were justified in attributing their findings only to the effects of anxiety. Perhaps their data should be viewed in part from the standpoint of the defenses which are automatically aroused by the anxiety stimulus.

The separation of the effects of anxiety from those of defense would have more than semantic importance. It is conceivable that anxiety affects performance through the mediation of drive increments and irrelevant responses (1), whereas defense may exert its influence through the mediation of cognitive rigidity and the narrowing of attention and associative processes.[3] Whether or not a particular task performance is affected by anxiety and defensiveness would then depend on the

[3] The effect of rigid defenses and controls on one phase of creative and inventive behavior has been discussed by Schafer (12).

effectiveness of an individual's defenses and on the vulnerability of the selected task to one or the other type of mediating mechanism. For instance, if performance of a task is most vulnerable to cognitive rigidity, then a subject who is only moderately defensive and experiences a good deal of distress will not be so severely penalized in his performance as another subject whose defenses are intensely and pervasively constricting and who is, therefore, free from experiences of overt distress and physiological stress. The analysis of intellectual functioning in different diagnostic groups tends to bear this out (8).

Little is known at the present time that would easily account for the improvement of the low defensive subjects. It is possible that unanxious, and therefore undistorted, experience of increased aggression provided them with greater energy, perhaps even with vindictive overtones. ("I'll show him who is immature!") Although the finding is not surprising in the light of clinical experience, there is little if any research support for the assumption that the aggressive drive can at times be utilized in this constructive way. Another possible explanation is that this added drive had merely a distracting effect on the low defensive subjects and that they overcame it by intensifying their efforts to attend only to the task. Whether or not *any* drive arousal will have such a facilitating effect on subjects who experience little anxiety about it is not known. It is quite possible that aggression, because of its nature, is more likely to have such energizing effects than is, say, an arousal of dependency needs. Furthermore, one of the criteria used for categorizing subjects as high defensive or low defensive was whether or not they made reference to active problem solving behavior on the part of the main figure in their story completions. The low defensive subjects' superiority on

the Anagrams test may be looked upon as another facet of their greater concern with or investment in problem solving. Just as these subjects involved their story figures in active problem solving attempts, so they became themselves involved in active attempts to restructure the anagram stimuli.

The findings of the experimental groups are interesting also in that they are consistent with economic considerations in psychoanalytic theory. It is assumed that the ego performs its adaptive functions, of which problem solving is one, with energy which is of instinctual origin but has undergone varying degrees of neutralization. The capacity to neutralize instinctual energy is thought to depend on the person's relative freedom from anxiety concerning the instinct in question. That is, defensiveness tends to preclude neutralization. The present findings can be explained as follows. The low defensive group had a greater quantity of neutralized, dischargeable energy available for problem solving and therefore showed an improvement, whereas the high defensive group had to block the aroused aggressive energy and therefore pre-empted it from adaptive utilization. These economic considerations seem the more applicable because the groups performed comparably in the absence of energic arousal and because the stimulus content was noncontributory to the observed effects.

An incidental observation needs to be mentioned in connection with the second finding. An analysis of the experimental subjects' verbal reactions to the experimental intervention revealed a tendency for high defensive subjects to object to the experimenter's accusation and arbitrariness more frequently than was true of low defensive subjects. Although this finding falls far short of statistical significance, failure to find a significant difference in the opposite direction serves as a reminder that one may not freely predict diffident and meek behavior from the presence of defensiveness in projective test responses. In many everyday situations, such defenses are overlaid with socially conditioned counterdefenses against passivity and timidity. In neurotic patients, considerable therapeutic work may often be required to bring to the surface the submissiveness which hides behind impressive swagger and assertiveness. However, this relationship between fantasy defensiveness and action assertiveness stands in need of further exploration.

The third finding suggests that theories derived from the phenomena of perceptual defense may not provide adequate explanations of the present observations. Apparently, psychological functions like those involved in the solution of anagrams can be subject to wholesale interference which transcends particular areas of tabu content. It is suggested that although anxiety is aroused by drives which have specifiable content, the effects, facilitating or inhibiting, of anxiety and defensiveness on performance may have a wider sphere of influence than the anxiety arousing content. There is no a priori reason to assume that anxiety will affect a given type of cognitive behavior differentially, depending on what drive gave rise to the anxiety. This too is borne out by the analysis of intellectual functions in patient groups (8).

Finally, it could be argued that the effect of the experimental intervention operated through a decrease in the cooperativeness or incentive of the high defensive subjects. The best reply to this and similar explanations is a question: Why should the experimental treatment have different effects on the cooperativeness of people who have high and low defensiveness ratings? The advantage of combining predispositional and experimental controls is that the number of plausible explanations of the obtained effects can be greatly reduced.

## SUMMARY

The psychoanalytic theory of anxiety and defense was reviewed. Following this, weaknesses were pointed out in experimental methods which apply the term "anxiety" to overt experiences of subjective distress accompanied by physiological distress symptoms, or which seek to control the level of anxiety by means of external threats. A new procedure was proposed and tested, consisting in the experimental arousal of a motive known to be psychologically unacceptable or dangerous for the subject. Anxiety is thought of as the automatic accompaniment of such arousals, regardless of its experiential conspicuousness to the subject himself.

A thematic test was utilized to assess defensiveness about aggression. Subsequently, an experimental intervention, designed to arouse aggression, was administered to the subjects, and the effects of this intervention on the performance of a problem solving task were measured. Findings were as follows:

1. Under drive arousal, high defensive subjects showed impairment and low defensive subjects improvement in performance.

2. Subjects did not differ in level of performance before drive arousal.

3. The content of the stimulus material used to measure problem solving ability did not seem to contribute to the vulnerability of performance to the effects of anxiety and defensiveness.

This reformulation of anxiety appears to hold promise for the conceptual and experimental separation of the effects of anxiety and defense.

## REFERENCES

1. CHILD, I. L. Personality. *Annu. Rev. Psychol.*, 5(1954), 149–170.

2. ERIKSEN, C. W. The case for perceptual defense. *Psychol. Rev.*, 61(1954), 175–182.

3. FARBER, I. E., and SPENCE, K. W. Complex learning and conditioning as a function of anxiety. *J. Exp. Psychol.*, 45(1953), 120–125.

4. FREUD, S. *The problem of anxiety.* (Originally published 1926) New York: Norton, 1936.

5. MALTZMAN, I., FOX, J., and MORRISETT, L., JR. Some effects of manifest anxiety on mental set. *J. Exp. Psychol.*, 46(1953), 50–54.

6. MANDLER, G., and SARASON, S. B. A study of anxiety and learning. *J. Abnorm. Soc. Psychol.*, 47(1952), 166–173.

7. MONTAGUE, E. K. The role of anxiety in serial rote learning. *J. Exp. Psychol.*, 45(1953), 91–96.

8. RAPAPORT, D., GILL, M., and SCHAFER, R. *Diagnostic psychological testing.* Vol. I. New York: International Univ. Press, 1945.

9. ROSENWALD, G. C. The effect of defensiveness on ideational mobility. Unpublished Ph.D. dissertation, Yale University, 1958.

10. SARASON, S. B., MANDLER, G., and CRAIGHILL, P. G. The effect of differential instructions on anxiety and learning. *J. Abnorm. Soc. Psychol.*, 47 (1952), 561–565.

11. SCHAFER, R. *Psychoanalytic interpretation in Rorschach testing.* New York: Grune & Stratton, 1954.

12. ———. Regression in the service of the ego: The relevance of a psychoanalytic concept for personality assessment. In G. Lindzey (Ed.), *The assessment of human motives.* New York: Rinehart, 1958. Pages 119–148.

13. SIEGEL, S. *Nonparametric statistics for the behavioral sciences.* New York: McGraw-Hill, 1956.

14. TAYLOR, JANET A. A personality scale of manifest anxiety. *J. Abnorm. Soc. Psychol.*, 48(1953), 285–290.

15. TAYLOR, JANET A., and SPENCE, K. W. The relationship of anxiety level to performance in serial learning. *J. Exp. Psychol.*, 44(1952), 61–64.

16. WECHSLER, D. *Wechsler Adult Intelligence Scale.* New York: Psychological Corporation, 1955.

17. WILSON, K. V. A distribution-free test of analysis of variance hypotheses. *Psychol. Bull.*, 53(1956), 96–101.

Joseph Wolpe

# Experimental Neuroses as Learned Behaviour

*Joseph Wolpe has risen in prominence in recent years as founder of one branch within a psychotherapeutic movement called behavior therapy. This approach emphasizes the understanding of the development and treatment of neurotic problems on the basis of learning principles uncovered in the psychology laboratory, often through work with animals. This paper includes Wolpe's analysis of the experiments of others which have produced "neurotic-like" behavior in animals as well as a report of his own work with such phenomena.*

Abridged from the British Journal of Psychology, 43(1952), 243–268 *with the permission of the Cambridge University Press and Dr. Wolpe.*

*This paper is significant because it presents a view of how neuroses develop which is quite different from the psychoanalytic position that preceded it and commanded a considerable following. Furthermore, it proposes a therapeutic approach which has come to attract considerable attention from researchers and therapists alike in recent years.*

*The editing done on this paper to conserve space eliminated part of Wolpe's comprehensive and detailed review of studies done in the area of experimental neurosis and his criticisms of previous theories developed to explain such phenomena. The reader who is interested in these details should consult the article in the original.*

## I. INTRODUCTION

In a recent issue of this *Journal* Russell (39) presented a very lucid review of experiments in which neuroses have been artificially produced, and of the theories that have been put forward in explanation. He did not pronounce on the relative merits of the theories, as he felt that further experimental and logical studies were prerequisite. In the present paper a new analysis is made of previously reported experimental neuroses; and then some new experiments are described which, it is believed, clarify our understanding of the mechanisms by which these conditions are produced. The study as a whole supports the conclusion that experimental neuroses constitute a variety of learned behaviour.

### Definition

An animal is said to have an experimental neurosis if it displays unadaptive responses that are characterized by anxiety, that are persistent, and that have been produced experimentally by behavioral means (as opposed to direct assault on the nervous system by chemical or physical agencies such as poisonings or extirpations).

An *adaptive response* is defined by Warren (41) as "any response which is appropriate to the situation, i.e. which favours the organism's life proc-

esses." This implies that it is a response that has the *effect* of leading directly or indirectly to the reduction of the organism's needs or to the prevention of pain or fatigue. An *unadaptive response*, on the other hand, does not lead to either.

## II. ANALYSIS OF PREVIOUS EXPERIMENTAL FINDINGS

Russell (39), like previous reviewers (5, 22), seems to have been too ready to accept without question the interpretations the various experimenters have given of their own work. It will be seen in the paragraphs that follow that these interpretations often ignore important factors in the experiments, and that if these factors are consistently taken into account all the neuroses so far recorded can be understood as being the outcome of one or other (perhaps sometimes both) of two basic situations —the exposure of the organism to ambivalent stimuli or its exposure to noxious stimuli, in either case under conditions of confinement. It will be argued that these two kinds of situation have an effect in common upon which the development of the neuroses depends.

In the account that follows the neuroses are grouped according to the basic situation which seems to have determined their production, and it will be seen repeatedly how experimental procedures may differ widely in other respects and yet provide the same kind of basic situation.

### (i) Neuroses Produced by Situations of Ambivalent Stimulation

An *ambivalent stimulus situation* is a situation to which opposing responses tend to be elicited simultaneously in more or less equal measure. The range of meaning is narrower than would be implied by "conflict situation," for not in every conflict are the opposing response tendencies equal. Examination of the literature reveals that three varieties of situatons involving ambivalent stimulation have been effective in producing experimental neuroses. These will be considered under their headings below.

(a) *Neuroses produced by difficult discriminations.* Although the expression "difficult discrimination" carries an unwanted suggestion of conscious weighing-up, it is a conveniently brief term of reference for the ambivalent stimulus situation that occurs under the following circumstances: a positive and a negative response having respectively been conditioned to two stimuli at different points on a continuum, the animal is confronted with a stimulus at an intermediate point on the continuum such that the opposing responses are evoked in more or less equal strength

Pavlov's experiment on neurosis-production based on difficult discrimination was the first to be reported (36, pp. 290–1). The projection of a luminous circle on to a screen in front of a dog was repeatedly followed by feeding. When the alimentary response to the circle was well established, an ellipse with semi-axes in the ratio of 2:1 began to be projected among presentations of the circle, and was never accompanied by feeding.

A complete and constant differentiation was obtained comparatively quickly. The shape of the ellipse was now approximated by stages to that of the circle (ratios of semi-axes of 3:2, 4:3 and so on) and the development of differentiation continued . . . with some fluctuation, progressing at first more and more quickly, and then again slower, until an ellipse with ratio of semi-axes 9:8 was reached. In this case, although a considerable degree of discrimination did develop, it was far from being complete. After three weeks of work upon this differentiation not only did the discrimination fail to improve, but it became considerably worse, and finally disappeared altogether. At the same time the whole behaviour of the animal underwent an abrupt change. The hitherto quiet dog began to squeal in its stand, kept wriggling about, tore off with its teeth the apparatus for mechanical stimulation of the skin, and bit through the tubes connecting the animal's room with the observer, a behaviour which never happened before. On being taken into the experimental room the dog now barked violently.

Because of its close resemblance to the circle the 9:8 ellipse presumably generated at least as great a positive ailmentary response tendency due to primary stimulus generalization (18, p. 184) from the circle as negative alimentary response tendency due to generalization from previous ellipses. Since primary stimulus generalization depends on the common neurones activated by similar stimuli (47), if the 9:8 ellipse activated a preponderating number of neurones in common with the circle, the negative response tendency to the ellipse could never become completely dominant, however often it were presented to the animal without reinforcement. Consequently, this ellipse would always evoke ambivalent response tendencies.

Karn (21) has described the production of a neurosis in a cat by a method that is of special interest in that a difficult discrimination of *intraorganismal cues* was involved. The animal was trained in a maze that was in effect a T-maze, with the left turn followed by two further left turns, and the right turn by two further right turns, all segments being the same length as the stem of the T. The only place where food was ever given was at the end of the final segment. The animal was required to learn at the choice point the double alternation—right, right, left, left. After 230 trials of the sequence it attained an average of 90% correct in the last 30 trials. During the 232nd trial, at its second arrival at the choice point, the animal hesitated much longer than usual, and then raced to the right end point. During the remainder of the trial it moved slowly, whimpering. From this time onwards the cat resisted being put into the maze, and mewed loudly and micturated at the choice point, especially at the second of the two occasions for a right turn. At later trials the signs of disturbance seemed to get worse, and accuracy of performance became progressively poorer. (In a later article, Karn (22) states that he and E. R. Malamud have produced a neurosis in a dog by the above technique, and that Keller has done likewise with a rat.)

It is reasonable to interpret the results as follows. Each time the cat arrived at the choice point the external cues were the same, and these were equally conditioned to a turn in either direction. In the case of a first arrival at the choice point the distinctive cue of a completely empty stomach must have become strongly conditioned to right-turning. Difficulty would occur at the second arrival, for the internal cues conditioned to right-turning would be the proprioceptive cues from the right-turning movements of one run, plus cues consequent on having eaten once;

while conditioned to left-turning would be the proprioceptive cues from the right-turning movements of two runs plus the internal cues consequent on having eaten twice. It is easy to believe that the difference between these two combinations of internal stimuli is minimal, so that at each second (and third) arrival at the choice point the right- and left-turning tendencies would be almost equal, constituting an ambivalent stimulus situation.

*(b) Neuroses produced by increasing the delay before reinforcement of a delayed conditioned response.* In Pavlov's laboratory (36, pp. 293–4), a dog with a predominant tendency of excitation had become conditioned to make the alimentary response to any of six stimuli. Food was presented when a stimulus had been acting for 5 sec. The duration of action of the conditioned stimulus before presentation of food was now prolonged by 5 sec. daily. All six stimuli were treated in this manner concurrently. When the delay reached 2 min., "the animal began to enter into a state of general excitation, and with a further prolongation of the delay to 3 min. the animal became quite crazy, increasingly and violently moving all parts of its body, howling, barking and squealing intolerably. All this was accompanied by an unceasing flow of saliva. . . ."

This neurosis is regarded as produced by ambivalent stimulation because of the following considerations. Pavlov (36, p. 92) found that when a delayed conditioned reflex has been established, salivation is delayed until some time after the commencement of the conditioned stimulus. Presumably, then, certain durations of the conditioned stimulus have become conditioned to an inhibition of the alimentary response, and other, longer durations to an excitation of that response. If the delay until presentation of food is now increased in stages, at each stage a duration of the stimulus which had previously stimulated the response would begin to be conditioned to an inhibition thereof. Whenever the positive and negative tendencies were more or less equal the stimulus would be an ambivalent one according to the definition given above.

(c) *Neuroses produced by rapid alternation of stimuli eliciting opposing responses.* In the two types of ambivalent stimulus situation just described the ambivalent effects are produced in the last resort by a single stimulus. The situation would be quite similar if the two opposing responses were elicited each by its own stimulus, provided that the stimuli followed each other rather closely. In one of Pavlov's dogs, among other positive and negative alimentary conditioned reflexes, conditioning was established positively to a tactile stimulation of 24 per minute and negatively to 12 per minute. One day the positive rate was made to follow the negative without any interval. For the first few days after this it was found that all positive conditioned reflexes had disappeared. This was followed by a period in which there were changing relations between the magnitudes of response to the various stimuli. The disturbances are said to have lasted 5½ weeks, but neither in Anrep's translation (36, pp. 301-2) nor in Gantt's (37, pp. 343-4) are any other changes in behaviour described.

(ii) Neuroses Produced by
Noxious Stimuli

A noxious stimulus is one that causes tissue disturbance of a kind that leads or tends to lead to withdrawal behaviour. In man it is correlated with the experience of pain or discomfort.

In certain experiments in which

noxious stimuli have been used to produce neuroses a "clash" between excitation and inhibition has been involved in one way or another. In other experiments, feeding reactions have been interfered with by the presentation of the noxious stimulus. Because in both categories conflict is in some sense present it has been regarded as the centre point of the aetiology in both. Nevertheless, these neuroses are grouped here among those due to noxious stimuli and not to ambivalent stimulation; the first category for reasons given below in the course of an examination of the experiments, the second for the following reasons. First, as was shown above, to result in a neurosis, conflicting tendencies must be of approximately the same strength at the same time, whereas when the reaction to a noxious stimulus has interfered with feeding it has been overwhelmingly stronger than the feeding tendency. Secondly, in experiments to be described below, the writer has found that noxious stimuli, alone and without the aid of any conflict, can be an entirely adequate cause of neurotic reactions. If anything, a more severe neurosis tends to be produced by shock alone than by shock associated with feeding.

In the following account of the various procedures that have been employed more specific comments will be made. To unify the commentary the procedures are grouped according to what the experimenter has believed to be the crux of his method.

(a) *Noxious stimuli in experiments involving 'clash' between excitation and inhibition.* The most extensive series of experiments coming under this heading has been reported from the Cornell Behaviour Farm by Liddell & Bayne (25), Anderson & Liddell (1), Anderson & Parmenter (2), and Liddell (24). Sheep, goats, dogs and pigs were used.

It will be noticed that some of the experiments parallel those of Pavlov, mentioned above, among the ambivalent stimulation neuroses, but the 'unconditioned response' is a shock-avoidance reaction in place of the alimentary reaction. The basic procedure is described as follows by Anderson & Liddell (1):

The sheep to be conditioned was led to the laboratory. It ascended a platform and stood on a table where it might eat from a basket of oats. Its freedom of movement was restricted by loops passing under the legs and attached to a beam overhead. With the incentive of food at the beginning and end of the experiment, the sheep within a few days would run on leash to the laboratory from the barn, mount the table and remain quietly for as long as two hours. A leather bracelet wrapped with brass wires was attached to the shaved skin of the upper part of the foreleg. . . . A brief tetanizing shock, not painful to the experimenter's touch . . . evoked a brisk flexion of the sheep's foreleg, after which the animal became quiet. . . . If the shock was regularly preceded by some neutral stimulus such as the ticking of a metronome, soon the ticking of the metronome would elicit movement of the leg in anticipation of the shock. . . . The signal that a shock was coming was invariably followed by the shock. The animal quieted down within a few seconds after the shock had been administered.

(b) *Noxious stimuli interrupting conditioned feeding responses.* Dimmick, Ludlow & Whiteman (8) were the first to produce animal neuroses by a method that falls under this heading, although they attributed their results to difficult discrimination—mistakenly, as will be shown. Using an experimental cage 36 × 28 × 16 in. they trained cats to raise the lid of a food-box in response to a lamp switched on simultaneously with the ringing of a bell. When 100% correct responses had been acquired the cat would be shocked through a grid on the floor of the cage if he opened the food-box at any time except while the conditioned stimuli lasted or 6 sec. thereafter. (This shocking, of course, constituted an interruption of the feeding response conditioned, incidentally, to such stimuli as the sight of the food-box.) A varying number of sessions after this was begun, it was found that the cat would stretch towards the food-box at the conditioned stimuli but not touch it. When this happened the animal would be shocked at the end of the "correct" period for opening the food-box. The effect of this was to produce progressively more negative behaviour towards the experimental situation, and such symptoms as yowling, crouching, and clawing at the sides of the cage developed as responses to the conditioned signals. Also, the cats became less friendly in their living quarters.

(c) *Noxious stimuli used alone.* The only previous report of neurosis production conforming to this heading appears to be that of Watson & Rayner (42). They found that a usually phlegmatic 11-month-old infant called Albert would react fearfully to the sound of an iron bar loudly struck behind his head. They contrived to strike the bar just as the child's hand touched a white rat. This was done 7 times and then repeated after a week. It was subsequently found that the child reacted with fear to the white rat, and also to a rabbit, a beaver fur, and a dog. A month later these fear reactions could still be elicited. After this the child was lost sight of.

## III. PRESENT EXPERIMENTS IN NEUROSIS PRODUCTION

These experiments were performed between June 1947 and July 1948 in the Department of Pharmacology of the University of the Witwatersrand. The present account is an abbreviated version of a more detailed one written in 1948 (43).

## (i) Subjects and Apparatus

The subjects were twelve domestic cats ranging in age from about 6 months to 3 years. They were housed in large, airy cages built into a brick cage-house on the roof of the department. When experimentation began an animal would have been in these quarters for at least 4 weeks. Experiments were always done between 11 a.m. and 1 p.m., when the animals had not eaten for 19–21 hr., except, occasionally, when prolonged observations were necessary.

The experimental centre was a laboratory on the floor below the cage house. Animals were carried to and from the laboratory in 'carrier cages' of which the dimensions were 9 × 9 × 16 in.

The experimental cage (40 × 20 × 20 in.) was practically identical with that of Masserman, except that the long sides and roof were made of stout ¾ in. wire-netting in the place of glass. A metal funnel delivered pellets of minced beef into the food-box as required. The conditioned signals used were auditory—a buzzer, and a whirring sound made by the armature of an automobile hooter (inaccurately referred to as a 'hoot'). The grid on the floor of the cage could be charged by depressing a telegraph key in the secondary circuit of an induction coil continuously vibrating 25 ft. away. The current delivered, being of high voltage but low amperage, was very uncomfortable to the human hand but not productive of tissue damage.

In the course of the experiments it became evident that the experimental laboratory, and, indeed, the experimenter himself, could well be regarded as part of the apparatus. For convenience the experimental laboratory was called room A. Experiments were also conducted in three other rooms which were labelled respectively B, C and D. These rooms, in the order stated, seemed, to the human eye and ear, to have decreasing degrees of resemblance to room A. Rooms A and B were both situated about 30 ft. above ground-level overlooking eastwards a fairly busy street, but room A was the brighter of the two, as it also had windows on its north side. Both rooms contained very dark laboratory furniture, the greater quantity being in room A. Room C faced south, was about half the size of A or B, and contained laboratory furniture lighter in colour and less in quantity than that in B. It was out of earshot of the street. Room D was situated on the roof of the Medical School, and was extremely bright with white-washed walls and large windows north and west. Besides a concrete trough and odd packages it contained only a light-coloured kitchen sink in one corner.

## (ii) Procedure

Experimentation was commenced only after an animal's original reactions had been recorded to the experimental cage, to the auditory signals and various other sounds, and to one or more of the rooms B, C and D. In all cases these reactions were found to be inconsequential.

Six experimental animals were subjected to the main experimental procedure (schedule I) and six to a control procedure (schedule II). In brief, it may be said that schedule II corresponds to the method for producing neuroses described by Masserman (29), and schedule I differs from it in omitting what Masserman would regard as an essential step—the conditioning of a feeding response.

*Schedule I.* Not more than 2 days after the control observations detailed above, the cat was reintroduced into the experimental cage and given five to ten grid-shocks, each immediately preceded by a "hoot" lasting 2 to 3 sec. The grid shocks were separated by irregular intervals ranging from 15 sec. to 2 min. With the exception of cat 8 who received five shocks in all, these animals were subjected to a second series of shocks 1 to 3 days later.

*Schedule II.* The first part of this schedule consisted of conditioning animals to perform food-approach responses to the buzzer. There were two variations differing from each other in a minor respect. Four of the six animals were trained to raise the lid of the food-box to the stimulus, the other two to orientate themselves to the *open* food-box. When either response had been strongly reinforced over eight to sixteen experimental sessions each consisting of about twenty reinforcements, each animal would be subjected to shocks from the floor of the cage, as follows. The buzzer had just sounded, the cat had made its learned response, the pellet had fallen into the food-box, and now the animal was moving forward to seize it. Before the pellet could be reached a grid-shock was passed into the cat which immediately recoiled, howling. Shocking under these conditions was repeated until the cat ceased to make its previous conditioned response to the buzzer. Two or three shocks were usually sufficient to accomplish this, but one cat required nine shocks distributed over three separate sessions.

### (iii) Immediate Effects of the Shock

The immediate responses to shock followed the same pattern in all cats,

whether they had previously acquired a feeding response in the experimental situation or not. This pattern was made up of various combinations of the following symptoms—rushing hither and thither, getting up on the hindlegs, clawing at the floor, roof and sides of the experimental cage, crouching, trembling, howling, spitting; mydriasis, rapid respiration, pilo-erection, and, in some cases, urination or defecation.

### (iv) Lasting Effects of the Shock

*(a) Effects noted in the experimental cage.* When tested at subsequent sessions, *all* animals, irrespective of the schedule employed, displayed neurotic symptoms in the sense of the definition given at the beginning of this paper. The effects of the two schedules were broadly the same, but a few differences will be mentioned below. Three manifestations were constant and common to all animals: (1) resistance to being put into the experimental cage; (2) signs of anxiety when inside the cage (muscular tension and mydriasis were invariable); (3) *refusal to eat meat pellets anywhere in the cage even after 1, 2 or 3 days' starvation.*

Quantitative change in general activity was almost invariable. An increase or decrease was usually constant for an individual animal. Increased activity took the forms of restless roving, clawing at the wire-netting, butting the roof with the head, and ceaseless vocalizing. Decreased activity varied between tense infrequent movements in the standing posture and very intense immobile crouching.

Symptoms that were observed intermittently in all animals were hypersensitivity to "indifferent" stimuli, pilo-erection, howling, crouching, and rapid respiration.

Certain cats displayed special symptoms in addition to those that were common to all. The respiratory rate of cat 9 always rose from about 30 to about 60 as soon as he was put into the cage. Cat 15, who had micturated while being shocked, invariably micturated a few seconds after being placed in the cage. Cat 6 manifested almost continuous trembling. Cat 8 developed a symptom that it seems permissible to call hysterical. He jerked his shoulders strongly every few seconds in the experimental cage, and also in his living cage *if the experimenter entered it.* This jerking suggested an abortive jumping movement, and may well have had its origin in the fact that on the first occasion on which this animal was shocked he jumped through a hatch in the roof of the cage that had been left open inadvertently. It is worth noting that all but the first-mentioned of these four cats had been through schedule I.

Whatever symptoms an animal showed in the experimental cage were invariably *intensified by presentation of the auditory stimulus* that had been contiguous with the occurrence of the shock.

*(b) Generalization of neurotic responses outside experimental cage.* All cats showed some symptoms outside the experimental cage of the same kind as inside it. In two schedule I animals and four schedule II animals these effects were limited to slight tenseness and fluctuating mydriasis in the experimental room, together with inhibition of feeding responses anywhere in the room at the sound of the buzzer or "hooter" as the case might be. However, in the remaining six cats (four of schedule I, and two of schedule II) such symptoms were very marked, and were observed also outside the confines of the experimental laboratory. That is to say, they were observed in one or more of the rooms B, C and D. One

animal also refused meat pellets in the passage in front of the living cages. Any animal that showed symptoms of tension in room D showed them more strongly in room C, and still more in room B. A cat free of symptoms in room B would also be free in rooms C and D. Thus it would appear that the anxiety-producing effect of these various rooms was a function of their resemblance to room A as judged in a rough way by the human eye and ear. More exactly, the magnitude of the anxiety response in room C, for instance, seems to have depended upon the number of stimuli common to rooms A and C. As will be seen below, the successful use of these rooms to build up a conditioned inhibition of the anxiety responses provides strong support for this supposition.

*(c) Neurotic responses to the experimenter.* Three schedule I animals developed phobic reactions towards the experimenter which were manifested even in the living cages. The jerking shoulders of cat 8 when the experimenter entered his cage have already been mentioned. Two others would crouch with pupils widely dilated as soon as they saw even his entry into the cage-house. Such effects were never noted in schedule II animals.

*(d) A note on some differences between the effects of the two schedules.* The general similarity between the effects of the two schedules has been mentioned. However, it is only to be expected that the preliminary conditioning of feeding reactions in schedule II animals would result in some differences. The fact that only schedule I animals became phobic towards the experimenter was noted in the last paragraph. The explanation seems to be that for schedule II cats "approach" attitudes towards the experimenter had at first been built up as a result of his previous association with feeding re-

sponses; and at the time of shocking, the experimenter was relatively remote as a stimulus since the animal was usually almost continuously orientated towards the food-box. Schedule II animals were alone found to show phobic responses to meat pellets dropped in front of them wherever they might be —starting with pupils widely dilated. This is easily understood, as these animals were responding strongly to the sight and smell of these pellets when they were shocked.

## IV. CURATIVE MEASURES INVOLVING RECIPROCAL INHIBITON

The fact that the neurotic reactions of the cats were associated with inhibition of feeding suggested that under different conditions feeding might inhibit the neurotic reactions: in other words, that the two reactions might be reciprocally inhibitory.

In order actively to inhibit the anxiety reactions the feeding would have to occur in the presence of anxiety-producing stimuli. Either, then, some factor that would favour feeding had to be added to the stimulus situation in the experimental cage, or else feeding had to be attempted somewhere *outside* the experimental cage where anxiety-producing stimuli would be less numerous and less potent. Both principles were used, as described below.

### (i) The Addition to the Experimental Environment of a Factor Favouring Feeding

(a) *The human hand as a stimulus to feeding.* Since in their living cages the cats were accustomed to have food cast to them by the human hand, it was expected that the hand had become conditioned to evoke approach

responses to food. Consequently, the experiment was tried of placing an animal in the experimental cage and moving towards its snout pellets of meat on the flat end of a 4 in. rod held in the experimenter's hand, in the hope that the presence of the hand would overcome the inhibition to eating. This procedure was applied to nine animals (six schedule I, and three schedule II), and after some persistence four of them (three schedule I, and one schedule II) were induced to eat. These animals at first approached a pellet hesitantly, sometimes refusing it. But after several had been eaten, they ate fairly freely from the rod, and soon after would also now and then eat a pellet on the floor of the cage or in the food-box. In the case of cat 3, the only one of these four cats that had been through schedule II (in which shock interrupted a movement towards the food-box), eating out of the food-box did not occur until he had eaten more than fifty pellets on the floor of the cage in the course of several sessions. As the number of pellets eaten in the situation increased, each of these animals ate more freely, moved about the cage with greater freedom, and showed decreasing anxiety symptoms. By the time cat 10 had eaten about fifty pellets and cat 11 about eighty they were jumping spontaneously out of the carrier into the experimental cage; and inside the cage were showing no sign of anxiety whatever. Cat 8, who, it will be remembered, had the 'hysterical' jerking movement of the shoulders, lost all traces of his symptoms only after he had eaten 216 pellets in the experimental cage in the course of eleven sessions.

(b) *Masserman's "forced solution."* The three schedule II cats on which the human-hand technique was not tried were each subjected to procedures based on the "forced solution" described by Masserman (29, p. 75), with like results. The essence of this method is that a hungry neurotic cat in the experimental cage is gradually pushed by means of a movable barrier towards the open food-box which contains appetizing food. This accentuates the manifestations of anxiety, but after a while the animal snatches at the food in one or more hurried gulps. Repeating the procedure over several days has the effect of diminishing and then eliminating the neurotic reactions.

### (ii) Feeding in the Presence of Relatively Weak Anxiety Responses

It has already been stated that the inhibition of eating, together with the rest of the neurotic picture, occurred not only in the experimental cage but also anywhere in the experimental room and in other rooms resembling this room in various ways—an effect presumably due to primary stimulus generalization (18, p. 184; 47). The slighter the resemblance of a given room to the experimental room the less marked were the anxiety reactions. In the case of the five cats who had remained unaffected by the delivery of food in the experimental cage by the human hand, it was decided to try to obtain feeding responses in the rooms where the anxiety reactions were less marked. It was thought that somewhere in this "hierarchy" of rooms there would be found for each animal a place where the anxiety responses were mild enough to permit eating at least at times. Starting in the experimental room (room A), each cat was patiently plied with meat pellets on the floor. If it did not eat after about 30 min. the experiment was repeated on the following day in the next room lower in the "hierarchy." One cat ate initially in room A, one in room B, one in room C, and one in room D. The fifth animal could not be persuaded to eat even in room D, but did so eventually in the passage that separated room D from the living cages. Once an animal had eaten in a given place it was given about twenty pellets there, always responding to their presentation with increasing rapidity, and with decreasing signs of anxiety. The next day it was tested in the room next in order of resemblance to room A. (From time to time control tests of response in the experimental cage were also made.) By this method of gradual ascent all the animals were eventually enabled to eat in room A. Then, within the room, gradual approach was made to the experimental cage in similar fashion, the animal being fed on the floor increasingly close to the experimental table, then on the table next to the cage, on the roof of the cage, and at last inside the cage. It was found that when feeding became possible in the cage anxiety reactions were much more rapidly eliminated there when the pellets were tossed at widely distributed points than if they were confined to the food-box. Apparently, scattered placing of the pellets resulted in reciprocal inhibition of the anxiety responses to stimuli from all parts of the experimental situation, and this made possible the development of conditioned inhibition of the responses to all parts (according to the mechanism discussed below), so that after 50–100 pellets had been eaten in the cage, manifestations of anxiety ceased to be observed.

### (iii) The Elimination of Neurotic Responses to the Conditioned Auditory Stimuli

The fact that an animal, after subjection to the procedures just described, would behave without anxiety in the experimental cage can be attributed to the elimination of the neurotic responses that had previously been conditioned to the various visual (and olfactory) cues in the vicinity of the cage. But if the *auditory* stimulus that had preceded the shocks was now presented the animals again manifested a high degree of anxiety. The effect was such that the animal could be inhibited by the auditory stimulus from completing any movement towards a pellet of meat in the experimental cage, and, in most cases, at various points in the experimental room as well. The problem was to present the auditory stimulus in such a way that the anxiety reactions would be weak and there would be no inhibition of eating. There were two possible solutions to this: (1) diminishing the strength of the stimulus either by reducing its physical intensity or by increasing the distance between the animal and the stimulus; or (2) making use of the stimulus trace and the fact that the effects of a brief sensory stimulus on the nervous system gradually decline in intensity with passage of time (1). The first solution was applied to two animals and the second to seven.

*(a) Feeding in conjunction with the auditory stimulus at reduced strength.* Both cats upon whom this procedure was used had been through schedule I. The minimum distance at which cat 11 would eat with the conditioned auditory stimulus ("hooter") sounding continuously was found by trial and error to be 40 ft. Here, though continuously tense and mydriatic, the animal ate eight pellets, but would not eat at a point 10 ft. nearer. The next day, after two pellets at 40 ft., he ate ten at 30 ft., at first only when dropped a few inches away from him, but afterwards even at distances of 3 or 4 ft. Pellets were then dropped increasingly near the "hooter," and by the time eight more had been given he had eaten two only 17 ft. away. After eating each

pellet he would run back to the 30 ft. point, or even beyond it. Day by day, the distance at which the animal would eat was reduced. When he had had a total of 160 pellets at progressively decreasing distances he was at last able to eat inside the experimental cage during the sounding of the "hooter," although manifesting considerable anxiety. At the end of his fourth session spent in eating in the cage, by which time he had eaten a total of eighty-seven pellets there, the note was made, "There is now absolutely no sign of avoidance reaction or anxiety to the auditory stimulus."

Cat 8, whose anxiety responses to the auditory stimulus were much milder than those of cat 11 at the commencement of this procedure ate as little as 20 ft. away from the "hooter" in the beginning, and required only thirty-three pellets at decreasing distances to enable him to eat in the presence of the sound in the experimental cage. He lost all tenseness there after forty-five pellets given over four sessions.

*(b) Feeding in the presence of the trace of the conditioned auditory stimulus.* Four of the cats treated in this way had been through schedule I and the other three through schedule II. The animal was placed inside the experimental cage, and though showing no sign of disturbance was given one or two meat pellets on the floor of the cage. Then, after an interval of about a minute, the auditory stimulus was sounded for about one-fifth of a second, and *immediately afterwards* a pellet was dropped in front of the animal, who had in the meantime become tense and hunched-up, with piloerection and mydriasis. After a variable interval, usually about 30 sec., the animal would have lost most of its tenseness and would move forward cautiously to the pellet and eat it. Not less than 1 min. later, the auditory stimulus

would again be presented, making the cat tense, and be followed by a meat pellet, but this time the animal would eat after a shorter interval. This procedure was repeated 10 to 20 times during a session, and the interval before the eating of the pellet would gradually diminish until the animal ate without delay. In illustration of the above, the intervals recorded (in seconds) for one cat during the first session of this kind were: 40, 15, 20, 7, 5, 6, 6, 6, 4, 8, 8, 11, 4, 6, 4, 4, 5, 3, and 4. At the next session the intervals were 3, 3, 2, 3, 2 and 2 sec. for the first six presentations of stimulus, and thereafter she consistently responded practically at once.

The next step was *to increase the duration of the auditory stimulus*. First, every fourth or fifth stimulus was given a duration of about a second; and then, gradually, depending on the responses of the animal, the duration was increased. Eventually, the animal would show no vestige of anxiety even to a stimulus of 30 sec. duration, and would make alert food-seeking movements as soon as she heard the auditory stimulus.

(c) *Demonstration that the neurotic reactions were not merely overshadowed*. Whichever of the above two procedures had been employed, the question remained whether the neurotic reactions had really been eliminated or had merely been overshadowed by a stronger reaction of feeding beneath which they lay dormant. The decisive experiment was *to extinguish the food-seeking response to the auditory stimulus* and then observe whether or not the neurotic reactions were reinstated. Each of the animals was given thirty irregularly massed extinction trials on each of three successive days. Long before the end of the third day's session they all showed almost complete indifference to the auditory stimulus. Immediately after the conclusion of the

third extinction session the following test was made. A pellet was dropped on the floor of the experimental cage about 2 ft. away from the animal, and as he began to approach it the auditory signal was sounded continuously, to see if extinction had reinstated the inhibitory effect on eating that had originally been noted. *In no instance was there observed any semblance of the restoration of an anxiety response or any suggestion of an inhibition of eating*. Moreover, observation for many weeks afterwards never revealed recurrence of anxiety responses in any animal.

## V. INTERPRETATIONS OF THE PRESENT RESULTS

### (i) Conformity of the Behaviour Changes to Definition of Experimental Neurosis

According to the definition given at the beginning of this paper an experimental neurosis has to satisfy criteria of anxiety, unadaptiveness and persistence. The prominence of anxiety is sufficiently obvious from the account of the experiments and need not be discussed further.

Unadaptiveness was shown in two ways—the inhibition of feeding responses in a hungry animal in a situation in which feeding would not again be followed by shock (and in the case of schedule I animals had never been followed by shock); and the mere fact that the anxious responses were causing fatigue without in any way favouring the organism's life processes (i.e. were without reward).

The criterion of persistence was satisfied by: (1) maintenance of tenseness and other manifestations at an undiminishing level throughout a long session; (2) recurrence of manifestations at unabated strength session after session; and (3) re-evocation of manifestations after long periods free from experimentation, for example, in all of three cats rested for 6 months.

The following extract from the protocols of cat 7 (schedule I) illustrates the unremittingness of the neurotic tension and shows how complete the inhibition of feeding could be.

On September 1, 1947, seven days after she had been shocked, cat 7 was taken when hungry to the experimental laboratory. She resisted being put into the experimental cage. Inside the cage, she crouched with pupils widely dilated. She was kept there for 2 hours, during which her pupils remained dilated, although their size fluctuated a good deal, reaching a maximum at any sharp sound or sudden movement. At times she became very restless, mewed plaintively, and clawed at the sides of the cage. She showed no response at all to meat pellets put in front of her nose on an ebony rod, and left untouched a pellet which lay on the floor of the cage during the whole of her two hours' confinement.

## (ii) Why the Behavior Changes Are Regarded as Learned

In order to decide whether or not the neurotic behaviour was learned it is necessary first to define what is to be understood by the term *learning*. Learning may be said to have occurred if a response has been evoked in temporal contiguity with a given sensory stimulus, and it is subsequently found that the stimulus can evoke the response although it could not have done so before. If the stimulus could have evoked the response before but subsequently evokes it more strongly, then, too, learning may be said to have occurred.

In the case of our experimental cats there was no qualitative difference between the immediate responses to the shock and the later responses to the experimental environment. In other words, the responses produced by the shock in the originally "neutral" experimental environment were subsequently found to be producible by the experimental environment itself. This clearly implies the occurrence of learning as defined above. It was particularly well shown in the development of the "special" symptoms noted earlier. For example, the cat that displayed the jerking shoulders was the one that had once jumped out of the cage when shocked, and the one that regularly micturated in the experimental cage had micturated when shocked.

Furthermore, it will be seen below that these experiments embody other features that make the results easily explicable in terms of modern knowledge of the learning process.

## (iii) The Present Results in the Light of Modern Learning Theory

(a) *Preliminary remarks on modern learning theory.* By modern learning theory is meant the recently developed body of psychological theory associated largely with the name of C. L. Hull (18). Involving a rigorous scientific discipline and placing much emphasis on quantification, this body of theory has gone far towards raising the methodological level of psychology to that of the older sciences. To-day it increasingly dominates the literature of American experimental and theoretical psychology.

A few of the basic notions of modern learning theory must be briefly mentioned. They derive essentially from Hull's classic work (18), but are modified in certain respects out of consideration of recent neurophysiological knowledge (44, 45, 47, 48, 49).

In 1938, Culler (7) showed in dogs that when a semitendinosus response was established to a tone, stimulation of a point found by trial and error on the exposed cortex also evoked the response, and ceased to do so if the response to the tone was extinguished. This finding strongly supports the supposition that learning is subserved by the development of conductivity between neurones in anatomical apposition. Numerous experiments have demonstrated that in a given learning situation there is a direct quantitative relationship between the amount of learning that occurs and the magnitude of the associated drive reduction. It has been argued elsewhere (45) that if learning has a neural basis, then it is through reduction of a feature common to all drives—*central neural excitation*—that drive reduction subserves learning. The strength of central neural excitation can be appraised indirectly by knowledge of stimulus strength or of response strength. (In the case of human subjects, some indication of strength of drive can, of course, be obtained from reports of experience.)

The process of *elimination* of learned reactions is conceived to involve the weakening of neural connexions previously formed during learning. The process occurs in either of two ways— extinction or reciprocal inhibition, and in both of them drive reduction plays as important a part as in learning. In the case of *extinction* the drive concerned is the fatigue-associated state of disequilibrium having its origin in the effector organs subserving the response —the Mowrer-Miller hypothesis (18, p. 277; 32, 35). *Reciprocal inhibition* implies that in the presence of stimuli that would lead to the given response, another, incompatible and stronger response is enabled to occur, and the given response is inhibited (49). In such cases, an obvious drive reduction is always provided by the reciprocal inhibition of the excitation that would have led to the given response; and if

the response that was dominant is rewarded its drive is also reduced.

(b) *The learning process in the present experiments.* Reasons were given above for deciding that the neurotic reactions of our cats were learned. The high intensity of the reactions after very few shocks can be accounted for on the basis that a very powerful drive reduction occurred *at the cessation of each shock.* The responses occurring at the time of the cessation became strongly connected thereby to stimuli from the experimental environment. These responses comprised musculo-skeletal movements tending away from the situation and autonomic responses evidenced, for example, by muscular tenseness, mydriasis, and pilo-erection. The whole picture was one of "anxiety."

After the first shocking, stimuli from the experimental environment were already able to elicit some measure of anxiety responses, and these, of course, had an anxiety-drive state as an antecedent. In other words, the environmental stimuli had become able to arouse a secondary (i.e. learned) drive state. Reduction of this secondary drive by the removal of the animal from the experimental environment would further reinforce the anxiety responses as responses to the stimuli of that environment. O. H. Mowrer (33, 34) was the first to recognize the role of anxiety reduction as a reinforcing agent. Other workers who have demonstrated this are Farber (13), May (30), and Miller (31).

(c) *The factor of confinement.* Anderson & Liddell (1) have pointed out that all animal neuroses have been produced in conditions of confined space. Cook's experiments (6), employing different degrees of space constriction with other factors constant, indicate that it is a potent factor in neurosis production. There are at least three ways in which confinement could exert its influence. First, the prevention of an effective escape response allows the cumulative action on the animal of stimuli that have become conditioned to anxiety, so that there is a rising magnitude of potentially reducible anxiety drive. Secondly, the drive reductions occur in the presence of a limited number of stimuli, and the anxiety responses can be conditioned to these in greater strength than would be the case if the environment were a changing one. Thirdly, it seems likely that autonomic responses are stronger when freed from the reciprocally inhibiting effects of musculo-skeletal responses (51).

(d) The reason for persistence of the neurotic responses (resistance to extinction). As stated under (a), learned responses that are unrewarded (and so unadaptive) ordinarily undergo extinction by a mechanism that is associated with fatigue. Since fatigue occurs whether there is reward or not, there is always a fatigue-associated drive state that tends towards a weakening of the connexion between the response and the stimulus that led to it. But it is only when there is no significant reward that the connexion is actually weakened (18, p. 298). When reward counteracts this tendency towards weakening it does so through reducing the central drive state due to, say, hunger.

Now, the neurotic responses are unrewarded (unadaptive). Yet they necessarily have a central state of drive as an antecedent. This drive is automatically reduced by the retreat of the organism from the anxiety-producing stimulus, or by any other means that removes the organism from the action of this stimulus. Any responses that may be occurring at such a time will be reinforced, and their fatigue-associated tendency to be extinguished will be counteracted. Farber (13) has pre-sented a clear demonstration in rats of the manner in which anxiety drive reduction interferes with extinction.

Frequently repeated or continuous consequents of the anxiety drive (of which the autonomic responses are an example) are much more likely to coincide in time with drive reductions than are responses that occur only occasionally. That is why, in our experiments, the autonomic responses, whose evocation was continuous, were always persistent, whereas such intermittent responses as clawing the sides of the cage were soon extinguished. It is important to note that these autonomic responses were reinforced even though they did not themselves bring about removal from the shock.

(e) The mechanism of cure. The effectiveness of the procedures that overcame the neurotic responses can be accounted for as follows: in every instance feeding was made possible in the presence of stimuli conditioned to anxiety responses which, under other circumstances, inhibited feeding. When stimuli to incompatible responses are present simultaneously the occurrence of the response that is dominant in the circumstances involves the reciprocal inhibition of the other. As the number of feedings increased, the anxiety responses gradually became weaker, so that to stimuli to which there was initially a response of the anxiety pattern there was finally a feeding response with inhibition of anxiety. This "permanent" change implies a new positive conditioning pari passu with a conditioning of inhibition, and this could have been subserved by at least two drive reductions—hunger drive reduction, and reduction by the reciprocal inhibition itself of the drive antecedent to the anxiety responses. That the conditioned inhibition was due to a neural change and was not merely a correlate of the occurrence of the alternative response seems a clear inference from the fact that eventual extinction of the alternative response did not result in reinstatement of the original one. This mechanism has been more fully discussed elsewhere (49).

At this point it is necessary to comment on Masserman's interpretation of the cures obtained by the "forced solution." He states (29, p. 203) that with the cat maximally hungry and the food very attractive, at a certain proximity to the food, the food-approach drive reached such an intensity as to break through the animal's inhibitions; and 'once the motivational impasse was disrupted, the feeding behaviour soon became more natural . . . and the other neurotic manifestations rapidly diminished in intensity.' Now, it can scarcely be doubted that the creation of a very intense drive to feed makes it possible to overcome the inhibitory effects of the anxiety state at a given moment. But it is still necessary to explain how the feeding results in a "permanent" decrease in anxiety. It is by no means self-evident that the momentary overcoming of an inhibition implies the breaking of a *habit* of inhibition, as Masserman seems to think.

## VIII. CLINICAL IMPLICATIONS

Since 1947 the writer has studied a large number of human cases of neurosis with a view to determining to what extent their causation parallels that of the experimental neuroses. The findings of these investigations can only be summarily mentioned here.

From the outset, the fact that in human case-histories, too, conflict or trauma or both are invariably found seemed to support the idea of a common basis; and the experience of the past 4 years has encouraged belief in the hypothesis that experimental and clinical neuroses are parallel phenomena. Some of the similarities, discussed at some length in a dissertation (43), have been briefly reported (46).

The human subject is not often forced to undergo his conflicts or his traumata in physically confined space. He is usually kept in the anxiety-producing situation by the force of habits previously learned. For instance, a woman entangled in a humiliating marriage may be unable to get out of it because her earlier training has given a horror to the idea of divorce. Besides confining her within the marriage, this feeling of horror, being in conflict with escape tendencies, makes possible the development of a high level of emotional tension (anxiety). This tension becomes increasingly conditioned to contiguous stimuli through the drive reductions that follow every partial escape from the causative situation.

In therapy, the writer has concentrated on seeking means of obtaining reciprocal inhibition of anxiety responses, after the pattern that was so successful in animals. In the great majority of cases reciprocal inhibition of anxiety has in fact been procurable, either in the interview situation or the life situation, always with results that are beneficial, sometimes in a most dramatic way. The methods used and their effects are discussed in detail elsewhere (50). In an earlier communication (46) reasons were given for supposing that the similar amounts of success obtained by therapies differing widely in character are largely due to something common to all interview situations— reciprocal inhibition of anxiety responses by more powerful antagonistic emotional responses evoked in the patient by the therapist and by the interview situation in general.

# REFERENCES

1. ANDERSON, O. D., & LIDDELL, H. S. (1935). Observations on experimental neurosis in sheep. *Arch. Neurol. Psychiat.* xxxiv, 330–54.

2. ANDERSON, O. D., & PARMENTER, R. (1941). A long term study of the experimental neurosis in the sheep and dog. *Psychosom. Med. Monogr.* ii, nos. 3 and 4.

3. BABKIN, B. P. (1938). Experimental neuroses in animals and their treatment with bromides. *Edinb. Med. J.* xlv, 605–19.

4. BAJANDUROW, B. (1932). Zur Psychologie des Sehenanalysators bei Vogeln. *Z. vergl. Physiol.* xviii, 288–306. Quoted by Cook (5).

5. COOK, S. W. (1939). A survey of methods used to produce 'experimental neurosis.' *Amer. J. Psychiat.* xcv, 1259–76.

6. COOK, S. W. (1939). The production of 'experimental neurosis' in the white rat. *Psychosom. Med.* i, 293–308.

7. CULLER, E. (1938). Observations on direct cortical stimulation in the dog. *Psychol. Bull.* xxxv, 687–8.

8. DIMMICK, F. L., LUDLOW, N., & WHITEMAN, A. (1939). A study of 'experimental neurosis' in cats. *J. Comp. Psychol.* xxviii, 39–43.

9. DWORKIN, S. (1939). Conditioning neuroses in dog and cat. *Psychosom. Med.* i, 388–96.

10. DWORKIN, S., BAXT, J. O., & DWORKIN, E. (1942). Behavioural disturbances of vomiting and micturition in conditioned cats. *Psychosom. Med.* iv, 75–81.

11. DWORKIN, S., RAGINSKY, B. B., & BOURNE, W. (1937). Action of anaesthetics and sedatives upon the inhibited nervous system. *Curr. Res. Anaesth.* xvi, 238–40.

12. ESTES, W. K. (1944). An experimental study of punishment. *Psychol. Monogr.* lvii, no. 263.

13. FARBER, I. E. (1948). Response fixation under anxiety and non-anxiety conditions. *J. Exp. Psychol.* xxxviii, 111–31.

14. FENICHEL, O. (1945). *The Psychoanalytic Theory of Neurosis.* New York: Norton.

15. FINGER, F. W. (1945). Abnormal animal behaviour and conflict. *Psychol. Rev.* lii, 230–40.

16. GANTT, W. H. (1944). Experimental basis for neurotic behaviour. *Psychosom. Med. Monogr.* iii, nos. 3 and 4.

17. HEBB, D. O. (1947). Spontaneous neurosis in chimpanzees: theoretical relations with clinical and experimental phenomena. *Psychosom. Med.* ix, 3–16.

18. HULL, C. L. (1943). *Principles of Behaviour.* New York: Appleton.

19. ISCHLONDSKY, N. E. (1944). Quoted by Gantt (16), pp. 180–1.

20. JACOBSEN, C. F., WOLFE, J. B., & JACKSON, T. A. (1935). An experimental analysis of the functions of frontal association areas in primates. *J. Nerv. Ment. Dis.* lxxxii, 1–14.

21. KARN, H. W. (1938). A case of experimentally induced neurosis in the cat. *J. Exp. Psychol.* xxii, 589–92.

22. KARN, H. W. (1940). The experimental study of neurotic behaviour in infrahuman animals. *J. Gen. Psychol.* xxii, 431–6.

23. KRASNOGORSKI, N. I. (1925). The conditioned reflexes and children's neurosis. *Amer. J. Dis. Child.* xxx, 754–68.

24. LIDDELL, H. S. (1944). Conditioned reflex method and experimental neurosis. In Hunt, J. McV., *Personality and the Behaviour Disorders.* New York: Ronald Press.

25. LIDDELL, H. S., & BAYNE, T. L. (1927). The development of 'experimental neurasthenia' in sheep during the formation of difficult conditioned reflexes. *Amer. J. Physiol.* lxxxi, 494.

26. MAIER, N. R. F. (1949). *Frustration: The Study of Behaviour without a Goal.* New York: McGraw-Hill.

27. MAIER, N. R. F., & GLASER, N. M.

(1942). Studies of abnormal behaviour in the rat. IX. Factors which influence the occurrence of seizures during auditory stimulation. *J. Comp. Psychol.* xxxiv, 11–21.

28. MAIER, N. R. F., & LONGHURST, J. V. (1947). Studies of abnormal behaviour in the rat. XXI. Conflict and audiogenic seizures. *J. Comp. Psychol.* xl, 397–412.

29. MASSERMAN, J. H. (1943). *Behaviour and Neurosis.* Chicago: University of Chicago Press.

30. MAY, M. A. (1948). Experimentally acquired drives. *J. Exp. Psychol.* xxxviii, 66–77.

31. MILLER, N. E. (1948). Studies of fear as an acquirable drive. I. Fear as motivation and fear-reduction as reinforcement in the learning of new responses. *J. Exp. Psychol.* xxxviii, 89–101.

32. MILLER, N. E., & DOLLARD, J. (1941). *Social Learning and Imitation.* New Haven: Yale University Press.

33. MOWRER, O. H. (1939). A stimulus-response analysis of anxiety and its role as a reinforcing agent. *Psychol. Rev.* xlvi, 553–65.

34. MOWRER, O. H. (1940). Anxiety-reduction and learning. *J. Exp. Psychol.* xxvii, 497–516.

35. MOWRER, O. H., & JONES, H. M. (1943). Extinction and behaviour variability as a function of effortfulness of task. *J. Exp. Psychol.* xxxiii, 369–86.

36. PAVLOV, I. P. (1927). *Conditioned Reflexes.* Transl. G. V. Anrep. London: Oxford University Press.

37. PAVLOV, I. P. (1928). *Lectures on Conditioned Reflexes.* Transl. W. H. Gantt. New York: Liveright.

38. PETROVA, M. K. (1935). New data concerning the mechanisms of the action of bromides on the higher nervous

activity. Moscow. Quoted by Babkin (3).

39. RUSSELL, R. W. (1950). The comparative study of 'conflict' and 'experimental neurosis.' *Brit. J. Psychol.* xli, 95–108.

40. THORNDIKE, E. L. (1932). Reward and punishment in animal learning. *Comp. Psychol. Monogr.* viii, no. 39.

41. WARREN, H. C. (1935). *Dictionary of Psychology.* London: Allen and Unwin.

42. WATSON, J. B., & RAYNER, R. (1920). Conditioned emotional reactions. *J. Exp. Psychol.* iii, 1–14.

43. WOLPE, J. (1948). An approach to the problem of neurosis based on the conditioned response. M.D. Thesis, University of the Witwatersrand.

44. WOLPE, J. (1949). An interpretation of the effects of combination of stimuli (patterns) based on current neurophysiology. *Psychol. Rev.* lvi, 277–83.

45. WOLPE, J. (1950). Need-reduction, drive-reduction, and reinforcement: a neurophysiological view. *Psychol. Rev.* lvii, 19–26.

46. WOLPE, J. (1950). The genesis of neurosis: an objective account. *S. Afr. Med. J.* xxiv, 613–16.

47. WOLPE, J. (1952). Primary stimulus generalisation: a neurophysiological view. *Psychol. Rev.* lix, 8–11.

48. WOLPE, J. (1952). The neurophysiology of learning and delayed reward learning. *Psychol. Rev.* lix, 192–9.

49. WOLPE, J. (1952). The formation of negative habits: a neurophysiological view. *Psychol. Rev.* lix, 290–9.

50. WOLPE, J. (1952). Objective psychotherapy of the nueroses. *S. Afr. Med. J.* (In the press.)

51. WOLPE, J. (1952). Learning theory and 'abnormal fixations.' To be published.

Myer Mendelson,
Solomon Hirsch,
and Carl S. Webber

# A Critical Examination of Some Recent Theoretical Models in Psychosomatic Medicine

*Although the acceptance of the general idea that emotional factors play a role in the development of physical symptoms led to the prominence of psychosomatic medicine, there has hardly been unanimity in opinion about the specific nature of the relationship between emotional causes and symptoms. In this paper, Mendelson, Hirsch, and Webber review the more prominent theories that have been offered in an attempt to explain the nature of this relationship. Essentially, they are concerned with the answers that have been offered to two questions: (1) Why do certain people develop psychosomatic illnesses? (2) Why does illness arise in one organ rather than another? The theories presented in this paper represent a good summary of the current state of thinking about such answers.*

Theoretical models can play a useful role in scientific work. They may suggest underlying similarities in different phenomena and thereby bring order into a disorganized field. They may point out new avenues of research. They have an immediate practical use in providing for the practicing physician a conceptual framework which enables him to carry out his daily tasks with some degree of consistency and assurance.

The mark of the scientist is his continual exposure of his theoretical models to the critical impact of experience and observation. When hard facts do not fit in with the theoretical concept, the theory is changed. The new model gives rise to new observations, and these in turn result in further revision and expansion of concepts.

It may happen, however, that a theoretical model has an impeding or dele-terious effect on scientific progress. Owing to the prestige of its author, a theory may assume the force of a dogma—witness some of the teachings of Aristotle and Galen. In such a case, scientific work may degenerate into a sterile attempt to prove an a priori theory, and scientific workers may become blind to the data before their eyes. Investigation may then be conducted in the spirit of passionate partisanship rather than of detached appraisal.

In general, it may be said that scientific models are fruitful when they enable us to comprehend or predict or modify events. When they fail in this respect, they must be revised. Freud modified some of his most basic theories when clinical observations could not be reconciled with his previous formulations.

*Reprinted from* Psychosomatic Medicine, 18(1956), 363–373 *with the permission of Hoeber Medical Division, Harper & Row Publishers, Inc., and Dr. Mendelson.*

## "LACK OF CRITICAL CHALLENGE"

In the psychosomatic field, too, there have been successive theoretical models, each usually an advance on the old, and each occasioned by growing experience and continuing observation. And yet it is beginning to appear that there has too long existed among psychosomatic writers an attitude that more closely resembles the devout believer's than the skeptical scientist's. Grinker (16) refers to this when he writes:

. . . a lack of critical challenge to the few existing theories has made assumptions seem unassailable and hypotheses capable only of confirmation. As a result, psychosomatic formulations have become stereotypes into which each patient's life history and situation is molded by special focusing, selective interpretation, and omission or neglect of the incongruent.

This uncritical and indeed unscientific attitude has reflected seriously upon the reputation of psychiatric writers among their medical colleagues. Psychosomatic medicine has been very much of a borderline discipline. It has interested both internists and psychiatrists. Internists have often formed their opinion of psychiatric theory and psychiatric practice from their contacts with, and understanding of, what has come to be known as psychosomatic medicine. Medical people claim no special knowledge of psychiatric illness in general, and as a rule have no considered opinions about the ordinary neuroses and psychoses. They are quite prepared to accept the judgment of their psychiatric colleagues in the diagnosis and treatment of what they consider to be obvious psychiatric illness. However, from their own experience, they do claim to possess some special-

ized knowledge of that broad group of disorders and physiological disturbances that are commonly referred to as psychosomatic. Responsible psychiatrists have shared their dismay at the lack of scientific sophistication revealed in too many psychosomatic publications.

It is of interest, therefore, to examine critically one of the most recent psychosomatic models, and to inquire carefully into its meaning, usefulness and validity. First, however, several of the theoretical models which have proved useful in psychosomatic medicine will be briefly reviewed. No attempt will be made at comprehensiveness, since Grinker (16); Alexander; Macleod, Wittkower, and Margolin; and others have all presented adequate critical and historical reviews of the most important models.

## REVIEW OF THEORETICAL MODELS

### Conversion

One of the earliest of the psychiatric or psychoanalytic excursions into the field of psychosomatic medicine was the attempt to view psychophysiological disorders as conversion phenomena in which the symptom symbolized the repressed feeling. Ferenczi, for example, described what he considered to be the symbolic role of diarrhea. Melanie Klein thinks of psychosomatic phenomena as pre-genital conversions. More recently Garma has defended the position that peptic ulcer is the symbolic expression of an internalized aggressive mother.

### Personality Profiles

However, at the present time psychosomatic workers particularly in the United States are almost unanimous in refusing to accept the conversion theory of psychophysiological symptoms. Dunbar challenged this concept as early as 1935 and attempted to demonstrate, as an alternative way of understanding psychosomatic illness, that certain diseases have a high statistical correlation with certain specific personality types. She outlined personality profiles, for example, for sufferers from peptic ulcer, migraine, coronary occlusion, and many other illnesses. Her formulations had a superficial plausibility, but although personality profile studies of various illnesses continue to appear in the literature, further empirical observation has led most workers to question the validity of this conceptual model (2, 4).

*"Maternal-Personality" Profile.* Falling into the general category of personality profile studies, but with their observations including both participants in the mother-child unit, are the reports of Spitz (31) and Gerard (14). Their studies have led them to propose correlations between the type of character or behavior of the mother and certain psychosomatic disorders in the child. For example, Gerard, in her series, found that children with asthma "were mothered by dependent, demanding, ungiving mothers who in all cases were charming and socially wooing, presenting an external appearance of good adjustment." However, Dawes (5) gives voice to the skepticism shared by many observers about the validity of this type of correlation; and certainly convincing statistical validation is lacking.

## Conflict Situations and Specific Response

After Dunbar's, the most important contribution to psychosomatic theory was Alexander's. While agreeing with her that psychosomatic disorders were not symbolic conversion phenomena, he contradicted her main thesis by stating flatly that "a mysterious and vague correlation between personality and disease does not exist." His studies and the studies of his colleagues led him to conclude that it is not a personality type that is characteristic of a patient with a given disorder, but a typical conflict situation which can develop in individuals with varying personalities. He feels that in each psychosomatic illness there is a nuclear emotional conflict which is chronically present. He feels that each conflict has a specific physiological accompaniment,

. . . physiological responses to emotional stimuli, both normal and morbid, vary according to the nature of the precipitating emotional state. Laughter is the response to merriment, weeping to sorrow; . . . Increased blood pressure and accelerated heart action are a constituent part of rage and fear. . . . Attacks of asthma are correlated with an unconscious suppressed impulse to cry for the mother's help.

Alexander acknowledges that certain psychological influences like anxiety, repressed hostility, dependent cravings, inferiority feelings, and so on, are present in all psychosomatic disorders, but he argues:

. . . it is not the presence of any one or more of these psychological factors that is specific but the presence of the dynamic configuration in which they appear.

He emphasizes that the psychosomatic disorder or "vegetative neurosis," as he often refers to it, is not an expression or symbolization of an emotion, but is the physiological response of the organ to chronically present or periodically returning emotional states. He thus postulates the reverse of the classical causal sequence of disturbed structure resulting in disturbed function. He argues that it also happens that disturbed function results in disturbed structure. Thus, he states that in cases of peptic ulcer the patient's repressed longing for help and love are unconsciously equated with the longing for food, that most primitive form of sustenance and help. This mobilizes the innervations of the stomach which then "responds continuously as if food were being taken in or about to be taken in."

It is the continuous secretion which ensues, with its accompanying high acidity, that is claimed to be an important causative factor in ulcer formation. Similar sequences are described in the other so-called vegetative neuroses.

*Somatic Factors.* Alexander makes a point of stating specifically that he does not believe that the etiology of psychosomatic disorders is exclusively psychological:

The merely psychogenic explanation of such diseases as peptic ulcer cannot be defended in view of the fact that the typical emotional constellations found in patients suffering from ulcer are also observed in a large number of patients who do not suffer from ulcers. Local or general somatic factors, as yet ill defined, must be assumed, and only the coexistence of both kinds of factors, emotional and somatic, can account for ulcer formation. Equally important is the fact that in different cases the relative importance of somatic and emotional factors varies to a high degree.

Alexander's method of studying psychosomatic phenomena has been productive of much important investigation in the last two decades. Numerous studies have been published, delineating the specific conflict situation in dozens of psychosomatic illnesses. Nevertheless, a study of the literature in the last few years reveals an increasing skepticism of specificity theories, despite their alluring simplicity and plausibility. Binger has urged an increased sense of caution in the formulation of this type of correlation. More recently, Kubie and Grinker (16) have written about their difficulties in ac-

cepting the specificity theory of psychosomatic illness. And the reporter (1) of the 1952 panel on hypertension at the American Psychoanalytic Association meeting was struck by this observation:

[There was an] almost total absence of speculation concerning a correlation of a specific personality type with hypertension . . . [He found] equally impressive . . . the relative lack of interest in attempting a specific correlation with . . . particular unconscious conflicts . . . [the Round Table asserted] the need for a humble attitude concerning all that is not yet known, and the need for sharpening the research tools which seek to combine psychological and physiological measurements.

## Protective Adaptive Response

Wolff is the author of another significant contribution to psychosomatic theory. He postulates that the body reacts to stress with what he calls, more teleologically than is perhaps desirable, a protective adaptive response. He definitely disassociates himself from the "emotion-acting-on-the-body" language. He states quite clearly that protective reactions are not chain reactions in which the individual first feels some emotion such as fear or hostility which then results in altered function of the gut or heart or some other organ, and ultimately in abnormal behavior. He points out that altered feeling, bodily adjustments, and behavior all occur at the same time, though in varying relative amounts, and are all aspects of the individual's reaction to stress.

*Consistency in Response.* In contrast to Dunbar, who believes that it is the patient's personality which determines his response to stress, and to Alexander, who states that the response depends on the specific emotional conflict that is troubling the patient, Wolff feels that an individual responds somatically to stress and conflicts of many different kinds in a fashion that is consistent for him and which is determined on a hereditary basis.

The implication is that the individual and his clan meet life in a particular way, different from the members of other stocks. An individual may have been a potential "nose reactor" or "color reactor" all his life without ever having actually called upon a particular protective pattern for sustained periods because he did not need to. A given protective pattern may remain inconspicuous during long periods of relative security, and then with stress, become evident as a disorder involving the gut, the heart and the vascular system, the naso-respiratory apparatus, the skin or general metabolism.

Furthermore, he believes that along with the bodily change the patient experiences an associated and consistent emotional feeling tone or attitude. This causes his theory to bear some resemblance to Dunbar's concept of personality types. Wolff describes what he refers to as ulcerative types, colitis types, migraine types, and so on, by which he means individuals who react to stress with a particular constellation of bodily changes, feelings, and attitudes.

There are at least four implications that can be drawn from this theory: (1) that an individual reacts to stress of many different kinds in a similar way; (2) that the particular way an individual reacts to stress is similar to the way his stock (family) does; (3) that an individual reacts to stress of many different kinds with a characteristic set of bodily changes, feelings and attitudes; and (4) that different people who react to stress with the same bodily changes must also react to stress with the same emotional attitudes and feeling tones.

These are very interesting hypotheses and should be susceptible to statistical verification. Such genetic studies of psychosomatic illness as exist, however, are regrettably incomplete, and the necessary observational and statistical data that would corroborate these speculations have not yet been reported. The theory therefore remains an interesting and to some extent, even a very plausible one, but to claim more for it as yet would be premature.

## THE REGRESSION CONCEPT

A concept that is currently attracting the attention of a number of workers in the field of psychosomatic research is that of regression. Alexander had used the term "vegetative retreat" in speaking of a group of patients who, instead of actively facing stressful situations, withdraw into a type of behavior and bodily functioning more appropriate to the period of childhood.

### Physiological Regression

But it is Michaels who, in 1944, first more explicitly attempted to extend Freud's concept of regression to the field of physiology. He cited attempts made by authors as diverse as Spencer and Hughlings Jackson to apply analogous concepts to their own specialized fields. He made reference to the use of the concept of regression in general psychiatry and then posed the question:

Would it not be consistent to anticipate that the so-called functional symptoms of a psychosomatic disorder will express themselves in a manner which utilizes modes of reacting which were consonant and characteristic for previous earlier age periods . . . ? In other words, is it possible to regard the somatic expression of psychological disorder as a regression of the adult physiological level to an infantile physiological level?

After a brief survey of the various physiological systems of the body, he concluded that it was indeed possible to regard psychosomatic illnesses as regressions to infantile modes of physiological functioning. The characteristic feature of this infantile mode of functioning was described as being a relatively greater reactivity to stimuli, a quantitatively more marked distubance of homeostasis.

More recently the concept of physiological regression has been defended most ardently by Margolin, although Grinker too appears to subscribe to this hypothesis. Margolin's point of view has been clearly and succinctly formulated by Zetzel in these words:

It is suggested that in psychosomatic disease, a regressive process takes place, with the emergence of physiological responses, which, although they had been appropriate to the infantile situation, are no more appropriate to the adult than are the parallel manifestations of psychological regression. It is, moreover, impossible to separate the psychological from the physiological functions so that, on the one hand, profound physiological regressions predominantly precipitated by psychological events, and on the other hand, certain psychological manifestations of serious physical illnesses are both characterized by the appropriate physical and psychological symptomatology. In short, the psychotic features which have been recognized in certain serious psychosomatic diseases confirm the evidence that, in these illnesses, physiological regression to the mechanisms of a very early infantile level has taken place.

Margolin feels not only that regression occurs in psychosomatic disorders, in both the physiological and psychological spheres, but also that a close correlation between the degree of regression in these two spheres exists. He implies that those patients who have the highest degree of tissue pathology also have the highest degree of psychotic substrate, and that those patients with the least tissue pathology have the least psychotic substrate.

## Regressive Innervation

Szasz has also made extensive use of the concept of regression to explain psychophysiological phenomena. He introduces the concept of "regressive innervation," which he defines as "an increased state of excitation of functionally specific (localized) parasympathetic pathways." Because the parasympathetic nervous system develops earlier than the sympathetic, Szasz argues that an increased state of excitation of the parasympathetic division is regressive and represents a retreat to adaptation of stress. He states that Cannon overemphasized the role of the sympathetic nervous system and paid too little attention to the parasympathetic. Szasz feels that "the majority of syndromes encountered in clinical medicine represent chronic and localized parasympathetic excitation." He includes under diseases of regressive innervation hay fever, vasomotor rhinitis, common cold, asthma, peptic ulcer, diarrhea, ulcerative colitis, coronary diseases, heart block, urticaria, and others.

## Re-examination and Appraisal

What can be said about these attempts to understand psychophysiological phenomena as regressive shifts to immature modes of functioning? How valid are these generalizations and how useful is this particular conceptual model? How much does it help us to predict or to modify events? How productive is it of earnest and inspired investigation?

One is impressed by the scale of the conceptualizations which these authors have attempted. Each one has boldly sketched a design which is offered as a blueprint for the understanding of very complex psychosomatic phenomena. However, the manner of the execution of their task is open to serious reservations. Ideally, when proposing a theory, scientists bring up for consideration all evidence that is relevant to their hypotheses, whether it is favorable or not. Darwin is said to have made special notes of facts that appeared to contradict his theory of evolution because he was very much aware of the only too human propensity to overlook and to forget such facts. This kind of disinterested presentation of all the evidence available is not always to be found in the papers on physiological regression. Instead, random isolated supporting evidence is sometimes quoted, while the solid mass of experimental and clinical data that contravenes the thesis is ignored. The speculative nature of the hypotheses is most clearly underlined by the title of Michael's contribution, "A Psychiatric Adventure in Comparative Pathophysiology of the Infant and Adult." He implicitly acknowledges the logical looseness of his analysis, stating that he is cognizant of the fact that a good deal of the material presented "may consist of analogies and parallels." And in Margolin's paper, there is a regrettable blurring of Alexander's widely accepted distinction between hysterical and psychophysiological disorders which detracts from the relevance of some of the evidence he marshals in defense of his theory.

Whitehorn has very pertinently distinguished "meaning" from "cause," and Redlich has recently drawn attention to the distinction between phenomenological descriptions and etiological propositions. Szasz does not appear to have avoided the fallacy of confusing a way of describing psychophysiological phenomena with etiologic statements about these phenomena. He argues that the concept of regressive innervation *explains* "the majority of syndromes encountered in clinical medi-

cine" because he feels that the idea of regression *explains* the chronic and localized parasympathetic excitations, which these syndromes allegedly represent.

The word "allegedly" is used advisedly here because another criticism of Szasz's thesis forces itself upon the reader. Before resorting to a term like "regressive innervation" to "explain" certain facts, it must first be unquestionably shown these facts do indeed exist. It need hardly be pointed out that it is very far from generally accepted that ulcerative colitis, peptic ulcer, asthma, and coronary artery disease are caused by excessive parasympathetic innervation, as Szasz alleges. Engel (10) has recently given his critical attention to this matter, insofar as ulcerative colitis is concerned, and concludes with the statement that "concepts of 'parasympathetic overactivity' are thus meaningless."

*Development of Psychosomatic Diseases.* Margolin, and Alexander before him, have clearly distinguished two phases of psychosomatic illness. The first is a functional phase consisting of reversible, disproportionate, or inappropriate responses in an organ or in its constituent tissues. The second phase is the stage of irreversible tissue changes which result in the so-called psychosomatic disease. The thesis that psychosomatic illnesses develop in this two-phase manner—that is, that a psychosomatic disease results from tissue changes secondary to the chronic stimulation of an organ in a situation of unresolved emotional tension—has received widespread acceptance among workers in the field of psychosomatic medicine. Writers have devoted their attention to explaining the first phase and have more or less taken the second phase for granted, although in accounting for the fact that the second phase is not inevitable, other determinants such as constitution are usually invoked.

Margolin attempts to account for the development of the second phase by stating that the tolerance of tissues for physiological fluctuations decreases with age. He feels that physiological regression to modes of functioning characteristic of infancy exposes the organ involved to fluctuations greater than it can now tolerate, and that the tissue changes which then occur lead to one of the psychosomatic diseases. As an aid to the understanding of this sequence of events, it would appear that the concept of physiological regression has relevance only to the extent that it is clearly established that these diseases do indeed result from long-continued and excessive physiological fluctuations of a kind that are tolerated better in infancy.

*Hypertension.* But even in his original contribution, Michaels conceded that "one of the marked exceptions to the general consistency of the resemblance of the psychosomatic symptom of the adult and the physiological state of the infant is the state of hypertension in many neurotic individuals." More recently Engel has also challenged the specific relationship of fluctuations in blood pressure and essential hypertension (1). Alexander and others have long contended that fluctuations in blood pressure secondary to chronic inhibited rage are etiologically related to essential hypertension. But Engel points out "that even if rage or aggression do prove to be the specific psychic states associated with such pressure response, there are as yet no data to indicate how such fluctuations in measured blood pressure obtained during acute situations are related to the disease hypertension."

*Ulcerative Colitis.* More recently, in his comprehensive consideration of ulcerative colitis, Engel (9, 10) concludes that this disease is essentially a disorder of the vascular system of the mucosa and submucosa of the bowel. It is implied that it has no counterpart in normal infant physiology and that in fact when the infant's bowel is subject to the same somatic process it too develops ulcerative colitis.

*Peptic Ulcers.* Mirsky (26) has reported observations on gastric activity using blood and urine pepsinogen as a measure of gastric secretion. From his studies it would appear that there is a certain percentage of individuals of all age groups from infancy onward who are hypersecretors and that it is only in the presence of hypersecretion that peptic ulcers can develop. The studies, admittedly incomplete, would not seem to confirm the hypothesis that ulcer patients under stress regress physiologically to a mode of functioning that is normal in infancy but inappropriate for adult life. They would suggest rather that there are individuals who, from infancy onwards, are gastric hypersecretors and that these individuals when faced with particular kinds of stress *may* develop peptic ulcers. It also appears (15) that duodenal ulcer is commoner among children than has been suspected.

Thus, workers interested in three disorders which have long been regarded as among the most indisputable psychosomatic illnesses are beginning to express doubts about relationships that have almost been looked upon as beyond suspicion. In this period of critical reexamination of data and theories it would seem inappropriate to propose global hypotheses that largely depend for their support on the very relationships that are being rejected.

*Anxiety and Specificity.* If the concept of physiological regression has any validity it would seem to apply most readily to the manifestations of anxiety and not to those diseases which are presumed with no degree of certainty to result from the long continued discharge of these manifestations. Grinker

(17) states the situation graphically and succinctly:

Anxiety in an adult activates certain visceral patterns which are specific to the individual, no matter what the stress, in that each one has his particular way of feeling anxious. Some variations include sinking abdominal sensations, diarrhea, vomiting, dyspnea, sensation of lump in the throat, etc. Out of the generalized infantile precursors of expressions of anxiety, each person seems to have been conditioned to certain fragmentary visceral patterns which for him become accurate and faithful harbingers of intrapsychic changes. If the signal intensifies, more previously silent fragments appear until the old generalized infantile pattern is revived in its entirety under conditions of panic or catastrophe. Thus, here too a selective differentiation has occurred in development by some form of conditioning. Under severe stress the conditioned reflexes disappear and diffuse irradiation of excitation appears.

It will be remembered that Wolff too spoke of each person reacting to different kinds of stress in ways which were specific to the individual. And this specificity, according to Wolff, was determined by heredity. It might appear that not "regression" but "fixation," as constitutionally determined, would best describe this state of affairs. Hendrick has, as a matter of fact, anticipated this objection and refers not to "physiological regression," but to "physiological infantilism." But just to illustrate how fundamentally subjective and charged with value judgments terms like "regression" are, it is interesting to note that Wolff refers to those phenomena that others label "regression" as "protective adaptive reactions."

## Choice of Individual and Mode of Manifestation of Psychosomatic Disease

It might well be asked whether, even if it should be clearly shown that the concept of physiological regression has some validity as a descriptive term, it has any usefulness in increasing our understanding of psychophysiological disorders. Most psychosomatic theories attempt to provide answers for at least one of two main questions: (1) *Why do certain individuals develop psychosomatic illnesses?* (2) *What determines the choice of organ?* Let us see how other writers have attempted to answer these questions.

Ruesch attempts to answer the first question by postulating that immature individuals who do not, as a result of early defects in interpersonal relationships, master an adequate system of symbolic communication use the body for expression of tensions. Deutsch considered that psychosomatic disorders developed because there were intercurrent disturbances of physiological functioning at stressful periods in early development. Wolff answered the questions in terms of constitution and heredity.

In attempting to answer the second question, the various psychosomatic syndromes were correlated with personality types by Dunbar and with specific conflicts by Alexander. Deutsch felt that the choice of organ depended on the accidental association of some particular illness with some significant period in early life. It is difficult to see how the concept of physiological regression makes any meaningful contribution to the understanding of either of these issues.

*Relation of Psychoses.* However, another type of theoretical usefulness is claimed for this concept. Margolin suggests that the hypothesis of physiological regression provides us with a key to the understanding of the alleged relationship between the degree of tissue pathology and the degree of psychotic substrate. An alternation of psychosomatic disorder and psychosis has frequently been described. Some writers have been so impressed by this relationship that they have postulated reciprocal relationships between psychosomatic illness and psychosis.

Honig, in a recent consideration of the relationship between psychoses and peptic ulcer, reviews the conflicting literature and the case material in the Winter VA Hospital and finds that

. . . although alternation of psychosis and the psychosomatic disorder can be readily discerned in certain individual and isolated cases, it may not be as prevalent as much of the psychiatric literature seems to convey. On the contrary, it is apparent that psychosis and peptic ulcer are not incompatible but can frequently occur concurrently.

In a very comprehensive survey of the literature, Ross makes some very interesting observations about the relationship between psychosomatic illness and psychoses. He shows that the situation is much more complex than is reflected in facile, but statistically invalid, correlations and he states directly:

It appears that there are not simple, direct or inverse, relationships between "psychosomatic disorders" and psychoses. Some so-called "psychosomatic disorders" are less rare among psychotic patients than has been claimed, and "psychosomatic disorder" may accompany psychosis, as well as alternate with it.

Margolin states that patients with psychosomatic illness who are hospitalized are more psychotic than patients with the same disorder seen in outpatient departments or offices. This would seem to be an impressionistic conclusion and one that would require statistical validation. Just to illustrate how impressions can vary, Murphy, in contradistinction to Margolin's assumption, questions the belief that psychosomatic disorders are found among the weak and speculates rather as to whether they are actually the refuge of the

strong. Lhamon and Saul, in the same view, report it as their opinion that "not only does the psychosomatic symptom not necessarily signify an infantile personality, but often it signifies just the opposite," and they cite the high incidence of psychosomatic symptoms among high executives with heavy responsibilities.

## Physiological-Regression Concept in Therapy

There remains to be considered the usefulness of the physiological-regression concept for therapy. Margolin has reported an interesting technique of "anaclitic" therapy, which permits the severely ill, hospitalized psychosomatic patient to regress to a state of marked dependency in which it is attempted to gratify his wishes, both verbal and nonverbal. The patient is, in effect, on a demand-feeding schedule. The goal is to change the patient's mood, in order to effect physiological remission. This technique of therapy is still in the controversial stage and results have yet to be fully reported. But regardless of the degree of success, it would not appear that this type of therapy depends for its rationale on a physiological-regression hypothesis. It is the opinion of many observers that mood changes are important in the remission of psychosomatic disorders. Engel (8) has recently issued a timely appeal for the investigation of the physiology of moods and affects. It would seem that an attempt to understand what Engel (10) refers to as "the jump from the psychic phenomena to the physical phenomena at the end organ" is at the present time one of the most urgently required endeavors in psychosomatic medicine.

## COMMENT

It is easy to see why the concept of regression has proved so attractive to workers in psychosomatic medicine. It has had a useful career in general psychoanalytic theory. Sometimes adults behave (the word is used very broadly) in some of the ways they once did as small children. To label such behavior "regressive" is to call attention to the ways in which it resembles earlier behavior. This manner of describing behavior has proved useful in the development of psychiatric understanding of people. By analogy, to speak of physiological regression is to emphasize the ways in which pathophysiological phenomena presumably resemble earlier functioning. Even though it has by no means been clearly shown that psychosomatic diseases are simply the end products of infantile physiological phenomena, of anachronisms of physiology, as it were, it might perhaps be possible to defend the position that the symptoms of anxiety or panic do resemble infantile phenomena. But to what end? Is it really of any value to think of anaplastic cells as regressive phenomena? The cells may resemble embryonic cells, but merely to call attention to this fact by a special term hardly helps to solve the etiology of cancer. And we would mislead ourselves if we thought we had gained much insight into pathological EEG forms by emphasizing their resemblance to infantile patterns.

The hypotheses of Dunbar, Alexander, Deutsch, and Wolff have inspired an enthusiastic and productive era of investigation into psychosomatic phenomena. They have produced a rich harvest of valuable insights into the bodily manifestations of anxiety, conflict, rage, and despair. These studies, despite the presence of a certain uncritical trend, have nevertheless become increasingly marked by a more experienced, dispassionate, and sophisticated scientific temper. However, there remains very much work yet to be done. The compilation of statistical data to confirm or refute so many plausible hypotheses is itself an urgent and by no means negligible task. The physiology and pharmacology of affect are as yet rudimentary. Engel's (11) study of the effect of mood on gastric physiology is an example of the classic method of study with a refreshing scientific vigorousness. Studies are beginning to appear which reexamine textbook truisms, about the effects of drugs on mood. In all the investigation that remains to be done it does not seem that a term like "physiological regression" affords the investigator a new vantage point from which to observe data. Nor, as has been emphasized above, does it seem that this term contributes anything concrete to the understanding of psychophysiological phenomena. Neither does it seem to provide any useful insight to the therapist. New terms are poor substitutes for new information, and it is difficult to see that this term does anything other than to provide the illusion of knowledge.

## SUMMARY AND CONCLUSIONS

The unscientific attitudes of many psychosomatic publications are discussed.

Dunbar's "personality profiles," Alexander's "emotional specificity," and Wolff's "protective adaptive reaction" are presented as an introduction to the concept of "physiological regression" as discussed by Michaels, Margolin, Szasz, Hendrick, and Grinker. Various errors in the above theories are discussed and an attempt is made to show how they arose, why they are misleading and how they may be avoided. In doing this, the following are dealt with:

1. A tendency to biased selection of clinical and physiological data to prove a given point.

2. The confusion between phenomenological description and etiology.

3. The belief that there must be one, and only one, theory to "explain" the etiology of psychosomatic illnesses.

4. The questionable assumption that parasympathetic hyperactivity is synonymous with, or a necessary concomitant of, psychosomatic illness.

5. The analogical reasoning on which "regression terminology" has been founded.

6. The conceptual errors which result when psychosomatic illness and physiological malfunctioning are not properly differentiated.

7. The unproved assumption that psychoses and psychosomatic illness have a definite relationship.

We conclude that many of the above theoretical models have served to produce new terms only, and that they impart no useful or verifiable information, and that the main problems posed by psychosomatic illnesses will remain with us until painstaking empirical observations and factual report complement theorizing.

# REFERENCES

1. ACKERMAN, N. W. Problems of hypertension. *J. Am. Psychoanalyt. A.* 1:562, 1953.

2. ALEXANDER, F. *Psychosomatic Medicine.* New York, Norton, 1950.

3. BINGER, C. On so-called psychogenic influences in essential hypertension. *Psychosom. Med.* 13:273, 1951.

4. COBB, S. *Emotions and Clinical Medicine.* New York, Norton, 1950.

5. DAWES, LYDIA L. Discussion in DEUTSCH, F. (Ed.): *The Psychosomatic Concept in Psychoanalysis.* New York, Internat. Univ. Press, 1953.

6. DEUTSCH, F. The choice of organ in organ neuroses. *Internat. J. Psychoanal.* 20:252, 1939.

7. DUNBAR, H. F. *Emotions and Bodily Changes.* New York, Columbia Univ. Press, 1935.

8. ENGEL, G. L. Selection of clinical material in psychosomatic medicine. *Psychosom. Med.* 16:368, 1954.

9. ENGEL, G. L. Studies of ulcerative colitis: I. Clinical data bearing on the nature of the somatic process. *Psychosom. Med.* 16:496, 1954.

10. ENGEL, G. L. Studies of ulcerative colitis: II. The nature of the somatic process and the adequacy of psychosomatic hypotheses: A review. *Am. J. Med.* 16:416, 1954.

11. ENGEL, G. L. Paper presented at 1955 meeting of American Psychoanalytic Association in Atlantic City, N. J.

12. FERENCZI, S. *Further Contribution to the Theory and Technique of Psychoanalysis.* London, Hogarth, 1926.

13. GARMA, A. Gastric neurosis. *Internat. J. Psychoanal.* 31:53, 1950.

14. GERARD, MARGARET W. "Genesis of Psychosomatic Symptoms in Infancy." In DEUTSCH, F. (Ed.): *The Psychosomatic Concept in Psychoanalysis.* New York, Internat. Univ. Press, 1953.

15. GIRDENY, B. R. Personal communication to I. A. MIRSKY (26).

16. GRINKER, R. R. *Psychosomatic Research.* New York, Norton, 1953.

17. GRINKER, R. R. "Some Current Trends and Hypotheses of Psychosomatic Research." In DEUTSCH, F. (Ed.): *The Psychosomatic Concept in Psychoanalysis.* New York, Internat. Univ. Press, 1953.

18. HENDRICK, I. Discussion in DEUTSCH, F. (Ed.): *The Psychosomatic Concept in Psychoanalysis.* New York, Internat. Univ. Press, 1953.

19. HONIG, E. M. Psychosis and peptic ulcer. *Bull. Menninger Clin.* 19:61, 1955.

20. KLEIN, MELANIE. *Contributions to Psychoanalysis, 1921–45* London, Hogarth, 1948.

21. KUBIE, L. S. "The Problem of Specificity in the Psychosomatic Process." In DEUTSCH, F. (Ed.): *The Psychosomatic Concept in Psychoanalysis.* New York, Internat. Univ. Press, 1953.

these laws of thought: that is, it may think "illogically." With an important exception, Von Domarus, to be mentioned later, science has not gone much beyond this point. The lack of research in this field is partially due to a consuetudinary aversion which physicians in particular and biologists in general have for any method which is not strictly empirical. On the other hand, philosophers and logicians themselves have to be blamed and for the opposite reason—that is, on account of a nonpsychological attitude which to physicians seems almost untenable. Since they are interested in thought itself and not in the thinker, they naturally have ignored the condition of health, illness, age, and the environmental situation in which the thinker happens to be.

It is my contention that the study of logic in mental illnesses may clarify several problems which have not yet been clarified by other methods of research. Furthermore, it is contended that it is not even necessary to be a logician in order to undertake such study. It will be shown in this paper that the application of a few elementary principles will open new avenues of research, the value of which cannot be properly estimated perhaps at the present time.

In the last half century, medical psychology has felt more and more the impact of psychoanalysis. The attention of an increasing number of workers has been concentrated upon the dynamics of emotional factors, conscious or unconscious, and has been more or less detracted from other aspects of psychological problems. Freudian psychoanalysis has made it possible to interpret the symptoms of the patient as a result of emotional forces or as attempts by the patient to fulfill psychologically what otherwise would be unfulfillable wishes. This interpretation and its derivatives

have advanced tremendously knowledge and therapeutic means, especially in the field of psychoneuroses, but in the psychoses have led to a standstill. For instance, psychoanalysis may explain why a deluded patient wishes unconsciously that his delusion be reality, but has not explained how it is that he intellectually accepts his delusion as reality, in spite of contradictory evidence. An obsessive patient who has, let us say, the obsession that if he does not wear a special suit, his mother is going to die, recognizes fully the absurdity of such an idea. It is true that he will continue to wear that special suit, but he knows that the idea is illogical. He has retained sufficient logical power to recognize the unreal nature of such obsession. Psychoanalysis will help in explaining what unconscious emotional factors and dissociated ideas have determined this symptom. In the case of the deluded patient also, psychoanalysis may explain what unconscious emotional factors have determined the delusional idea but will not explain why such an idea is accepted as reality. It does not explain what change has occurred in the logic powers of the patient so that he is not able any longer to test reality. To say that the patient's ego is disintegrating is to satisfy oneself with obscure words.

In another publication (4), I have suggested that the schizophrenic does not think with ordinary logic. His thought is not illogical or senseless, but follows a different system of logic which leads to deductions different from those usually reached by the healthy person. The schizophrenic is seen in a position similar to that of a man who would solve mathematical problems not with our decimal system but with another hypothetic system and would consequently reach different solutions. In other words, the schizophrenic seems to have a faculty of conception which is constituted differently from that of the normal man. It was further demonstrated that this different faculty of conception or different logic is similar to the one which is followed in dreams, in other forms of autistic thinking, and in primitive man. It was consequently called paleologic, to distinguish it from our usual logic which is generally called Aristotelian, since Aristotle was the first to enunciate its laws. It is not meant in this article that Aristotelian logic is correct in an absolute sense. The author is aware of the criticisms to which this logic has been subjected. Aristotelian logic is used only as a frame of reference, and only *relatively* to paleologic thinking.

In this paper the laws of paleologic, as they are deduced especially from the study of schizophrenic thought and dreams, will be examined in detail. I will then discuss in what situations and why a person may abandon a system of logic and adopt one which, as a rule, is repressed. This contribution should be considered preliminary in nature; further research is necessary to differentiate other laws of this archaic type of logic.

## VON DOMARUS' PRINCIPLE

Paleologic is to a great extent based on a principle enunciated by Von Domarus (5, 6). This author, as a result of his studies on schizophrenia, formulated a principle which, in slightly modified form, is as follows: *Whereas the normal person accepts identity only upon the basis of identical subjects, the paleologician accepts identity based upon identical predicates.* For instance, the normal person is able to conclude "John Doe is an American citizen," if he is given the following information: "Those who are born in the United States are American citizens; John Doe

was born in the United States." This normal person is able to reach this conclusion because the subject of the minor premise, "John Doe," is contained in the subject of the major premise, "those who are born in the United States."

On the other hand, suppose that the following information is given to a schizophrenic: "The President of the United States is a person who was born in the United States. John Doe is a person who was born in the United States." In certain circumstances, the schizophrenic may conclude: "John Doe is the President of the United States." This conclusion, which to a normal person appears as delusional, is reached because the identity of the predicate of the two premises, "a person who was born in the United States," makes the schizophrenic accept the identity of the two subjects, "the President of the United States" and "John Doe."

The mechanisms or successive steps of this type of thinking are not necessarily known to the schizophrenic who thinks in this way automatically, as the normal person applies automatically the Aristotelian laws of logic even without knowing them. For instance, a schizophrenic patient thinks without knowing why that the doctor in charge of the ward is her father and that the other patients are her sisters. A common predicate—a man in authority—leads to the identity between the father and the physician. Another common predicate —females in the same position of dependency—leads the patient to consider herself and the other inmates as sisters.

At times the interpretation of this type of thinking requires more elaboration. For instance, a patient of Von Domarus' (5) thought that Jesus, cigar boxes, and sex were identical. Study of this delusion disclosed that the common predicate, which led to the identification, was the state of being encircled.

According to the patient, the head of Jesus, as of a saint, is encircled by a halo, the package of cigars by the tax band, and the woman by the sex glance of the man.

At times paleologic thought is even more difficult to interpret because the principle of Von Domarus is applied only partially; that is, some partial identity among the subjects is based upon partial or total identity of the predicate. For instance, a person who is conceived by a schizophrenic as having a quality or characteristic of a horse may be thought of with a visual image consisting of part man and part horse. In this case one subject, the person, is partially identified with the other subject, the horse, because of a common characteristic—for instance, strength. It is well known how frequently similar distortions and condensations appear in hallucinations and drawings of schizophrenics. Similar conceptions appear in mythologies of ancient people and of primitives of today. As a matter of fact, anthropologic studies may disclose to the careful reader how often the principle of Von Domarus is applied in primitive thinking. Numerous studies, outstanding among which is the one by Storch (7), have emphasized the similarities between primitive and schizophrenic thought, but the common underlying principles of logic which rule this thought have received no mention. Werner (8) writes: "It is one of the most important tasks of the developmental psychology to show that the advanced form of thinking characteristic of Western civilization is only one form among many, and that more primitive forms are not so much lacking in logic as based on logic of a different kind. The premise of Aristotelian logic that, when a thing is A it cannot at the same time be B, will not hold through for the primitive. . . ." Werner, however, does not attempt to enunciate the

principles of a different logic. He does not add that for the primitive A may be B if A and B have only a quality (predicate) in common, although in his outstanding book, *Comparative Psychology of Mental Development*, he gives numerous examples proving this fundamental fact.

A step forward toward the interpretation of this way of thinking has been made by Max Levin (9) who compares schizophrenic thought to that of young children. Levin concludes that the patient as well as the young child "cannot distinguish adequately between a symbol and the object it symbolizes." For example, a middle-aged schizophrenic, speaking of an actor whom she admired, said, "He was smiling at me." The patient had seen on the cover of a magazine a picture of the actor in the act of smiling. Thus she had confused a picture of the actor with the actor himself. Levin reports that a 27-month-old child, drinking milk while looking at the picture of a horse, said, "Give milk to the horse." At 25 months, the same child, looking at the picture of a car, tried to lift the car from the picture and said to his father, "Daddy, get car out." For the child the pictured objects were real. Levin is correct in his observations. However, he has not been able to see them in the light of Von Domarus' principle. What appears to us as a symbol of the object is not a symbol for the schizophrenic or for the child but a duplication of the object. The two objects have been identified on account of the similar appearance. Levin makes other exceptionally interesting observations which, however, do not receive complete interpretation, and he is led to the conclusion that infantile and schizophrenic concepts "are the result of amusing mixtures of relevant and irrelevant." For instance, he reports that "a child of two knew the word 'wheel' as applied, for example, to the wheel of a toy car. One day, at twenty-five months, as he sat on the toilet, the white rubber guard (supplied with little boys' toilet seats to deflect the urine) came loose and fell into the toilet bowl; pointing to it, he exclaimed, 'broke, wheel!' In explanation it is to be noted that he had many toy cars whose wheels, when of rubber, were always of white rubber. Thus he came to think that the word 'wheel' embraced not only wheels but also anything made of white rubber." Levin concludes that this example "shows how associations of the most ephemeral nature are permitted to enter into a concept when the child is too young to appreciate the non-essentiality." In view of what has been said before, it is obvious that an identification had occurred because of the same characteristic "white rubber."

The same principle of Von Domarus is applied in dreams. Freud (10) has demonstrated that a person or object A having a certain characteristic of B may appear in the dream as being B or a composite of A and B. In the first case there is identification; in the second, composition. The whole field of Freudian symbolism is based, from a formal point of view, on Von Domarus' principle. A symbol of X is something which stands for X, but also something which retains some similarity with X—common predicate or characteristic. For instance, penis may be identified with snake on account of the elongated shape of both, father with king on account of the position of authority they both enjoy, and so on. The reason why certain symbols are specific only for one person will be discussed later. It has to be pointed out again that what one, using psychiatric terminology, calls a symbol is not a symbol for the schizophrenic or for the dreamer, but is, consciously or unconsciously, a duplication of the object symbolized.

The study of Von Domarus' principle in schizophrenia, in primitive thought, and in dreams requires that more consideration be paid to the predicate which determines the identification. In fact it is obvious that the predicate is the most important part in this type of thinking. Since the same subject may have numerous predicates, it is the choice of the predicate in the paleologic premises which will determine the great subjectivity, bizarreness, and often unpredictability of autistic thinking. For instance, in the quoted example of Von Domarus, the characteristic of being encircled was the identifying quality. Each of the three subjects which were identified—Jesus, cigar boxes, and sex—had a potentially large number of predicates, but the patient selected one which was completely unpredictable and bizarre. The predicate which is selected in the process of identification is called the "identifying link." Why a certain predicate should be selected out of numerous possible ones as the identifying link will be discussed shortly. A predicate is, by definition, something which concerns the subject. One is used to recognizing as predicates abstract or concrete qualities of the subject or something which in a certain way resides or is contained in the subject—for instance, being white, red, fluid, friendly, honest, suspicious, having a tail, and infinite other possibilities. These are called predicates of quality. There are, however, other characteristics which are paleologically conceived as pertaining to the subjects and, therefore, considered predicates, although they are not contained in the subject—for instance, the characteristic of occurring at a certain time or at a given place. For example, two completely different subjects may have as a common predicate the fact that they occur simultaneously or successively or in the same place. For instance, if a patient accidentally ate a certain exotic food on a day in which he had a pleasant experience, he may dream of eating again that special food because he wishes to revive the pleasant experience. Special food and pleasant experience are in the dream identified because they happen to be perceived at the same time. The identifying link in this case is a predicate of temporal contiguity. The predicate of contiguity may be not only temporal but also spatial. For instance, a patient may dream of being in her summer home in Connecticut. Nearby in Connecticut lives a man she loves. Home in Connecticut and loved man are identified because they both have the characteristic of residing in the same place. In this case the identifying link is a predicate of spatial contiguity. Two different subjects may be identified also because they originated from the same source or will give origin to the same event or to the same emotional reaction. For instance, a patient dreams of undressing a woman, with sexual intentions. In the dream he suddenly realizes that her vagina looks like an umbilicus. In his associations he remembers that when he was a child he thought that children were born from the umbilicus. In this dream vagina and umbilicus are identified because they both were thought of by the patient as organs which give birth to children. In this case the identifying link is a predicate of finality. In many cases the identifying link is a mixture of predicates of different types.

From the foregoing it appears that paleologic thinking is much less exact than Aristotelian. In the latter, only identical subjects may be identified. The subjects are immutable; therefore, only a few and the same deductions are possible. In paleologic thinking, on the other hand, the predicates lead to the identification. Since the predicates may be extremely numerous and one does not know which one may be chosen by the patient, this type of thought becomes unpredictable, individualistic, and often incomprehensible. If the identifying link is a predicate of quality, it will be relatively easy to understand the meaning of what the patient expresses. What are referred to in psychoanalytic literature as universal symbols are generally objects whose identifying link is a predicate of quality and, less frequently, of finality. If, however, the identifying link is an accidental predicate of contiguity, obviously the symbol is specific for the individual and many details concerning his life history are necessary in order to understand its meaning.

The unconscious choice of the predicate which is used as the identifying link, out of numerous possible ones, is often determined by emotional factors. In other words, emotional currents may determine which one of the predicates will be taken as the identifying characteristic. This extremely important point has been examined in detail in another of my publications (4) and will not be rediscussed here. It is obvious that if John Doe thinks that he is the President of the United States because he was born in the United States, he wishes to think so. His increased narcissistic requirements direct him toward the selection of that predicate—being born in the United States—out of many other possibilities. The same emotional factors described by Freud (11) in "Psychopathology of Everyday Life" and by Jung (12) in *Psychology of Dementia Praecox* are, of course, valid for paleologic thinking, also. However, these emotional factors do not explain the formal manifestations of this type of thinking. Conscious or unconscious emotions may be the directing motivation or the driving force of these thought processes, but the fact cannot be denied that these thoughts are molded according to a special pattern, which is conferred by the adoption of a different logic.

From the foregoing, the reader may have deduced the tremendous rôle played by Von Domarus' principle in non-Aristotelian thinking—a rôle whose importance escaped perhaps Von Domarus himself. For those interested in the problem mainly from a point of view of formal logic, I may add that of the four Aristotelian laws of thought —law of identity, law of contradiction, law of excluded middle, law of sufficient reason—the first three are annulled by Von Domarus' principle. In one of the following paragraphs, it will be shown how the fourth law also is altered.

## CONNOTATION, DENOTATION, VERBALIZATION

Before proceeding with this examination of paleologic thinking, I have to remind the reader of what is traditionally meant in logic by different aspects of terms, that is, by connotation and denotation. Let us take, for instance, the term *table*. The connotation of this term is the meaning of the term, that is, the concept *article of furniture with flat horizontal top, set on legs*. The denotation of the term is the object meant, that is, the table as a physical entity. In other words, the term *table* may mean table in general or it may mean any or all particular tables. Every term has both these aspects. It means certain definite qualities or attributes and it also refers to certain objects or, in the case of a singular term, to one object which has those qualities. The connotation is in a certain way the definition of the object and includes the whole class of the object, without any reference to a concrete embodiment of the object.

I feel that, in addition to the two

aspects of the terms which are traditionally considered in logic, one has to consider a third aspect, if he wants to understand better the problem from a psychological point of view. This is the verbal aspect of the term, the term as a word or verbal symbol. I propose to call this aspect of the term *verbalization*. For instance, the term *table* may be considered from three aspects: its connotation, when one refers to its meaning; its denotation, when one refers to the object meant; its verbalization, when one considers the word as a word, that is, as a verbal representation or symbol of the object table or of the concept table.

Now it is possible to formulate a second important principle of paleologic. Whereas the healthy person in a wakened state is mainly concerned with the connotation and the denotation of a symbol but is capable of shifting his attention from one to another of the three aspects of a symbol, the autistic person is mainly concerned with the denotation and the verbalization, and experiences a total or partial impairment of his ability to connote. In view of this principle, two phenomena have to be studied in schizophrenia and other types of autistic thinking: first, the reduction of the connotation power; second, the emphasis on the verbalization.

### Reduction of Connotation Power

For the person who thinks paleologically, the verbal symbols cease to be representative of a group or of a class, but only of the specific objects under discussion. For instance, the word "cat" cannot be used as relating to any member of the feline genus, but a specific cat, like "the cat sitting on that chair." Oftener there is a gradual shifting from the connotation to the denotation level.[1] This gradual regression is apparent if we ask a not too deteriorated schizophrenic to define words. For instance, following are some words which a schizophrenic was asked to define and her replies:

Q. Book.
A. It depends what book you are referring to.
Q. Table.
A. What kind of a table? A wooden table, a porcelain table, a surgical table, or a table you want to have a meal on?
Q. House.
A. There are all kinds of houses, nice houses, nice private houses.
Q. Life.
A. I have to know what life you happen to be referring to—Life magazine or to the sweetheart who can make another individual happy and gay.

From the examples it is obvious that the patient, a high school graduate, is unable to define usual words. She cannot cope with the task of defining the word as a symbol of a class or a symbol including all the members of the class, like all books, all tables, and so on. She tries first to decrease her task by limiting her definition to special subgroups or to particular members of the class. For instance, she is unable to define the word "table" and attempts to simplify her problem by asking whether she has to define various subgroups of tables—wooden tables, surgical tables, and so on. In the last example, she wants to know whether I am referring to two particular instances, Life magazine or to the life of the sweetheart. This reply, which reveals impairment of connotation power, is complicated also by the emphasis on the verbalization, as will be demonstrated in the following paragraph.

This tightness to the denotation prevents the schizophrenic from using figurate or metaphorical languages, contrary to what it may seem at first impression. It has already been stated by Benjamin (13) that the schizophrenic is unable to interpret proverbs correctly. He will give always a more or less literal interpretation of them. Figurate language increases the use of the term which acquires an unusual denotation and connotation. If one says, "When the cat's away, the mice will play," a normal listener will understand that by cat is meant a person in authority. A schizophrenic patient gave the following literal interpretation of that proverb: "There are all kinds of cats and all kinds of mice, but when the cat is away, the mice take advantage of the cat." In other words, for the schizophrenic the word "cat" could not acquire a special connotation.

The inability of the schizophrenic to use metaphorical language is revealed also by the following replies of a patient who was asked to explain what was meant when a person was called by the names of various animals, for instance:

Q. Wolf.
A. Wolf is a greedy animal.

[1] The statement made by many logicians that there is an inverse ratio between connotation and denotation does not hold true if the problem is considered from a psychological point of view. In other words, a decrease in the connotation power is not accompanied by an increase in the denotation power and vice versa. Many logicians, too, have criticized this concept of inverse ratio, because objects (denotation) can be enumerated, but qualities and meanings cannot be measured mathematically. I might add that the study of primitive thought discloses that what would be called terms with great connotation (with meaning of specific objects) preceded terms with greater denotation, which originated at a higher level of development.

Q. Fox.
A. A fox and a wolf are two different animals. One is more vicious than the other, more and more greedy than the other.
Q. Parrot.
A. It all depends what the parrot says.
Q. Peacock.
A. A woman with beautiful feathers. By the way, *Woman* is a magazine.

Many beginners in the field of psychiatry get the impression that schizophrenic language and thought are highly metaphorical and poetic. In reality it is not so. This impression is due to misinterpretation of the phenomena which were explained above in terms of Von Domarus' principle. For instance, a schizophrenic will be able to *identify* a man with a wolf on account of a common characteristic, greediness, but will not be able to accept the concept *wolf* as a symbol of greedy men. Two different mechanisms are employed. In the first instance, a very primitive paleologic mechanism is necessary; in the second instance a high process of abstraction is at play. If one understands fully this point, he understands also one of the fundamental differences between schizophrenic artistic productions and some manifestations of art of normal persons.

This restriction of the denotation power and decrease of the connotation power is very apparent in many instances reported by Goldstein (14). In the color sorting test, one of Goldstein's patients picked out various shades of green, but in doing so he named them—peacock green, emerald green, taupe green, bright green, bell green, baby green. He could not say that all might be called green. Another patient of Goldstein's said in the same situation: "This is the color of the grass in Virginia, this is the color of the grass in Kentucky, this is the color of the bark of the tree, this is the color of the leaves." The words used by the patients in naming colors belonged to a definite situation. "The words," Goldstein writes, "have become individual words, i.e., words which fit only a specific object or situation." In other words, the meaning or the connotation of the word includes not a class but only a specific instance. There is therefore a definite restriction of the connotation power.[2] Goldstein calls these phenomena expressions of "concrete attitude."

## Emphasis on Verbalization

Whereas the word is normally considered just as a symbol to convey a meaning, in the autistic person it acquires a greater significance. In many cases the attention of the schizophrenic is focused not on the connotation or denotation of the term, but just on its verbal expression—that is, on the word as a word, not as a symbol. Other paleologic processes may take place after the attention has been focused on the verbalization. For instance, a schizophrenic examined during the past war said that the next time the Japanese would attack the Americans it would be at Diamond Harbor or Gold Harbor. When she was asked why, she replied: "The first time, they attacked at Pearl Harbor; now they will attack at Diamond Harbor or at Sapphire Harbor." "Do you think that the Japanese attacked Pearl Harbor because of its name?" I asked. "No, no," she replied, "it was a *happy* coincidence." Note the inappropriateness of the adjective *happy*. It was a happy coincidence for her, because she could prove thereby

---

[2] Many logicians, on the other hand, would say that the connotation is increased. This point of view is psychologically wrong. Reference footnote 1.

the alleged validity of her paleophrenic thinking.

From this example, and from others which will follow, it is to be deduced that Von Domarus' principle is often applied when the emphasis is on the verbalization. Different objects are identified because they have names which have a common characteristic. The identification is very easily made if the terms are homonyms. Two otherwise different things are identified, or considered together, because they have the same verbalization, that is, the same phonetic or written symbol. In one of the examples mentioned above, the patient put together *Life* magazine and the life of the sweetheart. Another schizophrenic was noticed to have the habit of wetting her body with oil. Asked why she would do so she replied: "The human body is a machine and has to be lubricated." The word *machine*, applied in a figurative sense to the human body, had led to the identification with man-made machines. It is obvious that for the schizophrenic and, to a minor degree, for persons who are in other autistic conditions, the term is considered not as a symbol but as a characteristic, a quality or a predicate of the object which is symbolized. The identification, due to the similar or common verbal expression, is based not only on Von Domarus' principle but also on the second principle of paleologic, that is, the emphasis on the verbalization and the decreased importance of the connotation.

Werner (8) thinks that a name is not merely a sign for the primitive; it is part of the object itself. The verbalization thus is conceived as part of the denotation. The word does not have the same connotation for the primitive as for the civilized man; the meaning is often restricted to the specific instance which is denoted.

Children, too, experience names as fused in the object they denote. Piaget (15) has illustrated this phenomenon very well. When he asked children not older than six, "Where is the name of the sun?" he elicited the following responses: "Inside! Inside the sun" or "High up in the sky!"

The emphasis on the verbalization together with the application of Von Domarus' principle may also be found in normal adults in the technique of jokes and witticisms. Some of the examples mentioned above, such as the schizophrenic who was wetting her body with oil, have definite comical characteristics. The important point, however, is that what is comical for the healthy person is taken seriously by the schizophrenic. In a future publication the relation between wit and paleologic rules will be discussed. Freud (16) also, in his important monograph on wit, has described many mechanisms involved in the technique of witticisms but could not reduce them to the few principles of paleologic.

The emphasis on verbalization appears also in many dreams, as revealed first by Freud (10) in his monograph on dream interpretation. I report here one of the numerous examples he gives. C. dreams that on the road to X he sees a girl, bathed in a white light and wearing a white blouse. The dreamer began an affair with a Miss White on that road.

## CAUSALITY

I mentioned before that the first three laws of thought of traditional logic were eliminated by Von Domarus' principle. On the other hand, there is retained in paleologic thinking the fourth law, the law of sufficient reason: "We must assume a reason for every event." The methods, however, by which a reason for, or a cause of, an event is searched are different from those used by the normal mind. The works of Piaget (17, 15) on the mentality of the child help in understanding this problem. The autistic person, as well as the child, confuses the physical world with the psychological. Instead of finding a physical explanation of an event, the child, as well as the primitive and the autistic, looks for a motivation or an intention as the cause of an event. Every event is interpreted as caused by the will of an animated being. Of course, similar explanations of incidents are justified many times. For instance, if one says "I read this book of geometry because I want to learn this subject," this psychological causality is justified. The child, however, invokes to a much larger extent motives and intentions as causes of phenomena. He is always in search for a motivation which leads to an action. Children, examined by Piaget in Switzerland, thought that God made the thunder in the sky, that the Negroes were made in that way because they were naughty when they were little and God punished them; that there were a great and a little Salève lakes, because some people wanted to go into the little one and some into the great one. Werner (8) reports other examples. A boy, five years of age, thought that in the evening it got dark because people were tired and wanted to sleep. The same child thought that the rain was due to the fact that the angels swept the heavens with their brooms and lots of water.

The intentions are ascribed first to other people, then to things. The moon follows the child, the sun goes up in the sky, the rivers run. The world becomes peopled in various degrees.

An animistic and anthropomorphic conception of the world thus originates. Many works of anthropology and comparative psychology fully illustrate how the same conception of psychological causality is present in the primitive of today and in the mythology of ancient peoples.

In dreams, too, events are engendered by wishes, intentions, or psychological motivations. Paranoiacs and paranoids interpret almost everything as manifesting a psychological intention or meaning related to their delusional complexes.

One may conclude therefore that whereas the normal person is inclined to explain phenomena by logical deductions, often implying concepts involving the physical world, the autistic person, as well as the primitive and the child, is inclined to give a psychological explanation to all phenomena.

Between causality by psychological explanation and causality by logical deduction there are many other intermediate types of explanation which are described by Piaget. For instance, moral causality, magical causality, and so on. In a future contribution I will deal with this difficult problem.

## CONCEPTION OF TIME

This subject will be dealt with very briefly here, because it was elaborated in one of my previous publications (18). Whereas the normal adult is able to think of the present, to revive the past, and to anticipate the future, or, in other words, is able to transport chronologically remote phenomena to the only possible subjective or psychologic tense—present—the autistic person thinks mostly about the present.

Animals are unable to prospect a distant future. Experiments with delayed reactions have disclosed that they cannot keep in mind future events for more than a few minutes (19, 20).

They can foresee only the very immediate future—that is, only the reaction to a stimulus as long as the stimulus is present or was present not longer than a few minutes before. Prehuman species may be called biologic entities without psychic tomorrow. Cattle go to the slaughterhouse without feelings of anxiety, being unable to foresee what is going to happen to them. In humans, ability to anticipate the future begins during the anal period. At that stage of development the child becomes able to postpone immediate pleasure for some future gratification. In other words it is when the ability to anticipate is developed that "the reality principle" originates.

Phylogenetically, anticipation appeared at the primordial eras of humanity when man became interested not only in cannibalism and hunting, which are related to immediate present necessities, but also in agriculture and in hoarding in order to provide for future needs. It is in this period that culture—that is, knowledge to be used in future times or to be transmitted to future generations—originated. A person who would be able to conceive mentally only the present time would aim only toward what Sullivan (21) calls "satisfaction." A person who is able to prospect the future as well would aim also toward what Sullivan calls "security."

Autistic phenomena always occur as present phenomena without any reference to the future, although they may be motivated by wishes for the future. As Freud has emphasized, in dreams the situation is always lived in the present. In schizophrenia too, there is what I have called a "restriction of the psycho-temporal field." The patient withdraws more or less to a narcissistic level, and his temporal orientation becomes also more and more similar to that of the narcissistic period, that is, related to the present time. Balken (22), in her study with the Thematic Apperception Test, found that the schizophrenic does not distinguish between past, present, and future. According to her, the schizophrenic, in the attempt "to relieve the tension between the possible and the real" clings "desperately and without awareness to the present." In early schizophrenia, however, and especially in the paranoid type, the patient is still able to concern himself with past and future. Some delusions, especially with persecutory content, may involve the future rather than the present. The more the illness progresses, however, the more grandiose and related to the present time the delusions become. "I *am* the emperor of China; I *am* a millionaire."

To use Sullivan terminology, the schizophrenic, in a desperate attempt to regain security, uses more and more autistic mechanisms.

## PERCEPTUALIZATION OF THE CONCEPT

From the foregoing the reader has certainly inferred that the autistic person has the tendency to live in a world of perception rather than in a world of conception. The more autistically a person thinks, the more deprived he becomes of concepts or of Plato's universals. His ideas become more and more related to specific instances, and not concerned with classes, groups, or categories. Naturally, all gradations are possible and could be retraced in primitives.

When the pathologic process progresses further, the ideational formations will contain more and more concrete elements, representing reality as it appears to the senses rather than to the intellect. Perceptual elements finally eliminate completely higher thought processes. Storch (3) has demonstrated that the same process of perceptualization is found in the primitive as in the schizophrenic. Ideas are represented by sensory images. The wealth of vivid sensory images which are found in old myths was not the work of art but of necessity. The normal artist, too, uses perceptualization of concepts in his artistic productions but retains that ability to abstract which has not yet been acquired by the primitive and which has been lost by the schizophrenic. Perceptualization of the concept has its fullest expression in dreams and in hallucinations. As Freud and others have pointed out, the dream is just a translation of thoughts into visual images. Thoughts become visual perceptions. If the dreamer thinks about himself he sees himself in the dream. He sees himself as a physical entity or as a visual image, not as an abstract concept symbolized by the pronoun "I." These visual images use sensorial material. Since, for anatomical reasons, nobody can see his own face, the dreamer cannot recall the visual image of his face. This explains why the dreamer usually sees himself in the dream, but not his face. The sensorial material is revisualized and elaborated in accordance with paleologic and other archaic mechanisms. The same things could be repeated about hallucinations, except that in them auditory images are by far more common than visual.

This paragraph can therefore be summarized by stating that in autistic thought concepts have the tendency to disappear as concepts, inasmuch as their content tends to assume a perceptual expression. This process of perceptualization is completed in dreams and in hallucinations.

## FURTHER APPLICATION AND LIMITATION OF PALEOLOGIC RULES—REFERENCE TO MORE PRIMITIVE MECHANISMS

The few principles of paleologic thought which were expounded above have a much vaster application than it may seem from the few examples given. The whole way of thinking may be entirely transformed as to become completely inaccessible.

Von Domarus' principle may lead to what may be called self-identification. Self-identification, or identification of the self with another person, may occur unconsciously in normal and in neurotic persons, or consciously as in the delusional psychotics. The formal mechanism is the following: "If X will be identified with Y, because they have a common quality, it will be sufficient for me to acquire a quality of the person I want to be identified with, in order to become that person."

The very common hysterical identifications follow this mechanism. Freud's patient, Dora, developed a cough like that of Mrs. K. with whom she wanted to identify (23). A patient, mentioned by Fenichel (24), felt an intense pain in one finger. She felt as if she had her finger cut with a knife. She identified herself with her loved cousin, a medical student, who, she imagined, might have cut himself while dissecting.

The deluded patient discovers in himself a quality possessed also by a hero, a saint, a general, and identifies himself with the person who has that given quality. Other deluded patients try to acquire or to confer on others identifying qualities. A paranoid schizophrenic wanted her child to become an angel. Since angels are nourished only "by spiritual food," she did not feed her child for a few days—that is, until her relatives became aware of her acutely developed condition.

Von Domarus' principle in reverse is also applied in paleologic thinking as well as in primitive and infantile thinking. If A has not a given quality of A', A cannot be A'. I shall resort again to one of the very interesting examples given by Levin (25), although he has not fully interpreted it.

A bright six-year-old boy asked Levin whether twins are always boys. He replied that they may be either boys or girls, or a girl and a boy. When the child heard that twins may be a girl and a boy, he asked with surprise: "Then how could they wear the same clothes?" Levin concludes that the child had seen identical twins dressed alike, and his concepts of twins included an irrelevant detail, identity of raiment. If we apply Von Domarus' principle in reverse, the mental mechanism seems to be the following: "Twins have a common quality—identical raiment. If two people have not or cannot have identical raiment, they cannot be twins."

The five principles mentioned above —namely, (1) Von Domarus' principle, (2) the changed emphasis on the connotation, denotation, and verbalization of symbols, (3) psychological causality, (4) the narrower conception of time, and (5) the tendency to perceptualize concepts—obviously have a tremendous importance. These specific principles are representative of a power of perception and conception completely different from those usually possessed by the normal modern adult in waking status. These mechanisms offer to the thinker a completely different vision of the external universe as well as of his own inner experiences.

Throughout this paper the reader has probably been impressed by the continuous references to primitive and infantile thought. This has been done

to convey the notion that the type of thought which uses a non-Aristotelian logic is representative of a certain stage of phylogenetic and ontogenetic development. Unfortunately, many modern studies of anthropology and of child psychology, influenced by orthodox Freudian psychoanalysis, have not gone at all into this type of research. The character structure of a primitive society is interpreted by some orthodox analysts as due to a reproduction at a phylogenetic level of an ontogenetic Freudian complex such as in Freud's "Totem and Taboo" (26). Fromm (27) rightly calls this method the naive Freudian approach to anthropology. Other orthodox psychoanalysts, like Róheim (28) and Kardiner (29), interpret the character structure and the whole primitive culture as the result of the special upbringing of children in that given culture. The fact that the primitive interprets the world paleologically and therefore has a completely different vision of the universe, and that this completely different vision of the universe, in its turn, has its influence upon the upbringing of children, is completely ignored by these orthodox authors. For instance, the projective mechanisms described by Kardiner have not been interpreted as at least partially due to a different type of causality—namely, to that psychological causality mentioned in a previous paragraph of this paper.

Since I have mentioned that this type of paleologic thinking is typical in autistic states and especially in schizophrenics, does it follow that the characteristics of schizophrenic thought can all be interpreted in view of the paleologic principles expounded above?

These principles explain a great deal but certainly cannot explain every characteristic of schizophrenia or even of schizophrenic thought. This limitation is due to two different reasons. The first one is that not all paleologic rules have yet been discovered. For instance, some of the paleologic laws, discussed above, may explain the formal mechanisms of delusions of misidentification or of grandeur, but cannot explain why the homosexually loved person is transformed into the persecutor. The emotional mechanism, which is at play in this transformation, is understood very well because of the contributions of Freud, and especially his work on the Schreiber case (30). The concomitan paleologic mechanism is not yet clear, although some hypotheses are now under study.

The other reason is that schizophrenia involves the resurgence of archaic mechanisms, some of which are even more primitive than the paleologic. Paleologic thought is, by definition, thought that follows an archaic type of logic, which phylogenetically preceded the Aristotelian. However, not all thought is logical; primitive forms of thought follow no logic whatsoever, either Aristotelian or paleologic, but only associations. Associational thought, in contrast to logic thought, shows no signs of direction toward an end or conclusion. It consists generally of recollections which are at the mercy of the laws of association [3] and of primitive emotions.

Mrs. Nickleby, Dickens' character, is certainly remembered by the reader for her sparing use of logical processes in her conversational activities and for her conspicuous use of associational thought. In this type of thought ideas are expressed as they are recalled; they follow no logic rules but only the laws of associations—laws of contiguity and similarity—and underlying emotional currents. In advanced schizophrenia, impairment is to be noted, not only in logic thought, but also in associational thought. Even the simplest ideas cannot associate properly, as pointed out by Bleuler (31).

## PALEOLOGIC AND PSYCHOPATHOLOGICAL STATES

Now that the principal known laws of paleologic have been examined, it is appropriate to consider in what circumstances and why the normal adult abandons the Aristotelian way of thinking and adopts a more primitive type.

As mentioned before, logic (Aristotelian) thought is rigid and exact. In this type of thought only identical subjects can be identified. A is only A and cannot be B. The immutability of the subjects and the other characteristics de-

---

[3] Many readers may be surprised that I dare to mention the laws of association of ideas. Some psychological schools have tried to get rid of two fundamental characteristics of psychological phenomena: consciousness, denied by the behaviorists; and association of ideas, denied by those who are obsessively afraid of mental atomism. Nobody today would deny any longer that consciousness is a quality of some psychological processes. A two-minute observation can convince anyone of the fact that ideas do associate. I see my old high school and think of my adolescence; I hear somebody mention the name of Chopin, and I think immediately of an acquaintance of mine who is a pianist. The psychoanalytic treatment is based on free *associations* of ideas. In reality, associations in the analytic situation are free only from (Aristotelian) logic; they are not free from emotional currents, from paleologic mechanisms, and from the laws of association.

In a future contribution the transition will be studied from associational to paleologic thought. It will be demonstrated that the "associational link" becomes "the identifying link" in paleologic thought. In associational thought, if the associational link is a predicate of contiguity, the two ideas associate because of the law of contiguity. If the associational link is a predicate of quality, the ideas associate because of the law of similarity.

scribed above make only few deductions possible. The person who thinks logically may find reality very unpleasant as long as he continues to think so. John Doe cannot think that he is the President of the United States just because he was born in the United States, but he may think so if he abandons this method of logic and embraces a new one. Once he sees things in a different way, with a new logic, no Aristotelian persuasion will convince him that he is wrong. He is right, according to his own logic.

The maiden may not dare to think that she wishes sexual relations, but if in the dream the penis assumes the form of a terrifying snake, her objections will be temporarily removed. These examples disclose that one has the tendency to resort to paleologic thinking when one's wishes cannot be sustained by normal logic. If reality cannot grant gratification of wishes, a new system of logic, which will transform reality into a more complacent form may be adopted.

This tendency, which each person has, to think paleologically, is, of course, usually corrected by Aristotelian thought. The laws of paleologic are unconsciously applied in neurotic manifestations and in dreams, but are rejected by the patient and by the waking person. This is possible because the neurotic and the waking person retain their normal Aristotelian logic. Only dissociated tendencies in the neurotic retain autistic mechanisms.

In schizophrenia, instead, the paleologic way of thinking has the upper hand and seems to the patient a sound interpreter of reality. Because of the above-described, individual, and often unpredictable characteristics of this type of thinking, the schizophrenic will not be able to obtain consensual validation, but will reach that inner security derived by the newly-established agree-

ment between his logic and his emotions. He will have to withdraw more and more from this Aristotelian world, but will be finally at peace with himself.

The situation is not so clear-cut in the beginning of schizophrenia. The important contributions of Sullivan about the onset of schizophrenia will help one understand what is taking place at this stage of the illness.

After the state of panic which the new schizophrenic has undergone, the patient becomes aware of dissociated tendencies. He becomes aware not only of what was accepted and incorporated in his self-system but also of another and great part of his personality which was obscure to him.

It appears natural to Sullivan that the patient does not accept immediately this state of affairs, this new personality, and suffers terrifying experiences: "The structure of his world was torn apart and dreadful, previously scarcely conceivable, events injected themselves" (21). This description of Sullivan's is even better understood if one accepts the fact that the new schizophrenic realizes that his mind has started to think in a different way, obscure to him. He realizes that he is inclined to interpret the world in a different way, at variance from his previous way of thinking and from that of other people, and he is afraid that he will become insane. The schizophrenic fear of becoming insane is not just the phobic idea of insanity found in neurotics, but is a realization that some change in his way of thinking is actually taking place. At this stage the patient is able to think at the same time logically and paleologically, but his logic is not able any more to control the paleologic thoughts. Paleologic thinking will be first limited only to ideas connected with the patient's complexes, especially if the illness takes a paranoid course. The more progressed is the illness, however, the greater will be the percentage of paleologic thinking in the schizophrenic mixture of these two types of thoughts. Finally, when hebephrenic dilapidation approaches, there is a resurgence of thought mechanisms even more primitive than the paleologic.

# REFERENCES

1. WHITE, W. A. The language of schizophrenia. In Schizophrenia (dementia praecox). New York: Paul Hoeber, 1928. Pages 323–343.
2. VIGOTSKY, L. S. Thought in schizophrenia. Arch. Neurol. and Psychiat., 31(1934), 1036.
3. KASANIN, J. S. (ed.). Language and thought in schizophrenia: collected papers. Univ. of California Press, 1944.
4. ARIETI, S. Autistic thought: its formal mechanisms and its relations to schizophrenia. J. Nerv. and Ment. Disease, 111(1950), 288–303.
5. VON DOMARUS, E. Uber die Beziehung des normalen zum schizophrenen Denken. Arch. Psychiat., 74(1925), 641. Berlin.
6. KASANIN, J. S. (ed.). The specific laws of logic in schizophrenia. Language and thought in schizophrenia: collected papers. Univ. of California Press, 1944.
7. STORCH, A. The primitive archaic forms of inner experiences and thought in schizophrenics. New York and Washington: Nervous and Mental Disease Publishing Company, 1924.
8. WERNER, H. Comparative psychology of mental development. New York: Harper & Brothers, 1940.
9. LEVIN, M. Misunderstanding of the pathogenesis of schizophrenia, arising from the concept of "splitting." Amer. J. Psychiatry, 94(1938), 877–889.
10. FREUD, S. The interpretation of dreams. In S. Freud, The basic writings of Sigmund Freud. New York: Modern Library, 1938.
11. ———. Psychopathology of everyday life. Ibid.
12. JUNG, C. G. The psychology of dementia praecox. New York: Nervous and Mental Disease Monograph Series No. 3, 1936.
13. BENJAMIN, J. D. A method for distinguishing and evaluating formal thinking disorders in schizophrenia. In Kasanin, S. J. (ed.). Language and thought in schizophrenia: collected papers. Univ. of California Press, 1944.
14. GOLDSTEIN, K. The significance of psychological research in schizophrenia. J. Nerv. and Ment. Disease, 97(1943), 261–279.
15. PIAGET, J. The child's conception of the world. London: Routledge and Kegan Paul Ltd., 1929.
16. FREUD, S. Wit and its relation to the unconscious. In S. Freud, The basic writings of Sigmund Freud. New York: Modern Library, 1938.
17. PIAGET, J. The language and thought of the child. London: Routledge and Kegan Paul Ltd., 1948. Also, The child's conception of physical causality. London: Kegan, Trench, Trubner, 1930.
18. ARIETI, S. The processes of expectation and anticipation. J. Nerv. and Ment. Disease, 100(1947), 471–481.
19. HUNTER, W. S. The delayed reaction in animals and children. Behavior monographs, 2(1913), 86.
20. HARLOW, H. F., WEHLING, H., and MASLOW, A. H. Comparative behavior of primates: delayed reaction tests on primates. J. Comp. Psychol., 13(1932), 13.
21. SULLIVAN, H. S. Conceptions of modern psychiatry. Washington, D.C.: The William Alanson White Psychiatric Foundation, 1946.
22. BALKEN, E. R. A delineation of schizophrenic language and thought in a test of imagination. J. Psychol., 16 (1943), 239.
23. FREUD, S. Fragment of an analysis of a case of hysteria (1905). In Collected papers. Volume III. London: Hogarth Press, 13(1946), 146.

24. FENICHEL, O. The psychoanalytic theory of neurosis. New York: W. W. Norton & Co., 1945.
25. LEVIN, M. On the causation of mental symptoms. J. Mental Science, 82 (1938), 1–27.
26. FREUD, S. Totem and taboo. In S. Freud, The basic writings of Sigmund Freud. New York: Modern Library, 1938.
27. FROMM, E. Unpublished lectures given at seminar on social psychology. New York: William Alanson White Institute of Psychiatry, 1948.
28. RÓHEIM, G. The riddle of the sphinx.

London: International Psycho-analytical Library, No. 25, 1934.
29. KARDINER, A. The individual and his society. New York: Columbia Press, 1939.
30. FREUD, S. Psychoanalytic notes upon an autobiographical account of a case of paranoia (dementia paranoides) (1911). In S. Freud, Collected papers. Volume III. London, Hogarth Press, 1946. Pages 387–470.
31. BLEULER, E. Dementia praecox, oder Gruppe der Schizophrennen. Leipzig and Wien. Franz-Deutsche, 1911.

Margaret Thaler Singer
and Lyman C. Wynne

# Differentiating Characteristics of Parents of Childhood Schizophrenics, Childhood Neurotics, and Young Adult Schizophrenics

In recent years, researchers interested in schizophrenia have turned to a study of family interaction patterns in the hope that the illness can be understood as a product of such factors. In this very exciting research study by Singer and Wynne, efforts were made to distinguish among a large group of parents having either childhood schizophrenic, childhood neurotic, or young adult schizophrenic children on the basis of the way these parents related to people. The style of relating was inferred from responses on a Thematic Apperception Test. The hypotheses guiding the distinctions made by the authors derived from their observations of the family relations of schizophrenics. The fact that the authors could successfully determine which parents had offspring suffering from each type of disorder is more than a parlor trick. It can be taken as a validation of the parental behavioral styles that seem to be related to the development of such disorders.

During the course of a long-range research program on the family relations of schizophrenics, we have developed criteria by which families with late adolescent and young adult schizophrenic offspring can be differentiated from families whose offspring have other kinds of psychiatric disturbances

Reprinted from the American Journal of Psychiatry, 120(1963), 234–243 with the permission of the American Psychiatric Association and Dr. Singer. Copyright 1963, the American Psychiatric Association.

(1–5). In this paper we shall present data from parents of child psychiatric patients, and compare the findings with those from the parents of patients studied earlier.

Our research has assumed that innate and experiential factors are codeterminants of behavior. Additionally, we have hypothesized that certain parental forms of focusing attention, communicating and interpersonal "relating" are intimately linked to the forms of ego impairment found in offspring. *Form* or style of parental behaving has been emphasized rather than the *content* of thoughts and attitudes.

Schizophrenia does not appear to be a single entity; rather, there are various forms of individual schizophrenic illness. Similarly, there is no single pattern for families of schizophrenics; instead, subgroups of schizophrenics have families which share similar characteristics. Thus, among adult patients, the family patterns of patients with different forms of thought disorder can be blindly distinguished (5). We hypothesized that the family relations of the various kinds of childhood schizophrenics would similarly differ from each other and from the parents of the various kinds of adult schizophrenics.

This paper delineates certain of these differences through the study of pro-jective test data from (a) the parents of 20 autistic, schizophrenic children, (b) 20 neurotic children (10 "acting-out," aggressive children and 10 withdrawn children), and (c) 20 schizophrenics who became overtly ill in late adolescence or young adulthood.[1]

*Selection of Subjects.* The parents of the two groups of child patients (median age, 8 years) had been selected for another study (6) in the following way:[2] First, the parents of the schizophrenic children were selected. A clinical consensus in the diagnosis of "schizophrenic reaction, childhood type," was used, with cases eliminated having any serious physical illness, demonstrable neurological findings,[3] or recognizable mental deficiency.

Our review of the clinical records following the test analyses indicated that 14 of the "childhood schizophrenic" patients clearly fell into the group originally described by Kanner (7) under the heading of "early infantile autism" and recently reviewed by Rimland (8). The other 6 patients fitted the designation "childhood schizophrenia with autistic traits." Eighteen had clear-cut autistic symptoms well before age 2, and the other 2 clearly had these symptoms soon after their second and third birthdays. At ages 4–7 most of these children were without communicative speech, had

[1] Similar data from the parents of 20 chronically physically ill children and 20 asthmatic children, along with additional material about various kinds of adult schizophrenics and neurotics, will be reported subsequently.

[2] We wish to express our appreciation to Drs. Jeanne Block and Virginia Patterson, who made available to us a major portion of the tests from the parents of the young children. The schizophrenic children were patients of the Langley Porter Children's Service, San Francisco. Dr. S. A. Szurek, Director, and Dr. A. J. Gianascol gave access to the clinical records on these patients and families after the test analyses were completed. Responsibility for the interpretation of the data rests with the authors. The families of the neurotic and other children were secured from various clinics in the San Francisco area.

[3] Although none of the patients had neurological findings on examination, 7 histories (5 in an early infantile autism group) revealed an unusually difficult pregnancy or delivery; 2 of these, plus one other patient, all in the early infantile autism group, later had a history of seizures.

almost no contact with people, and showed idiosyncratic repetitive behavior, such as unscrewing screws, twiddling paper, and stacking items. All patients would be in the group described by Mahler (9) as "autistic psychoses" rather than "symbiotic psychoses." The findings reported in this paper should not be assumed to be generally applicable to the families of other varieties of patients.

These families were used as the base for selecting comparison families. The families of the schizophrenic and the neurotic children were individually matched using the method of "precision controls" (10) for the following 5 variables: (a) age of child within 3 years; (b) age of parents in relation to child; (c) number of children in family (the parents of an only child were matched with parents of an only child; where there was more than 1 child, the number was held roughly equivalent); (d) educational and occupational level of parents; (e) participation of at least the mother in a psychotherapeutic relation. Fifteen of the 20 schizophrenic children were also matched with 15 of the neurotic children on the basis of sex. Thirty-three of the child patients were male and 7 were female (S : 6 female, 14 male; N : 1 female, 19 male).

The families of the young adult schizophrenics [4] could not, of course, be matched so well with respect to age. The median age of the young adult patients was 23 years, and 56 years for their parents. The median age of the parents of the child patients was 37 years. In other respects, including size of family, and educational and occu-pational level, the parents of the young adult patients were comparable. It is important to note that in all the families the parents themselves had raised the children.

## PROCEDURES

1. Using general hypotheses drawn from earlier work, the projective test data from the 40 pairs of parents of the childhood schizophrenics (CS) and childhood neurotics (CN) were studied blindly in a preliminary fashion. The Thematic Apperception Test and the Rorschach were the main tests used in this study. Preliminary groupings of the parents into predicted CS and CN groups were rank-ordered by one of us (MTS) in terms of the degree of confidence with which the designations were made. Dr. Virginia Patterson,[4] who held the code of correct classification of these parents, indicated that the first 5 CS and the first 5 CN designations were correct.

2. These 10 sets of tests were then used for developing more specific criteria differentiating the CS and CN parents. In the second phase of the blind differentiations, the remaining 30 sets of tests from the child patients were blindly differentiated, first, into the CS and CN groups.

3. The tests from those parents who were correctly identified as having neurotic children were blindly differentiated with respect to whether their offspring were in the acting-out group or the withdrawn neurotic group.

4. Criteria were specified for the differences in the TAT test behavior

[4] We also wish to express our appreciation to Dr. Theodore Lidz of Yale University, who made available tests from 9 pairs of parents of the young adult schizophrenics. The parents of the other adult schizophrenic patients were tested at the NIMH by Mr. Charles Odell and Mr. George Usdansky. The parents of the adult patients constitute only an early portion of the NIMH data which was specifically comparable to the data from the families of the child patients.

of the 4 sets of parents—the parents of the childhood schizophrenics, the acting-out children, the withdrawn neurotic children, and the young adult schizophrenics.

5. Finally, various special Rorschach ratings were analyzed and compared statistically for the 4 groups of parents: (a) thinking disorder and related schizophrenic features; (b) genetic-level scores; (c) affective symbolism, particularly hostility scores and the presence of a hostile or threatening component to the first Rorschach response of each individual.

## RESULTS

1. In the preliminary blind differentiation and rank-ordering of the projective tests from the parents of the child patients, the Rorschach and TAT tests from each marital pair were considered simultaneously as a family unit. Most studies have considered fathers and mothers separately; the present study is concerned with what emerged when both parents' tests were examined in relation to each other and were considered together as compounding, confusing, or correcting the impact of each parent as an individual.

Selecting the 10 sets of tests which could be designated with the greatest confidence as belonging in either the CS or CN groups, resulted in an entirely accurate differentiation. That is, the 5 pairs of parents which were expected to have schizophrenic children were all designated correctly, and the 5 sets of parents which were predicted to have neurotic children were also designated correctly, with no errors. Using Fisher's exact test for categorical data, this differentiation is significant statistically $(p = .004)$.[5]

2. In the second phase of the blind differentiations, the remaining 30 sets of tests from the parents of the child patients were differentiated using the more detailed criteria developed on the basis of the 10 most distinctive sets of tests. Twenty-four of the 30 sets of parents were then correctly identified either as parents of autistic schizophrenic or of neurotic children. Twelve of 15 in both the schizophrenic and the neurotic groups were correctly placed, giving a statistically significant level of accuracy ($p < .005$, using Fisher's exact test).

3. The next stage of the blind differentiation combined the 5 sets of parents of the neurotic children who were used in the preliminary development of criteria and the 12 others who were correctly predicted as having neurotic children. The rater did not know which were parents of acting-out or withdrawn children. Thirteen of the 17 sets of parents were blindly labeled correctly; parents of 7 acting-out children out of a total of 9 were correctly designated; and the parents of 6 withdrawn children out of 8 were correctly designated (using Fisher's exact test, $p = .044$).

*TAT Criteria for Differentiation.* On theoretical grounds we expected that the parents of autistic schizophrenic children would be different from the parents of young adult schizophrenics previously studied. Contrasting core problems exist. The autistic children do not appear to relate to others, or do so in extremely restricted ways; the young adult schizophrenics have thinking and experiencing disorders. If learning, "conditioning" and experiential factors are related to the behavior of autistic children and of adult schizophrenics, then, in far over simplified terms, the role of *relating* is crucial in families with autistic children and the

[5] We wish to express our appreciation to Dr. Donald Morrison, Biometrics Branch, NIMH, for his invaluable assistance in the statistical analysis of the data of this study.

parental contribution to *thinking and attention defects* is central in the families of those who become designated as schizophrenic at a later age. The parents of autistic, childhood schizophrenics, we surmised, have forms of behavior which would rebuff, impair, and interfere with the very beginnings of relationships they might have with the child, and would continue to do so later.

In the earlier studies of the families of adult schizophrenics who had grown up in intact families, we had been impressed by a family subculture in which the parent-child relationships are not by any means prevented from developing nor are they totally shattered. Rather, the focusing of attention and the achievement of subjectively meaningful experience are impaired, blurred, and fragmented but with enduring parent-child relatedness.[6] The *content* of what these parents say is not so critical as the level at which focal attention [7] is impaired. Criteria which have been helpful in identifying the parents of the young adult schizophrenics include such maneuvers as amorphously and implicitly shifting the area to which attention is given, vaguely shifting the context of reference, externalizing the sources of attention, scattering and fragmenting attention over such a large series of items that meaningfulness cannot be integrated, *etc.* (5).

The further study of the CS and CN criterion groups highlighted two major distinguishing qualities in the TAT be- havior of the parents of these autistic children: *disaffiliation* and *dissatisfaction* as characteristic and pervasive expectancies about the way any interaction is going to turn out.[8]

## A. Parents of Autistic Childhood Schizophrenics

*Disaffiliation.* Persons are seen moving away from each other, moving out of relationships, and avoiding closeness. Interactions appear inherently unpleasant and failing to satisfy. Relationships are viewed with cynicism, distrust and pessimism. At best there is something uncomfortable about interacting with others.

At least four pathways to disaffiliation are discernible. In each pair of the CS parents, both have some of the following qualities, which appear *either* within the TAT stories, or in the manner of telling the story and interacting with the examiner.

1. *Cynical outlook.* Approximately 70% of the CS parents were in this group. They expect the worst possible motivation in people. They sound embittered, disenchanted, and describe warmth, closeness and tender motivations with contempt, skepticism, or scorn. Often their criticism conveys an active, destructive quality, with a sadistic finality about people leaving one another.

In their TAT stories these CS parents were vindictive toward persons for trying to establish and maintain relationships. They doubt the worthwhileness of relating and interacting; people disaffiliate into empty lives. Some indicate "things are not as they seem," not true or real. Some

---

[6] Earlier communications from the larger NIMH research group have used such terms as pseudomutuality and pseudohostility to characterize the essence of the oddly held-together relationships of these families(1, 3).

[7] The term focal attention is used here as described by Schachtel(11): acts of attention appear directional, specific, aim at mental grasp via a sustained approach and with renewed approaches to the object or thought, and flexibly exclude extraneous stimuli (p. 253).

[8] A partial replication based upon these criteria and utilizing the TAT parental tests alone was carried out by another rater (LCW). Nine out of 10 cases of the child patients (5 autistic and 5 neurotic withdrawn) were correctly differentiated in this replication.

parents of CN children and parents of young adult schizophrenics are pessimistic but imply one keeps on trying to establish relationships, and to trust people.

Certain CS parents covertly imply that nothing endures, and therefore one should not affiliate or attach oneself to people or objects.

2. *Passivity and apathy about interacting.* Others convey resignation, withdrawal, disinterest and avoidance when characterizing interactions between persons. They imply, "Why bother interacting. It's useless and going to turn out poorly anyhow." They create an air of passive pessimism.

3. *Superficiality.* Certain parents treat potentially moving, touching scenes with great superficiality. They seem unable to sense the persons in the cards might be involved in touching, feelingful experiences. They treat everything in a superficial "surfacey" way. Nothing has depth or poignancy and only the most blatant, overt, concrete actions are noted. When they try to describe close, tender and warm human transactions, their stories become parodies and travesties. Sometimes there is a seeming mockery present.

Facetiousness appears particularly in the tests of parents who might be classed as either cynical or superficial. Both imply there is a lack of genuineness about tender, positive scenes and they facetiously flaunt and degrade tenderness, closeness and positive emotions and interactions. They doubt their genuineness, imply they denote weakness, are maudlin and to be scorned.

4. *Obsessive, intellectualized distance.* Some parents convey a sense of disaffiliation via detachment and intellectualized distance. This has to be differentiated from certain CN parents who are obsessive and intellectualizing but who seem to bury themselves in busily trying to figure out what is going on in a transaction, but become obsessively involved and participating in the test task, rather than dismissing it.

*Dissatisfaction.* Overlapping with disaffiliation is dissatisfaction, a quality which is pervasive, but difficult to characterize briefly because it hinges upon reading and analyzing whole tales or the over-all test protocol. Disaffiliation can be described via actions and expectancies. Dissatisfaction is seen in TAT characters having lives that are non-rewarding. Their efforts, work, and patterns of life are chronically dissatisfying.

Praise, recognition, and admiration are almost absent from the CS parent tales.[9] Often when they see a person striving, they impute selfish motives, and predict that he will be punished or will collapse. For example, one card shows a man climbing a rope. The CS parents deride his physique and his mentality, impute self-centered motives, and usually have him fall or injure himself for showing off, trying to be strong, *etc.*

In one way or another most of the stories of these parents are negatively toned. Certain CS parents create a relatively positive story, but append side comments, bored yawns, and add denouements which ruin the impact of any pleasant content by a final coup de grâce which belies sincerity or belief in the content of the story.

When parents with these intense, disaffiliating, distancing, unempathic tendencies have an infant with a low innate capacity to elicit appropriate responsiveness, transactional failures crippling to ego development will necessarily begin at birth. Parents who are psychologically able to stand apart from others, including their infant, will be relatively objective, clear and definite in their thinking, and in their capacity to differentiate self and other, and in their capacity to direct their activities, including telling TAT stories, with

---

[9] Boatman and Szurek(12), summarizing clinical impressions from more than 200 childhood schizophrenics and their parents, including those whose tests are used here, noted (p. 415), "Exchange of tender words, admiration and approbation is also scanty."

relative coherence, unity, and point. Diversions do occur, but these parents manage to convey that they have maintained or can return to an over-all point. They seem to "remember" where they came from and where they are going with their stories. Thus, they do not ordinarily shown significant attention defects.

## B. Parents of Young Adult Schizophrenics

In contrast, the TATs of these parents of the young adult schizophrenics are marked by a failure to develop and hold a set, to focus and sustain attention. Their stories neither unfold with coherence nor with a clear sense of point and meaningfulness, nor conclude with closure.

The persons in these stories are not depicted as disaffiliated and detached but as interacting in frustrated or pointless ways. Sometimes the persons are together in parallel, each doing something but failing to interact productively. Others have people in the tales intruding into other persons, trying to control and manipulate them, usually to no avail. They convey feelings of aloneness, frustration, and meaninglessness about transactions even though the persons are together.

1. *Fragmentation.* Tangential ideas, side themes, and distracting comments are prominent. Their tales are replete with fragments of alternative meanings and alternative feelings, usually none of which are selected and completed. Often when the examiner asks for further steps or details, as well as when the teller recalls the instructions, there is a "jump" or almost non-sequitur appending of the next part. The teller seems to fail to realize he needs to move the listener with him to a conclusion or next step. Frequently words and phrases are omitted. This is especially apparent in verbatim, tape-recorded tests. Non-sequiturs and misperceptions seem to occur because intrusive, secondary

associations get into these parents' main stream of attention.

2. *Perseveration.* Concomitant with the fragmented quality of these attention-meaning defects, mild to open perseverative tendencies may be present. These parents' attention does not focus flexibility. Occasionally there is a failure to "clear" either a detail or a global essence from a previously attended idea; this influences subsequent perceptions and associations unduly.

3. *Pointlessness.* There is a feeling upon reading most of the stories that a point really never was developed. Even if apparent closure is achieved, the reader is left with a sense of pointlessness. Various wordy trappings often conceal that the production is merely a card description or "filler material."

4. *Indefinite referents.* A subgroup of these parents gives stories which seem relatively concise and with closure, but inspection reveals a great non-specificity about the referents of experience.

## C. Parents of Acting-Out Children

The TAT stories of the parents of the aggressive, acting-out children are distinctive from either of the schizophrenic groups. There is an absence of thought disorders, rambling communication, fragmented attention, low mood tones, anergy, and pessimism. They are not concerned about doing well. They fail to strive, in contrast to the parents of the CS who show contempt for others' striving. Some fail to sense tacit implications of social behavior. The following qualities do stand out:

1. *Facetiousness.* They directly or indirectly taunt about authority. They are facetious toward rules and amenities, while the autistic children's parents are facetious toward feelings, especially positive and tender ones.

2. *High activity.* They sound like active, energetic persons and have strong empathies with persons seen. In comparison with the parents of CS children and young adult

schizophrenics, they are more likely to stimulate action in others.

3. *Clear communication.* Percepts are relatively clear, ideas conventional, language orderly and concise. Almost none have genuinely obsessive tests. They have a lack of concern about doing well. They fail to strive, in contrast to the parents of the CS who show contempt for others' striving. Some fail to sense tacit implications of social behavior.

4. *Relatively "normal" tests.* In general their tests are those of active, somewhat hostile persons. Yet their hostile tales do not convey the sadism implied in the records of certain parents of CS children. Additionally, a sparseness of conflictual content conveys an aura of "normalcy" even though raters can detect propensities for disturbed moods and impulses.

## D. Parents of Withdrawn Neurotic Children

1. *Lower mood.* In contrast to the tests from the parents of acting-out children, these tests contain lower mood tones, less open energy, and less acting-out potentials.

2. *Coherence.* In contrast to TATs from parents of young adult schizophrenics, these parents do not have gross attention difficulties, nor do they feel resigned or deeply pessimistic. A few low-mood tone parents are moderately fragmentary, and their tests may seem "schizoid." However, they have people relating and staying together in spite of adversities. Some may talk in generalities and abstractions (masculinity versus femininity, viewing the sky equals thinking of the future, *etc.*), but do it within a framework of relating, striving, and attempts at coherence and cohesiveness.

3. *Affiliation and satisfaction.* In contrast to tests from parents of autistic children, these tests express a belief in the "basic goodness of men and life in general" even though mood tones may be low. There is a minimum of disaffiliation. When someone gets rejected, these parents have identified with the rejectee and not the rejector (as with autistic parents) and imply they would want to go back into the relationship and are sad over its loss. People may feel anxious, inadequate, or ambivalent, but

they strive to maintain relationships. They recognize it is best to comply, even though they may not want to. Inner drives may tempt one to do evil, but these should be overcome. Control is often an issue—one person over another, nature over man, *etc.* Control can be seen as intrusive, but it keeps children and others close. Satisfactions, accomplishments and pleasure from work can come to people.

Table 1 contrasts the TAT characteristics of the four groups of parents. These are expressed in terms of TAT features of prototypic parents. The underlined items are considered particularly distinctive qualities.

## Rorschach Measures

A. *Thinking Disorders.* These formulations have generated further specific hypotheses which we have tested with measures from the Rorschach protocols of these four parent groups. In work with the families of young adult schizophrenics, we have been impressed with striking links between the underlying form of thinking of parents and their offspring. We attempted to evaluate this question from Rorschach data through criteria developed by M. T. Singer, using cues from Benjamin (13) and Rapaport (14). We compared the frequency and kinds of thinking disorder and related schizophrenic features in the various groups of parents studied. Hypothetically, in terms of the considerations discussed from the TAT data, the parents of the acting-out children, would be most free of thinking disorders amongst these four parent groups. The next clearest thinking group would be the parents of the autistic schizophrenic children and the most disturbed in thinking processes would be the parents of the young adult schizophrenics. Considering that the withdrawn children were perhaps a somewhat heterogeneous nosologic

## TABLE 1. Summary of TAT Features of Parents

### Parents of Autistic Children
* 1. Feel dissatisfied, bitter, critical.
2. Disaffiliate via many modes.
3. Tell coherent tales with a point and unity.
4. Have clear percepts; depict people, events, feelings, consequences clearly compared to parents of adult schizophrenics.

### Parents of Withdrawn Children
1. Feel sad, with low mood.
2. Seek to stay in relationships, despite the mood tone.
3. Have a point and unity to stories.
4. Have relatively clear, specified percepts; may, however, dwell obsessively on details or on abstract qualities; appear introspective.

### Parents of Adult Schizophrenics
1. Feel unhappy, hopeless, resigned.
2. Have frustrating interaction, experienced as pointless.
3. Convey over-all sense of directionlessness; tell stories in which closure not achieved, without unity.
4. Have people, events, feelings, consequences remain global, abstract, overly general; attention appears fragmented or amorphous.

### Parents of Acting-Out Children
1. Have various moods, including orneriness, rebelliousness, sadness; are active, energetic.
2. Have people relate and interact to an ordinary level—not an outstanding feature.
3. Tell unified stories; do not strive to do outstandingly well on tests.
4. Have well defined, clear percepts; do not appear genuinely introspective.

* 1. Mood.
2. Relationship Style.
3. Capacity for Over-all Point and Coherence.
4. Clarity of Percept and Thought.

group, we expected that the parents of these patients would be intermediate in frequency and severity of thinking disorders.

As Table 2 indicates, the predicted ranking of Rorschach-rated thought disorder and schizophrenic features in the four groups of parents was confirmed. Ratings by independent psychologists [10] using Singer's criteria, achieved perfect agreement on the tests from the parents of the adult patients and the neurotic children with some disagreement among raters on 6 of the 40 parents of the autistic children. These 6 cases were resolved by consensus. Nearly all of the parents of the young adult schizophrenics had evidence of thought disorder in their Rorschach records, while almost none of the parents of the acting-out children had such features, with the other two groups intermediate in the predicted direction. These groups were significantly different (p = .001) (chi square test of homogeneity).

These differences were still more sharply apparent in terms of the severity of disorder. Briefly, the forms of thinking seen in the Rorschachs of the parents of the adult schizophrenics reflected relatively severe forms of rambling, loose, paralogical thought disorders, with marked attention problems

[10] We wish to thank Dr. Jerome Fisher and Mr. Frank Gorman of the Langley Porter Neuropsychiatric Institute and Dr. George DeVos of the University of California for their test evaluations.

TABLE 2. Schizophrenic Features, Especially Thought Disorder,
in Rorschachs of Parents

| Percent of Parents with Schizophrenic Rorschach Features Parental Pairs | Parents of Young Adult Schizophrenics (20 Pairs) | Parents of Withdrawn Children (10 Pairs) | Parents of Autistic Schizophrenic Children (20 Pairs) | Parents of Acting-Out Children (10 Pairs) |
|---|---|---|---|---|
| Neither parent | 0% | 20% | 50% | 90% |
| One parent | 5 | 20 | 30 | 10 |
| Both parents | 95 | 60 | 20 | 0 |
| Individual Parent Totals | 38/40 (95%) | 14/20 (70%) | 14/40 (35%) | 1/20 (5%) |

and peculiar content, sufficiently prominent so that the raters had easily noted these features. The CS parents showed a fairly large number of mild features, but rarely loose, scattered, or fragmented forms of thinking. The features found in their records included: pseudoprofundity, forms of concreteness, original but rather odd contents, and repetitious returns to particular themes. They cut off secondary confabulatory associations and focused attention in a relatively constricted, orderly fashion without rambling or loose associations.

B. *Genetic-Level Rorschach Scores.* Another way of scoring Rorschach data which is relevant to our conceptualizations is in terms of degree of psychological differentiation, the "genetic" level of perceptual development, as suggested by Heinz Werner's theory (15). Using Becker's method for Rorschach Genetic-level scoring (16), the parents of the four groups, treated as pairs, differentiate in a multi-variate analysis of variance at the 0.01 level of confidence (See Table 3).

The higher the genetic-level score is, the more mature the perceptual quality of the over-all responses. The parents of the young adult schizophrenics who are prone to blur and fragment

attention, give responses of a significantly less differentiated and less integrated quality than found in the other parents. They are not, however, a homogeneous group. We have noted elsewhere the importance of distinguishing the parents of schizophrenics who are especially amorphous and undifferentiated in their thinking from those who are relatively better differentiated but still fragmented and unintegrated (5).

TABLE 3. Genetic-Level Rorschach Scores

| Group | Mothers | | Fathers | |
|---|---|---|---|---|
| | Mean | SD | Mean | SD |
| Acting-out children (N = 20) | 3.70 | 0.369 | 3.71 | 0.302 |
| Schizophrenic young children (N = 40) | 3.45 | 0.319 | 3.59 | 0.373 |
| Withdrawn children (N = 20) | 3.29 | 0.291 | 3.06 | 0.508 |
| Schizophrenic young adults (N = 40) | 3.11 | 0.553 | 3.08 | 0.512 |

The acting-out children, where one expects little ego impairment of this basic labeling of "reality," had parents who tended to give the most articulated and integrated percepts. The parents of the autistic schizophrenic children show a higher level of psychological differentiation than the parents of either the withdrawn neurotic or the young adult schizophrenic groups. This finding appears to be consistent with the Rorschach ratings of thought disorder in that the frequency of thought disorder in the various parent groups increased in the same order: acting-out children, autistic children, withdrawn neurotic children, and young adult schizophrenics.

C. *Hostile Affect.* We have described our impression that the parents of the autistic schizophrenic children tend to disrupt actively and hostilely the very beginnings of transactions and relationships. It appears possible to be openly disaffiliating only if relatively clear capacity for self-other differentiation has been achieved. Among the group of parents of autistic children, those who seem most explicitly and, often, brutally disaffiliating have relatively clear, genetically "mature" perceptions and little indication of schizophrenic Rorschach features.

The parents of the young adult schizophrenics are rarely so openly and directly disaffiliative as the parents of most of the autistic children. They may be hostile, but are more prone to stay in a transaction, even if only as inert spectators. Although not all parents of the autistic children use a hostile path to disaffiliation, the impression of a greater frequency of this trend in these parents seemed worth while checking out statistically.

Over-all hostile affect: As a partial measure of this tendency, each parent's Rorschach responses were scored for affective symbolism (17). Each response was scored either neutral, hostile, anxious, body preoccupation, dependency, positive, or miscellaneous affect.[11] We reasoned that the CS parents would show the highest hostility scores, with the parents of the acting-out children next, but the parents of the young adult schizophrenics and the withdrawn children were expected to be lower. For the mothers, this hypothesis (child schizophrenic and acting-out parent groups > adult schizophrenic and neurotic withdrawn) was confirmed at the 0.01 level of confidence; for the fathers, at the 0.05 level of confidence. Within the schizophrenic groups alone, the parents of the child patients also had significantly higher hostility scores than the parents of the adult schizophrenics.

Initial hostile responses: It also seemed reasonable to hypothesize that the CS parents, if they characteristically disrupted transactions from their beginnings, would introduce hostile or threatening content very early in associations. A tally of the affective symbolism assigned each parent's very first Rorschach response revealed that 40% of the parents of the child schizophrenics (8 mothers and 8 fathers), but only 15% in each of the other three groups (4 mothers and 2 fathers of young adult schizophrenics, and 1 mother and 2 fathers each of the acting-out and withdrawn groups) had a hostile or threatening component to their first response. (Comparing parents of adult and child schizophrenics, chi square, 5.08, p. < .025.) A larger portion of the parents of child schizophrenics had

[11] Dr. Joseph C. Speisman, NIMH, independently scored the records for genetic-level and affective symbolism, achieving 89% agreement with the previous scores. We appreciate his assistance.

this initial tendency to think of a hostile or threatening association. This quick arousal of hostile or threatening content, association with a general presence of greater hostility content among the CS parents, is suggestive that not only the presence of hostile associations, but where they enter in the transaction seems relevant.

## SUMMARY

Research at the NIMH on the families of schizophrenics is broadened in this study to include the parents of child psychiatric patients. Previous studies in this program (5) have demonstrated that the families of young adult schizophrenics can be blindly differentiated from the families of young adult neurotics when criteria are used which emphasize form or style of thinking and focusing attention. In the present study we show that relationship disorders, rather than the thinking disorders which are so prominent in the families of the adult schizophrenics, are especially pertinent to the differentiation of families of autistic schizophrenic children from families of neurotic children.

The criteria for predicting autistic illness in an offspring from parental data were derived from the psychodynamic hypothesis that primary disruption and impairment in the child's relationship to parental figures is crucial in early autistic disorders. We have assumed that an infant's congenital incapacity can contribute to such relationship failure. Nevertheless, in this series of families it has been possible to distinguish blindly those parents who have autistic children from the manner in which they appear to rebuff, impair, and interfere with the very beginning of any tender or nurturant relationship, as judged from projective test protocols.

The parents of 20 autistic children were blindly differentiated at a statistically significant level of accuracy from sociologically matched parents of 20 neurotic children. The parents of the neurotic children, half withdrawn and half aggressive, acting-out, were in turn successfully differentiated into these two groups on the basis of the parental projective tests.

This research suggests the importance of considering mental disorders, including schizophrenia, both in childhood and later, as heterogeneous, and studying the links between definable varieties of individual mental disorder and definable varieties of family patterns.

Criteria applicable to TAT data for distinguishing the parents of the three varieties of child patients and the parents of young adult schizophrenics were described. The disaffiliative tendencies of the parents of the autistic young children were especially significant, while the parents of patients whose schizophrenia did not become overt until late adolescence or young adulthood appeared to let relationships develop but distorted and impaired the focusing of attention and the acquisition of clear meanings. The parents of the acting-out children in this series were active and energetic in their relationships, though often with various disturbed moods and impulses, and were relatively well-defined and clear in their percepts. Parents of a group of withdrawn neurotic children showed especially sadness, together with serious strivings to maintain relationships. The behavior of the offspring in all of these families appeared "logical" and developmentally meaningful in the sense that the forms of behavior seen in the patient-offspring would fit in with major formal transactional patterns seen in the parents.

The formulations made in this paper are applicable, we wish to stress, only to those varieties of patients and families which we have thus far studied; we do not regard these findings as applicable, for example, to the families of childhood schizophrenics who have gross neurological impairment (18).

These formulations generated additional hypotheses which were tested through blind ratings of Rorschach data from these parents. It was found that the frequency of thinking disorders, genetic-level of psychological differentiation, and frequency of expressions of over-all and initial hostile affect found in the four groups of parents were in predicted directions.

The data presented here support a developmental theory of familial contributions to ego impairment which is being evolved in the family studies at the NIMH. The present data especially emphasize parental *styles* of thinking and relating as a crucial co-determinant —other experiential and innate factors are also co-determinants—of enduring patterns of behavior in offspring.

## REFERENCES

1. WYNNE, L. C., *et al.*: Psychiatry, **21**: 205, 1958.
2. RYCKOFF, I. M., DAY, J., and WYNNE, L. C.: A.M.A. Arch. Psychiat., **1**:93, 1959.
3. WYNNE, L. C.: The Study of Intrafamilial Alignments and Splits in Exploratory Family Therapy. *In* Ackerman, N. W., *et al.* (Eds.): Exploring the Base for Family Therapy. New York: Fam. Service Asso., 1961.
4. SCHAFFER, L., *et al.*: Psychiatry, **25**:32, 1962.
5. WYNNE, L. C., and SINGER, M. T.: Thought Disorder and the Family Relations of Schizophrenics: I, II, III, and IV. Arch. Gen. Psychiat. In press, 1963.
6. BLOCK, J., *et al.*: Psychiatry, **21**:387, 1958.
7. KANNER, L.: Am. J. Orthopsychiat., **19**: 416, 1949.
8. RIMLAND, B.: Early Infantile Autism: Review, Theory and Implications. New York: Appleton-Century-Crofts, 1963.
9. MAHLER, M. S.: Psychoanal. Study Child, **7**:286, 1952.
10. Some Observations on Controls in Psychiatric Research. Group Advance. Psychiat. Report No. 42, 1959.
11. SCHACHTEL, E. G.: Metamorphosis. New York: Basic Books, 1959.
12. BOATMAN, M. J., and SZUREK, S. A.: A Clinical Study of Childhood Schizophrenia. *In* Jackson, D. D. (Ed.): The Etoi̇ogy of Schizophrenia. New York: Basic Books, 1960.
13. BENJAMIN, J.: Personal Communication, 1950–1954.
14. RAPAPORT, D.: Diagnostic Psychological Testing, Vol. II. Chicago: Year Book Publishers, 1946.
15. WERNER, H.: Comparative Psychology of Mental Development. New York: Science Editions, 1961.
16. BECKER, W. C.: J. Abnorm. Soc. Psychol., **53**:29, 1956.
17. DeVos, G. A.: J. Proj. Techniques, **16**:133, 1952.
18. MEYER, D., and GOLDFARB, W.: Am. J. Psychiat., **118**:902, 1962.

George H. Frank

# The Role of the Family in the Development
# of Psychopathology

*Those psychologists who assume that psychopathology is determined largely by a person's life experiences regard the early family life as quite a crucial factor in mental illness. In order to substantiate the importance of early experiences in the family, it is necessary to determine that certain parent-child interaction patterns characterize those who manifest certain disorders and that such patterns are unique to people suffering that disorder; that is, they are not found in people who fail to manifest such illness. In Frank's paper, an extensive review is made of the studies of the past 40 years which have been attempting to relate family patterns to various types of psychopathology.*

As psychopathology came to be viewed as the consequence of the emotional experiences to which the individual was exposed, interest was focused on the earliest of such experiences, those that occur in the family. The human infant is born incapable of sustaining its own life for a considerable length of time following birth, and is, in consequence, dependent upon the mother or a mother substitute for its very existence. There is no wonder, therefore, that the mother-child relationship is a close one and is expected to be influential with regard to the psychological development of the child. Some explanations for the development of psychopathology have therefore focused on this particular relationship as the major etiological factor. Levy (1931, 1932, 1937, 1943) has described a pattern centering around "maternal overprotection," involving a constellation of attitudes which he felt contributed to the development of neurotic disorders, and Despert (1938) focused on a kind of mother-child relationship which seemed to her to be closely associated with the development of schizophrenia, a pattern which has come to be termed the "schizophrenogenic mother."

The hypothesis that the emotional climate of the interpersonal relationships within the family—and between the child and its mother in particular—has a decisive part in the development of the personality of the child would seem to have face validity. In part, support for this hypothesis may be gleaned from the data demonstrating the devastating effects of being brought up in the extreme interpersonal isolation that comes from *not* having a family (Beres & Obers, 1950; Brodbeck & Irwin, 1946; Goldfarb, 1943a, 1943b, 1943c, 1945a, 1945b; Lowrey, 1940; Spitz, 1945) or extreme social isolation within a family (Bartmeier, 1952; Davis, 1940). Moreover, it has been demonstrated that various specific emotional behaviors of the child seem to be correlated causally with factors in the home. For example, children who could be described as emotionally im-

Reprinted from Psychological Bulletin, 64(1965), 191–205, with the permission of the American Psychological Association and Dr. Frank. Copyright 1965 by the American Psychological Association.

mature, who are dependent, fearful, negativistic, emotionally labile, etc., have had mothers described as warriors (Pearson, 1931), overattentive (Hattwick, 1936; Hattwick & Stowell, 1936), or punitive (McCord, McCord, & Howard, 1961; Sears, Whiting, Nowlis, & Sears, 1953; Watson, 1934). Children who were described as being overly aggressive were described as having come from homes where mothers were seen as overcontrolling (Bishop, 1951) or punitive (McCord et al., 1961; Sears, 1961).

The evidence thus far suggests that there is, in fact, a correlation between events in the parent-child relationship and resultant personality *traits*. The question arises as to whether there is evidence which supports the hypothesis that there is a correlation between events in the parent-child relationship and the resultant complex patterns of behavior which have been termed personality. More specifically, in light of the theories which relate personality development to social (i.e., interpersonal) learning, the question is raised as to whether there is any consistent relationship between the emotional experience the child may have in the home and the development of personality pathology, that is, schizophrenia, neurosis, and behavior disorders. Towards this end, the findings of the research that has explored the psychological characteristics of the parents of these people will be analyzed in order to isolate those consistent characteristics of the parents that may emerge from study to study. The analysis will be done with regard to each major type of psychopathology as a group. Moreover, because psychological test data might yield different information than case history analysis, or direct observation of familial interaction as compared to attitudes as elicited by questionnaire, an attempt will be made to analyze the

information gleaned from the studies in terms of the method of data collection within the specific psychopathological groupings.

## SCHIZOPHRENIA

### Case History

One of the classical methods of data collection in the study of psychiatric illness is the case history, the information for which has generally been gathered by other professionals. The individual conducting a piece of research notes the material in the folders and draws conclusions from the collation of these observations.

In so doing, Despert (1938) observed that approximately 50% of the mothers of a sample of schizophrenic children, generally between the ages of 7 and 13, had been described as aggressive, overanxious, and oversolicitous and were considered to be the dominant parent. Clardy (1951) noted that 50% of the 30 cases of children between the ages of 3 and 12 diagnosed as schizophrenic had families characterized as overprotective and yet basically rejecting. Frazee (1953) noted the presence of this constellation particularly when the families of schizophrenics were compared with the families of children diagnosed as behavior disorders. Canavan and Clark (1923) and Lampron (1933) noted that 30% of the children of psychotics were themselves emotionally disturbed. Huschka (1941) and Lidz and Lidz (1949) noted that over 40% of their sample of schizophrenics had parents who were psychotic or neurotic. Bender (1936, 1937) and Frazee (1953) noted the high incidence of psychopathology in the children of psychotic parents. Preston and Antin (1932), on the other hand, found no significant differences in the incidence of psychosis and neurosis as a function of parents who were psychotic as compared to parents who were "normal," and Fanning, Lehr, Sherwin, and Wilson, (1938) found that 43% of the children of mothers who were psychotic were observed to be making an adequate social and personal adjustment, with only 11% of that sample classified as maladjusted.

Lidz and Lidz (1949) found that 40% of their sample of schizophrenic patients were deprived of one parent by divorce or separation before they were 19. Plank (1953) found that 63% of his sample of schizophrenics had families where one parent was absent either due to death or marital separation. Wahl (1954, 1956) found that there was a greater incidence of parental loss and rejection early in life for schizophrenics as compared to normals, and Barry (1936) found that from the case histories of 30 rulers adjudged, post facto, insane, 80% of them had lost one of their parents by the time they were 18. However, Barry and Bousfield (1937) found that the incidence of orphanhood in a psychiatric population (19 out of 26) was not much different from the incidence of orphanhood in a normal population (19 out of 24). Moreover, Oltman, McGarry, and Friedman (1952) found that the incidence of broken homes and parental deprivation in the families of schizophrenics (34%) was not very different from that found in the families of hospital employees (32%), alcoholics (31%), and manic-depressives (34%); indeed, in their sampling, neurotics (49%) and psychopaths (48%) showed a greater incidence. Other studies have found that the incidence of broken homes in the history of neurotics is between 20% (Brown & Moore, 1944) and 30% (Madow & Hardy, 1947; Wallace, 1935), and Gerard and Siegel (1950) found no

particular incidence of broken homes in the family history of their sample of schizophrenics.

## Psychiatric Interview

Another classical method of obtaining information regarding the individual with whom patients have been living is by having interviews with them directly. The quality of the mother-child relationship is then inferred from what the interviewee says. From this research, an overwhelming number of studies (Despert, 1951; Gerard & Siegel, 1950; Guertin, 1961; Hajdu-Gimes, 1940; Kasanin, Knight, & Sage, 1934; Lidz, Cornelison, Fleck & Terry, 1957a, 1957b, 1957c; Lidz, Cornelison, Terry, & Fleck, 1958; Lidz & Lidz, 1949; Lidz, Parker, & Cornelison, 1956; Tietze, 1949; Walters, 1938) describe a familial pattern characterized by a dominant, overprotective, but basically rejecting mother and a passive, ineffectual father. Yet the data in the study by Schofield and Balian (1959) reflected similarity rather than differences in the families of schizophrenic and nonpsychiatric (general medical) patients, and the data of Gerard and Siegel (1950) indicated that the schizophrenics in their study, according to interpretation of the data gleaned from the interviews, received adequate breast feeding, had no history of particularly difficult toilet training or of obvious feeding problems, did not come from broken homes, and apparently were not unduly rejected or punished. Another factor which seems to emerge from the studies is that a dominant characteristic of the family life of schizophrenics is a quality of inappropriateness of thinking and behaving which seems to infiltrate the entire atmosphere (Fleck, Lidz, & Cornelison, 1963; Lidz et al., 1957b, 1957c; Stringer, 1962). Meyers and Goldfarb (1962), however, found that only 28%

of the mothers of 45 children diagnosed as schizophrenic and only 12% of the fathers were themselves manifestly schizophrenic.

## Psychological Evaluation

*Attitude Questionnaires.* One of the most widely used questionnaires in this area of research has been the Shoben (1949) Parent-Child Attitude Survey. The Shoben scale consists of 148 items which measure the dimensions of parental rejection, possessiveness, and domination. From the administration of this attitude survey, Mark (1953) and Freeman and Grayson (1955) reported significant differences in attitudes toward child rearing between mothers of schizophrenics and mothers of normal children. In comparison with the mothers of the control subjects, the mothers of schizophrenic patients (Mark, 1953) were revealed as inconsistent in their methods of control. They described themselves as being, at times, overrestrictive and controlling of behavior, but in some instances lax. They frowned on sex play and tended to keep information regarding sex from their children; they also seemed to frown on friends for their children. Their relationship to their children appeared inconsistent; they described what could be interpreted as excessive devotion and interest in the child's activities while at the same time revealing a notable degree of "cool detachment." Freeman and Grayson (1955) found that in comparison to mothers of students in an undergraduate course, mothers of 50 hospitalized schizophrenics (ages 20 to 35) tended to reveal themselves to be somewhat more possessive, but inherently rejecting of their children, and particularly disturbed about sexual behavior in their children. However, according to these same data, the mothers of schizophrenic

patients did not reveal themselves to be more dominant, dogmatic, or inconsistent in their attitude than the controls. But most important was the fact that item analysis of these data revealed that the attitudes of the mothers of the schizophrenics and of the controls were distinguished on only 14 of the items, and then, in general, there was so much overlap that even on these items the statistical significance was contributed by a small percentage of each group. Freeman, Simmons, and Bergen (1959) included four items from the Shoben scale among a larger sample of questions posed to parents. These items had been derived from a previous study (Freeman & Simmons, 1958) and were included in the second study because they were the only ones in the first study which were found to discriminate between the attitudes of mothers of schizophrenic patients and those of mothers of normals. The items are:

1. Parents should sacrifice everything for their children.
2. A child should feel a deep sense of obligation always to act in accord with the wishes of his parents.
3. Children who are gentlemanly or lady-like are preferable to those who are tomboys or "regular guys."
4. It is better for children to play at home than to visit other children.

Freeman et al. (1959) found no capacity for these items to differentiate the attitudes of the mothers of schizophrenics from those of other individuals with severe functional disorders.

Zuckerman, Oltean, and Monashkin (1958) utilized another attitude scale, the Parental Attitude Research Inventory (PARI, developed by Schaefer and Bell in their work at the Psychology Laboratory at NIMH). The PARI was administered to mothers of schizophrenics, and it was found that only one item distinguished between their attitudes and those of mothers of normal children. The mothers of schizophrenics tended to describe themselves as being stricter than did the mothers of nonschizophrenic children.

The minimal discrimination value of the several attitude scales should be noted. This would seem to reflect either minimal capacity of the scales to make such distinctions or little in the way of measurable differences between the groups. In either case, it is very difficult to evaluate the meaning of these data since the attitudes of the mothers of schizophrenics seemed to be distinguished from the attitudes of the mothers of neurotics on only a few items (the obtained number of differences did not even exceed that expected by chance alone).

*Projective Tests.* Several studies presented Rorschach data on the mothers of schizophrenic patients (Baxter, Becker, & Hooks, 1963; Prout & White, 1950; Winder & Kantor, 1958). In comparison to those of the mothers of normals, the Rorschach protocols of the mothers of the schizophrenic patients were undistinguished as regards the general degree of immaturity (Winder & Kantor, 1958) and the use of defenses which are essentially reality distorting, namely, denial and projection (Baxter et al., 1963).[1] However, Prout and White did find more pure color

without form and less human and animal movement and shading responses in the Rorschach protocols of mothers of schizophrenic boys as compared to the mothers of a comparable group of boys randomly selected from the community. Perr (1958) found that the parents of schizophrenic children gave responses to the Thematic Apperception Test (TAT) little distinguished from those of parents of normal children, and Fisher, Boyd, Walker, and Sheer (1959) found that the TAT and Rorschach protocols of the parents of schizophrenic patients were measurably different from those of the parents of nonpsychiatric (general medical) patients, but they were not distinguishable from the protocols of the parents of neurotic patients. The mothers of the schizophrenics revealed a higher degree of perceptual rigidity, greater incidence of indicators of maladjustment on the Rorschach, and less definitely conceived parental images on the TAT than the mothers of the normals.

*Direct Observation of Interpersonal Behavior.* Attempts have been made to study the interpersonal behavior of families of schizophrenics *in vivo;* some investigators have gone into the home, others have brought the family into a hospital setting and observed the interaction between family members for an hour or so at a time, others have brought

---

[1] The conclusion that the Rorschach protocols of the mothers of schizophrenics were undistinguished from the Rorschach protocols of the mothers of normals (as in the research by Winder & Kantor, 1958, Baxter et al., 1963) is an interpretation of the results made by the present author. In fact, in both of these articles, the authors conclude that there *are* significant differences. However, in the article by Winder and Kantor, the mean rating of the degree of maturity of personality development for the mothers of the schizophrenics was 2.89, for the mothers of the normals, 2.43. In the article by Baxter et al., the means of the ratings of the degree of utilization of psychologically immature defenses on the Rorschach by the parents of poor premorbid schizophrenics, good premorbid schizophrenics, and neurotics are, respectively, 19.43, 19.62, and 19.49. Though in both of these investigations valid statistical significance was demonstrated between the obtained means, the actual means, in both researches, are so similar to each other that the interpretation of *psychologically* significant differences between groups on the basis of the obtained *statistically* significant differences seemed a highly doubtful conclusion.

the family into a laboratory setting (National Institute of Mental Health) where the family lives under actual but known conditions for months at a time.

In the study of the interpersonal relationships in the actual home setting, Behrens and Goldfarb (1958) observed that the personality of the mother seemed to set the tone of the family milieu and that there seemed to be a direct relationship between the degree of pathology that could be seen in the family setting and the degree of psychopathology demonstrated by the child. The homes they observed appeared physically deteriorated and crowded. There was a basic isolation between the mother and father, and the fathers were basically passive. Confusion and disorganization characterized the family atmosphere, with the family demonstrating inadequate mechanisms to handle emotional flareups. The intensive observation of one mother-child interaction (Karon & Rosberg, 1958) yielded the observation that the mother was unempathic. She blocked verbalizations of emotions and tended to live vicariously through the child, but her relationship to the child appeared to involve a basic, though unconscious, hostility and rejection. The mother was an obsessive-compulsive personality, dominated the home, and was unable to accept herself as a woman. The intensive observation of 51 families (Donnelly, 1960) tends to confirm this finding. Observing the mother-child interaction in the home, utilizing the Fels Parent Behavior Scales, Donnelly found that mothers treated a psychotic child differently than their other nonpsychotic children. To the psychotic child, the mother was generally less warm, less accepting, less empathic, more punitive, more controlling, and more overprotective. The father was passive, but more rational than the mother in relation to the child. Psychotic children

tended to come from homes characterized as less well adjusted, full of discord, and low in sociability. However, in comparing the family interaction of schizophrenic patients with those of normal controls, both Perr (1958) and Meyers and Goldfarb (1961) found little that could stand as a valid measure of distinction between the two groups of families. Perr found that the parents of schizophrenics tend to show more self-deception and to describe themselves as being more hostile. Meyers and Goldfarb found that the mothers of schizophrenic children appeared less capable of formulating a consistent definition of the world for the child.

A method of directly assessing the interpersonal behavior of husband and wife was introduced by Strodtbeck (1951). He posed questions to each parent individually, then he brought them together and had them discuss those points where their attitudes differed. Farina and his associates (Bell, Garmezy, Farina, & Rodnick, 1960; Farina, 1960; Farina & Dunham, 1963) utilized this method to study the families of schizophrenic patients. The questionnaire they used was the PARI. They found that they could distinguish the interpersonal behavior of schizophrenics otherwise described as having good or poor premorbid adjustment. In these studies, mother dominance was discerned in the families of the poor premorbid group only, with interpersonal conflict greatest in that group. In comparing the family interaction of the schizophrenic patient with those of normal controls, Bell et al. (1960) found that in the family constellation of normals, authority tended to be shared by both parents, and parental conflict was at a minimum, although even here there was a trend towards maternal dominance.

Bishop (1951) reported a method of studying the mother-child interaction under live, yet controlled, conditions. The mother and child were brought into a play room where the interpersonal behavior was observed directly. In 1954, Bowen introduced the principle of this technique to the study of families of schizophrenics. Families were brought into what came to be known as the Family Study Section of NIMH (National Institute of Mental Health), and there they were observed living under actual but known conditions for long periods of time (6 months–2 years). Observations based on families living under these conditions revealed that the mothers of schizophrenics showed extremely domineering, smothering, close relationships with the child (Dworin & Wyant, 1957), with the mothers utilizing threat of deprivation to control the child. Bowen, Dysinger, and Basamanie (1959) observed the presence of marked emotional distance and intense conflict between the parents. The fathers were emotionally immature and unable to define their role in the family and unable to make decisions; the mothers were usually the dominant ones, affecting a close relationship with the child to the exclusion of the father. Brodey (1959) found that the behavior of the families of schizophrenics was characterized by a selective utilization of reality, particularly the use of externalization, and that the interpersonal relationships were highly narcissistic.

*Perception of Parental Behavior by Patients.* Several studies have indicated that schizophrenics tend to have experienced their mother as having been rejecting (Bolles, Metzger, & Pitts, 1941; Lane & Singer, 1959; Singer, 1954), and dominant, demanding, and overprotective (Garmezy, Clarke, & Stockner, 1961; Heilbrun, 1960; Kohn & Clausen, 1956; McKeown, 1950; Reichard & Tillman, 1950; Schofield & Balian, 1959). However, when one compares the perception of their mothers by normals (Garmezy et al., 1961; Heilbrun, 1960; Lane & Singer, 1959; Singer, 1954) the uniqueness of these attitudes toward the mothers of schizophrenics disappears. Recollections of dominance and overprotectiveness are common for both schizophrenics and normals. Although Heilbrun, Garmezy et al., and Bolles et al. report data which have shown that there is a greater incidence of a feeling of having been rejected on the part of a group of psychiatric patients when compared to medical-surgical controls, the actual incidence of this even in the psychiatric group was only 15% as compared to 1% in the controls. Moreover, Singer and Lane and Singer found that perception of parental relationships during childhood was more a function of the subjects' socioeconomic level than was psychopathology, paralleling a finding by Opler (1957) that familial patterns (parental dominance and attitudes) are a function of cultural factors (Italian versus Irish origin) rather than of psychopathology.

## NEUROSIS

As compared to the research in the area of schizophrenia, investigations of the dynamics of the family life of neurotics are few and generally restricted to data gleaned from case histories. From these studies it appears that the neurotic behavior of the child is a direct function of the neurotic behavior of the mother (e.g., Fisher & Mendell, 1956; Ingham, 1949; Sperling, 1949, 1951; Zimmerman, 1930). Neurotic behavior in children has been seen to have been related to maternal overprotection (Holloway, 1931; Jacobsen, 1947; Zimmerman, 1930), maternal domination (Mueller, 1945), maternal rejection (Ingham, 1949; Newell, 1934,

1936; Silberpfennig, 1941), separation from the mother during the first 3 years of life (Bowlby, 1940; Ribble, 1941), and oral deprivation (Childers & Hamil, 1932). Neurotic involvement with the mother, where the mother needs the child for the satisfaction of her own needs and discourages the development of emotional separation between the child and herself, has been associated with the development in the child of psychosomatic disorders (Miller & Baruch, 1950; Sperling, 1949) and school phobia (e.g., Davidson, 1961; Eisenberg, 1958; Estes, Haylett, & Johnson, 1956; Goldberg, 1953; Johnson, Falstein, & Suzurek, 1941; Suttenfield, 1954; Talbot, 1957; van Houten, 1948; Waldfogel, Hahn, & Gardner, 1954; Wilson, 1955).

Neurosis in children has also been associated with such factors in the home as poverty (Brown & Moore, 1944; Holloway, 1931) and broken homes (Ingham, 1949; Madow & Hardy, 1947; Wallace, 1935). Silverman (1935), however, found that 75% of the children from broken homes were essentially "normal"; 16% were described as conduct disorders, and only 9% were classifiable as personality problems.

Of the studies that did not use the case history method of data collection, McKeown (1950) found that neurotic children perceive their mothers as demanding, antagonistic, and setting inordinately high standards for them to meet. Stein (1944) found that neurotics tended to perceive themselves as having been rejected, particularly as compared to the perception of their family life held by normals (Bolles et al., 1941). Although Kundert (1947) found that whether justified by experience or not (e.g., separation due to hospitalization of mother or child), emotionally disturbed children, in general, fear being deserted by their mothers and cling to them compulsively.

The Rorschach protocols of mothers of neurotics reveal that they tend to utilize psychological mechanisms which abbrogate reality, for example, denial and projection (Baxter et al., 1963).

## BEHAVIOR DISORDER

The research on the family background of individuals whose personality problems take the form of antisocial behavior is scanty. Shaw and McKay (1932) found no differences in the incidence of broken homes from cases referred to Cook County Juvenile Court (36%) as compared to a random sample of children in the Chicago public school system (42%). Behavior disorders in children have been seen to have been related to neurotic behavior in their parents (Field, 1940; Huschka, 1941), primarily involving maternal rejection, overt and covert. In line with a social learning hypothesis, another interesting finding is that a correlation has been found between antisocial behavior in children and the children's perception of parents' antisocial behavior (Bender, 1937; K. Friedlander, 1945; Williams, 1932).

## DISCUSSION

Let us now summarize what conclusions can be drawn from these data which illuminate the role of the family in the development of psychopathology. As regards the families of schizophrenics, from an overview of the research which has investigated the pattern of parent-child interaction of this pathological group considered without reference to any other pathological or control group, several factors emerge which seem to characterize this group, regardless of the method of data collection, that is, whether by case history, interview, psychological test, or direct observation. Families of schizophrenics seem to be characterized by mothers who are dominant, fathers who are passive, and considerable family disharmony. The mother is overprotective, overpossessive, and overcontrolling, yet basically, albeit unconsciously, rejecting. These mothers frown on sex, are inconsistent in their methods of discipline, and introduce modes of thinking, feeling, and behaving which are not reality oriented. In light of the fact that these patterns emerge as a function of almost all methods of data collection, these results seem very impressive. Had our review of these data stopped here, we would have had apparent verification of the thesis that certain kinds of mother-child relationships and family atmospheres indeed account for the development of schizophrenia in the offspring. However, when each of these parental characteristics is compared with those which emerge from the analysis of the family situation of the normal (apparently nonpsychiatrically-involved) individual, each characteristic that is found to be typical of the families of schizophrenics is found to exist in the families of the controls as well. Furthermore, research which has attempted to make direct comparisons between the families of children in different categories of psychopathology (e.g., Baxter et al., 1963; Fisher et al., 1959; Frazee, 1953; Freeman et al., 1959; D. Friedlander, 1945; Inlow, 1933; McKeown, 1950; Oltman et al., 1952; Pollack & Malzberg, 1940; Pollack, Malzberg, & Fuller, 1936) reveals no significant or consistent differences in the psychological structure of the families.

The results are the same with regard to the families of the neurotics as well. At first glance, it appears that the mother's neurotic involvement with the child is causally associated with the neurotic behavior of the child. However, the

essential characteristics of this involvement—maternal overprotectiveness, maternal domination, maternal rejection, deprivation and frustration, and the mothers fostering an almost symbiotic relationship between themselves and their children—are basically the same as those found in the families of schizophrenics and of children with behavior disorders. Moreover, in many respects, it would be hard, on blind analysis, to distinguish the family which produced an emotionally disturbed child from that which produced the so-called normal or well-adjusted child.

It seems apparent that the major conclusion that can be drawn from these data is that there is no such thing as a schizophrenogenic or a neurotogenic mother or family. At least these data do not permit of the description of a particular constellation of psychological events within the home and, in particular, between mother and child that can be isolated as a unique factor in the development of one or the other kind of personality disorder. If one is looking for *the* factor to account for the development of neurosis or schizophrenia, that one factor does not appear to exist as a clear cut finding in the research.

It is incumbent upon us to wonder why the research literature does not permit support of a hypothesis regarding parental influence on the psychological development of children in the manner we hypothesized. One of the major problems with which we must contend is that human behavior is a very complicated event, determined by many factors, and not clearly understood out of the context in which it occurs, and, in this regard, not everyone reacts in a like manner to similar life experiences. For example, strict discipline is reacted to differently when this occurs in a "warm" or "cold" home atmosphere (Sears, 1961); maternal rejection is reacted to differently where the father is accepting and warm (Mc-Cord et al., 1961) as well as where the father can be a buffer between the child and the overprotective mother (Witmer, 1933). Emphasizing the multivariate aspect of the determinants of behavior, one notes that Madow and Hardy (1947) reported that of the soldiers who broke down with neurotic reactions there was a high incidence of those coming from broken homes. Amongst those soldiers who did not break down, the incidence of coming from a broken home was 11–15%; the incidence of broken homes in the history of soldiers who did break down was 36%. Statistically, there is a significant difference between these percentages; however, even the 36% datum leaves 64% of the soldiers who broke down *not* coming from a broken home. Huschka (1941) reported that the incidence of neurotic mothers of problem children is high (42%); however, this leaves 58% of the group *not* accounted for by this factor. Brown and Moore (1944) commented that the incidence of excessive poverty, drunkenness, and family conflict in soldiers who broke down was significant, but this accounted for only 20% of the cases. Although between 30% (Canavan & Clark, 1923; Lampron, 1933) and 40% (Huschka, 1941; Lidz & Lidz, 1949) of the children born to mothers who are psychotic become psychotic themselves, these percentages do not account for the majority of children born to these mothers. Indeed, Fanning et al. (1938) found that 43% of the children born to mothers who were psychotic were observed to be making an adequate social and personal adjustment; only 11% of that sample of children was not. It should be noted that only half of the samples of mothers studied by Despert (1938) and Clardy (1951) resembled the traditional pattern of what has come to be known as

the "schizophrenogenic mother." Finally, Beres and Obers (1950) observed that there is a wide reaction to an experience of emotional deprivation (in this instance, institutionalization) ranging from the development of a schizoid personality to schizophrenia itself, and including neurotic reactions and character disorders. Indeed, 25% of their sample of children who were brought up in institutions appeared to be making a satisfactory adjustment in spite of this ostensibly devastating experience.

Over and above the complexity of human behavior contributing to the inconclusiveness of the results, one must look at the way in which these data have been collected. It might be that the criterion measure, that is, the diagnosis, did not provide the investigator with meaningful groupings of subjects so that consistent findings *could* be obtained. As regards the method of data collection: Case histories may be inadequate in providing basic data; Information can be gross and/or inaccurate; The informant has to rely on memory, and this memory might be consciously or unconsciously selective, or the informant might not be aware of the import of or feel shame in giving certain data. Yet, despite the many limitations of this mode of data collection, some of the primary research in schizophrenia has utilized this method, and almost all of the data with respect to the family life of neurotics and behavior disorders were gathered in this way. These same limitations apply to data that are gathered when the informant is asked to fill out an attitude questionnaire. Surely the data on parents elicited from the children are susceptible to distortion even when given by normal children, no less those who already tend to consciously or unconsciously confound their perception of reality with fantasy. The psychiatric interview is a much more sensitive procedure than the case history or attitude questionnaire. Either structured or open-ended interviews enable the interviewer to follow up leads and possibly detect where information is being omitted for one reason or another. The problem here, however, is that there is always the possibility that distorted or inaccurate data are gathered by the interviewer, either through the kinds of questions asked, or the perception of the answer or of the individual being interviewed. For example, it is interesting to note that although the majority of psychiatric interviewers experienced the mothers of schizophrenics as matching the model of the schizophrenogenic mother —the dominant, overprotective, but basically rejecting mother who induces inappropriateness of thinking in her children—the psychological test evaluation of mothers of schizophrenics failed to confirm these findings. One explanation for this is that the interviewer, already acquainted with the literature regarding the mother of schizophrenics, anticipating to experience the mothers in terms of the ideas about schizophrenogenic mothers, did, indeed, experience them in that way, whereas a more objective evaluation of the patterns of thinking and feeling of these mothers did not confirm the more subjective impression.

In order to try and avoid the pitfalls inherent in data gleaned through case history or interview, investigators hypothesized that direct observation of the mother-child interaction might yield more valid information. Unfortunately, here, too, limitations inherent in the mode of data collection become apparent. Observations of the mother-child interaction in the home or in an observation room in a hospital or clinic are generally restricted to a limited time segment, for example, 1 hour once a week. This factor, in and of itself, limits the observations to a fairly restricted aspect of the spectrum of the interaction between mother and child. Here, too, the behavior to which the observer is exposed may be influenced by the conscious or unconscious attitudes and motives of the parent being observed. It is not too difficult for the parent to present only that behavior which, for one reason or another, she feels it safe to display and to control the presence of other behaviors. Direct observation of the family for extensive periods of time, that is, months, and under controlled but as natural as possible living conditions (as in the Family Study Section of NIMH) avoids the restrictiveness and overcomes, to one degree or another, the artificiality of the relatively brief observation. However, the family is still aware that they are being observed and may, to one degree or another, be unable to act "natural." Moreover, unless the observations are independently made by several people whose reliability of observation has already been established, they may also be influenced by the Zeitgeist and perceive the family as being "schizophrenogenic" whether it is or not, mutually reinforcing each other's expectations. A more pressing consideration in evaluating the validity of these kinds of observations is the fact that the interaction, no matter how natural, takes place after the development of the psychopathology. It is quite possible that the aspects of the interpersonal relationship within the family, or between the mother and child in particular, that eventuated in the development of the patterns of thinking, feeling, and behaving characteristic of the schizophrenic or the neurotic, are no longer present; they may have occurred at a time of the child's life long since past and/or under conditions of intimacy not even accessible to the observer. There is no reason to assume that the etiological factors are still functioning or that they will be available to the trained observer even over the course of 6 months. Of course, it might be that whatever differentiates the psychological existence of the schizophrenic from that of the neurotic or of the normal might be so subtle that it is imperceptible to the participants themselves or even the trained observer and, hence, escape notice. Here, one is reminded of Freud's comment that "the years of childhood of those who are later neurotic need not necessarily differ from those who are later normal except in intensity and distinctness [Freud, 1938 (Orig. publ. 1910), p. 583]."

Theorizing about the etiology of psychopathology has characteristically been of the either/or variety. Nineteenth century scientists sought explanations for neurotic and psychotic disorders in the heredity background of their patients, working from the assumption that many directly inherited the neurotic or psychotic "illness." On the other hand, the scientist of the twentieth century has sought explanations for psychopathology in the experiential aspect of man's life, in his emotional and interpersonal learning. As with most events in our life, the truth is probably somewhere in between these two positions. Indeed, in spite of the emphasis that is placed on the role of experience in the development of personality in psychoanalysis, Freud did not think, at least as regards the etiology of psychopathology, in such categorically black and white terms. He was able to bridge the gap between the nature-nurture extremes:

We divide the causes of neurotic disease into those which the individual himself brings with him into life, and those which life bring to him—that is to say, into con-

stitutional and accidental. It is the interaction of these that as a rule first gives rise to illness [Freud, 1950b (Orig. publ. 1913), p. 122].

Let us bear clearly in mind that every human being has acquired, by the combined operation of inherent disposition and of external influences of childhood, a special individuality in the exercise of his capacity to love—that is, in the conditions which he sets up for loving, in the impulses he gratifies by it, and in the aims he sets out to achieve in it. . . . We will here provide against misconceptions and reproaches to the effect that we have denied the importance of the inborn (constitutional) factor because we have emphasized the importance of infantile impressions. Such an accusation arises out of the narrowness with which mankind looks for causes, inasmuch as one single causal factor satisfies him, in spite of the many commonly underlying the face of reality. Psycho-Analysis has said much about the "accidental" component in aetiology and little about the constitutional, but only because it could throw new light upon the former, whereas of the latter it knows no more so far than is already known. We deprecate the assumption of an essential opposition between the two series of aetiological factors; we presume rather a perpetual interchange of both in producing the results observed [Freud, 1950a (Orig. publ. 1912), p. 312].

Other psychoanalysts have followed Freud in the presumption of an inherent, predetermined characteristic functioning of the nervous system of the human organism which determines reactions to stimuli pre- and postnatally (e.g., Greenacre, 1941).

Augmenting the clinical observations of psychoanalysis, one must juxtapose the experimental evidence in psychology which indicates that (a) individuals reflect characteristic patterns of autonomic activity which are stable and which are typical of them as individuals (Grossman & Greenberg, 1957; Lacey,

1950; Richmond & Lustman, 1955; Wenger, 1941), (b) the characteristic patterns of neural activity are identifiable prenatally and are consistent with the patterns of activity observable postnatally (Richards & Newbery, 1938), (c) these characteristic patterns of autonomic activity consistently emerge in a factor of lability and balance in which specific personality factors are consistently highly loaded (Darling, 1940; Eysenck, 1956; Eysenck & Prell, 1951; Theron, 1948; van der Merwe, 1948; van der Merwe & Theron, 1947), (d) there is greater similarity of autonomic reactivity between identical twins than fraternal twins or ordinary siblings (Eysenck, 1956; Eysenck & Prell, 1951; Jost & Sontag, 1944), and (e) there is a selective influence on personality functioning due to the sex of the individual per se. For example, generally boys outnumber girls 2–1 in being referred for psychological help (Bender, 1937; Wile & Jones, 1937). Sears (1961) found a significant difference in the basic mode of self-reported expression of aggression between boys and girls: Girls appeared higher in socially acceptable forms of aggression and high in anxiety regarding hostility, while boys were significantly higher in aggression that was directed against social control. Sears also found that the more punitive the mother is, the more dependent the son becomes but the less dependent the daughter becomes. Newell (1936) found that maternal rejection affected males more than females: Marked increase in aggressive behavior was noted in the boys who experienced rejection, not so with the females. Baruch & Wilcox (1944) noted that interparental tensions lead to different reactions in boys as compared to girls; in boys, it led to ascendance-submission problems, in girls to an experience of lack of affection.

We end this survey by concluding that we have not been able to find any unique factors in the family of the schizophrenic which distinguishes it from the family of the neurotic or from the family of controls, who are ostensibly free from evidence of patterns of gross psychopathology. In short, we end by stating that the assumption that the family is the factor in the development of personality has not been validated. It is interesting to note that Orlansky (1949), in his review of the literature exploring the relationship between certain childhood experiences, for example, feeding, toilet training, thumbsucking, the degree of tactile stimulation by the mother, etc., upon the development of personality characteristics, was also forced to conclude that the data failed to confirm an invariant relationship between the experience in infancy and the resultant personality. Of course, it might well be that the reality of the family is not the important dimension in determining the child's reactions; rather, it might be the perception of the family members, and this might often have little or no relation to the people as they really are. This would mean, then, that in many instances, the important variables in the development of psychopathology might be factors which the child brings to the family, the functioning of the nervous and metabolic systems and the cognitive capacity to integrate stimuli into meaningful perceptual and conceptual schema. Indeed, we are left to wonder, as do the psychoanalysts, whether the proclivity towards fantasy distortion of reality might not be the factor in the development of psychopathology, and this proclivity might not be always determined by the child's experiences per se.

Obviously, questions regarding the etiology of patterns of personality behavior which are regarded as pathological, unadaptive, or unadjusted cannot be met with simple answers. Apparently, the factors which play a part in the development of behavior in humans are so complex that it would appear that they almost defy being investigated scientifically and defy one's attempts to draw meaningful generalizations from the exploration which has already been done. It is, of course, conceivable that human behavior is so complex that it cannot be reduced to simple terms or be expected to yield unalterable patterns of occurrences. It might also be that what produces psychopathological reactions in one individual does not in another. All this would be understandable in light of the complexity that is the human being, neurologically as well as socially, but it is unfortunate as regards research endeavors. In 1926, Freud wrote:

Anxiety is the reaction to danger. One cannot, after all, help suspecting that the reason why the affect of anxiety occupies a unique position in the economy of the mind has something to do with the essential nature of danger. Yet dangers are the common lot of humanity; they are the same for everyone. What we need and cannot lay our fingers on is some factor which will explain why some people are able to subject the affect of anxiety, in spite of its peculiar quality, to the normal workings of the mind, or which decides who is doomed to come to grief over the task [Freud, 1936, p. 64].

We end this review of forty years of research without being able to feel that we are any closer to an answer than was Freud.

## REFERENCES

Ayer, Mary E., & Bernreuter, R. G. A study of the relationship between discipline and personality traits in little children. *Journal of Genetic Psychology*, 1937, **50**, 165–170.

Barry, H. Orphanhood as a factor in psychoses. *Journal of Abnormal and Social Psychology*, 1936, **30**, 431–438.

Barry, H., & Bousfield, W. A. Incidence of orphanhood among fifteen hundred psychotic patients. *Journal of Genetic Psychology*, 1937, **50**, 198–202.

Bartmeier, L. H. Deprivations during infancy and their effects upon personality development. *American Journal of Mental Deficiency*, 1952, **56**, 708–711.

Baruch, Dorothy W., & Wilcox, J. Annie. A study of sex differences in preschool children's adjustment coexistent with inter-parental tensions. *Journal of Genetic Psychology*, 1944, **64**, 281–303.

Baxter, J. C., Becker, J., & Hooks, W. Defensive style in the families of schizophrenics and controls. *Journal of Abnormal and Social Psychology*, 1963, **66**, 512–518.

Behrens, Marjorie L., & Goldfarb, W. A study of patterns of interaction of families of schizophrenic children in residential treatment. *American Journal of Orthopsychiatry*, 1958, **28**, 300–312.

Bell, R. Q., Garmezy, N., Farina, A., & Rodnick, E. H. Direct study of parent-child interaction. *American Journal of Orthopsychiatry*, 1960, **30**, 445–452.

Bender, Lauretta. Reactive psychosis in response to mental disease in the family. *Journal of Nervous and Mental Disease*, 1936, **83**, 143–289.

Bender, Lauretta. Behavior problems in the children of psychotic and criminal parents. *Genetic Psychology Monographs*, 1937, **19**, 229–339.

Beres, D., & Obers, S. J. The effects of extreme deprivation in infancy on psychic structure in adolescence: A study in ego development. *Psychoanalytic Study of the Child*, 1950, **5**, 212–235.

Bishop, Barbara M. Mother-child interaction and the social behavior of children. *Psychological Monographs*, 1951, **65**(11, Whole No. 328).

BOLLES, MARJORIE M., METZGER, HARRIET F., & PITTS, MARJORIE W. Early home background and personal adjustment. *American Journal of Orthopsychiatry*, 1941, 11, 530–534.

BOWEN, M., DYSINGER, R. H., & BASAMANIE, BETTY. The role of the father in families with a schizophrenic patient. *American Journal of Psychiatry*, 1959, 115, 1017–1020.

BOWLBY, J. The influence of early environment in the development of neurosis and neurotic character. *International Journal of Psychoanalysis*, 1940, 21, 154–178.

BRODBECK, A. J., & IRWIN, O. C. The speech behavior of infants without families. *Child Development*, 1946, 17, 145–156.

BRODEY, W. M. Some family operations in schizophrenia. *Archives of General Psychiatry*, 1959, 1, 379–402.

BROWN, W. T., & MOORE, M. Soldiers who break down—family background and past history. *Military Surgeon*, 1944, 94, 160–163.

CANAVAN, MYRTELLE M., & CLARK, ROSAMOND. The mental health of 463 children from dementia-praecox stock. *Mental Hygiene*, 1923, 7, 137–148.

CHILDERS, A. T., & HAMIL, B. M. Emotional problems in children as related to the duration of breast feeding in infancy. *American Journal of Orthopsychiatry*, 1932, 2, 134–142.

CLARDY, E. R. A study of the development and course of schizophrenic children. *Psychiatric Quarterly*, 1951, 25, 81–90.

DARLING, R. P. Automatic action in relation to personality traits of children. *Journal of Abnormal and Social Psychology*, 1940, 35, 246–260.

DAVIDSON, SUSANNAH. School phobia as a manifestation of family disturbance: Its structure and treatment. *Journal of Child Psychology and Psychiatry*, 1961, 1, 270-287.

DAVIS, K. Extreme social isolation of a child. *American Journal of Sociology*, 1940, 45, 554–565.

DESPERT, LOUISE J. Schizophrenia in children. *Psychiatric Quarterly*, 1938, 12, 366–371.

DESPERT, LOUISE J. Some considerations relating to the genesis of autistic behavior in children. *American Journal of Orthopsychiatry*, 1951, 21, 335–350.

DONNELLY, ELLEN M. The quantitative analysis of parent behavior toward psychotic children and their siblings. *Genetic Psychology Monographs*, 1960, 62, 331–376.

DWORIN, J., & WYANT, O. Authoritarian patterns in mothers of schizophrenics. *Journal of Clinical Psychology*, 1957, 13, 332–338.

EISENBERG, L. School phobia: A study in the communication of anxiety. *American Journal of Psychiatry*, 1958, 114, 712–718.

ESTES, H. R., HYLETT, CLARICE H., & JOHNSON, ADELAIDE M. Separation anxiety. *American Journal of Psychotherapy*, 1956, 10, 682–695.

EYSENCK, H. J. The inheritance of extraversion-introversion. *Acta Psychologica*, 1956, 12, 95–110.

EYSENCK, H. J., & PRELL, D. B. The inheritance of neuroticism: An experimental study. *Journal of Mental Science*, 1951, 97, 441–465.

FANNING, ANEITA, LEHR, SARA, SHERWIN, ROBERTA, & WILSON, MARJORIE. The mental health of children of psychotic mothers. *Smith College Studies in Social Work*, 1938, 8, 291–343.

FARINA, A. Patterns of role dominance and conflict in parents of schizophrenic patients. *Journal of Abnormal and Social Psychology*, 1960, 61, 31–38.

FARINA, A., & DUNHAM, R. M. Measurement of family relationships and their effects. *Archives of General Psychiatry*, 1963, 9, 64–73.

FIELD, MINNA A. Maternal attitudes found in twenty-five cases of children with primary behavior disorders. *American Journal of Orthopsychiatry*, 1940, 10, 293–311.

FISHER, S., BOYD, INA, WALKER, D., & SHEER, DIANNE. Parents of schizophrenics, neurotics, and normals. *Archives of General Psychiatry*, 1959, 1, 149–166.

FISHER, S., & MENDELL, D. The communication of neurotic patterns over two and three generations. *Psychiatry*, 1956, 19, 41–46.

FLECK, S., LIDZ, T., & CORNELISON, ALICE. Comparison of parent-child relationships of male and female schizophrenic patients. *Archives of General Psychiatry*, 1963, 8, 1–7.

FRAZEE, HELEN E. Children who later became schizophrenic. *Smith College Studies in Social Work*, 1953, 23, 125–149.

FREEMAN, R. V., & GRAYSON, H. M. Maternal attitudes in schizophrenia. *Journal of Abnormal and Social Psychology*, 1955, 50, 45–52.

FREEMAN, H. E., & SIMMONS, O. G. Mental patients in the community: Family settings and performance levels. *American Sociological Review*, 1958, 23, 147–154.

FREEMAN, H. E., SIMMONS, O. G., & BERGEN, B. J. Possessiveness as a characteristic of mothers of schizophrenics. *Journal of Abnormal and Social Psychology*, 1959, 58, 271–273.

FREUD, S. *Inhibitions, symptoms, and anxiety.* London: Hogarth Press, 1936.

FREUD, S. Three contributions to the theory of sex. In A. A. Brill (Ed.), *The basic writings of Sigmund Freud.* (Orig. Publ. 1910) New York: Modern Library, 1938. P. 583.

FREUD, S. The dynamics of the transference. (Orig. publ. 1912) In, *Collected papers.* Vol. 2. London: Hogarth Press, 1950. Pp. 312–322. (a)

FREUD, S. The predisposition to obsessional neurosis. (Orig. publ. 1913) In, *Collected papers.* Vol. 2, London: Hogarth Press, 1950. Pp. 122–132. (b)

FRIEDLANDER, D. Personality development of twenty-seven children who later became psychotic. *Journal of Abnormal and Social Psychology*, 1945, 40, 330–335.

FRIEDLANDER, KATE. Formation of the antisocial character. *Psychoanalytic Study of the Child*, 1945, 1, 189–203.

GARMEZY, N. CLARKE, A. R., & STOCKNER, CAROL. Child rearing attitudes of mothers and fathers as reported by schizophrenic and normal patients. *Journal of Abnormal and Social Psychology*, 1961, 63, 176–182.

GERARD, D. L., & SIEGAL, L. The family background of schizophrenia. *Psychiatric Quarterly*, 1950, 24, 47–73.

GOLDBERG, THELMA B. Factors in the development of school phobia. *Smith College Studies in Social Work*, 1953, 23, 227–248.

GOLDFARB, W. The effects of early institutional care on adolescent personality (graphic Rorschach data). *Child Development*, 1943, 14, 213–223 (a)

GOLDFARB, W. Infant rearing and problem behavior. *American Journal of Orthopsychiatry*, 1943, 13, 249–266. (b)

GOLDFARB, W. The effects of early institutional care on adolescent personality. *Journal of Experimental Education*, 1943, 12, 106–129. (c)

GOLDFARB, W. Psychological depriviation in infancy. *American Journal of Psychiatry*, 1945, 102, 19–33. (a)

GOLDFARB, W. Psychological privation in infancy and subsequent adjustment. *American Journal of Orthopsychiatry*, 1945, 15, 247–255. (b)

GREENACRE, PHYLLIS. The predisposition to anxiety. *Psychoanalytic Quarterly*, 1941, 10, 66–94.

GROSSMAN, H. J., & GREENBERG, N. H. Psychosomatic differentiation in infancy. I. Autonomic activity in the newborn. *Psychosomatic Medicine*, 1957, 19, 293–306.

GUERTIN, W. H. Are differences in schizophrenic symptoms related to the mother's avowed attitudes toward child rearing? *Journal of Abnormal and Social Psychology*, 1961, 63, 440–442.

HAJDU-GRIMES, LILLY. Contributions to the etiology of schizophrenia. *Psychoanalytic Review*, 1940, 27, 421–438.

HATTWICK, BERTA W. Interrelations between the preschool child's behavior and certain factors in the home. *Child Development*, 1936, 7, 200–226.

HATTWICK, BERTA W., & STOWELL, MARGARET. The relation of parental overattentiveness to children's work habits and social adjustment in kindergarten and the first six grades of school. *Journal of Educational Research*, 1936, 30, 169–176.

HEILBRUN, A. B. Perception of maternal childbearing attitudes in schizophrenics. *Journal of Consulting Psychology*, 1960, 24, 169–173.

HOLLOWAY, EDITH. A study of fifty-eight problem children, with emphasis upon the home situation as a causative factor in producing conflict. *Smith College Studies in Social Work*, 1931, 1, 403.

HUSCHKA, MABEL. Psychopathological disorders in the mother. *Journal of Nervous and Mental Disease*, 1941, 94, 76–83.

INGHAM, H. V. A statistical study of family relationships in psychoneurosis. *American Journal of Psychiatry*, 1949, 106, 91–98.

INLOW, RUBY S. The home as a factor in the development of the psychosis. *Smith College Studies in Social Work*, 1933, 4, 153–154.

JACOBSEN, VIRGINIA. Influential factors in the outcome of treatment of school phobia. *Smith College Studies in Social Work*, 1947, 19, 181–202.

JOHNSON, ADELAIDE M., FALSTEIN, E. I., SZUREK, S. A., & SVENDSEN, MARGARET. School phobia. *American Journal of Orthopsychiatry*, 1941, 11, 702–711.

JOST, H., & SONTAG, L. W. The genetic factor in autonomic nervous system function. *Psychosomatic Medicine*, 1944, 6, 308–310.

KARON, B. P., & ROSBERG, J. Study of the mother-child relationship in a case of paranoid schizophrenia. *American Journal of Psychotherapy*, 1958, 12, 522–533.

KASANIN, J., KNIGHT, ELIZABETH, & SAGE, PRISCILLA. The parent-child relationship in schizophrenia. *Journal of Nervous and Mental Disease*, 1934, 79, 249–263.

KOHN, M. L., & CLAUSEN, J. A. Parental authority behavior and schizophrenia. *American Journal of Orthopsychiatry*, 1956, 26, 297–313.

KUNDERT, ELIZABETH. Fear of desertion by mother. *American Journal of Orthopsychiatry*, 1947, 17, 326–336.

LACEY, J. I. Individual differences in somatic response patterns. *Journal of Comparative and Physiological Psychology*, 1950, 43, 338–350.

LAMPRON, EDNA M. Children of schizophrenic parents. *Mental Hygiene*, 1933, 17, 82–91.

LANE, R. C., & SINGER, J. L. Familial attitudes in paranoid schizophrenics and normals from two socioeconomic classes. *Journal of Abnormal and Social Psychology*, 1959, 59, 328–339.

LEVY, D. M. Maternal overprotection and rejection. *Archives of Neurology and Psychiatry*, 1931, 25, 886–889.

LEVY, D. M. On the problem of delinquency. *American Journal of Orthopsychiatry*, 1932, 2, 197–211.

LEVY, D. M. Primary affect hunger. *American Journal of Psychiatry*, 1937, 94, 643–652.

LEVY, D. M. *Maternal overprotection.* New York: Columbia Univer. Press, 1943.

LIDZ, T., CORNELISON, ALICE R., FLECK, S., & TERRY, DOROTHY. The intrafamilial environment of the schizophrenic patient: I. The father. *Psychiatry*, 1957, 20, 329–342. (a)

LIDZ, T., CORNELISON, ALICE R., FLECK, S., & TERRY, DOROTHY. The intrafamilial environment of the schizophrenic patient: II. Marital schism and marital skew. *American Journal of Psychiatry*, 1957, 114, 241–248. (b)

LIDZ, T., CORNELISON, ALICE R., FLECK, S., & TERRY, DOROTHY. The intrafamilial environment of the schizophrenic patient. *Psychiatry*, 1957, 20, 343–350. (c)

LIDZ, T., CORNELISON, ALICE, TERRY, DOROTHY, & FLECK, S. Intrafamilial environment of the schizophrenic patient: VI. The transmission of irrationality. *Archives of Neurology and Psychiatry*, 1958, 79, 305–316.

LIDZ, RUTH W., & LIDZ, T. The family environment of schizophrenic patients. *American Journal of Psychiatry*, 1949, 106, 332–345.

LIDZ, T., PARKER, NEULAH, & CORNELISON, ALICE. The role of the father in the family environment of the schizophrenic patient. *American Journal of Psychiatry*, 1956, 113, 126–137.

LOWREY, L. G. Personality distortion and early institutional care. *American Journal of Orthopsychiatry*, 1940, 10, 576–585.

MADOW, L., & HARDY, S. E. Incidence and analysis of the broken family in the background of neurosis. *American Journal of Orthopsychiatry*, 1947, 17, 521–528.

MARK, J. C. The attitudes of the mothers of male schizophrenics toward child behavior. *Journal of Abnormal and Social Psychology*, 1953, 48, 185–189.

McCORD, W., McCORD, JOAN, & HOWARD, A. Familial correlates of aggression in nondelinquent male children. *Journal of Abnormal and Social Psychology*, 1961, 62, 79–93.

McKeown, J. E. The behavior of parents of schizophrenic, neurotic, and normal children. *American Journal of Sociology,* 1950, **56,** 175–179.

Meyers, D. I., & Goldfarb, W. Studies of perplexity in mothers of schizophrenic children. *American Journal of Orthopsychiatry,* 1961, **31,** 551–564.

Meyers, D., & Goldfarb, W. Psychiatric appraisals of parents and siblings of schizophrenic children. *American Journal of Psychiatry,* 1962, **118,** 902–908.

Miller, H., & Baruch, D. A study of hostility in allergic children. *American Journal of Orthopsychiatry,* 1950, **20,** 506–519.

Mueller, Dorothy D. Paternal domination: Its influence on child guidance results. *Smith College Studies in Social Work,* 1945, **15,** 184–215.

Newell, H. W. The psycho-dynamics of maternal rejection. *American Journal of Orthopsychiatry,* 1934, **4,** 387–401.

Newell, H. W. A further study of maternal rejection. *American Journal of Orthopsychiatry,* 1936, **6,** 576–589.

Oltman, Jane E., McGarry, J. J., & Friedman, S. Parental deprivation and the "broken home" in dementia praecox and other mental disorders. *American Journal of Psychiatry,* 1952, **108,** 685–694.

Opler, M. K. Schizophrenia and culture. *Scientific American,* 1957, **197,** 103–110.

Orlansky, H. Infant care and personality. *Psychological Bulletin,* 1949, **46,** 1–48.

Pearson, G. H. Some early factors in the formation of personality. *American Journal of Orthopsychiatry,* 1931, **1,** 284–291.

Perr, H. M. Criteria distinguishing parents of schizophrenic and normal children. *Archives of Neurology and Psychiatry,* 1958, **79,** 217–224.

Plank, R. The family constellation of a group of schizophrenic patients. *American Journal of Orthopsychiatry,* 1953, **23,** 817–825.

Pollock, H. M., & Malzberg, B. Hereditary and environmental factors in the causation of manic-depressive psychoses and dementia praecox. *American Journal of Psychiatry,* 1940, **96,** 1227–1244.

Pollock, H. M., Malzberg, B., Fuller, R. G. Hereditary and environmental factors in the causation of dementia praecox and manic-depressive psychoses. *Psychiatric Quarterly,* 1936, **10,** 495–509.

Preston, G. H., & Antin, Rosemary. A study of children of psychotic parents. *American Journal of Orthopsychiatry,* 1932, **2,** 231–241.

Prout, C. T., & White, Mary A. A controlled study of personality relationships in mothers of schizophrenic male patients. *American Journal of Psychiatry,* 1950, **107,** 251–256.

Reichard, Suzanne, & Tillman, C. Patterns of parent-child relationships in schizophrenia. *Psychiatry,* 1950, **13,** 247–257.

Ribble, Margarethe A. Disorganizing factors of infant personality. *American Journal of Psychiatry,* 1941, **98,** 459–463.

Richards, T. W., & Newbery, Helen. Studies in fetal behavior: III. Can performance on test items at six months postnatally be predicted on the basis of fetal activity? *Child Development,* 1938, **9,** 79–86.

Richmond, J. B., & Lustman, S. L. Autonomic function in the neonate: I. Implications for psychosomatic theory. *Psychosomatic Medicine,* 1955, **17,** 269–275.

Schofield, W., & Balian, L. A comparative study of the personal histories of schizophrenic and nonpsychiatric patients. *Journal of Abnormal and Social Psychology,* 1959, **59,** 216–225.

Sears, R. R. Relation of early socialization experiences to aggression in middle childhood. *Journal of Abnormal and Social Psychology,* 1961, **63,** 466–492.

Sears, R. R., Whiting, J. W. M., Nowlis, V., & Sears, Pauline S. Some child-rearing antecedents of aggression and dependency in young children. *Genetic Psychology Monographs,* 1953, **47,** 133–234.

Shaw, C. R., & McKay, H. D. Are broken homes a causative factor in juvenile delinquency? *Social Forces,* 1932, **10,** 514–524.

Shoben, E. J. The assessment of parental attitudes in relation to child adjustment. *Genetic Psychology Monographs,* 1949, **39,** 101–148.

Silberpfenning, Judith. Mother types

encountered in child guidance clinics. *American Journal of Orthopsychiatry*, 1941, 11, 475–484.

SILVERMAN, B. The behavior of children from broken homes. *American Journal of Orthopsychiatry*, 1935, 5, 11–18.

SINGER, J. L. Projected familial attitudes as a function of socioeconomic status and psychopathology. *Journal of Consulting Psychology*, 1954, 18, 99–104.

SPERLING, MELITTA. The role of the mother in psychosomatic disorders in children. *Psychosomatic Medicine*, 1949, 11, 377–385.

SPERLING, MELITTA. The neurotic child and his mother: A psychoanalytic study. *American Journal of Orthopsychiatry*, 1951, 21, 351–362.

SPITZ, R. A. Hospitalism: An inquiry into the genesis of psychiatric conditions in early childhood. *Psychoanalytic Study of the Child*, 1945, 1, 53–74.

STEIN, LUCILLE, H. A study of over-inhibited and unsocialized-aggressive children. *Smith College Studies in Social Work*, 1944, 15, 124–125.

STRINGER, JOYCE R. Case studies of the families of schizophrenics. *Smith College Studies in Social Work*, 1962, 32, 118–148.

STRODTBECK, F. L. Husband-wife interaction over revealed differences. *American Sociological Review*, 1951, 16, 468–473.

SUTTENFIELD, VIRGINIA. School phobia: A study of five cases. *American Journal of Orthopsychiatry*, 1954, 24, 368–380.

TALBOT, MIRA. School Phobia: A workshop: I. Panic in school phobia. *American Journal of Orthopsychiatry*, 1957, 27, 286–295.

THERON, P. A. Peripheral vasomotor reaction as indices of basic emotional tension and lability. *Psychosomatic Medicine*, 1948, 10, 335–346.

TIETZE, TRUDE. A study of mothers of schizophrenic patients. *Psychiatry*, 1949, 12, 55–65.

VAN DER MERWE, A. B. The diagnostic value of peripheral vasomotor reactions in the psychoneuroses. *Psychosomatic Medicine*, 1948, 10, 347–354.

VAN DER MERWE, A. B., & THERON, P. A. A new method of measuring emotional stability. *Journal of General Psychology*, 1947, 37, 109–124.

VAN HOUTEN, JANNY. Mother-child relationships in twelve cases of school phobia. *Smith College Studies in Social Work*, 1948, 18, 161–180.

WAHL, C. W. Some antecedent factors in the family histories of 392 schizophrenics. *American Journal of Psychiatry*, 1954, 110, 668–676.

WAHL, C. W. Some antecedent factors in the family histories of 568 male schizophrenics of the United States Navy. *American Journal of Psychiatry*, 1956, 113, 201–210.

WALDFOGEL, S., HAHN, PAULINE B., & GARDNER, G. E. A study of school phobia in children. *Journal of Nervous and Mental Disease*, 1954, 120, 399.

WALLACE, RAMONA. A study of the relationship between emotional tone of the home and adjustment status in cases referred to a travelling child guidance clinic. *Journal of Juvenile Research*, 1935, 19, 205–220.

WALTERS, JEAN H. A study of the family relationships of schizophrenic patients. *Smith College Studies in Social Work*, 1939, 9, 189–191.

WATSON, G. A. A comparison of the effects of lax versus strict home training. *Journal of Social Psychology*, 1934, 5, 102–105.

WENGER, M. A. The measurement of individual differences in autonomic balance. *Psychosomatic Medicine*, 1941, 3, 427–434.

WILE, I. S., & JONES, ANN B. Ordinal position and the behavior disorders of young children. *Journal of Genetic Psychology*, 1937, 51, 61–93.

WILLIAMS, H. D. Causes of social maladjustment in children. *Psychological Monographs*, 1932, 43(1, Whole No. 194).

WILSON, MARGARET J. Grandmother, mother, and daughter in cases of school phobia. *Smith College Studies in Social Work*, 1955, 25, 56–57.

WINDER, C. L., & KANTOR, R. E. Rorschach maturity scores of the mothers of schizophrenics. *Journal of Consulting Psychology*, 1958, 22, 438–440.

WITMER, HELEN L. Parental behavior as

an index to the probable outcome of treatment in a child guidance clinic. *American Journal of Orthopsychiatry,* 1933, **3**, 431–444.

ZIMMERMAN, ANNA C. Parental adjustments and attitudes in relation to the problems of five- and six-year-old children. *Smith College Studies in Social Work,* 1930, **1**, 406–407.

ZUCKERMAN, M., OLTEAN, MARY, & MONASHKIN, I. The parental attitudes of mothers of schizophrenics. *Journal of Consulting Psychology,* 1958, **22**, 307–310.

Paul E. Meehl

## Schizotaxia, Schizotypy, Schizophrenia

*In this paper by Meehl, a case is made for the clearer recognition of the importance of both physiological and environmental factors in the development of schizophrenia. It was written as an address to psychologists who have largely been committed to understanding schizophrenia as caused by the environment. Meehl's point of view is that experience can play a key causal role in schizophrenia only when the appropriate organic state prevails.*

*The importance of organic or constitutional factors is suggested to Meehl by the findings of studies done with identical twins. In such pairs the genetic makeup is quite similar. Therefore, if one member of such a twin pair were to become schizophrenic, and constitutional factors are important determiners of the disorder, the other should also succumb to the illness. Such a finding would be particularly impressive if the twins involved were reared apart, since one could argue that identical twins reared together share a similar environment and schizophrenia might be caused by that factor instead of by the constitution. Understandably, cases of identical twins reared apart in which at least one member becomes schizophrenic are rare indeed, so that this kind of crucial study really has not been done. However, many twin studies have been reported, in some of which the concordance rates of schizophrenia between members of the pair were very high, and in all of which such rates are far above those for nonidentical twins and ordinary siblings.*

*Omitted in the editing of this paper are Meehl's speculations on nervous-system states that might account for the traits typifying schizophrenia. The reader who is interested in these should consult the original paper.*

In the course of the last decade, while spending several thousand hours in the practice of intensive psychotherapy, I have treated—sometimes unknowingly except in retrospect—a considerable number of schizoid and schizophrenic patients. Like all clinicians, I have formed some theoretical opinions as a result of these experiences. While I have not until recently begun

*Abridged from* American Psychologist, *17(1962), 827–838 with the permission of the American Psychological Association and Dr. Meehl. Copyright 1962 by the American Psychological Association.*

any systematic research efforts on this baffling disorder, I felt that to share with you some of my thoughts, based though they are upon clinical impressions in the context of selected research by others, might be an acceptable use of this occasion.

Let me begin by putting a question which I find is almost never answered correctly by our clinical students on PhD orals, and the answer to which they seem to dislike when it is offered. Suppose that you were required to write down a procedure for selecting an individual from the population who would diagnosed as schizophrenic by a psychiatric staff; you have to wager $1,000 on being right; you may not include in your selection procedure any behavioral fact, such as a symptom or trait, manifested by the individual. What would you write down? So far as I have been able to ascertain, there is only one thing you could write down that would give you a better than even chance of winning such a bet—namely, "Find an individual X who has a schizophrenic identical twin." Admittedly, there are many other facts which would raise your odds somewhat above the low base rate of schizophrenia. You might, for example, identify X by first finding mothers who have certain unhealthy child-rearing attitudes; you might enter a subpopulation defined jointly by such demographic variables as age, size of community, religion, ethnic background, or social class. But these would leave you with a pretty unfair wager, as would the rule, "Find an X who has a fraternal twin, of the same sex, diagnosed as schizophrenic" (Fuller & Thompson, 1960, pp. 272–283; Stern, 1960, pp. 581–584).

Now the twin studies leave a good deal to be desired methodologically (Rosenthal, in press); but there seems to be a kind of "double standard of methodological morals" in our profession, in that we place a good deal of faith in our knowledge of schizophrenic dynamics, and we make theoretical inferences about social learning factors from the establishment of group trends which may be statistically significant and replicable although of small or moderate size; but when we come to the genetic studies, our standards of rigor suddenly increase. I would argue that the concordance rates in the twin studies need not be accepted uncritically as highly precise parameter estimates in order for us to say that their magnitudes represent the most important piece of etiological information we possess about schizophrenia.

It is worthwhile, I think, to pause here over a question in the sociology of knowledge, namely, why do psychologists exhibit an aversive response to the twin data? I have no wish to argue *ad hominem* here—I raise this question in a constructive and irenic spirit, because I think that a substantive confusion often lies at the bottom of this resistance, and one which can be easily dispelled. Everybody readily assents to such vague dicta as "heredity and environment interact," "there need be no conflict between organic and functional concepts," "we always deal with the total organism," etc. But it almost seems that clinicians do not fully believe these principles in any concrete sense, because they show signs of thinking that *if* a genetic basis were found for schizophrenia, the psychodynamics of the disorder (especially in relation to intrafamilial social learnings) would be somehow negated or, at least, greatly demoted in importance. To what extent, if at all, is this true?

Here we run into some widespread misconceptions as to what is meant by *specific etiology* in nonpsychiatric medicine. By postulating a "specific etiology" one does *not* imply any of the following:

1. The etiological factor always, or even usually, produces clinical illness.

2. If illness occurs, the particular form and content of symptoms is derivable by reference to the specific etiology alone.

3. The course of the illness can be materially influenced only by procedures directed against the specific etiology.

4. All persons who share the specific etiology will have closely similar histories, symptoms, and course.

5. The largest single contributor to symptom variance is the specific etiology.

In medicine, not one of these is part of the concept of specific etiology, yet, they are repeatedly invoked as arguments against a genetic interpretation of schizophrenia. I am not trying to impose the causal model of medicine by analogy; I merely wish to emphasize that *if* one postulates a genetic mutation as the specific etiology of schizophrenia, he is not thereby committed to any of the above as implications. Consequently such familiar objections as "Schizophrenics differ widely from one another" or "Many schizophrenics can be helped by purely psychological methods" should not disturb one who opts for a genetic hypothesis. In medicine, the concept of specific etiology means the *sine qua non*—the causal condition which is necessary, but not sufficient, for the disorder to occur. A genetic theory of schizophrenia would, in this sense, be stronger than that of "one contributor to variance"; but weaker than that of "largest contributor to variance." In analysis of variance terms, it means an interaction effect such that no other variables can exert a main effect when the specific etiology is lacking.

Now it goes without saying that "clinical schizophrenia" as such cannot be inherited, because it has behavioral and phenomenal contents which are learned. As Bleuler says, in order to have a delusion involving Jesuits one must first have learned about Jesuits. It seems inappropriate to apply the geneticist's concept of "penetrance" to the crude statistics of formal diagnosis —if a specific genetic etiology exists, its phenotypic expression in *psychological* categories would be a quantitative aberration in some parameter of a behavioral acquisition function. What could possibly be a genetically determined functional parameter capable of generating such diverse behavioral outcomes, including the preservation of normal function in certain domains?

The theoretical puzzle is exaggerated when we fail to conceptualize at different levels of molarity. For instance, there is a tendency among organically minded theorists to analogize between catatonic phenomena and various neurological or chemically induced states in animals. But Bleuler's masterly *Theory of Schizophrenic Negativism* (1912) shows how the whole range of catatonic behavior, including diametrically opposite modes of relating to the interpersonal environment, can be satisfactorily explained as instrumental acts; thus even a convinced organicist, postulating a biochemical defect as specific etiology, should recognize that the causal linkage between this etiology and catatonia is indirect, requiring for the latter's derivation a lengthy chain of statements which are not even formulable except in molar psychological language.

What kind of behavioral fact about the patient leads us to diagnose schizophrenia? There are a number of traits and symptoms which get a high weight, and the weights differ among clinicians. But thought disorder continues to hold its own in spite of today's greater clinical interest in motivational (especially interpersonal) variables. If you are inclined to doubt this for yourself, consider the following indicators: Patient experiences intense ambivalence, readily reports conscious hatred of family figures, is pananxious, subjects therapist to a long series of testing operations, is withdrawn, and says, "Naturally, I am growing my father's hair."

While all of these are schizophrenic indicators, the last one is the diagnostic bell ringer. In this respect we are still Bleulerians, although we know a lot more about the schizophrenic's psychodynamics than Bleuler did. The significance of thought disorder, associative dyscontrol (or, as I prefer to call it so as to include the very mildest forms it may take, "cognitive slippage"), in schizophrenia has been somewhat deemphasized in recent years. Partly this is due to the greater interest in interpersonal dynamics, but partly also to the realization that much of our earlier psychometric assessment of the thought disorder was mainly reflecting the schizophrenic's tendency to underperform because uninterested, preoccupied, resentful, or frightened. I suggest that this realization has been overgeneralized and led us to swing too far the other way, as if we had shown that there really *is* no cognitive slippage factor present. One rather common assumption seems to be that if one can demonstrate the potentiating effect of a motivational state upon cognitive slippage, light has thereby been shed upon the etiology of schizophrenia. Why are we entitled to think this? Clinically, we see a degree of cognitive slippage not found to a comparable degree among nonschizophrenic persons. Some patients (e.g., pseudoneurotics) are highly anxious and exhibit minimal slippage; others (e.g., burntout cases) are minimally anxious with marked slippage. The demonstration that we can intensify a particular patient's cognitive dysfunction by manipulating his affects is not really very

illuminating. After all, even ordinary neurological diseases can often be tremendously influenced symptomatically via emotional stimuli; but if a psychologist demonstrates that the spasticity or tremor of a multiple sclerotic is affected by rage or fear, we would not thereby have learned anything about the etiology of multiple sclerosis.

Consequent upon our general assimilation of the insights given us by psychoanalysis, there is today a widespread and largely unquestioned assumption that when we can trace out the motivational forces linked to the content of aberrant behavior, then we understand why the person has fallen ill. There is no compelling reason to assume this, when the evidence is mainly our dynamic understanding of the patient, however valid that may be. The phrase "why the person has fallen ill" may, of course, be legitimately taken to include these things; an account of how and when he falls ill will certainly include them. But they may be quite inadequate to answer the question, "Why does X fall ill and not Y, granted that we can understand both of them?" I like the analogy of a color psychosis, which might be developed by certain individuals in a society entirely oriented around the making of fine color discriminations. Social, sexual, economic signals are color mediated; to misuse a color word is strictly taboo; compulsive mothers are horribly ashamed of a child who is retarded in color development, and so forth. Some color-blind individuals (not all, perhaps not most) develop a color psychosis in this culture; as adults, they are found on the couches of color therapists, where a great deal of *valid* understanding is achieved about color dynamics. Some of them make a social recovery. Nonetheless, if we ask, "What was basically the matter with these patients?" meaning, "What is the specific etiology of the color psychosis?" the answer is that mutated gene on the X chromosome. This is why my own therapeutic experience with schizophrenic patients has not yet convinced me of the schizophrenogenic mother as a specific etiology, even though the picture I get of my patients' mothers is pretty much in accord with the familiar one. There is no question here of accepting the patient's account; my point is that *given* the account, and taking it quite at face value, does not tell me why the patient is a patient and not just a fellow who had a bad mother.

Another theoretical lead is the one given greatest current emphasis, namely, *interpersonal aversiveness*. The schizophrene suffers a degree of social fear, distrust, expectation of rejection, and conviction of his own unlovability which cannot be matched in its depth, pervasity, and resistance to corrective experience by any other diagnostic group.

Then there is a quasi-pathognomonic sign, emphasized by Rado (1956; Rado & Daniels, 1956) but largely ignored in psychologists' diagnostic usage, namely, *anhedonia*—a marked, widespread, and refractory defect in pleasure capacity which, once you learn how to examine for it, is one of the most consistent and dramatic behavioral signs of the disease.

Finally, I include *ambivalence* from Bleuler's cardinal four (1950). His other two, "autism" and "dereism," I consider derivative from the combination of slippage, anhedonia, and aversiveness. Crudely put, if a person cannot think straight, gets little pleasure, and is afraid of everyone, he will of course learn to be autistic and dereistic.

If these clinical characterizations are correct, and we combine them with the hypothesis of a genetic specific etiology, do they give us any lead on theoretical possibilities?

Granting its initial vagueness as a construct, requiring to be filled in by neurophysiological research, I believe we should take seriously the old European notion of an "integrative neural defect" as the only direct phenotypic consequence produced by the genic mutation. This is an aberration in some parameter of single cell function, which may or may not be manifested in the functioning of more molar CNS systems, depending upon the organization of the mutual feedback controls and upon the stochastic parameters of the reinforcement regime. This neural integrative defect, which I shall christen *schizotaxia*, is all that can properly be spoken of as inherited. The imposition of a social learning history upon schizotaxic individuals results in a personality organization which I shall call, following Rado, the *schizotype*. The four core behavior traits are obviously not innate; but I postulate that they are universally learned by schizotaxic individuals, given any of the actually existing social reinforcement regimes, from the best to the worst. If the interpersonal regime is favorable, and the schizotaxic person also has the good fortune to inherit a low anxiety readiness, physical vigor, general resistance to stress and the like, he will remain a well-compensated "normal" schizotype, never manifesting symptoms of mental disease. He will be like the gout-prone male whose genes determine him to have an elevated blood uric acid titer, but who never develops clinical gout.

Only a subset of schizotypic personalities decompensate into clinical schizophrenia. It seems likely that the most important causal influence pushing the schizotype toward schizophrenic decompensation is the schizophrenogenic mother.

I hope it is clear that this view does not conflict with what has been established about the mother-child interaction. If this interaction were totally free of maternal ambivalence and aversive inputs to the schizotaxic child, even compensated schizotypy might be avoided; at most, we might expect to find only the faintest signs of cognitive slippage and other minimal neurological aberrations, possibly including body image and other proprioceptive deviations but not the interpersonal aversiveness which is central to the clinical picture.

Nevertheless, while assuming the etiological importance of mother in determining the course of aversive social learnings, it is worthwhile to speculate about the modification our genetic equations might take on this hypothesis. Many schizophrenogenic mothers are themselves schizotypes in varying degrees of compensation. Their etiological contribution then consists jointly in their passing on the gene, *and* in the fact that being schizotypic, they provide the kind of ambivalent regime which potentiates the schizotypy of the child and raises the odds of his decompensating. Hence the incidence of the several parental genotypes among parent pairs of diagnosed proband cases is not calculable from the usual genetic formulas. For example, given a schizophrenic proband, the odds that mother is homozygous (or, if the gene were dominant, that it is mother who carries it) are different from those for father; since we have begun by selecting a decompensated case, and formal diagnosis as the phenotype involves a potentiating factor for mother which is psychodynamically greater than that for a schizotypic father. Another important influence would be the likelihood that the lower fertility of schizophrenics is also present, but to an unknown degree, among compensated schizotypes. Clinical experience suggests that in the semicompensated range, this lowering of fertility is greater among males, since many schizotypic women relate to men in an exploited or exploitive sexual way, whereas the male schizo-

type usually displays a marked deficit in heterosexual aggressiveness. Such a sex difference in fertility among decompensated cases has been reported by Meyers and Goldfarb (1962).

Since the extent of aversive learnings is a critical factor in decompensation, the inherited anxiety readiness is presumably greater among diagnosed cases. Since the more fertile mothers are likely to be compensated, hence themselves to be relatively low anxiety if schizotaxic, a frequent parent pattern should be a compensated schizotypic mother married to a neurotic father, the latter being the source of the proband's high-anxiety genes (plus providing a poor paternal model for identification in male patients, and a weak defender of the child against mother's schizotypic hostility).

These considerations make ordinary family concordance studies, based upon formal diagnoses, impossible to interpret. The most important research need here is development of high-validity indicators for compensated schizotypy. I see some evidence for these conceptions in the report of Lidz and co-workers, who in studying intensively the parents of 15 schizophrenic patients were surprised to find that "minimally, 9 of the 15 patients had at least one parent who could be called schizophrenic, or ambulatory schizophrenic, or clearly paranoid in behavior and attitudes" (Lidz, Cornelison, Terry, & Fleck, 1958, p. 308). As I read the brief personality sketches presented, I would judge that all but two of the probands had a clearly schizotypic parent. These authors, while favoring a "learned irrationality" interpretation of their data, also recognize the alternative genetic interpretation. Such facts do not permit a decision, obviously; my main point is the striking difference between the high incidence of parental schizotypes, mostly quite decompensated (some to the point of diagnosable psychosis), and the zero incidence which a conventional family concordance study would have yielded for this group.

Another line of evidence, based upon a very small sample but exciting because of its uniformity, is McConaghy's report (1959) that among nondiagnosed parent pairs of 10 schizophrenics, subclinical thought disorder was psychometrically detectable in at least one parent of every pair. Rosenthal (in press) reports that he can add five tallies to his parent-pair count, and suggests that such results might indicate that the specific heredity is dominant, and completely penetrant, rather than recessive. The attempt to replicate these findings, and other psychometric efforts to tap subclinical cognitive slippage in the "normal" relatives of schizophrenics, should receive top priority in our research efforts.

Summarizing, I hypothesize that the statistical relation between schizotaxia, schizotypy, and schizophrenia is class inclusion: All schizotaxics become, *on all actually existing social learning regimes*, schizotypic in personality organization; but most of these remain compensated. A minority, disadvantaged by other (largely polygenically determined) constitutional weaknesses, and put on a bad regime by schizophrenogenic mothers (most of whom are themselves schizotypes) are thereby potentiated into clinical schizophrenia. What makes schizotaxia etiologically specific is its role as a *necessary* condition. I postulate that a nonschizotaxic individual, whatever his other genetic makeup and whatever his learning history, would at most develop a character disorder or a psychoneurosis; but he would not become a schizotype and therefore could never manifest its decompensated form, schizophrenia.

# REFERENCES

ANGYAL, A., & BLACKMAN, N. Vestibular reactivity in schizophrenia. *Arch. Neurol. Psychiat.*, 1940, 44, 611–620.

ANGYAL, A., & BLACKMAN, N. Paradoxical reactions in schizophrenia under the influence of alcohol, hyperpnea, and $CO_2$ inhalation. *Amer. J. Psychiat.*, 1941, 97, 893–903.

ANGYAL, A., & SHERMAN, N. Postural reactions to vestibular stimulation in schizophrenic and normal subjects. *Amer. J. Psychiat.*, 1942, 98, 857–862.

ARNHOFF, F., & DAMIANOPOULUS, E. Self-body recognition and schizophrenia: An exploratory study. *J. abnorm. soc. Psychol.*, in press.

BLEULER, E. *Theory of schizophrenic negativism.* New York: Nervous and Mental Disease Publishing, 1912.

BLEULER, E. *Dementia praecox.* New York: International Universities Press, 1950.

CLEVELAND, S. E. Judgment of body size in a schizophrenic and a control group. *Psychol. Rep.*, 1960, 7, 304.

CLEVELAND, S. E., FISHER, S., REITMAN, E. E., & ROTHAUS, P. Perception of body size in schizophrenia. *Arch. gen. Psychiat.*, 1962, 7, 277–285.

COLBERT, G., & KOEGLER, R. Vestibular dysfunction in childhood schizophrenia. *AMA Arch. gen. Psychiat.*, 1959, 1, 600–617.

COLLINS, W. E., CRAMPTON, G. H., & POSNER, J. B. The effect of mental set upon vestibular nystagmus and the EEG. *USA Med. Res. Lab. Rep.*, 1961, No. 439.

DELAFRESNAYE, J. F. (Ed.) *Brain mechanisms and learning.* Springfield, Ill.: Charles C Thomas, 1961.

DELGADO, J. M. R., ROBERTS, W. W., & MILLER, N. E. Learning motivated by electrical stimulation of the brain. *Amer. J. Physiol.*, 1954, 179, 587–593.

FISH, BARBARA. The study of motor development in infancy and its relationship to psychological functioning. *Amer. J. Psychiat.*, 1961, 117, 1113–1118.

FREEMAN, H., & RODNICK, E. H. Effect of rotation on postural steadiness in normal and schizophrenic subjects. *Arch. Neurol. Psychiat.*, 1942, **48**, 47–53.

FULLER, J. L., & THOMPSON, W. R. *Behavior genetics.* New York: Wiley, 1960. Pp. 272–283.

HOSKINS, R. G. *The biology of schizophrenia.* New York: Norton, 1946.

KING, H. E. *Psychomotor aspects of mental disease.* Cambridge: Harvard Univer. Press, 1954.

LEACH, W. W. Nystagmus: An integrative neural deficit in schizophrenia. *J. abnorm. soc. Psychol.*, 1960, **60**, 305–309.

LIDZ, T., CORNELISON, A., TERRY, D., & FLECK, S. Intrafamilial environment of the schizophrenic patient: VI. The transmission of irrationality. *AMA Arch. Neurol. Psychiat.*, 1958, **79**, 305–316.

MCCONAGHY, N. The use of an object sorting test in elucidating the hereditary factor in schizophrenia. *J. Neurol. Neurosurg. Psychiat.*, 1959, **22**, 243–246.

MEYERS, D., & GOLDFARB, W. Psychiatric appraisals of parents and siblings of schizophrenic children. *Amer. J. Psychiat.*, 1962, **118**, 902–908.

OLDS, J., & MILNER, P. Positive reinforcement produced by electrical stimulation of septal area and other regions of rat brain. *J. comp. physiol. Psychol.*, 1954, **47**, 419–427.

PAYNE, R. W. Cognitive abnormalities. In H. J. Eysenck (Ed.), *Handbook of abnormal psychology.* New York: Basic Books, 1961. Pp. 248–250.

PAYNE, R. S., & HEWLETT, J. H. G. Thought disorder in psychotic patients. In H. J. Eysenck (Ed.), *Experiments in personality.* Vol. 2. London: Routledge, Kegan, Paul, 1960. Pp. 3–106.

POLLOCK, M., & KRIEGER, H. P. Oculomotor and postular patterns in schizophrenic children. *AMA Arch. Neurol. Psychiat.*, 1958, **79**, 720–726.

RADO, S. *Psychoanalysis of behavior.* New York: Grune & Stratton, 1956.

RADO, S., & DANIELS, G. *Changing concepts of psychoanalytic medicine.* New York: Grune & Stratton, 1956.

RAMEY, E. R., & O'DOHERTY, D. S. (Ed.) *Electrical studies on the unanesthetized brain.* New York: Hoeber, 1960.

ROSENTHAL, D. Problems of sampling and diagnosis in the major twin studies of schizophrenia. *J. psychiat. Res.*, in press.

STERN, K. *Principles of human genetics.* San Francisco: Freeman, 1960. Pp. 581–584.

Sarnoff A. Mednick

# A Longitudinal Study of Children with a High Risk for Schizophrenia

*Among the variety of approaches being devoted to the study of schizophrenia, that which is described by Mednick in this paper is among the most exciting. It involves careful studies of adolescents who are "high risks" for becoming schizophrenic because their mothers are schizophrenic, and concurrent studies of a large group of adolescents having nonschizophrenic mothers. It has been found that roughly 15 per cent of the offspring of schizophrenic mothers become schizophrenic, whereas the incidence of schizophrenia in families where the mother is not schizophrenic is much lower. Eventually, therefore, Mednick can expect to have a sample of 20 to 30 schizophrenic subjects who were care-*

*Reprinted from* Mental Hygiene, *50(1966), 522–535 with the permission of the National Association for Mental Health and Dr. Mednick.*

*fully studied before they became ill and for whom "control" subjects are available for comparison. This rare opportunity will make it possible for Mednick to attempt to determine ways in which the schizophrenic differs from the non-schizophrenic prior to becoming overtly psychotic and, hopefully, to obtain some more precise ideas about the etiology of the illness.*

*The editing of this article has involved the omission of an appendix in which actual data are presented deriving from the psychophysiologic tests that are referred to in the text. The reader who is interested in these details should consult the original article.*

We have examined 207 "normally" functioning children who have chronically and severely schizophrenic mothers. On the basis of the literature on psychiatric genetics (notably work by Kallmann (1)) and a study of the morbidity risk in a sample of adults with schizophrenic mothers (2), we estimate that this group of 207 children contains about 23 to 32 who will some day be hospitalized for schizophrenia. We intend to follow these children closely for the next fifteen to twenty years. When some appreciable number becomes schizophrenic, we will be able to look back at our current measures and see how those who became schizophrenic differed in childhood from those who did not. If within the span of our current examinations there are some measures related to factors predisposing to schizophrenia, then it is possible that we will be able to devise a battery of tests that will effectively preidentify children who have an extremely high risk of becoming schizophrenic. This is our central aim.

The study is prospective. We are testing subjects and interviewing relatives, teachers, and friends before there is any knowledge that the subject is going to be mentally ill. The observations of our interviewees concerning subjects who will some day be hospitalized for mental illness are no more distorted or selective than their observations concerning children who will some day constitute our control group. In addition, the information we receive is current. We are not asking informants to think back ten or fifteen years before the hospitalization of a subject in reporting the subject's behavior. A large part of our inquiry concerns current social and intellectual functioning. (Further, that part of our inquiry that is retrospective is less so than it would be if the subjects were adults.) The responses of the subject himself are not clouded by his being a patient in a mental hospital, nor are they colored by the failures and miseries that may precede his breakdown.

Our data are also uniformly and systematically obtained. In all cases the information has been gathered in a standard manner—in *almost* all cases by the same examiner. In contrast, information drawn retrospectively from clinical records is always spotty, not to the point, and provided by numbers of different examiners with different viewpoints and different vocabularies.

We believe we are gathering and reporting information that cannot be secured reliably in any other manner. Interestingly enough, a similar prospective study has recently been successfully conducted in the field of heart disease. Here the investigators carried out a standard examination of a large group of adult males who had no history of heart ailment. They then followed this sample for some years and noted which individuals later suffered heart attacks. They compared the stricken group with a matched control group on the basis of the data collected at the onset of the study, before the incidence of morbidity. The investigators report a number of different indices that are, in effect, very early predictors of heart disease. These indicants can now be used to select individuals for preventive therapy and research. An index predicting schizophrenia could also be used in this manner if it were possible to devise one.

We first attempted this study in Michigan, in 1960 (3). We abandoned the attempt because the hospital records proved inadequate and the high residential mobility rate made it improbable that we could follow our subjects for any appreciable amount of time. Fifty per cent of the entire Detroit population moves every four years. When we examined the mobility patterns for persons in the age range of greatest danger of schizophrenia, we found that 47 per cent change address every year. This figure is even greater for the low-income non-home-owner; the group of greatest interest is also the most mobile, according to reports of the U. S. Bureau of Census (1956) and to the Detroit Area Study of 1956. If ten of our subjects were to move to California, for example, we would be hard pressed to locate them there; and, if we were able to do so, it would cost us up to $5,000 to bring them, with a responsible adult, for one day of testing. On the basis of these data and other considerations, we made the decision not to continue the study. Anything less than certainty of 90 per cent follow-up success was unacceptable.

Such certainty seemed unattainable until an address by Professor Erik Strömgren, a Danish research worker in psychiatric genetics, directed my attention to opportunities for research in Scandinavia. As an example, Fremming (4) carried out a 60-year follow-up of 5,500 persons, and was successful in locating 92 per cent of his sample. Clearly, the study I had just abandoned as impractical was feasible in Scandinavia.

Further investigation and a visit to Scandinavia in the summer of 1961 revealed that the epidemiologic aspects of schizophrenia there are about what we find here in the United States (5). A tour of the mental hospital system in Denmark suggested that the clinical picture was not essentially different from what we observe in our own hospitals. The national psychiatric register would greatly facilitate various aspects of the study; and the Folkeregister, which maintains an up-to-date record of the current home address of every person living in Denmark and which helped to explain the excellent record of the longitudinal research by Fremming, would be extremely valuable.

What further recommended Denmark as a site for the proposed research was the compact size of the country: half the population is concentrated in greater Copenhagen, which tends to minimize the distance that subjects must be transported.

The major loss of subjects in a longitudinal study in Denmark is through external emigration. If any subjects from our sample do emigrate, an attempt could be made to locate them. However, the low rate of emigration of Danes suggests that, in any case, this will not be a serious problem in our research (6).

The theory that guides this project (7) posits that the pre-schizophrenic has three predisposing characteristics: (1) abnormally great autonomic responsiveness, (2) abnormally slow recovery from response to stress, and (3) excessive stimulus generalization reactiveness. The theory suggests that, when the person is subjected to a series of stresses, these three factors can augment each other so as to raise the person's state of autonomic arousal and generalization to disruptive levels. Disturbances of perception and thought will result from the elevated gradients of associative and stimulus generalization. The resultant behavioral disturbances might lead to hospitalization for acute reactive schizophrenia.

Process or chronic schizophrenia is seen as the result of learning to avoid stressful stimulation by means of avoidant associative mechanisms. During some periods of high anxiety, tangential associations occur that momentarily replace anxiety-laden thought with less-anxiety-laden thought. This process is followed by anxiety reduction, which reinforces the remote, tangential, avoidant thought transition. After many such trials, the tangential thought will become a conditioned avoidance response, defending the person from stimuli that might elicit anxiety. When presented with such stimuli, the person can escape by means of an avoidant associative transition.

In this theoretical context, the process schizophrenic is one who has the three predisposing characteristics and who has also learned the avoidant thought mechanism early in life. This is perhaps due to his having been born into a stressful family situation, which would foster learning of avoidance in a sensitive child. In adolescence we would expect this person to show the classic withdrawal syndrome.

The reactive schizophrenic, also characterized by the same three predisposing characteristics, is born into a relatively unstressful family situation; thus, he is not forced to learn the avoidant associative mechanisms. However, having the same predisposing characteristics, he is prone to an acute breakdown if he suffers from a series of trauma. In adolescence we would expect to find him emotionally reactive but without pathologic manifestations.

We chose to study children whose *mothers* are *process* schizophrenics for a number of reasons:

1. According to Kinsey, paternity is sometimes questionable in normal middle-class families. It might be difficult to be quite sure of our major independent variable with alleged fathers, especially if they were schizophrenic.

2. Schizophrenic women have more children than schizophrenic men (8), affording us the luxury of a larger pool of subjects.

3. Psychodevelopmentally, mothers presumably play a greater role in shaping children. Using mothers has permitted us to carry out research on the effects of being reared by a schizophrenic mother.

4. Offspring of process (typical) schizophrenic mothers yield a higher rate of schizophrenia (9–11).

There are elements of family dynamics that will be biased in our study because of the choice of mothers, however. For example, Rosenthal (12) has shown that, in a family with a schizophrenic, the family members of the same sex are more likely to be concordant for schizophrenia. We shall expect more girls than boys in our experimental group to become schizophrenic.

Two experienced psychiatrists trained together and then independently tested their reliability in making judgments, from hospital records, for the form prepared to record the mothers' symptoms. They merely had to judge whether the mothers were typical schizophrenics; they were instructed to discard any questionable cases. Their agreement as to diagnosis on 20 test cases was found to be 100 per cent. Following this test of reliability, only one psychiatrist has checked each record.

For each mother a precoded form has been filled out that lists her symptoms, provides information concerning her dates of hospitalization, and makes some notation as to her clinical status. The hospital records are always easily available for further examination in case of need.

The high-risk subjects (that is, children with schizophrenic mothers) have been set off into pairs very carefully matched for age, sex, father's occupational status, rural or urban residence, years of formal education, and institutional versus family rearing conditions. We have selected a control subject for each pair of high-risk subjects. The control subject has been matched with the high-risk pair for all the aforementioned variables.

The control subjects come from families in which there has been no incidence of hospitalization for mental illness in the immediate family for two generations—parents and grandparents on both sides. (This determination can be made on the basis of unique records existing in Denmark.) As a consequence, we expect no more than a "normal" yield of schizophrenia in this group. This control group will serve a number of functions:

1. If the two groups are well matched and if the matching variables are relevant to schizophrenia, then the chief difference between the groups lies in their risk of becoming schizophrenic. If we do have two groups that differ only in their risk of becoming schizophrenic, then any differences we observe between them may relate to factors predisposing or leading to schizophrenia. The control group, then, makes possible interesting cross-sectional comparisons at this point.

2. The low-risk group has been matched with the high-risk group for "per cent of group raised in children's homes" and "number of years in children's homes." This will help us to evaluate the influence of grossly disrupted home life, which is in general more characteristic of our high-risk sample—that is, if differences between the entire high-risk and entire low-risk groups also hold up in the subgroups that have been raised in children's homes, then these differences are not easily ascribable to the more disturbed home life of the high-risk groups.

3. The control group provides us with an index of normal functioning and normal development. Thus, in one substudy, conducted by Higgins (13), we have compared children who were born to, and raised by, schizophrenic mothers with children who were born to schizophrenic mothers but raised by normal foster parents. Through the years that this study will be continuing, the control group will serve for many such investigations.

In what follows we center our discussion on the psychophysiologic results thus far obtained. The methodology and findings are described in some detail, specific data on the latter being presented in an appendix.

## MATERIAL AND METHODS

### The sample and Its procurement

Our procedure entailed several steps. We first sent social workers to state hospitals, where they obtained lists of resident female patients who had children between the ages of 10 and 18. These lists were checked with the University Institute for Human Genetics and the Folkeregister. The mothers' hospital records were examined by two psychiatrists, who certified chronic schizophrenia. (As noted above, when almost perfect reliability had been established, only one psychiatrist was used.)

Social workers then went to the homes of the children and enlisted their co-operation and that of the responsible adults. The children were then scheduled for testing.

After some children with schizophrenic mothers (the experimental group) had been tested, we began forming *pairs* of matched experimental subjects. When some of the experimental subjects begin to become schizophrenic, we shall already have made an unbiased selection of comparison subjects who did not become schizophrenic.

The pairs of experimental subjects were matched with respect to sex, age, father's occupation (the best single measure of social class in Denmark (14)), rural or urban residence, years of education, and upbringing in a children's home versus family life.

Next, a single control subject was selected who was matched on these same variables, "individual for individual," with each experimental pair. We wrote to a school attended by one or both of the experimental subjects and asked for the names of children, at that school, meeting all the matching criteria. The school typically would send through some names. These were then sent to the Institute for Human Genetics, which returned a report on each child concerning any history of psychiatric hospitalization or civil disturbance for the child, his parents, or his grandparents on either side. For example, we may have learned that child A's grandfather on his mother's side had been hospitalized for two months in 1937 for severe depression, whereas child B's record was "clean." We would, of course, choose child B as our control subject. A social worker would visit child B's home and engage the co-operation of the child and his guardians.

If a child in the experimental group was in a children's home, he would be paired with another child in a children's home. Control children were also sampled from children's homes. They, too, were checked through by the Institute for Human Genetics. In most cases the parents of these control children had divorced, died, or were alcoholics or criminals. These children's homes controls will be examined carefully in the analysis of the data. In any case, they represent some degree of control with respect to aspects of the study dealing with broken homes.

Socio-economic status of the children was rated according to the occupation of the head of the household. The criteria were taken from Svalastoga (14). The adaptation of his system resulted in an eight-point scale ranging from 0 (e.g., shoe shiner) to 7 (e.g., professor). Following detailed instruction in the use of the scale, two judges independently rating a series reached a satisfactorily high agreement: in 60 test cases,

a disagreement of only one class in one case was noted. In instances in which the child had lived in more than one household, we scored the child on the basis of the household in which he had spent the most time. If a child had spent more time in a children's home than with any family, he was coded "0" for social class.

An initial letter was sent to the families informing them of the project and the fact that they had been included in the sample. Both control and experimental families were told that we were interested in the effect of "nervous breakdown" on the members of the family. They were also informed of our need for normal families. We did not identify to which group we thought they belonged, but this was usually obvious to them.

Below is a summary of the identifying characteristics of the two groups of children:

| | Control | Experimental |
|---|---|---|
| Number of subjects | 104 | 207 |
| Boys | 59 | 121 |
| Girls | 45 | 86 |
| Mean age (to nearest whole year) | 15.1 | 15.1 |
| Mean social class (see above) | 2.3 | 2.2 |
| Mean year of education | 7.3 | 7.0 |
| Per cent of group in children's homes * | 14 | 16 |
| Mean number of years in children's homes * | 8.5 | 9.4 |
| Per cent of group considered rural residents † | 22 | 26 |

* We considered experience in children's homes of only five years or greater duration. Many of the children in the experimental group had been in children's homes for brief periods while their mothers were hospitalized. These experiences were seen as quite different from the experience of children who actually had to make a children's home their home until they could go out and earn their own living.

† A rural resident was defined as one living in a town with a population of 2,500 persons or fewer.

## Test procedure

Until testing was complete, none of the researchers was informed as to whether the children tested on a particular day were control or experimental subjects. The social worker scheduled all visits. The test procedure was identical for subjects from both groups.

Testing began at 8 A.M. First the subject had his height and weight taken. He was then escorted to the psychophysiologic laboratory, where he underwent mild stress, conditioning, and stimulus generalization procedures. He then took psychologic tests: a full Wechsler Intelligence Scale for Children (WISC) and an abbreviated Minnesota Multiphasic Personality Inventory (MMPI) test. Then came lunch. After lunch the subject took two word association tests (single word response and continual association) and completed an adjective check list describing himself. He returned for a second psychophysiologic session, in which he underwent mild stress, semantic conditioning, and mediated generalization procedures. Finally, the subject was interviewed by a psychiatrist and given an honorarium.

*Psychophysiologic procedure.* Recording was done on an Offner Type R Dynograph. Before each session, the apparatus was calibrated and the electrodes and leads were inspected. We made use of a device designed in Ax's psychophysiology laboratory to reverse polarity of the electrodes every 1.2 seconds.

The psychophysiology laboratory is in the basement of a hospital, in a room separated by two tight-fitting doors from a lightly traveled corridor. Signs caution quiet. The humidity and temperature of the laboratory are relatively constant, but were recorded before and after each session.

After the points of electrode placement had been washed and sponged with alcohol, the subject reclined on a hospital bed and was asked to relax. Respiration, heart rate, galvanic skin reflex (GSR), and electromyographic (EMG) results were recorded. (Only the morning GSR results are reported in this paper.) GSR electrodes consisted of zinc, 7 mm. in diameter, embedded

in a plastic cup. Small sponges saturated in zinc sulfate solution were inserted into the plastic cup. When the transducers were attached, recording was started and was continuous until the conclusion of the generalization testing. The subject was permitted to relax for 15 minutes, and then the earphones were attached.

Approximately 30 seconds after the tape recorder was started, the subject heard instructions about the procedure to follow. At the end of the instructions there was a silence of 70 seconds, followed by eight presentations of the conditioned stimulus (tone of 1,000 cycles per second). These eight presentations were included to desensitize the subject to the conditioned stimulus, and varied from 5 to 11 seconds. (All intervals reported are measured from "offset" of one stimulus to "onset" of the subsequent stimulus.) Nine seconds after the final "desensitization trial," conditioning trials began.

The unconditioned stimulus was an irritating noise of 96 decibels (a decibel equalling 0.0002 dynes per square centimeter) presented for 4.5 seconds following half a second after the onset of the conditioned stimulus (54 decibels). There were 14 partial reinforcement trials (9 conditioned stimulus-unconditioned stimulus pairings and 5 interspersed presentations of the conditioned stimulus alone). The trials were separated by intervals varying from 17 to 77 seconds.

Following the final conditioning trial, there was an interval of 3 minutes, after which conditioning and stimulus generalization testing began. Generalization stimuli were tones of 1,311 cycles per second ($GS_1$) and 1,967 ($GS_2$). There were nine trials, three each of conditioned stimulus, $GS_1$, and $GS_2$. The duration of each was 2 seconds, and stimuli were separated by intervals varying from 10 to 18 seconds. The order of the conditioned stimulus, $GS_1$, and $GS_2$ was counterbalanced.

The final conditioning and stimulus generalization testing trial marked the end of the morning session, which required approximately 50 minutes. The subject was disconnected from the apparatus and escorted from the laboratory.

*Psychologic tests.* The children were subjected to a battery of psychologic tests, as indicated above. Included were a Danish translation of the Wechsler Intelligence Scale for Children, in common use in Denmark; a Danish translation of the Minnesota Multiphasic Personality Inventory, shortened to 304 items by removing those deemed inappropriate or offensive to children (it should be noted that no scales for this test have been developed in Denmark); and word association tests. A Danish version of the Kent-Rosanoff Test was among the latter. The word "mutton" was omitted since it is extremely unusual in Danish; the words "sun" and "star" were added, to make a total of 101 words. The words were read to the subject with the instruction to respond to each word with the first word that came to mind. Latency of response was recorded.

The subjects were also presented with 30 other words and asked to associate continually to them for one minute. Responses and latencies in response were recorded. We attempted to avoid associative chaining by having the stimulus word on a card before the subject during the entire minute period.

A specially constructed adjective check list of 241 items was administered to each subject with instructions to use it to describe himself. The interviewing psychiatrist and the administrators of the WISC and the word association tests also used this check list to describe each subject.

*Psychiatric interview.* Each subject underwent a 30- to 40-minute psychiatric interview to assess his current diagnostic status. The interview was largely precoded and highly structured. The questions concerned the subject's mental status, social history, and attitudes.

*Other measures obtained.* The social workers interviewed the person responsible for the child on questions concerning the child's current behavior, social development, parental behavior, school behavior, and parents' socio-economic status. The interview was highly structured.

A questionnaire was mailed to each subject's school. Items concerned the subject's relationship with teacher and classmates as well as academic achievement. The questionnaire was filled out by the teacher most familiar with the subject.

## RESULTS

### Psychophysiologic findings

Extremely consistent and highly significant differences have been observed in the latency of the galvanic skin reflex (GSR) response. These differences, however, seem to be rather complex. Unequivocally and without exception, the experimental group responds with a shorter period of latency to the stress stimuli. In every case the differences are significant and marked. This short period of latency suggests that the experimental group is characterized by a volatile autonomic nervous system that is easily and quickly aroused by threat.

The differences between the two groups in latency of response to more neutral stimuli are not as marked. Although, in general, the experimental group continues to respond much more quickly, there are some instances in which this trend becomes reversed.

We predicted differences in amplitude of response, speed of recovery, and generalization responsiveness. The two predictions concerning amplitude of response and generalization were strongly supported. The experimental group responds with much greater amplitude to the stress and to the generalization stimuli than does the control group.

The big surprise in the data is the fairly consistent finding that the experimental group recovered from its response to the stress stimuli at a relatively greater rate of speed. For the past ten years our hypothesis in research in schizophrenia has been that the preschizophrenic should show slower recovery from stress. Our data seem definitely to contradict this hypothesis.

This is especially puzzling in view of the earlier findings with already quite schizophrenic populations showing slower recovery rates (15–18). It is difficult to abandon the hypothesis of a slower recovery rate in the pre-schizophrenic. It has always suggested itself as the method of differentiating between the pre-neurotic and the pre-schizophrenic. What is immediately indicated is a retesting of the subjects, with even more careful attention being given to an analysis of their recovery rates. However, in the interim it is interesting to speculate on what role quicker recovery could play in the development of schizophrenia.

The theory outlined above suggests that schizophrenia is a learned thought disorder. The thought disorder is learned at those times when a pre-schizophrenic or schizophrenic facing an anxiety-provoking thought or situation escapes from this anxiety by thinking of an irrelevant, or relatively irrelevant, idea. This irrelevant association will tend to remove the person, momentarily, from the anxiety-provoking stimulation. This will result in a reduction in anxiety level that will reinforce the anxiety-irrelevant-response associative link. After many such trials, the schizophrenic will have built up a large repertoire of responses that will have the ability to remove him from anxiety-provoking stimulation.

One of the difficulties that has consistently been raised by critics of this theoretical position has been that, if the pre-schizophrenic recovers more slowly from anxiety-provoking stimulation, then the reinforcement he will receive as a result of "thinking away" from anxiety-provoking events will be less than that a normal person might receive. Why, then, should he learn to think irrelevant thoughts more than a normal person might? The finding that the experimental group in this study shows quicker recovery than the control group suggests a possible answer

to this question, namely, that perhaps one of the determining features of the pre-schizophrenic is his relative ease in finding immediate surcease from anxiety-provoking events by means of avoidant thought. This might explain why this mechanism is seized upon by the schizophrenic; it might explain why this mechanism is so common in schizophrenia.

## Other Findings

We summarize the non-psychophysiologic findings informally by a narrative, interpretative description of the features of the members of the experimental group that, statistically, distinguish them from members of the control group. A word of caution is in order, however: we have combined many individual findings as though all of them were characteristic of all members of the experimental group. It is possible, if not likely, that separate subgroups were responsible for separate findings. Thus, by weaving them all together with a narrative threat, we are doubtless doing some violence to the facts. In any case, each statement reflects a statistically significant, empirical result.

The first characteristic that all of the experimental subjects have in common, of course, is that they have mothers who are schizophrenic. Their home life has not been harmonious, but has been marked by frequent parental quarrels. The mother has apparently been relatively dominant in the home. However, her influence has not been benign; the child sees her as scolding and unreliable and not worthy of his confidences.

This difficult environment has been imposed upon (or perhaps has been responsible for producing) a child whose autonomic nervous system is highly labile, reacting to threat abnormally quickly and with abnormal amplitude. To make things still more difficult, reactions are not specific, but overgeneralized. This serves to broaden the range of stimuli that are adequate to provoke this sensitive autonomic nervous system.

In school, the child's teachers recognize his tendency to get upset easily. He seems to react to excitement by withdrawing. He handles peer relations and classroom challenges by passivity. Perhaps this mode of reaction is learned, since it is usually followed by the reduction of his anticipatory fear. Despite the use of passivity and withdrawal, the child is still approachable and is performing relatively adequately. Still, he *shows* his "nervousness" enough for his teacher to remark on it. However, having begun to learn avoidance behavior, it is difficult for the child to stop, since this takes him away from the very social situations in which he might learn more direct means of dealing with his anticipatory anxiety. His recovery being more rapid, his withdrawal is even more effectively rewarded. Since he withdraws, his peers reject him; and the circle gets tighter and more difficult to break out of.

Although, in general, the child performs adequately, he has already learned to effect momentary withdrawal responses whenever pressures build up. In tasks that require continuous concentration and effort (arithmetic, coding in the WISC), his performance will begin to slip.

The child is a "loner" much of the time. He does not share associations with his peer group as much as does his schoolmate. In addition, he is beginning to learn to escape from autonomic arousal by drifting off into idiosyncratic thoughts.

# REFERENCES

1. KALLMANN, F. J.: American Journal of Psychiatry, 103:309, 1946.
2. REISBY, N.: Acta Psychiatrica Scandinavica (in press).
3. MEDNICK, S. A.: Schizophrenia: A. Learned Thought Disorder. In Nielsen, G. (ed.): Clinical Psychology (Proceedings of the XIV International Congress of Applied Psychology). Copenhagen, Munksgaard, 1962.
4. FREMMING, K. H.: Papers on Eugenics, No. 7. London, The Eugenics Society, 1951.
5. LEMKAU, P. V., and CROCETTI, G. M.: Vital Statistics of Schizophrenia. In Bellak, L. (ed.): Schizophrenia. New York, Logos, 1958.
6. STATISTISKE MEDDELELSER: Befolkningens Bevaegelser, 1959. Copenhagen, Det Statistike Department, 1961.
7. MEDNICK, S. A.: Psychological Bulletin, 55:316, 1958.
8. GOLDFARB, C., and ERLENMEYER-KIMLING, L.: Changing Mating and Fertility Patterns in Schizophrenia. In Kallmann, F. J. (ed.): Expanding Goals of Genetics in Psychiatry. New York, Grune & Stratton, 1962.
9. SCHULZ, B.: Zeitschrift fur die gesamte Neurologie und Psychiatrie, 165:97, 1939.
10. SCHULZ, B.: Zeitschrift fur die gesamte Neurologie und Psychiatrie, 168:332, 1940.
11. LEWIS, A. J.: Acta genetica, 7:309, 1957.
12. ROSENTHAL, D.: Psychological Bulletin, 59:401, 1962.
13. HIGGINS, J.: Psychiatric Research (in press).
14. SVALASTOGA, K.: Prestige, Class and Mobility. Copenhagen, Gyldendal, 1959.
15. AX, A. F., et al.: Psychophysiological Patterns in Chronic Schizophrenia. Paper read at the meeting of the Society of Biological Psychiatry, 1961.
16. DeVAULT, S. H.: Physiological Responsiveness in Reactive and Process Schizo-

phrenia. Unpublished Ph.D. disserta-
tation, Michigan State University,
1955.
17. SHIPLEY, W. C.: Psychiatric Quarterly,
8:736, 1934.
18. WHATMORE, G. B., and ELLIS, R. M.:
American Journal of Psychiatry, 114:
882, 1958.
19. ZAHN, T. P.: Psychiatric Research Reports of the American Psychiatric Association, 19:156, 1964.

20. MEDNICK, S. A.: Journal of Abnormal
and Social Psychology, 51:536, 1958.
21. GAINES, J., MEDNICK, S. A., and
HIGGINS, J.: Acta Psychiatrica Scandinavica, 39:601, 1964.
22. GARMEZY, N., and RODNICK, E. H.:
An Experimental Approach to the
Study of Motivation in Schizophrenia.
In Jones, M. R. (ed.): Nebraska Symposium on Motivation. Lincoln, University of Nebraska Press, 1957, pp.
109–184.

Mabel Blake Cohen,

Grace Baker,

Robert A. Cohen,

Frieda Fromm-Reichmann,

and Edith V. Weigert

# An Intensive Study of Twelve Cases
# of Manic-Depressive Psychosis

*While a variety of approaches have been taken in the study of schizophrenia, relatively little research has been done to uncover the etiology of manic-depressive psychosis. This paper by Cohen, Baker, Cohen, Fromm-Reichmann, and Weigert is one of the few energetic attempts to work on this problem. They have been concerned with an intensive study of twelve patients diagnosed as manic-depres- sive in order to be able to arrive at a detailed description of how the disorder develops. They have not been content with older theories that merely tend to characterize the personality of such patients as excessively oral or dependent, for example. Their concern is with why and how he got that way.*

The purpose of this study is to examine the manic-depressive character
by means of the intensive psychoanalytic psychotherapy of a number of
patients. We feel this to be potentially
useful, since the newer understanding
of interpersonal processes and of problems of anxiety has not hitherto been
brought to bear on this group of patients. The older psychoanalytic studies
of the psychopathology of the manic
depressive have largely described the
intrapsychic state of the patient and
left unexplained the question of how
the particular pattern of maladjustive
behavior has arisen. Thus, to use a
simple example, the manic depressive is
said to have an oral character. However,

Abridged from an article appearing in Psychiatry, 17(1954), 103–137, with the special permission of The William Alanson White Psychiatric Foundation, Inc., holder of the copyright, and Dr. Mabel Blake Cohen.

the question of how or why he developed an oral character is left unconsidered, except that such factors as a constitutional overintensity of oral drives, or overindulgence or frustration during the oral phase, are mentioned. Our purpose is to delineate as far as possible the experiences with significant people which made it necessary for the prospective manic depressive to develop the particular patterns of interaction which comprise his character and his illness. To this end, neither constitutional factors nor single traumata are stressed in this report, although we do not deny their significance. Rather, we have directed our attention to the interpersonal environment from birth on, assuming that it has interacted with the constitutional endowment in such a way as to eventuate in the development of a manic-depressive character in the child. In other words, the personality of the parents, the quality of their handling of the child, and the quality of the child's response to this handling have played an important part in the development of a characteristic pattern of relating to others and reacting to anxiety-arousing situations which we call typical of the manic-depressive character.

Such a study has many implications for the improvement of the therapeutic approach to the patient. We follow the basic premise of psychoanalytic theory —that in the transference relationship with the therapist the patient will repeat the patterns of behavior which he has developed with significant figures earlier in his life. By studying the transference, we can make inferences about earlier experiences; conversely, by understanding the patient historically, we can make inferences about the transference relationship. As our grasp of the patient's part of the pattern of interaction with his therapist improves, we can gain some concept of what goals

of satisfaction he is pursuing, as well as of what sort of anxieties he is striving to cope with. We may then intervene through our part in the interaction to assist him more successfully to achieve his goals of satisfaction and to resolve some of the conflicts which are at the source of his anxiety.

In this research project, a total of twelve cases were studied. They were all treated by intensive psychoanalytic psychotherapy for periods ranging from one to five years. Nine of the cases were presented and discussed in the original research seminar from 1944 to 1947. During 1952 and 1953, the present research group studied three additional cases in great detail; the members of the group met in three-hour sessions twice monthly during that period. All twelve of the cases are referred to in brief throughout the report, and extracts are used from the last three cases (namely, Miss G, Mr. R, and Mr. H) to illustrate various points.

## FAMILY BACKGROUND AND CHARACTER STRUCTURE

### Family Background

For all of the twelve patients studied, a consistant finding was made in regard to the family's position in its social environment. Each family was set apart from the surrounding milieu by some factor which singled it out as "different." This factor varied widely. In many instances it was membership in a minority group such as the Jews, as in the case of Mr. H. In others it was economic; for example, one patient's family had lost its money and was in a deteriorating social position, and in Mr. R's case, the father's illness and alcoholism had put the family in poor economic circumstances and in an anomalous social position. In another case, the difference resulted from the mother's being hospitalized for schizophrenia.

In every case, the patient's family had felt the social difference keenly and had reacted to it with intense concern and with an effort, first, to improve its acceptability in the community by fitting in with "what the neighbors think," and, second, to improve its social prestige by raising the economic level of the family, or by winning some position of honor or accomplishment. In both of these patterns of striving for a better social position, the children of the family played important roles; they were expected to conform to a high standard of good behavior, the standard being based largely on the parents' concept of what the neighbors expected. Thus Mr. R's mother was greatly overconcerned that he not walk in front of company in the living room, and Mr. H's mother threatened him with severe punishment when he misbehaved while out on the street with her. One mother described her early attitudes toward her child as follows:

I was always an independently minded person, not very demonstrative, so therefore most affection I may have had for anyone wasn't exactly worn on my sleeve. Kay I always loved and there was nothing I didn't try to get for her. My first thought, in most all my selfish material gains, was to get her things I had wanted or didn't have; to go places that I always longed to go to. Hasn't she ever told you of all the good times she has had? College proms, high school parties, dances, rides, silly girl incidents? I can remember so many she has had. Those were the things I had worked for her to have, and believe me, I had to fight to get them. . . . If you could have just an inkling of the unhappiness I have had trying to give her the material things I thought she wanted, for she never showed any love to me, perhaps you would understand my part. I always tried to protect her from the hurts that I had. . . .

These attitudes on the part of the parents—chiefly the mother—inculcated in the child a strict and conventional concept of good behavior, and also one which was derived from an impersonal authority—"they." The concept seemed to carry with it the connotation of parents whose own standards were but feebly held and poorly conceptualized, but who would be very severe if the child offended "them."

In addition to the depersonalization of authority, the use of the child as an instrument for improving the family's social position again acted as a force devaluing the child as a person in his own right. Not "who you are" but "what you do" became important for parental approval. Getting good grades in school, winning the approval of teachers and other authorities, receiving medals of honor, winning competitions, and being spoken of as a credit to the parents were the values sought by the parents from the child. In a few cases the family's isolation seemed to stem from the fact that they were "too good" for the neighboring families, due to the fact that they had more money or greater prestige. But here, too, the child's role was seen as being in service of the family's reputation.

In a number of cases, the child who was later to develop a manic-depressive psychosis was selected as the chief carrier of the burden of winning prestige for the family. This could be because the child was the brightest, the best looking, or in some other way the most gifted, or because he was the oldest, the youngest, or the only son or only daughter.

The necessity for winning prestige was quite frequently inculcated most vigorously by the mother. She was usually the stronger and more determined parent, whereas the father was usually the weakling, the failure who was responsible for the family's poor fortunes.

This was not invariably the case; thus one patient's mother had been hospitalized with schizophrenia from the patient's babyhood on. However, in the more typical cases, the mother was an intensely ambitious person, sometimes directly aggressive, at other times concealing her drive beneath a show of martyrdom. She tended to devalue the father and to blame his weakness, lack of ambition, or other fault for the family's ill fortune. The mother of the patient referred to as Kay wrote in the following terms:

About Kay's father, I'm afraid I can't tell you too much about him, because I was away a good deal, and didn't see too much of him. But as I remember him, I guess he was sort of a pathetic person, or at least I always had a feeling of pity. He had no real home; no immediate family; no decent jobs, at least in my opinion, and no real character.

This blaming of the father for the family's lack of position is in all likelihood due to the fact that in this culture the father is customarily the carrier of prestige, as well as being due to the peculiarities of the mother's relationship with him. The mother was usually thought of by the child as the moral authority in the family, and his attitude toward her was usually cold and unloving, but fearful and desirous of approval. Blame was also leveled at the mothers by the fathers for their coldness and contemptuousness. It seemed that the consistent use of blaming attitudes was of importance in establishing the child's patterns of self-evaluation.

The fathers in the cases studied were thought of by their children as weak but lovable. Two fathers were unsuccessful doctors, one an unsuccessful lawyer, one an unsuccessful tailor, another simply a ne'er-do-well, and so on. By and large they earned some kind of a living for their families and did not desert them but they were considered failures because of their *comparative* lack of success in relation to the standard the family *should* have achieved. The fathers usually were dependent on their wives, although they sometimes engaged in rather futile rebellious gestures against the pressures put on them —as when Mr. H's father spent the evenings playing pool and gambling with his men friends instead of at home listening to his wife's nagging. But, on the whole, they apparently accepted the blame visited upon them and thus implied to their children, "Do not be like me." Each patient, in general, loved his father much more warmly than his mother, and often attempted to defend and justify the father for his lack of success; but in the very defense of the father the patient demonstrated his acceptance of his mother's standards. This pattern was seen to occur regardless of the patient's sex.

Another important contrast in the child's attitude toward his parents was that in his eyes the mother was the reliable one. Thus the child faced the dilemma of finding the unreliable and more-or-less contemptible parent the lovable one, and the reliable, strong parent the disliked one. This pattern also was quite consistent in most of the families of these patients, whether the patient was a boy or a girl. The attitude of the mother toward the father served in addition as a dramatic example of what might happen to the child should he fail to achieve the high goals set by the mother.

### Early Development of the Child

Present-day concepts of the development of personality in infancy and early childhood no longer assume that the infant has no relationships with the people around him until he has reached the age of a year or so. Rather, it is believed that object relations develop from birth on, although it is obvious that early relationships must be quite different in quality from those experienced later on. Much evidence on infantile development in the early postnatal period [1] demonstrates that the infant reacts selectively to various attitudes in the mothering one. He thrives in an atmosphere of warmth, relaxation, and tenderness while he experiences digestive disorders, shows a variety of tension disorders, and even may die of marasmus in an atmosphere of tension, anxiety, and physical coldness. Under these circumstances, a vague, chaotic, and somewhat cosmic concept of another person—the mothering one—very soon begins to develop, and to this person the infant attributes his feelings of well-being or ill-being; this person is experienced as being extremely powerful.

We have compared the reports of the inner experiences of manic-depressives with those given by schizophrenic patients in regard to the times of greatest anxiety in each. While it is manifestly impossible to make specific constructions on the basis of such accounts, it is nevertheless our impression that they support the conception that the major unresolved anxiety-provoking experiences of the manic-depressive patient occur at a later stage in the development of interpersonal relationships than is the case with the schizophrenic. In the schizophrenic, a conception of self clearly differentiated from the surrounding world does not seem to have been developed, and the patient in panic believes that others are completely aware of his feelings, and that their actions are undertaken with this knowl-

edge. The manic depressive seems not to experience this breaking down of the distinction between himself and others in times of intense anxiety; rather, he mobilizes defenses which preserve the awareness of self as distinct from others. This formulation has much in common with that of Melanie Klein.

The common experience of therapists with the two disorders is to find the manic depressive much more irritating but much less frightening to work with than the schizophrenic. This may be related to the different concepts of self and others that the two groups of patients have.[2]

Figure 1 is intended to show pictorially the difference in interpersonal closeness and object relations between the schizophrenic and the manic-depressive characters.

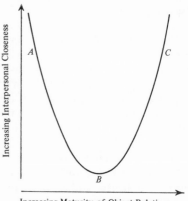

Points A, B, and C represent successive stages in development. At and soon after birth (A), other persons—chiefly the mother—are hardly recognized as such; interpersonal closeness is great but is based upon the intense dependence of the infant upon his

[1] See particularly Margaret Ribble, *The rights of infants*; New York: Columbia Univ. Press, 1943. See also Spitz, R. Anaclitic Depression. In *The psychoanalytic study of the child*, Vol. II. New York: International Universities Press, 1946.

[2] For further discussion of this point see a later section of this paper on Differential Diagnosis of the Manic-Depressive.

mother. As relationships develop, the primary closeness based upon identification diminishes (B). Later, a more mature closeness begins to develop (C), in which the self is at last perceived as distinct and separate from other persons. It is evident that a critical phase in development (point B on the graph) occurs when the closeness with the mother based upon identification has begun to disappear, but the more mature type of relationship based on recognition of others as whole, separate persons has not as yet developed to any great degree.

We conceive of the major unresolved anxiety-provoking experiences of the schizophrenic patient as occurring at point A. At this phase of personality development, closeness is based upon identification, and relationships are partial in character. In the manic-depressive patient, these experiences would occur at point B, at a time when identification is less frequently used, but when the ability to relate to others as individuals distinct from one's self is in the earliest stage of development. Consequently, although relationships at point B are more mature than at point A, the individual in another sense is in a more isolated position, since he no longer employs the mechanism of identification to the degree that he did in earlier infancy but has yet to develop the capacity for a higher level of interpersonal relatedness. At this time, therefore, the developing child could be expected to feel peculiarly alone and consequently vulnerable to any threat of abandonment. We would conceive of the neurotic individual as having experienced his major unresolved anxiety experiences at point C, when interpersonal, relatedness is more advanced than at B.

While reliable data about infancy are extremely difficult to gather, our series of manic-depressive patients show a preponderance of normal infancies, with one major exception, Mr. R, who was a feeding problem and was malnourished and fretful for the first several months of his life. The mothers of these patients appear to have found the child more acceptable and lovable as infants than as children, when the manifold problems of training and acculturation became important. Our impression is that it was the utter dependence of the infant which was pleasurable to the mother, and that the growing independence and rebelliousness of the early stage of childhood were threatening to her. Unconforming or unconventional behavior on the part of the child was labelled as "bad" by the mother, and she exerted great pressure to stamp it out. Thus, the heretofore loving and tender mother would rather abruptly change into a harsh and punishing figure, at about the end of the first year. The child, under the stress of anxiety, would have difficulty integrating the early good mother and the later bad mother into a whole human being, now good, now bad. While a similar difficulty in integration may face all children, this split in attitude toward authority, in the more fortunate, is eventually resolved as the personality matures; but it remains with the manic depressive for the rest of his life unless interrupted by life experience or therapy. An important authority is regarded as the source of all good things, provided he is pleased; but he is thought of as a tyrannical and punishing figure unless he is placated by good behavior. These early experiences probably lay the groundwork for the manic depressive's later ambivalence.

## Later Development of the Child

In later childhood, when the child's personality traits and role in the family have begun to crystallize, the manic depressive may be likened to Joseph in the Bible story. Joseph was his father's favorite son. The envy of his eleven brothers was aroused by his father's giving him a multicolored coat, and was increased after they heard of two of Joseph's dreams. The first dream was about eleven sheaves bent down, and one standing upright; everybody knew that this represented Joseph with his eleven brothers bowing to him. In the other dream, eleven stars, the sun, and the moon were bowing to the twelfth star, and everybody agreed that this represented the mother, the father, and the eleven brothers bowing before Joseph. His envious brothers decided to kill him, but one of them, finding himself unable to agree to killing his own flesh and blood, influenced the others to throw him into a pit in the wilderness, and finally to sell him to a passing merchant from a foreign land. After his separation from his family, and his arrival in the foreign land, Joseph immediately grew in stature, and quickly rose to the position of the Pharaoh's first adviser. By his skill and foresight, he averted the evil effects of a threatening famine, not only in Egypt, but also in the neighboring countries.

This story can be used to illustrate some aspects of the manic depressive's relationship to his family. Many of these patients are the best-endowed members of their families, excelling in some cases in specific creative abilities over their siblings, and over one or both of their parents. Some of them have a special place in the family as a result of their own ambitious strivings as, for example, Mr. H. Others are the favorites of one or both parents for other reasons, sometimes because they are the only one of their sex among the siblings, as in one of our patients. All this makes for their enviously guarding their special position in the family group, despite their being burdened with great responsibilities in connection with their special position. It also subjects them to the envy of their siblings, and, quite often, to the competition of one or both parents. Neither the patients themselves nor the family members are, generally speaking, aware of their mutual envy and competition. Mr. H's difficulties with envy were particularly acute. His therapist reported as follows:

Mr. H suffers from extreme feelings of envy toward his male contemporaries who have been more successful than he. The envy is so acute and painful that it is for the most part kept out of awareness. It occasionally forces itself upon his attention, particularly at times when some one of his contemporaries has received a promotion or other sign of success. The patient always feels that he deserves the promotion more than the other person and believes that his illnesses are the stumbling block in the way of his receiving it, or, at times, that the lack of recognition is due to anti-Semitism. While he is an extremely intelligent and able person who does his work adequately; except in periods of emotional disturbance, he does not visualize himself as succeeding on the basis of his productivity, and he makes little effort to succeed on the basis of doing a better job than his competitors. His efforts toward success are directed toward getting to be the friend of the boss, becoming a companion of the boss in sports or games, or going to the races with the boss. By getting the boss to like him especially or find him pleasant and agreeable to be with, he hopes to interest the boss in promoting his future. During his psychotic episodes this pattern increases in its scope and becomes a grandiose fantasy in which he is being groomed for the Presidency of the United States or in which the eye of some mysterious person is watching over him. He once said, for instance, "There is an organization, the FBI, which is set up to find the bad people and put them where they can't do any harm. Why should there not be a similar organization which has been set up to find the good people and see to it that they are put in a position of importance?"

As mentioned previously, manic depressives usually come from families who are in minority groups because of their social, economic, ethnic, or religious status. The family members in these minority groups cling together in group-conscious mutual love and acceptance, and in the wish and need to maintain and raise their family prestige in their groups, and their group prestige before an adverse outer world. There is little room for, or concern with, problems of interpersonal relatedness. Under the all-important requirement of seeking and maintaining high prestige, it seldom occurs to any member of these groups to think in terms other than "we belong together." This, then, is a background in which neither the active nor the passive participants in developments of envy and competition are aware of these developments. Yet, without being aware of it, the best-endowed children will spend quite a bit of energy to counteract the envy of the siblings, of which they are unconsciously afraid. Often the children are brought up, not only by their parents, but also by the joint endeavor of several other important older members of the clan. In spite of all this supervision, there is rarely an individual on whom a child can rely with confidence in a one-to-one relationship. In fact, it is frequently the case that the family group has a number of authority figures in it—grandparents, uncles, aunts, and so on—so that the child's experiences of authority are with multiple parent figures. In this setting, the manic depressive in very early childhood is frequently burdened with the family's expectation that he will do better than his parents in the service of the prestige of the family and

the clan; consequently, he may feel, or be made to feel, responsible for whatever hardship or failure occurs in the family. For example, one of our patients was held responsible by her sisters for her mother's death when the patient was eighteen months old—"Mother would still be here had you not been born"; for the failure of her father's second marriage, which had been made to provide a mother for the patient; and for her father's "ruined" feet, the result of tramping the streets as a salesman after his position of considerable prominence had ended in bankruptcy. Another patient at the age of three felt that he had to take over certain responsibilities toward the clan, sensing that his parents had failed in the fulfillment of these.

The special role in the family group which these patients hold is accentuated by the fact that they are, as a rule, pushed very early into unusual responsibility, or else themselves assume this role. As a result, their image of the significant people in the family usually differs considerably from that of the other siblings. With their different appraisal of one or both of their parents, from early childhood they are extremely lonely, in spite of growing up in the group-conscious atmosphere which we have described, where there is little feeling for privacy, and where the little-differentiated experiences of the various family members are considered in the light of the common good of the whole family, or the whole clan. In many cases these people are unaware of their loneliness, as long as they are well, because the sentiment of "we belong together" is fostered by their family.

As these people grow up, they remain extremely sensitive to envy and competition. They know what it is like to harbor it themselves and to be its target. One means of counteracting this envy, which early becomes an unconscious pattern, is to undersell themselves to hide the full extent of their qualifications. Another pattern which many of these patients develop to counteract feelings of envying and being envied is to be exceptionally helpful to their siblings, to other members of the early group, and, later on, to other people with whom they come in contact in various ways. They often use their talents for promoting other persons and their abilities. The price they unconsciously demand for this is complete acceptance and preference by the others. These traits are repeated in the transference situation during treatment.

For instance, a patient was brought to the hospital against her will, without any insight into her mental disturbance. Much to everybody's surprise, she most willingly entered treatment with one member of our group. Everything seemed to run in a smooth and promising way until suddenly, after about two weeks, the patient declared vehemently that she would continue treatment no longer. When she was asked for her reasons, she said that she had been under the impression that she might help her doctor, who was an immigrant, to establish herself professionally in the new country by allowing the doctor to treat her successfully. But during the two weeks she had been at the hospital, she had found that the doctor had already succeeded in establishing herself, and therefore the patient's incentive for treatment was gone.

## The Adult Character

As adults, persons with cyclothymic personalities continue to manifest many of the same traits that they exhibited in childhood. During the "healthy" intervals between attacks, they appear

from a superficial point of view to be relatively well adjusted and at ease with other people. A certain social facility is typical of the hypomanic, although it is not seen so clearly in the depressive person in his "healthy" intervals. For instance, the hypomanic typically has innumerable acquaintances with whom he appears to be on most cordial terms. On closer scrutiny of these relationships, however, it becomes apparent that they cannot be considered to be in any sense friendships or intimacies. The appearance of closeness is provided by the hypomanic's liveliness, talkativeness, wittiness, and social aggressiveness. Actually, there is little or no communicative exchange between the hypomanic and any one of his so-called friends. He is carrying out a relatively stereotyped social performance, which takes little or no account of the other person's traits and characteristics, while the other person, quite commonly, is allowing himself to be entertained and manipulated.

Both the hypomanic and the depressive share in their tendency to have one or a very few extremely dependent relationships. In the hypomanic this dependency is concealed under all his hearty good humor and apparent busyness, but it is quite clear in the depressive. The hypomanic or the depressive is extremely demanding toward the person with whom he has a dependent relationship, basing his claim for love and attention upon his need of the other, and making it a *quid pro quo* for his self-sacrifice. Demands are made for love, attention, service, and possessions. The concept of reciprocity is missing; the needs of the other for similar experiences are not recognized.[3]

[3] This formulation is similar to that made by O. Spurgeon English, who states, "Closely tied up with the matter of love is the patient's self-esteem or love of himself. The manic-depressive does not seem to have much feeling of love to give, and what he has he is afraid to give." English, Observation of trends in manic-depressive psychosis, *Psychiatry*, 12(1949), 129.

Yet the failure to recognize the needs of the other does elicit unconscious guilt which may be manifested by the manic depressive's consciously thinking of himself as having given a great deal. What the giving seems to amount to is a process of underselling himself. In the relationship the devaluation and underselling also indicate to the partner the person's great need of him, and serve to counteract the old, unconscious, fearful expectation of competition and envy from the important person. The cyclothymic person's own envy and competition, too, are hidden from his awareness, and take the form of feelings of inferiority and great need. The person conceives of himself as reaching success, satisfaction, or glory through the success of the other rather than by efforts of his own. Thus Mr. H made himself the stooge of the president of the class in high school, receiving as his reward the political plums that the president was able to hand out, and failing to recognize that what he actually wanted was to be class president himself. He continued this kind of relationship with some important figure—usually male—in every free period afterward, while in his psychotic attacks the wish to be president himself came to consciousness, and he made futile efforts to achieve it.

Thus, the process of underselling themselves, both for the sake of denying envy and in order to become the recipient of gifts from the other, often reaches the point where these persons actually paralyze the use of their own endowments and creative abilities. They themselves frequently believe that they have lost their assets or that they never had any. The process of underselling themselves, especially in depressives, also may convince other people in their environment of their lack of ability. At this point, they begin to hate these other people for being the cause of the vicious circle in which they are caught; and they hate themselves because they sense the fraudulence of their behavior in not having expressed openly all their inner feelings.

One patient said time and again during his depression, "I'm a fraud, I'm a fraud; I don't know why, but I'm a fraud." When he was asked why he felt fraudulent, he would produce any number of rationalizations, but at last it was found that the thing he felt to be fraudulent was his underselling of himself. This same patient got so far in his fraudulent attempt at denying his total endowment that he was on the verge of giving up a successful career—which, while he was well, held a good deal of security and satisfaction for him—in order to regain the love of an envious friend, which he felt he was in danger of losing because of his own greater success.

We see then, in the adult cyclothymic, a person who is apparently well adjusted between attacks, although he may show minor mood swings or be chronically overactive or chronically mildly depressed. He is conventionally well-behaved and frequently successful, and he is hard-working and conscientious; indeed, at times his overconscientiousness and scrupulousness lead to his being called obsessional. He is typically involved in one or more relationships of extreme dependence, in which, however, he does not show the obsessional's typical need to control the other person for the sake of power, but instead seeks to control the other person in the sense of swallowing him up. His inner feeling, when he allows himself to notice it, is one of emptiness and need. He is extremely stereotyped in his attitudes and opinions, tending to take over the opinions of the person in his environment whom he regards as an important authority. Again this contrasts with the outward conformity but subtle rebellion of the obsessional. It should be emphasized that the dependency feelings are largely out of awareness in states of well-being and also in the manic phase; in fact, these people frequently take pride in being independent.

His principal source of anxiety is the fear of abandonment. He is afraid to be alone, and seeks the presence of other people. Abandonment is such a great threat because his relationships with others are based upon utilizing them as possessions or pieces of property. If he offends them, by differing with them or outcompeting them, and they withdraw, he is left inwardly empty, having no conception of inner resources to fall back on. Also, if they offend him and he is compelled to withdraw, this leaves him similarly alone. In this situation of potential abandonment, the anxiety is handled by overlooking the emotional give-and-take between himself and others, so that he is unaware of the other person's feelings toward himself or of his feelings toward the other. This is clearly seen in the well-known difficulty which therapists have in terminating an hour with a depressive. Regardless of what has gone on during the hour, at the end of it the depressive stands in the doorway, plaintively seeking reassurance by some such question as "Am I making any progress, Doctor?" An attempt to answer the question only leads to another or to a repetition of the same one, for the patient is not seeking an answer—or rather does not actually believe there is an answer—but instead is striving to prolong his contact with the doctor. In carrying out this piece of stereotyped behavior, he is unaware of the fact of the doctor's mounting impatience and irritation, and overlooks its consequence—namely, that, instead of there being increasing closeness between patient and doctor, a situation has now been set up in which the

distance between them is rapidly increasing.

This character structure can be seen to have a clear-cut relationship to the infantile development which we have hypothesized for the manic depressive. According to this hypothesis, interpersonal relations have been arrested in their development at the point where the child recognizes himself as being separate from others, but does not yet see others as being full-sized human beings; rather he sees them as entities who are now good, now bad, and must be manipulated. If this is the case, then the adult's poorness of discrimination about others is understandable. His life and welfare depend upon the other's goodness, as he sees it, and he is unable to recognize that one and the same person may be accepting today, rejecting tomorrow, and then accepting again on the following day. Nor can he recognize that certain aspects of his behavior may be acceptable while others are not; instead, he sees relationships as all-or-none propositions. The lack of interest in and ability to deal with interpersonal subtleties is probably also due to the fact that the important persons in the child's environment themselves deal in conventional stereotypes. The child, therefore, has little opportunity at home to acquire skill in this form of communication.

We have said little in this report about the manic depressive's hostility. We feel that it has been considerably overstressed as a dynamic factor in the illness. Certainly, a great deal of the patient's behavior leaves a hostile impression upon those around him, but we feel that the driving motivation in the patient is the one we have stressed —the feeling of need and emptiness. The hostility we would relegate to a secondary position: we see hostile feelings arising in the patient as the result of frustration of his manipulative and exploitative needs. We conceive of such subsequent behavior, as demandingness toward the other or self-injury, as being an attempt to restore the previous dependent situation. Of course, the demandingness and exploitativeness are exceedingly annoying and anger-provoking to those around the patient— the more so because of the failure of the patient to recognize what sort of people he is dealing with. But we feel that much of the hostility that has been imputed to the patient has been the result of his annoying impact upon others, rather than of a primary motivation to do injury to them.

## The Psychotic Attack

The precipitation of the depressive attack by a loss is well known. However, there have been many cases in which attacks have occurred where there has been no loss. In some it has seemed that a depression occurred at the time of a promotion in job or some other improvement in circumstances. On scrutiny it can be seen that in those patients where a depression has occurred without an apparent change in circumstances of living, the change which has actually occurred has been in the patient's appraisal of the situation. The patient incessantly hopes for and strives for a dependency relationship in which all his needs are met by the other. This hope and the actions taken to achieve it are for the most part out of awareness since recognition of them would subject the person to feelings of guilt and anxiety. After every depressive attack, he sets forth upon this quest anew. In the course of time, it becomes apparent to him that his object is not fulfilling his needs. He then gets into a vicious circle: he uses depressive techniques—complaining or whining—to elicit the gratifications he requires. These become offensive to the other who becomes even less gratifying; therefore, the patient redoubles his efforts and receives still less. Finally, he loses hope and enters into the psychotic state where the pattern of emptiness and need is repeated over and over again in the absence of any specific object.

As to the person who becomes depressed after a gain rather than a loss, we interpret this as being experienced by the patient himself as a loss, regardless of how it is evaluated by the outside world. Thus a promotion may remove the patient from a relatively stable dependency relationship with his co-workers or with his boss, and may call upon him to function at a level of self-sufficiency which is impossible for him. Also, being promoted may involve him in a situation of severe anxiety because of the envious feelings which he feels it will elicit in others, the fear occurring as the result of his unresolved childhood pattern of envying those more successful than himself and, in return, expecting and fearing the envy of others at his success. Having made them envious, he may believe that he can no longer rely on them to meet his needs, whereupon he is again abandoned and alone. For example, an episode from Mr. R's life was described by his analyst as follows:

After about a year of treatment it was suggested to the patient by one of his fellow officers that he ought to apply for a medal for his part in the war and he found the idea very tempting. When this was discussed with me, I attempted to discourage it, without coming out directly with a strong effort to interfere, and the discouraging words I said were unheard by the patient. He went ahead with a series of manipulative acts designed to win the medal, and it was awarded to him. No sooner had he received it than he became acutely anxious and tense.

He began to suspect his compeers of envying him and plotting to injure him in order to punish him for having taken advantage of them by getting a medal for himself, and he thought that his superior officers were contemptuous of him for his greediness. His life became a nightmare of anxiety in which he misinterpreted the smiles, glances, gestures, hellos, and other superficial behavior of his fellow officers as signifying their hatred and disapproval of him.

The manic attack is similar to the depressive in following a precipitating incident which carries the meaning of a loss of love. It often happens that there is a transient depression before the outbreak of manic behavior. For instance, Mr. H. was mildly depressed at Christmas time; his behavior from then on showed increasing evidence of irrationality which, however, was not striking enough to cause alarm until June, when he developed a full-blown manic attack. We believe, from our experience with patients who have had repeated attacks, that the presence of depressive feelings prior to the onset of the manic phase is very common, and perhaps the rule.

It is well known that many manic patients report feelings of depression during their manic phase. As one of our patients put it, while apparently manic:

I am crying underneath the laughter. . . . Blues all day long—feelings not properly expressed. Cover up for it, gay front while all the time I am crying. Laughing too much and loud hurts more. Not able to cry it complete and full of hell. All pinned up inside but the misery and hatred is greater than the need to cry. Praying for tears to feel human. Wishing for pain in hopes that there is something left. Fright is almost indescribable.

We agree with Freud, Lewin, and others that dynamically the manic behavior can best be understood as a defensive structure utilized by the patient to avoid recognizing and experiencing in awareness his feelings of depression. The timing of the manic behavior varies widely: it may either precede the depression, in which case it can be understood as a defense which has eventually failed to protect the patient from his depression; or it may follow the depressive attack, when it represents an escape from the unbearable depressive state into something more tolerable. Subjectively, the state of being depressed is one of more intolerable discomfort than the state of being manic, since the patient in effect is threatened with loss of identity of his self.

There are personalities who are able to lead a life of permanent hypomania, with no psychotic episodes. Of course, many chronic hypomanics do have psychotic episodes, but there are some who never have to be hospitalized. Such a patient was Mr. R, who had a very narrow escape from hospitalization when he became agitatedly depressed at a time when several severely anxiety-producing blows occurred in rapid succession. On the whole, however, he maintained what appeared to be an excellent reality adjustment. Subjectively, he was usually constrained to avoid thinking of himself and his feelings by keeping busy, but when he did turn his attention inward, then intense feelings of being in an isolated, unloved, and threatened position would arise.

We have noted in our private practices a trend in recent years for an increased number of persons who utilize rather typical hypomanic defense patterns to enter into analytic therapy. These people tend in general to be quite successful in a material sense and to conceal their sense of inward emptiness and isolation both from themselves and from others. Probably their entering analysis in increasing numbers has some correlation with the popular success achieved by psychoanalysis in recent years in this country. Once committed to treatment, these so-called extraverts rapidly reveal their extreme dependency needs, and, on the whole, our impression has been that psychoanalysis has proven decidely beneficial to them.

In the light of the above discussion of the manic and depressive attacks, we have come to the conclusion that they need to be differentiated psychodynamically chiefly on the score of what makes the manic defense available to some patients while it is not so usable by others. Some investigators postulate a constitutional or metabolic factor here, but in our opinion adherence to this hypothesis is unjustified in the present state of our knowledge. We feel that further investigation of the manic defense is indicated before a reliable hypothesis can be set up.

We feel that the basic psychotic pattern is the depressive one. The onset of a depression seems understandable enough in the light of the patient's typical object-relation pattern described earlier. That is, becoming sick, grief-stricken, and helpless is only an exaggeration and intensification of the type of appeal which the manic depressive makes to the important figures in his life in the healthy intervals. When this type of appeal brings rejection, as it usually does when carried beyond a certain degree of intensity, then the vicious circle mentioned earlier can be supposed to set in, with each cycle representing a further descent on the spiral. At the end, the patient is left with his severely depressed feelings and with no feeling of support or relatedness from the people whom he formerly relied on. At this point, where the feelings of depression and emptiness are

acute, the patient may follow one of three courses: he may remain depressed; he may commit suicide; or he may regress still further to a schizophrenic state.

If he remains depressed, he carries on a chronic, largely fantastic acting-out of the pattern of dependency. There is no longer a suitable object. The members of the family who have hospitalized him are now only present in fantasy. The patient does, however, continue to address his complaints and appeals to them as though they were still present and powerful. In addition, he rather indiscriminately addresses the same appeal to all of those around him in the hospital. The appeal may be mute, acted out by his despair, sleeplessness, and inability to eat, or it may be highly vociferous and addressed verbally to all who come in contact with him, in the form of statements about his bowels being blocked up, his insides being empty, his family having been bankrupted or killed, and so on. The same pattern is developed with his therapist: instead of a therapeutic relationship in which he strives to make use of the doctor's skill with some confidence and notion of getting somewhere, the same empty pattern of mourning and hopelessness is set up, in which he strives to gain help by a display of his misery and to receive reassurance by repeatedly requesting it. It is notable and significant that his ability to work on or examine the nature of his relationships is non-existent; that difficulties with others are denied and self-blame is substituted. The major therapeutic problem with the depressive is actually the establishment of a working relationship in which problems are examined and discussed. Conversely, the major system of defenses which have to be overcome in order to establish such a working relationship lie in the substitution of the stereotyped complaint or self-accusation for a more meaningful kind of self-awareness. There seems to be a sort of clinging to the hope that the repetition of the pattern will eventually bring fulfillment. Relinquishing the pattern seems to bring with it the danger of suicide on the one hand, or disintegration on the other. It is our opinion that, in the situation in which the patient has given up his habitual depressive pattern of integration and has as yet not developed a substitute pattern which brings some security and satisfaction, he is in danger of suicide. The suicide, as has been well demonstrated by previous workers, has the meaning of a further, highly irrational attempt at relatedness. It can be thought of as the final appeal of helplessness. "When they see how unhappy I really am, they will do something." This fits in with the almost universal fantasy indulged in by most people in moments of frustration and depression of what "they" will say and do when I am dead. Along with this magical use of death to gain one's dependent ends, goes a fantasy of recapturing the early relationship by dying and being born again.

For instance, Miss G took an overdose of barbiturates as a last resort after her failure to persuade her father to accede to a request by other means. It appeared that in this case there was little intent to die, but that the action was resorted to because lesser means of convincing him had failed. Probably in this instance of a conscious suicidal gesture the manipulative goal is much more apparent and more clearly in awareness than with the majority of cases. On the other hand, self-destruction also has a more rational element; that is, it is the final expression of the feeling that all hope is lost, and the wish to get rid of the present pain. We are inclined to believe that the element of hopelessness in the act of suicide has

not been given sufficient weight in previous studies.

Sullivan, at the end of a great many years of studying the obsessional neurotic, came to the conclusion that many of the more severely ill cases were potentially schizophrenic in situations where their habitual and trusted obsessional defenses proved inadequate to deal with anxiety. This statement also applies to the depressive: if the defensive aspects of the depression become ineffectual, than a collapse of the personality structure can occur with an ensuing reintegration on the basis of a schizophrenic way of life rather than a depressive one.

## Guilt and the Superego

We have avoided using the term superego in this report, and have not involved the cruel, punishing superego in our attempted explanation of the depression. It is our opinion that utilization of the term superego in this way merely conceals the problem rather than explains it. There are several basic questions regarding the problems of conscience and guilt in the manic depressive. First, what influences account for the severe and hypermoral standards of these people? And second, what is the dynamic function of the self-punishing acts and attitudes which are engaged in during the periods of illness?

The overcritical standards of manic depressives are not explicable as a direct taking-over of the standards of the parents, since these patients in childhood have usually been treated with rather exceptional overindulgence. However, in the section on Family Background and Character Structure we have mentioned the peculiar combination of lack of conviction of worth and a standard of behavior in the family coupled with an intense devotion to conventional morality and to what other people think. It is logical that a child raised by an inconsistent mother who is at times grossly overindulgent and at others severely rejecting would be unable to build up a reasonable code of conduct for himself, and that his code —focussed around what an impersonal authority is supposed to expect of him and based on no concept of parental reliability or strength—would be both oversevere and frightening in its impersonality. In all probability, much of his moral code is based on the struggle to acquire those qualities of strength and virtue which he finds missing in his parents. Later in this report we will return to the problem of authority in the manic depressive. Suffice it to say here that in dealing with authority this type of patient shows a rigid preconception of what authority expects of him as well as a persistent conviction that he must fit in with these expectations which are beyond the reach of reason or experience. The authority appears, in our experience, at times as an incorporated superego and at other times as a projected, impersonal, but tyrannical force. Or rather, every significant person in the patient's social field is invested with the quality of authority.

In this relationship with authority, the self-punitive acts and experiencing of guilt can be understood as devices for placating the impersonal tyrant. The guilt expressed by the depressive does not carry on to any genuine feeling of regret or effort to change behavior. It is, rather, a means to an end. Merely suffering feelings of guilt is expected to suffice for regaining approval. On the other hand, it may also be seen that achieving a permanent, secure, human relationship with authority is regarded as hopeless. Therefore, no effort to change relationships or to integrate on a better level of behavior is undertaken,

and the patient merely resorts to the magic of uttering guilty cries to placate authority.

## DIFFERENTIAL DIAGNOSIS OF THE MANIC-DEPRESSIVE

Some observers have stated that in the intervals between attacks, the manic depressive has a character structure similar to that of the obsessional neurotic. It has also been asserted that in the psychotic phase the manic-depressive illness is essentially schizophrenic. This latter statement is supported by the fact that many manic depressives do, in the course of time, evolve into chronic schizophrenic psychoses, usually paranoid in character, and that there are many persecutory ideas present both in the manic attack and in the depression. In general, there has always been much uncertainty as to who should be diagnosed manic depressive—an uncertainty which is reflected in the widely differing proportions of manic depressives and schizophrenics diagnosed in different mental hospitals.

What, then, is the point of singling out a diagnostic category called manic depressive? In our opinion, the manic-depressive syndrome does represent a fairly clear-cut system of defenses which are sufficiently unique and of sufficient theoretical interest to deserve special study. We feel that equating the manic-depressive character with the obsessional character overlooks the distinguishing differences between the two. The obsessional, while bearing many resemblances to the manic depressive, uses substitutive processes as his chief defense. The manic, on the other hand, uses the previously mentioned lack of interpersonal awareness as his chief defense, together with the defensive processes which are represented by the manic and the depressive symptoms themselves. The object relations of the obsessional are more stable and well developed than those of the manic depressive. While the obsessional's relations are usually integrations in which there is an intense degree of hostility, control, and envy, they do take into consideration the other person as a person. The manic depressive, on the other hand, develops an intensely dependent, demanding, oral type of relationship which overlooks the particular characteristics and qualities of the other.

According to Sullivan's conceptualization of the schizophrenic process, the psychosis is introduced typically by a state of panic, in which there is an acute break with reality resulting from the upsurge of dissociated drives and motivations which are absolutely unacceptable and invested with unbearable anxiety. Following this acute break, a variety of unsuccessful recovery or defensive processes ensue, which we call paranoid, catatonic, or hebephrenic. These represent attempts of the personality to deal with the conflicts which brought about the panic: the paranoid by projection; the catatonic by rigid control; the hebephrenic by focussing on bodily impulses. According to this conception, the manic depressive can be differentiated from the schizophrenic by the fact that he does not exhibit the acute break with reality which is seen in the schizophrenic panic. On the other hand, his psychotic processes of depression, or of mania, can be thought of as serving a defensive function against the still greater personality disintegration which is represented by the schizophrenic state. Thus, in persons whose conflicts and anxiety are too severe to be handled by depressive or manic defenses, a schizophrenic breakdown may be the end result.

Contrasting the schizophrenic and the manic depressive from the point of view of their early relationships, we see that the schizophrenic has accepted the bad mother as his fate, and his relation to reality is therefore attenuated. He is inclined to withdraw into detachment. He is hypercritical of family and cultural values. He is sensitive and subtle in his criticisms, original but disillusioned. He is disinclined to rely on others and is capable of enduring considerable degrees of loneliness. His reluctance to make demands on the therapist makes the therapist feel more sympathetic, and therefore the therapist is frequently more effective. In addition, the schizophrenic patient is more effective in his aggression; he can take the risk of attacking, for he is less afraid of loneliness. He is more sensitively aware of the emotions of therapist, since the boundaries between ego and environment are more fluid. The schizophrenic is not inclined to pretend, and is not easily fooled by other people's pretenses. Dream and fantasy life are nearer to awareness, and guilt feelings are also more conscious than unconscious.

The typical manic depressive, on the other hand, has not accepted the "bad mother" as his fate. He vacillates between phases in which he fights with the bad mother, and phases in which he feels reunited with the good mother. In the manic phase, his relationship with reality is more tenuous; he shows a lack of respect for other people, and all reality considerations are dismissed for the sake of magic manipulation to make the bad mother over into a good mother. The manic depressive is, therefore, mostly a good manipulator, a salesman, a bargaining personality. He is undercritical instead of being hypercritical. He easily sells out his convictions and his originality in order to force others to love him, deriving from this a borrowed esteem. In the depressive phase, he sacrifices himself to gain a good mother or to transform the bad mother into a good one. In order to do this, he calls himself bad, and suffers to expiate his sins. But these guilt feelings are, in a sense, artificial or expedient, utilized in order to manipulate the bad mother into becoming a good mother. The depressive does not come to terms with realistic guilt feelings. Instead, he uses his self-accusations, which frequently sound hypocritical, to convince the mother or a substitute that his need to be loved has absolute urgency. He denies his originality because he is terribly afraid of aloneness. He is more of a follower than a leader. He is dependent on prestige, and is quite unable to see through the pretense of his own or other people's conventionalities. He shows a high degree of anxiety when his manipulations fail. His denial of originality leads to feelings of emptiness and envy. His lack of subtlety in interpersonal relationships is due to his overruling preoccupation with exploiting the other person in order to fill his emptiness. This operates as a vicious circle: he has to maintain his claims for the good fulfilling mother, but his search for fullness via manipulation of another makes him feel helpless and empty. This incorporation of another person for the purpose of filling an inward emptiness, of acquiring a borrowed self-esteem, is very different from the lack of ego boundaries in the schizophrenic. The schizophrenic is in danger of losing his ego, and he expresses this danger in fantasies of world catastrophe. The manic depressive is threatened by object loss, since he habitually uses the object to patch up his ego weakness. Object relations in the manic depressive are, therefore, clouded by illusions, but even when he wails, demands, and blames the frustrating object, he is—by this very agitated activity in behalf of his own salvation, ineffective as it may be—defended against the loss of the ego. When the manic depressive becomes schizophrenic, this defense breaks down.

It should be noted that the infantile dependency and manipulative exploitativeness seen in the manic depressive are not unique to this type of disorder. They occur, in fact, in many forms of severe mental illness. The hysteric, for instance, exemplifies infantile dependency and exploitativeness as dramatically as the manic depressive, and in *la belle indifférence* one may see a resemblance to the euphoria of the manic or hypomanic. However, the combination of the dependent and exploitative traits with the other outstanding characteristics of the cyclothymic personality—particularly the communicative defect and the accompanying inability to recognize other persons as anything but good-bad stereotypes and the conventional but hypermoralistic values—does become sufficiently distinct and unique to distinguish these patients characterologically from other types.

## SUMMARY AND CONCLUSIONS

An intensive study of twelve manic-depressive patients was made in order to reformulate and further develop the dynamics of the character structure of these patients in terms of their patterns of interpersonal relationships. In addition to further developing our knowledge of their psychodynamics, we hoped to arrive at therapeutic procedures which would prove more useful in interrupting the course of this kind of illness.

A comprehensive survey of the literature was made in order to determine the present state of development of psychopathology theory in regard to manic-depressive states.

The manic-depressive character was investigated from the point of view of (1) the patterns of interaction between parents and child and between family and community; (2) the ways in which these patterns influenced the character structure of the child and affected his experiencing of other people in his subsequent life; and (3) the way in which these patterns are repeated in therapy and can be altered by the processes of therapy.

## Psychopathology

Among the significant parent-child interactions, we found that the family is usually in a low-prestige situation in the community or socially isolated in some other way and that the chief interest in the child is in his potential usefulness in improving the family's position or meeting the parents' prestige needs. A serious problem with envy also grows out of the importance of material success and high prestige. We also found that the child is usually caught between one parent who is thought of as a failure and blamed for the family's plight (frequently the father) and the other parent who is aggressively striving, largely through the instrumentality of the child, to remedy the situation. And finally, the serious disturbance in the child's later value system (superego) is in part attributable to the lack of a secure and consistent authority in the home and to the tremendous overconcern of the parents about what "they" think.

A study of the major unresolved anxiety-provoking experiences of the manic depressive indicates that the crucial disturbance in his interpersonal relationship occurs at a time in his development when his closeness (identification) with his mother has diminished but his ability to reorganize others as whole, separate persons has not yet developed. This accounts for the perpetuation of his response to important figures in his later life as either good or bad, black

or white, and his inability to distinguish shades of grey.

## Therapy

As a result of our study of these patients, we found that our ability to intervene successfully in the psychosis improved. While all of the factors which contributed to successful therapy with these patients are by no means understood, we concluded that certain areas could be isolated, as follows:

*Communication.* The primary problem in therapy is establishing a communicative relationship, which is, of course, a reflection of the patient's basic life difficulty. The most characteristic aspect of the manic depressive's defenses is his ability to avoid anxiety by erecting conventional barriers to emotional interchange. We have learned to interpret this as a defense rather than a defect in the patient's experience, and we have found that when it is interpreted as a defense, he responds by developing a greater ability to communicate his feelings and to establish empathic relationships.

*Dependency.* A second major problem is that of handling the patient's dependency needs, which are largely gratified by successful manipulation of others. Since the manic depressive's relationships with others are chiefly integrated on the basis of dependency, the therapist is in a dilemma between the dangers of allowing himself to fit into the previous pattern of the dependency gratification patterns of the patient and of forbidding dependency *in toto.* Furthermore, the therapeutic relationship in itself is a dependent relationship. The therapist must be alert to the manipulative tendencies of the patient and must continually bring these into open discussion rather than permit them to go on out of awareness.

*Transference-countertransference.* The most significant part of treatment is, as always, the working through of the transference and countertransference problems. The patient's main difficulties with the therapist are those of dealing with him as a stereotype and as a highly conventionalized authority figure who is either to be placated or manipulated, and by whom all of his dependency needs are to be met. The main difficulties of the therapist are in the frustrations and helplessness of trying to communicate with the patient through his defensive barriers and the strain of constantly being the target for the manipulative tendencies. These problems inevitably involve the therapist in a variety of feelings of resentment and discouragement which must be worked through. We have found that a recognition of the ways in which transference-countertransference patterns manfest themselves and vary from the patterns found with other types of patients makes the working through of this problem possible.

*Problem of Authority and Defining Limits.* One of the great risks in therapy with the manic depressive is the danger of suicide when he is depressed or of the patient's damaging his economic and social security when he is in a manic phase. Much of the success in handling this destructive element must, of course, depend on successful therapy. However, we have found that a careful definition of limits and an appropriate expression of disapproval when the limits are violated is helpful.

## Further Areas for Study

We feel that the conclusions derived from our intensive study of twelve patients require confirmation by further investigation of a larger series. A thorough statistical study of the families of manic depressives is desirable in order to confirm and elaborate the picture of the family patterns as we have developed it. And finally, a more intensive study of psychotherapeutic interviews with manic-depressive patients is needed in order to define more clearly the characteristic patterns of communication and interaction between patient and therapist, and to contrast these with the interactions in other conditions. This is a logical next step in advancing our knowledge of the psychopathology of all mental disorders.

Norman Cameron

# The Paranoid Pseudo-Community Revisited

*One of the prominent theorists about paranoid disorders in recent years has been Dr. Norman Cameron. His concept of the pseudo-community as a feature of these disorders has been widely known. Here he reformulates that concept and in the process provides a good picture of the development of the paranoid disorder.*

Reprinted from the American Journal of Sociology, 65(1959), 52–58 by permission of The University of Chicago Press and Dr. Cameron.

A decade of experience with intensive clinical studies of paranoid thinking, in the course of psychoanalyzing psychoneurotics and in the long-term therapy of ambulatory psychotics, has led me to a reworking of the concept of the pseudo-community as formulated in this *Journal*[1] and further developed elsewhere.[2] The social aspects of the concept require little change. It is in its individual aspects—in a greater concern with the evidence of internal changes and with the signs that forces are operative which are not open to direct observation—that the pseudo-community acquires deeper roots and greater usefulness.

*Original presentation.* In the normal evolution and preservation of socially organized behavior the most important factor is the developing and maintaining of genuine communication. In each individual, language behavior grows out of preverbal interchange between infant and older person. It evolves in accordance with whatever traditional patterns prevail in the immediate environment, since communication is always, at first, between a child who operates at preverbal levels and older individuals whose language is already a highly organized interactive system. Through sharing continuously in such language and prelanguage interchange, each child develops shared social perspectives and skill in shifting from one perspective to another in time of need.

A highly significant result of this gradual process is that, as time goes on, the child normally acquires an increasingly realistic grasp of how other people feel, what their attitudes, plans, hopes, fears, and intentions are, and in what ways these all relate to his own. Eventually, he is able to take the roles of other people around him in imagination and to view things more or less realistically from their perspectives as well as from his own. In this way he also develops a workable degree of objectivity toward himself, learning to respond to his body, his personality, and his behavior more or less as others do. In the final product, there is considerable difference between the socialization achieved in behavior publicly shared and genuinely communicated and behavior that has remained private and little formulated or expressed in language.

The adult who is especially vulnerable to paranoid developments is one in whom this process of socialization has been seriously defective. His deficient social learning and poorly developed social skills leave him unable to understand adequately the motivations, attitudes, and intentions of others. When he becomes disturbed or confused under stress, he must operate under several grave handicaps imposed by a lifelong inability to communicate freely and effectively, to suspend judgment long enough to share his tentative interpretations with someone else, to imagine realistically the attitudes that others might have toward his situation and himself, and to imagine their roles and thus share their perspectives.

Left to his own unaided devices in a crisis, the paranoid person is able only to seek and find "evidence" that carries

---

[1] Norman Cameron, "The Paranoid Pseudo-Community," *American Journal of Sociology*, XLIX (1943), 32–38. Reprinted in A. M. Rose (ed.), *Mental Health and Mental Disorder: A Sociological Approach* (New York: W. W. Norton & Co., 1955).

[2] Norman Cameron, *The Psychology of Behavior Disorders: A Biosocial Interpretation* (Boston: Houghton Mifflin Co., 1947), and "Perceptual Organization and Behavior Pathology," in R. Blake and G. Ramsey (eds.), *Perception: An Approach to Personality* (New York: Ronald Press Co., 1951); and Norman Cameron and A. Magaret, *Behavior Pathology* (Boston: Houghton Mifflin Co., 1951), chap. xiii, "Pseudo-Community and Delusion."

him farther in the direction he is already going—toward a more and more delusional interpretation of what seems to be going on around him.[3] This process may culminate in a conviction that he himself is the focus of a community of persons who are united in a conspiracy of some kind against him. It is this supposed functional community of real persons whom the patient can see and hear, and of other persons whom he imagines, that we call the *paranoid pseudo-community*. It has no existence as a social organization and as soon as he attempts to combat it, or to flee, he is likely to come into conflict with his actual social community.

*Incompleteness of the descriptive pseudo-community.* This, in brief, is the background and structure of the paranoid pseudo-community, as originally described. As it stands, it still seems valid; but it is unnecessarily restricted. In the first place, the account of the delusional development pays scant attention to internal dynamics because of the limits imposed by a behavioristic orientation. Patients, of course, recognize no such limitations. In the course of long-term intensive therapy they can sometimes furnish important information about what is going on within them to a therapist who is ready to receive it. Some of this they describe as it happens, in their own terms, and often in their own idiom. Some of it one can infer from what is said and done, with the help of material communicated in parallel cases. Some of it one must postulate in an effort to make one's observations and direct inferences more intelligible, just as is done in other empirical sciences.

In the original account not enough emphasis was given to the positive achievements of delusion formation. As we shall see, the pseudo-community is the best means a paranoid patient has at the time for bridging the chasm between his inner reality and social reality. Its use for this purpose may lead to a progressive reduction in desocialization and the reappearance of more normal communicative channels.

And, finally, the concept of the pseudo-community needs a background of structural postulates. In order to make sense out of the experiences which people actually have in fantasies, daydreams, and psychoses, one is obliged to go beyond such impermanent concepts as perception, response, and behavior—upon which the writer earlier relied—and to assume probable forces and mechanisms operating within personality systems and interacting subsystems. Here, again, the patient often comes to the rescue with empirical data. And, every now and then, one comes across a patient who describes with naïve simplicity and directness—but consistently over a long period of time—phenomena which seem purely theoretical and highly abstruse, as reported in the literature. Exposed to such material the therapist may still be left with a sense of strangeness; but his previous feeling of their abstruseness and incredulity sooner or later vanishes.

*Paranoid loss of social reality.* Paranoid delusional development begins with an impairment of social communication. It is preceded by experiences of frustration to which, like many normal persons, the paranoid individual reacts by turning away from his surroundings, and taking refuge in fantasy and daydream. This is the phase of withdrawal and preoccupation which is sometimes obvious even to an untrained observer.

When a paranoid person withdraws like this, he is far more likely than a normal person to lose effective contact

---

[3] For a detailed discussion of this process of *desocialization* see "Desocialization and Disorganization," in Cameron and Magaret, *op. cit.*, pp. 448–517.

with his social environment (i.e., with social reality) and to undergo regression. If this happens, he may abandon social reality for a time completely and become absorbed in primitive regressive thinking and feeling. Occasionally, a patient openly expresses some of his regressive experiences at the time; more often they can be inferred only from what emerges later on.

*Precursors of the pseudo-community. I. Beginning restitution.* It is a fact, of both clinical observation and subjective report, that paranoid patients, while still withdrawn, preoccupied, and regressed, begin to make attempts to regain their lost relationships with social reality. We may conceptualize these as marking the tapering-off of regression and the beginning of the reintegration of personality. The attempts fail to recover the lost social reality, however, because the patient's internal situation is not what it was before his regression. It is no longer possible for him to regain social reality as, for example, a normal person does when he wakes up in the morning. Instead, as we shall see, paranoid reintegration involves a restitutive process, the construction of a pseudo-reality which culminates in the paranoid pseudo-community.

Paranoid personalities suffer all their lives from defective repressive defenses and a heavy reliance upon the more primitive defenses of denial and projection. If they undergo a psychotic regression, which involves partial ego disintegration, their repressive defenses become still more defective. Primitive fantasies and conflicts now begin to emerge and to threaten ego disruption. The patient is forced to deal with them somehow, if he is to preserve what personality integration he still has and avoid further regression. Since he cannot successfully repress them, he vigorously denies them and projects them. An im-

mediate result of the intense projective defense is that the products of the patient's emerging fantasies and conflicts now appear to him to be coming from outside him. Thus he seems to escape disintegration from within only to be threatened with destruction from without.

*Precursors of the pseudo-community. II. Estrangement and diffuse vigilance.* In the process of denying and projecting, the paranoid patient makes a start toward regaining contact with his surroundings. But this process neither simplifies nor clarifies the situation for him; and it does not bring about a return to social reality. On the contrary, the surroundings now seem somehow strange and different. Something has unquestionably happened. The patient misidentifies this "something" as basically a change in the makeup of his environment instead of what it actually is, a fundamental change within himself. If he expresses his feelings at this point, he is likely to say that things are going on which he does not understand; and this, of course, is literally true.

It is hardly surprising that the patient, finding himself in a world grown suddenly strange, should become diffusely vigilant. He watches everything uneasily; he listens alertly for clues; he looks everywhere for hidden meanings. Here his lifelong social incompetence makes matters still worse. He lacks even ordinary skill in the common techniques for testing social reality. He is unable to view his threatening situation even temporarily from the perspective of a neutral person. The more anxious and vigilant he grows, the less he can trust anybody, the less he dares to share with anyone his uneasiness and suspicion. He is condemned to pursue a solitary path, beset by primal fears, hates, and temptations which he cannot cope with nor escape.

*Precursors of the pseudo-community.
III. Increased self-reliance.* Strong tendencies toward self-reference are characteristic of paranoid personalities. When a paranoid adult becomes deeply and regressively preoccupied, his habitually egocentric orientation is greatly increased. And when he next resorts to wholesale projection, he in effect converts his environment into an arena for his projected fantasies and conflicts. This destroys whatever neutrality and objectivity the environment may have previously possessed for him. He is now engrossed in scrutinizing his surroundings for signs of the return of what he is denying and projecting. To these he has become selectively sensitive. He is watching out for something that will explain away the strangeness and enable him to escape his frightening sense of isolation.

It is an unfortunate fact that a badly frightened person—even a normal one—is likely to notice things and make interpretations that increase rather than diminish his fear. And this is especially the case if he feels alone, in strange surroundings, and threatened by an unknown danger. Many non-paranoid adults, for example, walking alone through a large cemetery at night, or lost at night in a forest, become extremely alert and feel personally threatened by harmless things wholly unrelated to them. The paranoid adult, who is peopling his surroundings with projected phantoms from his own past, likewise creates a situation in which everything seems somehow dangerously related to him. Since he cannot escape, he tries to understand the situation he has unconsciously created, in the vain hope that he may then be able to cope with it.

*Precursors of the pseudo-community.
IV. Preliminary hypotheses.* Being human, the paranoid patient is driven irresistibly to make hypotheses; but, having partially regressed, and being paranoid as well, he cannot test them. He tends, therefore, to pass from one guess or one suspicion to another like it. Using the materials provided by his environment and by his projected fantasies and conflicts, he constructs a succession of provisional hypotheses, discarding each as it fails to meet the contradictory demands of his internal needs and the environment. This is characteristic also of complex normal problem-solving. It is an expression of what is called the synthetic function of the ego.

Everyone who works with paranoid patients discovers that some kind of delusional reconstruction of reality is essential to their continued existence as persons. Even a temporary and unsatisfactory delusional hypothesis may be at the time a patient's sole means of bridging the gap between himself and his social environment. It gives a distorted picture of the world; but a distorted world is better than no world at all. And this is often a regressed person's only choice. To abandon his projected fears, hates, and temptations might mean to abandon all that he has gained in the reconstruction of reality, to have his world fall apart and fall apart himself. Patients sense this danger, even expressing it in these words, and they rightly refuse to give up their delusional reality. The fear is not unrealistic, for clinically such catastrophes actually occur, ending in personality disintegration.

A great many paranoid persons never go beyond the phase of making and giving up a succession of preliminary delusional hypotheses. Some of them regain a good working relationship with social reality, something approaching or equaling their premorbid status. Some are less successful and remain chronically suspicious, averse, and partially withdrawn but manage even so to go on living otherwise much as they had lived before. They may appear morose, irascible, and bitter; but they do not fix upon definite enemies or take definite hostile action. At most they suffer brief outbursts of protests and complaint without losing their ability to retreat from an angry delusional position. In this paper, however, we are concerned primarily with paranoid patients—by no means incurable—who go on to crystallize a more stable delusional organization.

*Final crystallization: the pseudo-community.* A great many paranoid persons succeed in crystallizing a stable conceptual organization, the pseudo-community, which gives them a satisfactory cognitive explanation of their strange altered world and a basis for doing something about the situation as they now see it. Their problem is exceedingly complex. It is impossible for them to get rid of the unconscious elements, which they have denied and projected, but which now return apparently from the outside. They cannot abandon or even ignore their environment without facing a frightening regression into an objectless world. Their task is somehow to integrate these internal and external phenomena which appear before them on a single plane into a unified world picture.

The human environment which others share (*social reality*) provides the patient with real persons having social roles and characteristics which he can utilize in making his delusional reconstruction. It also provides real interaction among them, including interaction with the patient himself. Many things actually happen in it, some of them in direct relation to the patient, most of them actually not.

Internal reality provides two sets of functions. One is made up of the pre-viously unconscious impulses, conflicts, and fantasies—now erupted, denied, and projected. This, as noted, introduces imagined motivation, interaction, and intentions into the observed activities of other persons. It gives apparent meaning to happenings which do not have such meaning for the consensus. The other set of functions is included in the concept of ego adaptation. It is the ego synthesis mentioned above, by means of which the demands of internal reality and the structure of social reality are integrated into a meaningful, though delusional, unity.

What the paranoid patient does is as follows: Into the organization of social reality, as he perceives it, he unconsciously projects his own previously unconscious motivation, which he has denied but cannot escape. This process now requires a perceptual and conceptual reorganization of object relations in his surroundings into an apparent community, which he represents to himself as organized wholly with respect to him (delusion of self-reference). And since the patient's erupted, denied, and projected elements are overwhelmingly hostile and destructive, the motivation he ascribes to the real persons he has now organized into his conceptual pseudo-community is bound to be extremely hostile and destructive.

To complete his conceptual organization of a paranoid conspiracy, the patient also introduces imaginary persons. He ascribes to them, as to real persons, imagined functions, roles, and motivations in keeping with his need to unify his restitutional conception and make it stable. He pictures helpers, dupes, stooges, go-betweens, and masterminds, of whose actual existence he becomes certain.

It is characteristic of the pseudo-community that it is made up of both real and imaginary persons, all of whom may have both real and imaginary functions and interrelations.[4] In form it usually corresponds to one or another of the common dangerous, hostile groups in contemporary society, real or fictional—gangs, dope and spy rings, secret police, and groups of political, racial, and religious fanatics. Many paranoid patients succeed in creating a restitutional organization which has well-formulated plans. The chief persecutor is sometimes a relative or acquaintance, or a well-known public figure, while the rest of the imaginary personnel forms a vague, sinister background. Sometimes one finds the reverse—the chief persecutor is unknown, a malevolent "brain" behind everything, while the known dangerous persons play supporting roles in the delusional cast.

The final delusional reconstruction of reality may fall into an integrated conceptual pattern that brings an experience of closure: "I suddenly realized what it was all about!" the patient may exclaim with obvious relief at sudden clarification. The intolerable suspense has ended; the strangeness of what has been "going on" seems to disappear, and confusion is replaced by "understanding," and wavering doubt by certainty. A known danger may be frightening; but at least it is tangible, and one can do something about it. In short, the pseudo-community reduces the hopeless complexity and confusion to a clear formula. This formula—"the plot"—the patient can now apply to future events as he experiences them and fit them into the general framework of his reconstruction.

The organization of a conceptual pseudo-community is a final cognitive step in paranoid problem-solving. It re-establishes stable object relations, though on a delusional basis, and thus makes integrated action possible. To summarize what this reconstruction of reality has achieved for its creator:

(a) *Reduction in estrangement.* As a direct result of paranoid problem-solving, experienced external reality is distorted so as to bring it into line with the inescapable projected elements. This lessens confusion and detachment and allows the patient to recover some of his lost sense of ego integrity. The world seems dangerous but familiar.

(b) *Internal absorption of aggression.* Construction and maintenance of a conceptual pseudo-community absorb aggression internally, in the same sense that organizing a baseball team, a political ward, or a scientific society absorbs aggression. This reduces the threat of ego disintegration which the id eruptions pose.

(c) *Basis for action.* Any new cognitive construct can serve as a basis for new action; in this respect the paranoid pseudo-community is no exception. It organizes the drive-directed cognitive processes, leads to meaningful interpretations in a well-defined pseudo-reality structure, and paves the way for overt action with a definite focus. The patient is enabled to go ahead as anyone else might who had powerful urges and felt sure that he was right.

(d) *Justification of aggressive action.* Finally, a persecutory pseudo-community justifies attack or flight, either of which involves a direct aggressive discharge in overt action. Fighting or running away is less disintegrative psychologically than prolonged frightened inaction. And under the circumstances, as the patient now conceptualizes them, he need feel neither guilt for attacking nor shame for fleeing.

[4] This is in contrast to the autistic community, which is composed of wholly imaginary persons (see "Autistic Community and Hallucination," in Cameron and Magaret, *op. cit.*, pp. 414–47.

*Paranoid cognition and paranoid action.* When a patient succeeds in conceptualizing a pseudo-community, he has taken the final cognitive step in paranoid problem-solving. He now "knows" what his situation is. But he is still faced with his need to do something about it. As a matter of fact, the crystallization of a hostile delusional structure usually increases the urge to take action. A circular process may quickly develop. The imagined threats of the now structured imaginary conspiracy seem to the patient concrete and imminent. They stimulate more and more his anxiety and defensive hostility—and the latter, being as usual projected, further increases the apparent external threat. Often this kind of self-stimulation spirals upward, while more and more "incidents" and people may be drawn into the gathering psychotic storm.

Paranoid action, however inappropriate it may be, still represents the completion of restitutional relationships and the fullest contact with his human environment of which the patient is capable at the time. He switches from his previous passive role of observer and interpreter, with all its indecision and anxiety, to that of an aggressive participant in what he conceives as social reality. For him this is genuine interaction, and he experiences the gratification that comes with certainty and with a massive discharge of pent-up aggressiveness. He may give a preliminary warning to the supposed culprits or make an appeal for intervention to someone in authority before taking direct action himself, which, when it comes, may be in the form of an attack or sudden flight, either of which may be planned and executed with considerable skill.

*Making social reality conform to the pseudo-community.* Paranoid patients who take aggressive action often achieve a pyrrhic victory. They succeed finally in making social reality act in conformity with the delusional reality which they have created. As long as a patient confines himself to watching, listening, and interpreting, he need not come into open conflict with the social community. But, when he takes overt action appropriate only in his private pseudo-community, a serious social conflict will arise.

Social reality is the living product of genuine sharing, communication, and interaction. Valid social attitudes, interpretations, and action derive continuously from these operations. The restitutional reality in which the patient believes himself to be participating has no counterpart outside of himself: it is illusory. Other persons cannot possibly share his attitudes and interpretations because they do not share his paranoid projections and distortions. Therefore they do not understand action taken in terms of his delusional reconstruction. The patient, for his part, cannot share their attitudes and interpretations because he is driven by regressive needs which find no place in adult social reality.

When an intelligent adult expresses beliefs and makes accusations which seem unintelligible to others, as well as threatening, he may make the people around him exceedingly anxious. This is particularly the case when his words tend to activate their unconscious fantasies and conflicts. And when such a person begins to take aggressive action, which seems unprovoked as well as unintelligible, he inevitably arouses defensive and retaliatory hostility in others. The moment the social community takes action against him, it provides him with the confirmation he has been expecting—that there is a plot against him.

Thus, in the end, the patient manages to provoke action in the social community that conforms to the expectation expressed in his pseudo-community organization. His own internal need to experience hostility from without—as a defense against being overwhelmed by internal aggression—is satisfied when actual persons behave in accordance with his projections. His need for a target against which to discharge hostility is also met. This is his victory and his defeat.

The defeat need not be final. Much will depend, of course, upon the patient's basic personality organization, particularly his emotional flexibility, his potentiality for internal change, and his residual capacity for establishing new ego and superego identifications. The depth and extent of his regression are also important, as are the fixity and the inclusiveness of his delusional structure. Much will also depend upon his potential freedom to communicate, to develop reciprocal role-taking skills with another person, and to include another's alternative perspectives in his own therapeutic orientation.

*Therapy.* The primary therapeutic consideration, of course, is not the character of the delusional structure but what makes it necessary. A reduction in anxiety is among the first objectives. The source of anxiety lies in the regressive changes and in the threat these have brought of an unconscious breakthrough. But it is also aggravated by anything in the environment which tends to increase the patient's hostility and fear. Once the setting has been made less anxiety-provoking, the most pressing need is for someone in whom the patient can ultimately put his trust —someone not made anxious by the patient's fear and hostility or driven to give reassurances and make demands.

For the paranoid patient who is ready to attempt social communication, an interested but neutral therapist can function as a living bridge between psychotic reality and social reality. Through interacting with such a person, who neither attacks the delusional structure nor beats the drums of logic, a patient may succeed in gaining new points of reference from which to build a new orientation. The therapeutic process now involves another reconstruction of reality, one which undoes the restitutional pseudo-community without destroying the patient's defenses and forcing him to regress further.

As anxiety and the threat of disintegration subside, paranoid certainty becomes less necessary to personality survival. The patient can begin to entertain doubts and consider alternative interpretations. Such changes, of course, must come from within if they are to come at all. If he is able to work through some of the origins and derivatives of his basic problems, the patient may succeed eventually in representing to himself more realistically than ever before how other people feel and think. In this way the conceptual structure of his pseudo-community may be gradually replaced by something approaching the conceptual structure of social reality.

Kurt Goldstein

# The Effect of Brain Damage on the Personality

*Kurt Goldstein was an eminent clinical neurologist who acquired a great deal of experience with patients suffering brain damage when he served as a German army physician during World War I. As a result of his observations of such patients, he became impressed with the very general disruptive effects brain damage had on personality and behavior, regardless of where it occurred and, within limits, how extensive it was. These common reactions of the brain-injured are described in this paper.*

When I was asked to speak before the Psychoanalytic Association about the changes of the personality in brain damage, I was somewhat hesitant because I was not quite sure that I would be able to make myself understood by an audience which thinks mainly in such different categories and speaks in such a different terminology from my own. I finally accepted the invitation, because I thought that members of the Association apparently wanted to hear what I think and because it brought me the opportunity to express an old idea of mine—the idea that it is faulty in principle to try to make a distinction between so-called organic and functional diseases, as far as symptomatology and therapy are concerned (1). In both conditions, one is dealing with abnormal functioning of the same psychophysical apparatus and with the attempts of the organism to come to terms with that. If the disturbances—whether they are due to damage to the brain or to psychological conflicts—do not disappear spontaneously or cannot be eliminated by therapy, the organism has to make a new adjustment to life in spite of them. Our task is to help the patients in this adjustment by

physical and psychological means; the procedure and goal of the therapy in both conditions is, in principle, the same.

This was the basic idea which induced a group of neurologists, psychiatrists, and psychotherapists—including myself—many years ago, in 1927, to organize the Internationale Gesellschaft für Psychotherapie in Germany and to invite all physicians interested in psychotherapy to meet at the First Congress of the Society. Psychotherapists of all different schools responded to our invitation, and the result of the discussions was surprisingly fruitful. At the second meeting in 1927, I spoke about the relation between psychoanalysis and biology (2). During the last twenty years, in which I have occupied myself intensively with psychotherapy, I have become more and more aware of the similarity of the phenomena of organic and psychogenic conditions.

It is not my intention to consider the similarities in this paper. I want to restrict myself to the description of the symptomatology and the interpretation of the behavior changes in patients with damage to the brain cortex,

Reprinted from Psychiatry, 15(1952), 245–260, by special permission of The William Alanson White Psychiatric Foundation, Inc., holder of the copyright.

particularly in respect to their personality, and would like to leave it to you to make comparisons.

The symptomatology which these patients present is very complex (3). It is the effect of various factors of which the change of personality is only one. Therefore, when we want to characterize the change of personality, we have to separate it from the symptoms due to other factors: (1) from those which are the effect of *disturbance of inborn or learned patterns* of performances in special performance fields—such as motor and sensory patterns; (2) from those which are the *expression of the so-called catastrophic conditions*; and (3) from those which are the *expression of the protective mechanisms* which originate from the attempt of the organism to avoid catastrophes.

In order to avoid terminological misunderstandings, I want to state what I mean by personality: Personality shows itself in behavior. Personality is the mode of behavior of a person in terms of the capacities of human beings in general and in the specific appearance of these capacities in a particular person. Behavior is always an entity and concerns the whole personality. Only abstractively can we separate behavior into parts—as for instance, bodily processes, conscious phenomena, states of feelings, attitudes, and so on (4, pp. 310 ff.).

According to my observation, all the phenomena of behavior become understandable if one assumes that all the behavior of the organism is determined by one trend (5), the *trend to actualize itself*—that is, its nature and all its capacities. This takes place normally in such harmony that the realization of all capacities in the best way possible in the particular environment is permitted. The capacities are experienced by a person as various *needs* which he is driven to fulfill with the cooperation of some parts of the environment and in spite of the hindrance by other parts of it.

Each stimulation brings about some disorder in the organism. But after a certain time—which is determined by the particular performance—the organism comes back, by a process of *equalization*, to its normal condition. This process guarantees the constancy of the organism. A person's specific personality corresponds to this constancy. Because realization has to take place in terms of different needs and different tasks, the behavior of the organism is soon directed more by one than by another need. This does not mean that organismic behavior is determined by separate needs or drives. All such concepts need the assumption of a controlling agency. I have tried to show in my book, *The Organism*, that the different agencies which have been assumed for this purpose have only made for new difficulties in the attempt to understand organismic behavior; they are not necessary if one gives up the concept of separate drives, as my theory of the organism does. All of a person's capacities are always in action in each of his activities. The capacity that is particularly important for the task is in the foreground; the others are in the background. All of these capacities are organized in a way which facilitates the self-realization of the total organism in the particular situation. For each performance there is a definite figure-ground organization of capacities; the change in the behavior of a patient corresponds to the change in the total organism in the form of an alteration of the normal pattern of figure-ground organization (4, p. 109).

Among patients with brain damage we can distinguish between alterations which occur when an area belonging to a special performance field—such as a motor or sensory area—is damaged somewhat isolatedly, and alterations which occur when the personality organization itself is altered. In lesions of these areas—according to a dedifferentiation of the function of the brain cortex (4, p. 131)—qualities and patterns of behavior (both those developing as a result of maturation and those acquired by learning) are disturbed. Indeed, these patterns never occur isolatedly. They are always embedded in that kind of behavior which we call personality. The personality structure is disturbed particularly by lesions of the frontal lobes, the parietal lobes, and the insula Reili; but it is also disturbed by diffuse damage to the cortex—for instance, in paralysis, alchoholism, and trauma, and in metabolic disturbances such as hypoglycemia. The effect of diffuse damage is understandable when we consider that what we call personality structure apparently is not related to a definite locality of the cortex (4, pp. 249 ff.) but to a particular complex function of the brain which is the same for all its parts. This function can be damaged especially by lesions in any of the areas I have mentioned. The damage of the patterns certainly modifies the personality too. Although for full understanding of the personality changes, we should discuss the organization of the patterns and their destruction in damaged patients, that would carry us too far and is not absolutely necessary for our discussion. I shall therefore restrict my presentation to consideration of the symptoms due to damage of the personality structure itself (6).

There would be no better way of getting to the heart of the problem than by demonstrating a patient. Unfortunately I have to substitute for this a description of the behavior of patients with severe damage of the brain cortex. Let us consider a man with an extensive lesion of the frontal lobes (7, 8). His customary way of living does not seem to be very much disturbed. He is a little slow; his face is rather immobile, rather rigid; his attention is directed very strictly to what he is doing at the moment—say, writing a letter, or speaking to someone. Confronted with tasks in various fields, he gives seemingly normal responses under certain conditions; but under other conditions he fails completely in tasks that seem to be very similar to those he has performed quite well.

This change of behavior becomes apparent particularly in the following simple test: We place before him a small wooden stick in a definite position, pointing, for example, diagonally from left to right. He is asked to note the position of the stick carefully. After a half minute's exposure, the stick is removed; then it is handed to the patient, and he is asked to put it back in the position in which it was before. He grasps the stick and tries to replace it, but he fumbles; he is all confusion; he looks at the examiner, shakes his head, tries this way and that, plainly uncertain. The upshot is that he cannot place the stick in the required position. He is likewise unable to imitate other simple figures built of sticks. Next we show the patient a little house made of many sticks—a house with a roof, a door, a window, and a chimney. After we remove it, we ask the patient to reproduce the model. He succeeds very well.

## IMPAIRMENT OF ABSTRACT CAPACITY

If we ask ourselves what is the cause of the difference in his behavior in the two tasks, we can at once exclude defects in the field of perception, action, and memory. For there is no doubt that copying the house with many details demands a much greater capacity in all these faculties, especially in memory, than putting a single stick into a position which the patient has been shown shortly before. A further experiment clarifies the situation. We put before the patient two sticks placed together so as to form an angle with the opening pointing upward (V). The patient is unable to reproduce this model. Then we confront him with the same angle, the opening downward this time (∧), and now he reproduces the figure very well on the first trial. When we ask the patient how it is that he can reproduce the second figure but not the first one, he says, "This one has nothing to do with the other one." Pointing to the second one, he says, "That is a roof"; pointing to the first, "That is nothing."

These two replies lead us to an understanding of the patient's behavior. His first reply makes it clear that, to him, the two objects with which he has to deal are totally different from one another. The second answer shows that he apprehends the angle with the opening downward as a concrete object out of his own experience, and he constructs a concrete thing with the two sticks. The two sticks that formed an angle with the opening upward apparently did not arouse an impression of a concrete thing. He had to regard the sticks as representations indicating directions in abstract space. Furthermore, he had to keep these directions in mind and rearrange the sticks from memory as representatives of these abstract directions. To solve the problem he must give an account to himself of relations in space and must act on the basis of abstract ideas. Thus we may conclude that the failure of the patient in the first test lies in the fact that he is unable to perform a task which can be executed only by means of a grasp of the abstract. The test in which the opening of the angle is downwards does

not demand this, since the patient is able to grasp it as a concrete object and therefore to execute it perfectly. It is for the same reason that he is able to copy the little house, which seems to us to be so much more complicated. From the result of his behavior in this and similar tasks we come to the assumption that these *patients are impaired in their abstract capacity.*

The term "abstract attitude," which I shall use in describing this capacity, will be more comprehensible in the light of the following explanation (9). We can distinguish two different kinds of attitudes, the concrete and the abstract. In the concrete attitude we are given over passively and bound to the immediate experience of unique objects or situations. Our thinking and acting are determined by the immediate claims made by the particular aspect of the object or situation. For instance, we act concretely when we enter a room in darkness and push the button for light. If, however, we reflect that by pushing the button we might awaken someone asleep in the room, and desist from pushing the button, then we are acting abstractively. We transcend the immediately given specific aspect of sense impressions; we detach ourselves from these impressions, consider the situation from a conceptual point of view, and react accordingly. Our actions are determined not so much by the objects before us as by the way we think about them: the individual thing becomes a mere accidental representative of a category to which it belongs.

The impairment of the attitude toward the abstract shows in every performance of the brain-damaged patient who is impaired in this capacity. He always fails when the solution of a task presupposes this attitude; he performs well when the appropriate activity is determined directly by the stimuli and when the task can be fulfilled by con-

crete behavior. He may have no difficulty in using known objects in a situation that requires them; but he is
totally at a loss if he is asked to demonstrate the use of such an object outside
the concrete situation, and still more
so if he is asked to do it without the
real object. A few examples will illustrate this:

The patient is asked to blow away a
slip of paper. He does this very well. If
the paper is taken away and he is asked
to think that there is a slip of paper
and to blow it away, he is unable to do
so. Here the situation is not realistically
complete. In order to perform the task
the patient would have to imagine the
piece of paper there. He is not capable
of this.

The patient is asked to throw a ball
into open boxes situated respectively at
distances of three, nine, and fifteen feet.
He does that correctly. When he is
asked how far the several boxes are from
him, he is not only unable to answer
this question but unable even to say
which box is nearest to him and which
is farthest.

In the first action, the patient has
only to deal with objects in a behavioral
fashion. It is unnecessary for him to be
conscious of this behavior and of objects
in a world separated from himself. In
the second, however, he must separate
himself from objects in the outer world
and give himself an account of his actions and of the space relations in the
world facing him. Since he is unable to
do this, he fails. We could describe this
failure also by saying that the patient
is unable to deal with a situation which
is only possible.

A simple story is read to a patient.
He may repeat some single words, but
he does not understand their meaning
and is unable to grasp the essential
point. Now we read him another story,
which would seem to a normal person
to be more difficult to understand. This

time he understands the meaning very
well and recounts the chief points. The
first story deals with a simple situation,
but a situation which has no connection with the actual situation of the
patient. The second story recounts a
situation he is familiar with. Hence one
could say the patient is able to grasp
and handle only something which is
related to himself.

Such a patient almost always recognizes pictures of single objects, even if
the picture contains many details. In
pictures which represent a composition
of a number of things and persons, he
may pick out some details; but he is
unable to understand the picture as a
whole and is unable to respond to the
whole. The patient's real understanding
does not depend on the greater or
smaller number of components in a
picture but on whether the components, whatever their number, hang together concretely and are familiar to
him, or whether an understanding of
their connection requires a more abstract synthesis on his part. He may lack
understanding of a picture even if there
are only a few details. If the picture
does not reveal its essence directly, by
bringing the patient into the situation
which it represents, he is not able to
understand it. Thus one may characterize the deficiency as an inability to discover the essence of a situation which
is not related to his own personality.

## Memory and Attention

This change in behavior finds its expression in characteristic changes in
memory and attention. Under certain
circumstances the faculty for reproduction of facts acquired previously may be
about normal. For example, things
learned in school may be recalled very
well, but only in some situations. The
situation must be suited to reawakening
old impressions. If the required answer

demands an abstract attitude on the part of a patient or if it demands that he give an account of the matter in question, the patient is unable to remember. Therefore he fails in many intelligence tests which may seem very simple for a normal person, and he is amazingly successful in others which appear complicated to us. He is able to learn new facts and to keep them in mind; but he can learn them only in a concrete situation and can reproduce them only in the same situation in which he has learned them. Because the intentional recollection of experiences acquired in infancy requires an abstract attitude toward the situation at that time, the patient is unable to recall infancy experiences in a voluntary way; but we can observe that the after-effect of such experiences sometimes appears passively in his behavior. Such a patient has the greatest difficulty in associating freely; he cannot assume the attitude of mind to make that possible. He is incapable of recollection when he is asked to recall things which have nothing to do with the given situation. The patient must be able to regard the present situation in such a way that facts from the past belong to it. If this is not the case, he is completely unable to recall facts which he has recalled very well in another situation. Repeated observation in many different situations demonstrates clearly that such memory failures are not caused by an impairment of memory content. The patient has the material in his memory, but he is unable to use it freely; he can use it only in connection with a definite concrete situation.

We arrive at the same result in testing attention. At one time the patient appears inattentive and distracted; at another time, he is attentive, even abnormally so. The patient's attention is usually weak in special examinations, particularly at the beginning before he has become aware of the real approach to the whole situation. In such a situation he ordinarily seems much distracted. If he is able to enter into the situation, however, his attention may be satisfactory; sometimes his reactions are even abnormally keen. Under these circumstances he may be totally untouched by other stimuli from the environment to which normal persons will unfailingly react. In some tests he will always seem distracted; for example, in those situations which demand a change of approach (a choice), he always seems distracted because he is incapable of making a choice. Consequently, it is not correct to speak of a change of attention in these patients in terms of plus or minus. The state of the patient's attention is but part of his total behavior and is to be understood only in connection with it.

## Emotional Responses

The same holds true if we observe the emotions of the patients. Usually they are considered emotionally dull and often they appear so, but it would not be correct to say simply that they are suffering from a diminution of emotions. The same patients can be dull under some conditions and very excited under others. This can be explained when we consider the patient's emotional behavior in relation to his entire behavior in a given situation. When he does not react emotionally in an adequate way, investigation reveals that he has not grasped the situation in such a way that emotion could arise. In fact, we might experience a similar lack of emotion through failing to grasp a situation. The patient may have grasped only one part of the situation—the part which can be grasped concretely—and this part may not give any reason for an emotional reaction. The lack of emotion appears to us inappropriate because we grasp with the abstract attitude the whole situation to which the emotional character is attached. This connection between the emotions and the total behavior becomes understandable when we consider that emotions are not simply related to particular experiences but are, as I have shown on another occasion (10), inherent aspects of behavior —part and parcel of behavior. No behavior is without emotion and what we call lack of emotion is a deviation from normal emotions corresponding to the deviation of behavior in general. From this point of view, one modification of reactions that is of particular interest in respect to the problem of emotions in general, becomes understandable. Often we see that a patient reacts either not at all or in an *abnormally quick manner*. The latter occurs particularly when the patient believes he has the correct answer to a problem. Although this behavior might seem to be the effect of a change in the time factor of his reactivity, it is rather the *effect of an emotional factor*—that is, it is the modification of his emotional feelings because of the impairment of his ability for abstraction—which in turn modifies the time reaction.

## Pleasure and Joy

These patients are always somewhat in danger of being in a catastrophic condition—which I shall discuss later —as a result of not being able to find the right solution to a problem put before them. They are often afraid that they may not be able to react correctly, and that they will be in a catastrophic condition. Therefore, when they believe they have the right answer, they answer as quickly as possible. Because of impairment of abstraction, they are not able to deliberate; they try to do what they can do as quickly as possible because every retardation increases the

tension which they experience when they are not able to. answer. The quick response is an effect of their *strong necessity to release tension;* they are forced to release tension because they cannot handle it any other way. They cannot bear anything that presupposes deliberation, considering the future, and so on, all of which are related to abstraction.

This difference in behavior between these patients and more normal people throws light on the nature of the *trend to release tension*. These patients must, so to speak, follow the "pleasure principle." This phenomenon is one *expression of the abnormal concreteness* which is a counterpart to the impairment of abstraction. The *trend to release tension appears to be an expression of pathology*—the effect of a protective mechanism to prevent catastrophic condition. To normal behavior belong deliberation and retardation; but in addition there is the ability to speed up an activity or a part of it to correspond to the requirements of the task, or at least part of the requirements, so that its performance guarantees self-realization. Sometimes the ability to bear tension and even to enjoy it are also a part of this normal behavior. In contrast, the patients that I am talking about are only able to experience the pleasure of release of tension; they never appear to enjoy anything—a fact which is often clearly revealed by the expression on their faces. This becomes understandable if we consider that immediate reality is transcended in any kind of joy and that joy is a capacity we owe to the abstract attitude, especially that part of it concerned with possibility. Thus brain-injured patients who are impaired in this attitude cannot experience joy. Experience with brain-injured patients teaches us that we have to distinguish between *pleasure by release of tension*, and the active *feeling of en-*

*joyment* and freedom so characteristic of joy. Pleasure through release of tension is the agreeable feeling which we experience on returning to a state of equilibrium after it has been disturbed —the passive feeling of being freed from distress. Pleasure lasts only a short time till a new situation stimulates new activity; we then try to get rid of the tension of the new situation which acts to shorten the span of pleasure. In contrast, we try to extend joy. This explains the different speeds of joy and pleasure. Because of the capacity for joy, we can experience the possibility of the indefinite continuation of a situation. The two emotions of joy and pleasure play essentially different roles in regard to self-realization; they belong to different performances or different parts of a performance; they belong to different moods. Pleasure may be a necessary state of respite. But it is a phenomenon of standstill; it is akin to death. It separates us from the world and the other individuals in it; it is equilibrum, quietness. In joy there is disequilibrium. But it is a productive disequilibrium, leading toward fruitful activity and a particular kind of self-realization. This difference in approach between the normal person and the brain-injured patient is mirrored in the essentially different behavior of the latter and the different world in which he lives. The different significance of the two emotional states in his total behavior is related to their time difference.

Edith Jacobson (11), in the outline of her paper presented to the Psychoanalytic Association, speaks about the speed factor in psychic discharge processes and comes to the conclusion that discharge is not the only process which produces pleasure—that we have to distinguish between different qualities of pleasure in terms of the slow rising and the quick falling of tension. That is very much in accordance with my con-clusions derived from experience with brain-injured patients. If one distinguishes two forms of pleasure, one should, for clarity's sake, use different names for them; I think that my use of pleasure and joy fits the two experiences. But I would not like to call them both discharge processes: the one is a discharge process; the other one a very active phenomenon related to the highest form of mental activity— abstraction. From this it becomes clear why they have such an essentially different significance in the totality of performance: the one is an equalization process which prepares the organism for new activity; the other one is an activity of highest value for self-realization. They belong together just as in general equalization process and activity belong together. Therefore they cannot be understood as isolated phenomena.

## The Phenomenon of Witticism

From this viewpoint of the emotions of brain-injured patients, the phenomenon of witticism appears in a new aspect. We can see that even though a patient makes witty remarks, he is not able to grasp the character of situations which produce humor in an average normal individual. Whether or not some situation appears humorous depends upon whether it can be grasped in a concrete way which is suited to producing the emotion of humor. In accordance with the impairment of his ability for abstraction, such a patient perceives many humorous pictures in a realistic way, which does not evoke the expected humor. But of course any of us who might at a given time perceive a humorous picture in a realistic way would respond similarly. On the other hand a patient may make a witty remark in relation to a situation which is not considered humorous by us, because he has experienced the situation in another way. Thus we should not speak of witticism as a special characteristic of these patients. It is but one expression of the change in their personality structure in the same way that their inability to understand jokes under other conditions expresses this change. Indeed, these patients are in general dull because of their limited experience, and their witticisms are superficial and shallow in comparison with those of normal people.

## Friendship and Love

The drive towards the release of tension, which I have already mentioned, is one of the causes of the strange behavior of these patients in friendship and love situations. They need close relationships to other people and they try to maintain such relationships at all cost; at the same time such relationships are easily terminated suddenly if the bearing of tension is necessary for the maintenance of the relationship.

The following example is illustrative: A patient of mine, Mr. A, was for years a close friend of another patient, Mr. X. One day Mr. X went to a movie with a third man. Mr. X did not take Mr. A along because Mr. A had seen the picture before and did not want to see it a second time. When Mr. X came back, my patient was in a state of great excitement and refused to speak to him. Mr. A could not be quieted by any explanations; he was told that his friend had not meant to offend him, and that the friendship had not changed, but these explanations made no impression. From that time on, Mr. A was the enemy of his old friend, Mr. X. He was only aware that his friend was the companion of another man, and he felt himself slighted. This experience produced a great tension in him. He regarded his friend as the cause

of this bad condition and reacted to him in a way that is readily understandable in terms of his inability to bear tension and to put himself in the place of somebody else.

Another patient never seemed to be concerned about his family. He never spoke of his wife or children and was unresponsive when we questioned him about them. When we suggested to him that he should write to his family, he was utterly indifferent. He appeared to lack all feeling in this respect. At times he visited his home in another town, according to an established practice, and stayed there several days. We learned that while he was at home, he conducted himself in the same way that any man would in the bosom of his family. He was kind and affectionate to his wife and children and interested in their affairs insofar as his abilities would permit. Upon his return to the hospital from such a visit, he would smile in an embarrassed way and give evasive answers when he was asked about his family; he seemed utterly estranged from his home situation. Unquestionably the peculiar behavior of this man was not really the effect of deterioration of his character on the emotional and moral side; rather, his behavior was the result of the fact that he could not summon up the home situation when he was not actually there.

Lack of imagination, which is so apparent in this example, makes such patients incapable of experiencing any expectation of the future. This lack is apparent, for instance, in the behavior of a male patient toward a woman whom he later married (12). When he was with the girl, he seemed to behave in a friendly, affectionate way and to be very fond of the girl. But when he was separated from her, he did not care about her at all; he would not seek her out and certainly did not desire to have a love relationship with her. When he was questioned, his answers indicated that he did not even understand what sexual desire meant. But in addition he had forgotten about the girl. When he met her again and she spoke to him, he was able immediately to enter into the previous relation. He was as affectionate as before. When she induced him to go to bed with her and embraced him, he performed an apparently normal act of sexual intercourse with satisfaction for both. She had the feeling that he loved her. She became pregnant, and they were married.

## Change in Language

Of particular significance in these patients is the change in their language because of their lack of abstract attitude (13, p. 56). Their words lose the character of meaning. Words are not usable in those situations in which they must represent a concept. Therefore the patients are not able to find the proper words in such situations. Thus, for instance, patients are not able to name concrete objects, since as shown by investigation, naming presupposes an abstract attitude and the abstract use of words. These patients have not lost the sound complex; but they cannot use it as a sign for a concept. On other occasions, the sound complex may be uttered; but it is only used at those times as a simple association to a given object, as a property of the object, such as color and form, and not as representative of a concept. If a patient has been particularly gifted in language before his brain is damaged and has retained many such associations or can acquire associations as a substitute for

naming something, then he may utter the right word through association, so that an observer is not able to distinguish between his uttering the sound complex and giving a name to something; only through analysis can one make this distinction (13, p. 61). Thus we can easily overlook the patient's defect by arriving at a conclusion only on the basis of this capacity for a positive effect. In the same way we can be deceived by a negative effect which may only be an expression, for instance, of the patient's fear that he will use the wrong word. I have used the term *fallacy of effect* to describe the uncertain and ambiguous character of a conclusion which is based only upon a patient's effective performance. This term applies not only to language but to all performances of the patients. It is the source of one of the most fatal mistakes which can be made in interpretation of phenomena observed in organic patients; incidentally, it is a mistake which can be made also in functional cases.

## Frontal Lobotomy

In reference to the fallacy of effect, I want to stress how easily one can be deceived about the mental condition of patients who have undergone frontal lobotomy. The results of the usual intelligence test, evaluated statistically, may not reveal any definite deviation from the norm; yet the patient can have an impairment of abstraction that will become obvious through tests which take into consideration the fallacy of effect.[1] My experience with frontal lobotomy patients and my eval-

[1] Thirty years ago we constructed special tests when we were faced with the problem of re-educating brain-injured soldiers. (See K. Goldstein and A. Gelb, "Über Farbennamen-amnesie," *Psychol. Forsch.* [1924] 6:127.) These tests, which were introduced in America by Scheerer and myself (reference 9), proved to be particularly useful not only for studying the problem of abstraction in patients, but also for the correct organization of treatment.

uation of the literature on frontal lobotomy leave no doubt in my mind that at least many of these patients show impairment of abstract capacity, although perhaps not to such a degree as do patients with gross damage of the brain. Because of the fallacy of effect, which tends to overlook the defect in abstraction, the reports of the relatives that the lobotomized patient behaves well in everyday life are often evaluated incorrectly by the doctor (14). In the sheltered, simple life that these patients have with their families, the patients are not often confronted with tasks which require abstract reasoning; thus the family is likely to overlook their more subtle deviations from the norm. Sometimes peculiarities of the patient are reported which definitely point to a defect in abstraction, which is more serious than it is often evaluated: for instance, a patient who in general seems to live in a normal way does not have any relationship with even the closest members of his family and manifests no interest in his children; another patient exists in a vacuum so that no friendship is possible with him.

A woman patient after lobotomy still knows how to set a table for guests, and how to act as a perfect hostess. Before lobotomy, she was always a careful housewife, deciding everything down to the last detail; but now she does not care how the house is run, she never enters the kitchen, and the housekeeper does all the managing, even the shopping. She still reads a great number of books, but she does not understand the contents as well as before.

A skilled mechanic, who is still considered an excellent craftsman, is able to work in a routine way; but he has lost the ability to undertake complicated jobs, has stopped studying, and seems to have resigned himself to being a routine worker; apparently all this is an effect of the loss of his capacity for abstraction, which is so necessary for all initiative and for creative endeavor. Thus we see that even when the behavior of the patients appears not to be overtly disturbed, it differs essentially from normal behavior—in the particular way which is characteristic of impairment in abstract attitude. Freeman (15), who was originally so enthusiastically in favor of the operation, has become more cautious about its damage to the higher mental functions. He writes:

The patients with frontal lobotomy show always some lack of personality depth; impulse, intelligence, temperament are disturbed; the creative capacity undergoes reduction—the spiritual life in general was affected. They are largely indifferent to the opinions and feelings of others.

He apparently discovered the same personality changes in his patients as those which we have described as characteristic of the behavior of patients with impaired capacity for abstraction. Thus we should be very careful in judging personality change following frontal lobotomy. Although I would not deny the usefulness of the operation in some cases, I would like to say, as I have before, that the possibility of an impairment of abstraction should always be taken into consideration before the operation is undertaken.

I would now like to present a survey of the various situations in which the patient is unable to perform. He fails when he has: (1) to assume a mental set voluntarily or to take initiative (for instance, he may even be able to perform well in giving a series of numbers, once someone else has presented the first number, but he cannot begin the activity); (2) to shift voluntarily from one aspect of a situation to another, making a choice; (3) to account to himself for his actions or to verbalize the account; (4) to keep in mind simultaneously various aspects of a situation or to react to two stimuli which do not belong intrinsically together; (5) to grasp the essence of a given whole, or to break up a given whole into parts, isolating the parts voluntarily and combining them into wholes; (6) to abstract common properties, to plan ahead ideationally, to assume an attitude toward a situation which is only possible, and to think or perform symbolically; (7) to do something which necessitates detaching the ego from the outer world or from inner experiences.

All these and other terms which one may use to describe the behavior of the patients basically mean the same. We speak usually, in brief, of an *impairment of abstract attitude*. I hope that it has become clear that the use of this term does not refer to a theoretical interpretation but to the real behavior of the human being and that it is suitable for describing both normal and pathological personality.

In brief, the patients are changed with respect to the most characteristic properties of the human being. They have lost initiative and the capacity to look forward to something and to make plans and decisions; they lack phantasy and inspiration; their perceptions, thoughts, and ideas are reduced; they have lost the capacity for real contact with others, and they are therefore incapable of real friendship, love, and social relations. One could say they have no real ego and no real world. That they behave in an abnormally concrete way and that they are driven to get rid of tensions are only expressions of the same defect. When such patients are able to complete a task in a concrete way, they may—with regard to the effect of their activity—not appear very abnormal. But closer examination shows that they are abnormally rigid, stereotyped, and compulsive, and abnormally bound to stimuli from without and within.

To avoid any misunderstanding, I would like to stress that the defect in patients with brain damage does not always have to manifest itself in the same way—not even in all frontal lobe lesions. To what degree impairment of abstraction appears depends upon the extensiveness, the intensity, and the nature of the lesion. To evaluate the relationship between a patient's behavior and his defect, we have to consider further that personal experience plays a role in determining whether a patient can solve a problem or not. One patient reacts well—at least at face value—when he is given a task, although another patient has failed the same task; to the first patient the task represents a concrete situation; for the second patient it is an abstract situation. But in both cases, the defect will always be revealed by further examination.

## CATASTROPHIC CONDITIONS

Impairment of abstraction is not the only factor which produces deviations in the behavior of patients, as I have stated before. Another very important factor is the occurrence of a catastropic condition (4, pp. 35 ff.). When a patient is not able to fulfill a task set before him, this condition is a frequent occurrence. A patient may look animated, calm, in a good mood, well-poised, collected, and cooperative when he is confronted with tasks he can fulfill; the same patient may appear dazed, become agitated, change color, start to fumble, become unfriendly, evasive, and even aggressive when he is not able to fulfill the task. His overt behavior appears very much the same as a person in a state of anxiety. I have called the state of the patient in the situation of success, *ordered condition;* the state in the situation of failure, *disordered or catastrophic condition.*

In the catastrophic condition the patient not only is incapable of performing a task which exceeds his impaired capacity, but he also fails, for a longer or shorter period, in performances which he is able to carry out in the ordered state. For a varying period of time, the organism's reactions are in great disorder or are impeded altogether. We are able to study this condition particularly well in these patients, since we can produce it experimentally by demanding from the patient something which we know he will not be able to do, because of his defect. Now, as we have said, impairment of abstractions makes it impossible for a patient to account to himself for his acts. He is quite unable to realize his failure and why he fails. Thus we can assume that catastrophic condition is not a reaction of the patient to failure, but rather belongs intrinsically to the situation of the organism in failing. For the normal person, failure in the performance of a nonimportant task would be merely something disagreeable; for the brain-injured person, however, as observation shows, any failure means the impossibility of self-realization and of existence. The occurrence of catastrophic condition is not limited therefore to special tasks; any task can place the patient in this situation, since the patient's self-realization is endangered so easily. Thus the same task produces anxiety at one time, and not at another.

## Anxiety

The conditions under which anxiety occurs in brain-injured patients correspond to the conditions for its occurrence in normal people in that what produces anxiety is not the failure itself, but the resultant danger to the person's existence. I would like to add that the danger need not always be real; it is sufficient if the person imagines that the condition is such that he will not be able to realize himself. For instance, a person may be in distress because he is not able to answer questions in an examination. If the outcome of the examination is not particularly important, then the normal person will take it calmly even though he may feel somewhat upset; because it is not a dangerous situation for him, he will face the situation and try to come to terms with it as well as he can by using his wits, and in this way he will bring it to a more or less successful solution. The situation becomes totally different, however, if passing the examination is of great consequence in the person's life; not passing the examination may, for instance, endanger his professional career or the possibility of marrying the person he loves. When self-realization is seriously in danger, catastrophe may occur together with severe anxiety; when this occurs, it is impossible for the person to answer even those questions which, under other circumstances, he could solve without difficulty.

I would like to clarify one point here —namely, that anxiety represents an emotional state which does not refer to any object. Certainly the occurrence of anxiety is connected with an outer or inner event. The organism, shaken by a catastrophic shock, exists in relation to a definitive reality; and the basic phenomenon of anxiety, which is the occurrence of disordered behavior, is understandable only in terms of this relationship to reality. But anxiety does not originate from the experiencing of this relationship. The brain-injured patient could not experience anxiety, if it were necessary for him to experience this relationship to reality. He is certainly not aware of this objective reality; he experiences only the shock, only anxiety. And this, of course holds true for anxiety in general. Observations of many patients confirm the interpretation of anxiety by philosophers, such as Pascal and Kierkegaard, and by psychologists who have dealt with anxiety—namely, that the source of anxiety is the inner experience of not being confronted with anything or of being confronted with nothingness.

In making such a statement, one must distinguish sharply between *anxiety* and *fear*—another emotional state which is very often confused with anxiety (4, p. 293; 16). Superficially, fear may have many of the characteristics of anxiety, but intrinsically it is different. In the state of fear we have an object before us, we can meet that object, we can attempt to remove it, or we can flee from it. We are conscious of ourselves, as well as of the object; we can deliberate as to how we shall behave toward it, and we can look at the cause of the fear, which actually lies before us. Anxiety, on the other hand, gets at us from the back, so to speak. The only thing we can do is to attempt to flee from it, but without knowing what direction to take, since we experience it as coming from no particular place. We are dealing, as I have shown explicitly elsewhere, with qualitative differences, with different attitudes toward the world. Fear is related, in our experience, to an object; anxiety is not—it is only an inner state.

What is characteristic of the object of fear? Is it something inherent in the object itself, at all times? Of course not. At one time an object may arouse only interest, or be met with indifference; but at another time it may evoke the greatest fear. In other words, fear must be the result of a specific relationship between organism and object. What leads to fear is nothing but the experience of the possibility of the onset of anxiety. What we fear is the impending

anxiety, which we experience in relation to some objects. Since a person in a state of fear is not yet in a state of anxiety but only envisions it—that is, he only fears that anxiety may befall him—he is not so disturbed in his judgment of the outer world as the person in a state of anxiety. Rather, driven as he is by the tendency to avoid the onset of anxiety, he attempts to establish special contact with the outer world. He tries to recognize the situation as clearly as possible and to react to it in an appropriate manner. Fear is conditioned by, and directed against, very definite aspects of the environment. These have to be recognized and, if possible, removed. Fear sharpens the senses, whereas anxiety renders them unusable. Fear drives to action; anxiety paralyzes.

From these explanations it is obvious that in order to feel anxiety it is not necessary to be able to give oneself an account of one's acts; to feel fear, however, presupposes that capacity. From this it becomes clear that our patients do not behave like people in a state of fear—that is, they do not intentionally try to avoid situations from which anxiety may arise. They cannot do that because of the defect of abstraction. Also from our observation of the patients we can assume that they do not experience fear and that they only have the experience of anxiety.

Anxiety, a catastrophic condition in which self-realization is not possible, may be produced by a variety of events, all of which have in common the following: There is a discrepancy between the individual's capacities and the demands made on him, and this discrepancy makes self-realization impossible. This may be due to external or internal conditions, physical or psychological. It is this discrepancy to which we are referring when we speak of "conflicts." Thus we can observe anxiety in infants, in whom such a discrepancy must occur frequently, particularly since their abstract attitude is not yet developed, or not fully. We also see anxiety in brain-injured people, in whom impairment of abstraction produces the same discrepancy. In normal people, anxiety appears when the demands of the world are too much above the capacity of the individual, when social and economic situations are too stressful, or when religious conflicts arise. Finally we see anxiety in people with neuroses and psychoses which are based on unsolvable and unbearable inner conflicts.

## THE PROTECTIVE MECHANISMS

The last group of symptoms to be observed in brain-injured patients are the behavior changes which make it possible for the patient to get rid of the catastrophic condition—of anxiety (4, pp. 40 ff.). The observation of this phenomenon in these patients is of special interest since it can teach us how an organism can get rid of anxiety without being aware of its origin and without being able to avoid the anxiety voluntarily. After a certain time these patients show a diminution of disorder and of catastrophic reactions (anxiety) even though the defect caused by the damage to the brain still exists. This, of course, can occur only if the patient is no longer exposed to tasks he cannot cope with. This diminution is achieved by definite changes in the behavior of the patients: They are withdrawn, so that a number of stimuli, including dangerous ones, do not reach them. They usually stay alone; either they do not like company or they want to be only with people whom they know well. They like to be in a familiar room in which everything is organized in a definite way. They show extreme orderli-

ness in every respect; everything has to be done exactly at an appointed time— whether it is breakfast, dinner, or a walk. They show excessive and fanatical orderliness in arranging their belongings; each item of their wardrobe must be in a definite place—that is, in a place where it can be gotten hold of quickly, without the necessity of a choice, which they are unable to make. Although it is a very primitive order indeed, they stick fanatically to it; it is the only way to exist. Any change results in a state of very great excitement. They themselves cannot voluntarily arrange things in a definite way. The orderliness is maintained simply because the patients try to stick to those arrangements which they can handle. This sticking to that which they can cope with is characteristic for their behavior; thus any behavior change can be understood only in terms of this characteristic behavior.

An illustration of this characteristic behavior is the fact that they always try to keep themselves busy with things that they are able to do as a protection against things that they cannot cope with. The activities which engross them need not be of great value in themselves. Their usefulness consists apparently in the fact that they protect the patient. Thus a patient does not like to be interrupted in an activity. For instance, although a patient may behave well in a conversation with someone he knows and likes, he does not like to be suddenly addressed by someone else.

We very often observe that a patient is totally unaware of his defect—such as hemiplegia or hemianopsia—and of the difference between his state prior to the development of the symptoms and his present state. This is strikingly illustrated by the fact that the disturbances of these patients play a very small part in their complaints. We are not dealing simply with a subjective lack of awareness, for the defects are effectively excluded from awareness, one might say. This is shown by the fact that they produce very little disturbance —apparently as the result of compensation. This exclusion from awareness seems to occur particularly when the degree of functional defect in performance is extreme. We can say that defects are shut out from the life of the organism when they would seriously impair any of its essential functions and when a defect can be compensated for by other activities at least to the extent that self-realization is not essentially disturbed.

One can easily get the impression that a patient tries to deny the experience of the functional disturbance because he is afraid that he will get into a catastrophic condition if he becomes aware of his defect. As a matter of fact, a patient may get into a catastrophic condition when we make him aware of his defect, or when the particular situation does not make possible an adequate compensation. Sometimes this happens—and this is especially interesting—when the underlying pathological condition improves and with that the function.

A patient of mine who became totally blind by a suicidal gunshot through the chiasma opticum behaved as if he were not aware of his blindness; the defect was compensated for very well by his use of his other senses, his motor skill, and his knowledge and intelligence. He was usually in a good mood; he never spoke of his defect, and he resisted all attempts to draw his attention to it. After a certain time, the condition improved; but at the same time he realized that he could not recognize objects through his vision. He was shocked and became deeply depressed. When he was asked why he was depressed, he said, "I cannot see." We might assume that

in the beginning the patient denied the defect intentionally because he could not bear it. But why then did he not deny it when he began to see? Or we might assume that in the beginning he did not deny his blindness, but that in total blindness an adjustment occurred in terms of a change of behavior for which vision was not necessary; and because of this it was not necessary for him to realize his blindness. The moment he was able to see, he became aware of his defect and was no longer able to eliminate it. The exclusion of the blindness defect from awareness could thus be considered a secondary effect of the adjustment. But in this patient who was mentally undisturbed a more voluntary denial cannot be overlooked. A voluntary denial is not possible in patients with impairment of abstraction as in brain-injured patients. Here the unawareness of the defect can only be a secondary effect—an effect of the same behavior, which we have described before, by which the brain-injured person is protected against catastrophes which may occur because of his defect. As we have said, the patient, driven by the trend to realize himself as well as possible, sticks to what he is able to do; this shows in his whole behavior. From this point of view, the patient's lack of awareness of his defect, as well as his peculiarities in general, becomes understandable. For instance, in these terms, it is understandable why an aphasic patient utters a word which is only on the normal fringe of the word that he needs; for the word that he needs to use is a word that he cannot say at all or can say only in such a way that he could not be understood and would as a result be in distress (13, p. 226). Thus a patient may repeat "church" instead of "God," "father" instead of "mother," and so on; he considers his reaction correct, at least as long as no one makes him aware of the fact that his reaction is wrong. This same kind of reaction occurs in disturbances of recognition, of feelings, and so on.

One is inclined to consider the use of wrong words or disturbances of recognition, actions, and feelings as due to a special pathology; but that is not their origin. Since these disturbances are reactions which represent all that the individual is able to execute, he recognizes them as fulfillment of the task; in this way, these reactions fulfill this need to such a degree that no catastrophe occurs. Thus the protection appears as a passive effect of an active "correct" procedure and could not be correctly termed denial, which refers to a more intentional activity, "conscious" or "unconscious."

This theory on the origin of the protective behavior in organic patients deserves consideration, particularly because the phenomena observed in organic patients shows such a similarity to that observed in neurotics. One could even use psychoanalytic terms for the different forms of behavior in organic patients. For instance, one might use the same terms that Anna Freud (17) uses to characterize various defense mechanisms against anxiety. Both neurotic and organic patients show a definite similarity in behavior structure and in the purpose served by that structure. In organic patients, however, I prefer to speak of protective mechanisms instead of defense mechanisms; the latter refers to a more voluntary act, which organic patients certainly cannot perform, as we have discussed earlier. In neurotics, the development of defense mechanisms generally does not occur so passively through organismic adjustment, as does the development of protective mechanisms in the organic patients; this is in general the distinction between the two. It seems to me that this distinction is not

true in the case of neurotic children, however; some of these children seem to develop protective mechanisms in a passive way, similar to organic patients. Such mechanisms can perhaps be found in other neurotics. Thus, in interpreting these mechanisms, one should take into account the possibility of confusing the neurotic patient with the organic patient.

I would like to add a last word with regard to the restrictions of the personality and of the world of these patients which is brought about by this protective behavior. The restrictions are not as disturbing in the brain-injured patients as is the effect of defense mechanisms in neuroses. In a neurotic, defense mechanisms represent a characteristic part of the disturbances he is suffering from; but the organic patient does not become aware of the restriction since his protective mechanisms allow for some ordered form of behavior and for the experience of some kind of self-realization—which is true, of course, only as long as the environment is so organized by the people around him that no tasks arise that he cannot fulfill and as long as the protecting behavior changes are not hindered. This is the only way the brain-damaged person can exist. The patient cannot bear conflict—that is, anxiety, restriction, or suffering. In this respect he differs essentially from the neurotic who is more or less able to bear conflict. This is the main difference which demands a different procedure in treatment; in many respects, however, treatment can be set up in much the same way for both (18). In treating these patients, it is more important to deal with the possible occurrence of catastrophe rather than with the impairment of abstraction, for my observations of a great many patients for over ten years indicate that the impairment of abstraction cannot be alleviated unless the brain damage from which it originated is eliminated. There is no functional restitution of this capacity by compensation through other parts of the brain. Improvement of performances can be achieved only by the building up of substitute performances by the use of the part of concrete behavior which is preserved; but this is only possible by a definite arrangement of the environment.

I am well aware that my description of the personality change in brain damage is somewhat sketchy. The immense material and the problems involved, so manifold and complex, make a more satisfactory presentation in such a brief time impossible. I hope that I have been successful in outlining, to the best of my ability, the essential phenomena and problems of these patients. In addition, I trust that I have shown how much we can learn from these observations for our concept of the structure of the personality, both normal and pathological, and for the treatment of brain-damaged patients and also, I hope, of patients with so-called psychogenic disorders.

# REFERENCES

1. GOLDSTEIN, K. Ueber die gleichartige functionelle bedingtheit der symptome in organischen und psychischen krankheiten. *Montschr. f. Psychiat. u. Neurol.*, 57(1924), 191.

2. ———. Die beziehungen der psychoanalyse zue biologie, in *Verhandlungen d. congresses für psychotherapie in nauheim*. Leipzig: Hirzel, 1927.

3. ———. *Aftereffects of brain injuries in war*. New York: Grune & Stratton, 1942.

4. ———.*The organism: a holistic approach to biology*. New York: American Book Co., 1939.

5. ———.*Human nature in the light of psychopathology*. Cambridge: Harvard Univ. Press, 1940. Page 194.

6. ———.*Handbuch der normalen und pathologischen physiologie*. Berlin: J. S. Springer, 1927. Volume 10, pages 600 ff. and 813.

7. ——— The significance of the frontal lobes for mental performances. *J. Neurol. & Psychopathol.*, 17(1936), 27–40.

8. ——— The modifications of behavior consequent to cerebral lesions. *Psychiat. Quart.*, 10(1936), 586.

9. ——— and Scheerer, M. *Abstract and concrete behavior*. Psychol. Monogr. No. 239, 1941.

10. GOLDSTEIN, K. On emotions: considerations from the organismic point of view. *J. Psychol.*, 31(1951), 37–49.

11. JACOBSON, EDITH. The speed pace in psychic discharge processes and its influence on the pleasure-unpleasure qualities of affects. Paper read before the American Psychoanalytic Association, May, 1952.

12. GOLDSTEIN, K., and STEINFELD, J. I. The conditioning of sexual behavior by visual agnosia. *Bull. Forest Sanit.*, 1 (1942), no. 2, pp. 37–45.

13. GOLDSTEIN, K., *Language and language disturbances*. New York: Grune & Stratton, 1948.

14. ———.Frontal lobotomy and impairment of abstract attitude. *J. Nerv. & Ment. Dis.*, 110(1949), 93–111.

15. FREEMAN, W., and WATTS, J. *Psychosurgery*, 2nd ed. Springfield, Ill.: Thomas, 1950.

16. GOLDSTEIN, K. Zum problem der angst. *Allg. ärztl. Ztscher. f. Psychotherap. u. psych. Hygiene*, 2(1929), 409–437.

17. FREUD, A. *The ego and the mechanisms of defense*. New York: Internat. Univ. Press, 1946.

18. GOLDSTEIN, K. The idea of disease and therapy. *Rev. Religion*, 14(1949), 229–240.

# Chapter 5

# Personality Disorders

The diagnosis of personality disorder is rapidly becoming the most popular available label in the out-patient situation, and by virtue of this is losing a good deal of meaning. Just as it was once popular to call any behavioral peculiarity "neurotic," more sophisticated individuals now point to these difficulties as personality or character problems. At one time this label was reserved for individuals with behavior problems that led them into difficulties with the law. The diagnostic category that is now used in such a case is sociopathic personality disturbance. Currently, references to personality disorders are more widely used to describe individuals technically diagnosed as personality trait disturbance or personality pattern disturbance. The common feature that cuts across these categories is that the individuals have developed a way of life that creates disharmony in their personal relationships. Instead of placing emphasis on their symptoms or on their subjective discomfort, the focus is on how they get along with others, and in this we usually find some inadequacy, although the patient may not always recognize it as such and often does not recognize his role in disrupting his relationships.

Gerald S. Blum

## Adult Character Structure

At the outset, the psychoanalyst viewed his therapeutic task as relatively simple and straightforward. Neurosis was thought to stem from unconscious conflict and thus it was necessary to uncover what was unconscious, deal directly with the conflict, and arrive at acceptable ways of gratifying impulses. In effect, Freud's famous dictum "Where id is, ego shall be" set the tone of therapy. As analysts accumulated experience, however, they began to find the road to the unconscious laden with obstacles erected by the ego. Essentially the same barriers that had been erected to deny impulses either conscious or motor expression were directed against the uncovering efforts of the therapist. These barriers are what have come to be called "character" and certain character styles came to be described. In this paper, a chapter from a book by Gerald S. Blum, there is a good discussion and description of the types of character structure that have been identified.

Abridged from Chapter 8 in Psychoanalytic Theories of Personality by G. S. Blum. Copyright, 1953, McGraw-Hill, Inc. Used by permission of McGraw-Hill Book Company, Inc. and the author.

The experiences of the first two decades of life all contribute to the gradual emergence in the individual of characteristic ways of thinking, feeling, and behaving. Every adult man or woman comes to acquire a particular constellation of traits, a unique style of living. However, psychoanalytic theories of adult personality, apart from those dealing with pathology, tend to stress common patterns. The various theoretical views presented in this chapter, therefore, are concerned mainly with "types" of character structure.

## ORTHODOX POSITION

### Definition and Classification of "Character"

Fenichel (3) describes character as "the ego's habitual modes of adjustment to the external world, the id and the superego, and the characteristic types of combining these modes with one another." This youngest branch of psychoanalysis, so-called "ego psychology," had its origins in two factors: first the growing awareness in psychotherapy of the necessity to analyze the patient's resistances and ego defenses; and second, the greater prominence of defenses in the clinical picture of the neuroses. The historical development, remarks Fenichel, is easy to understand, since psychoanalysis began with the study of unconscious phenomena, alien to the ego, and proceeded only gradually to consider character or the customary mode of behavior.

Character, however, has a broader scope than the defense mechanisms, for it includes the positive, organizing functions of the ego. Through the defense mechanisms the ego protects the organism from external and internal stimuli by blocking reactions. But the ego also serves to sift and organize stimuli and impulses. Some are permitted direct expression, others indirect. Hartmann (6), enumerating ego functions, includes reality testing, the control of motility and perception, action and thinking, inhibition and delay of discharge, anticipatory signaling of danger, and a synthetic or organizing function.

Instinctual demands are always bound up in the character structure, according to Fenichel. The organization, direction, and sifting of impulses, which must be made consonent with demands of the external world, constitute the attitudes of the ego. Likewise the superego is decisive in forming character, for the individual sets up habitual patterns based on what he considers good or bad. In the latter connection the adoption and modification of ideals in later life are also of importance. The other source of influence, the external world, is crucial in the sense that man's character is said to be socially determined. In Fenichel's words: (3, p. 464):

The environment enforces specific frustrations, blocks certain modes of reaction to these frustrations, and facilitates others: it suggests certain ways of dealing with the conflicts between instinctual demands and fears of further frustrations; it even creates desires by setting up and forming specific ideals. Different societies, stressing different values and applying different educational measures, create different anomalies. Our present unstable society seems to be characterized by conflicts between ideas of individual independence (created during the rise of capitalism and still effective) and regressive longings for passive dependence (created by the helplessness of the individual with respect to security and gratifications as well as by active educational measures which are the outcome of the social necessity of authoritative influences).

The relative constancy of character is presumed to depend on three facets: partly on the hereditary constitution of the ego, partly on the nature of the instincts against which the defense is directed, and mainly on the special attitude forced on the individual by the external world.

Fenichel classifies character traits into two broad categories—sublimation and reactive. In the sublimation category the original instinctual energy is discharged freely as a result of an alteration in aim. The "genital character" belongs here. The conditions underlying the formation of sublimation traits are felt to be obscure. In general such traits are fostered by the absence of fixations, plus favorable environmental conditions for providing substitute channels of expression.

Instinctual energy in the case of the reactive category is constantly held in check by countercathexes. Attitudes are concerned with avoidance (phobic) or opposition (reaction formation). Fatigue, inhibition, rigidity, and inefficiency are common. The flexibility of the person is limited, for he is capable neither of full satisfaction nor of sublimation. Some persons develop a defensive attitude only in certain situations; others have to protect themselves continually. The latter are said to employ "character defenses," which are unspecific and maintained indiscriminately toward everyone. For example, they may always be either impudent or polite, empty of emotions or ever ready to blame others. Reactions to conflict in the area of self-esteem manifest themselves in arrogant behavior to hide deep inferiority feelings; ambitious behavior to cover inadequacy; and so on. The development of reactive traits is said to be fostered by early psychosexual fixations.

Reich (8), a pioneer in the field of character analysis, describes reactive traits in terms of "character armor." A chronic alteration in the ego serves to protect against external and internal dangers. The armor, originally forged as a result of the conflict between instinctual demands and the frustrating outer world, gets its strength and reason for existence from continuing actual conflicts between these same opposing forces. Character grows out of the attempted solution of the Oedipus complex, with the subsequent hardening of the ego being accounted for by three processes: (1) identification with the main person who represents frustrating reality, (2) aggression turned inward as an inhibitory force, and (3) formation by the ego of reactive attitudes toward the sexual impulses. Thus, the armor serves to strengthen the ego by alleviating the pressure from repressed libidinal impulses. At the same time, though, it operates to insulate the person from external stimuli and renders him less susceptible to education.

## Character Types

Orthodox psychoanalytic literature contains descriptions of a wide variety of types—oral, anal, urethral, phallic, genital, compulsive, hysterical, phobic, cyclic, schizoid, and others. However, organization of these types into a meaningful classification has remained elusive. Fenichel expresses his own discontent in the following words (3, p. 527):

The differentiation of individual character traits into those of the sublimation types and reactive ones is not of much value in judging personalities, since every person show traits of both kinds. And still it seems the relatively most useful approach to distinguish personalities in whom the sublimation type of traits prevails from those that are predominantly reactive. It had become customary to distinguish genital from pregenital characters; however, although the traits of anal or oral characters consist of both sublimations and reaction formations, pregenital traits become predominant only in cases in which countercathexes suppress still operative pregenital impulses; in other words, pregenital characters, as a rule, are also reactive characters, whereas the attainment of genital primacy is the best basis for the successful sublimation of the remaining pregenital energies.

One source of confusion lies in the attempt to distinguish the more or less "normal" types from those which are primarily "neurotic." The problem becomes especially acute when, as in this text, the area of psychopathology has been excluded from consideration. A solution suggested by common practice is to designate arbitrarily the various pregenital types and the genital type as falling within the normal range and hence eligible for detailed discussion here. The psychoanalysts, in addition to Freud, who contributed heavily to the original formulation of these characterizations were Abraham, Jones, Glover, and Reich (1, 7, 5, 8).

*The Oral Character.* The oral character is one whose habitual mode of adjustment contains strong elements of oral fixations produced in early childhood. He is extremely dependent on others for the maintenance of his self-esteem. External supplies are all-important to him, and he yearns for them passively. The mouth serves an especially significant function. When he feels depressed, he eats to overcome the emotion. Oral preoccupations, in addition to food, frequently revolve around drinking, smoking, and kissing. As a consequence of the infantile association in the feeding situation, love is equated with food. Conflicted longings for love and narcissistic supplies may even generate physiological effects, such as the increased secretion of gastric juices observed in peptic ulcer cases.

Fenichel (3) links oral overindulgence in infancy to a later feeling of optimism and self-assurance, provided that the external environment does not threaten the individual's security. Early oral deprivation is said to determine a pessimistic or sadistic attitude. Persons in whom the oral-sadistic component is marked are aggressive and biting in their relationships. They continually demand supplies in a vampirelike fashion and affix themselves by "suction."

The passive-dependent, receptive orientation to life brings with it a number of other related personality characteristics. All positive or negative emphasis on taking and receiving is said to indicate an oral origin. Marked generosity and niggardliness both stem from oral eroticism. Generous persons sometimes betray their original stinginess, just as stingy ones occasionally resort to exceptional generosity. Gifts assume unusual importance. The particular form of behavior depends upon the ratio between sublimation and reaction formation in the handling of oral drives.

Some individuals manifest their dependent needs directly and insatiably by begging or even demanding to be cared for. According to Fenichel, the demanding tone prevails in persons who are incapable of getting sufficient reassurance, so that every real gift makes them long for more. The begging tone occurs in persons who actually are satisfied when taken care of, and who willingly sacrifice ambition and comfort in order to buy the necessary affection. Others tend to overcompensate for their unconscious passive longings by behaving in an extremely active and masculine fashion, under the pretense of being entirely independent. Alexander (2) describes the latter constellation as typical of the ulcer personality.

Another common form of behavior in oral characters is identification with the object by whom they want to be fed. Certain individuals always act like nursing mothers, showering everyone with presents and help. The attitude has the magical significance of "As I shower you with love, I want to be showered." Under favorable circumstances, this may serve a truly altruistic function. More often, it tends to be annoying. In contrast, some identify with a frustrating rather than a giving mother. Here the behavior is completely selfish and stingy, implying "Because I was not given what I wanted, I shall not give other people what they want." Additional oral traits described by Fenichel include curiosity (as a displacement of "hunger"), volubility, restlessness, haste, and a tendency toward obstinate silence.

*The Anal Character.* Traits associated with anal fixations were Freud's (4) first insights in the area of character structure. Personality features are said to grow out of the conflicts around toilet training, since the child, as we have seen earlier, has opportunities to please or defile his parents and also to gain physiological pleasure from elimination and retention. The predominant adult anal traits are known as the three "P's"—parsimony, petulance, and pedantry, or, as phrased more commonly, frugality, obstinacy, and orderliness. Fenichel (3) describes frugality as a continuation of the habit of anal retentiveness, sometimes motivated by the fear of losing, sometimes more by erogenous pleasure. Based on the equating of feces with money, attitudes toward money become irrational, as were the original anal instinctual wishes. No longer viewed as an objectively useful thing, money is retained and hoarded or sometimes carelessly thrown away. Similar attitudes exist toward time, so that the anal character may be punctual to the fraction of a minute or grossly unreliable.

Obstinacy is a passive type of aggression, stemming from the child's refusal to produce when his parents were intent upon his doing so. After a while

this "magical" superiority or feeling of power is replaced by a "moral" superiority in which the superego plays a decisive part. Stubbornness in the behavior of adults is explained as an attempt to use other persons as instruments in the struggle with the superego. By provoking people to be unjust, such individuals strive for a feeling of moral superiority which serves to increase self-esteem and to counterbalance pressure from the superego. The stubborn person considers himself to have been unfairly treated and often elicits affection forcibly by making his antagonist feel sorry afterward. Thus, says Fenichel, obstinacy, which originally is the combative method of the weak, later becomes a habitual method of struggle for maintaining or restoring self-esteem. Excessive orderliness arises from compliance and obedience to parental demands. Tidiness, punctuality, meticulousness, and propriety are all said to signify a displacement of compliance with the environmental requirements in regard to defecation.

The mechanism of reaction formation is frequently apparent in anal traits, for the scrupulously clean and orderly individual may at certain times be astonishingly messy and disorganized. Another example is painting, which in some cases represents a reaction formation to the unconscious desire for anal smearing. The artist who is not sublimating effectively often fails in his work or becomes inhibited in his ability to paint. Other anal characteristics manifest themselves as displacements to speech and thinking in the irrational modes of retaining or expelling words and thoughts. All anal traits are said to contain a sadistic element, in accordance with the original ambivalent object relations of the anal stage.

*The Urethral Character.* The outstanding personality features of the urethral character are ambition and competitiveness, both of which are presumed to be reactions against shame. The child who wets his pants is often made an object of ridicule and shame. In response to this feeling he later develops ambitious desires in order to prove that there is no longer any need for him to be ashamed. Another contributing element is the original competition with respect to urination, e.g., who can direct a longer stream.

Fenichel (3) also discusses the various displacements and secondary conflicts created by urethral ambition. The latter may be condensed with trends derived from earlier oral sources or, under the influence of the castration complex, may be displaced to the anal field. This is especially characteristic in girls because of the futility of urethral competition. Too, the reassurances which ambition and success provide against the idea of being castrated may be turned into prohibitions if they acquire, in connection with the Oedipus complex, the unconscious meaning of killing the father.

*The Phallic Character.* The phallic character behaves in a reckless, resolute, and self-assured fashion, mainly as a wish-fulfilling reaction to castration anxiety. The overvaluation of the penis and its confusion with the whole body, typical of the early phallic stage, are reflected by intense vanity, exhibitionism, and sensitiveness. These individuals usually anticipate an expected assault by attacking first. They appear aggressive and provocative, not so much from what they say or do, but rather in their manner of speaking and acting. Wounded pride, according to Reich (8), often results in either cold reserve, deep depression, or lively aggression. The resentment of subordination and the tendency to dominate others are both grounded in fear. Overtly courageous behavior, as exhibited by the motorcycle daredevil, is said to represent an overcompensation.

Basically the phallic character is extremely oral-dependent, and his narcissistic orientation precludes the establishment of mature relationships with others. The male, driven to attempts to demonstrate his masculinity, is nevertheless contemptuous and hostile toward women. The phallic female, motivated by strong penis envy, assumes the masculine role and strives for superiority over men. Narcissism is again a central characteristic.

*The Genital Character.* Fenichel (3) himself states that the normal "genital" character is an ideal concept. However, the achievement of genital primacy is presumed to bring a decisive advance in character formation. The ability to attain full satisfaction through genital orgasm makes the physiological regulation of sexuality possible and thus puts an end to the damming up of instinctual energies, with its unfortunate effects on the person's behavior. It also makes for the full development of love and the overcoming of ambivalence. Furthermore, the capacity to discharge great quantities of excitement means the end of reaction formations and an increase in the ability to sublimate. Emotions, instead of being warded off, are used constructively by the ego as part of the total personality. The formation of traits of the sublimation type thus becomes possible. Pregenital impulses are mostly sublimated, but some are also incorporated into the forepleasure mechanisms of the sexual act.

# REFERENCES

1. ABRAHAM, K. *Selected papers on psychoanalysis.* London: Hogarth, 1927.
2. ALEXANDER, F. Psychologic factors in gastrointestinal disturbances. *Psychoanal. Quart.,* 3(1934), 501–588.
3. FENICHEL, O. *The psychoanalytic the-*

ory of neurosis. New York: Norton, 1945.

4. Freud, S. Character and anal eroticism. In Collected papers, Vol. II. London: Hogarth, 1948. Pages 45–50.

5. Glover, E. Notes on character formation. Int. J. Psychoanal., 6(1925), 131–154.

6. Hartmann, H. Comments on the psychoanalytic theory of neurosis. Psychoanalytic Study of the Child, 5(1950), 74–96.

7. Jones, E. Papers on psychoanalysis. New York: Wood, 1913.

8. Reich, W. Character-analysis. New York: Orgone Institute Press, 1945.

George C. Rosenwald,
Gerald A. Mendelsohn,
Alan Fontana,
and Alexis T. Portz

# An Action Test of Hypotheses Concerning the Anal Personality

*Psychoanalytic theories about character structure have described a number of character types. These have been classified in terms of clusters of habits that are expected to be found in such types. It is hypothesized that a diversity in types arises as a result of the fact that different individuals have particular adjustment problems at different stages in development. Depending upon the stage that one has special problems with, one or another character type will result. In this paper by Rosenwald, Mendelsohn, Fontana, and Portz, a test situation was used to identify subjects having problems with anal impulses— in effect, subjects who might be described as anal personalities. Subjects so identified were then compared with other subjects who were not seen as anal personalities on several tasks in which other characteristics of the anal personality could be manifested. It was expected that such characteristics should be more prevalent in the former group than in the latter.*

Psychoanalytic study of individuals with prominent fixations on the anal stage of psychosexual development has yielded the impression that their characteristic defense tactics frequently result in an intellectualized approach to life problems, emotional issues, and interpersonal relationships. It seems, furthermore, that while the mere presence of anal fixations may lead to a sound, creative, and subtle *intellectual mentality*, the latter may decompensate into an *intellectual disturbance* marked by emptiness, ritualism, and pedantry, when defensive efforts are weakened or impulses gain in strength. This has been observed in adolescents in particular (A. Freud, 1936). A second normal compulsive trait often discerned in anally fixated people is that of cool and

Reprinted from the Journal of Abnormal and Social Psychology, 71(1966), 304–309 with the permission of the American Psychological Association and Dr. Rosenwald. Copyright 1966 by the American Psychological Association.

impassive *deliberateness* in taking action and in making decisions. Its pathological extreme are the paralyzing doubt and *indecisiveness* resulting from decompensated or overly rigid defenses against anal impulses. Normal intellectuality and deliberateness are usually ego-syntonic and adaptive personality traits, whereas their pathological extremes are often experienced as symptoms requiring amelioration. The present study reports an action test of the prediction that relatively ineffective defenses against anal impulses are associated with indecisiveness and intellectual disturbance.

Previous research dealing with anal personality traits has, on the whole, been discouraging. Although one or two factor-analytic investigations have isolated *traits* corresponding closely to the informal impressions reported in the clinical literature, it has not been possible to assign individuals to an anal *type* in accordance with casual clinical usage.

Barnes (1952) isolated two factors, one of orderliness, reliability, and law abidance, the other of sadism, and this accords well with the psychoanalytic formulation. Earlier still, Sears (1936), in his study of trait attribution, discovered that the traits of stinginess, obstinacy, and disorderliness tended to be correlated in the evaluation of subjects by their peers. This too is theoretically consistent.

Schlesinger recently (1963) collated anality questionnaires employed in various experimental investigations, including that reported in the present study, and submitted a total of 154 items to factor analysis. Among the first 12 factors which she extracted were regularity and meticulousness, retentiveness as a style of life, obstinacy, frugality, concern about dirt and contamination, anxiety over possible loss of control, and sensitivity to smells. Once

again, the intercorrelations of factor loadings tend to confirm clinical and theoretical preconceptions, and the extracted factors led to telling results in an investigation of personality and vocational choice.

Although these findings suggest that a single questionnaire could be constructed for the assessment of anal personality characteristics, this would not serve the purposes of the present study, since the qualitative analysis of defensive operations is the chief variable under consideration.

The action test utilized in the present study consists of a fecal-like stimulus and yields a measure of the effectiveness with which the subject coped with the stimulus. This performance criterion was employed to measure defense effectiveness because, according to psychoanalytic theory, effective defenses, in addition to reducing anxiety, also promote adaptation, whereas ineffective defenses do neither. Accordingly, relative task success was taken to reflect an adaptive strength, and relative failure, an adaptive weakness. Another part of the study made use of a questionnaire assessing anxiety about anal stimuli. In this way, defense effectiveness could be approached from both sides. More specifically, the action test does not attempt to determine whether the subject is anally fixated or even whether he is in conflict about anal impulses. Rather, it seeks to evaluate the adequacy with which he resolves whatever anal conflicts are present. Thus, it makes no distinction between individuals without noteworthy anal fixation and individuals who are flexibly defended against anal impulses. The questionnaire already mentioned does, however, make this distinction by means of items which tap stable anal character traits. Finally, it should be noted that rather different personality pictures result from the *choice* as well as the *effectiveness* of various defense mechanisms. However, no effort is made in the present study to compare, say, repression with reaction formation or projection. Only the degree of defense effectiveness, in terms of performance success, is measured.

## METHOD

The subjects were 48 male college freshmen and sophomores enrolled in an introductory psychology course. They were obligated to participate in the study as a course requirement. All subjects were first tested in a group session and then individually. In the group session, a modified form of the Remote Associates Test (RAT) was administered (Mednick, 1962). This test is said to yield a measure of creative thinking and seems manifestly to demand a certain flexibility of associative processes. In the context of the present study, it seemed a suitable measure of conceptualization and could serve to evaluate intellectual functioning of the kind which is hypothetically vulnerable to ineffective anal defenses. Its specially adapted form consisted of one part of 10, and a second part of 20 items. The first 10 required neutral solutions; the remaining 20 items were mixed, 10 requiring neutral and 10, anal solutions, appearing in random order. Both sets of neutral items were matched for difficulty. The instruction to the test was as follows: "In this test you will be presented with three words and asked to give the word *related* to *all three*." For example, "sweet" is the solution word for COOKIES, SIXTEEN, and HEART. No anal illustration item was, however, presented. A sample anal item is SHOOT, HORSE, HOUSE—SHIT (SHOOT THE SHIT, HORSESHIT, SHITHOUSE).

Fifteen minutes were allowed for the first 10 items and 30 for the other 20. The test was scored for the number of items solved correctly.

The second task administered in the group session was a specially prepared questionnaire which contained 18 items tap-ping a variety of anal anxieties, 16 items tapping anal character traits, and 9 items tapping nonanal anxieties. Twenty-five neutral items were added to these. Of the anal character traits and anxiety items, about half dealt directly with matters of the toilet or feelings about dirt and cleanliness, and half with more derived traits and preoccupations commonly associated with anal character structure, according to the clinical literature (e.g., Reich, 1949). Examples of anal anxiety items are: "Handling wet and slimy things upsets me," and "I get upset when I realize how much time I waste that should be used for study." Examples of anal character traits are: "I bathe (or shower) frequently," and "I am a punctual person." An example of a nonanal anxiety is: "I fear that I am mentally ill." The subjects endorsed each item on an 11-point scale from "very characteristic of me" to "not characteristic of me." In this way, every subject earned scores for anal anxiety, anal character, and nonanal anxiety. Thus, in addition to the measure of adaptive strength drawn from the action test, the questionnaire provided the second common criterion of defense effectiveness, freedom from anxiety.[1]

The individual session was begun with a Dot Estimation task. This test was administered to evaluate the subject's decisiveness in making simple judgments. Fifteen cards, 8 x 11½ inches in size, with random arrays of dots, from 19 to 267 in number, were exposed to the subject for 2 seconds at the rate of one card every 5 seconds. During the 3 seconds intervening between exposures he was to write down his "estimate of the number of exposed dots." In a second trial, the subject was to repeat the procedure with the difference that he himself would determine when the next card was to be exposed. He was informed that in this trial his "score would be equally weighted for accuracy and speed of estimation."

Subsequent to this task, the action test assessing the effectiveness of defenses against anal stimulation was administered. The subject's task required that he immerse his arm, up to the elbow, into a bucket filled with

---

[1] Further factor-analytic information concerning this questionnaire may be obtained from Schlesinger (1963).

water at room temperature which was hidden from his view by a curtain. Three irregularly shaped flat bits of aluminum, larger than those commonly used in jigsaw puzzles, had been dropped by the experimenter to the bottom of the bucket. A card with the outlines of six such pieces was displayed in full view of the subject. The instruction was to explore the contours of the three pieces, one after another, and to decide as quickly as possible to which of the displayed outlines it corresponded. The subject was required to leave his arm immersed until he had reached a decision. Then he was to remove the piece and place it on the table beside the bucket so that the experimenter might record the results. Four trials of three judgments each were administered using water as a medium. This was followed by four trials in a mixture of used crankcase oil and two pounds of flour. This dirty and odorous medium was assumed to arouse anxieties and other responses similar to those commonly attached to feces. While there were marked individual differences in response to this task—some subjects had had experience working in gas stations—it was quite clear from most subjects' behavior and verbal report that they found it decidedly unpleasant. Different aluminum figures were used in the water and oil trials. The number of correct judgments and the time required for each trial were recorded. To keep up their interest, subjects were informed of the number of correct judgments made in each trial.

## RESULTS

Each subject's performance on the action test was expressed in quotients of time-required-per-correct-matching in water and in oil. A subject whose efficiency in oil was less than it had been in water was said to be defending relatively ineffectively against the presumed anal stimulation of the oil medium. However, since the entire sample showed an average increase in efficiency from water to oil, the subjects were divided at the median of efficiency shift

scores (the difference between water and oil efficiency). Those below the median are referred to as good defenders (GD), implying that they either had no noteworthy conflict about anal stimulation or were dealing effectively with whatever conflict they had. Those above the median are referred to as poor defenders (PD).

The prediction that ineffective defenses against anal stimulation would be associated with indecisiveness was borne out by a sign-test evaluating the estimation latencies for Part II of the Dot task. On 11 out of the 15 stimulus cards the PDs' latencies were longer than the GDs' ($p = .006$). There are no consistent differences in accuracy of dot estimation between GD and PD subjects.

In order to test the prediction that ineffective defenses against anal stimulation would be associated with an intellectual disturbance, the relationship between action test and RAT performance was examined. The product-moment correlation between number of anal items solved and efficiency shift scores on the action test was $r = -.29$ ($p = .05$) indicating that GDs tend to solve more such items. But the correlation of action test with neutral RAT solutions was $r = -.01$. That anal and neutral items tap fairly distinct psychological functions is further suggested in that the number of anal RAT solutions was only slightly correlated with the number of neutral ones ($r = .13$).

It was a matter of interest to compare performance on the newly developed action test with questionnaire ratings, a more conventional instrument for the assessment of character traits and anxieties. Whether a measure of performance which did not aim directly at measuring the conscious experience of anxiety yielded the same results as a measure based on the subject's report of such manifest anxiety, would also be of theoretical interest. Accordingly, two groups of 12 subjects each were randomly chosen from the extremes of the anxiety questionnaire. The range of anxiety scores for the high-anxious group was from 14 to 7 and that for the low-anxious group from 0 to 3 with a possible maximum score of 18. These two groups performed differently on the action test, high anal-anxious scorers showing deterioration in the oil medium, and low scorers showing improvement ($t = 2.06$, $p < .05$). This indicates that subjects who describe themselves as *anxious* about anal concerns, show relative impairment of performance when the water medium is replaced by the oil medium. Neither anal *character* nor nonanal anxiety showed such an association with the action test. For each of these latter comparisons, $r = .02$. The differential association of anal anxiety and character traits with the performance criterion is quite in keeping with theoretically grounded expectations and will be discussed below. The questionnaire measures of anal anxiety and anal character were, however, significantly correlated with each other ($r = .32$, $p < .05$).

Would the anal anxiety questionnaire have served as well as the action test in confirming the predictions about indecisiveness and intellectual disturbance? To deal with this question, parallel computations were made. The measures of anal anxiety drawn from the questionnaire were positively correlated with the Dot latencies. On 13 of the 15 stimulus cards, the high-anxious subjects had longer average latencies than the low-anxious ones ($p = .002$). However, it was not found that they solved more anal RAT items, as was the case in comparing GDs and PDs. The action measure, therefore, yielded a correlation that would not have been obtained from the questionnaire.

## DISCUSSION

Performance of the action test, as a sample of the subject's adaptive potential in response to anal stimuli, was expected to hinge on the effectiveness of his defense, not on the relative importance of anal eroticism in his personality make-up. This expectancy is borne out in that stable character traits commonly thought to be derived from anal interests were not correlated with efficiency shift scores while self-reported *anxiety* about anal impulses did predict these scores. Both anxiety and inadequate adaptation are generally deemed to be consequences of ineffective defenses. Since anal character traits are, however, also known to occur in more or less stable people, free of anxiety, one would expect a far from perfect correlation between anal character and anal anxiety in the population at large. An underlying assumption, as yet to be specifically tested, is that while anal anxiety ought to be found only when evidence of anal character traits is also present, it is quite common to find the latter without the former. The statistical correlation should therefore be moderate, as it was in the present sample ($r = .32$). This permits the interpretation that there may have been well-functioning anal personalities among the GDs. From a theoretical standpoint, the distinction between having no anal conflicts and having anal conflicts, but resolving them successfully, is dubious. In principle, it is impossible to avoid dealing with erotic and aggressive impulses in oneself. The above distinction, therefore, refers mainly to the degree in which the successful resolution is evident to an observer or so deeply repressed or fully integrated as to escape notice.

Although the reported findings seem to bear out clinical impressions of the

obsessive-compulsive personality constellation, especially of the linkage between an involvement with dirt and a
characterological emphasis on intellectualization and action inhibition, the
findings can be explained in at least
two ways. The first explanation is based
on the presumed causal sequence of insufficient or undependable defensive
efforts failing to suppress the mounting
anxiety which is triggered by unacceptable anal impulses. This leads to functional disruption. A more detailed account of this is given elsewhere
(Rosenwald, 1961).

A second explanation is possible. The
PDs' relative impairment in the oil
medium may not have resulted from
anxiety, but from a playful lingering
over a substance which, in the case of
these subjects, was enjoyable precisely
because it lends itself to implicit anal
experiences or fantasies. In other words,
a kind of self-indulgence, rather than
anxiety, may have retarded their performance. This would be consistent
with the clinical understanding of anal,
or compulsive, personalities. Even severely neurotic individuals who observe
stringent taboos against anal temptations frequently betray a fascination
with dirt and destructiveness. However,
in the present context, playfulness or
fascination constituted an adaptive
weakness because all subjects knew that
they were being timed. The instructions
to the action test as well as to the previously administered Dot task had set
a competitive pace for the entire session. Furthermore, that the action test
was positively related to the anxiety
questionnaire lends additional credence
to the broad maladaptation hypothesis,
whether the inefficiency in the oil medium is interpreted as resulting from
functional disruption, playful lingering,
or a combination of both these factors.

The RAT findings also suggest that
sensitization factors, that is, factors of
fantasy or other symbolic activity, contributed to the action test performance.
The negative correlation between anal
RAT solutions and efficiency shift scores
may be explained by reference to the
PDs' sensitivities to anal stimuli: Just
as they were captivated and/or hindered
by the anal appeal of the oil medium,
so they were also alert to the opportunities for a symbolic anal response to
the relevant RAT items. In other words,
neither sensitization nor disruption
through anxiety can be ruled out from
the available data. The concatenation
of erotic and anxiety factors is a frequently observed clinical phenomenon
and can be conceived as an outcome
of ineffective defenses.

Several ambiguities arise in considering each of the employed measures
separately. For instance, the drop in
efficiency from the water to the oil
medium may reflect a generalized discomfort reaction to unfamiliar stimuli
or an aspect of tactile insensitivity
rather than a functional disruption
caused by attitudes toward dirt. It is
also possible that Dot Estimation scores
are related to psychophysical acuity. It
may, therefore, be hypothesized that
subjects whose sensory receptivity for
tactile cues is easily disturbed also show
a judgmental distractibility in response
to visual cues. That is to say, subjects
who were disturbed in one situation
were also disturbed in another. Similarly, it is possible that the correlation
between anal anxiety scores on the questionnaire and efficiency shift scores is
not mediated by particular impulse defense patterns. All one need assume is
that a subject will respond accurately
when asked whether he likes or dislikes
a mess. Those who say they dislike it,
prove to be consistent in that they perform poorly under messy conditions.
Finally, one can dispense with the defense theory in explaining the PDs'

advantage on anal RAT items. One can say that those subjects who had the greatest tolerance for the dirty medium, that is, the least squeamish subjects, also have fewer inhibitions against somewhat improper solution words.

However, when considered simultaneously, these various reinterpretations are not so persuasive. Taken together, they would imply that the action test is at once a measure of the subject's distractibility under the stress of unfamiliar conditions, of the subject's squeamishness about impropriety, and of the subject's positive liking for messiness. Although one cannot rule out that sensory acuity (and tactile sensitivity specifically) affects performance on the action test, this alone could not account for the correlation of the action test with the RAT, with the questionnaire, or perhaps even with the DOT task. Furthermore, while the action test and the Dot task have a sensory dimension and a concentration factor in common, this is not the case for the anal anxiety scores on the questionnaire, which were related both to the action test and to the Dot Estimation scores. All in all, it seems more parsimonious to abide with the theory and with the clinical observations which prompted this experiment. But further research linking the action test and questionnaire with factors like stubbornness, emotional constriction, and stinginess, will perhaps provide a more cogent demonstration of the cluster of anal traits.

Although the RAT is supposedly a measure of creative thought, the superior performance of the PDs may be viewed apart from considerations of creativity because their advantage was confined to anal items. The lack of correlation between these and the neutral RAT items suggests that solution of anal items is not so much a sign of creativity, as of a readiness for the ex-

pression of anal symbols and themes. On the other hand, the PDs' intellectual disturbance did not cause them any disadvantage in comparison with GDs' RAT performance.

In the past, researchers have often assumed that an emotional conflict and the resulting defensive efforts necessarily entail the eclipse of the relevant symbols and ideas from the subject's mind. However, especially in the case of anal characters, clinicians often remark on a rather eager, though incomplete, expression of libidinally or aggressively charged ideas. Defenses such as projection, reaction formation, and isolation and a host of so-called counterdefenses avert unconscious psychic dangers by modifying the content of forbidden wishes, rather than by eradicating them altogether. This phenomenon is reminiscent of a recent study in which lowered perceptual thresholds were observed in subjects with a preference for "externalizing" defenses (Lewit, Brayer, & Leiman, 1962).

An extreme form of intellectual disturbance found in compulsion neurosis is the emergence into awareness of unacceptable dirty or destructive ideas. Further research may show whether the present RAT finding is a mild form of such a disturbance. Because particular defenses are associated with particular contents, great care must be taken in generalizing the present RAT results. For instance, ineffective resolution of conflicts about dependency might be associated with predominantly avoidant defenses rather than counterdefenses. The result might be a suppression of, rather than a sensitization to, pertinent symbols and ideas. In brief, the hypothesis concerning intellectual disturbance in PDs is supported inasmuch as they show a bias which sensitizes them to drive-related, but not to neutral, associative contents.

# REFERENCES

BARNES, C. A statistical study of the Freudian theory of levels of psychosexual development. *Genetic Psychology Monographs*, 1952, **45**, 115–175.

FREUD, A. *The ego and the mechanisms of defense*. New York: International Universities Press, 1946 (orig. pub. 1936).

LEWIT, D. W., BRAYER, A. R., & LEIMAN, A. H. Externalization in perceptual defense. *Journal of Abnormal and Social Psychology*, 1962, **65**, 6–13.

MEDNICK, S. A. The associative basis of the creative process. *Psychological Review*, 1962, **69**, 220–232.

REICH, W. *Character-analysis*. New York: Orgone Institute Press, 1949.

ROSENWALD, G. C. The assessment of anxiety in psychological experimentation: A theoretical reformulation and test. *Journal of Abnormal and Social Psychology*, 1961, **62**, 666–673.

SCHLESINGER, V. J. Anal personality traits and occupational choice: A study of accountants, chemical engineers, and educational psychologists. Unpublished doctoral dissertation, University of Michigan, 1963.

SEARS, R. Studies of projection: I. Attribution of traits. *Journal of Social Psychology*, 1936, **7**, 151–163.

## E. M. Jellinek

# Phases of Alcohol Addiction

*E. M. Jellinek was one of the most respected workers and theorists in the area of alcoholism. One of the projects for which he was best known is reported in this classic paper. Based on a survey of nearly 2000 alcoholics, it describes the behavioral stages through which a person passes as a full-blown addiction to alcohol develops.*

In 1946 E. M. Jellinek, on the basis of a questionnaire study of members of Alcoholics Anonymous, first formulated his concept of phases in the drinking history of alcoholics. With the original publication [1] of this concept Jellinek outlined a more detailed questionnaire, which in the intervening years has been administered to some 2,000 alcoholics. The elaboration of the phases concept resulting from analysis of these additional materials has been presented by Jellinek in lectures at the Yale Summer School of Alcoholic Studies (July 1951 and July 1952) and at the European Seminar on Alcoholism (Copenhagen, October 1951). The summary of these lectures, as published

*Reprinted from the* Quarterly Journal of Studies on Alcohol, *13(1952), 673–684, with the permission of the Publications Division, Rutgers Center of Alcohol Studies.*

[1] Jellinek, E. M. Phases in the drinking history of alcoholics. Analysis of a survey conducted by the official organ of Alcoholics Anonymous. (Memoirs of the Section of Studies on Alcohol, Yale University, No. 5.) *Quart. J. Stud. Alc.*, 7(1946), 1–88. Published also as a monograph (Hillhouse Press, New Haven, 1946) under the same title; the monograph is now out of print.

under the auspices of the Alcoholism Subcommittee of the World Health Organization,[2] is reproduced here in full.

## INTRODUCTION

Only certain forms of excessive drinking—those which in the present report are designated as alcoholism—are accessible to medical-psychiatric treatment. The other forms of excessive drinking, too, present more or less serious problems, but they can be managed only on the level of applied sociology, including law enforcement. Nevertheless, the medical profession may have an advisory role in the handling of these latter problems and must take an interest in them from the viewpoint of preventive medicine.

The conditions which have been briefly defined by the Subcommittee as alcoholism are described in the following pages in greater detail, in order to delimit more definitely those excessive drinkers whose rehabilitation primarily requires medical-psychiatric treatment.

Furthermore, such detailed description may serve to forestall a certain potential danger which attaches to the disease conception of alcoholism, or more precisely of addictive drinking.

With the exception of specialists in alcoholism, the broader medical profession and representatives of the biological and social sciences and lay public use the term "alcoholism" as a designation for any form of excessive drinking instead of as a label for a limited and well-defined area of excessive drinking behaviors. Automatically, the disease conception of alcoholism becomes extended to all excessive drinking irrespective of whether or not there is any physical or psychological pathology involved in the drinking behavior.

Such an unwarranted extension of the disease conception can only be harmful, because sooner or later the misapplication will reflect on the legitimate use too and, more importantly, will tend to weaken the ethical basis of social sanctions against drunkenness.

## The Disease Conception of Alcohol Addiction

The Subcommittee has distinguished two categories of alcoholics, namely, "alcohol addicts" and "habitual symptomatic excessive drinkers." For brevity's sake the latter will be referred to as nonaddictive alcoholics. Strictly speaking, the disease conception attaches to the alcohol addicts only, but not to the habitual symptomatic excessive drinkers.

In both groups the excessive drinking is symptomatic of underlying psychological or social pathology, but in one group after several years of excessive drinking "loss of control" over the alcohol intake occurs, while in the other group this phenomenon never develops. The group with the "loss of control" is designated as "alcohol addicts." (There are other differences between these two groups and these will be seen in the course of the description of the "phases.")

The disease conception of alcohol addiction does not apply to the excessive drinking, but solely to the "loss of control" which occurs in only one group of alcoholics and then only after many years of excessive drinking. There is no intention to deny that the nonaddictive alcoholic is a sick person; but

[2] Expert Committee on Mental Health, Alcoholism Subcommittee, Second Report. Annex 2, The Phases of Alcohol Addiction. World Hlth. Org. Techn. Rep. Ser., No. 48, Aug. 1952.

his ailment is not the excessive drinking, but rather the psychological or social difficulties from which alcohol intoxication gives temporary surcease.

The "loss of control" is a disease condition per se which results from a process that superimposes itself upon those abnormal psychological conditions of which excessive drinking is a symptom. The fact that many excessive drinkers drink as much as or more than the addict for 30 or 40 years without developing loss of control indicates that in the group of "alcohol addicts" a superimposed process must occur.

Whether this superimposed process is of a psychopathological nature or whether some physical pathology is involved cannot be stated as yet with any degree of assurance, the claims of various investigators notwithstanding. Nor is it possible to go beyond conjecture concerning the question whether the "loss of control" originates in a predisposing factor (psychological or physical), or whether it is a factor acquired in the course of prolonged excessive drinking.

The fact that this "loss of control" does not occur in a large group of excessive drinkers would point towards a predisposing X factor in the addictive alcoholics. On the other hand this explanation is not indispensable as the difference between addictive and non-addictive alcoholics could be a matter of acquired modes of living—for instance, a difference in acquired nutritional habits.

## The Meaning of Symptomatic Drinking

The use of alcoholic beverages by society has primarily a symbolic meaning, and secondarily it achieves "function." Cultures which accept this custom differ in the nature and degree of the "functions" which they regard as legitimate. The differences in these "functions" are determined by the general pattern of the culture, e.g., the need for the release and for the special control of aggression, the need and the ways and means of achieving identification, the nature and intensity of anxieties and the modus for their relief, and so forth. The more the original symbolic character of the custom is preserved, the less room will be granted by the culture to the "functions" of drinking.

Any drinking within the accepted ways is symptomatic of the culture of which the drinker is a member. Within that frame of cultural symptomatology there may be in addition individual symptoms expressed in the act of drinking. The fact that a given individual drinks a glass of beer with his meal may be the symptom of the culture which accepts such a use as a refreshment, or as a "nutritional supplement." That this individual drinks at this given moment may be a symptom of his fatigue, or his elation or some other mood, and thus an individual symptom, but if his culture accepts the use for these purposes it is at the same time a cultural symptom.

In this sense even the small or moderate use of alcoholic beverages is symptomatic, and it may be said that all drinkers are culturally symptomatic drinkers or, at least, started as such.

The vast majority of the users of alcoholic beverages stay within the limits of the culturally accepted drinking behaviors and drink predominantly as an expression of their culture, and while an individual expression may be present in these behaviors its role remains insignificant.

For the purpose of the present discussion the expression "symptomatic drinking" will be limited to the predominant use of alcoholic beverages for the relief of major individual stresses.

A certain unknown proportion of these users of alcoholic beverages, perhaps 20 per cent, are occasionally inclined to take advantage of the "functions" of alcohol which they have experienced in the course of its "cultural use." At least at times, the individual motivation becomes predominant and on those occasions alcohol loses its character as an ingredient of a beverage and is used as a drug.

The "occasional symptomatic excessive drinker" tends to take care of the stresses and strains of living in socially accepted—i.e., "normal"—ways, and his drinking is most of the time within the cultural pattern. After a long accumulation of stresses, however, or because of some particularly heavy stress, his tolerance for tension is lowered and he takes recourse to heroic relief of his symptoms through alcoholic intoxication.[3] Under these circumstances the "relief" may take on an explosive character, and thus the occasional symptomatic excessive drinker may create serious problems. No psychological abnormality can be claimed for this type of drinker, although he does not represent a well-integrated personality.

Nevertheless, within the group of apparent "occasional symptomatic excessive drinkers" there is a certain proportion of definitely deviating personalities who after a shorter or longer period of occasional symptomatic relief take recourse to a constant alcoholic relief, and drinking becomes with them a "mode of living." These are the "alcoholics" of whom again a certain proportion suffer "loss of control," i.e., become "addictive alcoholics."

The proportion of alcoholics (addictive and nonaddictive) varies from country to country, but does not seem to exceed in any country 5 per cent or 6 per cent of all users of alcoholic beverages. The ratio of addictive to nonaddictive alcoholics is unknown.

## THE CHART OF ALCOHOL ADDICTION

The course of alcohol addiction is represented graphically in the Figure. The diagram is based on an analysis of more than two thousand drinking histories of male alcohol addicts. Not all symptoms shown in the diagram occur necessarily in all alcohol addicts, nor do they occur in every addict in the same sequence. The "phases" and the sequences of symptoms within the phases are characteristic, however, of the great majority of alcohol addicts and represent what may be called the average trend.

For alcoholic women the "phases" are not as clear-cut as in men and the development is frequently more rapid.

The "phases" vary in their duration according to individual characteristics and environmental factors. The "lengths" of the different phases on the diagram do not indicate differences in duration, but are determined by the number of symptoms which have to be shown in any given phase.

The chart of the phases of alcohol addiction serves as the basis of description, and the differences between addictive and nonaddictive alcoholics are indicated in the text.

### The Prealcoholic Symptomatic Phase

The very beginning of the use of alcoholic beverages is always socially motivated in the prospective addictive and nonaddictive alcoholic. In contrast to the average social drinker, however, the prospective alcoholic (together with

---

[3] This group does not include the regular "periodic alcoholics."

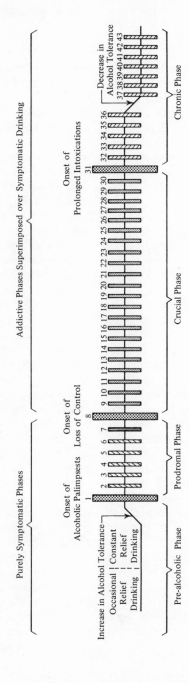

*The phases of alcohol addiction.* The large bars denote the onset of major symptoms which initiate phases. The short bars denote the onset of symptoms within a phase. Reference to the numbering of the symptoms is made in the text.

the occasional symptomatic excessive drinker) soon experiences a rewarding relief in the drinking situation. The relief is strongly marked in his case because either his tensions are much greater than in other members of his social circle, or he has not learned to handle those tensions as others do.

Initially this drinker ascribes his relief to the situation rather than to the drinking and he seeks therefore those situations in which incidental drinking will occur. Sooner or later, of course, he becomes aware of the contingency between relief and drinking.

In the beginning he seeks this relief occasionally only, but in the course of 6 months to 2 years his tolerance for tension decreases to such a degree that he takes recourse to alcoholic relief practically daily.

Nevertheless his drinking does not result in overt intoxication, but he reaches toward the evening a stage of surcease from emotional stress. Even in the absence of intoxication this involves fairly heavy drinking, particularly in comparison to the use of alcoholic beverages by other members of his circle. The drinking is, nevertheless, not conspicuous either to his associates or to himself.

After a certain time an increase in alcohol tolerance may be noticed, i.e., the drinker requires a somewhat larger amount of alcohol than formerly in order to reach the desired stage of sedation.

This type of drinking behavior may last from several months to two years according to circumstances and may be designated as the prealcoholic phase, which is divided into stages of occasional relief-drinking and constant relief-drinking.

## The Prodromal Phase

The sudden onset of a behavior resembling the "blackouts" in anoxemia marks the beginning of the prodromal phase of alcohol addiction. The drinker who may have had not more than 50 to 60 g. of absolute alcohol and who is not showing any signs of intoxication may carry on a reasonable conversation or may go through quite elaborate activities without a trace of memory the next day, although sometimes one or two minor details may be hazily remembered. This amnesia, which is not connected with loss of consciousness, has been called by Bonhoeffer the "alcoholic palimpsests," with reference to old Roman manuscripts superimposed over an incompletely erased manuscript.

*"Alcoholic palimpsests"* (1) [4] may occur on rare occasions in an average drinker when he drinks intoxicating amounts in a state of physical or emotional exhaustion. Nonaddictive alcoholics, of course, also may experience "palimpsests," but infrequently and only following rather marked intoxication. Thus, the frequency of "palimpsests" and their occurrence after medium alcohol intake are characteristic of the prospective alcohol addict.

This would suggest heightened susceptibility to alcohol in the prospective addict. Such a susceptibility may be psychologically or physiologically determined. The analogy with the "blackouts" of anoxemia is tempting. Of course, an insufficient oxygen supply cannot be assumed, but a malutilization of oxygen may be involved. The present status of the knowledge of alcoholism does not permit of more than vague conjectures which, nevertheless,

---

[4] The italicized figures in parentheses following the designations of the individual symptoms represent their order as given in Figure 1.

may constitute bases for experimental hypotheses.

The onset of "alcoholic palimpsests" is followed (in some instances preceded) by the onset of drinking behaviors which indicate that, for this drinker, beer, wine, and spirits have practically ceased to be beverages and have become sources of a drug which he "needs." Some of these behaviors imply that this drinker has some vague realization that he drinks differently from others.

*Surreptitious drinking* (2) is one of these behaviors. At social gatherings the drinker seeks occasions for having a few drinks unknown to others, as he fears that if it were known that he drinks more than the others he would be misjudged: those to whom drinking is only a custom or a small pleasure would not understand that because he is different from them alcohol is for him a necessity, although he is not a drunkard.

*Preoccupation with alcohol* (3) is further evidence of this "need." When he prepares to go to a social gathering his first thought is whether there will be sufficient alcohol for his requirements, and he has several drinks in anticipation of a possible shortage.

Because of this increasing dependence upon alcohol, the onset of *avid drinking* (4) (gulping of the first or first two drinks) occurs at this time.

As the drinker realizes, at least vaguely, that his drinking is outside of the ordinary, he develops *guilt feelings about his drinking behavior* (5) and because of this he begins to *avoid reference to alcohol* (6) in conversation.

These behaviors, together with an *increasing frequency of "alcoholic palimpsests"* (7), foreshadow the development of alcohol addiction; they are premonitory signs, and this period may

be called the prodromal phase of alcohol addiction.

The consumption of alcoholic beverages in the prodromal phase is "heavy," but not conspicuous, as it does not lead to marked, overt intoxications. The effect is that the prospective addict reaches towards evening a state which may be designated as emotional anesthesia. Nevertheless, this condition requires drinking well beyond the ordinary usage. The drinking is on a level which may begin to interfere with metabolic and nervous processes as evidenced by the frequent "alcoholic palimpsests."

The "covering-up" which is shown by the drinker in this stage is the first sign that his drinking might separate him from society, although initially the drinking may have served as a technique to overcome some lack of social integration.

As in the prodromal phase rationalizations of the drinking behavior are not strong and there is some insight as well as fear of possible consequences, it is feasible to intercept incipient alcohol addiction at this stage. In the United States of America, the publicity given to the prodromal symptoms begins to bring prospective alcoholics to clinics as well as to groups of Alcoholics Anonymous.

It goes without saying that even at this stage the only possible modus for this type of drinker is total abstinence.

The prodromal period may last anywhere from 6 months to 4 or 5 years according to the physical and psychological make-up of the drinker, his family ties, vocational relations, general interests, and so forth. The prodromal phase ends and the crucial or acute phase begins with the onset of loss of control, which is the critical symptom of alcohol addiction.

## The Crucial Phase

*Loss of control* (8) means that any drinking of alcohol starts a chain reaction which is felt by the drinker as a physical demand for alcohol. This state, possibly a conversion phenomenon, may take hours or weeks for its full development; it lasts until the drinker is too intoxicated or too sick to ingest more alcohol. The physical discomfort following this drinking behavior is contrary to the object of the drinker, which is merely to feel "different." As a matter of fact, the bout may not even be started by an individual need of the moment, but by a "social drink."

After recovery from the intoxication, it is not the "loss of control"—i.e., the physical demand, apparent or real—which leads to a new bout after several days or several weeks; the renewal of drinking is set off by the original psychological conflicts or by a simple social situation which involves drinking.

The "loss of control" is effective after the individual has started drinking, but it does not give rise to the beginning of a new drinking bout. The drinker has lost the ability to control the quantity once he has started, but he still can control whether he will drink on any given occasion or not. This is evidenced in the fact that after the onset of "loss of control" the drinker can go through a period of voluntary abstinence ("going on the water wagon").

The question of why the drinker returns to drinking after depeated disastrous experiences is often raised. Although he will not admit it, the alcohol addict believes that he has lost his will power and that he can and must regain it. He is not aware that he has undergone a process which makes it impossible for him to control his alcohol intake. To "master his will" becomes a matter

of the greatest importance to him. When tensions rise, "a drink" is the natural remedy for him and he is convinced that this time it will be one or two drinks only.

Practically simultaneously with the onset of "loss of control" the alcohol addict begins to *rationalize his drinking behavior* (9): he produces the well-known alcoholic "alibis." He finds explanations which convince him that he did not lose control, but that he had a good reason to get intoxicated and that in the absence of such reasons he is able to handle alcohol as well as anybody else. These rationalizations are needed primarily for himself and only secondarily for his family and associates. The rationalizations make it possible for him to continue with his drinking, and this is of the greatest importance to him as he knows no alternative for handling his problems.

This is the beginning of an entire "system of rationalizations" which progressively spreads to every aspect of his life. While this system largely originates in inner needs, it also serves to counter *social pressures* (10) which arise at the time of the "loss of control." At this time, of course, the drinking behavior becomes conspicuous, and the parents, wife, friends, and employer may begin to reprove and warn the drinker.

In spite of all the rationalizations there is a marked loss of self-esteem, and this of course demands compensations which in a certain sense are also rationalizations. One way of compensation is the *grandiose behavior* (11) which the addict begins to display at this time. Extravagant expenditures and grandiloquence convince him that he is not as bad as he had thought at times.

The rationalization system gives rise to another system, namely, the "system of isolation." The rationalizations quite naturally lead to the idea that the fault lies not within himself but in others, and this results in a progressive withdrawal from the social environment. The first sign of this attitude is a *marked aggressive behavior* (12).

Inevitably, this latter behavior generates guilt. While even in the prodromal period remorse about the drinking arose from time to time, now *persistent remorse* (13) arises, and this added tension is a further source of drinking.

In compliance with social pressures the addict now goes on *periods of total abstinence* (14). There is, however, another modus of control of drinking which arises out of the rationalizations of the addict. He believes that his trouble arises from his not drinking the right kind of beverages or not in the right way. He now attempts to control his troubles by *changing the pattern of his drinking* (15), by setting up rules about not drinking before a certain hour of the day, in certain places only, and so forth.

The strain of the struggle increases his hostility towards his environment and he begins to *drop friends* (16) and *quit jobs* (17). It goes without saying that some associates drop him and that he loses some jobs, but more frequently he takes the initiative as an anticipatory defense.

The isolation becomes more pronounced as his entire *behavior becomes alcohol-centered* (18), i. e., he begins to be concerned about how activities might interfere with his drinking instead of how his drinking may affect his activities. This, of course, involves a more marked egocentric outlook which leads to more rationalizations and more isolation. There ensue a *loss of outside interests* (19) and a *reinterpretation of interpersonal relations* (20) coupled with *marked self-pity* (21). The isolation and rationalizations have increased by this time in intensity and find their expression either in contem-

plated or actual *geographic escape* (22).

Under the impact of these events, a *change in family habits* (23) occurs. The wife and children, who may have had good social activities, may withdraw for fear of embarrassment or, quite contrarily, they may suddenly begin intensive outside activities in order to escape from the home environment. This and other events lead to the onset of *unreasonable resentments* (24) in the alcohol addict.

The predominance of concern with alcohol induces the addict to *protect his supply* (25), i.e., to lay in a large stock of alcoholic beverages, hidden in the most unthought-of places. A fear of being deprived of the most necessary substance for his living is expressed in this behavior.

*Neglect of proper nutrition* (26) aggravates the beginnings of the effects of heavy drinking on the organism, and frequently the *first hospitalization* (27) for some alcoholic complaint occurs at this time.

One of the frequent organic effects is a *decrease of the sexual drive* (28) which increases hostility towards the wife and is rationalized into her extramarital sex activities, which gives rise to the well-known *alcoholic jealousy* (29).

By this time remorse, resentment, struggle between alcoholic needs and duties, loss of self-esteem, and doubts and false reassurance have so disorganized the addict that he cannot start the day without steadying himself with alcohol immediately after arising or even before getting out of bed. This is the beginning of *regular matutinal drinking* (30), which previously had occurred on rare occasions only.

This behavior terminates the crucial phase and foreshadows the beginnings of the chronic phase.

During the crucial phase intoxication is the rule, but it is limited to the evening hours. For the most part of this phase drinking begins sometime in the afternoon and by the evening intoxication is reached. It should be noted that the "physical demand" involved in the "loss of control" results in continual rather than continuous drinking. Particularly the "matutinal drink" which occurs toward the end of the crucial phase shows the continual pattern. The first drink at rising, let us say at 7 A.M., is followed by another drink at 10 or 11 A.M., and another drink around 1 P.M., while the more intensive drinking hardly starts before 5 P.M.

Throughout, the crucial phase presents a great struggle of the addict against the complete loss of social footing. Occasionally the aftereffects of the evening's intoxication cause some loss of time, but generally the addict succeeds in looking after his job, although he neglects his family. He makes a particularly strong effort to avoid intoxication during the day. Progressively, however, his social motivations weaken more and more, and the "morning drink" jeopardizes his effort to comply with his vocational duties as this effort involves a conscious resistance against the apparent or real "physical demand" for alcohol.

The onset of the "loss of control" is the beginning of the "disease process" of alcohol addiction which is superimposed over the excessive symptomatic drinking. Progressively, this disease process undermines the morale and the physical resistance of the addict.

## The Chronic Phase

The increasingly dominating role of alcohol, and the struggle against the "demand" set up by matutinal drinking, at last break down the resistance of the addict and he finds himself for the first time intoxicated in the daytime and on a weekday and continues in that state for several days until he is entirely incapacitated. This is the onset of *prolonged intoxications* (31), referred to in the vernacular as "benders."

This latter drinking behavior meets with such unanimous social rejection that it involves a grave social risk. Only an originally psychopathic personality or a person who has later in life undergone a psychopathological process would expose himself to that risk.

These long-drawn-out bouts commonly bring about *marked ethical deterioration* (32) and *impairment of thinking* (33) which, however, are not irreversible. True *alcoholic psychoses* (34) may occur at this time, but in not more than 10 per cent of all alcoholics.

The loss of morale is so heightened that the addict *drinks with persons far below his social level* (35) in preference to his usual associates—perhaps as an opportunity to appear superior—and, if nothing else is available, he will *take recourse to "technical products"* (36) such as bay rum or rubbing alcohol.

A *loss of alcohol tolerance* (37) is commonly noted at this time. Half of the previously required amount of alcohol may be sufficient to bring about a stuporous state.

*Indefinable fears* (38) and *tremors* (39) become persistent. Sporadically these symptoms occur also during the crucial phase, but in the chronic phase they are present as soon as alcohol disappears from the organism. In consequence the addict "controls" the symptoms through alcohol. The same is true of *psychomotor inhibition* (40), the inability to initiate a simple mechanical act—such as winding a watch—in the absence of alcohol.

The need to control these symptoms of drinking exceeds the need of relieving the original underlying symptoms of the personality conflict, and the *drinking takes on an obsessive character* (41).

In many addicts, approximately 60 per cent, some *vague religious desires develop* (42) as the rationalizations become weaker. Finally, in the course of the frequently prolonged intoxications, the rationalizations become so frequently and so mercilessly tested against reality that the entire *rationalization system fails* (43) and the addict admits defeat. He now becomes spontaneously accessible to treatment. Nevertheless, his obsessive drinking continues as he does not see a way out.

Formerly it was thought that the addict must reach this stage of utter defeat in order to be treated successfully. Clinical experience has shown, however, that this "defeat" can be induced long before it would occur of itself and that even incipient alcoholism can be intercepted. As the latter can be easily recognized it is possible to tackle the problem from the preventive angle.

## THE "ALCOHOLIC PERSONALITY"

The aggressions, feelings of guilt, remorse, resentments, withdrawal, etc., which develop in the phases of alcohol addiction, are largely consequences of the excessive drinking, but at the same time they constitute sources of more excessive drinking.

In addition to relieving, through alcohol, symptoms of an underlying personality conflict, the addict now tends to relieve, through further drinking, the stresses created by his drinking behavior.

By and large, these reactions to excessive drinking—which have quite a neurotic appearance—give the impression of an "alcoholic personality," although they are secondary behaviors superimposed over a large variety of personality types which have a few traits in common, in particular a low capacity for coping with tensions. There does

not emerge, however, any specific personality trait or physical characteristic which inevitably would lead to excessive symptomatic drinking. Apart from psychological and possibly physical liabilities, there must be a constellation of social and economic factors which facilitate the development of addictive and nonaddictive alcoholism in a susceptible terrain.

## THE NONADDICTIVE ALCOHOLIC

Some differences between the nonaddictive alcoholic and the alcoholic addict have been stated passim. These differences may be recapitulated and elaborated, and additional differential features may be considered.

The main difference may be readily visualized by erasing the large bars of the diagram (see Figure 1). This results in a diagram which suggests a progressive exacerbation of the use of alcohol for symptom relief and of the social and health consequences incumbent upon such use, but without any clear-cut phases.

The prealcoholic phase is the same for the nonaddictive alcoholic as for the alcohol addict, i.e., he progresses from occasional to constant relief of individual symptoms through alcohol.

The behaviors which denote that alcohol has become a drug rather than an ingredient of a beverage (symptoms 2 to 6) occur also in the nonaddictive drinker, but, as mentioned before, the "alcoholic palimpsests" occur rarely and only after overt intoxication.

"Loss of control" is not experienced by the nonaddictive alcoholic, and this is the main differentiating criterion between the two categories of alcoholics. Initially, of course, it could not be said whether the drinker had yet reached the crucial phase, but after 10 or 12 years of heavy drinking without "loss of control," while symptoms 2 to 6 were persistent and "palimpsests" were rare and did not occur after medium alcohol intake, the differential diagnosis is rather safe.

The absence of "loss of control" has many involvements. First of all, as there is no inability to stop drinking within a given situation there is no need to rationalize the inability. Nevertheless, rationalizations are developed for justifying the excessive use of alcohol and some neglect of the family attendant upon such use. Likewise, there is no need to change the pattern of drinking, which in the addict is an attempt to overcome the "loss of control." Periods of total abstinence, however, occur as a response to social pressure.

On the other hand, there is the same tendency toward isolation as in the addict, but the social repercussions are much less marked as the nonaddictive alcoholic can avoid drunken behavior whenever the social situation requires it.

The effects of prolonged heavy drinking on the organism may occur in the nonaddictive alcoholic too; even delirium tremens may develop. The libido may be diminished and "alcoholic jealousy" may result.

Generally, there is a tendency toward a progressive dominance of alcohol resulting in greater psychological and bodily effects. In the absence of any grave initial psychopathy, however, the symptoms of the chronic phase as seen in addicts do not develop in the nonaddictive alcoholic. In the presence of grave underlying psychopathies a deteriorative process is speeded up by habitual alcoholic excess, and such a nonaddictive drinker may slide to the bottom of society.

Bernard C. Glueck, Jr.

# Psychodynamic Patterns in the Sex Offender

*Some forms of pathological behavior are particularly abhorrent to society. Sexual offenses are among these. They draw strong, angry reactions from both lay and professional people. As a result, certain stereotypes (generally uncomplimentary and pessimistic) about such offenders tend to be built up; these apply to both their superficial personality and to the prognosis for their future behavior. These stereotypes are often preserved because they help to perpetuate, or do little to contradict, the strong feelings stirred up by such odious actions. Glueck has had the opportunity to observe large numbers of individuals convicted of serious sexual crimes and incarcerated in Sing Sing Prison. In this paper, he presents both the typical stereotype of the sexual psychopath and a discussion of the degree to which the group that he observed conformed or failed to conform to that image.*

*This paper has been abridged by eliminating some case examples that the author presented. Readers interested in this material should consult the original paper.*

Abridged from Psychiatric Quarterly, 28(1954), 1–21 with the permission of State Hospitals Press, Utica, N. Y. and Dr. Glueck.

Of the many problems that plague our society, that of the sex offender is one of the most disturbing. Society reacts with greater fear, disgust, hysteria and anger to only one other crime, murder. Many explanations can be advanced for this intense emotional reaction, depending upon the particular frame of reference of the individual giving the interpretation. Thus we may have religious, moralistic, philosophical, sociological and psychological explanations, among others. In the course of the last 60 years, largely as a result of the pioneer efforts of Sigmund Freud, and those who followed the trail he blazed, a new approach to the age-old problem of understanding human behavior has been developed, the science of psychodynamics. This is the particular frame of reference for the present remarks.

In the years immediately following World War II, an increasing concern by society about the activities of "sex offenders," spotlighted by a furor in the press over "the depraved machinations of sex fiends," culminated in the establishment in New York State, among others, of a research project under the joint auspices of the commissioners of Correction and Mental Hygiene. Its purpose was to be "the development of information as to the underlying causes of sex crimes and the development of treatment for persons committing such crimes."

The raw material for this research was the group of men incarcerated at Sing Sing Prison, who had been convicted of sex felonies. Included in this group of felonies are: first and second degree rape, first and second degree sodomy, carnal abuse of a child under 10 years, carnal abuse of a minor between 10 and 16—if a second offense, and assault in the second degree with intent to rape, sodomize or carnally abuse. The lesser sexual offenses such as exhibitionism, voyeurism and statutory rape, are not considered felonies, so that men convicted of these offenses are not sentenced to Sing Sing Prison. This selective process has a very important bearing on the statistics gathered by the research group, since only the more serious sex offenses are represented in the men studied. This may account, at least in part, for the marked psychopathology found in the group.

In March 1950, a preliminary report (1) was issued on 102 men who had been studied up to that time. The general conclusions reached included a statement that every man studied suffered from some type of mental or emotional disorder, though not usually so pronounced as to meet the legal definition of mental illness. They were not, in other words, sufficiently psychotic to be certifiable. Additional information on the same men—coming from further psychiatric observation, psychological studies, and the changes in their adjustment to prison, or in a few cases, to parole—as well as information on new cases, confirm the psychopathology present in this group. The major question, at the present writing, is not: Does pathology exist? Instead, we are primarily concerned with an attempt at quantification of the pathology and the development of some kind of adequate diagnostic system which will reflect the psychodynamic aspects of each case, and give a more accurate description of the phenomena observed than the present diagnoses permit. It is unnecessary to stress the benefits from more accurate diagnosis. To mention only two points: There would be improved statistical reporting; and there are possible therapeutic and prognostic implications stemming from a given diagnosis. The last point has an added importance in dealing with psychiatric problems because of the rather divergent attitudes of the extremists who favor either psychotherapy or organic therapy as mutually exclusive techniques, and because of the rather nihilistic attitude of many psychiatrists where the diagnosis of schizophrenia is concerned.

Unquestionably, in the light of present therapeutic results, one tends to be somewhat pessimistic regarding the outcome when a diagnosis of schizophrenia or psychopathic personality is made. There is, however, sufficient evidence available, in the form of well-documented statistics collected over long periods, indicating a basic 30 to 35 per cent remission rate in schizophrenia, regardless of the type of psychosis or kind of treatment. We can, therefore, expect one out of every three schizophrenics to have a remission, even though nothing is done in terms of specific therapy. Furthermore the remission rate can be improved, if only for relatively short periods, by the various therapeutic approaches currently available. The writer is, therefore, of the opinion that the argument against making a diagnosis of schizophrenia, on the grounds of the "death sentence" implications of such a diagnosis, no longer applies, and should not influence decisions about diagnosis. Of even greater importance in forensic psychiatry, is the effect of the diagnosis, when made before trial or sentencing, on the disposition of the particular case.

The present legal interpretations of the terms "sane" and "insane" have been repeatedly challenged by both lawyers and psychiatrists, as being totally inadequate in the light of modern concepts of psychopathology and psychodynamics. The concern of the courts still centers, for the most part, around the need to punish the offender, and the fear that a plea of insanity will protect the "guilty" individual from the just retribution that society demands.

The discovery of extensive pathology in every individual studied by the research group has already been mentioned. All of the men in this first group of 102, covered in the research project's first report were, in spite of clear-cut clinical evidence of psychosis in several cases, and very suspicious symptoms in over half of the group, diagnosed as being without psychosis when examined psychiatrically before trial or sentencing. The same failure to detect overt psychotic symptoms and behavior has been apparent in many of the additional cases studied in the past three years. This has been true in both groups, those entering the prison under the usual short-term definite sentence, and those entering under provisions of the new, indeterminate-sentence law. Failure to establish an accurate diagnosis is especially disturbing in the second group of cases, since one of the provisions of the law is that, "No person convicted of a crime punishable in the discretion of the court with imprisonment for an indeterminate term, having a minimum of one day and a maximum of his natural life, shall be sentenced until a psychiatric examination shall have been made of him and a complete written report thereof shall have been submitted to the court." This examination is made according to certain paragraphs of the code of criminal procedure and involves observation and examination by two qualified psychiatrists.

In spite of these provisions, four men out of 46 who were received at Sing Sing Prison under the new law have been committed to Dannemora State Hospital with overt psychoses. Two of the four were committed within 60 days of reception at Sing Sing, and were held for that interval only to obtain a psychiatric appraisal for the research studies. A fifth individual was suspected of being feebleminded because of his general behavior in the prison community. On psychological testing he was found to have an IQ in the 60's and was committed to the state institution for defective delinquents.

How then can one explain the discrepancies between the pre-trial examination of these men, and the research findings, frequently within one or two weeks? One explanation can be considered and discarded in the same breath; that is the competence of the psychiatrists doing the examinations on these men. They are, for the most part, men of considerable clinical experience, especially in the rapid evaluation of patients hospitalized for psychiatric observation as potential psychotics. In many of the cases studied one finds, in the record, a rather extensive description of symptoms indicative of psychopathological processes, including statements about ideas of reference, persecutory ideas, extreme emotional lability and defective judgment; and yet the diagnosis of a psychotic illness, specifically schizophrenia, is avoided, and the individual is diagnosed as a psychopathic personality, a sexual psychopath, a psychopath with sexual perversions, and so forth. The writer believes that the critical factors influencing the judgment of these psychiatrists are three-fold: first, the patient's antisocial behavior, the fact that he has been indicted for a felony; second, stemming directly from the first, the concern that society, as represented by the prosecution and the court, will complain that the offender is being "protected medically" from receiving proper punishment if a diagnosis of psychosis is made; third, and here one treads on dangerous ground, the psychiatrist's own unconscious reaction to the sexual character of the felony, which may motivate him toward punishment rather than treatment in such a case.

In the writer's opening remarks, he indicated the horror, resentment, anger, fear and demand for retribution that make up society's response to a sexual offense. The reasons for this reaction cannot be gone into in this paper. But the writer does raise the question, on the basis of the psychiatric and psychological appraisals of the sex offenders studied at Sing Sing, of whether punishment is the optimum answer to this problem, or of whether a therapeutically-oriented program would not be preferable. Before arguing the pros and cons of this question, let us consider further the diagnostic problem in these cases.

If these men are psychopathic personalities, sexual or otherwise, they should show specific psychopathological characteristics that are the criteria for diagnosing this condition. In one of the widely-quoted books on the psychopath, Cleckley's *The Mask of Sanity* (2), the characteristics of this type of individual are given as follows, "Superficial charm and good intelligence, absence of delusions and other signs of emotional 'thinking,' absence of 'nervousness' or psychoneurotic manifestations, unreliability, untruthfulness and insincerity, lack of remorse or shame, inadequately motivated antisocial behavior, poor judgment and failure to learn by experience, pathologic egocentricity and incapacity for love, general poverty in major affective reactions, specific loss of insight, unresponsiveness in general interpersonal relations, fantastic and uninviting behavior, with drink and sometimes without, suicide rarely carried out, sex life impersonal, trivial, and poorly integrated, and lastly, failure to follow any life plan." Let us consider these 16 points, one by one, and see whether they fit the data collected from over 200 sex offenders during the course of the project's investigations.

*Superficial Charm and Good Intelligence.* The test scores of intelligence in the research project cases range from the middle 60's—four men were transferred to the institution for defective delinquents—to a high of 140, with the mean being slightly over 100. This would indicate that the sex offenders have the same intelligence spread as the general population, and do not fall into a high or low group. They are, however, anything but a charming group, even superficially. Many have definite physical deformities, and they all show marked social awkwardness, stemming from their withdrawn, isolated personality patterns.

*Absence of Delusions and Other Signs of Irrational Thinking.* The men studied do have the ability to cover up ideas and experiences that they have learned are not acceptable when related to their families, friends or others. The distortions in their perception of reality may be very subtle, requiring close contact with the inmate, over a considerable time, to detect. These perceptive disturbances can also be elicited, and this is particularly useful if the subject is trying to cover up, by the use of projective techniques, such as the TAT and the Rorschach examinations. It is the initial perceptive distortions, magnified and further altered by the disturbances of mood and affect, that in many instances lead to the antisocial sexual act; e.g., in the second case, B. relates his discouragement with women, their unreliability, and his lack of satisfaction from contact with them. In the light of his reality situation these would appear to be definite perceptual and reasoning distortions. Cleckley also speaks of the absence of valid depression. About 70 per cent of the cases in this study show mild to severe depression, with some expressing suicidal ideas.

*Absence of "Nervousness" or Psychoneurotic Manifestations.* The absence of anxiety and tension in the psychopath has been stressed repeatedly. In contrast, the writer has found moderate to severe anxiety in 90 per cent of the project cases, with little or no anxiety appearing only in those individuals with overt psychoses or marked organic cerebral impairment.

*Unreliability.* While this is the hallmark of the psychopath, particularly when subjected to the slightest pressure in the form of frustrations or obligations to perform, the opposite is true for the Sing Sing cases. The majority of these men are considered steady, reliable, even compulsive workers, especially in the older age groups, with the exception of their sexual behavior; and, in many of the cases studied, their difficulties with alcohol.

*Untruthfulness and Insincerity.* These qualities are extremely difficult to evaluate in individuals being studied in a prison setting, especially when they feel that their chances for parole may be influenced or determined by the information given to the investigator, a conviction that persists in spite of all reassurances to the contrary. Unquestionably, many of the men studied "put the best foot forward," in that they withhold information rather than concoct deliberate falsehoods. There is, however, a sizable group who persistently deny their guilt, in the face of overwhelming evidence in probation records and admissions of guilt at the time of arrest. These are, however, the more seriously-disturbed individuals, largely those with paranoid personality patterns, rather than the typical glib and very plausible psychopath.

*Lack of Remorse or Shame.* The amount of depression and guilt, already referred to, in the Sing Sing cases would indicate considerable shame and remorse as a consequence of the antisocial acts. While direct expressions of shame are obtained in less than half the cases studied, indirect evidence, such as the attempt to hide or deny the sex offense from the rest of the prison population, is rather common. This is true even in the group who deny their guilt, since the clinching argument for their innocence is often, "Why I couldn't do such a terrible thing, I'd feel too ashamed."

*Inadequately Motivated Anti-Social Behavior.* While many of the individuals in the Sing Sing group could give no immediate reason for committing their anti-social act or acts, in fact frequently asked for assistance in understanding their aberrant sexual behavior, immediate precipitating factors, such as sexual frustration by their wives, economic reverses, and other threats to status or security were found in about one-third of these men. The absence of such specific events does not, however, imply inadequate motivation. Overwhelmingly influential unconscious motivations can be discovered in these individuals, given an adequate—which does not of necessity mean lengthy—examination. The more bizarre and chaotic the sexual expression becomes, the more severe the degree of schizophrenic involvement, in the writer's experience.

*Poor Judgment and Failure to Learn by Experience.* This is another of the commonly-accepted characteristics of the psychopath, and is one of the factors that makes punishment for his activities so futile. While there are many recidivists in the sex offender group, and while many of them show remarkably poor judgment in the commission of their sexual acts, frequently choosing times and places that appear to invite detection and apprehension, this behavior, as already indicated, does not have the apparent purposelessness of the psychopath, as it is compulsively motivated in most instances. It is likely, however, that the apparent failure to learn by past experience, shown in the repetition of their sexual acts, is the

critical factor in determining the diagnosis of "sexual psychopath" made on 95 per cent of the men who have had psychiatric examinations before sentencing to Sing Sing.

*Pathologic Egocentricity and Incapacity for Love.* Superficial appraisal of the behavior of the "sexual psychopath," with its apparent concentration on the satisfaction of the individual's own sexual needs, to the exclusion of any and all other considerations, would seem to fit the Sing Sing offender into this category very neatly. When one looks beneath this superficial manifestation, however, the anti-social behavior is found to be the resultant of forces, largely unconscious, that have been in conflict for long periods, and that reach external expression—in the majority of the cases—only when the repressive factors are weakened by alcohol, organic brain damage, or the disorganization that accompanies an overt schizophrenic illness. The capacity for object relationships is certainly disturbed in these individuals, largely, one feels, as the result of incapacitating inhibitions and fears over establishing emotional contact and interpersonal give-and-take with others. It is the impression, however, that these disturbances result in a weakened, childish kind of behavior toward libidinal objects, rather than in the absence of capacity for object relationships that is described in the psychopath. Since therapeutic contact is dependent upon the ability to make some kind of object relationship, accurate estimation of this capacity in these individuals has an important bearing on the therapeutic possibilities and therefore on the ultimate prognosis.

*General Poverty in Major Affective Reactions.* In this area, as in the factor just considered, the importance of distinguishing between the "feebleness of affect" of the psychopath, and the affective blunting of the schizophrenic is emphasized by the superficial similarity of behavior in the two groups. This distinction has been attempted in the Sing Sing study by rating each case on "ability for emotional rapport and reactivity." None of the Sing Sing cases has been rated as having a "mature and adequate" ability. Approximately 50 per cent are rated as having ability "present but suppressed," 25 per cent as having "limited" ability, and 25 per cent as having "none or slight." This would indicate a disturbance of affect in all of these cases, the disturbance being both qualitative and quantitative, in contrast to the simple quantitative deficiency in the psychopath. These affective disturbances are interpreted as an indication of the fear experienced by these men when they attempt affective ties with others. As a defense against these fearful situations, they remain emotionally encapsulated, isolated and detached.

*Specific Loss of Insight.* Under this heading, Cleckley discusses the psychopath's inability "to see himself as others see him." This is in marked contrast to his perfect orientation, his ability to reason, and his freedom from delusions. The information on this point obtained by the estimate of insight in the Sing Sing prisoners studied, shows normal insight to be lacking. It is found, however, that one-third of the men have partial insight, another 50 per cent have some awareness of their difficulties, while less than 20 per cent are essentially without insight. This last group is comprised of the more overtly psychotic individuals in the series. The majority of the sexual offenders are keenly aware of the attitude of society in general, and prison society in particular, toward their sexual aberration; and they show, as has already been stated, varying degrees of shame and remorse.

*Unresponsiveness in General Inter-personal Relations.* The contrast is drawn here between the superficial ease and affability of the psychopath, and his basic lack of response to the usual emotional interplay existing in close interpersonal relationships. The difficulties in interpersonal relations seen in the Sing Sing cases stem, it is felt, from these offenders' marked anxiety and fear of close emotional contact with others, particularly with adults. This is a pervasive difficulty, so that these men show little social ability, and are a significantly isolated and withdrawn group. This isolation continues, even in the prison setting.

*Fantastic and Uninviting Behavior with Drink and Sometimes Without It.* The bizarre behavior in all areas of personality-functioning described under this heading in Cleckley's book has rarely been encountered in the Sing Sing cases. Again excluding overtly psychotic individuals, who may exhibit as bizarre behavior as can be imagined, the acting out seen in the majority of the men who were alcoholics tends to be confined to the specific area of their sexual difficulties. In addition, when sober, they are over-controlled, rigid conformists, for the most part.

*Suicide Rarely Carried Out.* In respect to suicide, the psychopath seems to resemble the Sing Sing sex offenders. One encounters mention of suicidal ideas or attempts infrequently, even though depression and guilt are relatively common. Again it is the more disturbed psychotics in the group who have shown the suicidal tendencies found. For example, B. speaks of suicide as an escape from the torment of his immediate situation.

*Sex Life Impersonal, Trivial, and Poorly Integrated.* This is the third, and perhaps most important area of agreement between the description of the psychopath and the Sing Sing group of sex offenders. In contrast to the generally accepted belief that the sexual offender is a "sex fiend," motivated by an uncontrollable need for sexual gratification, one finds that close to 90 per cent of the men studied show markedly impaired erotic drives. They are satisfying some need other than sexual while performing the aberrant sexual act—such as retaliation or revenge, for the trauma experienced with a hostile, rejecting or castrating mother or wife. There is also a marked lack of integration, extending to chaotic confusion, based primarily on the intense sexual fears generated by their traumatic childhood sexual experiences. A high percentage of such traumatic episodes is found in these men. Analysis of their sexual disturbances reveals a schizophrenic type of disorganization and shallowness, consistent with, and part of, the marked disturbances in interpersonal relationships already described.

*Failure to Follow Any Life Plan.* The inconsistency of the psychopath in working toward a definite goal or goals is seldom encountered in this group of offenders. A high percentage are compulsive workers, showing enormous energy and drive in their attempts to gain social and economic status and security. While there may be temporary interruptions because of alcoholism and anti-social sexual activities, they stick closely to patterns of achievement, and have very specific goals and objectives in all areas, including in some instances, fairly realistic sexual goals. Again those in the Sing Sing group who came closest to Cleckley's foregoing description are the more seriously disturbed, disintegrating schizophrenics, who may show very pointless, nomadic and irresponsible lives.

It is found, then, after careful scrutiny of the various characteristics of the psychopath, that the individuals in the present research group, most of them diagnosed as psychopathic personalities, show relatively few of the traits listed by Cleckley as typical of the true psychopath. In fact, in only five of the 16 characteristics given by Cleckley is there even superficial agreement. In four of the five—pathological egocentricity and incapacity for love; general poverty in major affective reactions; unresponsiveness in general interpersonal relations; and sex life impersonal, trivial and poorly integrated—the common psychodynamic denominator is the disturbance of affective capacity which manifests itself in impoverished emotional relationships, and a sharp dampening in external attachments and interests. This autistic withdrawal from interpersonal contacts is one of the earliest, and most significant symptoms of psychological decompensation, an indication of the dangerously narrow margin of competence remaining to the weakened and brittle ego structure of the individual. The fifth factor, poor judgment and failure to learn by experience, is an additional indication of the failure of the ego to perform satisfactorily in all three major areas of its function: the perceptive, integrative, and executive.

That the disintegration or collapse of ego function is not complete, thereby enabling the individual to maintain a façade of normal behavior, does not, in the writer's opinion, vitiate the diagnosis of a schizophrenic illness. The individual is not, to be sure, grossly decompensated, that is, overtly psychotic. But it is precisely because he maintains some semblance of normal behavior that he presents such a problem and threat to the community. The behavior disturbances of the overt psychotic cause him, as a general rule, to be detected rapidly and disposed of properly, in our highly-organized and complex modern society. It is the borderline individual, who can still maintain some semblance of control, but who loses this control episodically, or is about to lose control chronically, who winds up in prison, having had the opportunity to commit one or more anti-social acts, and who is diagnosed as "without psychosis, not mentally defective, psychopathic personality." It is the writer's contention that such a diagnosis does not indicate the true state of affairs, in fact effectively hides the psychodynamic status of the inmate, and causes confusion and apathy regarding treatment and eventual disposition of the inmate.

On the basis of clinical investigations on the Sing Sing sex offenders, corroborated by the findings on psychological examination, the writer would propose that these individuals be diagnosed, for the most part, somewhere along the continuum ranging from schizo-adaptive personality structure (3), through pseudoneurotic schizophrenia (4), pseudopsychopathic schizophrenia (5), and ambulatory schizophrenia to overt, clinically demonstrable schizophrenic psychosis. Without becoming involved in the controversy that is ever present regarding the genetic basis of schizophrenia, the usefulness of the concept of a schizotype—or to use Sandor Rado's term, a schizo-adaptive personality—in dealing with the problems of therapy and prognosis in this group of cases, has become increasingly evident over the past three years. In the field of therapy, for example, while the prognosis in schizophrenia is still not a rosy one, as has been mentioned, therapeutic techniques are available, and do modify the pattern of illness in many patients. On the other hand, there is a universal pessimism, and rightly so, about therapeutic efforts with the psychopath, and this may have an adverse effect upon the treatment of individuals so diagnosed.

In the field of prognosis, which in prison psychiatry includes not only a prediction about the medical future of the inmate patient, but also involves or implies a prediction about his future social behavior, the use of the diagnostic continuum just described, with its implication of movement in either direction, gives a flexibility to statements about therapeutic response that cannot be achieved using terms like "cured" or "improved." Every psychiatrist who has had to decide, or help decide on the ability of a hospitalized patient to adjust to life outside the institution is keely aware of the difficulties and problems surrounding such decisions. When the "patient" has committed an antisocial act, and may have a history of recidivism, the decision, from the psychiatric standpoint, on his suitability for release, is an even weightier one. The device of attaching a diagnostic label never suffices. The administrative officials in the probation offices, parole boards and courts are increasingly interested in a statement of the psychodynamics of the particular case, reduced of course to understandable lay terminology, and are willing, even eager, to be guided in their decisions by the implications about the future behavior of the individual that are contained in such a statement. In order, therefore, to meet most adequately the dual responsibility which medicine has always accepted—to society on the one hand, and to the individual patient on the other—and which has been intensified in recent years by the willingness of the courts and correctional authorities to accept medical, especially psychiatric, opinion about problems of human misbehavior, we must attempt as accurate a description as possible of the behavior pattern in question. This must be dynamically oriented, if a proper understanding of the motivational context, as well as the actual behavior, is to be achieved. Prediction of future behavior is dependent to a greater extent on a clear understanding of the motivations and goals, both conscious and unconscious, of the individual, than on any other factor.

## REFERENCES

1. Report on Study of 102 Sex Offenders at Sing Sing Prison. Albany. March 1950.
2. CLECKLEY, H.: The Mask of Sanity. Mosby. St. Louis. 1950.
3. RADO, SANDOR: Academic Lecture Am. J. Psychiat., 110:6, 406, December 1953.
4. HOCH, P., and POLATIN, P.: Pseudoneurotic forms of schizophrenia. Psychiat. Quart., 23, April 1949.
5. DUNAIF, S., and HOCH, P.: Pseudopsychopathic schizophrenia. Presentation at 1953 meeting of American Psychopathological Association.

# Chapter 6

# Children's Disorders

*There are many reasons why it is important to study the disorders of children apart from their adult counterparts. First of all, many workers feel that at least some disorders of childhood are unique to that period of life and could not appear at a later time. Furthermore, many events in childhood potentially can be expressed in adult behavior patterns. Lastly, those theorists who subscribe to a developmental personality theory feel that an understanding of childhood is essential to a full understanding of the adult.*

A. D. B. Clarke
and Ann M. Clarke

## Some Recent Advances in the Study of Early Deprivation

Most of the prominent theories of personality stress the importance of early life experiences as determiners of adult personality. Indeed, for some theories, like the psychoanalytic, the events of the first five years or so of life set a pattern that may be altered only with great difficulty later. In a sense, this notion is no more than an assumption until careful empirical studies are done to assess the effects of early experiences on later behavior. In this review by Clarke and Clarke, studies done on the effects of one class of early life experiences involving deprivations of important needs are surveyed. These are important for the study of abnormal psychology since the source of pathology in children and adults is often assumed to reside in such early need deprivation.

## INTRODUCTION

During the last 40 years there has been a growing awareness of the importance of early experiences in the development of later personality. The psychoanalysts were the first to stress this, but since then they have been joined by the learning theorists, notably Hebb, who indicated brilliantly that later stages of development depend on the integrity of preceding ones. More recently the ethologists have shown from the animal world that there exist critical periods of development—particularly in early life—during which the future of certain behaviour patterns is determined. These diverse trends indicate that from very different approaches a

*Reprinted from* Journal of Child Psychology and Psychiatry, *1(1960), 26–36 with the permission of Pergamon Press, Inc. and Dr. A. D. B. Clarke.*

similar stress is laid on the importance of early life experiences.

Much fascinating work on deprivation in animals has been produced by Lorenz, Tinbergen, Beach and others but one must beware of extending the results to man too readily, particularly where infra-primate organisms are concerned. Animals have, unlike man, a relatively short period of immaturity, and the part played during development by learning must be of correspondingly short duration. For survival, particularly in early life, the animal depends on predetermined modes of response, each triggered off by appropriate stimulation. During speedy development the organism tends to be particularly vulnerable, and early deprivation in animals may have very profound effects. For man the situation is different; prolonged development implies prolonged flexibility and hence, although deprivation effects in children may be considerable, there is a greater period for compensatory recovery, sometimes even up to about 30 years of age after which, as William James put it, man's personality tends to be set hard like a plaster cast.

There is theoretical interest in human deprivation because unusual experiences tend to have gross effects, and can therefore tell us something relevant to theories of normal development. The size of the problem is a more practical reason for studying this field. Take physical deprivation as an example: in England, where poverty is no longer a major problem, we tend to forget that well over half the world's children—in whom the foundations for later development are being laid—are at or below the poverty line, suffering from malnutrition. As Morgan (1959) recently put it, vast populations are "struggling with conditions that make sickness and undernourishment the normal state of life." In this country great improvement

in physical health has occurred but the same cannot be said for mental health; it is a well-worn statistic that about 44 per cent of our hospital beds are for mental cases. Any studies which throw light on this vast problem—and deprivation studies are one source—must therefore be worthwhile.

One great landmark in this field was Bowlby's (1951) monograph on *Maternal Care and Mental Health*, but its thesis already needs modification, and some advances in understanding have occurred. As will be remembered, Bowlby stated that "what is believed to be essential for mental health is that the infant and young child should experience a warm, intimate and continuous relationship with his mother (or permanent mother substitute) in which both find satisfaction and enjoyment. Given this relationship, the emotions of anxiety and guilt, which in excess characterize mental ill-health, will develop in a moderate and organized way. . . ." Bowlby's work has of course resulted in many humane changes in hospital practices.

Deprivation and separation from parents, however, tended to become interchangeable and synonymous terms, and much of his evidence implied far more than mere separation. Many studies, for example, concerned children who had suffered unfortunate experiences followed by removal from home and long periods in drab Dickensian institutions, which involved deprivation in a far wider sense than mere separation. Criticisms have been made along these lines by O'Connor (1956), and very recently by Barbara Wootton (1959), who rightly remarks that these findings highlight inadequate public care of children as much as the separation from the mother. Thus perhaps the most obvious feature of deprivation studies is the loose way in which the term is used, and that classification is almost nonexistent. We proposed to define deprivation widely as "any external event or constellation of events which significantly interferes with the child's normal developmental processes and which thus affects adversely his mental or physical status." Fig. 1 shows a simple scheme of classification of different types of deprivation.

This scheme is by no means comprehensive; we could add, for example, a large and important category of sensory deprivation. Moreover, each of these main types can and ought to be further subdivided. It will also be noted that from left to right there is a decrease in the severity of deprivation with, however, socioeconomic and cultural factors on their own on a rather different plane. Next, in Table 1, other important variables are noted.

**TABLE 1. Factors Relevant to Deprivation**

1. Duration
2. Intensity
3. Previous experiences
4. Age of occurrence
5. Constitutional vulnerability (modifiable by environment)
6. Experiences following deprivation
7. Constitutional resilience (modifiable by environment)
8. Aspects of personality affected

Perhaps the only point needing elaboration is the last one. Different aspects of personality may be damaged by diverse experiences or at different stages of development. For example, a child in a poverty-stricken family *may* be psychologically secure and suffer only physical effects: a child in a tense neurotic family may be intellectually unimpaired yet emotionally disturbed.

## SOME RECENT STUDIES

Each type of deprivation shown in Fig. 1 will now be considered briefly in connexion with some recent experiments which have added to our knowledge of this field.

### Social Isolation

Studies of social isolation are few and often anecdotal. Accounts of children reared by animals are usually suspect but it is possible that this has in fact happened, and that most, despite care and training, have remained at imbecile or idiot level. The first proper study of such a child was Itard's Wild Boy of Aveyron, itself a major step in the history of psychology, because for the first time a human being was investigated scientifically. The point is often made that such children must have been congenital imbeciles in the first place, but this is untenable. No

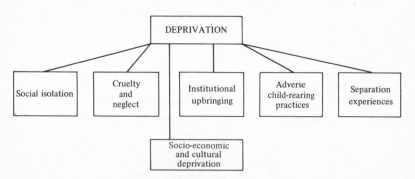

Fig. 1. Main types of deprivation.

genuine low-grade defective could survive the hazards of animal life or learn to adapt to animal ways.

There have been a few studies of illegitimate children locked away in attics for 5 to 6 years before discovery. Davis (1940, 1947), for example, reported two cases. When rescued, neither could talk and both functioned at idiot level. In spite of assiduous care one remained an idiot, but the other showed amazing resilience. Within 2 months she could speak in sentences, in 9 months she was reading and writing, and in 16 months had a vocabulary of 2000 words. After 2 years, by the age of 8, she was considered intellectually normal. It so happened that she had not been separated from her deaf mute mother but locked up with her in a darkened attic, while the first had been completely alone, and also had a defective mother.

More recently, Willis (1959, and personal communication) reported very briefly a case of a child kept locked in a hen house between the ages of 2 and 7.

This was the illegitimate son of a widow of 10 years' standing. Half-brothers and sisters on both maternal and paternal sides were normal. After a year of medical and surgical treatment following rescue, Miss Willis saw the child daily for a period of several months. He could not speak, never looked *at* any-one, smelt every new object and was uninterested in movement as such. But after 2 weeks' simple therapy he could be tested with Seguin Formboard and achieved a mental age of 6½–7 years, his age then being just over 8. The beginnings of the humanization process were observable, but the experiment was abruptly ended when hospital treatment was complete and he was removed to a children's home where at once he regressed—a human and a scientific tragedy.

To summarize, it is clear that extreme isolation can and usually does result in permanent severe intellectual impairment. In one or two cases, however, dramatic recovery has taken place.

## Cruelty and Neglect

It is well-known that cruelty and neglect may have very profound effects on young children, but there have been rather few systematic studies. An exception is Hilda Lewis's (1954) research on 500 deprived children in the county of Kent who had been sent to a Reception Centre. She showed the linkage between the child's background and the form of maladjustment exhibited, but Table 2 shows even more interesting data.

This shows the children's condition as assessed on reception and on follow up. In spite of gross deprivation, 40

TABLE 2. One Hundred Children Included in Special
Follow-Up Inquiry

| Condition of Children | At Reception | 2 Years Later |
|---|---|---|
| Good     .. .. | 15 ⎱ 40 | 39 ⎱ 75 |
| Fair     .. .. | 25 ⎰ | 36 ⎰ |
| Poor     .. .. | 39 | 22 |
| Very poor     .. | 21 | 3 |

After Table 50, Lewis (1954).

per cent were in good or fair psychological condition at reception, and, even more striking, this had increased to 75 per cent 2 years later. Not all children are equally damaged by similar experiences, and in many recovery tends to occur. Lewis points out that removal of children from very adverse homes and separation from bad mothers may be very essential for their mental health. "Some children long exposed to the dislike or indifference of their natural mothers," she writes, "gained rather than lost by separation, provided they passed into kind and sensible hands." This sort of statement tends to redress a common bias in favour of the natural mother, however bad. Similarly, studies at The Manor Hospital have indicated that subnormal deprived persons tend to make great progress after removal from severe deprivation experiences in their own homes.

## Institutional Upbringing

An excellent study of the effects of early institutionalization upon speech development in young children has been reported by Kellmer Pringle and Tanner (1958). The subjects were obtained from a day nursery and also from residential nurseries: it was possible to select eighteen reasonably matched pairs of 4–4½ year old children. The home backgrounds of both groups were very poor.

Careful measures of speech showed that in all cases the day nursery group living in their bad homes were in advance of the residential group to the extent, averaging four tests, of 10 months—all this at the early age of 4 years. Such differences in speech foundations are likely to increase with age, and reflect the typical child–other children relationship as against child–adult relationship which is typical for ordinary children. It should, however, be remembered that not all institutions are necessarily bad, and that in fact many are improving.

## Adverse Child-Rearing Practices

It is proposed to mention here adverse methods *within the limits of social acceptance*, and to report one of several promising approaches. Wittenborn (1956), for example, pointed out the difficulties in accepting at face value correlations between children and their parents where a quality with a possible hereditary basis was concerned; such relationships could be either genetic or environmental or both. However, if foster children were studied (to avoid the effects of selective placement) on nongenetic items of behaviour such as the presence or absence of phobias, then the relationship with the mother's attitude would be likely to be a causal one, and in fact small significant correlations were found between such behaviour and foster-mothers' unsympathetic and rejective attitude.

Several other studies have underlined general parental attitudes such as harshness as well as personal or marital instability as factors related to the child's maladjustment, but obviously nature and nurture intermingle in the natural family. Studies of foster children and their parents are clearly more useful.

## Separation Experiences

Much work on separation has been reported recently. Howells and Layng (1955), for example, established that, in a child guidance and a normal control group, about a third of both groups had experienced separation for more than 2 days under the age of 2 years. By the age of 5, about three-quarters of both groups had been separated from their mothers. A little over half the parents believed that harmful effects had resulted, but most thought these were temporary. The authors consider that much mental ill-health arises from the experience of being with unsatisfactory parents and, like Hilda Lewis, believe that some disturbed children may benefit from separation.

Douglas and Blomfield (1958) in their comprehensive study of 5000 randomly selected children, found that half the sample had experienced separation during the first 6 years of life. For 14 per cent this separation lasted for 4 weeks or more. These were carefully matched with a control group of non-separated children. Fairly crude measures of emotional disturbance (such as nightmares, enuresis and solitary play) were used. It was found that, where the child had been separated both from mother and from home, differences between the groups were apparent; 37 per cent of the separated group had nightmares versus 21 per cent of the controls. But where the child remained in his home during the separation period, no differences could be established. This seems a very important finding.

Schaffer (1958) has studied the effects of one or two weeks' hospital experience on seventy-six infants. The main finding at follow-up was the identification of two distinct syndromes (see Table 3), characteristic of the great majority of the children, and each associated with a particular age range—

either before or after the age of 7 months.

The main feature of the "global syndrome" was an extreme preoccupation with the environment. Sometimes for hours on end the infant would crane his neck, scanning his surroundings without apparently focusing on any particular feature. It was exceedingly difficult to "break through" this scanning behavior. The second symptom constellation—the "over-dependent syndrome"—is much more familiar to us, being characterized by unusual and excessive dependence, clinging almost continually, much crying and a fear of strangers.

Schaffer links these very distinct reactions with the different stages in the child's perceptual and conceptual development and cites Piaget's findings. It is only during the second half of the first year that a new type of cognitive structure emerges which enables the infant to make real relationships. The "global syndrome" is said to emerge as a response to the perceptual monotony of the hospital ward while the "over-dependent syndrome" results both from separation and the trauma of hospital experience.

Prugh et al. (1953) have studied reactions of children to hospitalization. A control and experimental group of 50 children each, the majority aged between 2 and 10 years, were selected. Most of these were admitted to hospital

TABLE 3. Syndromes Typical of 72 Per Cent of Infants Following Hospital Experience

| Type | Global | Over-dependent |
|---|---|---|
| Features | Extreme preoccupation with environment, "scanning," little vocalization | Excessive crying when mother out of sight, clinging, fear of strangers |
| Age range | Below 7 months | Above 7 months |
| Average duration | 3 days | 14 days |
| Range | 20 min–4 days | 1–80 days |

After Schaffer (1958).

for fairly short periods and for relatively acute illnesses. Matching of the two groups was reasonably successful except that the control group contained before admission a rather larger number of well-adjusted children.

The control group experienced ordinary ward routines and were assessed before, during and after their hospital experience. The experimental group, however, enjoyed special ward routines with visiting by parents at any time, psychological preparation, and support for unpleasant procedures, special play activities and so on. Table 4 shows some of the main results; it should be noted that Prugh's terms "maximal, limited, inadequate" for pre-hospital adjustment and "minimal, moderate, severe" for reactions to hospital, are really synonymous.

It will be seen that the control group showed a shift in the direction of moderate and severe maladjustment under orthodox conditions compared with pre-hospital adjustment. The experimental group under special conditions, however, showed a similar pattern of maladjustment and adjustment before and during their hospital experience.

The younger children were more disturbed than the older, and there was a correlation between previous adjustment and adjustment in hospital.

So far as follow-up is concerned, 92 per cent of the controls and 68 per cent of the experimental group showed significant disturbance of behaviour immediately after discharge. Three months later, the figures had dropped to 58 per cent and 44 per cent respectively. After 6 months 15 per cent of the controls and none of the experimental group showed continued disturbance. The authors have demonstrated without doubt the psychological value of the "humanized" hospital.

A recent paper by Bowlby et al. (1956) has considerably modified some of his earlier views. A group of 60 children admitted for long periods early in life to a T.B. sanatorium was followed up and contrasted with a control group selected as nearest in age to the subjects after their discharge, in their schools. There did appear to be small residual differences between the ex-sanatorium children and their controls but these might reside as much in the sort of home from which a tuberculous child is drawn as in the separation experiences. Bowlby goes on to say courageously that where his expectations proved most wrong was in the sanatorium children's capacity to make friends; unlike those reported on earlier, they appeared relatively normal in this respect. In fact one is able to infer from the data that there appeared to be only a 20 per cent greater incidence of maladjustment in the sanatorium as

TABLE 4. Pre-hospital Adjustment and the Reactions of Children to Hospital

| Control Group (Orthodox Conditions) | | | | Experimental Group ("Humanized" Conditions) | | | |
|---|---|---|---|---|---|---|---|
| Pre-Hospital Adjustment | | Reactions to Hospital | | Pre-Hospital Adjustment | | Reactions to Hospital | |
| Maximal | 56% | Minimal | 8% | Maximal | 34% | Minimal | 32% |
| Limited | 42% | Moderate | 56% | Limited | 54% | Moderate | 54% |
| Inadequate | 2% | Severe | 36% | Inadequate | 12% | Severe | 14% |

Data summarized from Prugh et al. (1953).

compared with control groups. In particular, Bowlby writes that the statements made earlier by him and by other workers, that children spending long periods in institutions *commonly* develop psychopathic or affectionless characters, are seen to be mistaken. Much will of course depend on the type of institution.

## Socio-economic Factors

The study of socio-economic factors in our own culture has provided material relevant to deprivation. For example, in the "Thousand Family Survey", Spence *et al.* (1954) found that half the unsatisfactory mothers came from Social Classes IV and V and that there was a tendency for children in such classes to suffer other handicaps, such as overcrowding and a greater number of illnesses. Douglas and Blomfield (1958) also point to social class differences in growth, health and maternal efficiency with much the same implications. It is clear that particularly the children of unskilled workers tend to start life with a number of handicaps and, in so far as this is true, are deprived.

It has long been known that there are class differences in average intelligence. Nowadays most of us believe that both nature and nurture are relevant, and recent work is giving an indication of some possible environmental mechanisms. Take language as an example: Luria (1959) has shown that language in the first few years of life is not merely a system for intercommunication; it has an additional function as externalized thinking needed for problem solving of all types. Now obviously language does not develop *in vacuo*—it is the result not only of neural maturation but also of language stimulation by parents and others. Hence a very poor language environment (see Kellmer Pringle and Tanner, 1958) is bound to retard the child's speech and hence certainly in early years, and perhaps later too, to affect the child's intellectual development. Moreover, Bernstein (1958), in an outstanding paper, has described two language systems—the concrete here-and-now "public language" and the "formal language" consisting of abstractions and cause-effect relationships. The public language is the main speech mode of lower socio-economic groups and certainly also occurs in the higher. But the formal language is the main speech mode of the higher groups and, reinforced by the more ambitious attitudes to children of middle-class parents, affects profoundly their language and hence their intellectual development, and this in turn has a bearing on responsiveness to education.

Thus culturally poor language environments must be considered as part of the deprivation problem.

## DISCUSSION AND CONCLUSIONS

An attempt will now be made to discuss and to draw together the threads of this exceedingly diverse material, and to state some general conclusions.

The first important point is that, apart from gross deprivation, studies of all other forms show considerable differences in individual vulnerability. Even in poor institutions it seems likely that only a minority develop those very severe disorders of conduct that caused Bowlby so much concern, although maladjustment is certainly a typical outcome. Separation itself is an immensely complex problem—much depends on previous experience and whether it is followed by traumatic situations. And, in spite of the analysts, the mother is not the only figure of importance. The child's conceptual and perceptual rigidity are such that removal from the familiar tends to produce stress, and the familiar includes the actual bricks, mortar and plaster of the particular home. As Woodward (personal communication) puts it, the child has learned expectancies, and depends upon these markedly.

What, then, are the factors determining differences in vulnerability? We know next to nothing about this, but here are some obvious suggestions: inherited predisposition, experiences preceding and circumstances surrounding the deprivation, and the child's personality *in toto*, in addition to the deprivation itself. In brief, environment does not operate in a mechanically similar way on all children, although there are of course strong "actuarial" tendencies of particular response to various types of severe or prolonged deprivation.

The second important point is that to varying extents there may be recovery from deprivation even of the most severe kind. This again is a highly complex process which among other things seems to involve a basic equality of the organism which we have termed resilience. Earlier there was certainly an error in supposing that deprivation effects were most likely to be permanent. On the contrary one is as much struck by the human being's resilience as by his tendency to break down. Until recently very few studies existed which showed adult outcome of early deprivation, and it is moreover obvious that we tend not to see professionally those who have recovered. Thus we cannot estimate their number completely. The fact that humans remain moderately flexible during the period of development, as mentioned, allows this possibility of compensatory recovery.

To underline this point we will refer briefly to some work carried out at The Manor Hospital. This concerns severely deprived adolescent and young adult defectives drawn either from adverse or exceptionally adverse backgrounds, often involving cruelty, neglect, separation, long periods in many institutions and so forth. This is therefore almost a pure culture (Clarke and Clarke, 1954, 1959; Clarke, Clarke and Reiman, 1958).

During our first year of work with these people we were struck by the frequency of large I.Q. increments particularly in the most deprived. After pilot experiments, all assessments and ratings of social histories were carried out independently, usually by colleagues who did not know the patients at all. Fig. 2 indicates some of the main results.

These graphs cut a very long story short. The vertical axis shows differing percentages of different but comparable groups. The horizontal axis shows test-retest time interval. It will be noted that a larger proportion of those from the most adverse homes had bigger increments, and that the longer the time interval the greater the proportion.

Our data suggest that these results represent recovery from past experiences rather than response to the present. And they seem to be paralleled by change in other aspects of personality. We believe that exceptionally adverse experiences in childhood prolong the immaturity of the organism, and that Hebb's (1949) work is particularly relevant. Many years are needed for learning, in its broadest sense, the experiences missed or disrupted. There is no way of knowing what these persons would have been like if brought up under good conditions—all we do know is that a very different prognostic picture is presented at 25 than at 15 (unless of course the social history is taken into account at the earlier age). This

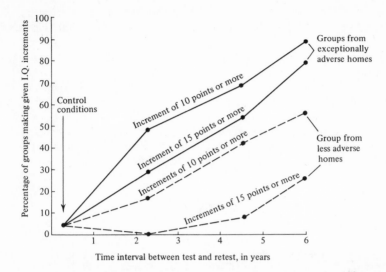

Fig. 2. Cognitive recovery from deprivation. This shows the increasing proportion of different but comparable groups of feebleminded patients exhibiting increments in I.Q. of 10 and 15 points with increase in time interval between test and retest. Increments of 20 points or more are not shown, but for the 6-year interval 33 per cent of the group from exceptionally adverse homes and 5 per cent of those from less adverse homes made gains of this order.

then is further evidence that very severe deprivation effects can fade.

Finally and briefly, some additional points:

(1) Perceptual and conceptual rigidity, a feature of infancy and childhood and very much a function of immature neural mechanisms, is likely to be an important causal factor in early adverse response to hospitalization and other separation experiences. There is also the likelihood, if this rigidity is not broken down by enriching stimulation—whether speech, educational or experiential—that it will continue to varying extents for longer periods than normal. The restricted informational experience of the institution where each drab day is like every other one, and where children's main source of stimulation is other impoverished children rather than adults, serves to retard or fixate perceptual and conceptual development.

(2) Cultures such as ours, which stress a nuclear family structure, are likely to increase the effects of separation in the child. There is some evidence from other societies, such as the Israeli kibbutzim, where the parents play a far less important role, that children grow up more independent and self-sufficient. ·

(3) One can expect the effects of deprivation to be severe and of long duration *either* when the child's personality before deprivation was poorly adjusted, *or* when the duration and intensity of the experience was great.

(4) Lastly, most deprivation experiences are likely to have an effect on mental health (ranging from transitory to permanent), but obviously mental ill-health has many causes additional to or different from deprivation. Deprivation is important because it is potentially so often preventable.

## SUMMARY

Deprivation is important not only in its own right as a vast world-wide problem but also in the general context of theories of personality development. This paper evaluates recent experimental literature with particular reference to individual differences in susceptibility to, and recovery from, the effects of

different types of deprivation. Gross deprivation, such as isolation, tends to have profound and usually permanent psychological effects. Earlier work, however, has tended to overestimate both the severity and permanence of the effects of milder and more common types of deprivation. One is as much struck by the human's resilence following suffering as by his tendency to break down.

## REFERENCES

BERNSTEIN, B. (1958) Some sociological determinants of perception. Brit. J. Sociol. 9, 159–74.

BOWLBY, J. (1951) Maternal Care and Mental Health. World Health Organization, Geneva.

BOWLBY, J., AINSWORTH, M., BOSTON, M., and ROSENBLUTH, D. (1956) The effects of mother-child separation: a follow-up study. Brit. J. Med. Psychol. 29, 211–247.

CLARKE, A. D. B., and CLARKE, A. M. (1954) Cognitive changes in the feeble-minded. Brit. J. Psychol. 45, 173–179.

CLARKE, A. D. B., and CLARKE, A. M. (1959) Recovery from the effects of deprivation. Acta Psychol. 16, 137–144.

CLARKE, A. D. B., CLARKE, A. M., and REIMAN, S. (1958) Cognitive and social change in the feebleminded: three further studies. Brit. J. Psychol. 49, 144–157.

DAVIS, K. (1940) Extreme social isolation of a child. Amer. J. Sociol. 45, 554–565.

DAVIS, K. (1947) Final note on a case of extreme isolation. Amer. J. Sociol. 52, 432–437.

DOUGLAS, J. W. B., and BLOMFIELD, J. M. (1958) Children under Five. Allen & Unwin, London.

HEBB, D. O. (1949) The Organization of Behaviour. Chapman & Hall, London.

HOWELLS, J. G., and LAYNG, J. (1955) Separation experiences and mental health. Lancet ii, 285–288.

KELLMER PRINGLE, M. L., and TANNER, M. (1958) The effects of early deprivation on speech development: a comparative

study of 4-year-olds in a nursery school and in residential nurseries. Language and Speech. 1, 269–287.

LEWIS, H. (1954) Deprived Children. Oxford University Press, London.

LURIA, A. R. (1959) The Role of Speech in the Formation of Mental Processes. London: Pergamon Press (in press).

MORGAN, M. (1959) Doctors to the World. Robert Hale, London.

O'CONNOR, N. (1956) The evidence for the permanently disturbing effects of mother–child separation. Acta Psychol. 12, 174–191.

PRUGH, D. G., STAUB, E. M., SANDS, H. H., KIRSCHBAUM, R. M., and LENIHAN, E. A. (1953) A study of the emotional reactions of children and families to hospitalization and illness. Amer. J. Orthopsychiat. 23, 70–106.

SCHAFFER, H. R. (1958) Objective observations of personality development in early infancy. Brit. J. med. Psychol. 31, 174–183.

SPENCE, J. WALTON, W. S., MILLER, F. J. W., and COURT, S. D. M. (1954) A Thousand Families in Newcastle upon Tyne. Oxford University Press, London.

WILLIS, B. E. (1959) A case of extreme isolation in a young child. Bull. Brit. psychol. Soc. 38, 68–69 (Abstract.).

WITTENBORN, J. R. (1956) A study of adoptive children. Psychol. Monog. 40, 1–115.

WOOTTON, B. (1959) Social Science and Social Pathology. Allen & Unwin, London.

O. Ivar Lovaas,
Benson Schaeffer,
and James Q. Simmons

# Building Social Behavior in Autistic Children
# by Use of Electric Shock

*The autistic child, as described by Eisenberg and Kanner (American Journal of Orthopsychiatry, 26 (1956), 556–566), is characterized by a number of distinct features: (1) extreme detachment from human relationships seemingly from birth; (2) failure to use speech to communicate; (3) little or no spontaneity and a preference for obsessive rituals; (4) an intense fascination for certain objects and many details about them; and (5) apparently high intellectual potential as judged from either the language they had managed to acquire or from motor facility. As can be imagined, such children are extraordinarily difficult to do therapy with since they are so encapsulated that the outsider can barely make a dent on them. This study by Lovaas, Schaeffer, and Simmons has received a great deal of attention and comment because it utilized pain associated with electric shock in order to "get through" to autistic children in an effort to begin shaping their behavior along desired lines. This approach is in keeping with many recently introduced therapeutic techniques based on laboratory studies of the learning process among animals.*

Psychological or physical pain is perhaps as characteristic in human relationships as is pleasure. The extensive presence of pain in everyday life may suggest that it is necessary for the establishment and maintenance of normal human interactions.

Despite the pervasiveness of pain in daily functioning, and its possible necessity for maintaining some behaviors, psychology and related professions have shied away from, and often condemned, the use of pain for therapeutic purposes. We agree with Solomon (1964) that such objections to the use of pain have a moral rather than a scientific basis. Recent research, as reviewed by Solomon, indicated that the scientific premises offered by psychologists for the

rejection of punishment are not tenable. Rather, punishment can be a very useful tool for effecting behavior change.

There are three ways pain can be used therapeutically. First, it can be used directly as punishment, i.e., it can be presented contingent upon certain undesirable behaviors, so as to suppress them. This is perhaps the most obvious use of pain. Second, pain can be removed or withheld contingent upon certain behaviors. That is, certain behaviors can be established and maintained because they terminate pain, or avoid it altogether. Escape and avoidance learning exemplify this. The third way in which pain can be used is the least well known, and perhaps the most intriguing. Any stimulus which is as-

*Reprinted from* Journal of Experimental Research in Personality, *1(1965), 99–109 with the permission of Academic Press and Dr. Lovaas.*

sociated with or discriminative of pain reduction acquires *positive* reinforcing (rewarding) properties (Bijou and Baer, 1961), i.e., an organism will work to "obtain" those stimuli which have been associated with pain reduction. The action of such stimuli is analogous to that of stimuli whose positive reinforcing properties derive from primary positive reinforcers.

These three aspects of the use of pain can be illustrated by observations on parent-child relationships. The first two are obvious; a parent will punish his child to suppress specific behaviors, and his child will learn to behave so as to escape or avoid punishment. The third aspect of the use of pain is more subtle, but more typical. In this case, a parent "rescues" his child from discomfort. In reinforcement, theory terms, the parent becomes discriminative for the reduction or removal of negative reinforcers or noxious stimuli. During the first year of life many of the interactions a parent has with his children may be of this nature. An infant will fuss, cry, and give signs indicative of pain or distress many times during the day, whereupon most parents will pick him up and attempt to remove the discomfort. Such situations must contribute a basis for subsequent meaningful relationships between people; individuals are seen as important to each other if they have faced and worked through a stressful experience together. It may well be that much of a child's love for his parents develops in situations which pair parents with stress reductions. Later in life, the normal child does turn to his parent when he is frightened or hurt by nightmares, by threat of punishment from his peers, by fears of failure in school, and so on.

In view of these considerations, it was considered appropriate to investigate the usefulness of pain in modifying the behaviors of autistic children. Autistic children were selected for two reasons: (1) because they show no improvement with conventional psychiatric treatment; and (2) because they are largely unresponsive to everyday interpersonal events.

In the present study, pain was induced by means of an electrified grid on the floor upon which the children stood. The shock was turned on immediately following pathological behaviors. It was turned off or withheld when the children came to the adults who were present. Thus, these adults "saved" the children from a dangerous situation; they were the only "safe" objects in a painful environment.

## STUDY 1

The objectives of Study 1 were (1) to train the children to avoid electric shock by coming to E when so requested; (2) to follow the onset of self-stimulatory and tantrum behaviors by electric shock so as to decrease their frequency; and (3) to pair the word "no" with electric shock and test its acquisition of behavior-suppressing properties.

### Method

*Subjects.* The studies were carried out on two identical twins. They were five-years old when the study was initiated and were diagnosed as schizophrenics. They evidenced no social responsiveness; they did not respond in any manner to speech, nor did they speak; they did not recognize each other or recognize adults even after isolation from people; they were not toilet trained; their handling of physical objects (toys, etc.) was inappropriate and stereotyped, being restricted to "fiddling" and spinning. They were greatly involved in self-stimulatory behavior, spending 70 to 80 per cent of their day rocking, fondling themselves, and moving hands and arms in repetitive, stereotyped manners. They engaged in a fair amount of tantrum behaviors, such as screaming, throwing objects, and hitting themselves.

It is important to note, in view of the moral and ethical reasons which might preclude the use of electric shock, that their future was certain institutionalization. They had been intensively treated in a residential setting by conventional psychiatric techniques for one year prior to the present study without any observable modification in their behaviors. This failure in treatment is consistent with reports of other similar efforts with such children (Eisenberg, 1957; Brown, 1960), which have suggested that if a schizophrenic child does not have language and does not play appropriately with physical objects by the age of three to five, then he will not improve, despite traditional psychiatric treatment, including psychotherapy, of the child and/or his family.

*Apparatus.* The research was conducted in a 12 x 12-foot experimental room with an adjoining observation room connected by one-way mirrors and sound equipment. The floor of the experimental room was covered by one-half inch wide metal tapes with adhesive backing (Scotch Tape). They were laid one-half inch apart so that when the child stepped on the floor he would be in contact with at least two strips, thereby closing the circuit and receiving an electric shock. A six-volt battery was wired to the strips of tape via a Harvard Inductorium. The shock was set at a level at which each of three Es standing barefoot on the floor agreed that it was definitely painful and frightening.

The Ss' behavior and the experimental events were recorded on an Esterline Angus pen recorder by procedures more fully described in an earlier paper (Lovaas *et al.*, 1965). The observer could reliably record both frequency and duration of several behaviors simultaneously on a panel of push-buttons. A given observer recorded at randomly selected periods.

*Pre-shock Sessions.* The Ss were placed barefoot in the experimental room with two Es, but were not shocked. There were two such pre-experimental sessions, each lasting for about 20 minutes. The Es would invite the Ss to "come here" about five times a minute, giving a total of approximately 100 trials per session. The observers recorded the amount of physical contact (defined as S's touching E with his hands), self-stimulatory and tantrum behavior, the verbal command "come here," and positive responses to the command (coming to within one foot of E within five seconds).

*First Shock Sessions.* The two pre-experimental sessions were followed by three shock sessions distributed over three consecutive days during which Ss were trained, in an escape-avoidance paradigm, to avoid shock by responding to E's verbal command according to the pre-established criterion. In the escape phase of the training, consisting of fifty trials, the two Es faced each other, about three feet apart, with S standing (held, if necessary) between them so that he faced one of the Es, who would lean forward, stretch his arms out, and say "come here." At the same time shock was turned on and remained on until S moved in the direction of this E, or, if S had not moved within three seconds, until the second E pushed S in the direction of the inviting E. Either type of movement of S toward the inviting E immediately terminated the shock. The S had to walk alternately from one E to the other.

In the avoidance sessions which followed, shock was withheld provided S approached E within five seconds. If S did not start his approach to the inviting E within five seconds, or if he was not within one foot of E within seven seconds, the shock was turned on and the escape procedure was reinstated for that trial.

During these avoidance sessions Es gradually increased their distance from each other until they were standing at opposite sides of the room. At the same time they gradually decreased the number of cues signaling S to approach them. In the final trials, Es merely emitted the command "come here," without turning toward or otherwise signaling S.

Shock was also turned on if S at any time engaged in self-stimulatory and/or tantrum behaviors. Whenever possible, shock was administered at the onset of such behaviors. Shock was never given except on the feet; no shock was given if S touched the floor with other parts of his body. In order to keep S on his feet, shock was given for any behavior which might have enabled him to avoid shock, such as beginning to sit down, moving toward the window to climb on its ledge, etc.

*Extinction Sessions.* The three shock sessions were followed by eleven extinction sessions distributed over a ten-month period. These sessions were the same as those in the previous sessions, except that shock and the command "no" were never delivered during this period.

*The Second Shock Sessions.* Three additional sessions terminated Study 1. In the first of these, S was brought into the experimental room and given a two-second shock not contingent upon any behavior of S or E. This was the only shock given. In all other respects these final sessions were similar to the preceding extinction sessions.

*Procedure for Establishing and Testing "No" as a Secondary Negative Reinforcer.* During the first shock sessions, shock had been delivered contingent upon self-stimulatory and/or tantrum behaviors. Simultaneous with the onset of shock Es would say

"no," thereby pairing the word "no" and shock. The test for any suppressing power which the word "no" had acquired during these pairings was carried out in the following manner. Prior to the shock sessions, Ss were trained to press a lever (wired to a cumulative recorder) for M & M candy on a fixed ratio 20 schedule. The sessions lasted for ten minutes daily. A stable rate of lever-pressing was achieved by the twelfth session, at which Es tested the word "no" for suppressing effects on the lever-pressing rate. The E delivered the "no" contingent upon lever-pressing toward the middle of each session, during three sessions *prior* to the shock sessions, and during three sessions *subsequent* to the shock sessions, i.e., after "no" had been paired with shock.

## Results and Discussion

Figure 1 gives the proportion of time Ss responded to Es' commands (proportion of Rs to $S^D$s). As can be seen, in the two pre-shock sessions Ss did not respond to Es' commands. During the

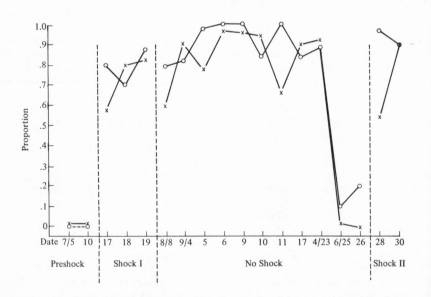

Fig. 1. Proportion of time Ss responded to Es commands—proportion of Rs to $S^D$s.

first three shock sessions (Shock I), Ss learned to respond to Es' requests within the prescribed time interval and thus avoided shock. This changed responsiveness of Ss to Es' requests was maintained for the subsequent nine months (no shock sessions). There was a relatively sudden decrease in Ss' responsiveness after nine months, i.e., the social behavior of coming to E extinguished. One non-contingent shock, however, immediately reinstated the social responsiveness (Shock II), suggesting that Ss responded to it as a discriminative stimulus for social behavior.

The data on Ss' pathological behaviors (self-stimulation and tantrums) and other social behaviors (physical contacts) are presented in Fig. 2. Prior to shock pathological behaviors occurred 65–85 per cent of the time; physical contacts were absent. Shock I suppressed the pathological behaviors immediately, and they remained suppressed during the following eleven months. In addition, social behaviors

replaced the pathological behaviors. This change was very durable (ten to eleven months), but did eventually extinguish. One non-contingent shock reinstated the social responsiveness and suppressed the pathological behaviors.

The data on the acquisition of "no" as a negative reinforcer are presented in Fig. 3. The records of bar-pressing for candy are presented as cumulative curves. The word "no" was presented contingent upon a bar-pressing response three sessions before and three sessions subsequent to shock, i.e., before and after the pairing of "no" with shock. The cumulative curves of the session immediately preceding and the session following shock to S1 is presented. The curves for the other sessions, both for S1 and S2, show the same effects. It is apparent upon inspection of Fig. 3 that the word "no" had no effect upon S1's performance prior to its pairing with shock, but that after such pairing it suppressed the bar-pressing response.

Observations of Ss' behaviors in the

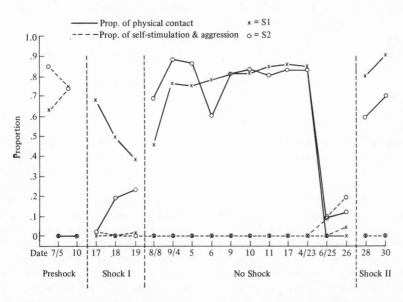

Fig. 2. Proportion of self-stimulation and tantrums (pathological behaviors) and physical contact (social behavior).

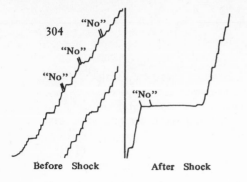

Fig. 3. Lever-pressing for candy as cumulative response curves: effect of "no" on lever-pressings by S1 before and after "no" was paired with shock.

Before Shock    After Shock

———— Prop. of R to $S^D$

$x = S1$
$o = S2$

experimental room indicated that the shock training had a generalized effect; it altered several behaviors which were not recorded. Some of these changes took place within minutes after the Ss had been introduced to shock. In particular, they seemed more alert, affectionate, and seeking of E's company. And surprisingly, during successful shock avoidance they appeared happy. These alterations in behavior were only partially generalized to the environment outside the experimental room. The changes in behaviors outside were most noticeable during the first fourteen days of the shock training, after which Ss apparently discriminated between situations in which they would be shocked and those in which they would not. According to their nurse's notes, certain behaviors, such as Ss' responsiveness to "come here" and "no" were maintained for several months, while others, such as physical contact, soon extinguished.

These observations formed the basis for the subsequent two studies. In Study 2 a more objective assessment of the changes in Ss' affectionate behavior toward adults was made, and a technique for extending these effects from the experimental room to the ward was explored. In Study 3 a test was made of any reinforcing power adults might have acquired as a function of their association with the termination of shock.

## STUDY 2

Study 2 involved two observations. One attempted to assess changes in Ss' affectionate behavior to E who invited them to kiss and hug him. The other observation was conducted by nurses who rated Ss on behavior change in seven areas (given below). Both observations incorporated measures of transfer of behavior changes to new situations brought about by the use of the remote control shock apparatus. Both observations were conducted immediately following the completion of Study 1.

*The "Kiss and Hug" Observations.* These observations consisted of six daily sessions. Three of the sessions (3, 5, and 6) are referred to as shock-relevant sessions. Sessions 3 and 5 were conducted in the experimental room where Ss had received shock during avoidance training. Three sessions (1, 2, and 4) are labeled control sessions. They took place in a room sufficiently different from the experimental room to minimize generalization of the shock effect. The last shock-relevant session (session 6) was conducted to test the changes produced by remotely controlled shock. This session was conducted in the same room as the previous control sessions. However, immediately preceding the session Ss received five shock-escape trials, similar to those of

Study 1. The shock was delivered from a Lee-Lectronic Trainer.[1] The S wore the eight-ounce receiver (about the size of a cigarette pack) strapped on his back with a belt. Shock was delivered at "medium" level over two electrodes strapped to S's buttock.

In order to minimize the effects of a particular observer's recording bias, two observers alternated in recording Ss' behavior. Each observer recorded at least one shock session. The sessions lasted for six minutes each. Every five seconds E would face S, hold him by the waist with outstretched arms, bow his head toward S, and state "hug me" or "kiss me." The E would alternate his requests ("hug me," "kiss me") every minute. The observer recorded (1) embrace (S placing his arms around E's neck), (2) hug and kiss (S hugging E cheek to cheek or kissing him on the mouth), (3) active physical withdrawal by S from E when held by the waist, and (4) E's requests.

## Results

Since Ss' behaviors on the test were virtually identical, their behaviors were averaged. The data are presented in Fig. 4. During the control sessions (sessions 1, 2, and 4) the proportion of time that Ss embraced, or hugged and kissed E was extremely low. Rather, they withdrew from him. During the shock-relevant sessions (sessions 3, 5, and 6) Ss' behavior changed markedly toward increased affection. In a situation where they had received shock-avoidance training they responded with affection to E and did not withdraw from him. The fact that this affectionate behavior maintained itself in session 6 demonstrates that the remotely controlled shock can produce transfer of behavior change to a wide variety of situations.

*Nurses' Ratings.* The nurses' ratings were initiated at the completion of the "kiss and hug" sessions. Four nurses who were familiar with Ss but unfamiliar with the experiment, and did not know that shock had been used, were asked to complete a rating scale pertaining to seven behaviors: (1) dependency on adults, (2) responsiveness to adults, (3) affection seeking, (4) pathological behaviors, (5) happiness and contentment, (6) anxiety and fear, and (7) overall clinical improvement. The scale was comprised of nine points, with the mid-point indicating no change. The nurses were asked to indicate whether they considered S to have changed (increased or decreased) in any of these

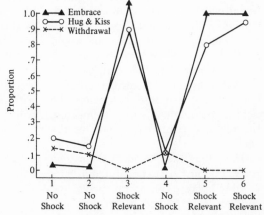

Fig. 4. Social reactions of Ss as a function of shock presentations. The "no shock" sessions (1, 2, 4) were run in a room where Ss had not been shocked. ("Shock" sessions (3, 5) were conducted in a room in which Ss had received shock-avoidance training. The last "shock" session (6) was conducted in the same room as the "no shock" sessions, but Ss had received remote controlled shock.)

[1] Lee Supply Co., Tucson, Arizona.

behaviors as compared to S's behaviors the preceding day or morning. The ratings were obtained under two conditions: (1) an experimental condition in which S, wearing the remote control unit on his belt underneath his clothing, was introduced to the nurses who "casually" interacted with him for ten minutes. S was not shocked while with the nurses, but he had been given a one-second, non-contingent shock immediately prior to his interaction with the nurses; (2) a control condition, which was run in the same manner as the experimental condition, except that S had no shock prior to the ratings.

The nurses rated changes in Ss under both conditions. They were not counter-balanced. The ratings from the control conditions were subtracted from the ratings based on the experimental conditions. The difference shows an increase in the ratings of all behaviors following the shock treatment, except for pathological behaviors and happiness-contentment, which both decreased. Only the ratings on dependency and affection seeking behaviors increased more than one point.

## STUDY 3

Study 3 showed the degree to which the association of an adult with shock reduction (contingent upon an approach response of the children) would establish the adult as a positive secondary reinforcer for the children. Increased resistance to extinction of a lever-pressing response producing the sight of the adult was used to measure the acquired reinforcing power of the adult.

The study was conducted in two parts. The first part constituted a "pre-training" phase. During this period the children were trained to press a lever to receive M & Ms and simultaneously see E's face. Once this response was acquired, extinction of the response was begun by removing the candy reinforcement, S being exposed only to E's face. The second part of the study constituted a test of the reinforcing power E had acquired as a result of having been associated with shock reduction. This association occurred when, immediately preceding several of the extinction sessions of the lever-press, Ss were trained to come to E to escape shock. The change in rate of responding to obtain a view of E during these sessions was used as a measure of E's acquired reinforcing power.

## Method

Study 3 was initiated after the completion of Study 2. It was conducted in an enclosed cubicle, four feet square, in which E and S sat separated by a removable screen. A lever protruded from a box at S's side. Lever-pressings were recorded on a cumulative recorder. An observer (O) looking through a one-way screen recorded the following behaviors of S as they occurred: (1) vocalizations (any sound emitted by S), and (2) standing on the chair or ledge in the booth. The latter measures were taken in a manner similar to that described in Study 1. These additional measures where obtained in an attempt to check on the possibility that an eventual increase in lever-pressing for E might be due to a conceivable "energizing" effect of shock, rather than to the secondary reinforcing power associated with shock reduction. This rationale will be discussed more fully below.

The first ten were labeled *pre-training* sessions. In each, a fifteen-minute acquisition preceded a twenty minute extinction of the lever-pressing response. During acquisition S received a small piece of candy and a five-second exposure to E (the screen was removed momentarily, placing E's face within S's view) on a fixed ratio 10 schedule. During extinction, S received only the five-second exposure to E on the same schedule as before. Both Ss reached a stable rate of about 500 responses during the first acquisition session.

The ten pre-training sessions were followed for S1 by nine *experimental* sessions. In these experimental sessions S never received candy. The sessions consisted only of a twenty-minute extinction period. An S's performance during the last extinction session of pre-training, labeled Session 1 in Fig. 5, served as a measure of the pre-experimental rate of lever-pressing. Electric shock was administered before the 2nd, 7th, and 9th experimental sessions, as follows: S was placed facing E in the room outside the cubicle. Shock was administered for two to four seconds, at which point E would tell S to "come here." S would invariably approach E and shock would be terminated. The E would then comfort S (fondle and stroke him) for one minute. This procedure was repeated four times. Immediately following this procedure, S was placed within his cubicle. E would repeat S's name every

five seconds. On the fixed ratio 10 schedule, the screen would open and E would praise S ("good boy") and stroke him.

The experimental treatment of S2 was identical to that of S1 with the following exceptions: (1) S2 received only seven experimental sessions; (2) shock preceded session 2, 6, and 8; (3) E did not call S2's name while he was in the cubicle; and (4) E was only visually exposed to S2 (E did not stroke or praise S2).

### Results and Discussion

The Ss' lever-pressing behavior is presented in Fig. 5 as cumulative curves. The last extinction curve from the pre-training is labeled one. This curve gives the rate of lever-pressing in the last extinction session preceding E's association with shock reduction. The upward moving hatchmarks on the curves show the occasions on which E was visually presented to S. The heavy vertical lines labeled shock, show shock-escape training preceding sessions 2, 7, and 9 for S1, and sessions 2, 6, and 8 for S2.

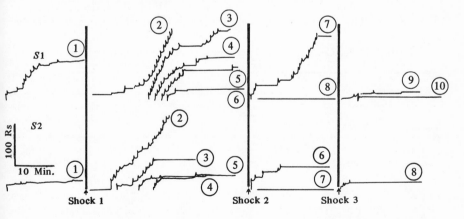

Fig. 5. The Ss' lever-pressing behavior for E as function of E's association with shock reduction. (Curve labelled "1" is the last extinction curve from the pretraining. Shock preceded sessions 2, 7, and 9 for S1, and sessions 2, 6, and 8 for S2. The upward moving hatchmarks on the curves indicate occasions at which E was visually presented to S.)

There was a substantial increase in rate of lever-pressing accompanying shock-escape training for both Ss. The curves also show the extinction of this response. The extinction is apparent in the falling rate between shock sessions (e.g., sessions 2 through 6 for S1 show a gradual decrease in rate of responding). A similar extinction is also manifested over the various shock sessions, i.e., the highest rate was observed after the first shock training, the next highest after the second shock training, and so on. The Ss' performances were very systematic and orderly.

Data based on the two additional measures, vocalization and standing on the chair or ledge, are presented in Table 1. The entries in the column labeled O1 can be compared to those in column O2. These data indicate that there was a high degree of agreement between the two observers rating amount of vocalizations of Ss. The O2's ratings were based on tape recordings taken from Ss while in the booth. It was physically impossible to have a second O assess the reliability of O1's ratings of climbing. However, because of the ease of recording such behavior it was judged unnecessary to check on its reliability. The agreement between Os on vocalizations was judged adequate for the purposes of this study.

If the increase in lever-pressing behavior was correlated with an increase in the two additional behaviors, then it might not be that shock-escape training had led to an increase in behavior toward people *per se*. Rather, it might have led to an "arousal" of many behaviors, asocial as well as social. As Table 1 shows, the two additional measures showed no systematic relationship to the shock-escape sessions for S2. In the case of S1 there is some possibility of *suppression* of vocalization and climbing subsequent to shock-escape sessions (sessions 2, 7, and 9). It is unlikely, then, that shock-escape training involving other people can be viewed simply as activating many behaviors; rather, such training selectively raised behavior which yielded a social consequence.

Thus it is concluded that this increase in behavior toward E subsequent to shock-escape training came about because E was paired with shock reduction, thereby acquiring reinforcing powers. This conceptualization is consistent with the findings of Studies 1 and 2, both of which demonstrated an increase in social and affectionate be-

**TABLE 1. Per Cent of Total Time Engaged in Vocalization and Climbing**

| | | S1 | | | S2 | | |
|---|---|---|---|---|---|---|---|
| | | Vocal. | | Climb. | Vocal. | | Climb. |
| Session | Shock | 01 | 02 | 01 | 01 | 02 | 01 |
| 1 | | 49 | | 0 | 27 | | 96 |
| 2 | S1 and S2 | 19 | 19 | 0 | 27 | | 0 |
| 3 | | 47 | | 0 | 20 | | 20 |
| 4 | | 25 | | 32 | 23 | | 0 |
| 5 | | 18 | | 65 | 26 | 29 | 0 |
| 6 | S2 | 22 | 23 | 97 | 22 | | 0 |
| 7 | S1 | 22 | 23 | 33 | 23 | 23 | 0 |
| 8 | S2 | 22 | | 83 | 22 | | 0 |
| 9 | S1 | 11 | | 0 | | | |
| 10 | | 13 | | 75 | | | |

haviors. The findings are similar to those reported by Risley (1964) who observed an increase in acceptable social behavior (eye-to-eye contact) in an autistic child to whom E had administered electric shock for suppression of behaviors dangerous to the child. The data are also consistent with the results of studies by Mowrer and Aiken (1954) and Smith and Buchanen (1954) on animals which demonstrated that stimuli which are discriminative for shock reduction take on secondary positive reinforcing properties. It is to be noted, however, that the data from the studies reported here also fit a number of other conceptual frameworks.

An apparent limitation in these data pertains to the highly situational and often short-lived nature of the effects of shock. This had definite drawbacks when one considers the therapeutic implications of shock. It is considered, however, that the effects of shock can be made much more durable and general by making the situation in which shock is delivered less discriminable from situations in which it is not. The purpose of the present studies was to explore certain aspects of shock for possible therapeutic use. Therefore, only the minimal amount of shock considered necessary for observing reliable behavior changes was employed. It is quite possible that the children's responsiveness to adults would have been drastically reduced if shock had been employed too frequently. It is worth making the point explicitly: a certain use of shock can, as in these studies, contribute toward beneficial, even therapeutic, effects; but it does not at all follow that a more widespread use of the same techniques in each case will lead to even better outcomes. Indeed, the reverse may be true. Recent studies with schizophrenic children in our laboratory have shown, tentatively,

that non-contingent shock facilitates performance of a well-learned task; however, such shock interferes with learning during early stages of the acquisition of new behaviors.

Certain more generalized effects of shock training, even though not recorded objectively, were noticed by Es and ward staff. First of all, Ss had to be trained (shaped) to come to E to escape shock. When shock was first presented to S2, for example, he remained immobile, even though adults were in the immediate vicinity (there was no way in which Ss could have "known" that Es presented the shock). This immobility when hurt is consistent with observations of Ss when they were hurt in the play-yard, e.g., by another child. But after Ss had been trained to avoid shock successfully in the experimental room, their nurses' notes state that Ss would come to the nurses when hurt in other settings.

Es had expected considerable expression of fear by Ss when they were shocked. Such fearful behavior was present only in the beginning of training. On the other hand, once Ss had been trained to avoid shock, they often smiled and laughed, and gave other signs of happiness or comfort. For example, they would "mold" or "cup" to E's body as small infants do with parents. Such behaviors were unobserved prior to these experiments. Perhaps avoidance of pain generated contentment.

In their day-to-day living, extremely regressed schizophrenic children such as these Ss rarely show signs of fear or anxiety. The staff who dealt with these children in their usual environments expressed concern about the children's lack of worry or anxiety. There are probably several reasons why children such as these fail to demonstrate anxiety. It is possible that their social and emotional development has been so curtailed and limited that they are unaffected by the fear-eliciting situations acting upon a normal child. For example, they do not appear to be afraid of intellectual or social inadequacies, nor are they known to experience nightmares. Furthermore, by the age of three or four, like normal children, these children appear less bothered by physiological stimuli, and unlike the small infant, are rather free of physiological discomforts. Finally, when these children are brought to treatment, for example in a residential setting, there is much effort made to make their existence maximally comfortable.

If it is the case, as most writers on psychological treatment have stated, that the person's experience of discomfort is a basic condition for improvement, then perhaps the failure of severely retarded schizophrenic children to improve in treatment can be attributed partly to their failure to fulfill this hypothesized basic condition of anxiety or fear. This was one of the considerations which formed the basis for the present studies on electric shock. It is important to note that the choice of electric shock was made after several alternatives for the inducement of pain or fear were tested and found wanting. For example, in the early work with these children we employed loud noise. Even at noise levels well above 100 decibels we found that the children remained unperturbed partic-

ularly after the first two or three presentations.

It seems likely that the most therapeutic use of shock will not lie primarily in the suppression of specific responses or the shaping of behavior through escape-avoidance training. Rather, it would seem more efficient to use shock reduction as a way of establishing social reinforcers, i.e., as a way of making adults meaningful in the sense of becoming rewarding to the child. The failure of autistic children to acquire social reinforcers has been hypothesized as basic to their inadequate behavioral development (Ferster, 1961). Once social stimuli acquire reinforcing properties, one of the basic conditions for the acquisition of social behaviors has been met. A more complete argument supporting this thesis has been presented elsewhere (Lovaas et al., 1964). A basic question, then, is whether it is necessary to employ shock in accomplishing such an end or whether less drastic methods might not suffice. In a previous study (Lovaas et al., 1964) autistic children did acquire social reinforcers on the basis of food delivery. However, the necessary conditions for the acquisition of social reinforcers by the use of food were both time-consuming and laborious, and by no means as simple as the conditions which were necessary when we employed shock reduction.

# REFERENCES

Bijou, S. W., and Baer, D. M. *Child Development; a systematic and empirical theory.* New York: Appleton-Century-Crofts, 1961.

Brown, Janet L. Prognosis from presenting symptoms of preschool children with atypical development. *American Journal of Orthopsychiatry*, 1960, **30**, 382–390.

Eisenberg, L. The course of childhood schizophrenia. *American Medical Association Archives for Neurology and Psychiatry*, 1957, **78**, 69–83.

Ferster, C. B. Positive reinforcement and behavioral deficits of autistic children. *Child Development*, 1961, **32**, 437–456.

Lovaas, O. I., Freitag, G., Gold, V. J., and Kassorla, I. C. A recording method and observations of behaviors of normal and autistic children in free play settings. *Journal of Experimental Child Psychology*, 1965, **2**, 108–120.

LOVAAS, O. I., FREITAG, G., KINDER, M. I., RUBENSTEIN, D. B., SCHAEFFER, B., AND SIMMONS, J. Q. Experimental studies in childhood schizophrenia—Establishment of social reinforcers. Paper delivered at Western Psychological Association, Portland, April, 1964.

MOWRER, O. H., AND AIKEN, E. G. Contiguity vs. drive-reduction in conditioned fear: temporal variations in conditioned

and unconditioned stimulus. *American Journal of Psychology*, 1954, **67**, 26–38.

RISLEY, TODD. The effects and "side effects" of the use of punishment with an autistic child. Unpublished manuscript, 1964. Florida State University.

SMITH, M. P., AND BUCHANEN, G. Acquisition of secondary reward by cues associated with shock reduction. *Journal of Experimental Psychology*, 1954, **48**, 123–126.

SOLOMON, R. L. Punishment. *American Psychologist*, 1964, **19**, 239–253.

David Elkind

# Middle-Class Delinquency

*Juvenile delinquency has always been a vexing problem involving, as it does, young people on the threshold of adulthood whose entire future may well be shaped by the way their adolescent acting-out problems are dealt with. It is an even more vexing problem when it arises among youngsters who have grown up in homes offering comforts and advantages that would seem to make delinquent behavior unnecessary. When a boy with a deprived background goes wrong we can readily relate it to unfulfilled needs and the frustrations offered by the circumstances of his life. When the delinquency occurs among the middle-class person, we are upset by both the antisocial nature of the behavior and our own inability to understand how it could come about. In this paper, Elkind, who has worked with such problems, offers an excellent discussion of the subtle interpersonal factors within the middle-class family which actually provoke such delinquency.*

The research literature on juvenile delinquency is already vast and continues to grow at an increasing pace (1). By and large, however, this research tends to deal with lower-class children living in slum areas of large cities. Much less is known about the young people from suburban, middle-class homes who also get into trouble with the law.

Some writers (2, 3) have suggested that delinquent youngsters from "respectable homes" are acting out the parents' repressed antisocial impulses and are subtly encouraged by the parents in this regard. Although this explanation probably holds true in a certain number of cases, my own experience (as consulting psychologist to a suburban juvenile court) suggests that

*Reprinted from* Mental Hygiene, **51**(1967), 80–84 *with the permission of the National Association for Mental Health and Dr. Elkind.*

the vicarious satisfaction of needs is but one of many forms of parental exploitation that can lead to delinquent behavior on the part of children. In what follows I shall elaborate on some of the forms of parental exploitation and some of the possible adolescent reactions to such exploitation.

Before proceeding, however, it is necessary to distinguish among three quite distinct groups of middle-class delinquents. There are, first of all, those adolescents whose delinquency is a direct manifestation of a long-standing emotional disturbance and for whom the remedy is usually psychiatric rather than probationary. Secondly, there are those young people who come before the court almost by accident—quite often for pulling some prank that turned out to be more serious than they had anticipated—and who are seldom, if ever, adjudicated for a second time. By far the largest group, however, are those adolescents who get into trouble more or less regularly and who have a series of past charges filed against them. Although these young people do not appear to have serious internalized conflicts, they are usually in quite open conflict with their parents.

It is with the etiology of delinquent behavior in this third group of young people that the present paper is primarily concerned.

## THE CONTRACT

The concept of parental exploitation makes sense only if there is an implicit contract between parents and their offspring. In middle-class families such a contract does exist. For their part, the parents agree to provide for the physical and emotional well-being of their children, who, in return, agree to abide by the norms of middle-class society.

Although minor infractions of this contract on the part of both parents and children are to be found in most middle-class families, they tend to be temporary. For the most part, the contract is honored on both sides.

This appears not to be true in the families of the delinquent children under discussion. If one inquires deeply enough into the family relationships of these children, one finds that the contract has been broken by one or both parents *over a prolonged period of time*. More particularly, that part of the contract is broken which ensures that the parent will take repsonsibility for the emotional well-being of his child. What one finds in these cases is that the parent not only puts his own needs before those of the child, but, more significantly, attempts to use the child as an instrument in the satisfaction of those needs. It is because the parent violates the contract with his child while demanding that the child hold to his end of the bargain that such violations are legitimately called "parental exploitation."

## FORMS OF PARENTAL EXPLOITATION

Although particular instances of parental exploitation are almost infinite in their variety, they can nonetheless be grouped under a few reasonably comprehensive headings. We have already noted that the *vicarious satisfaction of parental needs* is one frequent form of exploitation.

This form of exploitation is illustrated by a case in which a sexually frustrated mother encouraged her daughter to act out sexually. When the daughter returned from a date, the mother would demand a kiss-by-kiss description of the affair and end by calling the girl a tramp. When I saw the girl, who was being adjudicated for sexual vagrancy, she told me, "I have the name so I might as well play the role." When she left my office, her mother, who had been waiting outside, teasingly asked her how far she had gotten with the "cute psychologist."

A somewhat different form of parental exploitation might be called *ego bolstering*. In this category fall those parents who demand academic or athletic achievement far beyond what the young person is able, or has the capacity, to produce. This form of exploitation has an element of vicarious satisfaction in it, but the dominant affect seems to be the need to bolster flagging parental self-esteem. Although it is normal to want to take pride in one's child's achievements, it becomes pathologic when the parents' own needs to bask in reflected glory take precedence over the emotional welfare of the child.

A somewhat different variety of this form of exploitation is illustrated by the father who encouraged his 17-year-old son to drink, frequent prostitutes, and generally "raise hell." This particular father was awakened late one night by the police who had caught his son in a raid on a so-called "massage" parlor. The father's reaction was, "Why aren't you guys out catching crooks?" This same father would boast to his co-workers that his son was "all boy" and a "chip off the old block."

Still another form of parental exploitation occurs when parents use their youngsters as *slave labor*. In one instance, a father who owned a motel demanded that his son do all the lawn work and help to clean up the rooms and make the beds. To top it off, he insisted that the boy take the lids off all the cans in the trash barrels and then flatten the cans so that the volume of trash, and hence the cost of disposal,

would be lessened. The boy barely had time to do his homework, much less to visit with his friends. Mothers who get their teenage daughters to do more of the housework and the baby-sitting than is reasonable or equitable provide another example of slave labor exploitation.

A fourth form of parental exploitation is frequently encountered in broken homes in which the mother, who usually retains custody of the children, is relatively young and attractive. In one case a mother took a lover, much younger than herself, into her home over the protestations of her teenage daughter, who had to cope with the curiosity of friends and the indignation of neighbors. Another young divorcee had a baby out of wedlock whom she kept in the home without any explanation to her teenage children. Still another mother, who had lost her husband under tragic circumstances, took to drinking away her afternoons with a younger man, to whom she gave large sums of money. She could not understand why her teenage son ran off to Mexico.

In all such cases, the mothers demand not only that their children accept the situation, but that they condone it. By demanding that their children accept and condone their behavior, these mothers hope to use their children to *assuage their own consciences*.

One of the saddest forms of parental exploitation is engaged in by parents who are very much in the public eye, particularly school principals, clergymen (of whatever faith), and judges. If a parent in one of these professions see his child's behavior primarily in terms of what it means to his career, he may demand a degree of conformity to middle-class mores that is quite unreasonable from the young person's point of view. When young people of this kind get into trouble, it is not because the parents are too strict, but rather because the parents are using their children to *proclaim their own moral rectitude.* As in all cases of parental exploitation, the dominant affect in such children is not so much the feeling of being restricted as it is the feeling of being *used.*

## REACTIONS TO PARENTAL EXPLOITATION

When a worker is exploited he has at least four courses of action open to him. He can either quit, go out on strike, sabotage the plant, or passively submit to the exploitation.

Parallel types of reaction are found in middle-class delinquents. Some young people literally quit the scene. They may quit school and become truant, quit the home and become runaways, or quit the family psychologically and become incorrigible. Other adolescents go on strike. They continue to go to school, but refuse to perform; they stay in the home, but refuse to do their fair share of the chores; they stay out late, and they go with a group of whom the parents don't approve. In short, they defy parental authority generally. More serious reactions are observed in young people who wish to sabotage their parents. These kids get pregnant, steal cars, vandalize schools, get drunk, sniff glue, or take drugs. Such reactions cost the parents plenty in worry, time, money, and bad publicity. The saddest reaction of all is that of the youngsters who passively submit to parental exploitation in the hope of winning or regaining parental love.

Despite the variety of these reactions, they all have one feature in common: parental exploitation is essentially private and is seldom recognized by anyone outside the home. Whereas the worker often has a union to voice his grievances and to stand up for his rights, there are no unions for children. Consequently, the delinquent behavior of adolescents who are being exploited by their parents often serves as a kind of "cry for help." Put differently, delinquent behavior often has as one of its components the desire to make the exploitation public, to let the world know what is happening behind the drawn drapes and closed doors. The sad thing about such cries for help is that they are as injurious to the young person as they are to the parents.

## TREATMENT

To say that middle-class delinquency is difficult to treat psychotherapeutically is a gross understatement. The major reason for this is the fact that, *although the pathology exists in the parents, the symptoms appear in the children.* Since it is the children who are in trouble, the parents find it hard, except on a superficial basis, to accept their responsibility in the matter. Blind to their own violation of the parent-child contract, they insist that the young person live up to his side of the bargain. For his part, the young person feels that he has been used and abused and generally will not take responsibility for his actions.

With both parents and children blaming each other for the difficulty, there is little motivation for change on either side. Usually, however, the children are more tractable than the parents on this score. In many cases all that one can do is either remove the young person from the home, or help him to understand and deal with the exploitation in a more effective and less self-injurious way.

## SUMMARY AND IMPLICATIONS

In the foregoing discussion, I have argued that middle-class delinquency is essentially a reaction to parental exploitation and have tried to enumerate some of the forms of exploitation as well as some of the reactions to it. Such a position clearly places the burden of blame for middle-class delinquency upon the parents. To some extent, this is perhaps unjust, since children may encourage exploitation on their own behalf and may well exploit their parents in return. In many cases the exploitation is as likely to be circular as it is to be unidirectional. And yet, my impression is that in the majority of cases the parents are much more to blame than are their children.

It should be said, too, that I don't offer the notion of parental exploitation as a complete explanation of middle-class delinquency. It is probably true that many of these young people have ego and superego defects of long standing. It is also true that we don't know why one form of exploitation will lead to a particular kind of delinquency and not another. In some cases, the connections seem direct and clear-cut, whereas in others they remain obscure. Unknown, too, is how prolonged the exploitation must be and how much of it is needed to incite an adolescent to delinquent acting-out. Such threshold values are probably a joint function of the child's personality and the quality of parental exploitation.

In short, a detailed understanding of any particular case of middle-class delinquency will have to involve a psychodynamic evaluation of the personalities of both parent and child. On the other hand (or so it seems to me), a psychodynamic evaluation of the parent-child interaction, although provid-

ing an explanation in a particular case, may well miss the common theme that seems to run through all cases of middle-class delinquency, namely, parental exploitation. Taken together, however, the concept of parental exploitation and psychodynamic evaluations may well provide a general, as well as a specific, explanation for middle-class delinquency.

The value of such a general explanation of delinquency as parental exploitation is shown in the way it helps to make plausible why certain familial conditions are regularly associated with delinquent behavior. Broken homes, for example, have routinely contributed more than their fair share to the delinquent population (4–7). It seems reasonable to assume that in broken homes one is more likely to find unmet parental needs than would be the case in intact families. Under these conditions, the temptation to put one's own needs ahead of those of the child and to use the child as an instrument in the satisfaction of those needs would probably be greatly enhanced. In short, the concept of parental exploitation might allow one to predict, or at least hypothesize, the kinds of family constellations that would be most likely to produce delinquent behavior.

Before closing, I want to take up one more point that has been raised by those who attribute middle-class delinquency to the antisocial impulses of parents that are vicariously satisfied through the child. It has already been noted that the vicarious satisfaction of parental needs is indeed one form of parental exploitation. Where I disagree with this position is in the implication that middle-class delinquency is antisocial, regardless of whether or not this is true of the parental need. If antisocial means the intent to harm or injure society in general, then I do not believe middle-class delinquency is antisocial. I do believe it is antifamilial. Looked at from the point of view of the adolescent, and not necessarily from the point of view of society, delinquent behavior may be the most psychologically adaptive action a young person can take in the face of parental exploitation. Delinquent behavior not only calls attention to his plight, but also may remove him from the home on temporary or permanent basis.

Although I have limited the application of the concept of exploitation to the question of middle-class delinquency, it is possible that all delinquency is, at least in part, a reaction to exploitation and that society, as well as parents, can be culpable in this regard.

## REFERENCES

1. Quay, H. C. (ed.): Juvenile Delinquency. Princeton, Van Nostrand, 1965.
2. Giffin, M. E., Johnson, A. M., and Litin, E. M.: American Journal of Orthopsychiatry, 24:668, 1954.
3. Johnson, A. M., and Burke, E. C.: Proceedings of the Staff Meetings of the Mayo Clinic, 30:557, 1955.
4. Burt, C.: The Young Delinquent. New York, Appleton, 1929.
5. Glueck, S., and Glueck, E. T.: Unraveling Juvenile Delinquency. New York, Commonwealth Fund, 1950.
6. Monahan, T. P.: Social Forces, 35:250, 1957.
7. Nye, F. I.: Family Relationships and Delinquent Behavior. New York, Wiley, 1958.

# Section III
# Psychotherapy

*Any study of abnormality would seem incomplete without some mention of the means by which pathological patterns may be altered. This is essentially the business of psychotherapy, a procedure having its beginnings in the work of Freud, but one which has come, over the years, to be viewed differently by different theorists. Such diversity has probably stemmed from experiences with varying types of patients and the continued growth of our understanding about the forces that shape the individual's behavior. This section samples a number of diverse approaches to psychotherapy, ranging from classical psychoanalytic thinking to current developments in behavior modification and existential therapy. A controversy about the effectiveness of therapy and an interesting recent research paper also are presented.*

# Chapter 7

# Approaches and Research
# in Psychotherapy

*This chapter includes many different approaches to psychotherapy, both of a clinical and a research nature. This diversity should give some indication of the controversy and current state of flux which typifies current developments in this area.*

## Robert P. Knight

## A Critique of the Present Status
## of the Psychotherapies

*Dr. Knight presents a summary of a wide variety of approaches to psychotherapy. Most of these approaches have in common the fact that basically they are varieties of some form of psychoanalysis. When Knight refers to dynamic psychology, he is describing classical Freudian theory, and he sees good therapy as essentially developing from a Freudian framework. A number of radically different frameworks will be presented in later papers. Dr. Knight was a medically trained psychoanalyst, and it is interesting to note that he implies that the analyst must initially be a psychiatrist, and does not give very much attention to lay, or nonmedically trained, analysts. However, in describing the personal qualities that he feels are necessary for an analyst, he clearly argues that psychiatry is different from other medical specialties such as surgery, and describes characteristics such as personal integrity which clearly are not restricted to physicians.*

Before one can write a meaningful critical evaluation of the psychotherapies of today, he must attempt to define the types of treatment methods which are commonly assumed to be distinguishable varieties of psychotherapy. This is no easy task, for there exists no such generally accepted classi-fied listing of the psychotherapies. A motley array of adjectives is found to designate brands of psychotherapy which are supposedly different from each other but which actually overlap each other in manifold ways. It will be a necessary preliminary task for us to review the terms commonly used in

*Reprinted from the* Bulletin of the New York Academy of Medicine, *25(1949), 100–114, with the permission of The New York Academy of Medicine and Mrs. Adele B. Knight.*

psychiatric literature and in ordinary professional parlance to designate various types of psychotherapy.

In a survey of usages which probably falls short of being exhaustive, I have noted that the type of psychotherapy may be characterized from any one of a number of frames of reference:

1. With regard to the preponderant attitude taken or influence attempted by the therapist; e.g., suggestion, persuasion, exhortation, intimidation, counselling, interpretation, re-education, retraining, etc.

2. With regard to the general aim of the therapy; e.g., supportive, suppressive, expressive, cathartic, ventilative, etc.

3. With regard to the supposed "depth" of the therapy—superficial psychotherapy and deep psychotherapy.

4. With regard to the duration—brief psychotherapy and prolonged psychotherapy.

5. With regard to its supposed relationship to Freudian psychoanalysis, as, for example, orthodox, standard, classical, or regular psychoanalysis, modified psychoanalysis, wild analysis, direct psychoanalysis, psychoanalytic psychotherapy, psychoanalytically oriented psychotherapy, psychodynamic psychotherapy, psychotherapy using the dynamic approach, and psychotherapy based on psychoanalytic principles.

6. With regard to the ex-Freudian dissident who started a new school of psychotherapy. Thus we have Adler's individual psychology with its Adlerian "analysis," Jung's analytical psychology with its Jungian "analysis," the Rankian analysis, the Stekelian analysis, and the Horney modifications.

7. With regard to whether patients are treated singly or in groups—individual psychotherapy and group psychotherapy.

8. With regard to whether the psychotherapy is "directive" or "non-directive," an issue emphasized strongly by the Rogers group of psychologists.

9. With regard to the adjunctive technique which is coupled with psychotherapy; e.g., narcotherapy (narcoanalysis, narcosynthesis), and hypnotherapy (hypnoanalysis), the first using drugs and the second hypnosis for technical reasons to be discussed later.

It is not surprising that both physicians and the lay public regard this welter of terminology as something less than scientific, and that patients seeking help for emotional distress are often confused as to where to find that help and as to what type of psychotherapy to trust. In defense of the present confusion one can remind himself that although psychotherapy is said to be the oldest form of medical treatment, it is also one of the very latest to achieve a scientific, rational basis, i.e., to rest on a basic science of dynamic psychology. Because of its partial derivation from many unscientific and extra-scientific sources—primitive magical practices of tribal medicine men, religious rites, parental exhortations and commands, mysticism, commonsense advice and intuitive insights of friends, and downright quackery, to mention but a few—psychotherapy has among its practitioners today not only many lay fakirs but also a good many physicians whose training in dynamic psychology is grossly inadequate. Also, even among the best trained psychiatrists there exist some honest differences of opinion regarding principles and techniques of psychotherapy. However, research and experimentation continue to expand, and slowly the phenomena of artful and intuitive psychotherapeutic influences are translated into scientific principles and techniques.

It is impossible to overstate the importance of dynamic psychology as a basic science on which all competent psychotherapy must rest. Without an underlying structure of psychodynamics and psychopathology, in which the psychotherapist must be well trained, all psychotherapy is at best empirical, at the worst the blind leading the blind. No valid critique of the psychotherapies is possible except in relation to the penetrating understanding of human personality and behavior provided by dynamic psychology, the chief contributions to which have been made by psychoanalysis.

It seems necessary, therefore, to review for an essentially nonpsychiatric medical audience the theoretical essentials in modern dynamic psychology. The cornerstone of dynamic psychology is the concept of repression. As the psychic structure of the human personality develops in infancy and childhood, the primitive erotic and aggressive impulses come to be opposed by counter-impulses deriving from the child's training and adaptive experiences. The chief counter-impulse is repression, which banishes from consciousness—but not from continued active existence in the unconscious— those impulses, some native and some stimulated by specific experiences, which the child discovers are condemned and forbidden expression by its upbringers. Both the strength of the alien impulses and the child's capacity to oppose them are partially determined by his native constitution, partly by the nature of his early experiences, and partly by the character and upbringing methods of those adults who rear him. Some condemned impulses are simply repressed, along with their associated fantasies and affects; others are modified in partial expression and partial repression assisted by other defense mechanisms. Topographically the unconscious is regarded as the repository of repressed impulses and forgotten memories, the preconscious as that part of the mind in which reside the rememberable but currently unattended-to memories, and the conscious mind as the aware, focussing, thinking portion of the psychic structure. Viewed dynamically, the primitive impulses arise out of biological and psychological drives identified collectively as the Id, while the opposing, defensive forces arise from Ego, or organized part of the personality, and the Super-ego—roughly the conscience. The sum total of these dynamic internal and external interactions, plus constitution and native intellectual endowment, equals the developing personality in all of its individual uniqueness. While the major battle between opposing internal forces appears to be settled at about age five or six, thus forming the basic personality structure, there is a continuous internal interaction and a constant external adaptive attempt throughout life, with special crises during adolescence and in reaction to the Protean forms that stressful life experiences can take. Also, each individual, however healthy his adaption appears to be, has his own particular psychological areas of vulnerability to stress, and he may be precipitated into clinical neurotic or psychotic illness by experiences whose qualitative or quantitative nature exceed his capacity to master them through healthy adaptive methods.

This highly condensed exposition of dynamic psychology with its emphasis on the uniqueness of the individual will, I hope, be sufficient to serve as a background for the following proposition, namely, that competent treatment of a patient by psychotherapeutic means requires of the psychotherapist:

1. That he be thoroughly grounded in the basic science of dynamic psychology.

2. That he be well trained in clinical methods of evaluating the individual patient, not only in terms of general comparison with others presenting similar clinical pictures, but also in terms of the uniquely individual forces and factors in each individual patient.

3. That he then utilize, from among the available psychotherapeutic approaches and techniques, those particular ones which, according to his best clinical judgment, are most appropriate in a given case.

4. A fourth prerequiste does not follow logically from the previous argument but is of an importance at least equal to the other three, namely, that the psychotherapist be a person of integrity, objectivity, and sincere interest in people, and that he be relatively free from personal conflicts, anxieties, biases, emotional blind spots, rigidities of manner, and settled convictions as to how people should properly behave.

This last prerequisite for psychotherapeutic work requires some amplification. Unlike the situation in other fields of medical therapy, the man well grounded in the basic science underlying his therapy, well trained in diagnostic methods, and possessing technical competence to use the indicated therapy may still, in psychotherapy, be a poor practioner if he is personally anxious, rigid, or full of moral convictions. Other therapies in medicine can be competently performed, with good results on patients, without these personal qualities, largely because a great deal of medical and surgical treatment consists of doing something *to* the patient. To be sure the personal qualities in a physician which cause his patients to love and trust him are exactly the

ones which make him a real physician rather than a mechanical artisan; but far greater emotional demands are made on the psychotherapist. The nature of the subject material in psychotherapy, the intense personal give and take in the patient-therapist relationship, the enormously increased possibilities of anti-therapeutic personal involvement, the self knowledge in the therapist required both to understand his patients and to steer a sound therapeutic course with them, all require of the psychotherapist certain personal qualities not essential to other medical specialists. It is not particularly difficult for physicians to acquire protective attitudes of detachment in respect to those bodily elements and products—blood, pus, urine, diseased tissue, mucus, feces, guts—which so upset the squeamish layman, and this detachment serves the physician in good stead as he works coolly and efficiently at his therapeutic task. But this sort of detachment in a psychotherapist is not only no protection against the psychological products of his patients, it actually hampers and distorts his therapeutic work and, if extreme, even disqualifies him from undertaking to deal with psychopathology and psychotherapy. The counterphobic attitude may be sufficient for competent work in physiology, pathology, and surgery; it is a poor and brittle defense for work in psychiatry and psychotherapy.

Such personal considerations with regard to the psychotherapist raise important questions regarding selection of candidates for psychiatric training, and regarding the importance of personal psychoanalysis as a part of psychoanalytic and psychiatric training. Certainly every psychiatrist who wishes to do psychoanalytic therapy should have full psychoanalytic training, including, of course, the personal analysis. It might also be said that every psychiatrist who expects to practice major psychotherapy of any kind should have full psychoanalytic training, just as every physician who plans to do major surgery should have full surgical training.

I have so far attempted to show that the terminology designating supposed varieties of psychotherapy is very confusing because of the many frames of reference in which identifying adjectives were applied, and to indicate that a critique of these psychotherapies is not possible until a valid frame of reference is established. I then tried to show that familiarity with the basic science of dynamic psychology, and the clinical techniques derived from it is necessary to provide a valid frame of reference for a critique. This led to the collateral but vital point of the psychotherapist's personal suitability. It is necessary to establish one more phase of this frame of reference. This has to do with the nature and vicissitudes of the patient-physician relationship in psychotherapy.

Most physicians are not much concerned about the attitudes, emotions, and fantasies their patients have about them as long as the patients are cooperative, don't go to other physicians, and pay their bills for professional services. Occasionally physicians are startled to encounter outbursts of unprovoked hostility or professions of love or jealousy, or suspicion from their patients. I suppose the usual result is that the patient is then discharged by that physician in the event the physician cannot "talk him out of his nonsense." Many psychiatrists of the past (and some in the present) have been more concerned about emotional reactions of patients to them, but have thought of them in terms of "good rapport" or the lack of it, without paying much attention to the exact nature

of these reactions, whether friendly or hostile. Sigmund Freud, picking up a cue noted but abandoned by Josef Breuer, had the genius to follow through to a penetrating study of patients' emotional attitudes toward their doctors and to bring this group of phenomena into both the theoretical framework of dynamic psychology and the clinical framework of psychotherapy. He saw that whereas the various emotional reactions of the individual patient appeared at first to be irrational and unprovoked, actually these attitudes could be understood the same as other psychological phenomena in the patient could be understood, such as recovered memories, dreams, fantasies, and so on, and could, instead of being emotionally reacted to by the therapist, provide him with material for fresh insights into his patient. Freud called these reactions "transference" because of his understanding of them as emotions originally felt toward other significant persons in the patient's past experience, and now transferred to the doctor. He discovered that their nature could be interpreted to the patient, and that such interpretations, when correctly timed and accurately expressed, had significant therapeutic effect on the patient. Thus the theoretical understanding and clinical use of transference phenomena became one of the significant contributions of psychoanalysis to the field of psychiatry, and, indeed, to the practice of medicine in general, for transference reactions by patients are by no means limited to those being treated psychotherapeutically.

Freud also had the objectivity to observe and analyze his own reactions to patients, and concluded that all psychotherapists would have their own particular tendencies to react inappropriately (that is, inappropriately from the standpoint of correct therapeutic technique) to the material, or behavior, or persons of their patients. He called such reactions and reaction tendencies "counter-transference," and bade all analysts to be acutely observant of themselves in this regard so that they might analyze and dissipate these counter-transference reactions without letting themselves be unwittingly influenced by them to the detriment of their therapeutic efforts. Again, such counter-transference reactions are not confined to psychiatrists, psychoanalysts, or psychotherapists, but are present in all physicians toward their patients, albeit with considerably less significance, for the most part, in therapy other than psychotherapy. Once more, then, we see the importance for the psychotherapist of those personal qualities of integrity, objectivity, sincerity, and relative freedom from emotional blind spots.

I have now used almost half of my time to develop the background frame of reference in which any psychotherapy may properly be critically evaluated. The following elements have been emphasized:

1. The theoretical understanding of human personality provided by dynamic psychology.

2. The clinical evaluation of each individual patient—the nature and intensity of his internal and external conflicts, the genetic history of those conflicts, his particular defenses against anxiety, his strengths as shown by past adaptations and achievements, his vulnerabilities and weaknesses as shown by the extent of his decompensation, his way of relating initially to the therapist, his intelligence and its possible impairments, the intactness of his concept formation, his loyalty to reality, his capacity for introspection and self-confrontation, and so on.

3. The utilization of psychothera-

peutic techniques based on sufficient knowledge of dynamic psychology and applied appropriately to the individual case in the light of the clinical evaluation.

4. The personal qualifications and suitability of the psychotherapist, and, we may now add, his capacity to recognize and deal with transference manifestations in his patients and counter-transference tendencies in himself.

If these four criteria provide a valid frame of reference in which to evaluate psychotherapy, it is readily seen that those psychotherapists who have a fixed system of treatment for all patients who come to them are practicing poor psychotherapy. This is true whether it refers to those therapists who treat all patients with such banal exhortations as "Buck up," "Go home and forget it," "Stop worrying about that," "Pull yourself together," "Don't cross bridges until you come to them," and so on; to therapists who treat all patients by assigning reading for subsequent interview discussions in prepared booklets on how to live; to psychoanalysts who put all patients on the couch and tell them to free-associate; or to therapists who keep the syringe loaded with sodium pentothal for each patient, or who routinely start their hypnotic maneuvers promptly. One may give insulin to every diabetic, or operate every acute appendix, with, of course, some judgment as to dosage, timing, and collateral measures, but psychotherapy is, or should be, a highly individual matter for each patient. Far too often in current practice the type of psychotherapy used with the patient is determined solely by the limited training and ability of the psychotherapist rather than by either the type of illness the patient has or the type of patient that has the illness.

Of the various possible ways of classifying psychotherapeutic attempts, most psychiatrists would agree that two large groups could be identified—those which aim primarily at support of the patient, with suppression of his symptoms and his erupting psychological material, and those which aim primarily at expression. It is actually more appropriate to speak of a group of techniques utilized to accomplish suppression or expression than to speak of sub-groups of psychotherapies under each major heading. Suppressive or supportive psychotherapy, also called superficial psychotherapy, utilizes such devices as inspiration, reassurance, suggestion, persuasion, counselling, re-education, and the like and avoids investigative and exploratory measures. Such measures may be indicated, even though the psychotherapist is well trained and experienced in expressive techniques, where the clinical evaluation of the patient leads to the conclusion that he is too fragile psychologically to be tampered with, or too inflexible to be capable of real personality alteration, or too defensive to be able to achieve insight. Certain recovering schizophrenics or agitated depressions or children might illustrate the fragility; rigid character disorders, certain manics and hypomanics, and elderly patients might illustrate the inflexibility; and some paranoid states might illustrate the defensiveness. The decision to use suppressive measures is made actually because of contraindications to using exploratory devices. One can say, then, that supportive or suppressive psychotherapy, with its variety of techniques and devices for accomplishing support and suppression, is a valid psychotherapy provided it is applied on the basis of sound indications and not indiscriminately to all or most patients simply because the particular psychotherapist does not know how to do anything else with the patient, and provided the

psychotherapist realizes that transference and counter-transference manifestations can and do occur, and need to be handled, even in such superficial psychotherapy. Supportive psychotherapy may be brief or prolonged, as indicated, and may be carried out with individuals or with groups.

It is in the group of psychotherapies intended to be expressive that one encounters the various schools of thought, the adjunctive devices, the more frequent conflicts in theory, and the more significant question of personal suitability of the therapist. Expressive psychotherapies utilize such devices as exploratory probing through questioning, free-association, abreaction, confession, relating of dreams, catharsis, interpretation and the like, all with the purpose of uncovering and ventilating preconscious and unconscious pathogenic psychological material. Elements of support, reassurance, suggestion, advice, and direction are not necessarily excluded, and may, in fact, be consciously utilized. Expressive psychotherapy may be brief and intensive or prolonged, depending on the aims of the therapist and the response of the patient. Expressive psychotherapy is major psychotherapy and should not be undertaken without thorough grounding in dynamic psychology, adequate experience in clinical evaluation, practice under supervision, and personal suitability. Lacking this background, the psychotherapist is extremely likely to get into difficulties. He introduces topics for the patient to discuss without being aware that they are irrelevant to the matters pressing for expression within the patient, or that the patient cannot tackle a given topic until certain defenses are first pointed out and removed. He gives long and sententious theoretical explanations which he regards as interpretations, but which are either then learned as intellectual defenses by the patient or their content ignored while the patient basks in this verbal bath at the hands of the therapist. He permits himself unwittingly to be drawn into an active role as an ally in the patient's external interpersonal struggles, while remaining oblivious to the provocative shenanigans of the patient which keep these struggles going on. He pounces on dreams or slips of the tongue with ready and pat interpretations which miss the point. He focusses his attention on symptoms, and tries to treat them by interpretation, or special investigatory questioning. He becomes embroiled in transference-counter-transference jams and does not know how to extricate himself except by discontinuing the interviews for a while. I cite these common errors as illustrations of what may happen if the inadequately trained psychotherapist undertakes expressive psychotherapy. Needless to say such mishandling complicates the patient's illness exceedingly and renders more difficult the task of the inevitable subsequent psychotherapist.

Competent expressive psychotherapy may have goals which vary considerably. In cases where there has been an acute onset of neurotic symptoms in reaction to a discoverable precipitating event, and the patient's history shows a comparatively healthy course, the therapy may properly consist of thorough ventilation of the reaction to the upsetting event, with the therapist pointing out connections, relationships, and hidden motivations in the limited life area of the setting prior to the event, of the event itself, and of the patient's immediate and later reactions to the event. In skillful hands this is a most rewarding type of expressive psychotherapy. Recovery may be achieved in a very few interviews and the patient is restored to his previous good functioning with insights he would not otherwise have achieved. In such instances there is no therapeutic aim of exhaustive investigation, recovery of infantile memories, or altered ego structure. In other cases which may at first seem similar, the early clinical evaluation uncovers more neurotic difficulties than were at first apparent, and it becomes clear that the patient's adjustment prior to the precipitating event was a precarious one at best. The therapeutic aim may now change to one of more thoroughgoing alteration of the neurotic personality structure, and the expressive techniques lead into psychoanalysis. If the psychotherapist is competent to conduct psychoanalysis as well as the shorter expressive therapies with limited aim, he will have so handled the early therapy that the analytic techniques are a logical continuation of his early therapeutic work. If he is not so trained, he should at this point refer the patient to a suitable analyst.

Freudian psychoanalysis—and psychoanalysis actually implies "Freudian" —is a major, time-consuming, and therefore expensive, type of psychotherapy. It is by no means a panacea, and its most competent practitioners would readily concede that as a method of therapy it has limited application in the vast field of human psychological distress. (As a dynamic psychology and as a method of investigation it is, of course, invaluable, and possesses almost unlimited applicability.) Its limitations as a method of therapy do not depend merely on such factors as its duration (twelve to eighteen months as a minimum; four to five years as a maximum), its cost to the patient, and the availability of analysts (approximately 500 in the United States, with one-fourth of these in New York City). There is also a considerable list of special indications and contraindications, as, for example:

1. The patient should be of at least bright normal intelligence on the Bellevue-Wechsler scale (115 to 120 IQ).

2. The suitable age range for adults is about 20 to 50, with certain exceptions to be made at either end of this range.

3. There must be some capacity for introspection, and some awareness of nuances of feeling in himself and in others.

4. There must be sufficient motivation in terms of initial distress and strong desire to change.

5. The patient must possess sufficient intactness of personality so that this intact portion may become allied with the analyst in the analytic work.

6. In general, patients with unalterable physical handicaps are not suitable subjects for psychoanalysis.

7. The general field for psychoanalytic therapy includes the psychoneuroses, character disorders, some of the perversions, neurotic depressions, anxiety states, and some of the psychoses. Patients in the midst of acute external turmoil should not begin psychoanalysis as such until their life situations are more stable.

With all of its limitations, however, psychoanalytic therapy is, in well-trained hands, a highly effective procedure for achieving in patients a profound alteration in their neurotic personality structure and developing otherwise latent potentialities for achievement and responsible living.

The Freudian school of psychoanalysis is the main stream of the psychoanalytic movement. There have, in the past, been several split-offs from the main stream which resulted in transient and minor developments of non-Freudian schools. The school of the late Alfred Adler took one aspect of psychoanalysis, namely, the methods of the ego in dealing with external forces,

and attempted to develop it into a system called individual psychology. The central theme of this psychology was that of inferiority feelings and the drive for power. This psychology and system of therapy died out with its leader. Carl Jung, also an early pupil and associate of Freud, split with him and developed a school of "analytical psychology" which emphasized symbolism and religious beliefs and which explained mental disorders, especially those of middle life and after, in terms of regressions to a collective unconscious, or racial heritage. His school still persists but his incorporation of Nazi racial ideology into his psychological theories has caused him to be severely criticized. The late Otto Rank, also an early pupil of Freud's, developed a system of therapy which emphasized the transference and the uncovering and working through of birth anxiety in a three months' period of treatment. There were many short Rankian analyses in the 1920's, but this system is now also extinct. The late Wilhelm Stekel, a remarkably intuitive man and a prolific writer, attracted a few followers to his technique of rapid and early deep interpretations of symbolic and unconscious meanings. His influence has now become almost nil. Karen Horney, originally a Freudian with many fine contributions to the literature, has led a movement in the last decade to eliminate a number of the fundamental concepts of psychoanalysis and to focus attention on current cultural conflicts as the main source of personality disorders. She rejects the libido theory, the significance of early psychosexual development, and in general takes a stand against genetic psychology in favor of culturalism.

There are other deviations from orthodox psychoanalytic techniques which are not represented by their practitioners nor regarded by others as separate dissident schools of psycho-analysis, but which are modifications of technique to meet the therapeutic problems in patients who are too ill to cooperate in the usual analytic procedure. These modifications are used chiefly with psychotics and involve approaches by the analyst which actively cultivate a treatment relationship, communication with the sick patient being established on whatever level is possible in the individual case. The success of such attempts depends on the resourcefulness of the analyst in coping with the patient's inaccessibility and his capacity for empathy and intuition in understanding what is communicated by the patient's verbalizations, behavior, and attitudes. Long periods of careful therapeutic work are required but the results are often very rewarding. As the patient improves the treatment may merge into a more regular psychoanalytic procedure.

A special type of analytic psychotherapy developed by Rosen, for which the designation "direct psychoanalysis" has been made, deserves some comment. Rosen has reported a striking series of recoveries of severe and chronic schizophrenias. His method consists of repeated, prolonged sessions with the patient in which deep interpretative activity is carried out fearlessly and relentlessly. Interpretations are based on psychoanalytic theory, and sometimes on insights provided by other schizophrenics. The usual cautions and tentative approaches which have characterized others' work with psychotics are abandoned, and direct, deep interpretations are made promptly when the therapist believes he understands. The therapist also, when necessary to make contact, takes the roles of powerful figures in the patient's delusions and shouts denials, reassurances, and interpretations. Remarkable results are reported, and this work is now undergoing study under research conditions. It promises much but is at present difficult to evaluate.

The school of Adolf Meyer, identified as psychobiology, emphasized the sound concept of all-embracing study of man in his totality. He developed a new system of nomenclature which did not achieve significant acceptance, and termed his treatment "distributive analysis and synthesis." This psychotherapy aimed at exhaustive collecting of data regarding the patient's life, past and present, utilized diagrams to depict life influences, and assigned to the therapist the role of educator and explainer of the experiences and reactions in the patient's life. This procedure may be criticized as being far too theoretical and intellectual to influence many patients, and as having almost totally ignored the elements of transference and counter-transference in the relationship between therapist and patient. As a school of psychotherapy, it probably has a diminishing number of adherents.

All of the major psychotherapies—i.e., those which aim at significant alterations in personality structure rather than at symptomatic relief—have encountered the phenomenon discovered by Freud and termed by him "resistance." This refers to those partly conscious and partly unconscious tendencies in patients to resist self-knowledge and change, as manifested in their inability to remember the past or to capture for therapeutic use the current unconscious content. Resistance produces a marked slowing down of progress, often approaching stalemate, while symptoms continue unaltered. Technical problems of resistance are among the most difficult to solve, and the long duration of major psychotherapy is attributable chiefly to this phenomenon.

In order to shorten the duration of therapy many attempts have been made to circumvent resistence. Chief among these techniques have been the use of hypnosis and certain sedative drugs. Under hypnosis or narcosis (also mild elation or light anesthesia) some patients are able to gain access to and to verbalize with affect otherwise unconscious memories, and to profit from the ventilation and abreaction and the interpretations of the therapist associated with this therapeutic experience. During World War II there was widespread use of intravenous sodium amytal and sodium pentothal as well as of hypnosis to produce dissolution of the resistance barriers against recalling overwhelming traumatic experiences. There often resulted clear recall and reliving of the traumatic experiences, with associated assimilation of the overstressful event and great diminution or relief of the symptoms. It was found that early treatment was essential, delay resulting in the building of stronger barriers against recall and fixing of the symptomatology, to which was then added the exploitation of secondary gains. These psychotherapeutic procedures had enormous significance in military psychiatry, but, as sole treatment attempts, have proved to be disappointing in civilian psychiatry except with early traumatic neuroses in civil life. Such techniques of reducing resistance through hypnosis or narcosis do not constitute separate systems of psychotherapy, so that it is incorrect to speak of narcoanalysis, narcosynthesis, hypnotherapy, and hypnoanalysis as psychotherapies. They are adjuvant techniques to be used as a preliminary step in overcoming an initial impasse, or as devices to be introduced during psychotherapy when strong resistance blocks further progress.

The attempts to shorten the duration of psychotherapy have led to other techniques which make use of psychoanalytic principles but which try to achieve faster results especially through manipulation of the transference, role-taking by the therapist in order to provide a corrective emotional experience, and interruptions of treatment to avoid a difficult dependent transference. Alexander, French, and others who report this work maintain that their therapy is entitled to be called psychoanalysis—psychoanalysis with more flexible utilization of techniques. Many critics insist that the techniques as reported represent abandonment of fundamental analytic principles and that the goals of such therapy have become relief of symptoms and conventional social adaptation instead of the goals of structural personality alterations of psychoanalysis. Many other studies of short psychotherapy using psychoanalytic principles have been reported in the literature, and it seems well established that the whole field of psychotherapy has been greatly enriched by contributions from psychoanalysis.

In the last analysis there is only one psychotherapy, with many techniques. This one psychotherapy must rest on a basic science of dynamic psychology, and those techniques should be used which are clinically indicated for each individual patient—certain appropriate techniques for the initial stages and others later as the continuous clinical evaluation proceeds pari passu with therapy, and the goals and potentialities for the patient become more clearly delineated through his responses to therapy. And, finally, it is important to recognize that techniques as such are hardly separable from the individual who uses them. Psychotherapy is an enormously complex intercommunication and emotional interaction between two individuals, one of whom seeks help from the other. What is done and said by the one who tries to give help is inevitably his personal version of technique. Beyond all knowledge of dynamic psychology and training in techniques is his own individual personality, with its inevitable variables as to sex, physical appearance, depth of understanding, ability to communicate ideas, tone of voice, set of values, and all of the other highly individual elements which differentiate one therapist from another. The utmost impersonality and analytic incognito cannot exclude the effect of such individual elements. Hence we may say that in addition to a critique of psychotherapy one must also make a critique of the psychotherapist.

Albert Bandura

# Psychotherapy as a Learning Process

*A radically different approach to psychotherapy is embodied in a school known as behavior modification. This school seeks to apply scientifically established laws of learning in the psychotherapy session, so that attempts to modify the patient's behavior are based on principles of broad generality and sound evidence. In this paper, Bandura reviews a number of the principles that are utilized by behavior therapists. The counterconditioning approach is most closely identified with the work of Dr. Joseph Wolpe, and the technique of systematic desensitization is its leading application. Many of the other principles are outgrowths of the approach taken in the laboratory by Dr. B. F. Skinner, and are more closely related to operant conditioning than to classical conditioning.*

While it is customary to conceptualize psychotherapy as a learning process, few therapists accept the full implications of this position. Indeed, this is best illustrated by the writings of the learning theorists themselves. Most of our current methods of psychotherapy represent an accumulation of more or less uncontrolled clinical experiences and, in many instances, those who have written about psychotherapy in terms of learning theory have merely substituted a new language; the practice remains essentially unchanged (Dollard, Auld, & White, 1954; Dollard & Miller, 1950; Shoben, 1949).

If one seriously subscribes to the view that psychotherapy is a learning process, the methods of treatment should be derived from our knowledge of learning and motivation. Such an orientation is likely to yield new techniques of treatment which, in many respects, may differ markedly from the procedures currently in use.

Psychotherapy rests on a very simple but fundamental assumption, i.e., human behavior is modifiable through psychological procedures. When skeptics raise the question, "Does psychotherapy work?" they may be responding in part to the mysticism that has come to surround the term. Perhaps the more

*Reprinted from the* Psychological Bulletin, *58(1961), 143–159 with the permission of the American Psychological Association and Dr. Bandura. Copyright 1961 by the American Psychological Association.*

meaningful question, and one which avoids the surplus meaning associated with the term "psychotherapy," is as follows: Can human behavior be modified through psychological means and if so, what are the learning mechanisms that mediate behavior change?

In the sections that follow, some of these learning mechanisms will be discussed, and studies in which systematic attempts have been made to apply these principles of learning to the area of psychotherapy will be reviewed. Since learning theory itself is still somewhat incomplete, the list of psychological processes by which changes in behavior can occur should not be regarded as exhaustive, nor are they necessarily without overlap.

## COUNTERCONDITIONING

Of the various treatment methods derived from learning theory, those based on the principle of counterconditioning have been elaborated in greatest detail. Wolpe (1954, 1958, 1959) gives a thorough account of this method, and additional examples of cases treated in this manner are provided by Jones (1956), Lazarus and Rachman (1957), Meyer (1957), and Rachman (1959). Briefly, the principle involved is as follows: if strong responses which are incompatable with anxiety reactions can be made to occur in the presence of anxiety evoking cues, the incompatible responses will become attached to these cues and thereby weaken or eliminate the anxiety responses.

The first systematic psychotherapeutic application of this method was reported by Jones (1924b) in the treatment of Peter, a boy who showed severe phobic reactions to animals, fur objects, cotton, hair, and mechanical toys. Counterconditioning was achieved by feeding the child in the presence

of initially small but gradually increasing anxiety-arousing stimuli. A rabbit in a cage was placed in the room at some distance so as not to disturb the boy's eating. Each day the rabbit was brought nearer to the table and eventually removed from the cage. During the final stage of treatment, the rabbit was placed on the feeding table and even in Peter's lap. Tests of generalization revealed that the fear responses had been effectively eliminated, not only toward the rabbit, but toward the previously feared furry objects as well.

In this connection, it would be interesting to speculate on the diagnosis and treatment Peter would have received had he been seen by Melanie Klein (1949) rather than by Mary Cover Jones!

It is interesting to note that while both Shoben (1949) and Wolpe (1958) propose a therapy based on the principle of counterconditioning, their treatment methods are radically different. According to Shoben, the patient discusses and thinks about stimulus situations that are anxiety provoking in the context of an interpersonal situation which simultaneously elicits positive affective responses from the patient. The therapeutic process consists in connecting the anxiety provoking stimuli, which are symbolically reproduced, with the comfort reaction made to the therapeutic relationship.

Shoben's paper represents primarily a counterconditioning interpretation of the behavior changes brought about through conventional forms of psychotherapy since, apart from highlighting the role of positive emotional reactions in the treatment process, no new techniques deliberately designed to facilitate relearning through counterconditioning are proposed.

This is not the case with Wolpe, who has made a radical departure from tradition. In his treatment, which he calls reciprocal inhibition, Wolpe makes systematic use of three types of responses which are antagonistic to, and therefore inhibitory of, anxiety. These are: assertive or approach responses, sexual responses, and relaxation responses.

On the basis of historical information, interview data, and psychological test responses, the therapist constructs an anxiety hierarchy, a ranked list of stimuli to which the patient reacts with anxiety. In the case of desensitization based on relaxation, the patient is hypnotized and given relaxation suggestions. He is then asked to imagine a scene representing the weakest item on the anxiety hierarchy and, if the relaxation is unimpaired, this is followed by having the patient imagine the next item on the list, and so on. Thus, the anxiety cues are gradually increased from session to session until the last phobic stimulus can be presented without impairing the relaxed state. Through this procedure, relaxation responses eventually come to be attached to the anxiety evoking stimuli.

Wolpe reports remarkable therapeutic success with a wide range of neurotic reactions treated on this counterconditioning principle. He also contends that the favorable outcomes achieved by the more conventional psychotherapeutic methods may result from the reciprocal inhibition of anxiety by strong positive responses evoked in the patient-therapist relationship.

Although the counterconditioning method has been employed most extensively in eliminating anxiety-motivated avoidance reactions and inhibitions, it has been used with some success in reducing maladaptive approach responses as well. In the latter case, the goal object is repeatedly associated with some form of aversive stimulus.

Raymond (1956), for example, used nausea as the aversion experience in the treatment of a patient who presented a fetish for handbags and perambulators which brought him into frequent contact with the law in that he repeatedly smeared mucus on ladies' handbags and destroyed perambulators by running into them with his motorcycle. Though the patient had undergone psychoanalytic treatment, and was fully aware of the origin and the sexual significance of his behavior, nevertheless, the fetish persisted.

The treatment consisted of showing the patient a collection of handbags, perambulators, and colored illustrations just before the onset of nausea produced by injections of apomorphine. The conditioning was repeated every 2 hours day and night for 1 week plus additional sessions 8 days and 6 months later.

Raymond reports that, not only was the fetish successfully eliminated, but also the patient showed a vast improvement in his social (and legal) relationships, was promoted to a more responsible position in his work, and no longer required the fetish fantasies to enable him to have sexual intercourse.

Nauseant drugs, especially emetine, have also been utilized as the unconditioned stimulus in the aversion treatment of alcoholism (Thirmann, 1949; Thompson & Bielinski, 1953; Voegtlen, 1940; Wallace, 1949). Usually 8 to 10 treatments in which the sight, smell, and taste of alcohol is associated with the onset of nausea is sufficient to produce abstinence. Of 1,000 or more cases on whom adequate follow-up data are reported, approximately 60% of the patients have been totally abstinent following the treatment. Voegtlen (1940) suggests that a few preventive treatments given at an interval of about 6 months may further improve the results yielded by this method.

Despite these encouraging findings,

most psychotherapists are unlikely to be impressed since, in their opinion, the underlying causes for the alcoholism have in no way been modified by the conditioning procedure and, if anything, the mere removal of the alcoholism would tend to produce symptom substitution or other adverse effects. A full discussion of this issue will be presented later. In this particular context, however, several aspects of the Thompson and Bielinski (1953) data are worth noting. Among the alcoholic patients whom they treated, six "suffered from mental disorders not due to alcohol or associated deficiency states." It was planned, by the authors, to follow up the aversion treatment with psychotherapy for the underlying psychosis. This, however, proved unnecessary since all but one of the patients, a case of chronic mental deterioration, showed marked improvement and were in a state of remission.

Max (1935) employed a strong electric shock as the aversive stimulus in treating a patient who tended to display homosexual behavior following exposure to a fetishistic stimulus. Both the fetish and the homosexual behavior were removed through a series of avoidance conditioning sessions in which the patient was administered shock in the presence of the fetishistic object.

Wolpe (1958) has also reported favorable results with a similar procedure in the treatment of obsessions.

A further variation of the counterconditioning procedure has been developed by Mowrer and Mowrer (1938) for use with enuretic patients. The device consists of a wired bed pad which sets off a loud buzzer and awakens the child as soon as micturition begins. Bladder tension thus becomes a cue for waking up which, in turn, is followed by sphincter contraction. Once bladder pressure becomes a stimulus for the more remote sphincter control response, the child is able to remain dry for relatively long periods of time without wakening.

Mowrer and Mowrer (1938) report complete success with 30 children treated by this method; similarly, Davidson and Douglass (1950) achieved highly successful results with 20 chronic enuretic children (15 cured, 5 markedly improved); of 5 cases treated by Morgan and Witmer (1939), 4 of the children not only gained full sphincter control, but also made a significant improvement in their social behavior. The one child with whom the conditioning approach had failed was later found to have bladder difficulties which required medical attention.

Some additional evidence for the efficacy of this method is provided by Martin and Kubly (1955) who obtained follow-up information from 118 of 220 parents who had treated their children at home with this type of conditioning apparatus. In 74% of the cases, according to the parents' replies, the treatment was successful.

## EXTINCTION

"When a learned response is repeated without reinforcement the strength of the tendency to perform that response undergoes a progressive decrease" (Dollard & Miller, 1950). Extinction involves the development of inhibitory potential which is composed of two components. The evocation of any reaction generates reactive inhibition ($I_r$) which presumably dissipates with time. When reactive inhibition (fatigue, etc.) reaches a high point, the cessation of activity alleviates this negative motivational state and any stimuli associated with the cessation of the response become conditioned inhibitors ($_sI_r$).

One factor that has been shown to influence the rate of extinction of maladaptive and anxiety-motivated behavior is the interval between extinction trials. In general, there tends to be little diminution in the strength of fear-motivated behavior when extinction trials are widely distributed, whereas under massed trials, reactive inhibition builds up rapidly and consequently extinction is accelerated (Calvin, Clifford, Clifford, Bolden, & Harvey, 1956; Edmonson & Amsel, 1954).

An illustration of the application of this principle is provided by Yates (1958) in the treatment of tics. Yates demonstrated, in line with the findings from laboratory studies of extinction under massed and distributed practice, that massed sessions in which the patient performed tics voluntarily followed by prolonged rest to allow for the dissipation of reactive inhibition was the most effective procedure for extinguishing the tics.

It should be noted that the extinction procedure employed by Yates is very similar to Dunlap's method of negative practice, in which the subject reproduces the negative behaviors voluntarily without reinforcement (Dunlap, 1932; Lehner, 1954). This method has been applied most frequently, with varying degrees of success, to the treatment of speech disorders (Fishman, 1937; Meissner, 1946; Rutherford, 1940; Sheehan, 1951; Sheehan & Voas, 1957). If the effectiveness of this psychotherapeutic technique is due primarily to extinction, as suggested by Yates' study, the usual practice of terminating a treatment session before the subject becomes fatigued (Lehner, 1954), would have the effect of reducing the rate of extinction, and may in part account for the divergent results yielded by this method.

Additional examples of the therapeutic application of extinction procedures are provided by Jones (1955), and most recently by C. D. Williams (1959).

Most of the conventional forms of psychotherapy rely heavily on extinction effects although the therapist may not label these as such. For example, many therapists consider *permissiveness* to be a necessary condition of therapeutic change (Alexander, 1956; Dollard & Miller, 1950; Rogers, 1951). It is expected that when a patient expresses thoughts or feelings that provoke anxiety or guilt and the therapist does not disapprove, criticize, or withdraw interest, the fear or guilt will be gradually weakened or extinguished. The extinction effects are believed to generalize to thoughts concerning related topics that were originally inhibited, and to verbal and physical forms of behavior as well (Dollard & Miller, 1950).

Some evidence for the relationship between permissiveness and the extinction of anxiety is provided in two studies recently reported by Dittes (1957a, 1957b). In one study (1957b) involving an analysis of patient-therapist interaction sequences, Dittes found that permissive responses on the part of the therapist were followed by a corresponding decrease in the patient's anxiety (as measured by the GSR) and the occurrence of avoidance behaviors. A sequential analysis of the therapeutic sessions (Dittes, 1957a), revealed that, at the onset of treatment, sex expressions were accompanied by strong anxiety reactions; under the cumulative effects of permissiveness, the anxiety gradually extinguished.

In contrast to counterconditioning, extinction is likely to be a less effective and a more time consuming method for eliminating maladaptive behavior (Jones, 1924a; Dollard & Miller, 1950); in the case of conventional interview therapy, the relatively long intervals between interview sessions, and the ritualistic adherence to the 50-minute hour may further reduce the occurrence of extinction effects.

## DISCRIMINATION LEARNING

Human functioning would be extremely difficult and inefficient if a person had to learn appropriate behavior for every specific situation he encountered. Fortunately, patterns of behavior learned in one situation will transfer or generalize to other similar situations. On the other hand, if a person overgeneralizes from one situation to another, or if the generalization is based on superficial or irrelevant cues, behavior becomes inappropriate and maladaptive.

In most theories of psychotherapy, therefore, discrimination learning, believed to be accomplished through the gaining of awareness or insight, receives emphasis (Dollard & Miller, 1950; Fenichel, 1941; Rogers, 1951; Sullivan, 1953). It is generally assumed that if a patient is aware of the cues producing his behavior, of the responses he is making, and of the reasons that he responds the way he does, his behavior will become more susceptible to verbally-mediated control. Voluntarily guided, discriminative behavior will replace the automatic, overgeneralized reactions.

While this view is widely accepted, as evidenced in the almost exclusive reliance on interview procedures and on interpretative or labeling techniques, a few therapists (Alexander & French, 1946) have questioned the importance attached to awareness in producing modifications in behavior. Whereas most psychoanalysts (Fenichel, 1941), as well as therapists representing other points of view (Fromm-Reichmann, 1950; Sullivan, 1953) consider insight

a precondition of behavior change, Alexander and French consider insight or awareness a result of change rather than its cause. That is, as the patient's anxieties are gradually reduced through the permissive conditions of treatment, formerly inhibited thoughts are gradually restored to awareness.

Evidence obtained through controlled laboratory studies concerning the value of awareness in increasing the precision of discrimination has so far been largely negative or at least equivocal (Adams, 1957; Erikson, 1958; Razran, 1949). A study by Lacy and Smith (1954), in which they found aware subjects generalized anxiety reactions less extensively than did subjects who were unaware of the conditioned stimulus provides evidence that awareness may aid discrimination. However, other aspects of their findings (e.g., the magnitude of the anxiety reactions to the generalization stimuli were greater than they were to the conditioned stimulus itself) indicate the need for replication.

If future research continues to demonstrate that awareness exerts little influence on the acquisition, generalization, and modification of behavior, such negative results would cast serious doubt on the value of currently popular psychotherapeutic procedures whose primary aim is the development of insight.

## METHODS OF REWARD

Most theories of psychotherapy are based on the assumption that the patient has a repertoire of previously learned positive habits available to him, but that these adaptive patterns are inhibited or blocked by competing responses motivated by anxiety or guilt. The goal of therapy, then, is to reduce the severity of the internal inhibitory controls, thus allowing the healthy patterns of behavior to emerge. Hence, the role of the therapist is to create permissive conditions under which the patient's "normal growth potentialities" are set free (Rogers, 1951). The fact that most of our theories of personality and therapeutic procedures have been developed primarily through work with oversocialized, neurotic patients may account in part for the prevalence of this view.

There is a large class of disorders (the undersocialized, antisocial personalities whose behavior reflects a failure of the socialization process) for whom this model of personality and accompanying techniques of treatment are quite inappropriate (Bandura & Walters, 1959; Schmideberg, 1959). Such antisocial personalities are likely to present *learning deficits*, consequently the goal of therapy is the acquisition of secondary motives and the development of internal restraint habits. That antisocial patients prove unresponsive to psychotherapeutic methods developed for the treatment of oversocialized neurotics has been demonstrated in a number of studies comparing patients who remain in treatment with those who terminate treatment prematurely (Rubenstein & Lorr, 1956). It is for this class of patients that the greatest departures from traditional treatment methods is needed.

While counterconditioning, extinction, and discrimination learning may be effective ways of removing neurotic inhibitions, these methods may be of relatively little value in developing new positive habits. Primary and secondary rewards in the form of the therapist's interest and approval may play an important, if not indispensable, role in the treatment process. Once the patient has learned to want the interest and approval of the therapist, these rewards may then be used to promote the ac-

quisition of new patterns of behavior. For certain classes of patients such as schizophrenics (Atkinson, 1957; Peters, 1953; Robinson, 1957) and delinquents (Cairns, 1959), who are either unresponsive to, or fearful of, social rewards, the therapist may have to rely initially on primary rewards in the treatment process.

An ingenious study by Peters and Jenkins (1954) illustrates the application of this principle in the treatment of schizophrenic patients. Chronic patients from closed wards were administered subshock injections of insulin designed to induce the hunger drive. The patients were then encouraged to solve a series of graded problem tasks with fudge as the reward. This program was followed 5 days a week for 3 months.

Initially the tasks involved simple mazes and obstruction problems in which the patients obtained the food reward directly upon successful completion of the problem. Tasks of gradually increasing difficulty were then administered involving multiple-choice learning and verbal-reasoning problems in which the experimenter personally mediated the primary rewards. After several weeks of such problem solving activities the insulin injections were discontinued and social rewards, which by this time had become more effective, were used in solving interpersonal problems that the patients were likely to encounter in their daily activities both inside and outside the hospital setting.

Comparison of the treated group with control groups, designed to isolate the effects of insulin and special attention, revealed that the patients in the reward group improved significantly in their social relationships in the hospital, whereas the patients in the control groups showed no such change.

King and Armitage (1958) report a

somewhat similar study in which severely withdrawn schizophrenic patients were treated with operant conditioning methods; candy and cigarettes served as the primary rewards for eliciting and maintaining increasingly complex forms of behavior, i.e., psychomotor, verbal, and interpersonal responses. Unlike the Peters and Jenkins study, no attempt was made to manipulate the level of primary motivation.

An interesting feature of the experimental design was the inclusion of a group of patients who were treated with conventional interview therapy, as well as a recreational therapy and a no-therapy control group. It was found that the operant group, in relation to similar patients in the three control groups, made significantly more clinical improvement.

Skinner (1956b) and Lindsley (1956) working with adult psychotics, and Ferster (1959) working with autistic children, have been successful in developing substantial amounts of reality-oriented behavior in their patients through the use of reward. So far their work has been concerned primarily with the effect of schedules of reinforcement on the rate of evocation of simple impersonal reactions. There is every indication, however, that by varying the contingency of the reward (e.g., the patient must respond in certain specified ways to the behavior of another individual in order to produce the reward) adaptive interpersonal behaviors can be developed as well (Azran & Lindsley, 1956).

The effectiveness of social reinforcers in modifying behavior has been demonstrated repeatedly in verbal conditioning experiments (Krasner, 1958; Salzinger, 1959). Encouraged by these findings, several therapists have begun to experiment with operant conditioning as a method of treatment in its own right (Tilton, 1956; Ullman, Krasner,

& Collins, in press; R. I. Williams, 1959); the operant conditioning studies cited earlier are also illustrative of this trend.

So far the study of generalization and permanence of behavior changes brought about through operant conditioning methods has received relatively little attention and the scanty data available are equivocal (Rogers, 1960; Sarason, 1957; Weide, 1959). The lack of consistency in results is hardly surprising considering that the experimental manipulations in many of the conditioning studies are barely sufficient to demonstrate conditioning effects, let alone generalization of changes to new situations. On the other hand, investigators who have conducted more intensive reinforcement sessions, in an effort to test the efficacy of operant conditioning methods as a therapeutic technique, have found significant changes in patients' interpersonal behavior in extra-experimental situations (King & Armitage, 1958; Peters & Jenkins, 1954; Ullman et al., in press). These findings are particularly noteworthy since the response classes involved are similar to those psychotherapists are primarily concerned in modifying through interview forms of treatment. If the favorable results yielded by these studies are replicated in future investigations, it is likely that the next few years will witness an increasing reliance on conditioning forms of psychotherapy, particularly in the treatment of psychotic patients.

At this point it might also be noted that, consistent with the results from verbal conditioning experiments, content analyses of psychotherapeutic interviews (Bandura, Lipsher, & Miller, 1960; Murray, 1956) suggest that many of the changes observed in psychotherapy, at least insofar as the patients' verbal behavior is concerned, can be accounted for in terms of the therapists' direct, although usually unwitting, reward and punishment of the patients' expressions.

## PUNISHMENT

While positive habits can be readily developed through reward, the elimination of socially disapproved habits, which becomes very much an issue in the treatment of antisocial personalities, poses a far more complex problem.

The elimination of socially disapproved behaviors can be accomplished in several ways. They may be consistently unrewarded and thus extinguished. However, antisocial behavior, particularly of an extreme form, cannot simply be ignored in the hope that it will gradually extinguish. Furthermore, since the successful execution of antisocial acts may bring substantial material rewards as well as the approval and admiration of associates, it is extremely unlikely that such behavior would ever extinguish.

Although punishment may lead to the rapid disappearance of socially disapproved behavior, its effects are far more complex (Estes, 1944; Solomon, Kamin, & Wynne, 1953). If a person is punished for some socially disapproved habit, the impulse to perform that act becomes, through its association with punishment, a stimulus for anxiety. This anxiety then motivates competing responses which, if sufficiently strong, prevent the occurrence of, or inhibit, the disapproved behavior. Inhibited responses may not, however, thereby lose their strength, and may reappear in situations where the threat of punishment is weaker. Punishment may, in fact, prevent the extinction of a habit; if a habit is completely inhibited, it cannot occur and therefore cannot go unrewarded.

Several other factors point to the futility of punishment as a means of correcting many antisocial patterns. The threat of punishment is very likely to elicit conformity; indeed, the patient may obligingly do whatever he is told to do in order to avoid immediate difficulties. This does not mean, however, that he has acquired a set of sanctions that will be of service to him once he is outside the treatment situation. In fact, rather than leading to the development of internal controls, such methods are likely only to increase the patient's reliance on external restraints. Moreover, under these conditions, the majority of patients will develop the attitude that they will do only what they are told to do—and then often only half-heartedly—and that they will do as they please once they are free from the therapist's supervision (Bandura & Walters, 1959).

In addition, punishment may serve only to intensify hostility and other negative motivations and thus may further instigate the antisocial person to display the very behaviors that the punishment was intended to bring under control.

Mild aversive stimuli have been utilized, of course, in the treatment of voluntary patients who express a desire to rid themselves of specific debilitating conditions.

Liversedge and Sylvester (1955), for example, successfully treated seven cases of writer's cramp by means of a retraining procedure involving electric shock. In order to remove tremors, one component of the motor disorder, the patients were required to insert a stylus into a series of progressively smaller holes; each time the stylus made contact with the side of the hole the patients received a mild shock. The removal of the spasm component of the disorder was obtained in two ways. First, the patients traced various line patterns (similar to the movements required in writing) on a metal plate with a stylus, and any deviation from the path produced a shock. Following training on the apparatus, the subjects then wrote with an electrified pen which delivered a shock whenever excessive thumb pressure was applied.

Liversedge and Sylvester report that following the retraining the patients were able to resume work; a follow-up several months later indicated that the improvement was being maintained.

The aversive forms of therapy, described earlier in the section on counterconditioning procedures, also make use of mild punishment.

## SOCIAL IMITATION

Although a certain amount of learning takes place through direct training and reward, a good deal of a person's behavior repertoire may be acquired through imitation of what he observes in others. If this is the case, social imitation may serve as an effective vehicle for the transmission of prosocial behavior patterns in the treatment of antisocial patients.

Merely providing a model for imitation is not, however, sufficient. Even though the therapist exhibits the kinds of behaviors that he wants the patient to learn, this is likely to have little influence on him if he rejects the therapist as a model. Affectional nurturance is believed to be an important precondition for imitative learning to occur, in that affectional rewards increase the secondary reinforcing properties of the model, and thus predispose the imitator to pattern his behavior after the rewarding person (Mowrer, 1950; Sears, 1957; Whiting, 1954). Some positive evidence for the influence of social rewards on imitation is provided by Bandura and Huston (in press) in a recent study of identification as a process of incidental imitation.

In this investigation preschool children performed an orienting task but, unlike most incidental learning studies, the experimenter performed the diverting task as well, and the extent to which the subjects patterned their behavior after that of the experimenter-model was measured.

A two-choice discrimination problem similar to the one employed by Miller and Dollard (1941) in their experiments of social imitation was used as the diverting task. On each trial, one of two boxes was loaded with two rewards (small multicolor pictures of animals) and the object of the game was to guess which box contained the stickers. The experimenter-model (M) always had her turn first and in each instance chose the reward box. During M's trial, the subject remained at the starting point where he could observe the M's behavior. On each discrimination trial M exhibited certain verbal, motor, and aggressive patterns of behavior that were totally irrelevant to the task to which the subject's attention was directed. At the starting point, for example, M made a verbal response and then marched slowly toward the box containing the stickers, repeating, "March, march, march." On the lid of each box was a rubber doll which M knocked off aggressively when she reached the designated box. She then paused briefly, remarked, "Open the box," removed one sticker, and pasted it on a pastoral scene which hung on the wall immediately behind the boxes. The subject then took his turn and the number of M's behaviors performed by the subject was recorded.

A control group was included in order to, (a) provide a check on whether the subjects' performances reflected genuine imitative learning or merely the chance occurrence of behaviors high in the subjects' response hierarchies, and (b) to determine whether subjects would adopt certain aspects of M's behavior which involved considerable delay in reward. With the controls, therefore, M walked to the box, choosing a highly circuitous route along the sides of the experimental room; instead of aggressing toward the doll, she lifted it gently off the container.

The results of this study indicate that, insofar as preschool children are concerned, a good deal of incidental imitation of the behaviors displayed by an adult model does occur. Of the subjects in the experimental group, 88% adopted the M's aggressive behavior, 44% imitated the marching, and 28% reproduced M's verbalizations. In contrast, none of the control subjects behaved aggressively, marched, or verbalized, while 75% of the controls imitated the circuitous route to the containers.

In order to test the hypothesis that children who experience a rewarding relationship with an adult model adopt more of the model's behavior than do children who experience a relatively distant and cold relationship, half the subjects in the experiment were assigned to a nurturant condition; the other half of the subjects to a nonnurturant condition. During the nurturant sessions, which preceded the incidental learning, M played with subject, she responded readily to the subject's bids for attention, and in other ways fostered a consistently warm and rewarding interaction with the child. In contrast, during the nonnurturant sessions, the subject played alone while M busied herself with paperwork at a desk in the far corner of the room.

Consistent with the hypothesis, it was found that subjects who experienced the rewarding interaction with M adopted significantly more of M's behavior than did subjects who were in the nonnurturance condition.

A more crucial test of the transmission of behavior patterns through the process of social imitation involves the delayed generalization of imitative responses to new situations in which the model is absent. A study of this type just completed, provides strong evidence that observation of the cues produced by the behavior of others is an effective means of eliciting responses for which the original probability is very low (Bandura, Ross, & Ross, in press).

Empirical studies of the correlates of strong and weak identification with parents, lend additional support to the theory that rewards promote imitative learning. Boys whose fathers are highly rewarding and affectionate have been found to adopt the father-role in doll-play activities (Sears, 1953), to show father-son similarity in response to items on a personality questionnaire (Payne & Mussen, 1956), and to display masculine behaviors (Mussen & Distler, 1956, 1960) to a greater extent than boys whose fathers are relatively cold and nonrewarding.

The treatment of older unsocialized delinquents is a difficult task, since they are relatively self-sufficient and do not readily seek involvement with a therapist. In many cases, socialization can be accomplished only through residential care and treatment. In the treatment home, the therapist can personally administer many of the primary rewards and mediate between the boys' needs and gratifications. Through the repeated association with rewarding experiences for the boy, many of the therapist's attitudes and actions will acquire secondary reward value, and thus the patient will be motivated to reproduce these attitudes and actions in himself. Once these attitudes and values have been thus accepted, the boy's inhibition of antisocial tendencies will function independently of the therapist.

While treatment through social imitation has been suggested as a method for modifying antisocial patterns, it can be an effective procedure for the treatment of other forms of disorders as well. Jones (1924a), for example, found that the social example of children reacting normally to stimuli feared by another child was effective, in some instances, in eliminating such phobic reactions. In fact, next to counterconditioning, the method of social imitation proved to be most effective in eliminating inappropriate fears.

There is some suggestive evidence that by providing high prestige models and thus increasing the reinforcement value of the imitatee's behavior, the effectiveness of this method in promoting favorable adjustive patterns of behavior may be further increased (Jones, 1924a; Mausner, 1953, 1954; Miller & Dollard, 1941).

During the course of conventional psychotherapy, the patient is exposed to many incidental cues involving the therapist's values, attitudes, and patterns of behavior. They are incidental only because they are usually considered secondary or irrelevant to the task of resolving the patient's problems. Nevertheless, some of the changes observed in the patient's behavior may result, not so much from the intentional interaction between the patient and the therapist, but rather from active learning by the patient of the therapist's attitudes and values which the therapist never directly attempted to transmit. This is partially corroborated by Rosenthal (1955) who found that, in spite of the usual precautions taken by therapists to avoid imposing their values

on their clients, the patients who were judged as showing the greatest improvement changed their moral values (in the areas of sex, aggression, and authority) in the direction of the values of their therapists, whereas patients who were unimproved became less like the therapist in values.

## FACTORS IMPEDING INTEGRATION

In reviewing the literature on psychotherapy, it becomes clearly evident that learning theory and general psychology have exerted a remarkably minor influence on the practice of psychotherapy and, apart from the recent interest in Skinner's operant conditioning methods (Krasner, 1955; Skinner, 1953), most of the recent serious attempts to apply learning principles to clinical practice have been made by European psychotherapists (Jones, 1956; Lazarus & Rachman, 1957; Liversedge & Sylvester, 1955; Meyer, 1957; Rachman, 1959; Raymond, 1956; Wolpe, 1958; Yates, 1958). This isolation of the methods of treatment from our knowledge of learning and motivation will continue to exist for some time since there are several prevalent attitudes that impede adequate integration.

In the first place, the deliberate use of the principles of learning in the modification of human behavior implies, for most psychotherapists, manipulation and control of the patient, and control is seen by them as antihumanistic and, therefore, bad. Thus, advocates of a learning approach to psychotherapy are often charged with treating human beings as though they were rats or pigeons and of leading on the road to Orwell's *1984*.

This does not mean that psychotherapists do not influence and control their patients' behavior. On the contrary. In any interpersonal interaction, and psychotherapy is no exception, people influence and control one another (Frank, 1959; Skinner, 1956a). Although the patient's control of the therapist has not as yet been studied (such control is evident when patients subtly reward the therapist with interesting historical material and thereby avoid the discussion of their current interpersonal problems), there is considerable evidence that the therapist exercises personal control over his patients. A brief examination of interview protocols of patients treated by therapists representing differing theoretical orientations, clearly reveals that the patients have been thoroughly conditioned in their therapists' idiosyncratic languages. Client-centered patients, for example, tend to produce the client-centered terminology, theory, and goals, and their interview content shows little or no overlap with that of patients seen in psychoanalysis who, in turn, tend to speak the language of psychoanalytic theory (Heine, 1950). Even more direct evidence of the therapists' controlling influence is provided in studies of patient-therapist interactions (Bandura et al., 1960; Murray, 1956; Rogers, 1960). The results of these studies show that the therapist not only controls the patient by rewarding him with interest and approval when the patient behaves in a fashion the therapist desires, but that he also controls through punishment, in the form of mild disapproval and withdrawal of interest, when the patient behaves in ways that are threatening to the therapist or run counter to his goals.

One difficulty in understanding the changes that occur in the course of psychotherapy is that the independent variable, i.e., the therapist's behavior, is often vaguely or only partially defined. In an effort to minimize or to deny the therapist's directive influence on the patient, the therapist is typically depicted as a "catalyst" who, in some mysterious way, sets free positive adjustive patterns of behavior or similar outcomes usually described in very general and highly socially desirable terms.

It has been suggested, in the material presented in the preceding sections, that many of the changes that occur in psychotherapy derive from the unwitting application of well-known principles of learning. However, the occurrence of the necessary conditions for learning is more by accident than by intent and, perhaps, a more deliberate application of our knowledge of the learning process to psychotherapy would yield far more effective results.

The predominant approach in the development of psychotherapeutic procedures has been the "school" approach. A similar trend is noted in the treatment methods being derived from learning theory. Wolpe, for example, has selected the principle of counterconditioning and built a "school" of psychotherapy around it; Dollard and Miller have focused on extinction and discrimination learning; and the followers of Skinner rely almost entirely on methods of reward. This stress on a few learning principles at the expense of neglecting other relevant ones will serve only to limit the effectiveness of psychotherapy.

A second factor that may account for the discontinuity between general psychology and psychotherapeutic practice is that the model of personality to which most therapists subscribe is somewhat dissonant with the currently developing principles of behavior.

In their formulations of personality functioning, psychotherapists are inclined to appeal to a variety of inner explanatory processes. In contrast, learning theorists view the organism as a far more mechanistic and simpler system, and consequently their formulations tend to be expressed for the most part in terms of antecedent-consequent relationships without reference to inner states.

Symptoms are learned S-R connections; once they are extinguished or deconditioned treatment is complete. Such treatment is based exclusively on present factors; like Lewin's theory, this one is a-historical. Non-verbal methods are favored over verbal ones, although a minor place is reserved for verbal methods of extinction and reconditioning. Concern is with *function*, not with *content*. The main difference between the two theories arises over the question of "symptomatic" treatment. According to orthodox theory, this is useless unless the underlying complexes are attacked. According to the present theory, there is no evidence for these putative complexes, and symptomatic treatment is all that is required (Eysenck, 1957, pp. 267–268). (Quoted by permission of Frederick A. Praeger, Inc.)

Changes in behavior brought about through such methods as counterconditioning are apt to be viewed by the "dynamically-oriented" therapist, as being not only superficial, "symptomatic" treatment, in that the basic underlying instigators of the behavior remain unchanged, but also potentially dangerous, since the direct elimination of a symptom may precipitate more seriously disturbed behavior.

This expectation receives little support from the generally favorable outcomes reported in the studies reviewed in this paper. In most cases where follow-up data were available to assess the long-term effects of the therapy, the patients, many of whom had been treated by conventional methods with little benefit, had evidently become considerably more effective in their social, vocational, and psychosexual adjustment. On the whole the evidence, while open to error, suggests that no matter what the origin of the maladap-

tive behavior may be, a change in behavior brought about through learning procedures may be all that is necessary for the alleviation of most forms of emotional disorders.

As Mowrer (1950) very aptly points out, the "symptom-underlying cause" formulation may represent inappropriate medical analogizing. Whether or not a given behavior will be considered normal or a symptom of an underlying disturbance will depend on whether or not somebody objects to the behavior. For example, aggressiveness on the part of children may be encouraged and considered a sign of healthy development by the parents, while the same behavior is viewed by school authorities and society as a symptom of a personality disorder (Bandura & Walters, 1959). Furthermore, behavior considered to be normal at one stage in development may be regarded as a "symptom of a personality disturbance" at a later period. In this connection it is very appropriate to repeat Mowrer's (1950) query: "And when does persisting behavior of this kind suddenly cease to be normal and become a symptom" (p. 474).

Thus, while a high fever is generally considered a sign of an underlying disease process regardless of when or where it occurs, whether a specific behavior will be viewed as normal or as a symptom of an underlying pathology is not independent of who makes the judgement, the social context in which the behavior occurs, the age of the person, as well as many other factors.

Another important difference between physical pathology and behavior pathology usually overlooked is that, in the case of most behavior disorders, it is not the underlying motivations that need to be altered or removed, but rather the ways in which the patient has learned to gratify his needs (Rotter, 1954). Thus, for example, if a patient displays deviant sexual behavior, the goal is not the removal of the underlying causes, i.e., sexual motivation, but rather the substitution of more socially approved instrumental and goal responses.

It might also be mentioned in passing, that, in the currently popular forms of psychotherapy, the role assumed by the therapist may bring him a good many direct or fantasied personal gratifications. In the course of treatment the patient may express considerable affection and admiration for the therapist, he may assign the therapist an omniscient status, and the reconstruction of the patient's history may be an intellectually stimulating activity. On the other hand, the methods derived from learning theory place the therapist in a less glamorous role, and this in itself may create some reluctance on the part of psychotherapists to part with the procedures currently in use.

Which of the two conceptual theories of personality—the psychodynamic or the social learning theory—is the more useful in generating effective procedures for the modification of human

behavior remains to be demonstrated. While it is possible to present logical arguments and impressive clinical evidence for the efficiency of either approach, the best proving ground is the laboratory.

In evaluating psychotherapeutic methods, the common practice is to compare changes in a treated group with those of a nontreated control group. One drawback of this approach is that, while it answers the question as to whether or not a particular treatment is more effective than no intervention in producing changes along specific dimensions for certain classes of patients, it does not provide evidence concerning the relative effectiveness of alternative forms of psychotherapy.

It would be far more informative if, in future psychotherapy research, radically different forms of treatment were compared (King & Armitage, 1958; Rogers, 1959), since this approach would lead to a more rapid discarding of those of our cherished psychotherapeutic rituals that prove to be ineffective in, or even a handicap to, the successful treatment of emotional disorders.

# REFERENCES

ADAMS, J. K. Laboratory studies of behavior without awareness. *Psychol. Bull.*, 1957, 54, 393–405.

ALEXANDER, F. *Psychoanalysis and psychotherapy.* New York: Norton, 1956.

ALEXANDER, F., & FRENCH, M. T. *Psychoanalytic therapy.* New York: Ronald, 1946.

ATKINSON, RITA L. Paired-associate learning by schizophrenic and normal subjects under conditions of verbal reward and verbal punishment. Unpublished doctoral dissertation, Indiana University, 1957.

AZRAN, N. H., & LINDSLEY, O. R. The reinforcement of cooperation between children. *J. abnorm. soc. Psychol.*, 1956, 52, 100–102.

BANDURA, A., & HUSTON, ALETHA C. Identification as a process of incidental learning. *J. abnorm. soc. Psychol.*, in press.

BANDURA, A., LIPSHER, D. H., & MILLER, PAULA E. Psychotherapists' approach-avoidance reactions to patient's expressions of hostility. *J. consult. Psychol.*, 1960, 24, 1–8.

BANDURA, A., ROSS, DOROTHEA, & ROSS, SHEILA A. Transmission of aggression through imitation of aggressive models. *J. abnorm. soc. Psychol.*, in press.

BANDURA, A., & WALTERS, R. H. *Adolescent aggression.* New York: Ronald, 1959.

CAIRNS, R. B. The influence of dependency-anxiety on the effectiveness of social reininforcers. Unpublished doctoral dissertation, Stanford University, 1959.

CALVIN, A. D., CLIFFORD, L. T., CLIFFORD, B., BOLDEN, L., & HARVEY, J. Experimental validation of conditioned inhibition. *Psychol. Rep.*, 1956, 2, 51–56.

DAVIDSON, J. R., & DOUGLASS, E. Nocturnal enuresis: A special approach to treatment. *British med. J.*, 1950, 1, 1345–1347.

DITTES, J. E. Extinction during psychotherapy of GSR accompanying "embarrassing" statements. *J. abnorm. soc. Psychol.*, 1957, 54, 187–191. (a)

DITTES, J. E. Galvanic skin responses as a measure of patient's reaction to therapist's permissiveness. *J. abnorm. soc. Psychol.*, 1957, 55, 295–303. (b)

DOLLARD, J., AULD, F., & WHITE, A. M. Steps in psychotherapy. New York: Macmillan, 1954.

DOLLARD, J., & MILLER, N. E. *Personality and psychotherapy*. New York: McGraw-Hill, 1950.

DUNLAP, K. *Habits, their making and unmaking*. New York: Liveright, 1932.

EDMONDSON, B. W., & AMSEL, A. The effects of massing and distribution of extinction trials on the persistence of a fear-motivated instrumental response. *J. comp. physiol. Psychol.*, 1954, 47, 117–123.

ERICKSON, C. W. Unconscious processes. In M. R. Jones (Ed.), *Nebraska symposium on motivation*. Lincoln: Univer. Nebraska Press, 1958.

ESTES, W. K. An experimental study of punishment. *Psychol. Monogr.*, 1944, 57 (3, Whole No. 363).

EYSENCK, H. J. *The dynamics of anxiety and hysteria*. New York: Praeger, 1957.

FENICHEL, O. *Problems of psychoanalytic technique*. (Trans. by D. Brunswick) New York: Psychoanalytic Quarterly, 1941.

FERSTER, C. B. Development of normal behavioral processes in autistic children. *Res. relat. Child.*, 1959, No. 9, 30. (Abstract)

FISHMAN, H. C. A study of the efficiency of negative practice as a corrective for stammering. *J. speech Dis.*, 1937, 2, 67–72.

FRANK, J. D. The dynamics of the psychotherapeutic relationship. *Psychiatry*, 1959, 22, 17–39.

FROMM-REICHMANN, FRIEDA. *Principle of intensive psychotherapy*. Chicago: Univer. Chicago Press, 1950.

HEINE, R. W. An investigation of the relationship between change in personality from psychotherapy as reported by patients and the factors seen by patients as producing change. Unpublished doctoral dissertation, University of Chicago, 1950.

JONES, E. L. Exploration of experimental extinction and spontaneous recovery in stuttering. In W. Johnson (Ed.), *Stuttering in children and adults*. Minneapolis: Univer. Minnesota Press, 1955.

JONES, H. G. The application of conditioning and learning techniques to the treatment of a psychiatric patient. *J. abnorm. soc. Psychol.*, 1956, 52, 414–419.

JONES, MARY C. The elimination of childrens' fears. *J. exp. Psychol.*, 1924, 7, 382–390. (a)

JONES, MARY C. A laboratory study of fear: The case of Peter. *J. genet. Psychol.*, 1924, 31, 308–315. (b)

KING, G. F., & ARMITAGE, S. G. An operant-interpersonal therapeutical approach to schizophrenics of extreme pathology. *Amer. Psychologist*, 1958, 13, 358. (Abstract)

KLEIN, MELANIE. *The psycho-analysis of children*. London: Hogarth, 1949.

KRASNER, L. The use of generalized reinforcers in psychotherapy research. *Psychol. Rep.*, 1955, 1, 19–25.

KRASNER, L. Studies of the conditioning of verbal behavior. *Psychol. Bull.*, 1958, 55, 148–170.

LACEY, J. I., & SMITH, R. I. Conditioning and generalization of unconscious anxiety. *Science*, 1954, 120, 1–8.

LAZARUS, A. A., & RACHMAN, S. The use of systematic desentization in psychotherapy. *S. Afr. med. J.*, 1957, 32, 934–937.

LEHNER, G. F. J. Negative practice as a psychotherapeutic technique. *J. gen. Psychol.*, 1954, 51, 69–82.

LINDSLEY, O. R. Operant conditioning methods applied to research in chronic schizophrenia. *Psychiat. res. Rep.*, 1956, 5, 118–138.

LIVERSEDGE, L. A., & SYLVESTER, J. D. Conditioning techniques in the treatment of writer's cramp. *Lancet*, 1955, 1, 1147–1149.

MARTIN, B., & KUBLY, DELORES. Results of treatment of enuresis by a conditioned response method. *J. consult. Psychol.*, 1955, 19, 71–73.

MAUSNER, B. Studies in social interaction: III. The effect of variation in one partner's prestige on the interaction of observer pairs. *J. appl. Psychol.*, 1953, 37, 391–393.

MAUSNER, B. The effect of one partner's success in a relevant task on the interaction of observer pairs. *J. abnorm. soc. Psychol.*, 1954, 49, 557–560.

MAX, L. W. Breaking up a homosexual fixation by the conditioned reaction technique: A case study. *Psychol. Bull.*, 1935, 32, 734.

MEISSNER, J. H. The relationship between voluntary nonfluency and stuttering. *J. speech Dis.*, 1946, 11, 13–33.

MEYER, V. The treatment of two phobic patients on the basis of learning principles: Case report. *J. abnorm. soc. Psychol.*, 1957, 55, 261–266.

MILLER, N. E., & DOLLARD, J. *Social learning and imitation.* New Haven: Yale Univer. Press, 1941.

MORGAN, J. J. B., & WITMER, F. J. The treatment of enuresis by the conditioned reaction technique. *J. genet. Psychol.*, 1939, 55, 59–65.

MOWRER, O. H. *Learning theory and personality dynamics.* New York: Ronald, 1950.

MOWRER, O. H., & MOWRER, W. M. Enuresis—a method for its study and treatment. *Amer. J. Orthopsychiat.*, 1938, 8, 436–459.

MURRAY, E. J. The content-analysis method of studying psychotherapy. *Psychol. Monogr.*, 1956, 70(13, Whole No. 420).

MUSSEN, P., & DISTLER, L. M. Masculinity, idenitfication, and father-son relationships. *J. abnorm. soc. Psychol.*, 1959, 59, 350–356.

MUSSEN, P., & DISTLER, L. M. Child-rearing antecedents of masculine identification in kindergarten boys. *Child Develpm.*, 1960, 31, 89–100.

PAYNE, D. E., & MUSSEN, P. H. Parent-child relationships and father identification among adolescent boys. *J. abnorm. soc. Psychol.*, 1956, 52, 358–362.

PETERS, H. N. Multiple choice learning in the chronic schizophrenic. *J. clin. Psychol.*, 1953, 9, 328–333.

PETERS, H. N., & JENKINS, R. L. Improvement of chronic schizophrenic patients with guided problem-solving motivated by hunger. *Psychiat. Quart. Suppl.*, 1954, 28, 84–101.

RACHMAN, S. The treatment of anxiety and phobic reactions by systematic desensitization psychotherapy. *J. abnorm. soc. Psychol.*, 1959, 58, 259–263.

RAYMOND, M. S. Case of fetishism treated by aversion therapy. *Brit. med. J.*, 1956, 2, 854–857.

RAZRAN, G. Stimulus generalization of conditioned responses. *Psychol. Bull.*, 1949, 46, 337–365.

ROBINSON, NANCY M. Paired-associate learning by schizophrenic subjects under conditions of personal and impersonal reward and punishment. Unpublished doctoral dissertation, Stanford University, 1957.

ROGER, C. R. *Client-centered therapy.* Boston: Houghton Mifflin, 1951.

ROGERS, C. R. Group discussion: Problems of controls. In E. H. Rubinstein & M. B. Parloff (Eds.), *Research in psychotherapy.* Washington, D. C.: American Psychological Association, 1959.

ROGERS, J. M. Operant conditioning in a quasi-therapy setting. *J. abnorm. soc. Psychol.*, 1960, 60, 247–252.

ROSENTHAL, D. Changes in some moral values following psychotherapy. *J. consult. Psychol.*, 1955, 19, 431–436.

ROTTER, J. B. *Social learning and clinical psychology.* Englewood Cliffs, N. J.: Prentice-Hall, 1954.

RUBENSTEIN, E. A., & LORR, M. A comparison of terminators and remainers in outpatient psychotherapy. *J. clin. Psychol.*, 1956, 12, 345–349.

RUTHERFORD, B. R. The use of negative practice in speech therapy with children handicapped by cerebral palsy, athetoid type. *J. speech Dis.*, 1940, 5, 259–264.

SALZINGER, K. Experimental manipulation of verbal behavior: A review. *J. gen. Psychol.*, 1959, 61, 65–94.

SARASON, BARBARA R. The effects of verbally conditioned response classes on post-conditioning tasks. *Dissertation Abstr.*, 1957, 12, 679.

SCHMIDBERG, MELITTA. Psychotherapy of juvenile delinquents. *Int. ment. hlth. res. Newsltr.*, 1959, 1, 1–2.

SEARS, PAULINE S. Child-rearing factors related to playing of sex-typed roles. *Amer. Psychologist*, 1953, 8, 431. (Abstract)

SEARS, R. R. Identification as a form of behavioral development. In D. B. Harris (Ed.), *The concept of development: An issue in the study of human behavior.* Minneapolis: Univer. Minnesota Press, 1957.

SHEEHAN, J. G. The modification of stuttering through non-reinforcement. *J. abnorm. soc. Psychol.*, 1951, 46, 51–63.

SHEEHAN, J. G., & VOAS, R. B. Stuttering as conflict: I. Comparison of therapy techniques involving approach and avoidance. *J. speech Dis.*, 1957, 22, 714–723.

SHOBEN, E. J. Psychotherapy as a problem in learning theory. *Psychol. Bull.*, 1949, 46, 366–392.

SKINNER, B. F. *Science and human behavior.* New York: Macmillan, 1953.

SKINNER, B. F. Some issues concerning the control of human behavior. *Science*, 1956, 124, 1057–1066. (a)

SKINNER, B. F. What is psychotic behavior? In, *Theory and treatment of psychosis: Some newer aspects.* St. Louis: Washington Univer. Stud., 1956. (b)

SOLOMON, R. L., KAMIN, L. J., & WYNNE, L. C. Traumatic avoidance learning: The outcomes of several extinction procedures with dogs. *J. abnorm. soc. Psychol.*, 1953, 48, 291–302.

SULLIVAN, H. S. *The interpersonal theory of psychiatry.* New York: Norton, 1953.

THIRMANN, J. Conditioned-reflex treatment of alcoholism. *New Engl. J. Med.*, 1949, 241, 368–370, 406–410.

THOMPSON, G. N., & BIELINSKI, B. Improvement in psychosis following conditioned reflex treatment in alcoholism. *J. nerv. ment. Dis.*, 1953, 117, 537–543.

TILTON, J. R. The use of instrumental motor and verbal learning techniques in the treatment of chronic schizophrenics. Unpublished doctoral dissertation, Michigan State University, 1956.

ULLMAN, L. P., KRASNER, L., & COLLINS, BEVERLY J. Modification of behavior in group therapy associated with verbal conditioning. *J. abnorm. soc. Psychol.*, in press.

VOEGTLEN, W. L. The treatment of alcoholism by establishing a conditioned reflex. *Amer. J. med. Sci.*, 1940, 119, 802–810.

WALLACE, J. A. The treatment of alcoholics by the conditioned reflex method. *J. Tenn. Med. Ass.*, 1949, 42, 125–128.

WEIDE, T. N. Conditioning and generalization of the use of affect-relevant words. Unpublished doctoral dissertation, Stanford University, 1959.

WHITING, J. W. M. The research program of the Laboratory of Human Development: The development of self-control. Cambridge: Harvard University, 1954. (Mimeo)

WILLIAMS, C. D. The elimination of tantrum behaviors by extinction procedures. *J. abnorm. soc. Psychol.*, 1959, 59, 269.

WILLIAMS, R. I. Verbal conditioning in psychotherapy. *Amer. Psychologist*, 1959, 14, 388. (Abstract)

WOLPE, J. Reciprocal inhibition as the main basis of psychotherapeutic effects. *AMA Arch. Neurol. Psychiat.*, 1954, 72, 205–226.

WOLPE, J. *Psychotherapy by reciprocal inhibition.* Stanford: Stanford Univer. Press, 1958.

WOLPE, J. Psychotherapy based on the principle of reciprocal inhibition. In A. Burton (Ed.), *Case studies in counseling and psychotherapy.* Englewood Cliffs, N. J.: Prentice-Hall, 1959.

YATES, A. J. The application of learning theory to the treatment of tics. *J. abnorm. soc. Psychol.*, 1958, 56, 175–182.

Bernard Weitzman

# Behavior Therapy and Psychotherapy

The psychoanalytic approach to individual psychotherapy is the oldest and most traditional approach. The behavior modification approach is a very recent development in the field of individual psychotherapy. Many psychoanalysts criticize behavior therapists as cold, unfeeling, and machinelike people who ignore the richness of human personality and see only the superficial symptoms. In return, many behavior therapists criticize psychoanalysts as muddleheaded practitioners of an art rooted in fantasy. Such conflict typically produces more heat than light. In this paper, Weitzman looks at some of the convergences between the two approaches, and attempts to see how each approach can be better understood in view of the findings of the other. Particular attention is given to the problem of symptom substitution, a situation in which the relief of a symptom—without attention to a possible underlying cause—is postulated to result in the development of new symptoms. This is an area of particular conflict between the two approaches, since psychoanalysts believe strongly in underlying causes, while behavior therapists see symptoms as learned maladaptive habits. This selection is the first half of Dr. Weitzman's paper, with the remainder devoted to examination of further intersections of the two approaches, along with some illustrative case material. The reader who is interested in the omitted material should consult the original article.

A number of procedures which would, a decade ago, have claimed the status of "psychotherapies" (cf., e.g., Wolpe, 1958) have in the recent past characterized themselves as "behavior therapies." It is intended by its users that this nomenclature shall be pregnant with meaning (cf. Eysenck, 1960). Properly understood, it reflects the long-resisted penetration of clinical practice by that form of "scientism" which, earlier, had a hand in leading academic "psychologists" to their sea change into "behavioral scientists." While attempts to articulate the historical factors which underlie such transformations are always speculative, there seems little doubt that, in the case of clinical practice, the publication of Wolpe's psychotherapeutic manual is one causal nexus. The apparent effectiveness of the techniques devised by Wolpe, in particular the procedure called "systematic desensitization" (cf. Grossberg, 1964), has won him a following, and has invited the use of an argument of virtue by association in a bid to legitimize the host of procedures calling themselves "behavior therapies."

Many psychologists in clinical practice have found quite irresistible the promise of quick and effective results which Wolpe's procedure holds forth, despite a host of objections to it which arise from the various "dynamic" orientations. Others, feeling tempted, have resisted the demons of mechanization and dehumanization, and the

Abridged from the Psychological Review, 74(1967), 300–317 with the permission of the American Psychological Association and Dr. Weitzman. Copyright 1967 by the American Psychological Association.

danger of "loss of soul" which is understood to be implicit in the Weltanschauung of behaviorism. This resistance is buttressed by theoretical allegiances and made to seem necessary by a variety of therapeutic rubrics, for example, the expectation of symptom substitution, a problem which will be treated in some detail later.

The rejection, on grounds of principle, of behavior therapy by the clinical community, and the derogatory treatment of dynamic therapies by behavior therapists, have had the inevitable consequence of generating premature crystallizations of positions in both camps. The lines of battle have been most sharply and articulately drawn in the writings of Eysenck (1960), who asserts:

. . . behavior therapy is an alternative type of treatment to psychotherapy [ie., it is not ancillary], . . . it is a *superior* type of treatment, both from the point of view of theoretical background and practical effectiveness; . . . in so far as psychotherapy is at all effective, it is so in virtue of certain principles which can be *derived from learning theory* . . . psychotherapy itself, when shorn of its inessential and irrelevant parts, can usefully be considered as a minor part of behavior therapy [p. ix].

While the position taken by Eysenck is more extreme than other behavior therapists might prefer, its clarity makes it a useful target for analysis. Some comments on the contents of Eysenck's statement will clear the way for the major substance of this essay, that is, an examination of the grounds upon which clinicians have based their rejection of behavior therapy.

## THE THEORETICAL BACKGROUND OF BEHAVIOR THERAPY

The evidence of the practical effectiveness of behavior therapy, while not conclusive, is indeed impressive. However, if one notes (as Eysenck does) that the term "behavior therapy" refers to a large and diverse group of treatment methods, clarity requires that the question of effectiveness must be put to each method. If one extracts from the mass of data the results of systematic desensitization therapy, one is left with an impression which is rather different from that intended by Eysenck. The residue, that is, the evidence of the practical effectiveness of behavior therapies other than systematic desensitization, while interesting, would excite the enthusiasm of few clinicians (cf. Grossberg, 1964). As a first step then, the accuracy of Eysenck's statement might be increased by appropriately reading "systematic desensitization" where he has written "behavior therapy." This sharpening of focus permits a more cogent appraisal of the evidence, and a more lucid analysis of the problems.

An issue of considerable importance is raised by Eysenck's claim of theoretical superiority for behavior therapy. It has been pointed out, from both camps, that analytic theory requires that symptom substitution or recurrence must attend a symptomatic treatment which, by definition, does not affect the dynamic sources of the symptoms. The evidence is rather impressive that neither substitution nor recurrence typically follows treatment by systematic desensitization. When occasional recurrences are reported, they are described as being of low intensity and, apparently, never catastrophic. Wolpe and Eysenck have both explicitly contended that this evidence constitutes a decisive empirical argument against psychoanalysis. A detailed analysis of the theoretical grounds upon which this contention is based will be undertaken later in this discussion. At this point, however, it must be noted that a crucial logical alternative, that is, that systematic desensitization does, as a technique, in some way affect the total psychological matrix, has not been given due theoretical consideration by behavior therapists or by psychotherapists. Attempts have been made to demonstrate, *empirically*, the specificity of the effects of systematic desensitization, that is, to demonstrate that desensitization is confined, in the locus of its effects, to the undoing of specific conditioned associations. The evidence, however, is not altogether convincing and certainly not conclusive. As long as the issue is empirically open, the *logical* analysis must be allowed.

When this analysis is undertaken it appears that there are implications of the data for Eysenck's theoretical model which have not been examined, and which seem to indicate that the Eysenckian position is vulnerable to criticisms similar to those leveled at psychoanalysis. Eysenck (1957) views neuroticism as a genetically determined constitutional predisposition. That is, all else being equal, there is a genetic determination of the likelihood that one individual will develop neurotic symptoms more readily than will another individual. Obviously, behavior therapy, in removing symptoms, cannot be expected to alter this genetic base. Thus, the likelihood of developing symptoms, insofar as this is genetically given, will remain constant. It would seem reasonable to assume that, in statistical mass, the number of patients treated as neurotics in any therapeutic setting will contain a disproportionately large number of individuals high in genetically determined neuroticism. If this reasoning is correct, Eysenck's model would seem to predict a high incidence of new symptom formations in patients who have already been treated for neurotic symptoms. Indeed, if one takes seriously the reports of almost total absence of new symptoms in patients treated by systematic de-

sensitization, a problem of some difficulty arises for the Eysenckian model. On the one hand there are difficulties in attempting to solve the problem by entertaining the speculation that a lasting transformation of learning processes has been achieved by this technique if one is determined to deny that there are any nonspecific characterological consequences attending its application. (An analysis of some of the conceptual difficulties for S-R theories in ". . . explaining how *generality* of behavior results from specific learning experiences" has been presented by Breger and McGaugh, 1965, p. 348.) On the other hand, if it is granted that there are such nonspecific consequences, the genetic hypothesis must be formulated in a manner which makes such consequences intelligible. The alternatives for Eysenck would seem to entail a surrender, both of the current conception of genetically determined neuroticism and of the insistence upon the specificity of the effects of desensitization.

Eysenck's intention, however, is not to burden his own theory with the support of his claim to theoretical superiority for behavior therapy. Rather, the burden falls more broadly on something called "learning theory." An issue which exists for many clinicians seems to pivot about the intrinsic relation which is claimed to exist between behavior therapy and this "learning theory." The clinician is asked to agree that if he accepts the method as therapeutically valid and gives credence to the data which support assertions of its effectiveness, he must "buy" some "S-R" model of man. But what model of man is, in fact, required? A number of comments on this relationship may be helpful.

In the foreword to a volume reporting the outcome of a summer symposium on learning theory (Estes, Koch, MacCorquodale, Meehl, Mueller,

Schoenfeld, & Verplanck, 1954), the editor writes:

It might be supposed that there would crystallize out from such a critical and unbiased analysis of theories and the experimental evidence on which they rest, some one basic theory of the learning process which all reasonable persons could accept. If there were any such expectations among the members of the group, they were soon dissipated. Each theory appeared to exist within its own closed system and to defy direct comparison and the pooling of data. Concepts, techniques, apparatus, units of measurement, and definitions of terms were peculiar to a given theory and could not safely be lifted out of their own frame of reference. Each theory, then, had to be examined and analyzed separately for internal consistency and the degree to which it satisfied the logic of science [p. vii].

In the context of a discussion similar to the present one Breger and Mc-Gaugh (1965, p. 341) conclude that "The claim to scientific respectability by reference back to established laws of learning is . . . illusory." In light of these reports it seems somewhat misleading to speak as if there were a monolithic system properly called "learning theory." Indeed, Eysenck (1960) concedes this point. To the objection that "learning theorists are not always in agreement with each other," he answers:

. . . those points about which argument rages are usually of academic [theoretical] interest rather than of practical importance. Thus, reinforcement theorists and contiguity theorists have strong differences of view about the necessity of reinforcement during learning and different reinforcement theorists have different theories about the nature of reinforcement. Yet there would be general agreement in any particular case about the optimum methods of achieving a quick rate of conditioning . . . [p. 15].

In fact, only an eclectic learning theory which systematically avoids examination of the relations between its own assumptions—that is, a nontheoretical amalgamation of pragmatic principles—can hope to derive the effects of a behavioral setting as complex as the therapeutic interview. Whether or not the methodological consensus which Eysenck assumes really exists (the reader is referred once more to the quotation from Estes et al., 1954), the theoretical limitation which is acknowledged must be as constraining for those procedures called "behavior therapy" as for psychotherapy. That is, if there is no "learning theory" competent to handle the data of behavior therapy, there is no "learning theory" competent to handle the data of psychotherapy. If, then, one accepts the data of behavior therapy, one is faced, not with a set of necessary theoretical conclusions, but with a set of theoretical problems.

## THE METHOD OF SYSTEMATIC DESENSITIZATION: AN INQUIRY

Since the most impressive data have been produced by Wolpe's method, it will be worthwhile to turn now to a more detailed consideration of systematic desensitization, and the relation of its practical methodology to Wolpe's conception of it.

Wolpe (1962) has described the genesis of systematic desensitization in discussing his replication of Masserman's (1943) study. Masserman produced "neurotic" behavior in cats by directing blasts of air at the animals as they began to eat. Wolpe, in his replication, demonstrated that the confrontation of appetitive and avoidant drive states is not a necessary condition for eliciting this symptomatology; that is, he obtained apparently the same form of neurotic behavior by shocking cats in the absence of food. (It is worth noting, en passant, that Wolpe has claimed that this demonstration undermines the psychoanalytic theory of the relation of symptom and conflict. While his study does seem to provide evidence concerning necessary conditions, it is not relevant to the premise that drive conflict is a *sufficient* condition for symptom formation.)

Wolpe then "deconditioned" the fear reaction by a procedure in which a gradual, stepwise approach was made to the feared stimuli (the experimental cage and room), each step accompanied by feedings. Feedings, sometimes repeated at a given step, led to extinction of the fear response at that level of approach and permitted feeding to be initiated at the next step. The animals were, finally, free of any signs of neurotic behavior. This result was rationalized by the assumption that the eating response inhibits the occurrence of anxiety and leads to the extinction of the anxiety response to the stimuli which are present at a given step.

Wolpe reasoned that eating is only one of a variety of behaviors which may be used to inhibit anxiety. This thinking led to the application of the procedure to human subjects. Relaxation was substituted for eating as the anxiety-inhibiting response, and the resulting method was called "systematic desensitization."

A description of this method sounds strikingly like the method used by Wolpe to cure his cats: The human subject is trained, by a short form of the Jacobson (1938) method, to develop high-strength relaxation responses. He is then, while in a relaxed condition, presented, one at a time, with preselected stimuli, known to produce anxiety and arranged in a series of intensity or approach steps. When, after one or a number of presentations, a given step elicits no anxiety response, the next stimulus in the intensity hierarchy is presented, until the most intense stimulus produces no anxiety.

In this description, however, is hidden a form of analogy-making which gives comfort to the behavior therapist but which obscures differences of profound significance between the systematic desensitizations of cats and men. The reaction of the clinician, that "they are treating patients the way they treat cats," fails to penetrate the flaws of the analogy. (It is not entirely beside the point to note that this reaction implicitly grants the legitimacy of the behavioristic interpretation of cat behavior. The necessity of that interpretation is, of course, open to question.) It is crucial that the above, stylized description of systematic desensitization be concretized and given a more detailed procedural analysis.

The human subject is trained in voluntary relaxation. The training directs the subject to careful observation of certain internal states, to the discrimination of tensions in the major muscle groups of the body, and to the voluntary cessation of muscular responding. When this highly complex "response" has been acquired, a stimulus is presented. That is to say, the patient is directed by the therapist to *imagine a stimulus* which he has previously described to the therapist and which he has placed, for the use of the therapist, among other anxiety-producing stimuli in a given hierarchical position. The patient is, in fact, required to produce a vivid visualization of a scene. It is this visualization which is the "stimulus" bandied about in discussions of systematic desensitization. As Breger and McGaugh (1965, p. 340) have put it, ". . . the use of the terms stimulus and response are only remotely allegorical to the traditional use of these terms in psychology." The importance of this characterization of the stimulus is underlined by the fact that *inability to produce such visualizations is grounds for rejecting a patient for treatment by this method.* Having "presented a stimulus," the therapist lapses into silence for periods of up to 1 minute. *Any stimulus present in this situation is produced by the patient's internal processes.*

The therapeutic effect of systematic desensitization thus seems to be produced in periods of silence. That is, the therapist describes a scene which, presumably, sets a process in motion. So long as this process continues neither therapist nor patient speaks, and neither acts. There is, thus, for the content of the therapeutic process itself, no response of record. In other words, the question of what transpires during these silences is not, and has not been, asked. In reaction to the formulation of this question, and to frequent spontaneous reports from patients who were concerned that their inability to maintain static visualizations of the scene described by the therapist might hamper therapy, the author undertook regular inquiry into the contents of these silences. Six patients being treated by the method of systematic desensitization were interviewed. An interview was conducted at the end of each session of desensitization, providing a sample of approximately 200 interviews. Without exception, when closely questioned, patients reported a flow of visual imagery. The imitating scene, once visualized, shifted and changed its form. Moreover, these transformations took place continuously and, when the imagining was terminated by the therapist, had produced images which were quite removed in their content from the intended stimulus. These contents, and the transformations they exhibit, compel a characterization as a form of spontaneous and apparently autonomous fantasy familiar to many dy-

namically oriented therapists and, in fact, a therapeutic focus for those analysts who use Jung's (1959) method of active imagination. (While there is one report in the literature—Weinberg & Zaslove, 1963—of " 'involuntary' manipulations of the imaginal process," during treatment by systematic desensitization, the observed shifts in the intended stimulus are understood by the authors as a form of "resistance" to the treatment.)

What emerges from this inquiry is the information that the initiating scene presented by the therapist undergoes a series of transformations and elaborations which are under the control of the patient's internal, psychological processes. With this information in hand, it is not surprising, to a dynamically oriented therapist, to find that a wealth of dynamically rich and exciting material results from desensitizations obtained with Wolpe's method. For example, in one case, immediately upon conclusion of a densitization series dealing with the patient's fears about the eventual death of his mother, he spontaneously reported:

It was as if my feelings about my mother were transformed. Whenever I thought about her dying what I really felt was a fear of my being deserted by her. Now if I think of her dying I feel sorry for *her* [patient's emphasis]. For the first time I feel sorry for her instead of for myself.

Such a reminder of the fact that one is engaging processes of profound depth and complexity is hardly unique in the writer's experience. Opportunities for similar observations will probably present themselves to any behavior therapist who is willing to listen, and might be expected to serve as a caution against the simplistic view that only a stimulus-response connection is being affected by the therapy.

To note that the stimulus of record

in this procedure is a self-produced visualization, and then to observe that the period in which the therapeutic effect is produced is characterized by a flow of images and symbolic materials, stretches the analogy to Wolpe's procedure with the cats rather thin. The grounding of behavior therapy in the history of the past decade of experimental psychology, which behavior therapists hope has elevated them above the analytic schools and made a science of therapy, is placed in jeopardy by this finding. I am not aware of the existence, in the literature of experimental psychology generated by learning theories, of anything more than an unpaid promissory note in regard to conceptualizations of this form of cognitive activity.

When one notes, in addition, that in this procedure an internally produced, imagined representation of a stimulus has a reality, in terms of its observable and specifiable behavioral consequences, equal to what one might expect of an externally produced stimulus, it is clear that the current conceptual horizons of S-R learning theories have been passed. What in fact seems to be demanded by these data is a conceptualization geared to understanding man as a cognitive being.

In all fairness to behavior therapists it should be noted that Wolpe has offered demonstrations of effectiveness for other procedures, including in vivo presentations of actual stimuli, based on his general principle of reciprocal inhibition, and using responses other than relaxation for the inhibition of anxiety. In addition, other behavior therapies have used therapeutic analogues which are, at least without closer scrutiny, better approximations of laboratory procedures with animals. The present critique, however is, justified by the status of systematic desensitization therapy, and does not require modification if its applicability to behavior therapies is not universal. In other words, the writer is not willing to prejudge the question of whether a single set of processes is responsible for the successes reported by every therapeutic school.

## DEFENSE OF PSYCHOTHERAPY

Neither cognitive psychologists nor psychoanalysts have yet seized upon the data of systematic desensitization as providing an opportunity for theoretical growth. Nor have dynamically oriented therapists fulfilled their professional responsibility, which, or so it appears to me, requires the most careful investigation of a method which makes and supports claims to therapeutic efficacy. Here I am in full agreement with Eysenck (1960) when he says:

. . . I have noted with some surprise that many psychotherapists have refused to use such methods [behavior therapies] . . . on *a priori* grounds, claiming that such mechanical methods simply could not work, and disregarding the large body of evidence available . . . only actual use can show the value of one method of treatment as opposed to another [p. 14].

An attempt to weaken the claims of behavior therapists of the theoretical superiority of their position by a critical attack may be welcomed by analytically oriented psychologists but is not likely to prove constructive. It is, rather, necessary to turn attention to the attacks made upon psychotherapy and to seek out the legitimate sources of its defense. While this examination is cast in a theoretical context, it should be noted that there is also at issue, waiting offstage but providing a background of urgency, a question of therapeutic responsibility; that is, what degree of theoretical certainty justifies withholding an available therapeutic method from a client?

## The Therapy-Theory Distinction

There are two issues, typically confounded in the literature, which need to be separated before an intelligible analysis can proceed. It is claimed by behavior therapists that the clinical success of behavior therapy invalidate psychoanalysis. Statistics on rates of "cure" are adduced in support of the claim that behavior therapy is more effective than psychoanalysis. Whatever the persuasiveness of these statistics, final judgment is a complex matter. Definitions of therapeutic practice and diagnostic criteria remain inadequate. The uses of the word "cure" by behavior therapists and psychotherapists are often incommensurable. Regardless, however, of history's verdict on the value of psychoanalytic therapy as it is practiced today, the problem will remain that psychoanalysis as a theory requires evaluation by criteria different from those by which therapy is evaluated.

There appears in many places in the analytic literature the articulation of an awareness of Freud's intention to consider analytic theory and therapy as distinct endeavors. The metapsychology incorporates analytically derived data but goes, with full comprehension of this step, far beyond the data. On the other hand, the metapsychology requires, if it is to be properly implemented in practice, procedures which have not yet been invented. Thus Reich (1949) wrote:

All problems of techniques converge in the one basic question whether and how an unequivocal technique of analytic therapy can be derived from the therapy of the nueroses. . . . Ample experience[s] . . . have shown that we have hardly made a beginning at this task [p. 3].

A responsible critique of psychoanalysis by behavior therapists would need to make this distinction clear. The adequate response from psychoanalysts would also make this distinction. If behavior therapy is indeed the more effective instrumentality, this fact should instigate a reexamination of the untapped technical resources of analytic theory. One cannot expect progress to follow from defensive denials.

## The Problem of Symptom Substitution

On other fronts, genuinely theoretical attacks have been leveled at psychoanalysis. The most potent of these is the claim that, according to analytic theory, symptom substitution or recurrence *must* follow a course of treatment which removes a symptom by treating it directly, that is, without altering the underlying source of the symptom. In fact, analysts have tended to the belief that symptomatic treatment may be worse than no treatment at all, that is, that it may be dangerous. Both Eysenck and Wolpe have stated that psychoanalytic theory is decisively undermined by the failure of this prediction. The expectation of symptom substitution is a clinical prejudice of long standing, but the data seem to require a reevaluation.

Freud (1936) considered the possibility that a symptom may be a behaviorally fixed pattern which has inherited the total cathectic energy of the impulse which existed at its time of origin:

. . . of the repressed instinctual impulse itself we assumed that it persisted unchanged for an indefinite period in the unconscious. Now our interest shifts to the fate of the repressed, and we begin to feel that this persistence, unchanged and unchanging, is not a matter of course, is perhaps not even the rule. . . . Do there therefore still exist the old desires, of the earlier existence of which analysis informs us? The answer appears obvious and certain. The old repressed desires must still persist in the unconscious, since we find their lineal descendents, the symptoms, still alive. *But this answer is inadequate*; it does not make it possible to distinguish between the two possibilities that, on the one hand, *the old desire now operates only through its descendents*, the symptoms, *to which it has transformed all its cathectic energy*, or on *the other hand, that the desire itself persists in addition*. . . . There is much in the phenomena of both the morbid and the normal life of the psyche which seems to demand the raising of such questions. In my study of the breakdown of the Oedipus complex, *I became mindful of the distinction between mere repression and the true disappearance of an old desire or impulse* [p. 83; italics mine].

Successful symptomatic treatment may be taken as evidence for this second alternative, which might be extended and elaborated in ways entirely compatible with analytic theory.

On another level of analysis, Rapaport (1959) has noted that psychoanalysis is, essentially, a postdictive system. It can rationalize events after their occurrence, but cannot predict these events. This assertion is, in part, based upon Freud's conception of the energetic relations between the systems of the psychic economy. The originally unitary nature of the psychic structure is conceived as remaining, in certain essential characteristics, unalterable. Thus the energetics of those psychic systems which emerge in the course of the development of personality remain highly interactive. This interactivity makes it extraordinarily difficult to predict the consequences of alterations of energy distributions in one psychic system upon the other systems. Is it possible, then, to state what follows of theoretical necessity from the removal of a symptom? Such an alteration of experience and behavior is, after all, likely to involve a not inconsiderable redistribution of cathectic processes. From this vantage it would appear that predictions of symptom substitution follow from a clinical rubric, and not with strict necessity from the analytic theory of the neuroses.

These considerations can be carried still further. Another line of analysis arises from the consequences of the thesis that the ego depends, for its development, on the greater efficiency of the secondary, as compared to the primary, process. That is, because the operations of the secondary process lead to increasing mastery of the relation of the psychic structure to object reality, exercise of the secondary process results in the binding of libidinal energies to the service of the emerging ego. Among the services to which energy is bound is that termed "repression." If one now considers the consequences for the ego, in its relations with object reality, of the removal of a symptom, the strands of the analysis come together. The removal of a symptom typically involves an increased mastery of object relations; for example, in the case of the person who is freed to express love, or hostility, or the person who is able, for the first time in a decade, to climb a flight of stairs without trembling. Such increased mastery must lead to an increment in the bound energy available to ego functioning. Even if one must insist that the dynamic source of an original symptom formation remains unaffected by the removal of that symptom, the consideration that an increase in bound energy may well lead to an increase in the effectiveness of repressive cathexes should prohibit any *certain* prediction that symptom substitution must follow.

A final line of analysis of this problem is stimulated by a consideration of Freud's conception of symptoms in their relation to anxiety. It is useful to compare this conception with

Wolpe's behavioristic formulation. Wolpe conceives of anxiety as *the neurosis*. As such, it is simply an acquired, that is, learned, maladaptive response. In this formulation anxiety is not given a functional role in the psychic system. Freud, on the other hand, envisions symptoms, that is, maladaptive responses, as means used by the ego to protect itself from danger. Anxiety, in this context, serves as a signal to the ego that a dangerous instinctual demand is growing in strength. In response to this impending danger a symptomatic action is engaged which binds a portion of the energy available to the instinctual demand. This binding reduces the imperiousness of the instinctual demand and permits the ego to avoid engaging it. Thus conceived, the symptom is a behavior substituted for the behavior demanded by the instinctual arousal. It is a maladaptive substitute because the danger to the ego, which may, at the time of symptom formation, have been actual, no longer exists. The ego never discovers that the danger is past because every arousal of the instinct produces a signal of anxiety, which in turn produces a discharge of the instinctual energy through the substitutive action, that is, the symptom. Of immediate relevance to the problem in hand is that in order to bind, successfully, the energy of the instinct, the substitute formation must bear a certain meaningful relation to the original object of the instinct. That is, the symptom formation is governed by the same principles which govern every displacement from an original instinctual object. This is another way of saying that the symptom must contain, in some measure, a symbolically adequate representation of the original object. Thus, for example, an external, phobic stimulus must symbolically represent the meaning of the internal danger.

This analysis leads to another formulation of the belief that symptom substitution must follow symptom removal, but also contains a suggestion of the possible error of this belief. If a symptom is removed, it is argued, the instinctual demand is unaltered, but now the ego has been deprived of its safety valve, that is, of its means of binding the instinctual energy. Without a means of discharge available the urgency of the impulse will increase, anxiety signals will come more and more frequently, and in the end the ego will either be inundated or a new substitute formation, that is, a new symptom, will appear to bind the energy which is pressing forward.

Among the many assumptions, both explicit and implicit, in the above argument, the postulated relation between an instinctual demand and its object underpins both psychoanalytic method and theory. Every displacement of cathexis from an existing object is determined by, and participates in, a system of associative and symbolic meaningfulness. It is this fact which permits the reading of dynamic messages in the overt behaviors of people. It is this premise which permits psychoanalytic theory a solution of the problem of joining an apparently limitless field of variations in human behavior to a limited number of motivational sources. Thus, when a therapist confronts a symptom as a substitute formation he is, by definition, confronting the inner dynamic as well, albeit at a remove. Insight is, after all, conceived as the grasping of this relationship in a particular instance. To speak analytically of treating a symptom is theoretically inexact, unless one envisions the psychic equivalent of a scalpel which can enter a body of tissue, excise a desired portion, and leave lower tissue layers unaffected.

The treatment of a symptom by the

method of systematic desensitization has no sensible analogy to such an idealized surgical procedure. On the contrary, the entire ego system is engaged in an eidetic and introspective task. The patient confronts his fear and inhibits his flight reflex. His fear, then, decreases. This fact should not upset the analytic theorist. If, in treating a symptom, we are treating the symbolic carrier of a feared instinctual demand, it satisfies the "logic" of our understanding of unconscious processes to expect far-reaching effects. To the degree to which a substitute formation is an adequate binder of cathectic energy, we may expect that a reduction in the strength of the signal anxiety which sustains this formation will represent an increase in ego tolerance of the instinctual demand. Freedom from fear, theory leads us to expect, is characteristic of increased ego strength, and may signal the possibility of creating more adequate binding behaviors. Why then predict symptom substitution?

It would neither surprise nor distress the author if psychoanalytic theorists should find fault with the above arguments. If a critique leads to a more convincing and elegant penetration of the proper relationship between the data of behavior therapy and analytic theory, the intention of the present analysis will have been realized. What is of importance is that this relationship be examined. The considerations already outlined suggest the futility of the position taken by Wolpe and Eysenck. To maintain that the failure of symptom substitution to occur with any regularity following symptom removal by the interventions of behavioral therapists constitutes a decisive argument against the validity of psychoanalysis, is to seriously underestimate its theoretical resources. Similarly, the unexamined prediction that symptom substitution must occur, as the grounds for a refusal by clinicians to give the use of the technique of systematic desensitization due consideration, must be rejected.

## REFERENCES

ANDREWS, J. D. W. Psychotherapy of phobias. *Psychological Bulletin*, 1966, 66, 455–480.

BREGER, L., & McGAUGH, J. L. Critique and reformulation of "learning theory" approaches to psychotherapy and neurosis. *Psychological Bulletin*, 1965, 63, 338–358.

ESTES, W. K., KOCH, S., MacCORQUODALE, K., MEEHL, P. E., MUELLER, C. G., JR., SCHOENFELD, W. N., & VERPLANCK, W. S. *Modern learning theory*. New York: Appleton-Century-Crofts, 1954.

EYSENCK, H. J. *The dynamics of anxiety and hysteria*. New York: Praeger, 1957.

EYSENCK, H. J. (Ed.), *Behavior therapy and the neurosis*. New York: Pergamon Press, 1960.

FREUD, S. *The problem of anxiety*. New York: Norton, 1936.

GENDLIN, E. T. *Experiencing and the cre-ation of meaning*. New York: Free Press of Glencoe, 1962.

GROSSBERG, J. M. Behavior therapy: A review. *Psychological Bulletin*, 1964, 62, 73–88.

HILLMAN, J. *Emotion*. London: Routledge and Kegan Paul, 1960.

JACOBSON, E. *Progressive relaxation*. Chicago: University of Chicago Press, 1938.

JUNG, C. G. The spirit of psychology. In J. Campbell (Ed.), *Spirit and nature*. New York: Pantheon, 1954. Pp. 371–444.

JUNG, C. G. *The archetypes and the collective unconscious*. New York: Pantheon, 1959.

JUNG, C. G. *The psychogenesis of mental disease*. New York: Pantheon, 1960.

MASSERMAN, J. H. *Behavior and neurosis*. Chicago: University of Chicago Press, 1943.

RAPAPORT, D. The structure of psycho-analytic theory: A systematizing attempt. In S. Koch (Ed.), *Psychology: A study of a science*. Vol. 1. New York: Mc-Graw-Hill, 1959. Pp. 55–183.

REICH, W. *Character-analysis*. New York: Noonday, 1949.

SULLIVAN, H. S. *Conceptions of modern psychiatry*. New York: Norton, 1940.

WEINBERG, N. H., & ZASLOVE, M. "Resistance" to systematic desensitization of phobias. *Journal of Clinical Psychology*, 1963, **19**, 179–181.

WOLPE, J. *Psychotherapy by reciprocal inhibition*. Stanford: Stanford University Press, 1958.

WOLPE, J. The experimental foundations of some new psychotherapeutic methods. In A. J. Bachrach (Ed.), *Experimental foundations of clinical psychology*. New York: Basic Books, 1962. Pp. 554–575.

Thomas G. Stampfl
and Donald J. Levis

# Essentials of Implosive Therapy: A Learning-Theory-Based Psychodynamic Behavioral Therapy

*One feature of the behavior modification approach is that it has given rise to numerous and varied techniques of treatment. Investigators have devised many ingenious approaches, all of which, in theory, have in common their initial reliance on established principles of learning. A somewhat unusual development is the technique of implosive therapy, presented in this paper by Stampfl and Levis. They present the underlying laboratory evidence for their approach, and then go to outline the clinical technique that they have developed. The unusual feature of this technique is the conscious attempt on the part of the therapist to arouse anxiety in the patient. The anxiety is induced in measured doses, and the basic theory is that if the anxiety appears along with typical anxiety-arousing stimuli, but in the absence of any gain to the patient from the anxiety, eventually the stimuli will no longer arouse anxiety, and the patient will be able to respond to those stimuli in a more comfortable manner.*

Behavioral or learning-theory approaches to psychotherapy may be divided into several distinct orientations.[1] Differences among the various behavioral methods arrange themselves along both theoretical and applied lines of cleavage. For one group, the emphasis has been placed upon the establishment of empirically derived techniques, which are developed relatively inde-

*Reprinted from the* Journal of Abnormal Psychology, *72(1967), 496–503 with the permission of the American Psychological Association and Dr. Stampfl. Copyright 1967 by the American Psychological Association.*

[1] This paper is not intended as a complete presentation of the theoretical framework of implosive therapy. Unfortunately, the complexities of features involving both the learning model and certain subtleties associated with the therapeutic technique precluded a completely exhaustive treatment of these issues in the space limitations of this article.

pendently of any specific theoretical system (e.g., Ayllon, 1963; Krasner, 1958; Lindsley, 1956; Skinner, 1956). For another group (Dollard & Miller, 1950; Rotter, 1954; Shoben, 1949), the orientation has been predominantly theoretical. For this group, the emphasis has been upon reinterpreting conventional therapeutic strategies and goals from a learning-theory framework. Such fresh looks have generated a number of new hypotheses and concepts which illuminate the basic processes and principles essential for behavioral change. Still a third group is concerned not only with theoretical advances, but also with applying their learning-theory orientation directly to the development of new techniques and approaches (Salter, 1949; Wolpe, 1958; Yates, 1958). Although it is not the purpose of this paper to review the above orientations (for a detailed analysis see Bandura, 1961; Breger & McGaugh, 1965; Grossberg, 1964), such a review points to at least four distinct assets of learning-oriented approaches to the study of psychopathology: (a) It identifies psychotherapy with an objective, experimental discipline that provides a model susceptible to generating testable hypotheses; (b) it establishes a common language between the basic research and applied areas which should in turn enhance communication and the generation of new ideas; (c) it highlights the vast amounts of human and subhuman learning research which have frequently been overlooked by the clinician; (d) it provides a foundation for the development of new treatment techniques.

## Integration of Learning Principles with Psychopathology

The thrust of learning-oriented therapies, for reasons not entirely clear, has been biased heavily toward non-psychodynamic approaches to the problems of psychopathology. The writings of Salter, Wolpe, and advocates of the Skinnerian methods are almost completely antithetical to conventional psychodynamic approaches. The traditionally oriented practitioners may well be dismayed at the celerity and ease with which the standard dynamic approaches, born of decades of experience, are dispensed. Not fully appreciated and frequently overlooked by both the traditional and behavioral therapists, however, are the numerous analyses proposed by non-applied-learning theorists which are quite consistent with a more dynamic approach to treatment (Brown, 1961; Dollard & Miller, 1950; Holland & Skinner, 1961; Kimble, 1961; Mednick, 1958; Mowrer, 1953; Shoben, 1949). The main disadvantage associated with these analyses is that little effort was made to extend their treatment beyond the area of theory into the realm of practice (Bandura, 1961; Grossberg, 1964).

It is believed (and it is the main purpose of this paper to show) that a better integration between the principles and theory of learning, on the one hand, and traditional dynamic approaches to psychotherapy, on the other, can be effected. Implosive therapy (IT) is an approach which incorporates formulations inherent to dynamic systems of treatment retranslated and reapplied in terms of learning principles; dynamically oriented clinicians need not relinquish their fundamental conceptions of the human situation to use it. The IT technique not only provides a new theoretical orientation, but also alters and in some cases drastically modifies existing treatment procedures and suggests new lines of experimentation with animals. Utilization of principles derived from such research can be used advantageously in the development of new techniques for application to problems of human pathology.

## Laboratory Evidence

Two-factor theory (Mowrer, 1960) states that an organism can be made to respond emotionally to an originally "neutral" stimulus by pairing the "neutral" stimulus with a noxious stimulus. A typical procedure is simply to pair a tone with electric shock. Subsequently, the organism responds to the tone with objectively verifiable changes in his physiological state, such as changes in blood sugar, heart rate, and skin resistance. Descriptively, this state can be labeled as fear or anxiety, and the stimulus which produces the physiological state can be construed to function as a danger signal or warning stimulus. The fear or anxiety state functions as a motivator of behavior, and the reduction or elimination of the fear state serves as a reinforcer of behavior. If the tone is conditioned to produce fear, then any action taken which terminates the tone will be strengthened automatically. A danger signal paired with another neutral stimulus will transfer some of its fear-eliciting properties to the new neutral stimulus (higher-order conditioning). It is important, however, to note that the stimulus preceding noxious stimulation whether applied to subhuman or human fear conditioning ordinarily involves multiple-stimulus patterns sequentially organized in time. Thus, in a sense it is misleading to say that a single discrete stimulus elicits the fear reaction. (For a further discussion and elaboration of the role of contextual and sequential cues, see Levis, 1966; Stampfl, 1960.)

Many studies conducted in the laboratory indicate that Ss can learn a wide variety of responses in order to terminate feared stimuli. In addition, fear states can be developed in the organism leading to behavior which is labeled as neurotic, psychosomatic, or even psychotic (e.g., Brady, Porter, Conrad, & Mason, 1958; Liddell, 1965; Masserman & Pechtal, 1953; Wolpe, 1958). It seems reasonable to assume that many if not all of the anxiety states experienced in the human are a product of numerous conditioning experiences in the life of the individual which can be understood in terms of the conditioning model of the laboratory. Past specific experiences of punishment and pain confer strong anxiety reactions to initially neutral stimuli. These experiences are represented neurally and the neural engram (memory, image) may be considered as possessing the potential to function as a stimulus. The imagery, thoughts, or other stimuli correlated with the past experience of pain will be avoided, and whatever action or mechanism which prevents them from reoccurring will be learned and maintained on the basis of anxiety reduction. Ideational representation (level of awareness) of the dangerous associations need not be present to function as an elicitation of the anxiety state. Thus, a subliminal area of neural functioning is necessary to account for all of the phenomena associated with the defensive avoidance maneuvers of the individual. Any stimulus object or event in the external environment (e.g., a phobic object) or response-produced stimulation such as the impulse to act sexually or aggressively (or even the impulse to act morally) if associated on a stimulus continuum with the stimulus pattern originally paired with pain will tend to reactivate or reintegrate the anxiety-arousing associations or memories (originally neutral stimuli). The defensive maneuvers of the patient are then seen as a means of avoiding the dangerous associations. Such a viewpoint incorporates many dynamic notions such as placing repression and anxiety as central concepts in the explanation of psychopathology, and points in the direction psychotherapy might proceed.

The question which may then be raised is simply how best the therapist might proceed to divest the anxiety-eliciting stimuli of their potential. Fortunately, both laboratory methods of effective procedures of extinction and evidence which has accrued from the wealth of information available from psychodynamic practice indicate clearly one way in which therapeutic practice might be developed.

## Experimental Extinction

One of the more reliable formulations of laboratory research is the original principle of Pavlov that presentation of the conditioned stimulus (CS) without the unconditioned stimulus (UCS) will lead to the extinction of the learned response. An enormous amount of evidence is available which indicates that this principle is a valid one whether overt action or emotional states have been learned.

The knowledge that a CS followed by nonreinforcement leads to extinction of the emotional response has led various writers in the field of learning to describe models for psychotherapy which are based on this principle. Kimble (1961) said:

The analysis of maladjustment in terms of conflict, anxiety, and repression points the direction in which therapy might proceed. Its method might be to bring traumatic events to consciousness so that the fear they evoke might extinguish [p. 476].

Holland and Skinner (1961) devoted considerable space to the adoption of the same principle to account for traditional methods of psychotherapy—the therapist constitutes a nonpunishing audience so that emotional responses evoked in the patient extinguish by nonreinforcement. Solomon and Wynne (1954, p. 381) pointed out that the transference relationship developed in dynamic therapy duplicates parts of the CS patterns associated with original traumatic experiences to which the emotional responses are attached and thereby leads to extinction. Miller (1951) stated that: "Experimental extinction is more effective when the animal is in the original punished situation that evokes the most intense fear [p. 453]." Since the procedures employed in IT depend very heavily on this principle, it is interesting to observe that Solomon, Kamin, and Wynne (1953) have based their conservation of anxiety hypothesis on exactly the same principle:

. . . the best way to produce extinction of the emotional response would be to arrange the situation in such a way that an extremely intense emotional reaction takes place in the presence of the CS. This would be tantamount to a reinstatement of the original acquisition situation, and since the US is not presented a big decremental effect should occur [p. 299].

A number of experimental studies have corroborated this interpretation. Studies by Black (1958), Denny, Koons, and Mason (1959), Hunt, Jernberg, and Brady (1952), Knapp (1965), Weinberger (1965), and others indicated that extinction of a learned emotional response proceeds with greatest rapidity when the organism is exposed to stimulus conditions most closely approaching those which were originally associated with painful stimulation. A corollary to this principle is reflected in the experimental studies of Lowenfeld, Rubenfeld, and Guthrie (1956) and Wall and Guthrie (1959) which indicated that the more clearly an S perceives anxiety-eliciting stimuli when followed by nonreinforcement, the more rapid the extinction of the emotional response will be.

## THERAPY

The fundamental hypothesis is that a sufficient condition for the extinction of anxiety is to re-present, reinstate, or symbolically reproduce the stimuli (cues) to which the anxiety response has been conditioned, in the absence of primary reinforcement. In a controlled laboratory situation where naïve subhuman animals serve as $S$s, the above objective presents little challenge to $E$. In the case of a human patient, however, the contingencies of the conditioning history usually are unknown. The therapist, in his attempt to restructure the conditioning paradigms, is forced to rely mainly upon verbal reports. Considerable time is needed in treatment before sufficient information is available for the reconstruction of the important contingencies. Moreover, the accuracy of the reconstruction is questionable. Thus, at first glance, it would appear that the task of using an extinction procedure is infeasible for a short-term therapeutic approach.

Nevertheless, despite the apparent difficulty of determining the conditioning paradigms, most trained therapists, after only a few diagnostic interviews, usually find themselves speculating upon the etiology of the patient's present pathology; that is, a "good guess" about the significant personal, environmental, and dynamic interactions shaping the patient's behavior often can be made within a relatively short time. In many cases, as therapy progresses, these hypotheses are supported by the verbal report of the patient. Although these initial hypotheses are conceived only as approximations of the original conditioning paradigm, it is quite conceivable that they incorporate a number of the more significant CS components.

Unfortunately, these cues are not presented systematically by the therapist using conventional techniques until he believes the patient is ready to accept them in the form of an interpretation.

However, in the implosive procedure, the emphasis is not upon the acceptance of interpretations, but rather upon the extinction of anxiety-evoking conditioned stimuli (cues) which provide both motivational and reinforcing properties for perpetuating the patient's symptoms (avoidance responses). It would also follow from the learning model that it would be irrelevant whether or not the patient "understood" or "accepted" the significance of these cues. All that is necessary for effective treatment is to re-present these conditioned cues in the absence of primary reinforcement. Since the task of accurately establishing the original conditioning cues is difficult, the presentation of hypothesized cues serves as an excellent substitute. Complete accuracy is not essential since some effect, through the principle of generalization of extinction, would be expected when an approximation is presented. The more accurate the hypothesized cues and the more realistically they are presented, the greater the extinction effect would be.

The above analysis is essentially the strategy employed by implosive therapists. Hypotheses are developed about the important cues involved, and these are presented to the patient in the most vivid or realistic manner possible. Because many of the cues presented are believed originally to involve not only auditory but also visual and tactual modalities, an attempt to produce the cues in the patient's imagery, rather than a simple verbal reproduction, seems worthwhile.

The selection of hypotheses can be determined operationally by the therapist. If the cues selected elicit anxiety, the assumption is that the patient has been conditioned to them previously. The greater the degree of anxiety elicited, the greater the reason for continuing the presentations of anxiety-eliciting stimuli. To define the anxiety response, either psychophysiological techniques (e.g., GSR, heart rate) or behavioral observation (e.g., sweating, flushing of the face, increased motor behavior) can be used. In the majority of the cases, for clinical purposes, the latter method is both quite adequate and easily observable. Experience indicates that there is little difficulty in determining whether the patient is anxious. If the hypothesis presented is not confirmed by the patient's reactions, a new hypothesis is selected.

## PROCEDURE

Two or three standard clinical diagnostic interviews with the patient usually provide sufficient information to begin IT. A lengthy and detailed dynamic analysis of the patient's difficulties usually is not necessary, as additional information relating to the dynamic motivation of the patient emerges through the implosive process. As treatment progresses, further interviewing may prove beneficial. After a few sessions, patients frequently report recalling various memories which previously had evaded them. Following the initial interviews, the patient is instructed in the implosive procedure. He is asked to play act various scenes which will be presented to him by the therapist. Once the implosive procedure is begun, every effort is made to encourage the patient to "lose himself" in the part that he is playing and "live" the scenes with genuine emotion and affect. He is asked, much like an actor, to portray certain feelings and emotions and to experience them as an important part of the process. The patient is instructed to play the part of himself. Belief or acceptance, in a cognitive sense, of the themes introduced by the therapist is not requested, and little or no attempt is made to secure any admission from the patient that the cues or hypotheses actually

apply to him. This factor seems to be especially important in permitting, in a short time, the restatement of cues which are analogous to "depth" interpretations of dynamically oriented therapies.

The scenes which contain the hypothesized cues are described at first by the therapist. The more involved and dramatic the therapist becomes in describing the scenes, the more realistic the presentation, and the easier it is for the patient to participate. At each stage of the process an attempt is made by the therapist to attain a maximal level of anxiety evocation from the patient. When a high level of anxiety is achieved, the patient is held on this level until some sign of spontaneous reduction in the anxiety-inducing value of the cues appears (extinction). The process is repeated, and again, at the first sign of spontaneous reduction of fear, new variations are introduced to elicit an intense anxiety response. This procedure is continued until a significant diminution in anxiety has resulted. After a few repetitions of a particular scene, the patient is given an opportunity to act out the scene by himself. He is encouraged especially to verbalize his own role-playing behavior. Between sessions the patient is instructed to reenact in his imagination the scenes which were presented during the treatment session. This homework provides additional extinction trials. As therapy progresses he is given more instructions on how to handle fearful situations through use of the implosive process. It is hoped that at the termination of treatment the patient will be able to handle new anxiety-provoking situations without the therapist's help.

At no time throughout the procedure is the patient told or encouraged to suppress whatever symptoms he may have. The basic premise is that anxiety is a learned response to sets of cues based on previous trauma in the patient's life. If these cues elicit the anxiety response in the absence of primary reinforcement, the anxiety response will extinguish after repeated evocations. The assumption made here is that these cues essentially consist of avoided (repressed) aspects of the personality, and that by approximating the past dangerous situations and associations without primary reinforcement extinction may be achieved.

## Avoidance Serial Cue Hierarchy

The cues selected for reproduction are derived both from an analysis of the patient's present behavior and from dynamic areas thought relevant to the basic problems of the patient. The patient is presumed to be avoiding (repressing) these cues precisely because they have anxiety-evoking value. Since it is maintained that the patient's maladaptive behavior is based on the secondary-drive value of these cues, it follows that reduction or elimination, through extinction, of the drive value of the cues should lead to a proportional reduction or elimination of the maladaptive behavior which was based upon the cues. At the same time, since the anxiety level itself is being reduced, substitute symptom formation (new avoidance responses) should not occur.

The question asked continually by the therapist is, "What are the exteroceptive and interoceptive conditioned stimuli that the patient is avoiding?" The assumption is made that these cues are multiple, involve varied forms of stimulation, and are possibly interdependent. They are believed to be ordered in a serial hierarchy in terms of the extent to which they are avoided (repressed). Those cues highest on the Avoidance Serial Cue Hierarchy (ASCH) have the highest anxiety loading because they are believed to be the cues previously most closely associated with trauma (primary reinforcement). Furthermore, since these cues are the most completely avoided, their infrequent exposure protects the main source of secondary drive from undergoing extinction (Solomon & Wynne's, 1954, conservation of anxiety hypothesis). The cues low on the ASCH have less of an anxiety loading. They are usually more accessible and identifiable by the patient. They can be deduced usually from a purely descriptive analysis of the patient's behavior.

### Symptom-Contingent Cues

The hypothesized cues which are believed to be low on the ASCH are presented first. Many of these cues can be identified as symptom-contingent cues. These are the situational or environmental cues which are highly correlated with the occurrence of the patient's symptom. They can be identified by analyzing the contingencies surrounding the occurrence of the symptom. For example, in the case of a phobic reaction, the symptom-contingent cues might involve the sight of a tall building, the driving of a car, or being confined to a small enclosed space. Whether the symptom involves a compulsive ritual, an obsessive thought, a hysterical fit, or a conversion reaction the strategy is essentially the same, that is, the identification of as much of the stimulus complex as possible surrounding the occurrence of the symptom.

Once the cues associated with the anxiety-evoking situation are deduced, the therapist can attempt to extinguish their anxiety-eliciting properties by verbally describing in detail to the patient the sequence in which the cues occur. At the same time the patient is encouraged to visualize the cues in imagery. Scenes are described to the patient in which he is asked to imagine himself being unable to elaborate his symptom while in the anxiety-eliciting situation. For example, he might be asked to imagine himself climbing the stairs of a feared tall building, being unable to perform his compulsive ritual, or having to visualize the acting out of his feared obsession. In a sense, the therapist forces the patient to be exposed to some of the anxiety-provoking cues that he partially avoids outside of the treatment session by means of his symptom. Therefore, with the avoidance response circumvented, greater exposure to the cues will occur, and subsequently greater extinction will be effected.

Frequently, with this reduction in anxiety, the patient will report a number of other anxiety-eliciting situations in his life which he maintains he previously had forgotten completely. Such information provides further cues. The assumption made is that anxiety which is extinguished to one set of cues will, through the principle of generalization of extinction, make the next set of cues which have higher anxiety-eliciting value more accessible.

## Hypothesized Sequential Cues

When the symptom-contingent cues have been extinguished, the hypothesized sequential cues (those hypothesized avoided cues comprising the rest of the total stimulus complex) are introduced. These cues are assumed to be higher on the patient's ASCH and are believed mainly to incorporate the dynamic areas thought relevant to the basic problems of the patient. The cues found most anxiety eliciting usually center about the expression of hostility and aggression directed toward parental figures, retaliation for aggressive acts by the patient with cues depicting various degrees of bodily injury, and those related to experiences of rejection, deprivation, abandonment, helplessness, guilt, shame, and sex. Oedipal, anal, oral, sibling-rivalry, primal scene, and death-wish impulse themes are worked into the hypothesized ASCH, along with the introduction of "acceptance of conscience" cues and other areas somewhat neglected by psychodynamically oriented therapies.

For didactic purposes, the areas which usually incorporate the hypothesized sequential cues can be categorized under the following 10 major headings:

*Aggression.* Scenes presented in this area usually center around the expression of anger, hostility, and aggression by the patient toward parental, sibling, spouse, or other significant figures in his life. Various degrees of bodily injury are described including complete body mutilation and death of the victim.

*Punishment.* The patient is instructed to visualize himself as the recipient of the anger, hostility, and aggression of the various significant individuals in his life. The punishment inflicted in the scene is frequently a result of the patient's engaging in some forbidden act.

*Oral material.* In this category oral incorporative and destructive scenes involving, for example, eating, biting, spitting, cannibalism, and sucking are introduced.

*Anal material.* Anal retentive and expulsive scenes comprising a variety of excretory and related anal situations are described.

*Sexual material.* In this area a wide variety of hypothesized cues related to sex are presented. For example, primal and Oepidal scenes and scenes of castration, fellatio, and homosexuality are presented.

*Rejection.* Scenes where the patient is rejected, deprived, abandoned, shamed, or left helpless are enacted.

*Bodily injury.* Scenes involving mutilation and death of the patient are introduced where fear of injury appears dominant (e.g., in phobic reactions such as falling off a high building, being hit by a car, dying from an infection). This procedure is followed also in cases where suicidal fantasies are present.

*Loss of control.* Scenes are presented where the patient is encouraged to imagine himself losing impulse control to such an extent that he acts out avoided sexual or aggressive impulses. These scenes usually are followed by scenes where the individual is directed to visualize himself hospitalized for the rest of his life in a back ward of a mental hospital as a result of his loss of impulse control. This area is tapped primarily with patients who express fear of "becoming insane" or concern about being hopeless and incurable.

*Acceptance of conscience.* Scenes are portrayed in which the patient confesses, admits, and believes he is responsible and guilty for all sins and wrongdoings (as portrayed in scenes from other categories) throughout his life. The surrounding may be described as involving a courtroom scene with all the patient's family and loved ones present. After his confession he is convicted by the court, sentenced to death, and executed. In some cases, after death the patient is instructed to picture himself going before God, and the theme is essentially repeated with God condemning him to eternal suffering. An attempt is then made to fit the patient's "hell" to his "sins."

*ANS and CNS reactivity.* The sensory consequences of autonomic and central nervous system reactivity may function itself as a cue for anxiety. Scenes are introduced in which the patient is asked to visualize the sensory consequences of his own nervous system (e.g., heart pounding, perspiration increase, increase in muscular tension, involuntary discharge of the bladder or bowels).

In general, most of the above areas are touched upon at one point or another during the patient's treatment. The categories emphasized, and where they fall on the ASCH, will depend upon the patient's history and dynamics. The categories, of course, are not mutually exclusive or all inclusive. From a learning model many of the cues would be expected to occur within the same stimulus complex in which the original conditioning occurred. In practice, many of the scenes presented within a session include cues from more than one of the above categories. These scenes are presented from least to most feared in terms of the hypothesized ASCH. They are repeated until the anxiety reactions elicited by them are markedly reduced or eliminated.

To summarize, the first objective of the implosive procedure is to have the patient imagine and verbalize those important symptom-contingent cues and/or hypothesized sequential cues which, although possessing high-anxiety-eliciting value, are believed to be relatively low on the patient's ASCH. These cues are chosen from the real-life experiences of the patient in which objects or situations are known to have high-anxiety-eliciting value, as in specific traumatic situations, material produced in dreams, or symbolism of a psychoanalytic nature such as snakes, spiders, wolves, or other objects or animals thought to have stimulus-generalization properties (symbolically meaningful to the patient). As each theme is worked through and extinguished, hypothesized cues believed to be higher on the ASCH are introduced. This procedure is continued until all the areas desired to be worked through are extinguished.

## VALIDATION

It was developed by the first author in 1957 (see London, 1964). Since that time, the technique has been applied to a wide variety of psychopathological problems. It appears to be highly effective over a wide range of psychoneurotic disorders including anxiety, phobic, obsessive-compulsive, and depressive reactions and has been applied successfully to psychotic disorders including affective, schizophrenic, and paranoid reactions. It shows promise in the treatment of personality disorders including homosexuality, alcoholism, and speech disturbances. A striking feature of the therapy is the reduced treatment time needed to achieve marked changes in symptomatology (from 1 to 15 1-hr. sessions) with total treatment time rarely exceeding 30 implosive hr.

Since "new" therapies frequently appear to be more effective initially, it was thought desirable not to publish the above theoretical approach pending the completion of objective experimental studies. Such confirmation has been reported recently (see Hogan, 1966); Hogan & Kirchner, 1967; Kirchner & Hogan, 1966; Levis & Carrera, 1967). However, further research on the efficacy of the technique, theory, and interaction of the two is still needed before any definite claims can be made.

## REFERENCES

AYLLON, T. Intensive treatment of psychotic behavior by stimulus satiation and food reinforcement. *Behavior Research and Therapy*, 1963, 1(1), 53–61.

BANDURA, A. Psychotherapy as a learning process. *Psychological Bulletin*, 1961, 58, 143–157.

BLACK, A. H. The extinction of avoidance responses under curare-like drugs. *Journal of Comparative and Physiological Psychology*, 1958, 51, 519–525.

BRADY, J. V., PORTER, R. W., CONRAD, D. G., & MASON, J. W. Avoidance behavior and the development of gastroduodenal ulcers. *Journal of the Experimental Analysis of Behavior*, 1958, 1, 69–73.

BREGER, L., & McGAUGH, J. L. Critique and reformulation of "learning-theory" approaches to psychotherapy and neurosis. *Psychological Bulletin*, 1965, 63, 338–358.

BROWN, J. S. The motivation of behavior. New York: McGraw-Hill, 1961.

DENNY, M. R., KOONS, P. B., & MASON, J. E. Extinction of avoidance as a function of the escape situation. Journal of Comparative and Physiological Psychology, 1959, 52, 212–214.

DOLLARD, J., & MILLER, N. E. Personality and psychotherapy. New York: McGraw-Hill, 1950.

GROSSBERG, J. M. Behavior therapy: A review. Psychological Bulletin, 1964, 62, 73–88.

HOGAN, R. A. Implosive therapy in the short term treatment of psychotics. Psychotherapy: Theory, Research and Practice, 1966, 3, 25–32.

HOGAN, R. A., & KIRCHNER, J. H. Preliminary report of the extinction of learned fears via short-term implosive therapy. Journal of Abnormal Psychology, 1967, 72, 106–109.

HOLLAND, J. G., & SKINNER, B. F. The analysis of behavior. New York: McGraw-Hill, 1961.

HUNT, H. F., JERNBERG, P., & BRADY, J. V. The effect of electroconvulsive shock (ECS) on a conditioned emotional response: The effect of post-ECS extinction on the reappearance of the response. Journal of Comparative and Physiological Psychology, 1952, 45, 589–599.

KIMBLE, G. A. Hilgard and Marquis' Conditioning and learning. New York: Appleton-Century-Crofts, 1961.

KIRCHNER, J. H., & HOGAN, R. A. The therapist variable in the implosion of phobias. Psychotherapy: Theory, Research and Practice, 1966, 3, 102–104.

KNAPP, R. K. Acquisition and extinction of avoidance with similar and different shock and escape situations. Journal of Comparative and Physiological Psychology, 1965, 60, 272–273.

KRASNER, L. Studies of the conditioning of verbal behavior. Psychological Bulletin, 1958, 55, 148–170.

LEVIS, D. J. Effects of serial CS presentation and other characteristics of the CS on the conditioned avoidance response. Psychological Reports, 1966, 18, 755–766.

LEVIS, D. J., & CARRERA, R. N. Effects of ten hours of implosive therapy in the treatment of outpatients. Journal of Abnormal Psychology, 1967, 72, 504–508.

LIDDELL, H. S. The challenge of Pavlovian conditioning and experimental neurosis in animals. In J. Wolpe, A. Salter, & L. J. Reyna (Eds.), The conditioning therapies. New York: Holt, Rinehart & Winston, 1965. Pp. 127–148.

LINDSLEY, O. R. Operant conditioning methods applied to research in chronic schizophrenia. Psychiatric Research Reports, 1956, 5, 118–138.

LONDON, P. The modes and morals of psychotherapy. New York: Holt, Rinehart & Winston, 1964.

LOWENFELD, J., RUBENFELD, S., & GUTHRIE, G. M. Verbal inhibition in subception. Journal of General Psychology, 1956, 54, 171–176.

MASSERMAN, J. H., & PECHTEL, C. Neuroses in monkeys: A preliminary report of experimental observation. Annals of the New York Academy of Sciences, 1953, 56(2), 253–265.

MEDNICK, S. A. A learning theory approach to research in schizophrenia. Psychological Bulletin, 1958, 55, 316–327.

MILLER, N. E. Learnable drives and rewards. In S. S. Stevens (Ed.), Handbook of experimental psychology. New York: Wiley, 1951. Pp. 435–472.

MOWRER, O. H. Motivation and neurosis. In, Current theory and research in motivation—a symposium. Lincoln: University of Nebraska Press, 1953. Pp. 162–185.

MOWRER, O. H. Learning theory and behavior. New York: Wiley, 1960.

ROTTER, J. B. Social learning and clinical psychology. Englewood Cliffs, N. J.: Prentice-Hall, 1954.

SALTER, A. Conditioned reflex therapy. New York: Farrar, Straus & Cudahy, 1949.

SHOBEN, E. J. Psychotherapy as a problem in learning theory. Psychological Bulletin, 1949, 46, 366–392.

SKINNER, B. F. What is psychotic behavior? In, Theory and treatment of psychosis: Some newer aspects. St. Louis: Washington University Studies, 1956. Pp. 77–99.

SOLOMON, R. L., KAMIN, L. J., & WYNNE, L. C. Traumatic avoidance learning: The outcomes of several extinction procedures with dogs. Journal of Abnormal and Social Psychology, 1953, 48, 291–302.

SOLOMON, R. L., & WYNNE, L. C. Traumatic avoidance learning: The principles of anxiety conservation and partial irreversibility. *Psychological Review*, 1954, 61, 353–385.

STAMPFL, T. G. Avoidance conditioning reconsidered: An extension of Mowrerian theory. Unpublished manuscript, John Carroll University, 1960.

WALL, H. W., & GUTHRIE, G. M. Extinction of responses to subceived stimuli. *Journal of General Psychology*, 1959, 60, 205–210.

WEINBERGER, N. M. Effects of detainment on extinction of avoidance responses. *Journal of Comparative and Physiological Psychology*, 1965, 60, 135–138.

WOLPE, J. *Psychotherapy by reciprocal inhibition*. Stanford: Stanford University Press, 1958.

YATES, A. J. The application of learning theory to the treatment of tics. *Journal of Abnormal and Social Psychology*, 1958, 56, 175–182.

Rollo May

# Existential Bases of Psychotherapy

*Along with the traditional, deterministic psychoanalytic approaches and the newly developed, scientifically based, equally deterministic behavior modification approach, the last few years have seen the emergence of what has come to be known as a "third force." This is the humanistic, existential influence on psychotherapy. This school has been a very popular one for a long period of time in Europe, but its influence in the United States is quite recent, and rapidly growing. Its emphasis on immediacy of experience makes it a very exciting and compelling approach to a large number of therapists. However, others have criticized it as lacking in adequate theoretical or research underpinnings and, although not of necessity, tending to attract a number of undisciplined and antiscientific practitioners. In his paper, Dr. May gives a well-balanced presentation of the basic tenets of an existential approach, indicating areas of convergence and contrasts with more traditional approaches, and illustrating his remarks with appropriate case material.*

Though the existential approach has been the most prominent in European psychiatry and psychoanalysis for two decades, it was practically unknown in America until a year ago. Since then, some of us have been worried that it might become *too* popular in some quarters, particularly in national magazines. But we have been comforted by a saying of Nietzsche's, "The first adherents of a movement are no argument against it."

We have no interest whatever in importing from Europe a ready-made system. I am, indeed, very dubious about the usefulness of the much-discussed and much-maligned term "Existentialism." But many of us in this country have for years shared this approach, long before we even knew the meaning of that confused term.

On the one hand this approach has a deep underlying affinity for our American character and thought. It is very

Reprinted from American Journal of Orthopsychiatry, 30(1960), 685–695 Copyright, the American Orthopsychiatric Association, Inc. Reproduced by permission.

close, for example, to William James' emphases on the immediacy of experience, the unity of thought and action, and the importance of decision and commitment. On the other hand, there is among some psychologists and psychoanalysts in this country a great deal of hostility and outright anger against this approach. I shall not here go into the reasons for this paradox.

I wish, rather, to *be* existentialist, and to speak directly from my own experience as a person and as a practicing psychoanalytic psychotherapist. Some fifteen years ago, when I was working on my book *The Meaning of Anxiety*, I spent a year and a half in bed in a tuberculosis sanatorium. I had a great deal of time to ponder the meaning of anxiety—and plenty of firsthand data in myself and my fellow patients. In the course of this time I studied the two books written on anxiety up till our day, the one by Freud, *The Problem of Anxiety*, and the one by Kierkegaard, *The Concept of Dread*. I valued highly Freud's formulations: namely, his first theory, that anxiety is the reemergence of repressed libido, and his second, that anxiety is the ego's reaction to the threat of the loss of the loved object. Kierkegaard, on the other hand, described anxiety as the struggle of the living being against nonbeing which I could immediately experience there in my struggle with death or the prospect of being a lifelong invalid. He went on to point out that the real terror in anxiety is not this death as such but the fact that each of us within himself is on both sides of the fight, that "anxiety is a desire for what one dreads," as he put it; thus like an "alien power it lays hold of an individual, and yet one cannot tear one's self away."

What powerfully struck me then was that Kierkegaard was writing about *exactly what my fellow patients and I*

*were going through*. Freud was not; he was writing on a different level, giving formulations of the psychic mechanisms by which anxiety comes about. Kierkegaard was portraying what is immediately experienced by human beings in crisis—the crisis specifically of life against death which was completely real to us patients, but a crisis which I believe is not in its essential form different from the various crises of people who come for therapy, or the crises all of us experience in much more minute form a dozen times a day even though we push the ultimate prospect of death far from our minds. Freud was writing on the technical level, where his genius was supreme; perhaps more than any man up to his time, he *knew about* anxiety. Kierkegaard, a genius of a different order, was writing on the existential, ontological level; he *knew anxiety*.

This is not a value dichotomy; obviously both are necessary. Our real problem, rather, is given us by our cultural-historical situation. We in the Western world are the heirs of four centuries of technical achievement in power over nature, and now over ourselves; this is our greatness and, at the same time, it is also our greatest peril. We are not in danger of repressing the technical emphasis (of which Freud's tremendous popularity in this country were proof if any were necessary). But rather we repress the opposite. If I may use terms which I shall be discussing more fully presently, we repress the *sense of being*, the ontological sense. One consequence of this repression of the sense of being is that modern man's image of himself, his experience of himself as a responsible individual, his experience of his own humanity, have likewise disintegrated.

The existential approach, as I understand it, does not have the aim of ruling out the technical discoveries of

Freud or those from any other branch of psychology or science. It does, however, seek to place these discoveries on a new basis, a new understanding or rediscovery, if you will, of the nature and image of man.

I make no apologies in admitting that I take very seriously the dehumanizing dangers in our tendency in modern science to make man over into the image of the machine, into the image of the techniques by which we study him. This tendency is not the fault of any "dangerous" men or "vicious" schools; it is rather a crisis brought upon us by our particular historical predicament. Karl Jaspers, both psychiatrist and existentialist philosopher, holds that we in the Western world are actually in process of losing self-consciousness and that we may be in the last age of historical man. William Whyte in his *Organization Man* cautions that modern man's enemies may turn out to be a "mild-looking group of therapists, who . . . would be doing what they did to help you." He refers here to the tendency to use the social sciences in support of the social ethic of our historical period; and thus the process of helping people may actually make them conformist and tend toward the destruction of individuality. We cannot brush aside the cautions of such men as unintelligent or antiscientific; to try to do so would make *us* the obscurantists.

You may agree with my sentiments here but cavil at the terms "being" and "non-being"; and many of you may already have concluded that your suspicion was only too right, that this so-called existential approach in psychology is hopelessly vague and muddled. Carl Rogers remarked in his paper at the American Psychological Association convention last September in Cincinnati that many American psychologists must find these terms abhorrent

because they sound so general, so philosophical, so untestable. Rogers went on to point out, however, that he had no difficulty at all in putting the existential principles in therapy into empirically testable hypotheses.

But I would go further and hold that *without* some concepts of "being" and "non-being," we cannot even understand our most commonly used psychological mechanisms. Take for example, *repression, resistance* and *transference*. The usual discussions of these terms hang in mid-air, without convincingness or psychological reality, precisely because we have lacked an underlying structure on which to base them. The term "repression," for example, obviously refers to a phenomenon we observe all the time, a dynamism which Freud clearly described in many forms. We generally explain the mechanism by saying that the child represses into unconsciousness certain impulses, such as sex and hostility, because the culture in the form of parental figures disapproves, and the child must protect his own security with these figures. But this culture which assumedly disapproves is made up of the very same people who do the repressing. Is it not an illusion, therefore, and much too simple, to speak of the culture over against the individual in such fashion and make it our whipping boy? Furthermore, where did we get the ideas that child or adult are so much concerned with security and libidinal satisfactions? Are these not a carry-over from our work with the *neurotic, anxious* child and adult?

Certainly the neurotic, anxious child is compulsively concerned with security, for example; and certainly the neurotic adult, and we who study him, read our later formulations back into the unsuspecting mind of the child. But is not the normal child just as truly interested in moving out into the world, exploring, following his curiosity and sense of adventure—going out "to learn to shiver and to shake," as the nursery rhyme puts it? And if you block these needs of the child, you get a traumatic reaction from him just as you do when you take away his security. I, for one, believe we vastly overemphasize the human being's concern with security and survival satisfactions because they so neatly fit our cause-and-effect way of thinking. I believe Nietzsche and Kierkegaard were more accurate when they described man as the organism who makes certain values—prestige, power, tenderness—more important than pleasure and even more important than survival itself.

My implication here is that we can understand repression, for example, only on the deeper level of the meaning of the human being's potentialities. In this respect, "being" is to be defined as the individual's "pattern of potentialities." These potentialities will be partly shared with other persons but will in every case form a unique pattern in each individual. We must ask the questions: What is this person's relation to his own potentialities? What goes on that he chooses or is forced to choose to block off from his awareness something which he knows, and on another level *knows that he knows?* In my work in psychotherapy there appears more and more evidence that anxiety in our day arises not so much out of fear of lack of libidinal satisfactions or security, but rather out of the patient's fear of his own powers, and the conflicts that arise from that fear. This may be the particular "neurotic personality of our time"—the neurotic pattern of contemporary "outer-directed," organizational man.

The "unconscious," then, is not to be thought of as a reservoir of impulses, thoughts, wishes which are culturally unacceptable; I define it rather as *those potentialities for knowing and experiencing which the individual cannot or will not actualize.* On this level we shall find that the simple mechanism of repression is infinitely less simple than it looks; that it involves a complex struggle of the individual's *being* against the possibility of *non-being;* that it cannot be adequately comprehended in "ego" and "not-ego" terms, or even "self" and "not-self"; and that it inescapably raises the question of the human being's margin of freedom with respect to his potentialities, a margin in which resides his responsibility for himself which even the therapist cannot take away.

Let us now come back from theory to more practical matters. For a number of years as a practicing therapist and teacher of therapists, I have been struck by how often our concern with trying to understand the patient in terms of the mechanisms by which his behavior takes place blocks our understanding of what he really is experiencing. Here is a patient, Mrs. Hutchens (about whom I shall center some of my remarks this morning) who comes into my office for the first time, a suburban woman in her middle thirties who tries to keep her expression poised and sophisticated. But no one could fail to see in her eyes something of the terror of a frightened animal or a lost child. I know, from what her neurological specialists have already told me, that her presenting problem is hysterical tenseness of the larynx, as a result of which she can talk only with a perpetual hoarseness. I have been given the hypothesis from her Rorschach that she has felt all her life, "If I say what I really feel, I'll be rejected; under these conditions it is better not to talk at all." During this first hour, also, I get some hints of the genetic *why* of her problem as she tells me of her authoritarian relation with her mother and grandmother, and how she learned to guard firmly against telling any secrets at all. But if as I sit here I am chiefly thinking of these *why's* and *how's* concerning the way the problem came about, I will grasp everything except the most important thing of all (indeed the only real source of data I have), namely, this person now existing, becoming, emerging, this experiencing human being immediately in the room with me.

There are at present in this country several undertakings to systematize psychoanalytic theory in terms of forces, dynamisms and energies. The approach I propose is the exact opposite of this. I hold that our science must be relevant to the distinctive characteristics of what we seek to study, in this case the human being. We do not deny dynamisms and forces—that would be nonsense—but we hold that they have meaning only in the context of the existing, living person; that is to say, in the *ontological* context.

I propose, thus, that we take the one real datum we have in the therapeutic situation, namely, the *existing person* sitting in a consulting room with a therapist. (The term "existing person" is used here as our European colleagues use *Dasein.*) Note that I do not say simply "individual" or "person"; if you take individuals as units in a group for the purposes of statistical prediction— certainly a legitimate use of psychological science—you are exactly *defining out of the picture* the characteristics which make this individual an existing person. Or when you take him as a composite of drives and deterministic forces, you have defined for study everything except *the one to whom these experiences happen*, everything except the existing person himself. Therapy is one activity, so far as I can see, in

which we cannot escape the necessity of taking the subject as an existing person.

Let us therefore ask, What are the essential characteristics which constitute this patient as an existing person in the consulting room? I wish to propose six characteristics which I shall call principles,* which I find in my work as a psychotherapist. Though these principles are the product of a good deal of thought and experience with many cases, I shall illustrate them with episodes from the case of Mrs. Hutchens.

First, Mrs. Hutchens like every existing person is *centered in herself*, and an attack on this center is an attack on her existence itself. This is a characteristic which we share with all living beings; it is self-evident in animals and plants. I never cease to marvel how, whenever we cut the top off a pine tree on our farm in New Hampshire, the tree sends up a new branch from heaven knows where to become a new center. But this principle has a particular relevance to human beings and gives a basis for the understanding of sickness and health, neurosis and mental health. Neurosis is not to be seen as a deviation from our particular theories of what a person should be. *Is not neurosis, rather, precisely the method the individual uses to preserve his own center, his own existence?* His symptoms are ways of shrinking the range of his world (so graphically shown in Mrs. Hutchens' inability to let herself talk) in order that the centeredness of his existence may be protected from threat; a way of blocking off aspects of the environment that he may then be adequate to the remainder. Mrs. Hutchens had gone to another therapist for half a dozen sessions a month before she came to me. He told her, in an

* From a philosophical point of view, these are to be termed "ontological principles."

apparently ill-advised effort to reassure her, that she was too proper, too controlled. She reacted with great upset and immediately broke off the treatment. Now technically he was entirely correct; existentially he was entirely wrong. What he did not see, in my judgment, was that this very properness, this overcontrol, far from being things Mrs. Hutchens wanted to get over, were part of her desperate attempt to preserve what precarious center she had. As though she were saying, "If I opened up, if I communicated, I would lose what little space in life I have." We see here, incidentally, how inadequate is the definition of neurosis as a failure of adjustment. *An adjustment is exactly what neurosis is; and that is just its trouble.* It is a necessary adjustment by which centeredness can be preserved; a way of accepting *non-being*, if I may use this term, in order that some little *being* may be preserved. And in most cases it is a boon when this adjustment breaks down.

This is the only thing we can assume about Mrs. Hutchens, or about any patient, when she comes in: that she, like all living beings, requires centeredness, and that this has broken down. At a cost of considerable turmoil she has taken steps, that is, come for help. Our second principle thus, is: *every existing person has the character of self-affirmation, the need to preserve its centeredness.* The particular name we give this self-affirmation in human beings is "courage." Paul Tillich's emphasis on the "courage to be" is very cogent and fertile for psychotherapy at this point. He insists that in man being is never given automatically but depends upon the individual's courage, and without courage one loses being. *This makes courage itself a necessary ontological corollary.* By this token, I as a therapist place great importance upon expressions of the patients which

have to do with willing, decisions, choice. I never let little remarks the patient may make such as "maybe I can," "perhaps I can try," and so on slip by without my making sure he knows I have heard him. It is only a half truth that the will is the product of the wish; I wish to emphasize rather the truth that the wish can never come out in its real power except with will.

Now as Mrs. Hutchens talks hoarsely, she looks at me with an expression of mingled fear and hope. Obviously a relation exists between us not only here but already in anticipation in the waiting room and ever since she thought of coming. She is struggling with the possibility of participating with me. Our third principle is, thus: *all existing persons have the need and possibility of going out from their centeredness to participate in other beings.* This always involves risk; if the organism goes out too far, it loses its own centeredness—its identity—a phenomenon which can easily be seen in the biological world. If the neurotic is so afraid of loss of his own conflicted center that he refuses to go out but holds back in rigidity and lives in narrowed reactions and shrunken world space, his growth and development are blocked. This is the pattern in neurotic repressions and inhibitions, the common neurotic forms in Freud's day. But it may well be in our day of conformism and the outer-directed man, that the most common neurotic pattern takes the opposite form, namely, the dispersing of one's self in participation and identification with others until one's own being is emptied. At this point we see the rightful emphasis of Martin Buber in one sense and Harry Stack Sullivan in another, that the human being cannot be understood as a self if participation is omitted. Indeed, if we are successful in our search for these ontological principles of the existing person, it should be true that the omission of any one of the six would mean we do not then have a human being.

Our fourth principle is: *the subjective side of centeredness is awareness.* The paleontologist Pierre Teilhard de Chardin has recently described brilliantly how this awareness is present in ascending degrees in all forms of life from amoeba to man. It is certainly present in animals. Howard Liddell has pointed out how the seal in its natural habitat lifts its head every ten seconds even during sleep to survey the horizon lest an Eskimo hunter with poised bow and arrow sneak up on it. This awareness of threats to being in animals Liddell calls *vigilance,* and he identifies it as the primitive, simple counterpart in animals of what in human beings becomes anxiety.

Our first four characteristic principles are shared by our existing person with all living beings; they are biological levels in which human beings participate. The fifth principle refers now to a distinctively human characteristic, self-consciousness. *The uniquely human form of awareness is self-consciousness.* We do not identify awareness and consciousness. We associate awareness, as Liddell indicates above, with vigilance. This is supported by the derivation of the term—it comes from the Anglo-Saxon *gewaer, waer,* meaning knowledge of external dangers and threats. Its cognates are *beware* and *wary.* Awareness certainly is what is going on in an individual's neurotic reaction to threat, in Mrs. Hutchens' experience in the first hours, for example, that I am also a threat to her. Consciousness, in contrast, we define as not simply my awareness of threat from the world, but *my capacity to know myself as the one being threatened,* my experience of myself as the subject who has a world. Consciousness, as Kurt Gold-

stein puts it, is man's capacity to transcend the immediate concrete situation, to live in terms of the possible; and it underlies the human capacity to use abstractions and universals, to have language and symbols. This capacity for consciousness underlies the wide-range of possibility which man has in relating to his world, and it constitutes the foundation of psychological freedom. Thus human freedom has its ontological base and I believe must be assumed in all psychotherapy.

In his book, *The Phenomenon of Man,* Pierre Teilhard de Chardin, as we have mentioned, describes awareness in all forms of evolutionary life. But in man, a new function arises, namely, this self-consciousness. Teilhard de Chardin undertakes to demonstrate something I have always believed, that when a new function emerges the whole previous pattern, the total gestalt of the organism, changes. Thereafter the organism can be understood only in terms of the new function. That is to say, it is only a half truth to hold that the organism is to be understood in terms of the simpler elements below it on the evolutionary scale; it is just as true that every new function forms a new complexity which conditions all the simpler elements in the organism. *In this sense, the simple can be understood only in terms of the more complex.*

This is what self-consciousness does in man. All the simpler biological functions must now be understood in terms of the new function. No one would, of course, deny for a moment the old functions, nor anything in biology which man shares with less complex organisms. Take sexuality for example, which we obviously share with all mammals. But given self-consciousness, sex becomes a new gestalt as is demonstrated in therapy all the time. Sexual impulses are now conditioned by the *person* of the partner; what we think of the other male or female, in reality or fantasy or even repressed fantasy, can never be ruled out. The fact that the subjective person of the other to whom we relate sexually makes least difference in *neurotic* sexuality, say in patterns of compulsive sex or prostitution, only proves the point the more firmly; for such requires precisely the blocking off, the checking out, the distorting of self-consciousness. Thus when we talk of sexuality in terms of sexual *objects*, as Kinsey does, we may garner interesting and useful statistics; but we simply are not talking about human sexuality.

Nothing in what I am saying here should be taken as antibiological in the slightest; on the contrary, I think it is only from this approach that we *can* understand human biology without distorting it. As Kierkegaard aptly put it, "The natural law is as valid as ever." I argue only against the uncritical acceptance of the assumption that the organism is to be understood solely in terms of those elements below it on the evolutionary scale, an assumption which has led us to overlook the self-evident truth that what makes a horse a horse is not the elements it shares with the organisms below it but what constitutes distinctively "horse." Now *what we are dealing with in neurosis are those characteristics and functions which are distinctively human*. It is these that have gone awry in our disturbed patients. The condition for these functions is self-consciousness—which accounts for what Freud rightly discovered, that the neurotic pattern is characterized by repression and blocking off of consciousness.

It is the task of the therapist, therefore, not only to help the patient become aware; but even more significantly to help him to *transmute this awareness into consciousness*. Awareness is

his knowing that something is threatening from outside in his world—a condition which may, as in paranoids and their neurotic equivalents, be correlated with a good deal of acting-out behavior. But self-consciousness puts this awareness on a quite different level; it is the patient's seeing that *he is the one who is threatened*, that he is the being who stands in this world which threatens, he is the subject who *has* a world. And this gives him the possibility of *in-sight*, of "inward sight," of seeing the world and its problems in relation to himself. And thus it gives him the possibility of doing something about the problems.

To come back to our too-long silent patient: After about 25 hours of therapy Mrs. Hutchens had the following dream. She was searching room by room for a baby in an unfinished house at an airport. She thought the baby belonged to someone else, but the other person might let her take it. Now it seemed that she had put the baby in a pocket of her robe (or her mother's robe) and she was seized with anxiety that it would be smothered. Much to her joy, she found that the baby was still alive. Then she had a strange thought, "Shall I kill it?"

The house was at the airport where she at about the age of 20 had learned to fly solo, a very important act of self-affirmation and independence from her parents. The baby was associated with her youngest son, whom she regularly identified with herself. Permit me to omit the ample associative evidence that convinced both her and me that the baby stood for herself. The dream is an expression of the emergence and growth of self-consciousness, a consciousness she is not sure is hers yet, and a consciousness which she considers killing in the dream.

About six years before her therapy, Mrs. Hutchens had left the religious faith of her parents, to which she had

had a very authoritarian relation. She had then joined a church of her own belief. But she had never dared tell her parents of this. Instead, when they came to visit, she attended their church in great tension lest one of her children let the secret out. After about 35 sessions, when she was considering writing her parents to tell them of this change of faith, she had over a period of two weeks spells of partially fainting in my office. She would become suddenly weak, her face would go white, she would feel empty and "like water inside," and would have to lie down for a few moments on the couch. In retrospect she called these spells "grasping for oblivion."

She then wrote her parents informing them once and for all of her change in faith and assuring them it would do no good to try to dominate her. In the following session she asked in considerable anxiety whether I thought she would go psychotic. I responded that whereas anyone of us might at some time have such an episode, I saw no more reason why she should than any of the rest of us; and I asked whether her fear of going psychotic was not rather anxiety coming out of her standing against her parents, as though genuinely being herself she felt to be tantamount to going crazy. I have, it may be remarked, several times noted this anxiety at being one's self experienced by the patient as tantamount to psychosis. This is not surprising, for consciousness of one's own desires and affirming them involves accepting one's originality and uniqueness, and it implies that one must be prepared to be isolated not only from those parental figures upon whom one has been dependent, but at that instant to stand alone in the entire psychic universe as well.

We see the profound conflicts of the emergence of self-consciousness in three vivid ways in Mrs. Hutchens, whose chief symptom, interestingly enough, was the denial of that uniquely human capacity based on consciousness, namely, talking: 1) the temptation to kill the baby; 2) the grasping at oblivion by fainting, as though she were saying, "If only I did not have to be conscious, I would escape this terrible problem of telling my parents"; and 3) the psychosis anxiety.

We now come to the sixth and last ontological characteristic, *anxiety*. Anxiety is the state of the human being in the struggle against what would destroy his being. It is, in Tillich's phrase, the state of being in conflict with nonbeing, a conflict which Freud mythologically pictured in his powerful and important symbol of the death instinct. One wing of this struggle will always be against something outside one's self; but even more portentous and significant for psychotherapy is the inner side of the battle, which we saw in Mrs. Hutchens, namely, the conflict within the person as he confronts the choice of whether and how far he will stand against his own being, his own potentialities.

From an existential viewpoint we take very seriously this temptation to kill the baby, or kill her own consciousness, as expressed in these forms by Mrs. Hutchens. We neither water it down by calling it "neurotic" and the product merely of sickness, nor do we slough over it by reassuring her, "O.K., but you don't need to do it." If we did these, we would be helping her adjust at the price of surrendering a portion of her existence, that is, her opportunity for fuller independence. The self-confrontation which is involved in the acceptance of self-consciousness is anything but simple: it involves, to identify some of the elements, accepting the hatred of the past, her mother's against her and hers of her mother; accepting her present motives of hatred and destruction; cutting through rationalizations and illusions about her behavior and motives, and the acceptance of the responsibility and aloneness which this implies; the giving up of childhood omnipotence, and acceptance of the fact that though she can never have absolute certainty of choices, she must choose anyway. But all of these specific points, easy enough to understand in themselves, must be seen in the light of the fact that *consciousness itself implies always the possibility of turning against one's self, denying one's self*. The tragic nature of human existence inheres in the fact that consciousness itself involves the possibility and temptation at every instant of killing itself. Dostoevski and our other existential forebears were not indulging in poetic hyperbole or expressing the aftereffects of immoderate vodka when they wrote of the agonizing burden of freedom.

I trust that the fact that existential psychotherapy places emphasis on these tragic aspects of life does not at all imply it is pessimistic. Quite the contrary. The confronting of genuine tragedy is a highly cathartic experience psychically, as Aristotle and others through history have reminded us. Tragedy is inseparably connected with man's dignity and grandeur, and is the accompaniment, as illustrated in the dramas of Oedipus and Orestes *ad infinitum*, of the human being's moments of greatest insight.

I hope that this analysis of ontological characteristics in the human being, this search for the basic principles which constitute the existing person, may give us a structural basis for our psychotherapy. Thus the way may be opened for the developing of sciences of psychology and psychoanalysis which do not fragmentize man while they seek to study him, and do not undermine his humanity while they seek to help him.

Franz G. Alexander
and Sheldon T. Selesnick

# The Organic Approach

*Most of the therapeutic approaches that we have described are equally well practiced by well-trained therapists with backgrounds in psychiatry or psychology. There is one approach that is legally restricted to men with medical training, and that is the organic approach. Earlier versions of this were dramatic in their violent manner of dealing with the patient, with techniques such as shock therapy and psychosurgery common. Electric shock therapy, particularly with depressive patients, is still widely used. However, the major thrust of contemporary organic approaches is to replace these gross physical treatments with drugs. One*

Reprinted from The History of Psychiatry, by *Franz G. Alexander and Sheldon T. Selesnick (New York: Harper & Row, 1966), pp. 279–296. Copyright 1966 by the Estate of Franz Alexander, M.D. and Sheldon Selesnick, M.D. Reprinted by permission of Harper & Row, Publishers, and George Allen & Unwin Ltd., London.*

*of the major developments of the past decade has been in psychopharmacology, and the use of drugs, either as a method of treatment or as an adjunct to more traditional methods, has had enormous impact on the mental health field. It should be clear that drugs are frequently used along with psychotherapy, as a method of making the patient more comfortable and more accessible to psychotherapy. Drs. Alexander and Selesnick have written a comprehensive book detailing the history of developments in psychiatry. The selection presented here is that portion of the book discussing the organic approaches, but the reader is referred to the original volume for a fuller picture of historical developments in this area.*

## SHOCK TREATMENTS
## AND PSYCHOSURGERY

The isolation, in 1922, of insulin by Frederick Banting, C. H. Best, and J. R. MacLeod brought diabetes, one of man's most dread diseases, under control. It also inaugurated the first systematized biological approach to a somatic treatment for schizophrenia. It so happened that small dosages of insulin were often used to stimulate appetite in patients with chronic illnesses, including those who were hospitalized with severe mental illnesses. Although such physicians as H. Steck in Switzerland, C. Munn in America, and H. Haack in Germany had noted beneficial effects of these insulin doses on the moods of excited psychotic patients, the idea of using insulin in the treatment of psychotics was developed by Manfred Sakel (1900–1957). Sakel had treated patients recovering from morphine addiction at the Lichterfelde Hospital, Berlin, from 1927 to 1933 and had observed that morphine abstainers became overly excited. He considered this excitement to be caused by overactivity of the adrenal-thyroid endocrine systems and reasoned that a drug antagonistic to this system would also decrease the tone of the sympathetic nervous system, which enhances overactivity of this endocrine system. He experimented with insulin and found that high dosages did indeed

appear to diminish the overactive states. Sakel then decided to try using insulin in high enough dosages to produce coma in excited patients, especially those who had been diagnosed as schizophrenic. Late in 1933 Sakel reported his first experimental findings of beneficial results in schizophrenia following insulin shock.

Sakel's therapeutic endeavors were not unanimously accepted by the medical profession, in part because the theoretical rationale of his treatment method was vague. Although schizophrenic patients, especially those who had recently become ill, appeared to benefit by the treatment, it has been increasingly recognized over the years that schizophrenics in their early stage of illness respond to most treatments with benefit. Insulin, as well as other therapies, is less effective in the chronic stages of the illness. Because it was not an easy therapeutic regimen, the technique of the treatment came under attack. For maximum effect at least thirty to fifty hours of coma had to be produced; patients required continuous nursing care, and physicians had to be highly skilled in insulin administration in order to avoid such hazards as irreversible coma and circulatory and respiratory collapse. Exactly how insulin-shock treatment benefits the schizophrenic is still an open question. Recent speculations hold that the nucleoproteins in the neuron may be affected by the reduction in blood sugar caused by insulin or that the brain's enzyme systems are brought into better equilibrium, thus making the brain better able to utilize beneficial minerals circulating in the blood. These physiological hypotheses are, however, as yet unconfirmed.

Another explanation for the benefits of insulin shock depends on the idea that the reduced blood-sugar supply also reduces the amount of oxygen present in the bloodstream. If the highest brain centers require the greatest amount of oxygen, then the function of the cortex will be impaired first by any diminishment in the glucose supply, and the lower centers of the brain will thus be released from the inhibition of the cerebral cortex. In essence, then, insulin treatment encourages the individual to regress to lower and more primitive levels of adaptation. Viewed from a psychological standpoint, the patient awakens from an insulin coma in a regressed psychological state. He has to be fed intravenously or with a stomach tube and is extremely dependent on external help. This continuing physiological and psychological regression, it is presumed, gradually leads to a reshaping of higher physiological and psychological patterns as the patient responds to the great amount of attention and the hopefulness of the psychiatric team administering the insulin.

Because of its dangers, unreliable results, and high cost, insulin therapy was largely superseded during the 1940's by other forms of shocking the nervous

system. The next phase in shock treatment developed as a result of investigations of epilepsy, the "sacred disease" of the ancients. In the late 1920's Ladislaus Joseph von Meduna (1896–1964), then the superintendent of the Royal State Mental Hospital in Budapest, observed that the glial tissue, which connects the cell structures of the cortex, had thickened in epileptic patients. When he compared their brains with those of deceased schizophrenic patients he noted that the latter showed a deficiency of glial structure. On the basis of these findings (which have not been subsequently confirmed) Meduna became convinced that schizophrenia and epilepsy were incompatible diseases and that a convulsive agent administered to schizophrenics would therefore cure them.[1]

This technique was not original with Meduna, for convulsive agents had been used by previous investigators to treat severe mental states.[2] Not knowing of these earlier experiments, he decided in 1933 to test camphor and soon thereafter began to use a less toxic synthetic camphor preparation, Metrazol (also called Cardiazol). Metrazol had several practical shortcomings, among them an unpredictable time lag between injection and convulsion, during which the patient was fearful and uncooperative. Also, the convulsions frequently were severe enough to cause fractures.

In 1932 Ugo Cerletti (1877–1963), at the Neuropsychiatric Clinic in Genoa, was autopsying bodies of those

---

[1] In the late 1920's and early 1930's Meduna had read of statistical clinical studies purporting that schizophrenia and epilepsy rarely, if ever, occur in the same patient. These reports claimed that should a schizophrenic develop epilepsy, his psychosis could be cured.

[2] Dr. William Oliver in 1785 reported in a London medical journal that he had cured a case of mania by giving camphor (1). Dr. G. Burrows made a similar claim in a book, *Commentaries on the Causes, Forms, Symptoms, Treatment, Moral and Medical, of Insanity,* published in 1828 (2). And in the eighteenth century, Auenbrugger, the discoverer of auscultation, and a Dr. Weickhardt had also recommended camphor for the treatment of mental diseases (3).

who had died from epilepsy; he noted a hardening in a sector of the brain known as Ammon's horn. Cerletti decided to find out whether this hardening caused or was the result of epileptic attacks. Because he assumed that drugs used to produce experimental convulsions might have produced the hardening in the brain, he decided to use electrical stimulation instead. (4).[3]

Later, in Rome, in 1935, Cerletti began collaborating with L. Bini. Cerletti learned that hogs were killed at a Roman slaughterhouse after they had been stupefied by an electrical current; Bini used these hogs to establish a safe dosage of electricity, and on April 15, 1938, Cerletti and Bini administered their first electroshock treatment to a schizophrenic patient. It soon became evident that electroshock was superior to Metrazol, since it was less dangerous, less expensive, and produced a milder convulsion. Because of its simplicity of procedure and favorable results, electroshock had, by the 1940's, also widely replaced insulin-shock treatments in schizophrenia.

Shock treatment today consists of passing seventy to one hundred and thirty volts for one tenth to five tenths of a second through electrodes attached to the patient's head. Usually three treatments a week are given; anywhere from five to thirty-five treatments may be considered optimal. For such a relatively violent procedure the side effects are mild, and the patient experi-

ences no pain. The danger of bone fractures has been minimized by the use of curare-like drugs (by A. E. Bennet in 1941) that inhibit the production of acetylcholine at the neuromuscular junction and thus reduce muscular spasm. The patient loses consciousness immediately after the shock is administered and therefore resistance to further treatment is not connected with a recollection of physical trauma. The most striking feature of the post-treatment period is that the patient has a memory loss of a varying degree for recent events. This amnesia may last for several weeks or months following the treatment, but eventually memory is restored. Whatever brain changes do occur are reversible, and persisting brain damage is very rare.

Electroshock treatment has been proved a particularly effective measure for the severe depression—involutional melancholia—that appears in late middle age. On the other hand, shock treatments effect only a relief of symptoms. They do not reach the basic psychological disturbance underlying the illness, and patients who receive electroshock without psychotherapy—which reaches the source of the illness —frequently relapse, even those who have psychotic depressions, for which electroshock is most effective. Despite this drawback, it must be recognized that electroshock may be imperative in cases where symptoms must be alleviated immediately in order to protect

---

[3] The use of nonconvulsive electrotherapy as a method for alleviating symptoms through suggestion dates back to Scribonius Largus (c. A.D. 47), who treated the headaches of the Roman emperor with an electric eel. Nonconvulsive electrotherapy was in widespread use in the late nineteenth century, advocated by the German neurologist W. H. Erb and the French neurologist G. B. Duchenne. Probably the first electroconvulsive treatment for mental illness was administered by the French physician J. B. LeRoy in 1755 on a patient with a psychogenic blindness; almost a half century later F. L. Augustin of Germany reported a similar case. These were isolated experiments and were not followed up; the exact amount of electricity that produced convulsions without fatality was unknown. Cerletti was unfamiliar with these reports, but he did know that experimental convulsions had been produced in animals and that humans too had seizures after accidental electrical exposure (5).

the life of a suicidal patient or the lives of others exposed to an excessively aggressive patient.

Speculations about the mode of action of electroshock treatment fall roughly into two sets of theories, one set based on possible psychological reactions to the treatment, the other on possible physiological reactions. One psychological theory maintains that the patient is so fearful of the treatment that he "escapes into health" rather than face another treatment; another proposes that the treatment satisfies the patient's need for punishment. If this were true, however, beating or chaining the patients—as practiced in the Middle Ages—would more readily cure them. Metrazol produced a much more violent reaction and was more painful to the patient, yet its effects were inferior to electroshock. A third psychological theory holds that the patient releases his pent-up aggressive and hostile impulses through the violent muscular convulsions; but if this were true, running around the block or doing push-ups to the point of exhaustion should be equally effective. Still another psychological theory proposes that the patient experiences the electroshock as a threat to his life, against which his body mobilizes all its defenses. But if this theory were true, then psychotic patients in the analogous circumstances of facing death from cancer or other terminal illness should inevitably show signs of remission of their psychotic illness. Occasionally this does occur, but it is by no means frequent. Another theory holds that the patient's family, fearful of the treatment, gives the patient more attention and thus helps him to get better. But there are families who are consciously or unconsciously hostile to the sick person in their group and therefore would not be influenced by any such threat at all. In general it may be said that all these psychological

theories may be applicable to individual patients but that they cannot hold true for all individuals.

The physiological theories about electroshock are just as speculative. Claims that electroshock stimulates the hypothalamus and therefore the sympathetic nervous system or that it stimulates adaptive responses from the adrenal cortex suffer from the observation that specific sympathetic stimulators or adrenal-cortical hormones do not cure psychotic conditions. Perhaps a plausible explanation for the efficacy of shock is that it produces a slight brain damage and thus erases the most recent neurohistological changes in the highest brain area, which stores as memories those experiences which precipitated the psychosis. In other words, as the result of shock treatment the patient completely forgets the events leading up to his symptoms and thus is put back into a predepression psychological state. The best-substantiated facts of electroshock therapy are that amnesia occurs during this period and that when the temporary memory defect based on the patient's reversible brain damage is restored, illness is apt to reoccur. The exceptions are those lucky patients whose external-life situations fortuitously improve after the shock therapy.

One speculation about the way shock treatment operates involves the concepts of feedback and reverberating circuits. After Hans Berger's discovery of the electrical potentials of the brain and his inauguration of electroencephalography, some scientists began to view the brain as a series of electrical circuits. Norbert Wiener (1894–1964) compared the brain to an electrical computer governed by mechanisms— that is, self-regulating and self-corrective devices—that allow a machine to operate according to prearranged patterns. Negative feedback keeps a ma-

chine in a state of stability; positive feedback acts to increase instability of
whatever system it governs and in effect
causes a machine to develop what is
called a reverberating cycle in which internal control is lost. Some psychiatrists
have therefore suggested that electroshock therapy breaks up a reverberating
circuit in the brain that is caused by
positive feedback and thereby clears
the brain. The question of how far
the "neurotic machines" of Norbert
Wiener can be compared with a neurotic personality offers interesting areas
for further research. As of the moment,
the positive-feedback theory must remain in the realm of speculation.

The idea of a vicious cycle in which
morbid ideas become intensified if they
are not checked predated the concepts
of cybernetics and was one of the theoretical concepts that led to the development of psychosurgery. Egas Moniz
(1874–1955), clinical professor of neurology at the University of Lisbon,
believed that "morbid" ideas stimulate
and restimulate the neuron. Although
no pathological changes could be detected in the synapses or in the nerve
cells of patients suffering from functional psychoses, nevertheless Moniz
"was particularly struck by the circum-
stance that certain mental patients as
a type—I had in mind obsessive and
melancholic cases—have a circumscribed mental existence confined to a
limited cycle of ideas which, dominating all others, constantly revolved in
the patient's diseased brain" (6).
Moniz believed that if the frontal area
of the brain were to be altered, this
recurrence of unhealthy thoughts would
be interrupted. He decided that the
connection of the thalamus and the
frontal lobes would be the most logical
to work with because the thalamus is
the relay center of sensory impressions,
while the prefrontal lobe is concerned
with interpreting sensory experiences
and rendering them conscious.

Two studies influenced Moniz' interest in the prefrontal lobes. The functions of the frontal lobes had been
studied at Yale by Fulton and Jacobson, who noted that monkeys whose
prefrontal-lobe fibers had been severed
seemed to accept frustration better and
were easier to manage. Richard Brick-
ner had removed parts of frontal lobes
while removing a tumor and reported
that the patient subsequently seemed
less worried and less inhibited and did
not appear intellectually deteriorated
(7). A Swiss psychiatrist, Burckhardt,
in 1890 had also removed part of the
frontal lobe in a mental patient (8),
but the work was not followed up,
probably because of ethical pressure,
and Moniz was thus the first to operate on a large number of patients.

Moniz' first frontal lobotomy on a
psychiatric patient was performed in
1935 with the aid of Almeida Lima, a
Portuguese neurosurgeon; during the
1940's psychosurgery was often advocated for patients with irretractable
psychoses resistant to shock treatments.
Although mortality from prefrontal
operations was only one or two percent, loud protests were raised against
its use. Patients who had this kind of
surgery were not merely calmer—much
of the time they were reduced to being
placid "zombies." Many postoperative
patients lacked ambition, tact, and
imagination; although the patients
themselves may have felt more comfortable, their families did not. Anxiety
was relieved, but at the price of a loss
of self-respect and of empathy with
others. Furthermore, patients with re-
current severely morbid thoughts—that
is, with obsessional psychoses—were
not relieved of their symptoms. A major difficulty was that psychosurgery,
which mutilated irrevocably a part of
the brain, was final. Not a dispensable
part, such as the appendix, is removed,
but an area essential to the human
being—his personality—is forever de-

stroyed. Fortunately, before the brains of too many unapproachable psychotics could be operated upon, another approach was discovered to relieve insufferable anxiety and tension—psychopharmacology.

## PSYCHOPHARMACOLOGY

Primitive medicine men often used dry leaves, roots of plants, and fermented fruits to produce transient psychotic states as a way to heighten and intensify the experiences of religious ceremonials. However, only one of these naturally occurring drugs—opium, the product of poppy seeds—has been deliberately used throughout the centuries to reduce emotional stress. Theophrastus, the Greek physician-botanist, mentions opium's pain-relieving qualities; Paracelsus stored a bit of it in his walking cane; and Sydenham claimed that he could not practice medicine without it.

The drugs that have been used in medicinal therapy for disturbed emotional states can be categorized into five very general classes.

1. Drugs that do not act upon the central nervous system and do not produce changes in behavior, but that do act through suggestion—otherwise called the "placebo effect." Doctors of all periods have had their favorite remedies for ailments, and a doctor's belief that the drug will be helpful is transmitted to the patient.

2. Drugs that correct a deficiency or combat an infection that has led to disease of the central nervous system. Thyroxin, for example, helps the mental retardation occurring in myxedema and cretinism; and states of severe confusion caused by a vitamin-B deficiency have been corrected by proper administration of vitamins. Syphilis of the central nervous system has been cited as an infectious disease that can be cured by drug therapy. Drugs that are given for these specific causes are, however, ineffective for any other mental disorder.

3. Sedatives administered to convert excited states into quiescent ones and stimulants used to produce increased activity in depressed patients. Sedatives like chloral hydrate were first synthesized about 1870 and were used in psychiatric disorders, bromides were also prescribed extensively during the nineteenth century to produce heavy sedation, and in the early twentieth century barbiturates came into use for the same purpose. As for stimulants, the effects of alcoholic beverages and of caffeine have been known for centuries. Synthetic drugs used extensively during the 1930's to treat depression were the amphetamine derivatives (Benzedrine and Dexedrine), but their disagreeable side effects—they caused loss of appetite, palpitations, and an increase in heart rate and blood pressure—interfered with widespread acceptance. Stimulants, like sedatives, act for a limited period of time; they do not produce permanent changes of mood. In the first years of this century, on the assumption that excitement interferes with clear thinking, prolonged administration of barbiturates in excited states was proposed. In 1922 Jacob Klasi recommended prolonged sedative-induced sleep, on the basis that excitement was a result of an inflammatory process in the brain that could be relieved through rest, as other inflammatory conditions were (9). Prolonged-sleep treatment preceded insulin therapy and may be considered a forerunner of the shock treatments.

4. Drugs that facilitate verbal expression of emotions, often called narcotherapy. World War II patients suffering from traumatic war neuroses were given intravenous injections of barbiturates to help them relate the sensations they had experienced during combat.

Enough of the barbiturate was given to enable a patient to speak freely without putting him to sleep. Variants of this technique continued to be used throughout the 1940's, but it is generally conceded today that this kind of treatment helps the patient to express repressed feelings and has some value in relieving acute hysterical symptoms but that it is not suited to resolving underlying conflicts. Another drug used in narcotherapy is carbon dioxide, which has also proved to have the same kind of limited value.

5. Drugs used to test pet theories about mental illness. A list of all these would fill volumes, and indeed textbooks of psychiatry used to recommend many drugs, enzymes, concoctions, extracts, hormones, and vitamins for use in mental disorders. Many of them represent desperate attempts to validate an organic explanation for psychoses, and some of them should, of course, also be considered as drugs that work by suggestion.

In general the pattern of drug therapy for mental illness has been one of initial enthusiasm followed by disappointment. Twenty years after Balard discovered bromides (1826) they were widely used in psychiatric illnesses. During the latter part of the nineteenth century and in the early years of the twentieth, physicians found that uncontrollable states of excitement could be markedly relieved by the administration of bromides. By the mid-twenties, even some psychiatrists writing in the official journal of the American Psychiatric Association were claiming that finally a drug—bromide—had been discovered that could alleviate serious symptoms of disturbed behavior. The American public, following the lead of physicians, so desired bromides that by 1928 one out of every five prescriptions was for bromides. As is usual when drugs are hailed as the solution to

mental illness, disillusionment gradually set in. Patients had to be continuously maintained on bromides in order to show improvement. Nonetheless, despite the repeated shattering of the drug dream, physicians still hope eventually to alleviate man's inner strife by chemical means.

Since antiquity men have desired a state of perfect tranquillity—what the Epicureans called "ataraxia," a serene calmness. The Greeks used alcoholic beverages or narcotics to dull their senses into a state of relative peacefulness; but then, as now, they suffered eventually from confusion and hangover. In the tropical areas of the Orient, however, one drug was said to produce contentment without cloudiness. It was derived from a red-blossomed plant, about eighteen inches high, whose roots zigzagged along the ground like snakes. This plant's many names reflect its use both as an antidote for snakebite ("snakeroot plant," "serpentina," and "sarpagandha," or snake repellent) and as a treatment for moonsickness or insanity ("chabdra," or moon, and "pagla-ka-dawa," or insanity herb) (10).

The snakeroot plant was unknown to the Western world until early in the seventeenth century, when Plumier, a French botanist, first described it. He named it *Rauwolfia serpentina* after the German physician-botanist Leonard Rauwolf, who had, between 1573 and 1574, explored the medicinal plants of the orient. It was not until the 1930's however, that any serious scientific interest was given to its medical potential. In 1931 two Indian doctors, S. Siddiqui and Rafat Siddiqui, isolated five alkaloids from the snakeroot plant, and two other Indian scientists, Ganneth Sen and Katrick Bose, described the use of *Rauwolfia serpentina* in cases of high blood pressure and also in psychoses. By the 1950's *Rauwolfia's* ability to lower blood pressure and to calm excited patients without producing a state of confusion was known to Western physicians as well, and medication incorporating the alkaloids from its roots was being prescribed throughout the world (under many trade names, some of which are Moderil, Sandril, Serpasil, Reserpine, and Harmonyl).

Another group of potent tranquilizers, the phenothiazine derivatives, evolved as the product of meticulous laboratory investigation. One of these derivatives was used to combat parasitic worms in cattle; it also proved effective against malaria and trypanosomiasis— a form of sleeping sickness caused by a parasite in humans. Further investigation revealed that other phenothiazines were effective against some forms of allergies. In 1952 a French psychiatrist, Jean Delay, along with his coworker, Pierre Deniker, reported the beneficial results of using chlorpromazine, a phenothiazine, for treating psychotic patients. In the 1950's the derivatives of the snakeroot plant of ancient India and chemical compounds of this new drug (sold under the trade names Thorazine, Sparine, Compazine, Stelazine, etc.) seemed to combat everything from allergy to psychosis and competed for dominance in the medical journals. Then a third drug was introduced that was to challenge the other tranquilizers in sales as a psychopharmacological panacea. Mephenesin, a glycerol derivative, was known to have a marked muscle-relaxing effect and was used extensively in the treatment of muscle spasm in acute excited conditions like delirium tremens. F. M. Berger, medical director of Wallace Laboratories, realized that Mephenesin's action was of too short a duration and in the early 1950's synthetized a related chemical compound, meprobamate, that had a more lasting effect. Meprobamate (Miltown,

Equanil) had in its favor few side effects, and yet mildly tranquilized the patient.

Because these tranquilizing drugs do not significantly impair consciousness, memory, or intellectual functioning, the conclusion has been drawn that the cerebral cortext must be more or less unaffected and that the subcortical areas must be most implicated, in particular the hypothalamus, the limbic system, and the reticular-activating system.

The phenothiazines appear to inhibit significantly the alerting r.a.s., thereby diminishing awareness of disturbing stimuli. If a phenothiazine is given to a patient in a state of severe pain, for example, the patient continues to feel pain but is not as attentive to it, not as aware of it, and consequently not as troubled by it. For this reason the phenothiazines are widely used in obstetrics and surgery. These drugs are not merely effective against physical pain, however; they also reduce mental anguish and anxiety, so that individuals who usually would be driven by their inner impulses to excessive activity and excitement quiet down remarkably well after taking a phenothiazine derivative. The *Rauwolfia* compounds are less sedative than the phenothiazine derivatives and apparently have their most crucial effect upon the hypothalamus and the autonomic nervous system. They seem both to inhibit the sympathetic nervous system and stimulate the parasympathetic nervous system, which would account for some of their annoying side effects, such as pupillary constriction, increased motility of the gastrointestinal tract, and lowering of the blood pressure. Their most untoward side effect is that in many cases they produce depression.

The mildest tranquilizers, the meprobamates, seem to act in completely dissimilar fashion from both the *Rau-*

*wolfia* and the phenothiazines. They do not affect the hypothalamus or the r.a.s., but instead apparently slow down transmission of sensory impulses from the thalamus to the cortex. The exact manner of this inhibition is uncertain, and the suppression of impulses appears to be incomplete, since if it were complete the effect would be equivalent to a chemical lobotomy, which it is not. In general the tranquilizers, with a few exceptions, have proved to be safe with relatively few side effects.

The tranquilizers have proved least effective for cases of depression, which is not surprising. Any drug that tranquilizes or inhibits alertness to stimuli could scarcely have much value for patients who are already hypertranquilized, inattentive, and excessively limited in their activity. However, a group of stimulating drugs, the amine-oxidase inhibitors, have proved promising for lifting the spirits of depressed patients. Amphetamines had been used during the 1930's as antidepressants, but their undesirable side effects brought them into some disfavor. Then, in the 1950's, it was observed that a drug, Iproniazid, used in the treatment of tuberculosis appeared to elate the depressed tubercular patients who took it, and research work began on using similar compounds that were less toxic than Iproniazid in the treatment of depressions. These drugs, which do not have the same undesirable side effects as the amphetamines, apparently act by inhibiting an enzyme called amine-oxidase, which seems to destroy serotonin; consequently the body is able to store up reserves of serotonin in the body. In addition to the amine-oxidase inhibitors, there are several other classes of antidepressants that are presently under full-scale investigation.

The use of the new psychotropic drugs—tranquilizers and antidepressants—has opened up new horizons for psychiatry. They have the practical advantages that they neither affect the state of consciousness to the same degree as the traditional sedatives nor have the unpleasant side effects of the amphetamines; they offer physicians the opportunity to influence specific psychic functions and shift the equilibrium between inhibitions and excitations in the desired direction. Retarded depressive patients can be stimulated; excited manic patients can be tranquilized.

Although the mode of action of these drugs is not yet fully understood, it is well established that tranquilizing drugs act primarily on the midbrain, the reticular formation, and the vegetative centers. They do not interfere with cortical functions, nor do they induce excessive drowsiness like the barbiturates. The fact that they act on the lower centers renders them therapeutically more useful than drugs that have a direct effect upon the higher centers of the nervous system: they leave integrative and cognitive functions unaffected and thus allow drug treatment to be combined with psychotherapy, which of necessity has to rely on the integrative functions of the highest centers. The very limited therapeutic usefulness of hypnotherapy and narcotherapy has shown that a genuine reconstruction of a neurotic personality cannot be achieved without involvement of these integrative functions.

Used with psychotic patients, tranquilizers reduce anxiety, restlessness, hallucinations, and delusions, which are the outward manifestations of underlying disturbances that seriously interfere with the patient's human relationships, with his functioning in life, and with psychotherapy. The manifest florid symptoms, particularly anxiety, impair the higher integrative functions. Moreover, hallucinations and delusions make contact with others more difficult and induce further withdrawal from reality. This vicious cycle is broken when drug treatment is successful. Symptomatic improvements from drugs allow for further spontaneous ego development. However, since the drug does not change the underlying personality disturbance and merely reduces its secondary manifestations, psychotherapy remains still the most incisive tool. It is still not clear, though, how far systematic and expert psychotherapy can go with psychotic patients, even when drugs have made them more accessible to intensive psychological treatment.

Whether or not psychotropic drugs should be used in cases of neurosis is a controversial issue. The secondary symptoms, such as the disturbance of the sensorium and of the thought processes that makes the psychological approach to psychotics often impossible, are much less common in neurotic patients. Reduction of extreme anxiety remains a real indication for the use of drugs in the psychoneurotic, but treatment should focus on its essential target, the underlying personality disturbance. Some psychoanalysts combine their treatment with a judicious administration of psychotropic drugs, trying to create by the reduction of disturbing excessive anxiety more favorable conditions for the psychological approach; other psychoanalysts, more fundamentalistic in their approach, believe, for technical reasons, that the use of drugs seriously interferes with their therapeutic work. These psychoanalysts maintain that to give drugs is to play the role of the magician who is trying to relieve symptoms quickly, thereby hampering his role as a psychotherapist who is trying to help the patient reveal and understand himself.

There can be no question that the psychotropic drugs have great practical value. Their use has markedly shortened the hospital stay of severely disturbed patients and has also simplified the hospital management of these patients by making them more tractable. And what is most important, the more drastic methods of treating psychotics—electroshock, insulin therapy, and psychosurgery—are less frequently used. Unfortunately most severely depressed patients respond less rapidly to the antidepressant drugs than to electroshock; nonetheless, these drugs have made it possible to humanize the hospital treatment of psychotic patients by substituting chemical for corporal restraint.

It is most tempting for a person to get relief from the unavoidable burdens and anxieties of everyday life by taking a drug rather than by facing his actual problems realistically. However, psychological habituation to a chemically induced oblivion is an unrealistic solution and a basically unreliable crutch that only compounds the problems encountered in day-to-day living. Concern about real problems induces a person to plan and strive realistically. Anxiety mobilizes both biological and psychological defenses to ensure survival. Unquestionably, under certain extremely stressful life conditions and also in pathological states of mind, tension and anxiety may hamper effectual planning and concentration. Relief by tranquilizers, even temporary relief, in such conditions may allow the person to face more realistically his internal and external problems. Only an expert psychological evaluation of the situation can lead to the correct decision whether or not administration of drugs is indicated in an individual case. Meanwhile, indiscriminate use of psychotropic drugs constitutes a definite danger for proper psychiatric care as well as for mental hygiene in general.

New drugs will come to take over for older ones, and there will be many new drug trials. It does not seem foreseeable that one drug will solve the dilemma of mental illness, but the experimentation into how drugs act on the nervous system will aid us inestimably to understand better the functioning of the brain. As we learn more about the reticular-activating system, the limbic system, and the hypothalamus, and the enzymes and the neurohormones active in the nervous system, the gap between the mind and brain becomes narrowed. Already we suspect that the cerebral cortex can block through inhibitory discharges unpleasant stimuli reaching it from other neuronal centers. We call this psychological repression. We have noted that interruption of thalamic-cortical circuits, inhibition of the r.a.s. system, or reverberations set up in the limbic lobe are not dissimilar and occur with drug intervention. The day will arrive when the mind will come to its intended resting place, not as a structure of the brain, but as a function of it. How disturbing thoughts, feelings, and sensations, the psychological phenomenon called mind, are transmitted, stored as memories, and reacted to at a later time in life will be the legacy left by what appeared at one time to be psychopharmacological fads. Nevertheless, in the future we must be cautious lest we overevaluate valuable neurological data and claim from it more than is justified. In the final analysis, the situations that provoke emotional upsets and the subjective experience of psychic pain cannot be explained in terms of the nervous system but must be described in psychological language.

## THE HALLUCINOGENS AND EXPERIMENTAL PSYCHOSIS

The rediscovery of hallucinogens, drugs that produce transient psychotic states, has in recent years aroused the hope that chemical compounds may be found that will terminate not only experimentally induced psychoses, but other psychotic states as well. Man's attempt to produce states in himself in which he would have vivid and fantastic experiences long outdates man's attempt to cure psychosis. Over the ages men have looked for agents that would allow escape from life's pressures: opium, for instance, is such a drug, and so are alcohol and hashish. Marihuana, cohoba seed, mushrooms, and the buttons from the peyote cactus are others.

In the late nineteenth century an alkaloid isolated from the peyote cactus, mescaline, was found to produce intense perceptual disturbances, which have often been described by those who have taken it. During the 1950's mescaline was used experimentally to induce psychotic states; but also another compound, dissimilar in structure and ten thousand times more potent, lysergic acid diethylamide (LSD), has also been so used.

Lysergic acid is the active ingredient of ergot, a fungus that causes the rye cereal plant to decay. Its hallucinogenic quality was discovered by accident in 1943, when, working on the derivatives of the rye ergot, a Swiss chemist, Dr. A. Hofmann, accidentally sniffed one of the synthetic products he was using. He later wrote: "I was seized in the laboratory by a peculiar sensation of vertigo and restlessness. Objects in my vicinity and also the shape of my co-workers in the laboratory appeared to undergo optical changes. . . . In a dreamlike state I left the laboratory and went home where I was seized by an irresistible urge to lie down and sleep. Daylight was felt as being unpleasantly intense. I drew the curtains and immediately fell into a peculiar state of 'drunkenness,' characterized by an exaggerated imagination. With closed eyes, fantastic pictures of extraordinary plasticity and intensive kaleidoscopic colorfulness seemed to surge towards me. After two hours this state gradually subsided" (11). Further investigations in the 1940's and 1950's brought reports of perceptual distortions, mood modulations, multicolored illusionary and hallucinatory patterns made up of glowing and beautiful geometrical designs.

Investigators have so far been unable to establish the causes of the vivid experiences that mescaline and LSD produce; both compounds appear to have similar psychological effects in man and animals. It has been theorized but not confirmed that mescaline, which is similar in structure to adrenalin, becomes converted in the body to one of the breakdown products of adrenalin, adrenochrome, which produces hallucinogenic states. The entire problem of how adrenalin is metabolized in the body has been a major concern of biological research in the past several years.

LSD on the other hand, has an indole nucleus also present in serotonin and the Rauwolfia compounds; LSD seems to be antagonistic to serotonin, which perhaps may underlie its psychotomimetic qualities. However, we still do not know how abnormal quantities of serotonin are related to mental illness. Some investigators postulate that by combining LSD with psychotherapy, repression might be overcome so that unconscious conflicts would reach consciousness and be communicated. The use of LSD at this time is, however, in the experimental stage, and the neurophysiological and psychological phenomena produced by these drugs remain enigmatic.

H. J. Eysenck

# The Effects of Psychotherapy: An Evaluation

*While a large number of varying theories have been presented, each of which claims to hold the key to the treatment of the mentally ill, the amount of hard evidence supporting the clinical claims is usually disappointing. A number of years ago, Dr. Eysenck published a paper pointing out the lack of evidence supporting claims about the effectiveness of psychotherapy, and that paper is presented here. Since this paper was published, Dr. Eysenck has brought his argument up to date with continuous review of relevant research, but his conclusions have remained largely unchanged. It may be of some interest to the reader to know that Dr. Eysenck is a very strong proponent of the behavior modification approach, and finds the evidence in that area a good deal more satisfactory. It should be clear that Dr. Eysenck did not do any research to support his conclusions but, instead, came to these conclusions after reviewing a number of studies performed by others. It should also be clear that Dr. Eysenck*

Reprinted from the Journal of Consulting Psychology, 16(1952), 319–324, with the permission of The American Psychological Association and Dr. Eysenck. Copyright 1952 by the American Psychological Association.

*does not conclude that therapy has been demonstrated to be ineffective, but instead that it has not been demonstrated to be effective.*

The recommendation of the Committee on Training in Clinical Psychology of the American Psychological Association regarding the training of clinical psychologists in the field of psychotherapy has been criticized by the writer in a series of papers (10, 11, 12). Of the arguments presented in favor of the policy advocated by the Committee, the most cogent one is perhaps that which refers to the social need for the skills possessed by the psychotherapist. In view of the importance of the issues involved, it seemed worth while to examine the evidence relating to the actual effects of psychotherapy, in an attempt to seek clarification on a point of fact.

## BASE LINE AND
## UNIT OF MEASUREMENT

In the only previous attempt to carry out such an evaluation, Landis has pointed out that "before any sort of measurement can be made, it is necessary to establish a base line and a common unit of measure. The only unit of measure available is the report made by the physician stating that the patient has recovered, is much improved, is improved or unimproved. This unit is probably as satisfactory as any type of human subjective judgment, partaking of both the good and bad points of such judgments" (26, p. 156). For a unit Landis suggests "that of expressing therapeutic results in terms of the number of patients recovered or improved per 100 cases admitted to the hospital." As an alternative, he suggests "the statement of therapeutic outcome for some given group of patients during some stated interval of time."

Landis realized quite clearly that in order to evaluate the effectiveness of any form of therapy, data from a control group of nontreated patients would be required in order to compare the effects of therapy with the spontaneous remission rate. In the absence of anything better, he used the amelioration rate in state mental hospitals for patients diagnosed under the heading of "neuroses." As he points out:

There are several objections to the use of the consolidated amelioration rate . . . of the . . . state hospitals . . . as a base rate for spontaneous recovery. The fact that psychoneurotic cases are not usually committed to state hospitals unless in a very bad condition; the relatively small number of voluntary patients in the group; the fact that such patients do get some degree of psychotherapy especially in the reception hospitals; and the probably quite different economic, educational, and social status of the State Hospital group compared to the patients reported from each of the other hospitals—all argue against the acceptance of [this] figure . . . as a truly satisfactory base line, but in the absence of any other better figure this must serve (26, p. 168).

Actually the various figures quoted by Landis agree very well. The percentage of neurotic patients discharged annually as recovered or improved from New York state hospitals is 70 (for the years 1925–1934); for the United States as a whole it is 68 (for the years 1926 to 1933). The percentage of neurotics discharged as recovered or improved within one year of admission is 66 for the United States (1933) and 68 for New York (1914). The consolidated amelioration rate of New York state hospitals, 1917–1934, is 72 per cent. As this is the figure chosen by Landis, we may accept it in preference to the other very similar ones quoted. By and large, we may thus say that of severe neurotics receiving in the main custodial care, and very little if any psychotherapy, over two-thirds recovered or improved to a considerable extent. "Although this is not, strictly speaking, a basic figure for 'spontaneous' recovery, still any therapeutic method must show an appreciably greater size than this to be seriously considered" (26, p. 160).

Another estimate of the required "base line" is provided by Denker:

Five hundred consecutive disability claims due to psychoneurosis, treated by general practitioners throughout the country, and not by accredited specialists or sanatoria, were reviewed. All types of neurosis were included, and no attempt made to differentiate the neurasthenic, anxiety, compulsive, hysteric, or other states, but the greatest care was taken to eliminate the true psychotic or organic lesions which in the early stages of illness so often simulate neurosis. These cases were taken consecutively from the files of the Equitable Life Assurance Society of the United States, were from all parts of the country, and all had been ill of a neurosis for at least three months before claims were submitted. They, therefore, could be fairly called "severe," since they had been totally disabled for at least a three months' period, and rendered unable to carry on with any "occupation for remuneration or profit" for at least that time (9, p. 2164).

These patients were regularly seen and treated by their own physicians with sedatives, tonics, suggestion, and reassurance, but in no case was any attempt made at anything but this most superficial type of "psychotherapy" which has always been the stock-in-trade of the general practitioner. Repeated statements, every three months or so by their physicians, as well as independent investigations by the insurance company, confirmed the fact that these people actually were not engaged in productive work during the period of their illness. During their disablement, these cases received disability benefits. As Denker points out, "It is appreciated that this fact of disability income may have actually prolonged the total period of disability and acted as a barrier to incentive for recovery. One would, therefore, not expect the therapeutic results in such a group of cases to be as favorable as in other groups where the economic factor might act as an important spur in helping the sick patient adjust to his neurotic conflict and illness" (9, p. 2165).

The cases were all followed up for at least a five-year period, and often as long as ten years after the period of disability had begun. The criteria of "recovery" used by Denker were as follows: (a) return to work, and ability to carry on well in economic adjustments for at least a five-year period; (b) complaint of no further or very slight difficulties; (c) making of successful social adjustments. Using these criteria, which are very similar to those usually used by psychiatrists, Denker found that 45 per cent of the patients recovered after one year, another 27 per cent after two years, making 72 per cent in all. Another 10 per cent, 5 per cent, and 4 per cent recovered during the third, fourth, and fifth years, respectively, making a total of 90 per cent recoveries after five years.

This sample contrasts in many ways with that used by Landis. The cases on which Denker reports were probably not quite as severe as those summarized by Landis; they were all voluntary, non-hospitalized patients, and came from a much higher socioeconomic stratum. The majority of Denker's patients were clerical workers, executives, teachers, and professional men. In spite of these differences, the recovery figures for the two samples are almost identical. The most suitable figure to choose from those given by Denker is probably that for the two-year recovery rate, as follow-up studies seldom go beyond two years and the higher figures for three-, four-, and five-year follow-up would overestimate the efficiency of this "base line" procedure. Using, therefore, the two-year recovery figure of 72 per cent, we find that Denker's figure agrees exactly with that given by Landis. We may, therefore, conclude with some confidence that our estimate of some two-thirds of severe neurotics showing recovery or considerable improvement without the benefit of systematic psychotherapy is not likely to be very far out.

## EFFECTS OF PSYCHOTHERAPY

We may now turn to the effects of psychotherapeutic treatment. The results of nineteen studies reported in the literature, covering over seven thousand cases, and dealing with both psychoanalytic and eclectic types of treatment, are quoted in detail in Table 1. An attempt has been made to report results under the four headings: (a) cured, or much improved; (b) improved; (c) slightly improved; (d) not improved, died, discontinued treatment, etc. It was usually easy to reduce additional categories given by some writers to these basic four; some writers give only two or three categories, and in those cases it was, of course, impossible to subdivide further, and the figures for combined categories are given.[1] A slight degree of subjectivity inevitably enters into this procedure, but it is doubtful if it has caused much distortion. A somewhat greater degree

of subjectivity is probably implied in the writer's judgment as to which disorders and diagnoses should be considered to fall under the heading of "neurosis." Schizophrenic, manic-depressive, and paranoid states have been excluded; organ neuroses, psychopathic states, and character disturbances have been included. The number of cases where there was genuine doubt is probably too small to make much change in the final figures, regardless of how they are allocated.

A number of studies have been excluded because of such factors as excessive inadequacy of follow-up, partial duplication of cases with others included in our table, failure to indicate type of treatment used, and other reasons which made the results useless from our point of view. Papers thus rejected are those by Thorley and Craske (37), Bennett and Semrad (2), H. I. Harris (19), Hardcastle (17), A. Harris (18), Jacobson, and Wright (21), Friess and Nelson (14), Comroe (5), Wenger (38), Orbison (33), Coon and Raymond (6), Denker (8), and Bond and Braceland (3). Their inclusion would not have altered our conclusions to any considerable degree, although, as Miles et al. point out: "When the various studies are compared in terms of thoroughness, careful planning, strictness of criteria and objectivity, there is often an inverse correlation between these factors and the percentage of successful results reported" (31, p. 88).

Certain difficulties have arisen from the inability of some writers to make their column figures agree with their totals, or to calculate percentages accurately. Again, the writer has exercised his judgment as to which figures to accept. In certain cases, writers have

---

[1] In one or two cases where patients who improved or improved slightly were combined by the original author, the total figure has been divided equally between the two categories.

TABLE 1. Summary of Reports of the Results of Psychotherapy

| | N | Cured; Much Improved | Improved | Slightly Improved | Not Improved; Died; Left Treatment | Per Cent Cured; Much Improved; Improved |
|---|---|---|---|---|---|---|
| (A) Psychoanalytic | | | | | | |
| 1. Fenichel (13, pp. 28–40) | 484 | 104 | 84 | 99 | 197 | 39 |
| 2. Kessel and Hyman (24) | 34 | 16 | 5 | 4 | 9 | 62 |
| 3. Jones (22, pp. 12–14) | 59 | 20 | 8 | 28 | 3 | 47 |
| 4. Alexander (1, pp. 30–43) | 141 | 28 | 42 | 23 | 48 | 50 |
| 5. Knight (25) | 42 | 8 | 20 | 7 | 7 | 67 |
| All cases | 760 | 335 | | | 425 | 44 |
| (B) Eclectic | | | | | | |
| 1. Huddleson (20) | 200 | 19 | 74 | 80 | 27 | 46 |
| 2. Matz (30) | 775 | 10 | 310 | 310 | 145 | 41 |
| 3. Maudsley Hospital Report (1931) | 1721 | 288 | 900 | | 533 | 69 |
| 4. Maudsley Hospital Report (1935) | 1711 | 371 | 765 | | 575 | 64 |
| 5. Neustatter (32) | 46 | 9 | 14 | 8 | 15 | 50 |
| 6. Luff and Garrod (27) | 500 | 140 | 135 | 26 | 199 | 55 |
| 7. Luff and Garrod (27) | 210 | 38 | 84 | 54 | 34 | 68 |
| 8. Ross (34) | 1089 | 547 | 306 | | 236 | 77 |
| 9. Yaskin (40) | 100 | 29 | 29 | | 42 | 58 |
| 10. Curran (7) | 83 | 51 | | | 32 | 61 |
| 11. Masserman and Carmichael (29) | 50 | 7 | 20 | 5 | 18 | 54 |
| 12. Carmichael and Masserman (4) | 77 | 16 | 25 | 14 | 22 | 53 |
| 13. Schilder (35) | 35 | 11 | 11 | 6 | 7 | 63 |
| 14. Hamilton and Wall (16) | 100 | 32 | 34 | 17 | 17 | 66 |
| 15. Hamilton et al. (15) | 100 | 48 | 5 | 17 | 32 | 51 |
| 16. Landis (26) | 119 | 40 | 47 | | 32 | 73 |
| 17. Institute Med. Psychol. (quoted Neustatter) | 270 | 58 | 132 | 55 | 25 | 70 |
| 18. Wilder (39) | 54 | 3 | 24 | 16 | 11 | 50 |
| 19. Miles et al. (31) | 53 | 13 | 18 | 13 | 9 | 58 |
| All cases | 7293 | 4661 | | | 2632 | 64 |

given figures of cases where there was a recurrence of the disorder after apparent cure or improvement, without indicating how many patients were affected in these two groups respectively. All recurrences of this kind have been subtracted from the "cured" and "improved" totals, taking half from each. The total number of cases involved in all these adjustments is quite small. Another investigator making all decisions exactly in the opposite direction to the present writer's would hardly alter the final percentage figures by more than 1 or 2 per cent.

We may now turn to the figures as presented. Patients treated by means of psychoanalysis improve to the extent of 44 per cent; patients treated eclectically improve to the extent of 64 per cent; patients treated only custodially or by general practitioners improve to the extent of 72 per cent. There thus appears to be an inverse correlation between recovery and psychotherapy; the more psychotherapy, the smaller the recovery rate. This conclusion requires certain qualifications.

In our tabulation of psychoanalytic results, we have classed those who stopped treatment together with those not improved. This appears to be reasonable; a patient who fails to finish his treatment, and is not improved, is surely a therapeutic failure. The same rule has been followed with the data summarized under "eclectic" treatment, except when the patient who did not finish treatment was definitely classified as "improved" by the therapist. However, in view of the peculiarities of Freudian procedures it may appear to some readers to be more just to class those cases separately, and deal only with the percentage of completed treatments which are successful. Approximately one-third of the psychoanalytic patients listed broke off treatment, so that the percentage of successful treat-

ments of patients who finished their course must be put at approximately 66 per cent. It would appear, then, that when we discount the risk the patient runs of stopping treatment altogether, his chances of improvement under psychoanalysis are approximately equal to his chances of improvement under eclectic treatment, and slightly worse than his chances under a general practitioner or custodial treatment.

Two further points require clarification: (a) Are patients in our "control" groups (Landis and Denker) as seriously ill as those in our "experimental" groups? (b) Are standards of recovery perhaps less stringent in our "control" than in our "experimental" groups? It is difficult to answer these questions definitely, in view of the great divergence of opinion between psychiatrists. From a close scrutiny of the literature it appears that the "control" patients were probably at least as seriously ill as the "experimental" patients, and possibly more so. As regards standards of recovery, those in Denker's study are as stringent as most of those used by psychoanalysts and eclectic psychiatrists, but those used by the State Hospitals whose figures Landis quotes are very probably more lenient. In the absence of agreed standards of severity of illness, or of extent of recovery, it is not possible to go further.

In general, certain conclusions are possible from these data. They fail to prove that psychotherapy, Freudian or otherwise, facilitates the recovery of neurotic patients. They show that roughly two-thirds of a group of neurotic patients will recover or improve to a marked extent within about two years of the onset of their illness, whether they are treated by means of psychotherapy or not. This figure appears to be remarkably stable from one investigation to another, regardless of type of patient treated, standard of recovery employed, or method of therapy used. From the point of view of the neurotic, these figures are encouraging; from the point of view of the psychotherapist, they can hardly be called very favorable to his claims.

The figures quoted do not necessarily disprove the possibility of therapeutic effectiveness. There are obvious shortcomings in any actuarial comparison and these shortcomings are particularly serious when there is so little agreement among psychiatrists relating even to the most fundamental concepts and definitions. Definite proof would require a special investigation, carefully planned and methodologically more adequate than these ad hoc comparisons. But even the most modest conclusions that the figures fail to show any favorable effects of psychotherapy should give pause to those who would wish to give an important part in the training of clinical psychologists to a skill the existence and effectiveness of which is still unsupported by any scientifically acceptable evidence.

These results and conclusions will no doubt contradict the strong feeling of usefulness and therapeutic success which many psychiatrists and clinical psychologists hold. While it is true that subjective feelings of this type have no place in science, they are likely to prevent an easy acceptance of the general argument presented here. This contradiction between objective fact and subjective certainty has been remarked on in other connections by Kelly and Fiske, who found that:

One aspect of our findings is most disconcerting to us: the inverse relationship between the confidence of staff members at the time of making a prediction and the measured validity of that prediction. Why is it, for example, that our staff members tended to make their best predictions at a time when they subjectivity felt relatively unacquainted with the candidate, when they had constructed no systematic picture of his personality structure? Or conversely, why is it that with increasing confidence in clinical judgment . . . we find decreasing validities of predictions? (23, p. 406).

In the absence of agreement between fact and belief, there is urgent need for a decrease in the strength of belief, and for an increase in the number of facts available. Until such facts as may be discovered in a process of rigorous analysis support the prevalent belief in therapeutic effectiveness of psychological treatment, it seems premature to insist on the inclusion of training in such treatment in the curriculum of the clinical psychologist.

## SUMMARY

A survey was made of reports on the improvement of neurotic patients after psychotherapy, and the results compared with the best available estimates of recovery without benefit of such therapy. The figures fail to support the hypothesis that psychotherapy facilitates recovery from neurotic disorder. In view of the many difficulties attending such actuarial comparisons, no further conclusions could be derived from the data whose shortcomings highlight the necessity of properly planned and executed experimental studies into this important field.

## REFERENCES

1. ALEXANDER, F. Five year report of the Chicago Institute for Psychoanalysis. 1932–1937.
2. BENNETT, A. E., and SEMRAD, E. V. Common errors in diagnosis and treatment of the psychoneurotic patient— a study of 100 case histories. Nebr. Med. J., 21(1936), 90–92.

3. Bond, E. D., and Braceland, F. J. Prognosis in mental disease. *Amer. J. Psychiat.*, 94(1937), 263–274.
4. Carmichael, H. T., and Masserman, T. H. Results of treatment in a psychiatric outpatients' department. *J.A.M.A.*, 113(1939), 2292–2298.
5. Comroe, B. I. Follow-up study of 100 patients diagnosed as "neurosis." *J. Nerv. Ment. Dis.*, 83(1936), 679–684.
6. Coon, G. P., and Raymond, A. A review of the psychoneuroses at Stockbridge. Stockbridge, Mass.: Austen Riggs Foundation, Inc., 1940.
7. Curran, D. The problem of assessing psychiatric treatment. *Lancet*, II (1937), 1005–1009.
8. Denker, P. G. Prognosis and life expectancy in the psychoneuroses. *Proc. Ass. Life Insur. Med. Dir. Amer.*, 24 (1937), 179.
9. Denker, R. Results of treatment of psychoneuroses by the general practitioner. A follow-up study of 500 cases. *N. Y. State J. Med.*, 46(1946), 2164–2166.
10. Eysenck, H. J. Training in clinical psychology: an English point of view. *Amer. Psychologist*, 4(1949), 173–176.
11. ――― The relation between medicine and psychology in England. In W. Dennis, ed., *Current trends in the relation of psychology and medicine.* Pittsburgh: Univ. of Pittsburgh Press, 1950.
12. ――― Function and training of the clinical psychologist. *J. Ment. Sci.*, 96 (1950), 1–16.
13. Fenichel, O. *Ten years of the Berlin Psychoanalysis Institute. 1920–1930.*
14. Friess, C., and Nelson, M. J. Psychoneurotics five years later. *Amer. J. Ment. Sci.*, 203(1942), 539–558.
15. Hamilton, D. M., Vanney, I. H., and Wall, T. H. Hospital treatment of patients with psychoneurotic disorder. *Amer. J. Psychiat.*, 99(1942), 243–247.
16. Hamilton, D. M., and Wall, T. H. Hospital treatment of patients with psychoneurotic disorder. *Amer. J. Psychiat.*, 98(1941), 551–557.
17. Hardcastle, D. H. A follow-up study of one hundred cases made for the Department of Psychological Medicine, Guy's Hospital. *J. Ment. Sci.*, 90 (1934), 536–549.
18. Harris, A. The prognosis of anxiety states. *Brit. Med. J.*, 2(1938), 649–654.
19. Harris, H. I. Efficient psychotherapy for the large out-patient clinic. *New England J. Med.*, 221(1939), 1–5.
20. Huddleson, J. H. Psychotherapy in 200 cases of psychoneurosis. *Mil. Surgeon*, 60(1927), 161–170.
21. Jacobson, J. R., and Wright, K. W. Review of a year of group psychotherapy. *Psychiat., Quart.*, 16(1942), 744–764.
22. Jones, E. *Decennial report of the London Clinic of Psychoanalysis. 1926–1936.*
23. Kelly, E. L., and Fiske, D. W. The prediction of success in the VA training program in clinical psychology. *Amer. Psychologist*, 5(1950), 395–406.
24. Kessel, L., and Hyman, H. T. The value of psychoanalysis as a therapeutic procedure. *J.A.M.A.*, 101(1933), 1612–1615.
25. Knight, R. O. Evaluation of the results of psychoanalytic therapy. *Amer. J. Psychiat.*, 98(1941), 434–446.
26. Landis, C. Statistical evaluation of psychotherapeutic methods. In S. E. Hinsie, ed., *Concepts and problems of psychotherapy.* London: Heineman, 1938. Pages 155–165.
27. Luff, M. C., and Garrod, M. The after-results of psychotherapy in 500 adult cases. *Brit. Med. J.*, 2(1935), 54–59.
28. Mapother, E. Discussion. *Brit. J. Med. Psychol.*, 7(1927), 57.
29. Masserman, T. H., and Carmichael, H. T. Diagnosis and prognosis in psychiatry. *J. Ment. Sci.*, 84(1938), 893–946.
30. Matz, P. B. Outcome of hospital treatment of ex-service patients with nervous and mental disease in the U.S. Veteran's Bureau. *U.S. Vet. Bur. Med. Bull.*, 5(1929), 829–842.
31. Miles, H. H. W., Barrabee, E. L., and Finesinger, J. E. Evaluation of psychotherapy. *Psychosom. Med.*, 13 (1951), 83–105.
32. Neustatter, W. L. The results of fifty cases treated by psychotherapy. *Lancet*, I(1935), 796–799.
33. Orbison, T. J. The psychoneuroses:

psychathenia, neurasthenia and hysteria, with special reference to a certain method of treatment. *Calif. West. Med.*, 23(1925), 1132–1136.

34. Ross, T. A. *An enquiry into prognosis in the neurosis.* London: Cambridge Univ. Press, 1936.

35. SCHILDER, P. Results and problems of group psychotherapy in severe neuroses. *Ment. Hyg.*, N.Y., 23(1939), 87–98.

36. SKOTTOWE, I., and LOCKWOOD, M. R. The fate of 150 psychiatric outpatients. *J. Ment. Sci.*, 81(1935), 502–508.

37. THORLEY, A. S., and CRASKE, N. Comparison and estimate of group and indi-

vidual method of treatment. *Brit. Med. J.*, 1(1950), 97–100.

38. WENGER, P. Uber weitere Ergebnisse der Psychotherapie in Rahmen einer Medizinischen Poliklinik. *Wien. Med. Wschr.*, 84(1934), 320–325.

39. WILDER, J. Facts and figures on psychotherapy, *J. Clin. Psychopath.*, 7 (1945), 311–347.

40. YASKIN, J. C. The psychoneuroses and neuroses. A review of 100 cases with special reference to treatment and results. *Amer. J. Psychiat.*, 93(1936), 107–125.

Donald J. Kiesler

# Some Myths of Psychotherapy Research and the Search for a Paradigm

*H. J. Eysenck has written a widely quoted paper questioning the effectiveness of psychotherapy. The immediate impact of Dr. Eysenck's paper was the arousal of an enormous amount of hostility and opposition among psychotherapists. While he did not say that psychotherapy did not work, this inference was widely seen as stemming from the paper, and it seemed to run counter to the experience of many therapists. A number of psychotherapists dismissed the paper without much thought, since it did not support their views of psychotherapy. This reaction was not likely to add much to knowledge, and did not do Dr. Eysenck the justice of grappling with the critical problem that he raised. Other psychologists have examined Dr. Eysenck's argument carefully, and found a number of logical and methodological flaws. This selection from a longer paper by Dr. Kiesler summarizes the critical arguments about the Eysenck thesis. In the remainder of the original paper, Dr. Kiesler criticizes other approaches to psychotherapy, and the reader is referred to that paper.*

## THE SPONTANEOUS REMISSION MYTH

This second myth has been perpetuated primarily by Eysenck (1952, 1954, 1955a, 1955b, 1961, 1964).

Despite many refutations, it has continued to muddle research regarding the effectiveness of psychotherapy, and has fostered much of the pessimism that has more recently colored this research. Although this conception was restricted by Eysenck to psychoneurosis

*Abridged from the* Psychological Bulletin, *64(1966), 114–120 with the permission of the American Psychological Association and Dr. Kiesler. Copyright 1966 by the American Psychological Association.*

alone, its implications seem to have generalized to most of psychotherapy. Its more specific statement takes the following form (Eysenck, 1961): "We may conclude with some confidence that about two-thirds of severe psychoneurotics show recovery or considerable improvement without the benefit of systematic psychotherapy, after a lapse of two years from the time that their disorder is notified, or they are hospitalized [p. 711]." The clear implication of this proposition is that for psychotherapy to be proven worthwhile, it has to demonstrate it can beat this two-thirds percentage, since two-thirds of the patients improve without having anything done to or for them.

This percentage represents a rather severe standard, as the evidence, such as it is, has reflected. Without this base rate for comparison most therapists and laymen might be satisfied with a two out of three success rate. But with this base rate of spontaneous remission psychotherapy needs to be almost totally successful. Apparently the assumption has taken a rather tight hold on both practitioners and researchers of psychotherapy. Yet, the surprising fact is that the entire evidence for this assumption comes from the findings of two studies, which are, at best, ambiguous. Further, the assumption contradicts clinical experience as well as some of the experimental findings regarding human and animal learning, and has been refuted in the literature on several occasions. Unfortunately, these refutations focused on different aspects of the argument, and were obscured by their connection with the effectiveness-of-therapy polemic. Hence, it is necessary to separate the spontaneous remission argument from the latter polemic, and to integrate the various arguments against spontaneous remission. This section will, therefore, seriously reconsider this assumption with the hope that this refutation will bury it permanently.

In the first place, clinical lore indicates that the phenomenon of spontaneous remission has been observed for only three diagnostic categories. The first category is acutely reactive schizophrenics, who typically experience an abrupt onset of psychosis under usually specifiable traumatic conditions, and whose premorbid history is relatively free of gross pathology. Lasting recovery is generally rapid for these schizophrenics regardless of treatment. The other two diagnostic groups include the reactive and psychotic depressions. After temporary remission of their depressive symptoms these patients characteristically exhibit a regular course of recovery, ordinarily for a period of about 2 years, after which the depression recurs. It would obviously be essential in any studies evaluating therapy with any of these three groups that these remission characteristics be considered. But, as far as can be ascertained by this author, spontaneous remission as a typical phenomenon has not been clinically observed for other types of patients. In regard to psychoneurosis, moreover, clinical tradition indicates quite clearly that, rather than spontaneous recovery, increased rigidity of symptoms tends to be the rule when the patient remains untreated. Freud was so impressed by the rigidity of the resistance encountered in the treatment of psychoneurosis that he coined the term repetition compulsion to describe the process. Secondly, no attempt has been made to explain the phenomenon in other than quite gross terms. If spontaneous remission of neurosis occurs, it must occur via some psychological and/or physiological process. What is the nature of this process? What is the stimulus which initiates the process of recovery? Are the stimulus and the process the same for all psychoneurotics, or different for various types? How does it come about that attitudes and habit systems on which one has acted for much of his life are modified so easily without rather energetic intervention of some sort? What makes an habitual maladaptive pattern of behavior suddenly begin to disappear? These are crucial questions that need to be considered regarding spontaneous remission. Thirdly, how can one reconcile spontaneous remission with the evidence in the area of learning regarding habit strength and particularly the extreme difficulty of extinguishing avoidance responses?

Since this phenomenon seems counter to clinical experience, is only grossly explained, and contradicts evidence from learning research, it would seem that the empirical evidence for its existence needs to be quite impressive indeed before its generality can be accepted. Instead, the entire argument for spontaneous remission of neurotic patients comes from two survey studies cited by Eysenck (Landis, 1937; Denker, 1947), whose results are interpreted to meet the needs of his ineffectiveness-of-therapy polemic. Let us reexamine these two studies critically to see if Eysenck's conclusion is justified.

In approaching the problem of evaluating psychotherapy, in 1952 Eysenck searched in vain for a psychotherapy research study which had included a control group in its design. This was a legitimate search, since there is always the possibility in research that some variable other than the defined treatment variable is responsible for the effects observed for the experimental subjects. To remove this possibility of confounding, one traditionally uses a group of control subjects. In the present case, if therapy patients change significantly more than controls, one can legitimately conclude that some aspect of the treatment, ceteris paribus, is responsible for the differences.

But, as mentioned, Eysenck found it impossible to find any such study in his 1952 survey. Hence, as a substitute for the missing experimental control groups he looked for evaluative studies of untreated psychoneurotics (receiving no psychotherapy) where the patients had been followed up over time to determine what, if any, improvement occurred "spontaneously" as the result of the "natural healing process." Eysenck found two published studies which seemed to satisfy these criteria. He then abstracted and used the percentage of cases who improved over time from these two untreated samples as a base line with which to compare the changes observed in the reported studies of psychotherapy in the literature at that time.

The first of these base-line studies was that of Landis (1937) who reported the amelioration rate in state mental hospitals (in New York State as well as in the United States generally) for patients diagnosed under the heading of psychoneurosis. Because of the overcrowding of state hospitals and their chronic understaffing problem, it would seem extremely unlikely that these hospitalized neurotics received much, if any, therapy. Hence, any recovery observed for them could legitimately be considered as spontaneous. Landis reported that the percentage of patients "discharged annually as recovered or improved" was 70% for New York State (during the years 1925–1934) and 68% for the United States as a whole (1926–1933). Eysenck (1961) concludes from these data: "By and large, we may thus say that of severe neurotics receiving in the main custodial care, and very little if any psychotherapy, over two-thirds recovered or improved to a considerable extent." Quoting Landis, he continues: "Although this is not, strictly speaking, a basic figure for 'spontaneous' recovery, still any therapeutic method must show an appreciably greater size than this to be seriously considered." In

other words, Eysenck seems to be saying that although this is not a basic
figure for "spontaneous" remission, we
can still treat it as such.

The second base-line estimate which
Eysenck offers comes from a study by
Denker (1947). Denker's report concerns 500 disability claims taken from
the files of the Equitable Life Assurance Society of the United States.
These claims were made by persons
who reportedly had been ill of a neurosis for at least 3 months before their
claims were submitted. The claimants
came from all parts of the country, had
many different occupations, and included all types of psychoneuroses.
During their disability (defined as inability to carry on with any "occupation for remuneration or profit") these
patients were regularly treated only by
their local general practitioners "with
sedatives, tonics, suggestion, and reassurance, but in no case was any attempt made at anything but this most
superficial type of 'psychotherapy'
which has always been the stock-in-
trade of the general practitioner." The
disability benefits the patients received
ranged from $10 to $250 monthly.
Denker followed up these cases for at
least a 5-year period after their illness,
and often for as long as 10 years after
the period of disability had begun. The
criteria he used for "apparently cured"
were, (a) complaint of no further, or
very slight, difficulties, and (b) successful social and economic adjustment by
the patient.

Eysenck (1961) reports:

Using these criteria, which are very similar
to those usually used by psychiatrists,
Denker found that 45% of the patients recovered after one year, another 27% after
two years, making 72% in all. Another
10%, 5%, and 4% recovered during the
third, fourth, and fifth years respectively,
making a total of 90% recoveries after five
years [pp. 710–711].

These are certainly very striking figures.
Eysenck finally concludes:

If we take a period of about two years for
each baseline estimate, which appears to be
a reasonable figure in view of the fact that
psychotherapy does not usually last very
much longer than two years and may sometimes last less, we may conclude with some
confidence that about two-thirds of severe
neurotics show recovery or considerable improvement, without the benefit of systematic psychotherapy, after a lapse of two
years from the time that their disorder is
notified, or they are hospitalized [p. 711].

Is this conclusion justified from
Landis' and Denker's findings? Is
Eysenck correct when he states that
two-thirds of untreated psychoneurotics
will, over a 2-year period, experience
spontaneous remission of their neurotic
illnesses? Many individuals have questioned this conclusion, notably Rosenzweig (1954), as well as others (Cartwright, 1955; de Charms, Levy, &
Wertheimer, 1954; Dührssen & Jorswieck, 1962; Luborsky, 1954; Stevenson, 1959; Strupp, 1964a, 1964b). Let
us examine in detail these counter arguments.

Rosenzweig provides the most comprehensive and critical attack on the
conclusion Eysenck draws from the
Landis and Denker studies. His basic
argument is that before these two
studies can be considered as representing a base line for recovery for untreated psychoneurotics (thereby functioning as extrapolated control groups
for studies evaluating the effects of
psychotherapy) the data of these studies must show three experimental characteristics: (a) the patients used in
the Landis and Denker studies must
be comparable to those treated by
psychotherapy—that is, the definition
of psychoneurosis for the patients in
these studies must be the same as that
for patients in psychotherapy, and the

severity of the neurotic illness must be equivalent for the contrasted groups; (b) the Landis and Denker base-line groups must in fact have received no psychotherapy; otherwise the essential meaning of control group here is violated; and (c) the criteria for successful outcome or improvement need to be equivalent, so that recovery or improvement means the same thing for the Landis and Denker patients as for typical psychotherapy patients.

Rosenzweig then proceeds to argue that the Landis and Denker studies violate all three of these necessary conditions; therefore, Eysenck's conclusion of two-thirds spontaneous recovery is unwarranted. If Rosenzweig is correct, then the purported phenomenon of spontaneous recovery for psychoneurotic patients is indeed a myth, since the Landis and Denker studies are the only evidence offered for its existence. Let us look at Rosenzweig's and others' arguments in detail as to why the two studies do not meet the three essential conditions for a psychotherapy control group.

1. Are the Patient Groups Comparable? In the first place, the Patient Uniformity Myth is operative in this comparison. It is quite easy, but incorrect, to assume that patients labeled psychoneurotic are more alike than different, despite the fact that they are naturally selected in both the Landis and Denker studies. From an a priori basis alone the probability seems quite small that equivalent groups resulted from these several natural selection processes. Rosenzweig further argues that

The insurance disability cases were, as a whole, in all likelihood less severely ill than any of the others. Denker himself points out that in these cases where disability income was a factor the illness may have been prolonged by this tangible secondary gain [money]. By the same token the illness may very well have been initiated, or at least partly instigated, by conscious or unconscious prospects of such gains. To compare psychoneuroses of long standing, dating in many instances from early childhood (the typical case treated by psychoanalysis), with such disability neuroses is highly dubious, and the fact that the latter would have cleared up quickly after brief treatment by a general practitioner is thus not surprising [p. 300].

Cartwright (1955) further argues against the psychoneurotic status of Denker's insurance patients:

Denker's study was published in 1946, and all cases were followed-up for at least five years after recovery. If it is assumed that Denker's research took one year to carry out, then, since some cases were disabled for five years and others for only one, all these cases of neurosis had their onset between 1934 and 1940. In 1933 the economic depression was at its worst in the United States. From that time on, the country's economy tended to improve except for a partial relapse around 1937–38. . . . It is evident that this period (which overlapped the period of disability of Denker's subjects) was one of general growth from a condition of severe unemployment to a condition of plentiful employment throughout the United States. These data (i.e., employment rates from 1933 to 1944) suggest that it is reasonable to ask what proportion of the variance of Denker's results may be accounted for in terms of national recovery from economic depression rather than a personal recovery from neurosis [p. 292].

And Luborsky (1954) speculates still further about the lack of comparability of the Denker patients to psychotherapy patients:

Many of the "insurance" group would probably never have visited the doctor if it were not required. As a whole the group is probably of higher social and economic level than other groups (apparently since they were able to carry disability insurance in the first place). Very likely the choice of a general practitioner rather than a psychiatrist to treat their psychoneurosis reflects a not-to-be-ignored difference in an attitude to their illness [p. 129],

or as Cartwright has just argued, reflects the scarcity and relative expense of psychiatrists in depression years.

Regarding the lack of comparability of the patients in the Landis study, Rosenzweig makes the following comments:

Here one could reasonably expect that the neuroses must have been extraordinarily severe in order for these patients to have become eligible for admission to these crowded institutions. In these instances the outcome of treatment would be expected to be far less favorable than for either the Denker control group or the experimental groups [p. 300].

This of course argues for less spontaneous recovery for Landis' patients, which is inconsistent with the percentages reported, at least for the questionable criterion of recovery that Landis used.

Regarding both the Denker and Landis patient groups, Rosenzweig summarizes:

It may be concluded that, in general, the Denker base-line group was probably less seriously ill, the Landis control group more seriously ill" [than the patients who typically are seen in psychotherapy]. To the degree that this conclusion is sound it may be further inferred that the control and experimental groups fail to meet an essential criterion of comparability—illness severity [p. 300].

It seems quite clear from the above rebuttals how one can get into inextricable interpretive difficulties, by operating on a misconception as unfounded as the Patient Uniformity Assumption, (for those cases where patients are naturally selected for vari-

ous studies and where one attempts to compare results). It seems quite obvious that the above itemizations represent serious patient confoundings —possible secondary gain, a concomitantly improving economic milieu, and social-class contamination of the "psychoneurotic" patients in Denker's study and the more severely ill Landis patients—and indicate at the very least feasible alternatives to Eysenck's claim of comparability of the "control" patients to those usually seen in psychotherapy. Indeed, in view of these confounding factors, the probability that the groups are comparable seems quite low; and hence the use of the Denker and Landis patients as control groups for base-line comparisons with psychotherapy seems invalid. One can approximate comparability of groups only by random selection and random assignment of patients to treatments; or by careful matching of experimental and control patients on relevant variables; or by obtaining post facto measures of relevant patient characteristics, statistically controlling for their influence. These procedures represent the reasonable alternatives to the naive selection dictated by the Patient Uniformity Myth, as well as the recommended designs for any future studies attempting to arrive at a base line of "spontaneous remission" for psychoneurotic patients. The incomparability of the control groups vitiates the case for spontaneous remission of psychoneurotic disorders based on the Denker and Landis studies.

2. *Did the Two Groups of Patients Actually Receive No Psychotherapy?* Let us look first at the Denker group, and again quote Rosenzweig (1954):

In Eysenck's words these patients were "regularly seen and treated by their own physicians with sedatives, tonics, suggestion, and reassurance." . . . These various presumably nonpsychotherapeutic techniques mentioned include suggestions and reassurance—well-known methods of psychotherapy; and psychiatrists regularly use sedatives and tonics as adjuncts to their practice. . . . The only difference between the work of the general practitioner and of the eclectic psychiatrist that could be assumed, in the absence of detailed and specific knowledge, would be a difference in thoroughness or expertness, not a difference in kind [p. 300].

In other words, from the Denker data, legitimate comparison could be made between psychotherapy of different levels of expertness, with the prediction being that the more expert therapy would produce greater improvement than that of the general practitioner. But the crucial point is that the Denker group cannot properly be considered a control group for spontaneous recovery, since the patients admittedly receive some of the elements of psychotherapy.

Similar doubt is cast upon Landis' group. Again to quote Rosenzweig:

To maintain that neurotic patients admitted to state hospitals receive no psychotherapy is seriously open to doubt. These institutions, despite their notorious shortage of staff, usually make a special effort to treat their neurotic admissions, because these cases have a better prognosis, and because they are far more accessible to treatment [p. 301].

De Charms, Levy, and Wertheimer (1954) add: "Some of Landis' group did receive psychotherapy;" and suggest a further contamination in that "hospital confinement and treatment may themselves be therapeutic." Luborsky (1954) elaborates further on the same point:

Also as Landis points out (in objecting himself to the use of the consolidated amelioration rate as a base-line for "spontaneous" recovery) neurotics in state hospitals

are given a variety of treatments, including some psychotherapy. And, as they are relatively unusual occupants of state hospitals, they probably get unusual treatment [p. 131].

This point can be underscored further by adding that, since psychiatrists in state hospitals are very likely human, it would not be too unbelievable that they might seek out, and perhaps enjoy a little, some contact with a patient who was not divorced from reality, who could converse reasonably well, who presented some hope of recovery, and whose treatment-of-choice could appropriately be traditional psychotherapy.

One again is compelled by these arguments to agree with Rosenzweig (1954):

It must then be concluded that the control subgroups cited by Eysenck do not sharply differ from the experimental groups in respect to the important variable of having received psychotherapy. As before with regard to illness severity, the necessary contrast between the base line and the experimental groups becomes markedly attenuated [p. 301].

Further, since the spontaneous recovery phenomenon by definition requires that control patients not be treated, the violation of this essential condition by the Landis and Denker studies by itself negates their value as evidence for the Spontaneous Remission Assumption.

3. *Are the Criteria for Improvement or Recovery Used in the Denker and Landis Studies Comparable to Those Used to Evaluate Traditional Psychotherapy?* Can the degree of improvement or recovery reported in these two studies be regarded as equivalent to that reported for traditional psychotherapy? In the first place, it is important to note that terms like im-

provement or recovery are at best ambiguous. As Luborsky (1954) states:

The terms say nothing about what the patient was like at the beginning and end of treatment; they can be and are applied to patients at the entire range of mental health. A schizophrenic patient can be called "recovered"; so can a patient with a slight personality problem. Obviously the word "recovered" is used differently in each case [p. 130].

The criterion for improvement or recovery for Landis' state hospital patients was "favorable discharge" from the hospital. Rosenzweig (1954) reasons that the probability is quite low that the criteria used to come to a favorable discharge decision for hospital patients are the same as those used for termination of therapy outpatients.

In other words, while patients residentially treated are generally considered in terms of hospital discharge and return to the community, the criterion of social recovery being highly relevant, patients nonresidentially treated, as by psychoanalysis, live continuously in the community and are worked with in terms of radical therapy which, if successful, permits them to live not only with others but with themselves. This difference in therapeutic goal is so great that percentage figures for residential and nonresidential treatment are dubiously commensurable [p. 301].

It could be added, along similar lines, that it is not too unreasonable to assume that in many hospitals, especially for voluntary, noncommitted psychoneurotic patients, factors other than personality condition—such as daily patient quotas which determine the hospital budget, pressure from relatives, pressure from the patient himself, etc. —often come to bear on the decision to discharge a particular patient.

The criteria of recovery utilized by Denker are admittedly far superior to Landis' discharge rate. Recall that Denker used two basic indices: (a) complaint of no further, or very slight, difficulties, and (b) successful social and economic adjustments by the patient. Further, he followed up these patients for a 5 to 10 year period—a procedure that would have certainly strengthened Landis' outcome data. This seems to represent a careful and sophisticated attempt to evaluate the recovery of his insurance patients. However, Cartwright (1955) asks:

It is of some interest to speculate about what evidences were available in the files of the insurance company concerning successful *social* adjustments made by persons whose disability benefits had been terminated. Such termination must certainly be taken as evidence for the making of successful *economic* adjustments. But "complaint of no further, or very slight, difficulties" may represent little more than no further supportable claims against the company [p. 291].

In other words, what motive would make an insurance company collect careful and detailed records of social adjustment of patients *after* they had withdrawn their claims. If subjective report of the patients was given heaviest weight in these indices, as seems likely, then this report seems especially susceptible to the "hello-goodbye" effect (Hathaway, 1948), particularly if one recalls the above argument regarding secondary gain (money) for these patients.

These considerations compel one to agree with Rosenzweig, that "the standards of improvement and recovery in Eysenck's various patient groups, control and experimental, bear so little resemblance to each other that, once again, the basis of his comparisons has little demonstrable validity." Since the criteria of recovery for the Landis and

Denker groups seem quite divergent from those used for the evaluation of psychotherapy, the violation of this essential condition in the Landis study, and likely the violation in the Denker study as well, further destroys their utility as evidence for the Spontaneous Remission Assumption.

In summary, the discussion reported seems to lead unequivocally to the conclusion that there is no evidence for spontaneous remission of psychoneurosis. Hence, the belief seems to be nothing more than a myth propagated by a popularized and naive interpretation of two research studies. The patients used in the Landis and Denker studies and the percentages of recovery reported by these authors in no way can be considered evidence of spontaneous remission for untreated psychoneurotic patients. Consequently, Eysenck's use of these percentages as a base line of spontaneous recovery against which to compare the efforts of psychotherapy is invalid. The discussion above has shown that the control patients were very likely not comparable, in fact did receive some treatment (psychotherapy) and hence are not controls, and their recovery was very likely evaluated on significantly different criteria. As Cartwright (1955) concludes:

It is a regrettable accident that the question concerning the effectiveness of psychotherapy has been tied up with the question about spontaneous remission. It has been assumed that the question about therapy is dependent for its answer upon the answer to the question about spontaneous remission. The regrettable part of this is that the worse assumption has been made that the answer to the spontaneous remission question is already known. Of course, it is said, people do recover spontaneously from neurosis and other psychopathological states. Do they? How many? How quickly? Certainly there is no reliable evidence in the studies of Landis and Denker. Indeed, the general absence of such evidence leaves it possible to conclude that the statement asserting the existence of spontaneous remission phenomena in regard to neurosis is made on a priori grounds, rooted perhaps in loose analogy with the natural histories of coughs and colds. It seems to be an open question of fact as to whether or not there are spontaneous remission phenomena at all, and if so, what statistical characteristics they possess [pp. 294–295].

It should be pointed out that the spontaneous recovery rates reported for "psychoneurosis" are far from being reliable. Various survey studies do not agree with the two-thirds rate that Eysenck presents. As de Charms, Levy, and Wertheimer (1954) observe:

Eysenck (1952) also states that these results are typical and that they are "remarkably stable from one investigation to another." This statement is questionable in view of the reports of five year follow-ups such as (a) that of Friess & Nelson (1942) where one may interpret the results . . . to mean that 20% is the spontaneous remission rate, and (b) that of Denker (1946) where 90% is reported as the spontaneous remission rate for a five year follow-up. If these two studies differ so widely, it appears that existing figures for spontaneous remission rates are not at all consistent. Although Eysenck used a two year base, we see no reason why a five year base may not be taken in comparing two studies, especially since we found no other studies utilizing a two year follow-up with which to check Eysenck's claim of stability [pp. 234–235].

It can be added that two more recent follow-up studies report rates which are also quite different from Eysenck's two-thirds percentage (Hastings, 1958; Saslow & Peters, 1956).

Finally, it is important to emphasize that it would be quite a useful contribution if valid developmental data could be obtained for emotionally disturbed individuals. But the approach must be more sophisticated than those of Landis and Denker. One cannot operate on the Patient Uniformity Myth and report spontaneous remission rates for "psychoneurosis." Rather an attempt first must be made to develop reliable operations by which one can distinguish different types of psychoneurotics. Several more recent survey studies of remission have attempted this kind of differentiation (Hastings, 1958; Saslow & Peters, 1956), but unfortunately used traditional psychiatric nosologies (hysterics, obsessive-compulsives, etc.) which have been shown to be unreliable classifications (Arnhoff, 1954; Ash, 1949; Dayton, 1940; Doering & Raymond, 1934; Mehlman, 1952; Schmidt & Fonda, 1956; Wilson

& Deming, 1927). If reliable measures can be developed which meaningfully differentiate psychoneurotic patients, then ideally one could obtain developmental data covering the entire lifespan for these respective groups. That is, it would be useful not only to have data charting the course of an untreated disorder after it has become a debilitating problem, but also to obtain data reflecting the prior development of the disorder. With data of this kind one could not only more validly assess the effects of specific therapeutic interventions, but could also be able to predict which individuals will subsequently experience which kinds of disorders.

## REFERENCES

ARNHOFF, F. N. Some factors influencing the unreliability of clinical judgments. *Journal of Clinical Psychology*, 1954, 10, 272–275.

ASH, P. The reliability of psychiatric diagnoses. *Journal of Abnormal and Social Psychology*, 1949, 44, 27–277.

ASHBY, J. D., FORD, D. H., GUERNEY, B. G., JR., & GUERNEY, L. F. Effects on clients of a reflective and a leading type of psychotherapy. *Psychological Monographs*, 1957, 7 (24, Whole No. 453).

AULD, F., JR., & MURRAY, E. J. Content-analysis studies of psychotherapy. *Psychological Bulletin*, 1955, 52, 377–395.

BERDIE, R. F. Counseling. *Annual Review of Psychology*, 1959, 10, 345–370.

BORDIN, E. S., CUTLER, R. L., DITTMANN, A. T., HARWAY, N. I., RAUSH, H. L., & RIGLER, D. Measurement problems in process research on psychotherapy. *Journal of Consulting Psychology*, 1954, 18, 79–82.

BREGER, L., & McGAUGH, J. L. Critique and reformulation of "learning-theory" approaches to psychotherapy and neurosis. *Psychological Bulletin*, 1965, 63, 338–358.

CAMPBELL, D. T. Factors relevant to the validity of experiments in social situations.

*Psychological Bulletin*, 1957, 54, 297–312.

CAMPBELL, D. T. From description to experimentation: Interpreting trends as quasi experiments. In C. W. Harris (Ed.), *Problems in measuring change.* Madison: Univer. Wisconsin Press, 1963. Pp. 212–242.

CARTWRIGHT, D. S. Effectiveness of psychotherapy: A critique of the spontaneous remission argument. *Journal of Counseling Psychology*, 1955, 2, 290–296.

CARTWRIGHT, D. S. Annotated bibliography of research and theory construction in client-centered therapy. *Journal of Counseling Psychology*, 1957, 4, 82–100.

CHASSAN, J. B. Probability processes in psychoanalytic psychiatry. In J. Scher (Ed.), *Theories of the mind.* New York: Free Press of Glencoe, 1962. Pp. 598–618.

COLBY, K. M. Psychotherapeutic processes. *Annual Review of Psychology*, 1964, 15, 347–370.

DAYTON, N. A. *New facts on mental disorders.* Springfield, Ill.: Charles C Thomas, 1940.

DeCHARMS, R., LEVY, J., & WERTHEIMER, M. A note on attempted evolutions of psychotherapy. *Journal of Clinical Psychology*, 1954, 10, 233–235.

DENKER, P. G. Results of treatment of psychoneuroses by the general practitioner: A follow-up study of 500 cases. *Archives of Neurology and Psychiatry*, 1947, **57**, 504–505.

DOERING, C. R., & RAYMOND, ALICE F. Reliability of observations of psychiatric and related characteristics. *American Journal of Orthopsychiatry*, 1934, **4**, 249–257.

DÜHRSSEN, A., & JORSWIECK, E. Zur Korrektur von Eysenck's Berichterstattung über psychoanalytische Behandlungsergebnisse. *Acta Psychotherapeutica et Psychsomatica*, 1962, **10**, 329–342.

EDWARDS, A. L., & CRONBACH, L. J. Experimental design for research in psychotherapy. *Journal of Clinical Psychology*, 1952, **8**, 51–59.

EYSENCK, H. J. The effects of psychotherapy: An evaluation. *Journal of Consulting Psychology*, 1952, **16**, 319–324.

EYSENCK, H. J. A reply to Luborsky's note. *British Journal of Psychology*, 1954, **45**, 132–133.

EYSENCK, H. J. The effects of psychotherapy: A reply. *Journal of Abnormal and Social Psychology*, 1955, **50**, 147–148. (a)

EYSENCK, H. J. Review of C. R. Rogers & R. F. Dymond: *Psychotherapy and personality change*. *British Journal of Psychology*, 1955, **46**, 237–238. (b).

EYSENCK, H. J. The effects of psychotherapy. In H. J. Eysenck (Ed.), *Handbook of abnormal psychology: An experimental approach*. New York: Basic Books, 1961. Pp. 697–725.

EYSENCK, H. J. The outcome problem in psychotherapy: A reply. *Psychotherapy: Theory, Research and Practice*, 1964, **1**, 97–100.

FENICHEL, O. *Problems of psychoanalytic technique*. New York: Psychoanalytic Quarterly, 1941.

FENICHEL, O. *Collected papers*. New York: Norton, First Series (1922–36), 1953. Second Series (1936–46), 1954.

FRIESS, C., & NELSON, M. J. Psychoneurotics five years later. *American Journal of Mental Science*, 1942, **203**, 539–558.

GARDNER, G. G. The psychotherapeutic relationship. *Psychological Bulletin*, 1964, **61**, 426–437.

GENDLIN, E. T. The social significance of the research. In C. R. Rogers, E. T. Gendlin, D. J. Kiesler, & C. B. Truax, (Eds.), *The therapeutic relationship and its impact: A study of psychotherapy with schizophrenics*. Madison: Univer. Wisconsin Press, 1966, Ch. 21.

GILBERT, W. Counseling: Therapy and diagnosis. *Annual Review of Psychology*, 1952, **3**, 351–380.

GOLDSTEIN, A. P. *Therapist-patient expectancies in psychotherapy*. New York: Macmillan, 1962.

GROSSBERG, J. M. Behavior therapy: A review. *Psychological Bulletin*, 1964, **62**, 73–88.

HASTINGS, D. N. Follow-up results in psychiatric illness. *American Journal of Psychiatry*, 1958, **114**, 1057–1066.

HATHAWAY, S. R. Some considerations relative to nondirective counseling as therapy. *Journal of Clinical Psychology*, 1948, **4**, 226–231.

HERRON, W. G. The process-reactive classification of schizophrenia. *Psychological Bulletin*, 1962, **59**, 329–343.

HERZOG, ELIZABETH. *Some guidelines for evaluative research*. (United States Department of Health, Education and Welfare, Social Security Administration Children's Bureau, pamphlet) Washington, D. C.: Government Printing Office, 1959.

KIESLER, D. J. Some basic methodological issues in psychotherapy process research. *American Journal of Psychotherapy*, 1966, in press.

KIESLER, D. J., KLEIN, MARJORIE H., & MATHIEU, PHILIPP L. A summary of the issues and conclusions. In C. R. Rogers, E. T. Gendlin, D. J. Kiesler, & C. B. Truax (Eds.), *The therapeutic relationship and its impact: A study of psychotherapy with schizophrenics*. Madison: Univer. Wisconsin Press, 1966, in press. Ch. 12.

KRASNER, L. Group discussion: Therapist's contribution. In H. H. Strupp & L. Luborsky (Eds.), *Research in psychotherapy*. Vol. 2. Washington, D. C.: American Psychological Association, 1962. Pp. 103–104.

LANDIS, C. A. Statistical evaluation of psychotherapeutic methods. In L. E. Hinsie (Ed.), *Concepts and problems of psy-*

*chotherapy.* New York: Columbia Univer. Press, 1937. Pp. 155–169.

LEVINSON, D. J. The psychotherapist's contribution to the patient's treatment career. In H. H. Strupp & Luborsky (Eds.), *Research in psychotherapy.* Vol. 2. Washington, D. C.: American Psychological Association, 1962. Pp. 13–24.

LEVY, N. A. An investigation into the nature of psychotherapeutic process: A preliminary report. In J. H. Masserman (Ed.), *Psychoanalysis and social process.* New York: Grune & Stratton, 1961. Pp. 125–149.

LUBORSKY, L. A note on Eysenck's article "The effects of psychotherapy: An evaluation." *British Journal of Psychology,* 1954, **45,** 129–131.

LUBORSKY, L. Psychotherapy. *Annual Review of Psychology,* 1959, **10,** 317–344.

MARSDEN, G. Content-analysis studies of therapeutic interviews: 1954 to 1964. *Psychological Bulletin,* 1965, **63,** 298–321.

MATARAZZO, J. D. Psychotherapeutic processes. *Annual Review of Psychology,* 1965, **16,** 181–224.

MEEHL, P. E. Psychotherapy. *Annual Review of Psychology,* 1955, **6,** 357–378.

MEHLMAN, B. The reliability of psychiatric diagnoses. *Journal of Abnormal and Social Psychology,* 1952, **47,** 577–578.

PATTERSON, C. H. Matching vs. randomization in studies of counseling. *Journal of Counseling Psychology,* 1956, **3,** 262–272.

RAIMY, V. C. Clinical methods: Psychotherapy. *Annual Review of Psychology,* 1952, **3,** 321–350.

RAPAPORT, D. The structure of psychoanalytic theory: A systematizing attempt. *Psychological Issues,* 1960, **2,** 1–158.

ROGERS, C. R. The necessary and sufficient conditions of therapeutic personality change. *Journal of Consulting Psychology,* 1957, **21,** 95–103.

ROGERS, C. R. A tentative scale for the measurement of process in psychotherapy. In E. A. Rubinstein & M. B. Parloff (Eds.), *Research in psychotherapy.* Washington, D. C.: American Psychological Association, 1959. Pp. 96–107. (a)

ROGERS, C. R. A theory of therapy, personality, and interpersonal relationships as developed in the client-centered framework. In S. Koch (Ed.), *Psychology: A study of science.* Vol. 3. *Formulations of the person and the social context.* New York: McGraw-Hill, 1959. Pp. 184–256. (b)

ROGERS, C. R., & DYMOND, R. F. (Eds.), *Psychotherapy and personality change.* Chicago: Univer. Chicago Press, 1954.

ROGERS, C. R., GENDLIN, E. T., KIESLER, D. J., & TRUAX, C. B. *The therapeutic relationship and its impact: A study of psychotherapy with schizophrenics.* Madison: Univer. Wisconsin Press, 1966, in press.

ROGERS, C. R., WALKER, A., & RABLEN, R. Development of a scale to measure process change in psychotherapy. *Journal of Clinical Psychology,* 1960, **16,** 79–85.

ROSENZWEIG, S. A transvaluation of psychotherapy: A reply to Hans Eysenck. *Journal of Abnormal and Social Psychology,* 1954, **49,** 298–304.

ROTTER, J. B. Psychotherapy. *Annual Review of Psychology,* 1960, **11,** 381–414.

RUBINSTEIN, E. A., & PARLOFF, M. B. (Eds.), *Research in psychotherapy.* Washington, D. C.: American Psychological Association, 1959.

SANFORD, N. Clinical methods: Psychotherapy. *Annual Review of Psychology,* 1953, **4,** 317–342.

SASLOW, G., & PETERS, ANN D. A follow-up study of "untreated" patients with various behavior disorders. *Psychiatric Quarterly,* 1956, **30,** 283–302.

SCHMIDT, H. O., & FONDA, C. P. The reliability of psychiatric diagnosis: A new look. *Journal of Abnormal and Social Psychology,* 1956, **52,** 262–267.

SEEMAN, J. Psychotherapy. *Annual Review of Psychology,* 1961, **12,** 157–194.

STEIN, M. I. (Ed.) *Contemporary psychotherapies.* New York: Free Press of Glencoe, 1961.

STEVENSON, I. The challenge of results in psychotherapy. *American Journal of Psychiatry,* 1959, **116,** 120–123.

STIEPER, D. R., & WIENER, D. N. *Dimensions of psychotherapy: An experimental and clinical approach.* Chicago: Aldine, 1965.

STONE, L. Psychoanalysis and brief psychotherapy. *Psychoanalytic Quarterly*, 1951, 20, 215–236.

STRUPP, H. H. Psychotherapy. *Annual Review of Psychology*, 1962, 13, 445–478.

STRUPP, H. H. The outcome problem in psychotherapy revisited. *Psychotherapy: Theory, Research and Practice*, 1964, 1, 1–13. (a)

STRUPP, H. H. The outcome problem in psychotherapy: A rejoinder. *Psychotherapy: Theory, Research and Practice*, 1964, 1, 101. (b)

STRUPP, H. H. A *bibliography of research in psychotherapy*. Chapel Hill, N. C.: University of North Carolina, Department of Psychiatry, 1964.

STRUPP, H. H., & LUBORSKY, L. (Eds.). *Research in psychotherapy*. Vol. 2. Wash-

ington, D. C.: American Psychological Association, 1962.

UNDERWOOD, B. J. *Psychological research*. New York: Appleton-Century-Crofts, 1957.

WILSON, E. B., & DEMING, JULIA. Statistical comparison of psychiatric diagnosis in Massachusetts State Hospitals during 1925 and 1926. *Bulletin of Massachusetts' Department of Mental Disorders*, 1927, 11, 6–19.

WINDER, C. L. Psychotherapy. *Annual Review of Psychology*, 1957, 8, 309–330.

ZAX, M. & KLEIN, A. Measurement of personality and behavior changes following psychotherapy. *Psychological Bulletin*, 1960, 57, 435–448.

Ernest G. Poser

# The Effect of Therapists' Training on Group Therapeutic Outcome

*One of the most critical problems in the mental health field is in the area of manpower shortage. The number of well-trained psychotherapists does not nearly satisfy the need for such people. One reaction to this problem has been the development of a number of treatment paradigms that do not rely on the trained professional. Such novices as housewives, college students, and parents of disturbed children have been enlisted in an attempt to cope with manpower problems. This raises the question of whether these less well-trained people are competent to deal with the complex issues of treatment of the mentally ill. In this paper, Dr. Poser examines the efficacy of a group of untrained college students, as compared to professionals, in group therapy with schizophrenic patients, and finds the two groups to be similarly effective, with the advantage, although slight, resting with the nonprofessionals. Dr. Poser quite correctly indicates that it is impossible to draw conclusions from this research that go beyond the specific method of treatment and type of patient studied, but it is of interest that a good deal of other evidence supports the generality of the finding that nonprofessionals can be highly effective therapeutic agents.*

The present manpower shortage in the mental health professions has given new impetus to investigations concerned with therapist variables in

Reprinted from the Journal of Consulting Psychology, 30(1966), 283–289 with the permission of the American Psychological Association and Dr. Poser. Copyright 1966 by the American Psychological Association.

studies of therapeutic outcome. Hence, it is not surprising that recent work in this field, notably by Anker and Walsh (1961), Beck, Kantor, and Gelineau (1963), Rioch, Elkes, Flint, Usdansky, Newman, & Silber (1963), and Schofield (1964) should have focused attention on what appear to be the active therapeutic ingredients of the patient-therapist interaction. All of these authors suggest that effective therapy can be carried out by personnel without professional training, and most of them provide objective evidence in support of this view.

Truax (1963) and his associates also drew attention to nonacademic qualifications of therapists by their ingenious demonstration that those rated high with respect to certain human qualities, such as "accurate empathy," tend to improve the psychological functioning of schizophrenics, while therapists rated low in empathy actually impair the clinical status of their patients. The therapist's personality attributes with which Truax is concerned are essentially those previously elaborated by Rogers (1957), who does not feel that special intellectual professional knowledge—psychological, psychiatric, medical, or religious —is required of the therapist. In this context he observes that "intellectual training and the acquiring of information has, I believe, many valuable results—but becoming a therapist is not one of those results [p. 101].". This view is consistent with the speculation that nonprofessional workers, possibly selected in accordance with Truax's criteria, could do effective therapy, at least with certain types of patients.

There is urgent need for studies seeking to define those aspects of the treatment process which crucially affect therapeutic outcome. Without such information, it is difficult to distinguish between the necessary and the superfluous conditions of therapeutic

personality change. But it may be misleading to think of the variance accounting for therapeutic outcome only in terms of active versus inactive ingredients, if the term "active" is meant to imply the deliberate application of some theory or procedure to the conduct of psychotherapy. There may be a third source of therapeutic change related to the familiar placebo effect operative in most other forms of medical and psychiatric treatment. Because, strictly speaking, there is no such thing as "inert" psychotherapy in the sense that placebos are pharmacologically inert, the term "placeboid" might serve to describe this effect in psychotherapy.

Rosenthal and Frank (1956) have dealt with the placebo phenomenon in some detail and conclude that

. . . improvement under a special form of psychotherapy cannot be taken as evidence for: (a) correctness of the theory on which it is based; or (b) efficacy of the specific technique used, unless improvement can be shown to be greater than, or qualitatively different from that produced by the patients' faith in the efficacy of the therapist and his technique—"the placebo effect" [p. 300].

More recently, Frank, Nash, Stone, and Imber (1963) have shown that some psychiatric patients recover simply as a result of attending a clinic or receiving placebo, without psychotherapy or other treatment being given.

Such studies, however, do not bear on the crucial problem of placeboid effects in the psychotherapeutic interaction itself. They do not tell us whether some of the supposedly active ingredients of therapy, such as the theoretical training or experience of the therapist, for instance, are or are not relevant to therapeutic outcome. Could it be that such behavior change as does occur posttherapeutically is due to other factors not hitherto considered to be necessary antecedents of therapeutic change? Fiedler (1950) and others have already shown that adherents of widely disparate theoretical persuasions achieve much the same results in psychotherapy, and more recently similar findings have been reported by Gelder, Marks, Sakinofsky, and Wolff (1964) with respect to the comparative outcome of psychotherapy and behavior therapy. Though rich in implication, none of these studies were specifically designed to test for placeboid effects in therapeutic outcome. To do so, according to Rosenthal and Frank (1956), requires, in addition to the therapy under study, the application of

another form of therapy in which patients had equal faith, so that the placebo effect operated equally in both, but which would not be expected by the theory of therapy being studied to produce the same effects [p. 300].

The present study constitutes an attempt to provide a controlled experiment in line with the above suggestion.

The therapeutic technique under study was group therapy with chronic schizophrenics. The fact that such therapy is most often carried out by psychiatrists, social workers, occupational therapists, and psychologists (Poser, 1965) suggests that training in one of these professions is commonly regarded as an appropriate, if not essential, prerequisite for the successful group therapist. To test the validity of this assumption three treatment conditions were compared in this investigation.

In the first, group therapy was conducted by highly trained psychiatrists, social workers, and occupational therapists. In the second condition all therapists were undergraduate students without previous training or experience relevant to the care of mental patients. Because a comparison of two treatments in terms of their effectiveness would be meaningless without first demonstrating the validity of the outcome criterion to be applied, a control group of untreated patients was also included.

In terms of Rosenthal and Frank's statement cited above, the untrained therapists in the present investigation were thought to provide a form of treatment which, by virtue of their lacking professional sophistication, would prove to be less effective than that offered by trained personnel. This, at least, would be the prediction if it is true that training and experience are relevant to therapeutic outcome. At the same time, there was no reason to believe that the patients had more faith in the trained than the untrained therapists, since they were in the main unaware of this distinction. Hence placeboid effects, if any, could operate equally in both therapeutic situations. In fact, the untrained therapists are here conceptualized as contributing nothing but placeboid effect, much as the pharmacologically inert substance does in a placebo-controlled drug study. By corollary, the theoretical sophistication and past experience of a trained therapist is, for the purpose of this study, viewed as the active ingredient in the therapeutic process. In other words, it is proposed that such therapeutic effectiveness as untrained therapists do attain is attributable to nonspecific aspects of the helping relationship, such as activation, sympathy, opportunity for verbal ventilation, regularity of attendance, and the like. These would appear to be formally comparable to the nonspecific factors thought to underlie placebo responses as, for instance, attention giving, expectation inducing, pill ingestion, and many other situational variables familiar to the drug therapist. Many of these variables are highly effective in the treatment of certain physical disabilities, as placebo studies of patients with headaches (Jellinek, 1946) or the common cold (Diehl, Baker, and Cowan, 1940) have abundantly shown. A similar phenomenon may operate in psychotherapy, which would account for the near-ubiquitous two-thirds improvement rate consequent upon most forms of psychotherapy.

## METHOD

*Subjects.* A total of 343 male chronic schizophrenics was studied. They represent almost the entire male schizophrenic population of a 1,500-bed hospital, only assaultive patients and those suffering from known organic brain damage having been excluded. Their median age was 47 years (range 20–73). All of them had been hospitalized uninterruptedly for at least 3 years. Their median length of hospitalization was 14 years, with a range from 3 to 44 years.

The vast majority of these patients were receiving phenothiazine medication at the time of the study. This was continued throughout, and only in emergencies was medication changed during the course of the project.

*Therapists.* The untrained therapists consisted of 11 young women between the ages of 18 and 25. All were undergraduate students in one of Montreal's universities, and most had never had a course in psychology. None intended to enter a mental health profession, nor had any of them ever visited a mental hospital. No attempt was made to select a particular type of applicant. Anyone who expressed interest in the project and accepted the terms of employment was enrolled. They were paid at the standard rate for summer employment at that time and were asked to consent to the taking of numerous psychological tests which were to be used for a subsequent investigation. As an additional control, two inpatients—one an alcoholic and the other suffering from hysteria—were asked to act as untrained therapists.

The professional therapists were seven psychiatrists, six psychiatric social workers, and two occupational therapists. In addition to their formal professional qualifications, that is, certification in psychiatry, all the psychiatrists had had from 5 to 17 years of professional experience. All but one had previously done group psychotherapy, and three were specialized in this area. Their ages ranged from 35 to 50, and all were male.

All social workers had had postgraduate professional training leading to a degree and at least 5 years' professional experience. Two were specialized in group work, and all but two had had previous experience doing case or group work with psychotic patients. Their ages ranged from 36 to 43, and two out of the six were male.

The two occupational therapists had professional experience of 5 and 7 years' duration, respectively, and this included some mental hospital work. Both were female, one aged 27 and the other 30.

None of the therapists taking part in this project were on the staff of the hospital where this work was done, nor were any of the patients known to the therapists prior to the start of the project. All were paid at the rate appropriate to their profession.

*Tests.* Selection of these was guided by three considerations. First, the performance required had to be within the behavioral repertoire of chronic schizophrenic patients. Second, preference was given to tests which had previously been demonstrated to differentiate normals from psychotics. Since a large number of patients were involved, the third criterion was purely practical—those tests were chosen which could be administered in a relatively short space of time.

The final test battery consisted of two psychomotor, two perceptual, and two verbal tests, in addition to the Palo Alto Hospital Adjustment Scale (McReynolds & Ferguson, 1946), intended to provide a quantitative estimate of the patients' adjustment in the hospital. The tests were:

1. Speed of tapping (TAP). (The number of taps on a reaction key in 10 seconds.)

2. A test of visual reaction-time (RT) involving choice.

3. The Digit-Symbol test (DS) of the Wechsler-Bellevue Scale I.

4. A color-word conflict test (Stroop), in which the score reflects the time taken by the patient to read 100 color names under three conditions of increasing difficulty (Thurstone & Mellinger, 1953).

5. Verbal fluency (VF). (The number of different animals named in 1 minute.)

6. The Verdun Association List (VAL), a 20-item word-association test devised by Sigal (1956) to discriminate between working and nonworking mental hospital patients.

All of these tests were individually administered immediately before or after therapy. Occasionally a patient was found untestable before or after therapy. Such patients were seen by another examiner, so that no patient was given a zero score on any test unless he had been given two opportunities to take it from a different examiner on each occasion.

*Procedure.* The 343 patients were selected for this project by the psychiatric staff of the hospital. Each patient was assigned to a group in such a way that every unit of 10 patients would be matched as closely as possible with every other unit in terms of the patients' age, severity of illness, and length of hospitalization. Following this, the groups were compared with respect to their mean test performance prior to therapy. Where major disparities between groups were noted, individual patients were exchanged, so that all groups were roughly comparable with respect to age, clinical status, length of hospitalization, and test performance prior to therapy.

At this stage six groups (one of them composed of 13 patients) were picked at random to serve as untreated controls. Patients in these groups received the usual hospital care, but were excluded from all forms of group treatment other than routine occupational therapy. The remaining 28 groups were each assigned to a therapist picked at random from among the project staff available at the time. The project extended over three periods of 5 months. In the first of these, 11 untrained therapists took part; in the second, seven professional

and one untrained therapist; and in the final period, eight professional and one untrained therapist.

Each therapist met his or her group during 1 hour daily 5 days a week for a period of 5 months. A special attendant saw to it that patients would join their groups at the appropriate time and place. Even so, one or two patients in almost every group refused to attend regularly. Their absences were recorded, and only those patients who attended at least two-thirds of all available sessions were re-evaluated at the end of the 5-month period. This reduced the total number of patients included in the study from 343 to 295. At the time of the post-therapy retest no group had less than six members who met the attendance criterion.

Both the trained and untrained therapists were quite free to conduct their therapy sessions in any way they wished. Wherever possible, the materials or facilities they required were provided by the hospital, but at no time did the project director offer suggestions for procedure or in any way facilitate communication among therapists while the project was under way. To get some idea of each therapist's approach, a few sessions of every group were attended by an observer. Also, each therapist was asked to keep a daily record of his group's activities. Some therapists used only verbal communication during therapy; others arranged activities ranging from party games and dancing to "communal" painting and public speaking. All stressed interaction among members of their group.

## RESULTS

The pre- and post-therapy test scores of all patients were subjected to covariance analysis. The covariance adjusted posttherapy scores of the untreated control group were then compared to those of the patients treated by lay therapists (Table 1) and those of the professional therapists (Table 2), respectively. This was done for each of the six tests separately. On all tests, with the exception of the Stroop, a high score indicates

TABLE 1. Covariance Adjusted Posttherapy Scores of Untreated Patients and Those Treated by Lay Therapists

| Treatment | | TAP | VF | VAL | DS | RT | Stroop |
|---|---|---|---|---|---|---|---|
| Untreated | | | | | | | |
| controls | Mean | 45.763 | 11.699 | 26.218 | 20.428 | .169 | 2.508 |
| (N = 63) | SD | 9.772 | 4.449 | 6.580 | 7.204 | .054 | .768 |
| Treated by | | | | | | | |
| lay therapists | Mean | 49.735 | 12.600 | 28.786 | 24.135 | .197 | 1.025 |
| (N = 87) | SD | 10.222 | 4.370 | 8.264 | 6.812 | .063 | .698 |
| | t | 2.308 † | 1.295 | 1.801 * | 2.922 ** | 2.613 | 2.336 ‡ |

\* p < .10.
† p < .05.
‡ p < .02.
\*\* p < .01.

TABLE 2. Covariance Adjusted Posttherapy Scores of Untreated Patients and Those Treated by Professional Therapists

| Treatment | | TAP | VF | VAL | DS | RT | Stroop |
|---|---|---|---|---|---|---|---|
| Untreated | | | | | | | |
| controls | Mean | 45.763 | 11.699 | 26.218 | 20.428 | .169 | 2.508 |
| (N = 63) | SD | 9.772 | 4.449 | 6.580 | 7.204 | .054 | .768 |
| Treated by | | | | | | | |
| professional | | | | | | | |
| therapists | Mean | 46.372 | 10.948 | 28.104 | 23.187 | .154 | .835 |
| (N = 145) | SD | 9.894 | 3.061 | 6.950 | 5.612 | .049 | .579 |
| | t | .387 | 1.148 | 1.427 | 2.313 ‡ | 1.688 | 2.903 ** |

‡ p < .02.
\*\* p < .01.

better performance than a low score.[2] Similar comparisons were made between the posttherapy scores of patients receiving lay therapy and those treated by professionals (Table 3). Finally, in Table 4, interprofessional comparisons are made between the posttherapy test behavior of patients treated by social workers and psychiatrists.

It appears from these tables that the largest number of significant differences in test behavior occur between the untreated group and those groups treated by lay therapists. Four out of the six tests reflect significantly better performance by the patients of lay therapists. The VAL approaches significance in the expected direction.

On comparing the test behavior of the untreated with that of patients

---

[2] The reversal of direction in the Stroop test scores arises from the raw score's being expressed as a ratio.

TABLE 3. Covariance Adjusted Posttherapy Scores of Patients Treated by Lay and Professional Therapists

| Treatment | | TAP | VF | VAL | DS | RT | Stroop |
|---|---|---|---|---|---|---|---|
| Treated by lay therapists (N = 87) | Mean | 49.735 | 12.600 | 28.786 | 24.135 | .197 | 1.025 |
| | SD | 10.222 | 4.370 | 8.264 | 6.812 | .063 | .698 |
| Treated by professional therapists (N = 145) | Mean | 46.372 | 10.948 | 28.104 | 23.187 | .154 | .835 |
| | SD | 9.894 | 3.061 | 6.950 | 5.612 | .049 | .579 |
| | t | 2.331 † | 2.899 ** | .588 | .930 | 4.998 § | .356 |

† p < .05.
* p < .01.
§ p < .001.

TABLE 4. Covariance Adjusted Posttherapy Scores for Patients Treated by Social Workers and Psychiatrists

| Treatment | | TAP | VF | VAL | DS | RT | Stroop |
|---|---|---|---|---|---|---|---|
| Treated by social workers (N = 53) | Mean | 47.332 | 10.613 | 27.687 | 22.324 | .154 | 1.025 |
| | SD | 10.222 | 3.05 | 6.618 | 6.603 | .063 | .656 |
| Treated by psychiatrists (N = 60) | Mean | 46.252 | 11.212 | 28.011 | 23.307 | .151 | .755 |
| | SD | 8.978 | 3.162 | 7.899 | 5.459 | .040 | .561 |
| | t | .564 | .743 | .203 | .688 | .249 | .321 |

treated by professionals, only two out of the six tests show significant superiority of the latter group (Table 2).

A direct comparison of patients treated by lay and professional therapists reveals a significantly better performance on the part of those treated by the former on three of the six tests (Table 3). It is of interest to note that the standard deviation on every test is smaller for the group of patients treated by professional therapists.

Table 4 suggests that there is no significant difference between posttherapeutic test performance of patients treated by social workers and the performance of those treated by psychiatrists.

Because the study began with patients treated by lay therapists, it was possible before the end of the project to retest some of the patients and most of the untreated controls who took part in that first phase of the investigation. These scores, obtainable from 61 patients, constitute a 3-year followup and are presented in Table 5. To save time, only four of the original six tests were given in this part of the study, and a t test for correlated means was used to evaluate the difference between the two test sessions, separated

TABLE 5. Three-Year Follow-Up of Schizophrenics Treated by Lay Therapists
(N = 61)

| Stage | | TAP | VF | RT | VAL |
|---|---|---|---|---|---|
| Before treatment | Mean | 38.84 | 9.02 | 326.24 | 19.08 |
| | SD | 19.63 | 5.50 | 405.09 | 14.07 |
| Three years later | Mean | 48.15 | 10.52 | 183.07 | 24.20 |
| | SD | 17.50 | 6.43 | 320.04 | 14.53 |
| | t | 4.22 § | 2.58 ‡ | 3.61 § | 3.32 ** |

‡ $p < .02$.
** $p < .01$.
§ $p < .001$.

by 3 years. Table 5 shows that test performance after 3 years was still significantly better than it was before treatment on all of the tests used. That this result was not a function of greater familiarity with the tests at follow-up—by which time each patient had taken them twice before—is indicated by the result of retesting 23 untreated controls after 3 years. Only on the tapping test did they show significantly better performance on follow-up, much as they had done on the first retest after 5 months.

In an effort to get some measure of change in the patients' ward behavior, the Hospital Adjustment Scale was administered to 80 patients, all of whom had been treated by lay therapists. The scale was administered before treatment, and again after 5 months. On each occasion it was completed both by the nursing supervisor and an attendant familiar with the patients. The supervisor's ratings showed significant improvement between test and retest, but the attendants' ratings did not. It was felt that this equivocal result reflected little more than the greater ego-involvement of the supervisors, whose wish to see the project succeed might well have influenced their ratings.

Unfortunately it was not possible to have the scale completed by personnel sufficiently familiar with the patients to assess their behavior and yet unaware of their participation in the project. For this reason and also because of the ward staff's strong resistance to the time consuming task of filling out the scale it was not administered to subsequent therapy groups.

DISCUSSION

The objection may be made that changes in psychological test performance, as employed in this study, do not constitute a relevant criterion of therapeutic outcome. The usual alternatives are rating scales, questionnaires or the comparison of discharge rates before and after therapy. None of these seemed appropriate for the present patient population, consisting as it did of schizophrenics with many years of hospitalization. The behavioral repertoire of such patients is so limited that rating scales are difficult to complete as our own attempt at using the Hospital Adjustment Scale clearly showed. For the same reason, questionnaire completed by the patients would be hard to interpret. Discharge rates during and after therapy were compared but showed no significant difference between treated and untreated groups. Nor would this be expected in the light of previous findings, such as those of Beck et al. (1963). Their study showed that in a sample of 120 psychotics, those who were discharged during the Harvard undergraduate volunteer program had, on the average, been hospitalized for 4.7 years, whereas the undischarged patients had been hospitalized for 12.4 years. This is consistent with earlier studies, suggesting that after 4 years of hospitalization only 3% of patients are likely to be discharged.

With one exception (Stroop) the verbal and performance tests employed in the present investigation were known from earlier work to discriminate effectively between psychotics and normals. It therefore seems justified to interpret significant incremental change in the treated groups' test behavior as reflecting therapeutic gain. This conclusion is validated by the absence of such change in the untreated control group on five out of the six tests. That the TAP did show significant improvement on retest of the control group may reflect the greater emphasis placed on activity programs for mental patients in recent years. On the other hand, since tapping was the first test to be administered to each patient, initial performance on it may have been impaired by apparatus stress or the novelty effect of the test situation.

Why lay therapists should have done somewhat better than professional therapists in facilitating the test behavior of their patients remains a matter of conjecture. It seems likely that the naïve enthusiasm they brought to the therapeutic enterprise, as well as their lack of "professional stance" permitted them to respond more freely to their patients' mood swings from day to day. Certainly, the activities in which they engaged their patients had a less stereotyped character than that offered by their professional counterparts. On the other hand, the greater standard deviation in the test behavior of those treated by lay therapists suggests that they may have helped some of their patients at the expense of others. Professional therapy, by contrast, seems to have had a more even effect on all participants.

The 3-year follow-up data for the untrained group are highly encouraging and support the conclusion that the therapy given achieved more than transient activation. It is planned to carry out similar follow-up studies on the patients treated by professional therapists.

The groups treated by fellow patients were too small to make quantitative assessment very meaningful. Their results were, however, treated separately in the covariance analysis and showed no significant difference from patients treated by lay or professional therapists. They received excellent cooperation from their fellows, as evidenced by their group attendance record, which showed full attendance in one group and 8 out of 10 in the other. Those who knew the patient-therapists clinically agreed that participation in the project had enhanced their mental health. Both are now discharged after prolonged hospitalization.

To extend the conclusions from this study beyond its present context, that is, the outcome of group therapy with chronic schizophrenics, would clearly be premature. When viewed in relation to the literature reviewed at the outset of this paper, the present findings do, however, support the conclusion that traditional training in the mental health professions may be neither optimal nor even necessary for the promotion of therapeutic behavior change in mental hospital patients.

# REFERENCES

Anker, J. M., & Walsh, R. P. Group psychotherapy, a special activity program, and group structure in the treatment of chronic schizophrenics. *Journal of Consulting Psychology*, 1961, 25, 476–481.

Beck, J. C., Kantor, D., & Gelineau, V. A. Follow-up study of chronic psychotic patients "treated" by college case-aide volunteers. *American Journal of Psychiatry*, 1963, 120, 269–271.

Diehl, H. S., Baker, A. B., & Cowan, D. W. Cold vaccines, further evaluation. *Journal of the American Medical Association*, 1940, 115, 593–594.

Fiedler, F. E. A comparison of therapeutic relationships in psychoanalytic, non-directive and Adlerian therapy. *Journal of Consulting Psychology*, 1950, 14, 436–445.

Frank, J. D., Nash, E. H., Stone, A. R., & Imber, S. D. Immediate and long-term symptomatic course of psychiatric outpatients. *American Journal of Psychiatry*, 1963, 120, 429–439.

Gelder, M. G., Marks, I. M., Sakinofsky, I., & Wolff, H. H. Behavior therapy and psychotherapy for phobic disorders: Alternative or complementary procedures? Paper presented at the 6th International Congress of Psychotherapy, London, 1964.

Jellinek, E. M. Clinical tests on comparative effectiveness of analgesic drugs. *Biometrics Bulletin*, 1946, 2, 87.

McReynolds, P., & Ferguson, J. T. Clinical manual for the Hospital Adjustment Scale. Palo Alto: Consulting Psychologists Press, 1946.

Poser, E. G. Group therapy in Canada: A national survey. *Canadian Psychiatric Association Journal*, 1966, 11, 20–25.

Rioch, M. J., Elkes, C., Flint, A. A., Usdansky, B. S., Newman, R. G., & Silber, E. National Institute of Mental Health pilot study in training mental health counselors. *American Journal of Orthopsychiatry*, 1963, 33, 678–689.

Rogers, C. R. The necessary and sufficient conditions of therapeutic personality change. *Journal of Consulting Psychology*, 1957, 21, 95–103.

Rosenthal, D., & Frank, J. D. Psychotherapy and the placebo effect. *Psychological Bulletin*, 1956, 53, 294–302.

Schofield, W. *Psychotherapy: The purchase of friendship.* Englewood Cliffs, N. J.: Prentice-Hall, 1964.

Sigal, J. The Verdum Association List. Unpublished doctoral dissertation, University of Montreal, 1956.

Thurstone, L. L., & Mellinger, J. J. *The Stroop test.* University of North Carolina, The Psychometric Laboratory, 1953.

Truax, C. B. Effective ingredients in psychotherapy: An approach to unraveling the patient-therapist interactions. *Journal of Counseling Psychology*, 1963, 10, 256–263.

# Section IV

# Recent Issues and Trends

This is a time in the development of the field of abnormal psychology when some rather major innovative movements are under way. These represent much more than a simple case of a new way of looking at old problems, although there is certainly some of that taking place. The more innovative programs that are emerging are really addressing themselves to a problem that is different from the one that typically engaged the mental health professional up to recent years. Where the traditional worker adopted the stance of waiting for a person to come to him with a complaint that could be classified and worked on in some time-honored way, many who are concerned about helping psychology make an even greater impact on society's problems are redefining the object of their concern. For such people criminal behavior, doing poorly at school and dropping out, alcoholism, even failure to approach living up to one's potential are all problems that must be dealt with. In addition, the idea of attempting to prevent the development of problems that must be dealt with in the clinic or hospital is also prominent.

By redefining the problem in such a way, the mental health worker is called upon to re-examine many of the assumptions that had been fundamental to the way he worked traditionally. He must also begin to understand the problem he is grappling with in different terms and his own role must be redefined. Finally, he must develop entirely new vehicles through which services can be delivered to his target group. Most of the following papers deal with various aspects of these problems.

# Chapter 8

# Issues and Emergent Programs

*The papers in this chapter deal with the soil from which the community psychology approach grew, and some of the basic issues that must be grappled with in its development. In addition, examples are offered of specific programs that have been applied in different settings.*

Melvin Zax

## Recent Innovations in Dealing with Mental Health Problems in the U.S.A.

*This paper by Dr. Zax was written for a Danish psychology journal to acquaint its readers with some of the recent trends in clinical psychology and psychiatry in the United States. It characterizes a movement away from what had become traditional clinical techniques as a result of several factors: (1) dissatisfaction with effectiveness of old approaches; (2) forecasts of continuing failure to meet manpower needs; (3) evidence that the traditional clinician, already badly in short supply, is dealing only with a small proportion of people who need his services; and (4) a broadening redefinition of what constitutes a mental health problem, one that embraces a variety of phenomena ranging from delinquency and alcoholism to slow learning and chronic impoverishment. It is felt that this paper provides a good framework within which to understand the development of the variety of new programs that are emerging in the mental health fields.*

The "talking cure" introduced by Freud around the turn of the 20th century was probably embraced more enthusiastically in the United States than anywhere else in the world. The idea that deep personality change could be brought about through probing into the psychological forces, both conscious and particularly unconscious, which are theorized to cause emotional disorder found fertile soil in a young, vital country where innovation was not feared. As a result many European practitioners migrated to the United States, psychoanalytic institutes were set up, more and more American psychiatrists and psychologists were drawn into psychoanalytic training and the status of the analyst rose to a high level indeed.

One might include in this flowering of the psychoanalytic movement the development of briefer psychotherapies

*Reprinted from* Dansk Psykolognyt, 18(1967), 3–7, *with the permission of the Danish Psychological Association.*

ased on psychoanalytic principles. Though such approaches were intended ) be briefer, and perhaps more superficial in their goals, they owed much ) Freud's most basic principles. They ccepted the importance of early psychological experience rooted in a particular developmental paradigm, the importance of the unconscious, and the ssential idea that the uncovering and working through of the relevant forces was necessary for a cure to take place. Moreover, such treatments accepted implicitly, as did orthodox psychoanalysis and virtually all other psychologically based therapies, a few important ssumptions. The idea that psychotherapy was a very complex process which could only be practiced by certain highly trained individuals was one of these. Another was the notion that the proper role of the therapist was to offer services only to those who sought him out actively and possessed qualities which were regarded as essential to therapeutic movement such as a certain degree of intelligence, verbal facility, motivation to change, etc. This role is one which has been adapted from the example of medical practice and has come to be looked upon as the medical model."

The period, therefore, of the 1920's through the 1940's saw a steady growth f psychotherapeutic practice and a continuing consolidation of training ractices. Likewise the role of the therapist became more and more institutionalized and the psychological ublic in the United States seemed quite content with "the word" as handed down by Freud and as practiced by his disciples.

Perhaps the earliest signs of some discontent with the state of therapeutic ractice in the United States came in the early 1940's with the appearance of the writings of people like Carl Rogers (1942). He questioned many of the basic principles of psychoanalysis, asserted that psychotherapy itself and the training of therapists need not be as time-consuming and complex a process as analysts would have it. He also instituted a systematic research program for evaluating the process and outcome of psychotherapy as he practiced it. In his day Rogers' position seemed to burst upon a relatively tranquil scene but he has been joined by other innovators like Joseph Wolpe (1958) who have become openly disillusioned with the psychoanalytic psychotherapies on several counts. Thus, the earliest signs of a change that was to take place with respect to the way emotional illness was dealt with in the United States came about through disputes on theoretical and practical grounds with respect to the best established system.

Criticisms like those of Rogers were relatively mild, however, compared to those that were to be heard during the 1950's. By this time a good deal of research on the effects of psychotherapy, unsystematic to be sure, had accumulated. In a very controversial paper in 1952, Eysenck (1952) reviewed many such studies and concluded that the effectiveness of psychotherapy had not been established. He was promptly attacked in the journals for many other implications which one could, perhaps falsely, draw from his paper and on other grounds. Nevertheless, no one was able to make a case which would refute his basic assertion. The considerable research done on psychotherapy over a period of many years had not established its effectiveness. It is conceivable that the seed of Eysenck's distasteful conclusion had begun to grow in the minds of many psychologists and psychiatrists. The reaction made to his paper might, therefore, have been intensified by a combination of a few parts of agreement with his position and many parts of disagreement since it implied the necessity of throwing over an established order, one with which many practitioners had grown comfortable.

This seems plausible since, despite the angry feelings engendered by Eysenck's paper, his dubious attitude seems to have spread widely as evidenced by a variety of experimental programs which have been instituted in recent years. Many who are concerned with servicing the emotionally disturbed have become emboldened enough by their feeling that they are not doing as effective a job as they should to begin challenging some of the holiest principles of the orthodox dogma. For example, Margaret Rioch (1967) suggested that ordinary housewives without medical or psychological education could be trained to practice psychotherapy. She collected such a group of women, set up a training program, and has reported at its conclusion that her students were performing at the same level as advanced psychiatric residents. Another equally challenging movement involves the college students who, on a volunteer basis, have begun to visit hospitalized mental patients. Such a program originated among students at Harvard (Umbarger, Dalsimer, Morrison & Breggin, 1962) but quickly spread to many other locations and have been described widely in the literature. These are instances where the therapeutic agent is not only a lay person but one who is quite unsophisticated with respect to therapeutic theories and principles. Many other innovations have been introduced in the way services are delivered, such as through day hospitals or night hospitals, and in some programs individuals who would ordinarily be institutionalized are maintained in the community with the help of lay volunteers.

As radical as these innovations may seem, many still more radical by fa are beginning to appear, in keepin, with what amounts to an evolving re definition of the scope of function o the psychologist and psychiatrist. His torically, the profession devoted t dealing with the mentally ill emerge because it filled a role in society tha needed filling. In a sense society de fined a group which presented prob lems and such problems were what wa known as mental illness. For man thousands of years this definition in volved largely the very dramatic an often severe psychoses. It is really onl since the nineteenth century and par ticularly from the time of Freud tha neurosis has come to be regarded withi the purview of the servicer of the men tally ill. So, one major contributio of Freud was the redefinition an broadening of the problems confronte by the psychiatrist and psychologis For several reasons a further redefin tion of the problems that helping pr fessionals address themselves to is tak ing place in the United States to day.

Freud's theories of personality an others like his which placed the men tally healthy and unhealthy on a singl continuum was a major precursor t a further broadening of the scope o the mental health worker. If a set o developmental principles help us t understand psychoses and neuroses o the one hand and normal behavior o the other, might they not be equall useful in understanding the vast realn between these poles which encompasse after all, the largest percentage of so ciety? Relatively few people are net rotic or psychotic and relatively fev are as "happily normal" as they migh be. Most are more or less well ad justed. Most fall short in some wa in the goodness of their adaptation t their life conditions. Most fail to func tion anywhere near the upper limit o their potential effectiveness. In most societies this is a group that is easily ignored since, to a great extent, such individuals fail to recognize their own weaknesses and limitations. They tend to accept them as one of life's givens and to do their best to cope with a bad situation. Most of all, if they recognize any personal problems, they clearly do not feel that such problems are within the purview of the mental health worker who is seen as working traditionally with "nuts." On the other hand the neurotic and psychotic see themselves as ill or are clearly seen so by others and much clamor is raised by such groups for the services of the psychologist, psychiatrist and social worker.

Another good reason for ignoring this vast middle group is that the "medical model" as we have described it, the only one with which most mental health workers are familiar, doesn't prescribe a role for dealing with the person who won't regard himself as a patient, who seems relatively content with little education and a low station in life, who doesn't respect the therapist as a potentially helpful expert. Thus, if part of the problem is that the person with a more-or-less debilitating characterological defect doesn't know enough to ask for help or for what kind, it is at least equally true that most professionals avoid such problems. They simply haven't grown up with the equipment for working with such individuals and the inertia that must be overcome for "tooling up" for this new kind of work is not easily overcome. With the shortages that exist among mental health workers, there is plenty of work available if one concentrates on the more traditional patient. It is easy to dismiss the alcoholic, the criminal, the person who doesn't seem to be able to benefit from education, the chronically impoverished

as inferior organisms not suited to sophisticated therapeutic techniques which are the only ones available in the doctor's bag.

It has not been possible, however, to maintain such a bland rejection by the professions in the United States. There are several complicated reasons for this but certainly one of them is the fact that in the United States the gulf between the successful and the unsuccessful in life is extremely apparent. Traditionally, and even now, the opportunities to rise socially and economically have been very great. Accordingly, those who are equipped to benefit from the social and educational opportunities available to them do rise. Those who are not so equipped fail to rise but view clearly the better example of their more fortunate peers. This doubtless makes for great discontentment among the less successful in the lower classes and this feeling is reflected in high alcoholism and crime rates as well as in other symptoms like a scorn for the very institutions, such as the schools, which represent a major avenue for altering their unhappy lives. In any case, the discontent of the lower classes has been manifested in enough ways to prompt even smug, aloof psychologists, or at least some of them, to begin considering how what is known about human behavior and its development might be applied to such problems.

Another factor which has jarred the mental health worker out of his feelings of self-satisfaction with old role models and techniques is the growing realization that the professions, as they have functioned, cannot hope to keep up with the demand that is placed on their services. Surveys like the Midtown Manhattan study (Srole, Langner, Michael, Opler & Rennie, 1962) and some of those sponsored by the Joint Commission on Mental Illness and

Health (1961) indicate that, as busy as psychologists and psychiatrists are, they are seeing only a fraction of the people who need even traditional services. Albee (1959) has pointed out that traditional workers cannot possibly be trained in numbers vast enough to keep up with even projections of current demands.

The combination of such a shortage of mental health professionals and the need to attempt to deal with social problems which have not yet been encompassed within the scope of the mental health worker's function has prompted much thought about new approaches to mental health problems. The thinking of individuals concerned with either or both types of problems converges on the idea that concerted efforts must be made to prevent the development of serious disorders and that many services, either traditional ones or others, will have to be delivered directly by someone other than the traditional, highly trained professional. In effect this latter notion alters the role of the professional from that of the expert who sees the patient directly to that of a program organizer or designer who recruits, trains and supervises the work of people who, though not highly trained, are thought to possess qualities which will make them capable of performing important mental health functions. Emphasis on preventive efforts also alters the professional role in another way. It requires that one renounce the traditionally passive pose. Instead one must attempt to develop services among people who are not asking for help.

These types of role changes are just beginning to be instituted in a variety of programs. Some like those of Sanders (1967) and Holzberg & Knapp (1965) are based in the mental hospital. Others like those of Donahue & Nichtern (1965), Zax & Cowen (1967) and Iscoe, Pierce-Jones, Friedman & Mc-Gehearty (1967) are based in the schools. Still others like those of Riessman (1967) and Klein (1967) are based in underprivileged neighborhoods. All, whether oriented toward more traditional therapy or toward prevention, share the belief that the old order was inadequate and that many of its hallowed principles bear challenging.

It is difficult to predict what new professional and sub-professional role models will evolve to augment the more traditional ones. In the best of circumstances such a crystallization will not take place until the emerging programs have undergone appropriate tests of their effectiveness so that empirical results rather than simple faith in a theory can be used to mold the form of new approaches. With increasing government concern for the problems deriving from growing up in the midst of poverty and ignorance, it can be expected that the next several years will see much experimenting in such realms and very likely many of the most creative advances in thinking about the causes and treatment of psychological problems since the time of Freud.

# REFERENCES

ALBEE, G. W. *Mental health manpower trends.* New York: Basic Books, 1959.

COWEN, E. L., GARDNER, E. A. & ZAX, M.: *Emergent approaches to mental health problems.* New York: Appleton-Century-Crofts, 1967.

DONAHUE, G. T., and NICHTERN, S. *Teach-*ing the troubled child. New York: Free Press, 1965.

EYSENCK, H. J. The effects of psychotherapy: an evaluation. *Journal of Consulting Psychology,* 16(1962), 319–324.

HOLZBERG, J. D., and KNAPP, R. H. The social interaction of college students and chronically ill mental patients. *American Journal of Orthopsychiatry*, 35(1965), 487–492.

Iscoe, I., Pierce-Jones, I., Friedman, S. T., and McGehearty, L. Some strategies in mental health consultation: a brief description of a project and some preliminary results. In E. L. Cowen, E. A. Gardner, and M. Zax (eds.), *Emergent approaches to mental health problems*. New York: Appleton-Century-Crofts, 1967.

Joint Commission on Mental Illness and Health. *Action for mental health*. New York: Basic Books, 1961.

Klein, W. L. The training of human service aides. In E. L. Cowen, E. A. Gardner, and M. Zax (eds.), *Emergent approaches to mental health problems*. New York: Appleton-Century-Crofts, 1967.

Riessman, F. A neighborhood-based mental health approach. In E. L. Cowen, E. A. Gardner, and M. Zax (eds.), *Emergent approaches to mental health problems*. New York: Appleton-Century-Crofts, 1967.

Rioch, Margaret J. Pilot projects in training mental health counselors. In E. L. Cowen, E. A. Gardner, and M. Zax (eds.), *Emergent approaches to mental health problems*. New York: Appleton-Century-Crofts, 1967.

Rogers, C. R. *Counseling and psychotherapy*. Boston: Houghton-Mifflin, 1951.

Sanders, R. New manpower for mental hospital service. In E. L. Cowen, E. A. Gardner, and M. Zax (eds.), *Emergent approaches to mental health problems*. New York: Appleton-Century-Crofts, 1967.

Srole, L., Langner, T. S., Michael, S. T., Opler, M. K., and Rennie, T. A. C. *Mental health in the metropolis*, Vol. I. New York: McGraw-Hill, 1962.

Umbarger, C. C., Dalsimer, J. S., Morrison, A. P., and Breggin, A. S. *College students in a mental hospital*. New York: Grune & Stratton, 1962.

Wolpe, J. *Psychotherapy by reciprocal inhibition*. Stanford, Calif.: Stanford University Press, 1958.

Zax, M., and Cowen, E. L. Early identification and prevention of emotional disturbance in a public school. In E. L. Cowen, E. A. Gardner, and M. Zax (eds.), *Emergent approaches to mental health problems*. New York: Appleton-Century-Crofts, 1967.

Bernard L. Bloom

# The "Medical Model," Miasma Theory, and Community Mental Health

This paper by Dr. Bloom points up the similarity between the thinking and practices in the community mental health field today and in the early public health model. Both seem to operate on the basis of "miasma" theory, which lacked validity as a theory but which nevertheless prescribed practices useful for the prevention of physical illness. Another point of similarity between the public health and community mental health movement is that both eschew the "medical model," which has come under close scrutiny in recent years. It has been attacked as a theory of how illness is caused (see Szasz, The Myth of

*Reprinted from* Community Mental Health Journal, 1(1965), 333–338 *with the permission of Behavioral Publications, Inc. and Dr. Bloom.*

Mental Illness) *and as a way of practicing, although rarely both ways by the same people. The prevention-oriented and community-oriented person in the mental health field has found that the medical model, with its emphasis on waiting for people with fully developed illness to appeal for his help, is extremely limiting. His concern has been with preventing full-blown illness as it is viewed traditionally and to ameliorate or prevent many problems that have not been widely regarded as mental health problems either by professionals or even by the afflicted persons. This has forced the worker to adopt a more active role which brings him out of office practice and into key parts of the community where his influence can be felt by a significant proportion of individuals needing his service. Some of the specific programs described in this section will reflect this reaction against the medical model.*

Questions about the appropriateness of the so-called medical model in the field of the emotional disorders have long been voiced by professionals of many disciplines. The components of the medical model which have been especially singled out for comment by mental health practitioners include: (1) the belief that one is dealing with diseases or disease syndromes, each with a specific etiology, a disease-specific cure, and ultimately a disease-specific prevention; (2) the belief that the cause, as well as the appropriate prevention and treatment of emotional disorders, will ultimately be found in the biology of the organism, as opposed to its psychology or sociology; and (3) the belief that definitive treatment of emotional disorders takes place almost exclusively in the dyad between practitioner-patient. Perhaps the only characteristic of the medical model with which there appears to be general agreement, at least by the profession of psychology, is that one's formal training has not been completed until the title of "Doctor" has been earned.

The medical model grew out of and received its major impetus during the past century as a consequence of the extraordinary successes of germ theory and the doctrine of contagion in the field of the infectious diseases, and from the equally striking successes in the treatment and prevention of nutri-

tional disorders. In view of its characteristics as well as its historical development, this model should, perhaps more properly, be called the biological model. It is not surprising that the model has been applied to the field of the chronic diseases, including the emotional disorders. Yet there appears to be little convincing evidence that the model is appropriate for the emotional disorders. Since emotional disorders are still mainly conditions of unknown etiology and meaningful diagnostic nomenclature continues to be the object of considerable research and speculation, it seems therefore premature to most mental health professionals to give major emphasis for the amelioration of these disorders to the dyadic treatment model or to any other single treatment approach.

With the rapid current growth of the field of community mental health, particularly with its emphasis upon primary prevention, questions about the appropriateness of the biological model are being raised anew. Less is known about community dis-ease than about individual dis-ease. Techniques of prevention and treatment, imperfectly understood in the case of the individual, are even more tentative in the case of communities. Study of the community and of techniques for inducing community change so clearly involves the social sciences and group action that the unilateral emphasis on the patient-practitioner interaction seems foolhardy.

In this paper some beliefs and practices in the field of mental health in general, and in the field of community mental health in particular, will be considered in order to induce information about the apparent model being followed. In arguing inductively—that is, from the practice to the theory—it will be suggested: (1) that the biological model as defined above is not actually a major philosophical influence in the field of community mental health, and (2) that the model which is apparently employed is strikingly similar to the notions of miasma theory.

Miasma theory preceded germ theory as the major explanatory concept in the understanding of disease processes. It held that soil polluted with waste products of any kind gave off a "miasma" into the air, which caused many major infectious diseases of the day. This theory, which dated from the writings of Hippocrates, suggested that these "poisonous substances" rose up from the earth and were spread through the winds. People living near swamps, and thus particularly vulnerable to marsh gases, were thought to develop fever from these gases—a fever which came to be known as malaria (bad air). The doctrine of miasma, which will be further elaborated below, was preeminent until the end of the nineteenth century, by which time germ theory had become established as the prevailing explanation of the infectious diseases. The major differences between miasma theory and germ theory have implications for an analysis of current thought regarding the theory and practice of community mental health.

While miasma theory has been generally discredited, it possessed great utility at the time it was being applied. Many of the current concepts in community mental health appear to share this potential usefulness. In suggesting that these concepts are similar to miasma theory, no criticism of current practice is intended. Indeed, there is reason to believe that miasma theory provides a quite proper model to be followed.

## THE TAXONOMY OF DISEASE

The biological model holds that there are a large number, perhaps an unlimited number, of discrete, uniquely caused diseases. Diseases are, therefore, essentially independent of each other. Miasma theory, on the other hand, suggests that there are very few diseases, perhaps as few as one, and that disease states are quite interdependent and even interchangeable. Florence Nightingale, who is reputed to have founded the nursing profession as a protest against germ theory, and who was a confirmed miasmatist throughout her lifetime, wrote,

I was brought up . . . to believe that small-pox, for instance, was a thing of which there was once a first specimen in the world, which went on propagating itself, in a perpetual chain of descent. . . . Since then I have seen with my own eyes and smelt with my nose small-pox growing up in first specimens, either in close rooms or in over-crowded wards where it could not by any possibility have been "caught" but must have begun. Nay more, I have seen diseases begin, grow up, and pass into one another. I have seen, for instance, with a little overcrowding continued fever grow up; and with a little more, typhoid fever; and with a little more, typhus, and all in the same ward or hut [Cope, 1958, pp. 14–15].

Thus, different names were assigned to what was thought to be the same disorder as a function of its severity, much as in the South Pacific different names are assigned to the same fish as a function of its size.

There can be little question but that general thought in the field of mental health follows the miasma theory quite closely. While there is no single generally accepted theory of psychopathology, one commonly espoused point of view postulates that differences between normal and abnormal, between neurosis and psychosis are essentially quantitative in character—that a psychosis was once a neurosis. No psychiatric nomenclature suggests that each mental disorder is uniquely caused, however elaborate or sophisticated the nomenclature. Most proposals for the quantitative reporting of psychiatric hospitalizations take the position that there is only one emotional disorder. That is to say, in most suggested statistical reporting systems, a patient cannot be listed as being admitted for the first time for a condition different from the condition for which he was previously admitted. There has been no recognition of the logical possibility that within the same individual two or more different independent emotional disorders can arise, each requiring a first admission into a treatment facility.

## DIAGNOSIS AND TREATMENT

The biological model contends that etiology and treatment are disease-specific. Accordingly, the establishment of a diagnosis is generally necessary before appropriate treatment can be instituted. Since, according to miasma theory, diagnosis was essentially irrelevant, there was no particular relationship postulated between treatment and prior diagnosis. Actually, miasma theory offered little specific direction regarding treatment. It was primarily a theory aimed at the prevention of disease. Treatment was seen as making the pa-

tient as comfortable as possible and relying on the patient's own restitutive potential. That is, while the biological model views treatment as doing something to the patient, miasma theory proposed that treatment consisted of arranging optimal conditions for the patient to help himself. While the physician is thus the key treatment figure, according to the contemporary medical model, a century ago miasma theory accorded primary treatment responsibility to the nursing profession.

Most thinking in the field of mental health takes positions quite similar to miasma theory, both on the issue of diagnosis and on the relationship of diagnosis to rational treatment. While the hope is frequently expressed that a diagnostic system will ultimately be developed which will yield diagnosis-specific treatment procedures, many mental health practitioners doubt that this state of affairs can or will ever come to pass. Certainly, treatment for emotional disorders today can hardly be considered to be diagnosis-specific. And even the most physiologically oriented practitioner is aware that a major consideration in the successful treatment of mental disorders is to involve the patient actively in his own behalf. This situation is even more cogent when the patient is the community, that is, when community change is desired. To a considerable extent, then, current mental health practice seeks to utilize the same techniques as the bedside nurse of the last century, namely, to create a milieu which will facilitate natural forces bringing about restitution or change whether in the patient or in the community.

In the context of a discussion of the relationship between treatment of a disorder and one's understanding of its history or cause, it may be perhaps useful to note that the term "cause" as applied to diseases has two distinguishable meanings (Cassel, 1964). The onset of a disease is "caused," and a patient's lack of recovery from the disease is "caused," but there is no reason to believe that these two "causes" are identical. Understanding the first set of causes can help in the prevention of a particular disorder but may not be useful in treating an existing case. The practices of the miasmatists fell in this category. Alternatively, understanding the second set of causes can help in the treatment of a disorder, but not necessarily in its prevention. This occurs in the case, for example, of applying the known relationship between insulin metabolism and diabetes. The disease can be treated but not prevented. Questions can be raised not only about the extent of our valid knowledge of techniques for the treatment of emotional disorders, but also about the extent to which these techniques or their underlying theory can be appropriately applied in the task of primary prevention.

## PREVENTION AND THE DOCTRINE OF CONTAGION

The doctrine of contagion, without its biological implications, long predated miasma theory. All evil was considered contagious by early peoples, including misfortune, uncleanliness, wickedness, and disease (Singer, 1918). It was a habit of ancient literature, wrote Greenwood (1953),

to speak of seeds of pestilence, of victims struck down by the contagion, passing it on, infecting others. But there is no hint in the Greek or Roman writers that this notion of seeds was more than a metaphor, that arrows or particles might not have been substituted for seeds [p. 502].

With the development of miasma theory even the metaphorical use of the term "contagion" was rejected. The real triumph of the concept occurred subsequently when its essentially biological nature was finally recognized. With an understanding of the agent of disease transmission, a considerably more sophisticated view of disease prevention could develop.

Medico-biological theory now views disease as developing out of the interaction of host, agent, and environment. An appropriate modification of any one of these three factors can result in the prevention of disease. Not only has this three-factor theory been useful in the field of traditional diseases, but also the model is being effectively exploited in such related fields as accident prevention—the automobile driver is viewed as the host, the automobile as the agent, and the road and weather as examples of the relevant environment. Prevention of disease has been found feasible either by influencing the host, as by immunization against smallpox; or by direct action on the agent, as by the proper use of soap and water in the prevention of syphilis; or by modification of the environment, as by spraying mosquito-infested areas in the prevention of malaria and yellow fever. There is thus a relatively rich armamentarium of techniques available to the contemporary practitioner to control the development of infectious diseases.

In contrast, the miasmatist had but a single major avenue open to him to prevent disease. In the absence of the theory of contagion, and as a direct consequence of miasma theory itself, the major technique for disease prevention was to attempt to modify the environment by removing the sources of the miasma. The early miasmatists declared war on all refuse quite indiscriminately. Accumulated manure was considered just as dangerous as a cesspool which was contaminating a supply of drinking water. The public health movement had its beginnings with the early environmental and sanitary engineers who sought to prevent disease by removing and preventing the accumulation of filth. Indeed, physicians played a relatively small role in disease prevention, and the medical profession was not always represented on early national health boards. Secondary to modification of the environment, miasmatists sought, by public education, to alert the potential victims of disease—that is, the host—to the dangers of the environment in which they lived.

Except in a metaphorical sense, the concept of contagion plays little significant role in the considerations of mental health practitioners. Accordingly, theories in the field of primary prevention are relatively limited. Even today proposals about the prevention of mental disorder are mainly hypotheses to be tested, rather than established principles. These proposals include both direct environmental modification as well as certain attempts to improve individuals' resistance to deleterious psychic forces around them. In a manner of speaking, current concepts of primary prevention in the field of mental disorders appear to be designed to remove existing accumulations of psychic sewage and to develop improved techniques to prevent their further accretion, both in the individual and in the community. Representing the first category, modification of the environment, are such activities as mental health education, community organization, and administrative consultation. In the second category, modification of the host, are such activities as anticipatory guidance, crisis intervention, and case-centered or consultee-centered agency consultation. Thus, the theory of prevention underlying community mental health practice appears to be patterned after the model first proposed by the miasmatists.

## MIASMA THEORY AS A COMMUNITY MENTAL HEALTH MODEL

It may be discouraging to contemplate the fact that current concepts in community mental health closely follow a set of earlier ideas which have been shown to be without scientific validity. But it must not be supposed that miasma theory was methodologically unscientific or irrational or capricious. The sanitation movement was an entirely rational application of the then prevailing theory of disease. It was an attempt to deal with an extremely serious health situation and played a vital and stable role in the provision of health services of a century ago, particularly during the industrial revolution in Europe and the United States which, among other things, resulted in extreme overcrowding and uncleanliness in urban areas. There was an immense amount of sickness in the poorer crowded sections of most large cities (a situation not unlike estimates of mental disorders today); and it was felt that beyond any doubt, disease—particularly the communicable diseases—was due to the lack of drainage, water supply, and the means for removing refuse from houses and streets. Rene Dubois (1961) wrote:

To a group of public-minded citizens guided by the physician Southwood Smith and the engineer Edwin Chadwick, it appeared that, since disease always accompanied want, dirt, and pollution, health could be restored only by bringing back to the multitudes pure air, pure water, pure food, and pleasant surroundings. This simple concept was synthesized in the movement "The Health of Towns Association," the prototype of the present-day voluntary health associations throughout the world. Its aim was to "substitute health for disease, cleanliness for filth, order for disorder, . . . order for palliation, . . . enlightened self-interest for ignorant selfishness, and bring home to the poorest, . . . in purity and abundance, the simple blessings which ignorance and negligence have long combined to spoil—*Air, Water, Light!*" [pp. 127–8].

Scientists of a century ago were as concerned about the evaluation of their theory and practice as are mental health scientists today. For example, Lilienfeld (1958) has noted that an association was observed between elevation of residence and cholera mortality in London in 1848–49. With increasing elevation, there was decreasing cholera mortality. Cholera mortality was reported as 102 deaths per 10,000 inhabitants in homes located less than 20 feet above sea level, 65 deaths per 10,000 inhabitants in homes between 20–40 feet above sea level, with the mortality rate declining in a curvilinear fashion until at elevations of over 340 feet above sea level the mortality rate was 7 per 100,000. While this statistical association can now be understood in terms of the relationship of the purity of the water supply to the elevation of the pump, it was consistent with miasma theory as well, and was interpreted as confirmatory evidence for it.

It must also not be assumed that miasma theory, because it was ultimately discredited as theory, was not effective in practice. Shryock (1949), in commenting on the miasmatist's effectiveness in disease prevention in contrast to disease treatment, noted:

The conviction that the quickest way to improve the health of the poor was through sanitation received statistical verification during the 1850's when various British towns showed marked mortality declines following the establishment of sanitary controls. . . . At the same time that sanitation promised so much, direct medical care of the poor seemed to promise little. . . . It is no wonder that lay reformers . . . had more confidence in what mathematics could

do for the poor than they had in medicine [p. 41].

Under the leadership of Max von Pettenkofer, Munich began a city-wide cleanup and beautification program. Clean water was brought in from the surrounding mountains, and city sewage was diluted. As a consequence, typhoid mortality fell from 72 per million in 1880 to 14 per million in 1898. The incidence and mortality of yellow fever was significantly decreased in large Spanish cities following the anti-filth campaigns. Mortality from tuberculosis fell from a high of 500 per 100,000 in 1845 to 200 per 100,000 in 1900. Earlier, again as a direct consequence of the striving for cleanliness, maternal mortality had already been reduced from 24 per 1000 live births in 1750 to 3.5 per 1000 live births in 1800. Infant mortality rates had shown a parallel decrease. In addition, the sanitation movement resulted in major decreases in the morbidity and mortality associated with typhus and cholera. These successes, it should be remembered, occurred as a result of programs instituted by people who did not believe in contagion, let alone in the germ theory of disease, and occurred in the total absence of any disease-specific therapeutic or preventive techniques. While, as was already mentioned, miasma theory offered little direction for treatment, its contribution to disease prevention was no less than extraodinary.

Some future historian may look back at our beginning efforts in the prevention and early treatment of mental disorders with some of the same amused compassion that we feel in considering miasma theory of a century ago. But miasma theory and the practical programs which it generated have probably done more to raise the general level of health in the world than have the

programs instituted as a consequence
of germ theory. To quote again from
Dubois (1961),

It is easy to see how the appearance of the
new antibacterial drugs on the medical scene
gave rise to the illusion that the age-old
problem of infection had finally been solved.
A few diseases almost universally fatal could
now be cured. . . . The course of other
infectious processes could be interrupted
with incredible rapidity. . . . It is obvious
that these triumphs . . . are changing the
very pattern of disease in the Western
world, but there is no reason to believe
that they spell the *conquest* of microbial
diseases. While it is true that the mortality
of many of these afflictions is at an all-time
low, the amount of disease that they cause
remains very high. Drugs are far more effective in the dramatic acute conditions which
are relatively rare than in the countless
chronic ailments that account for so much
misery in everyday life. Furthermore, as we
have seen, the decrease in mortality caused
by infection began almost a century ago and
has continued ever since at a fairly constant
rate irrespective of the use of any specific
therapy. The effect of antibacterial drugs is
but a ripple on the wave which has been
wearing down the mortality caused by infection in our communities [pp. 136–7].

The model introduced by the practices of the miasmatists should be carefully considered by professionals entering the field of community mental
health. Its successes were outstanding,
albeit for the wrong reasons. As was
previously noted, the field of public
health was begun by miasmatists. While
the practice of community mental
health involves interaction with programs in welfare, in education, as well
as in general health, it represents, in
part, the application of basic public
health concepts to the mental disorders.
These concepts, introduced so usefully

more than a century ago, include: (1)
an emphasis upon primary prevention
rather than on treatment or rehabilitation; (2) an emphasis on the total
community rather than on the individual; and (3) the recognition that
progress is made by working with and
through community agencies, that is,
that communities are organized and
that this community organization is a
powerful and relevant force in the
service of improving a community's
emotional well-being.

In a sense, miasma theory suffered
from being insufficiently precise. Im-
bedded within its borders was a small
but important island of validity. Until
the reasons for their effectiveness were
properly understood, miasmatists were
concerned about much which, in retrospect, was not within their proper scope
of interest. This phenomenon has probably characterized many other theories
as well. Certainly the contemporary
community mental health professional
is being attacked for his involvement in
areas such as poverty, urban renewal,
and social disequilibrium, which people
consider outside the direct scope of
mental health. Yet, as one examines
the current state of knowledge in the
field and the array of hypotheses available to anyone particularly interested in
the prevention of emotional disorders,
the miasma model seems entirely appropriate. It may be that the theories
which lie behind the practice of community mental health—and this paper
has sought to show how similar these
theories actually are to those of the
miasmatists—may one day also be considered naive. But in return for results
equivalent to those obtained by the
sanitarians and engineers in the prevention of infectious diseases, we might
willingly pay the price.

## REFERENCES

CASSEL, J. Social science theory as source of hypotheses in epidemiological research. *Amer. J. publ. Hlth.*, 1964, **54**, 1482–1488.

COPE, Z. *Florence Nightingale and the doctors.* Philadelphia: Lippincott, 1958.

DUBOIS, R. *The mirage of health.* New York: Doubleday, 1961.

GREENWOOD, M. Miasma and contagion. In E. A. Underwood (Ed.) *Science, medicine and history.* Vol. II. London: Oxford Univ. Press, 1953.

LILIENFELD, A. M. Epidemiological methods and inferences in studies of noninfectious diseases. *Publ. hlth. Rep.*, 1958, **72**, 51–60.

SHRYOCK, R. H. In the 1840's. In I. Galdston (Ed.) *Social medicine: Its derivations and objectives.* New York: Commonwealth Fund, 1949.

SINGER, C. Discussion. *Proc. royal soc. Med.*, 1918–19, **12**, 71–72.

Arthur J. Bindman

# The Psychologist as a Mental Health Consultant

*In this paper by Dr. Bindman, the role of the psychologist as a mental health consultant is discussed. Such a role is a relatively new one for the mental health worker and is in keeping with a movement toward extending the influence of the scarce professional by using him as a consultant to key groups of individuals. It is hoped that such individuals—teachers, nurses, clergymen, and the like— in turn will be able to develop skills through the help of the consultant which will be usefully applied to the large number of people they contact each day who need assistance with psychological problems. It is the long-range hope that such efforts will ultimately reduce the number of individuals whose problems grow to such proportions that they require referral to the clinic or hospital. Another goal of such an approach is to enhance the capacity of some individuals to realize their own potentials as fully as possible.*

The psychologist as a mental health consultant is a relatively new role requiring a breadth of knowledge and experience culled from a number of fields and applied in a wide variety of areas. In the remarks which follow, the historical background of mental health consultation, as a specific technique, will be sketched and differentiated from other types of consultation. Its application by psychologists and the unique aspects of psychological training which enhance or detract from this method will be described. Suggestions for future developments in mental health consultation will also be made.

Consultation is not a new word in our vocabulary, although it has received little attention from psychological theory or research. Secondly, the types of consultation which can be provided have frequently become confused, not

*Reprinted from* Journal of Psychiatric Nursing, 2(1964), 367–380 *with the permission of Stuart James Publishing Co., Bordentown, N. J. and Dr. Bindman.*

only in the minds of those receiving consultation, but also among the various practitioners. If we think of our usual model of consultation, it is one of a professional asking another professional to see the former's client in order to make an appraisal and suggestions for problem resolution. The consultant may be called in because he is a specialist and can provide some specific knowledge or act in a technical assistant capacity. In the medical model, he may even follow through and provide a specific procedure.

Another type of consultation which is frequently noted in social agencies is the use made of one professional discipline, e.g., psychiatrists, who consult on cases or other problems, but who do not supervise these cases. Gilbert (1960) (8) has made this point quite clearly when she notes that a consultant in this latter role cannot become involved in the supervisory process if he is to remain a "pure" consultant, i.e., having no decision making power or administrative role.

A third type of consultant is the individual who works in a particular agency in an administrative position who provides consultation to line personnel, but who also may have administrative responsibilities for these same personnel. This type of consultant is frequently seen in public health agencies, departments of education, and in industrial settings where they are known as intramural consultants, in contrast to the extramural consultants who come "from the outside." The intramural consultant usually cannot divorce his supervisory and inspection roles from his consultation role, and in a sense he is, therefore, not a "pure" consultant.

A fourth example of consultation which gives more breadth to our discussion is the type of consultant who becomes involved in a counseling relationship with the consultee, whom he views as the client. I would submit that this example, frequently seen where psychologists have transferred their clinical and counseling skills to the industrial setting, would not fall into the generic category of what is called consultation, although it may be so labeled by some practitioners.

How does mental health consultation relate to the general area of consultation? Mental health consultation is a type of consultation aimed at the reduction of mental health problems by involving the participation of the professional caretakers who deal with these problems in their own professional roles. The mental health consultant deals particularly with problems that induce "crises," as well as providing assistance in early case-finding and special types of program consultation [Simmons (15)]. This is termed mental health case consultation which stresses work with a consultee around the problems of clients. Simmons points out that the consultant "is not viewed as a therapist or the giver of prescriptive advice. Instead, the consultant seeks to assist a co-professional deal more effectively with that segment of the population which he serves by helping the consultee solve those problems in his work which have mental health implications." The mental health consultant can also provide technical assistance regarding mental health problems, so that consultees can become more skillful and gain knowledge in dealing with problems which concern them [Bindman (2)].

The technique of mental health consultation takes its base from writings by members of the Wellesley Human Relations Service, such as Klein (9, 10, 11), Lindemann (12), and more recently Simmons (15). Vaughan (18) and Bindman (1, 2, 3) of the Massachusetts Department of Mental Health, where mental health consultation is part of the department's community mental health program, have written about particular applications of this method of mental health practice. Caplan (4, 5, 6, 7) of the Harvard School of Public Health has provided the best theoretical model as gleaned from his research and from in-service seminars he has conducted over a period of years with the Massachusetts Department of Mental Health. It may be of interest that the techniques of mental health consultation have received ever-widening attention and are being offered in the curriculum of the Postgraduate Center for Psychotherapy (13), as well as being the subject of a conference sponsored by NIMH (16). Mental health consultation has only recently received more attention from psychologists, as far as the technical literature is concerned, and training in the techniques of mental health consultation for psychologists have only been noted in recent years.

What is unique about mental health consultation? How does it differ from other interpersonal techniques? How well trained is the psychologist in applying these techniques, and what further training does he need? Perhaps a definition will help in focusing upon the process. It has been defined as "an interaction process or interpersonal relationship that takes place between two professional workers, the consultant and and the consultee, in which one worker, the consultant, attempts to assist the other worker, the consultee, to solve a mental health problem of a client or clients, *within the framework of the consultee's usual professional functioning*. The process of consultation depends upon the communication of knowledge, skills, and attitudes through this relationship, and therefore is dependent upon the degree of emotional and intellectual involvement of the two

workers. A secondary goal of this process is one of education so that the consultee can learn to handle similar cases in the future in a more effective fashion and thus enhance his professional skills" [Bindman (1, 2)].

It will be noted that stress has been placed on the words, "within the framework of the consultee's usual professional functioning." This implies that the consultant does not try to make a psychotherapist out of the consultee when the latter is confronted with a mental health problem. In fact, stress is placed upon the improvement of the consultee's use of his own professional skills in reducing mental health difficulties or in enhancing mental health in his client(s).

The definition of mental health consultation suggests that there is a relationship to education, psychotherapy, supervision and administration in this process. It is really none of these methods, although techniques may have been borrowed from each.

The following are some distinctive differences:

## EDUCATION AND MENTAL HEALTH CONSULTATION

Education generally emphasizes a long-term systematic approach; the curriculum is usually planned; the problem area is usually well-defined and delimited and the teacher may "feed" information to the student. In mental health consultation, there is no highly structured, pre-planned approach. The consultant uses whatever opportunities he can to form a relationship with the consultee and to focus upon the problem. The meetings are usually few in number, and thus difficulties may result in delimiting the problem too quickly in terms of an expected outcome. Finally, the consultant may advise, but he usually does so in a nondirective fashion and in no case does he implement a plan for problem solution himself. Caplan (7) suggests that consultation does come close to the methods of a problem centered seminar, individual tutorial or individual and group supervision.

## SUPERVISION AND MENTAL HEALTH CONSULTATION

There is an essential and basic difference between consultation and supervision. The supervisor must be responsible for the work of the supervised individual, but the consultant is not directly responsible. The supervisor directs the work of the supervisee and even assists him in a direct fashion, while the mental health consultant is problem-focused and is not expected to follow through to see if his suggestions are being used. This is a major difference; i.e., the supervisor must deal directly with the professional role of the person being supervised, while the consultant should remain focused on the problem if he is to maintain his role. As Rhodes (14) points out in writing about the process of consultation in general: Consultation . . . "does not explore or attempt to interact with other roles of the consultee. Whenever it does venture into other life roles of the consultee, it is no longer consultation." Perhaps a minor distinction between supervision and consultation is the frequency with which the consultant is from another professional discipline than the consultee. In mental health consultation he is usually from one of the so-called mental health professions and the consultee is not. In supervision, particularly in case work and nursing, the supervisor will be from the same profession. Finally, the consultee usually

initiates mental health consultation, while in supervision the supervisory relationship is initiated "from above."

## PSYCHOTHERAPY AND MENTAL HEALTH CONSULTATION

There are a number of differences between these two interpersonal methods. Psychotherapy is generally long term; it is concerned with a range of intrapsychic problems in a patient or client; it weakens or changes defenses; there may be interpretation and other psychological means of handling resistances. In mental health consultation, the time span is short and the consultant attempts to handle a specific problem of a client and then withdraws. Defenses are not weakened in the consultee, but rather they are bolstered and supported. The consultant rarely interprets and if he does it may be about the client's problems and not the consultee's.

Psychotherapy of the consultee should be avoided. The consultant may be aware of the consultee's personal difficulties, but he constantly focuses upon the problem, the client, or other aspects of the work situation and not upon the intrapsychic conflicts of the consultee. "If the consultant allows himself to get involved in the consultee's intrapsychic problems, he is falling into the trap which has been set for him; namely, that the consultee was not fully certain that he is to play the role of a patient, but now he has proved that he is to do so" [Bindman (1)]. Rhodes (14) also notes that there has been much confusion between these two methods. In fact, he remarks that consultants have been met with anger and rejection on the part of consultees when they have applied their therapeutic skills to the consultee's intrapsychic processes instead of being aware of the consultee's need to focus upon the problem situation or client.

On the other hand, one cannot deny that in mental health case consultation there is the need to develop a close relationship with the consultee, just as in other interpersonal modes, although the consultant must do this as quickly and efficiently as possible and without the depth noted in intensive psychotherapy. Secondly, corrective emotional experiences take place in both mental health case consultation and in psychotherapy, but once again in a much less intensive fashion in the former.

## ADMINISTRATION AND MENTAL HEALTH CONSULTATION

In administrative practice, the administrator assumes responsibility for taking specific action, making decisions, promulgating policy, and in general taking leadership. Administration implies that a subordinate will follow directions of the administrator. Mental health consultation is best carried out when the consultant can clearly communicate to the consultee that there is a "take it or leave it" characteristic to their relationship with each having the right to withdraw. The consultant does not make decisions, assume responsibility for follow-up of results, or take a leadership role. Towle (17) indicates that in a true consultation relationship the person seeking advice is a free agent and he alone holds the responsibility for using the advice. The distinction between administration and consultation may become particularly nebulous in program consultation where there may be problems related to administration. The consultant should be wary lest he become the administrator instead of merely assisting in ad-

ministrative planning. Of course, when the consultant is hired on an intramural basis this "pure" role of consultant may become impossible to maintain, especially when he acts in a line function and carries certain administrative responsibilities in his role. It would appear from our present knowledge that mental health consultation is best carried on in as "pure" a form as possible with the consultant on an extramural staff level.

One cannot discuss techniques of mental health consultation without relying heavily on the theoretical writings of Caplan (4, 5, 6, 7). He divides mental health case consultation into four major categories: case insight, action-help, consultee crisis, and social system consultation.

In case insight consultation, the consultee lacks understanding regarding a client's problems. The consultant attempts to increase the consultee's knowledge regarding the psychological functioning of the client, but in keeping with the consultee's professional background. One technique that is used is to jointly observe a client, and then discuss their perceptions. The hoped for result is that the consultee will then enhance the environment in such a way that it has a positive effect upon the client's behavior pattern. One example might be that of a teacher who does not understand why a child behaves aggressively on the playground in relation to younger children. She is helped by the consultant in her understanding of the child's sibling rivalry problems. The result is that she gives special attention to the child and helps him compensate for his feelings of rejection. Another example is that of a manager in industry who cannot understand why a particular subordinate is easily flustered and on the verge of tears at times. The mental health consultant might help the manager gain further understanding into the subordinate's feelings of low self-esteem and also provide suggestions which could help the employer become more effective.

In action-help consultation, the consultee lacks the skill or facilities in his work setting to deal with special mental health problems of a client. For example, he may not know what resource he can use in the community when a particular problem occurs. The mental health consultant collaborates with the consultee and assists him in working out a plan for the client. Nondirective techniques are used at first, but at a later stage the consultant may give more direct information in order to broaden the consultee's knowledge in assisting clients. In the long run, the consultee should become more effective in case finding and in the utilization of community resources in meeting the needs of his clients. One example is that of a school principal who is assisted by the mental health consultant in understanding a serious mental health problem of a child and how she can help the family to bring the child to a community health center. Another example in an industrial setting is that of a mental health consultant who helps a supervisor sharpen his skills in assessing problems of depression in older workers, and tells him how he can make inplant referrals for assistance or use outside facilities for referrals in some instances.

In consultee crisis consultation, a disturbed or disturbing situation in a client may trigger off a crisis in a consultee. Frequently, the client's behavior is the type which will cause similar problems which have been controlled to suddenly reemerge. The consultee may distort and stereotype his relationship with the client, the result being reduction in the consultee's effective functioning. The consultant uses two major techniques in working with the consultee. The first is "segmental tension reduction" (Caplan, 1959) (7) in which the consultant fosters discussion of the client's problems, which by implication are concerned with the consultee's problems. There is no explicit discussion of the consultee's feelings, but rather this implied method reduces the consultee's tension which in turn affects the client due to the close relationship between them. An example of this method might be the discussion of a child's mother by a teacher and mental health consultant, which in turn is meaningful for the teacher's own feelings in relation to the child.

The second method in crisis reduction is "dissipation of the stereotype" [Caplan (5, 6, 7)]. This consists of the consultant discussing with the consultee about the client's behavior in an attempt to encourage a more realistic appraisal and reduce stereotype. The aim is to have the consultee see the human aspects of the client as a person in need and not as a "monster" of some sort so that the crisis will be reduced. An example might be a hospital superintendent who stereotypes an aide as "shiftless and sloppy." The mental health consultant may use discussion and/or joint observation to help the superintendent see that this aide does not necessarily fit the pattern to which he has been relegated.

In social system consultation, one must consider whether crises or needs for action-help may have been engendered by difficulties in the social system of the consultee, such as communication problems, a vague or poor authority system, role conflicts, and disturbing personality problems. Usually, these problems have had a long history, but sudden changes in the equilibrium of the social system may require consultation. The consultant may use a case consultation approach, in which he is working indirectly, or he may work directly and provide administrative consultation in which organizational practices, personnel problems, and other management problems which may relate to the solving of a client's mental health problems will be discussed. An example of this approach would be mental health consultation with a superintendent of schools concerning the personnel practices in his school system which have resulted in an incompetent individual obtaining an important supervisory position which in turn is upsetting a very competent principal.

## TRAINING IN MENTAL HEALTH CONSULTATION

Although mental health consultation is not exclusively a psychologist's function, it would appear that psychological training, particularly in clinical and counseling psychology coupled with supervised experience, is a strong base for this work. A background in casework or psychotherapy would be essential in order that the practitioner be experienced with human dynamics and be sensitive to unconscious processes and interpersonal elements in a relationship. However, stress should be placed upon training and experience with so-called normal behavior and its vagaries rather than merely pathological functioning.

In an earlier paper, it was suggested that the psychologist should have the following [Bindman (2)]:

1. Thorough knowledge and experience in personality functioning and psychodynamics.

2. Thorough knowledge and experience in psychotherapy, both individual and group, and sufficient supervision in these methods so that he under-

stands himself and is able to control his relationships with others.

3. Thorough knowledge and experience in diagnostic appraisal and especially through the use of secondary cues and behavioral features.

4. Some training and experience in various aspects of educational methods, both in a didactic sense and in the use of other educational and promotional methods.

5. Some knowledge of social psychology and especially of social structures, communities, social groups institutional structures, and community organization.

A clinical psychologist with experience in a community mental health setting may frequently have much of the above, but in some areas the health educator, sociologist, social worker, or social psychologist will be more adequate. In addition, as the psychologist mental health consultant becomes more involved in administrative or social system consultation, he should be further trained in administrative principles, organization of community resources, industrial management, and mental health promotion techniques. In closing, let me add that there are still very few places where a psychologist can go to gain the necessary basic training and experience in mental health consultation, let alone advanced course work in this area.

## A NOTE FOR THE FUTURE

The part that psychologists—, as well as others working in the mental health field and functioning in a consultant capacity, are playing and will continue to play in developing, understanding, and evaluating mental health consultation would appear to be increasing. With the continuing demand for mental health services and the rapid burgeoning of community mental health programs, there is an ever increasing need for techniques which will possibly prevent problems in the mental health sphere, and to do this in a relatively quick and effective fashion. Mental health consultation may not be the complete panacea, but it does hold promise for positive change and deserves the interest of the professional psychologist. Although one should not make a prediction without sufficient data or at least a high degree of confidence in the data at hand, nevertheless the trend appears to be one of increased use of consultants in general and men-

tal health consultants in particular. Once again, psychologists are faced with a dilemma—how can they best train themselves for the application of these techniques, if there is this increased demand for services? Perhaps more post-graduate training centers (13) are the solution in combination with ongoing service programs. It is a difficult problem, and one which is barely being faced now. One wonders if this training opportunity will be grasped by psychology in the near future, or will it, like other chances, perish due to lack of interest.

# REFERENCES

1. BINDMAN, A. J.: Mental Health Consultation: Theory and Practice. *J. Consult. Psychol.*, 23: 473–482, 1959.
2. ———: Training in Mental Health Consultation. Paper read at the American Psychological Association Convention, Cincinnati, 1959.
3. BINDMAN, A. J., AND KLEBANOFF, L. B.: Administrative Problems in Establishing a Community Mental Health Program. *Amer. J. Orthopsychiat.*, 30: 696–711, 1960.
4. CAPLAN, G.: The Role of the Social Worker in Preventive Psychiatry. *Med. Soc. Wk.*, 4: 144–159, 1955.
5. ———: Mental Health Consultation in Schools. In *Elements of a Community Mental Health Program*. Milbank Memorial Fund, N. Y., pp. 77–85, 1956.
6. ———: *Mental Health Aspects of Social Work in Public Health*. U. S. Children's Bureau, Washington, D. C., 1956.
7. ———: *Concepts of Mental Health and Consultation*. U. S. Children's Bureau, Washington, D. C., 1959.
8. GILBERT, RUTH: Functions of the Consultant. *Teach. Coll. Rec.*, 61: 177–187, 1960.
9. KLEIN, D. C.: Training the Psychologist in a Community Mental Health Center. Paper read at the American

Psychological Association Convention, Chicago, 1956.
10. ———: Consultation in the Framework of Preventive Psychiatry. Paper read at the American Orthopsychiatric Association Annual Meeting, San Francisco, 1959.
11. ———: The Prevention of Mental Illness. *Ment. Hyg.*, 45: 101–109, 1961.
12. LINDEMANN, E.: The Wellesley Project for the Study of Certain Problems in Community Mental Health. In *Interrelations Between the Social Environment and Psychiatric Disorders*. Milbank Memorial Fund, N. Y., 1953.
13. *Postgraduate Center for Psychotherapy*. N. Y. Postgraduate Center for Psychotherapy, *Bulletin of Information*, 1960.
14. RHODES, W. C.: Training in Community Mental Health Consultation. Paper read at the American Psychological Association Convention, Chicago, 1960.
15. SIMMONS, A. J. Consultation Through a Community Mental Health Agency. Paper read at the American Psychological Association Convention, Chicago, 1960.
16. *The Psychologist and Consultation*. Report of the Consultation Subcommittee of the Conference of Chief Psychologists in State Mental Health Programs. NIMH, Bethesda, 1959.
17. TOWLE, CHARLOTTE: The Consultation

Process. Unpublished mimeographed
manuscript. University of Chicago,
1950.

18. VAUGHAN, W. T. Mental Health for
School Children. *Children*, **2**: 203–207,
1955.


Beryce W. MacLennan,
William Klein,
Arthur Pearl,
and Jacob Fishman

# Training for New Careers

*Fundamental to many programs that have been emerging in the prevention-and community-oriented mold is the idea that the manpower problem must be solved largely through the use of nonprofessionals. Much variety has been seen in the types of nonprofessionals which have been incorporated. In this paper, MacLennan, Klein, Pearl, and Fishman set out to train and supervise socially deprived young people to work as "human service aides." This is a program that is thought to have a double-barreled effect. The socially deprived individual is virtually always one who must settle for a low-level job that does nothing to enhance his esteem or to help him grow beyond the low station that he has always known. Often in such circumstances delinquency or existence on the welfare dole seems more desirable than taking a job. There is also little incentive for education or self-betterment. Work as a human service aide is an esteem-enhancing job involving some training and the development of personal skills, a rare opportunity indeed for the youth of the average lower-class community. Thus, the aide himself is helped by the program perhaps as much as those he is trained to service.*

*The other side of the coin is the growing feeling that if only there were people available to service the special needs of children, many problems they come to develop could be forestalled. In this respect the human service aide, properly trained and supervised, can provide a most important function.*

Population increase and the spread of automation has resulted in a lack of jobs for unskilled and semi-skilled workers while the accelerated demand for human services (U.S. Dept. Labor, 1963) has created a shortage of highly trained professionals. The New Careers concept (Pearl, 1964) is an attempt to alleviate these problems through the reorganization of professional roles to provide nonprofessional positions in such human service fields as education, recreation and child care. The concept has a potential for making employment, training, and advancement available to boys and girls who are currently under-educated and unskilled, and for freeing the professional to make even better use of his education and training.

Automation has drastically reduced

*Reprinted from* Community Mental Health Journal, *2(1966), 135–141 with the permission of Behavioral Publications, Inc. and Dr. MacLennan.*

the number of job opportunities for the semi-skilled, and the trend is likely to continue and intensify. Young people who live in the slums of big cities and grow up without adequate education and specialized training are particularly vulnerable. Today, it is not uncommon for between 40 and 60 percent of such youth to be unemployed. If a youth cannot reach a certain standard of education, he is dropped from school and is not eligible to enter specialized training. Without training he is hampered in acquiring skills and obtaining a meaningful job. Furthermore, no one feels responsible if a youth is fired for performing inadequately or behaving inappropriately on the job. Many in these circumstances exist on public relief, retreat into mental hospitals, or pass their lives in prison.

The demand for such human services as education, recreation, child and health care, and social science research has been expanding over the last few years and is likely to continue to grow. This is an important area of the employment structure where services are lacking and labor is in short supply. In the New Careers system, the responsibilities of the professional are redefined so that he undertakes the direction, supervision, and highly skilled technical tasks appropriate to his training and education, while nonprofessionals and subprofessional technicians undertake the simpler and more routine parts of the job requiring less skill, training, and judgment. In this way, many new jobs for the semi-skilled are created, the shortage of professionals is relieved, and the resources for service are increased.

This system entails the acceptance of the following concepts: First, society has a responsibility to see that everyone receives adequate education and training to be able to perform a job. Second, if training is to be meaningful, par-

ticularly to socially deprived youth, work experience, training and education should be carried on concurrently so that work is considered one aspect of training. Institutions, agencies, and individual employers must accept the fact that they have a responsibility to assist employees to perform adequately enough to hold the jobs for which they are being trained. Third, if New Careers are to be meaningful, permanent job positions have to be created and institutionalized, career lines established, channels for employment and educational advancement cleared, and social and trade union supports built in. The nonprofessional aide must easily be able to become the sub-professional technical assistant and to move from there into full professional status if he has the capabilities and desire.

Opportunity must be provided for the youth to obtain initial employment in spite of an unfavorable past. To deal with this problem, both the school and the service institutions in the community should redefine their functions and accept responsibility to engage and advance these youth to the point of independence and employability. This, in itself, would be a major service which the community should support.

One way to achieve this objective is to reverse current procedures and to make education and training an integral part of the job rather than to conceive of employment as dependent on prior education and training. Thus entry jobs become essentially one aspect of training for employment.

It is the purpose of this paper to consider specifically the requirements of a training program for Human Service Aides as they have been conceptualized at the Center for Youth and Community Studies, Howard University (MacLennan, 1964). Such a training program must include: (1) the definition of nonprofessional roles and work responsibilities with professional and agency administrators; (2) the selection and training of aides; (3) the selection and training of instructors and the training of on-the-job supervisors; (4) the orientation of agency administrators and staff to the particular problems which aides may present; (5) educational accreditation of the program, opportunity for the aides to obtain their high school diplomas or the equivalent, and further in-service training and education for the development of technical assistants; (6) consideration given to the kinds of training models required and where the programs should be housed—whether as vocational education in high school, as in-service training in the institutions, or in an independent center or community college; (7) finally, the provision of means to evaluate and refine the program, without which no such experimental effort can be complete.

Experimentation in aide training has been continuing at Howard University since March 1964 when the Center for Youth and Community Studies began a small project, financed jointly by the Office of Juvenile Delinquency and Youth Development and the National Institute of Mental Health (Center for Youth and Community Studies, 1965), to train school dropouts from poverty stricken backgrounds as Day Care, Recreation, and Research Aides. All 10 of these original aides completed the training program and nine out of 10 have been employed as Aides. In the ensuing 18 months, 35 youth have been trained as Aides, 65 older men and women as Community Organization Neighborhood Development Center workers, 25 young men and women between 20 and 30 years of age as subprofessional youth counsellors and aide trainers, funded by a complex of grants

from the Office of Education; the Office of Manpower, Automation and Training; and the Office of Juvenile Delinquency and Youth Development. Further, aides and youth counselors are being trained as jobs and career lines are established.

## JOB DEFINITION

Introduction of aides into any human service program necessitates a reorganization of the work of the professional and the creating of new jobs. At this early stage, it is important for the trainer to collaborate with the professional staff and agency administrators in the joint development of a new job description. In time, this job description may well be standardized and accepted as a country-wide classification, particularly in public agencies. In the meantime, this period of working together enables the institutional staffs who are going to employ the aides to feel that they have a major stake in the program and to understand some of the special problems related to the employment of disadvantaged youth. It is important for the successful employment of aides that the tasks which they will be required to perform are clearly specified and that adequate supervision is provided. Most of the young people from underprivileged backgrounds are not sophisticated in understanding and finding their way around institutional structures. They tend to give up when they meet with confusing situations and, unless carefully instructed, do not know how to get help when they encounter difficulties. They often do not expect sympathetic understanding and assistance, and consequently fail to try to communicate their needs; rather, they act out impulsively, so that crises readily occur if problems are not identified and solved at an early stage. Agency administrators and professional supervisors need to be alerted to these matters.

Working on job definition and conditions of employment offers the opportunity for agency staffs to become reconciled to some of the doubts which they have about the employment of nonprofessionals. Administrators are naturally concerned about the quality of their service. They worry about accepting boys and girls who have not given evidence of great responsibility. They distrust youth in general and are particularly anxious if there is evidence of past delinquency and school dropout. The idea of using supervised work experience as a period during which the young people will be trained how to hold a job and to become more responsible seems foreign to them at first, and they have to be convinced of its importance. The Neighborhood Youth Corps is helping to spread this idea but has so far, in most instances, failed to build in concurrent training, adequate job descriptions, or to push for the creation of permanent jobs. Very frequently, administrators express the idea they would only like to employ aides who are "poor but honest," or older people. They do not fully recognize the need to reinvolve alienated youth and to enable them to become a part of the regular work force.

## SELECTION

As present methods of predicting work performances or of selecting people for either professional or nonprofessional roles in human services are very unreliable, particularly for youth with a history of poor functioning, no specific criteria have yet been established in the Center for Youth and Community Studies training programs (MacLennan, 1964; Center for Youth and Community Studies, 1965) for aides, beyond the youths' expressed interest in taking part in the program, a poverty-stricken background, and a need for a job. Aides are interviewed together and separately and undergo a medical examination, so that anyone suffering from acute infectious diseases, or who has a court action pending, can be temporarily eliminated. However, records are being scrutinized so that, over time, dimensions may be identified which can predict suitability for human service fields. Meantime agencies for whom aides are being trained usually participate in the final selection of trainees.

One question which arises is how to provide these young people with sufficient information on which to make reasonable career choice. It has been found that most youngsters who have lived all their lives in the slums do not know what is entailed in selecting one career as against another. They cannot describe the functions of a day care or research worker. It would seem important that more effort be made in school to provide within the curriculum itself more knowledge of what different kinds of jobs entail and to carry out realistic vocational guidance. One method which has proved effective when only a small number of choices are offered is to rotate the trainees through the different jobs, expose them to the various routines, and then require them to help each other choose the occupation most suited to their interests and capabilities. Part time work and work study programs also offer the opportunity to try out different jobs.

## AIDE TRAINING

Many of those for whom the aide training programs are being designed come from very poor environments in which they have developed standards and values which are antagonistic to steady work. In general, low income youth are considered to suffer from a poor self-image and feelings of powerlessness, low frustration tolerance, and impulsivity. The Howard University programs have been established on the following assumptions:

It is assumed that the aides will need to revise and reconsider their customary standards and values in regard to employment, and they will have to learn how to comport themselves on the job. Many young people from disadvantaged backgrounds consider that to work hard is to be "square." They are unwilling to accept the fact that they have to dress appropriately, stick by the rules and routines, report punctually and regularly on the job, and even, perhaps, change their customary manner of speech. They do not know how to understand the institutional structure, to use supervision or get help if things go wrong.

Second, it is assumed that in order to counteract the poor self-image and low self-esteem the youngsters must be respected and valued; adequate standards of work and behavior must be expected of them, and they should feel that they are doing a meaningful job. It is believed important that they should be encouraged to take responsibility for themselves, participate in decision-making, and help each other attain satisfactory work habits.

Third, if people are going to learn easily they need to be told how their performance appears to others and must learn to face problems as they arise. Consequently, early feedback is considered essential.

Lastly, in the ever-changing state of the present-day world it is important to build flexibility into the training. The youth are encouraged to think of themselves as human service aides with specialization in one area, so that, if need arise, they can easily move from one specific field to another with a small amount of additional training.

For these reasons the Center's aide training programs have been constructed in the following way. The aides spend six weeks in intensive training which consists of half of each day spent in supervised work experience; skill workshops; and a daily "core group" which lasts two to three hours. This is followed by a three to six month period during which the Aides work under intensive supervision with two core group periods a week and continuing weekly workshops. Aides differ in the speed with which they develop adequate work habits and allowances should be made for this difference in flexibility.

## The Core Group

Core Groups serve as a major vehicle for the development of human service skills. They consist of 10 members who help each other learn how they function in relation to each other and on the job. They use their own group, the total aide program and their experiences in the community to examine how groups work, how the community is organized, and how to understand the meaning of behavior and their own reactions to life.

Each of these groups has a Core Trainer who works with them throughout the program, encourages members to use themselves for self-study, serves as liaison with the job supervisor, helps the group to develop programs in terms of the agenda, and is available as need arises for individual consultation.

Daily reporting from the job supervisors to the core group leader is a very important part of this program so that the leader can help the group examine the problems which they are facing on the job. From their experiences the Aides learn to understand how they react differently to different kinds of people. They learn how to analyze and cope with situations and know where and how to get help. Specifically, in relation to employment they learn how to apply for jobs, what a job description is and why it is important, the function of administrative structure, the use of supervision, the necessity of keeping to the rules of the job and the management of problems as they arise. They also study general techniques such as how to work as leaders and participants with different kinds of groups, how to observe and how to keep records.

Maximum opportunity is created for the group to take responsibility for themselves to make their own decisions and to establish the conditions under which they will operate. They are encouraged to feel that it is important that they help each other work out difficulties. Essentially, the Core Group should be seen as a new reference group in which the leader sets standards and confronts the members with the inappropriateness of inadequate and delinquent ways of dealing with situations.

General knowledge required of all human service personnel is also taught in the Core Group. The aides start from their own experience to examine the process of adolescence and the problems of living in poor areas of the city. As the groups progress, they draw in experts to study with them areas of knowledge of human services common to all. Some of the areas discussed are:

1. Human development, family life, childhood, adolescence, dating and marriage.

2. Common mental health problems, normalcy and deviance.

3. The structure and function of community institutions and their resources.

4. The special problems of socially deprived areas and minority groups.

5. Health care, common health problems and first aid.

6. The employment structure and labor organizations.

7. The law and the use of legal aid.

8. Credit unions, insurance, medical care programs.

9. Budgeting and the management of money.

All curriculum is taught in seminar fashion with maximal group discussion. Field visits, planned by the youth, are made to community institutions.

## Specialty Workshops

While the knowledge common to all human services is taught in the Core Group, each special service has theory and skills which are unique, and curriculum has to be developed for each. For instance, recreation aides need to know how to start a baseball league and to possess a repertoire of crafts and games which they can introduce into their groups. Day Care Aides must understand the uses of different kinds of play activities and be able to care for the children's physical needs. The aides are assembled in small groups in accordance with their specialty in order to take part in these workshops.

## Supervised On-the-Job Experience

When the aides are working on the job, emphasis is placed on the development of responsible work habits, on learning how to use supervision and on obtaining practice in the basic skills and routines of the particular service which the aide has chosen. It is important that the work is carefully planned so that the aides are able gradually to enlarge their experience and have opportunity to practice all essential routines and skills.

## TRAINING RESPONSIBILITIES

Responsibilities have been variously distributed. In one part of the program, the work supervisor also undertook the skill workshops. In another of the services, these workshops were conducted independently. In a future program, it is planned for a training coordinator to conduct the Core Group and the skill workshops as well as to maintain liaison with the work supervisors. These changes have been organized pragmatically in terms of the capacities of the personnel involved in the programs and the organization of the agencies concerned. No opinion has yet been formed of the relative values of these different arrangements. However, it is important that the basic philosophy and standards of the training staff and the cooperating agency are consistent.

## PROGRAM CLIMATE

It is believed that the climate of the training programs affects the outcome so that staff have attempted to generate an atmosphere of enthusiasm and interest and the value of the work of aides has been emphasized. At the same time, all participants have been asked to recognize that the future as yet holds no security for aides, that everyone has to be able to tolerate much uncertainty, and that no guarantees or promises can be made. Staff and aides have also been expected to face the fact that no one is perfect, that everyone makes mistakes, and that much learning takes place through the analysis of error. Thus, a high value has been placed on the capacity to be undefensive, flexible and free to examine one's own behavior in a critical fashion.

## REMEDIATION AND EDUCATION

Because so many children who grow up in the slums are lacking the basic skills of reading, writing, spelling, and counting, remedial activities have been incorporated into all aspects of the training. The aides are expected to write reports, transcribe materials from tapes, keep accounts of their observations, budget and read simple pamphlets and manuals. In this way, they not only obtain practice in basic skills but also perceive the relevance of formal education and become stimulated to request instruction in these subjects.

This leads to the question of the completion of high school education and the auspices under which aide training should be conducted. It is probable that the most convenient model for such programs would be to incorporate them as part of vocational education within the school system so that credit could automatically be obtained for all parts of the program. This would resemble the present work study arrangements except that education training and work experience would be closely related and have relevance for each other. Because many of these young people are disillusioned with formal education, a period of work experience and Core Group training outside the formal structure of the school may be necessary before they are sufficiently motivated to accept any formal classroom instruction. Our experience to date has been that the younger aides attend night school while those who are nearly 21 work for the High School Equivalency exam.

Aide training should not be limited to high school students, however, and it seems likely that institutions will find it convenient to develop their own post-high school in-service training programs which might be integrated with universities and community colleges and make a smooth transition to the training of technical assistants at the sub-professional level, where a model of continued supervised work experience, in-service training, and courses at the Associate of Arts and Bachelor's levels is already being tried in some places. The advantages of this arrangement are that agencies tend to be more interested in their own trainees, that such trainees can move more easily into the lower levels of the institutional hierarchy, and that channels for technical and educational advancement are already created.

## ROLE FLEXIBILITY AND THE IDENTITY OF THE HUMAN SERVICE AIDE

Although the idea of a specific aide training center as a permanent institution seems of doubtful value, the concept of a common Human Service Aide who can move with relative ease across the range of New Careers has considerable validity at the present time when the future of such aides is still quite uncertain. No one knows which services will accept such aides and how fast employment opportunities can be made available. With a common basic training, it is relatively simple for the aide to make such a transfer if additional specific training is provided.

A second reason for such role flexibility and common identity is related to the problems created for the aides by the change in their own attitudes and behavior. They tend to move away from their old associates on the streets, are not yet numerous enough to influence their own neighborhoods, and, by reason of disparate background and lesser education, are unlikely to be fully accepted as social equals by the professional. Consequently some Aide Center or Clubhouse where all can meet, socialize, and share experiences seems to be a valuable institution. Such an association also provides a nucleus for the development of credit unions and other material supports which serve to increase the stability of the aides.

## THE SELECTION AND TRAINING OF INSTRUCTORS AND SUPERVISORS

The quality of the Core trainers and supervisors is crucial in the training of aides and it is probable that the personalities and character of the staff are as important as their knowledge and skill.

Although selection criteria and procedures are still minimally developed, attempts have been made to hire people who are sincere, interested, and able to stimulate interest in others. They must be able to like and respect the aides or they cannot work with them. No educational criteria as yet have been set, and the Center is experimenting with the use of staff at different educational levels and from different backgrounds.

Although it is hard on the candidates, the best way known, at present, for predicting how people will perform in human services is to expose them to a diversity of human interactions such as taking part in a group and acting as interviewer in a simulated situation.

Training for instructors has included orientation to the New Careers concepts and aide training, the life styles of socially disadvantaged youth, the organization and resources of the community, the special problems of working with aides such as learning how to convey knowledge and skills in a form which is understandable to the aides, and developing the perceptiveness, sensitivity, undefensiveness, and techniques necessary to understand and conduct groups of aides. Training has been organized in a fashion similar to aide training with a central Core Group and supervised practical experience gained through working with aides. Staff aides take part in some of the group discussions and act as informants in some of the seminars.

## EVALUATION

Attempts are being made to conceptualize all activities in the program and to work out instruments to evaluate whether the program is being maintained within the range of these designated activities. Careful observation and feedback to staff and aides is arranged, both to evaluate and control the nature and quality of the training and to teach the importance of studying one's own performance. The kinds of youth who apply for the program, the affect of the program on their lives, the capacity of the youth to obtain and hold jobs as Aides after training, and the influence of New Careers on the services and structure of institutions, and the role of the professional are all important objects of the study.

## REFERENCES

BLOOMBERG, CLAIRE, & KLEIN, W. L. *Preschool aide training curriculum.* Washington, D. C.: Center for Youth and Community Studies, Howard Univ., 1965. (mimeo)

CENTER FOR YOUTH AND COMMUNITY STUDIES, *Training for new careers.* Washington, D. C.: President's Committee on Juvenile Delinquency and Youth Crime, June, 1965.

FISHMAN, J. R., PEARL, A., & MACLENNAN, BERYCE W. *New careers: ways out of poverty for disadvantaged youth, a conference report.* Washington, D. C.: Center for Youth and Community Studies, Howard Univ., 1965. (mimeo)

KLEIN, W. L., & MACLENNAN, BERYCE W. *Health aide training curriculum.* Washington, D. C.: Center for Youth and Community Studies, Howard University, 1964. (mimeo)

MACLENNAN, BERYCE W. *The training of community apprentices and of professional supervisors.* Washington, D. C.: Center for Youth and Community Studies, Howard Univ., 1964. (mimeo)

MACLENNAN, BERYCE W. &. KLEIN, W. L. Utilization of groups in job training with the socially deprived, *Internat. J. of Group Psychotherapy,* 1965, **15**, 4.

MACLENNAN, BERYCE W., et al., *Job descriptions of community aides.* Washington, D. C.: Center for Youth and Community Studies, Howard Univ., 1965. (mimeo)

PEARL, A., *Forging new careers: a new approach to the problem of poverty.* Washington, D. C.: Center for Youth and Community Studies, Howard Univ., 1964. (mimeo)

U. S. DEPARTMENT OF LABOR, *Manpower Report to the President.* Washington, D. C.: U. S. Government Printing Office, March, 1963.

Emory L. Cowen,
Melvin Zax,
and James D. Laird

# A College Student Volunteer Program
# in the Elementary School Setting

*Cowen, Zax, and Laird describe a program that utilizes nonprofessionals in a therapeutic and preventive role. These are college students who, in recent years, have been used in mental-hospital settings to enrich the program available to severely disturbed patients. In the program discussed, the college student was called upon to work in a one-to-one relationship with a primary-grade child who had been judged early as likely to develop psychological problems that would interfere with his school functioning. It was felt that giving the child the opportunity to develop a relationship with a warm, interested, enthusiastic young person would itself be beneficial. In addition, such a relationship would offer the faltering youngster a good model with which to identify and a chance to widen personal horizons that might be especially narrow because of the family's limitations.*

Increasingly in recent years, it has become apparent that existing resources within the mental health helping professions are insufficient to meet social needs. Such an awareness encourages consideration of new approaches for the resolution of real and pressing social problems. Whether one thinks in terms of shoring up present helping structures, of developing techniques better suited for the large masses who are seemingly unreached by present methods, or of considering models that emphasize early detection and prevention, one is led to question long-standing assumptions concerning the necessity of advanced, high-level professional training as a prerequisite for *all* those involved in mental health-type "helping" interactions.

One practical result has been the increased use, in a variety of mental health settings, of two types of non-professional personnel. One group, the subprofessionals, is characteristically paid and is given specific, focused, and time-limited training designed to fit them to some particular role and task (Project Re-Ed, 1964; Sanders, 1967). Another group of nonprofessionals is the volunteers, most often college students (Umbarger, Dalsimer, Morrison, & Breggin, 1962; Holzberg & Knapp, 1965), who receive little training and no pay.

While there has certainly been a proliferation of subprofessional and volunteer programs in the mental health sphere in recent years, such programs have, understandably, been primarily service oriented. If a sounder basis for reshaping mental health helping services is to be developed and if volunteer and subprofessional manpower is to have an increasingly important and extensive role in this

Reprinted from Community Mental Health Journal, 2(1966), 319–328 *with the permission of Behavioral Publications, Inc. and Dr. Cowen.*

"hypothetical new order," it becomes essential that such emergent programs be carefully researched in their multiple facets. Two notable exceptions to the general absence of research on these programs have been Kantor's (1962) evaluation of the effectiveness of the Harvard program, for the patients, and Holzberg's extensive program of research on the effects of participation in his program on the student volunteers themselves (Holzberg & Gewirtz, 1963; Holzberg, Gewirtz, & Ebner, 1964; Holzberg & Knapp, 1965; Knapp & Holzberg, 1964).

The program to be described in the present report involved college undergraduates working in the school setting with emotionally disturbed youngsters referred by teachers and other school personnel. The program was a relatively modest one, which operated for a very short period of time, and was set up primarily as a first step in evolving a model for this type of activity that might be effectively integrated with a long-range program for early detection and prevention of emotional disorders in the school setting. Despite these limitations of size and duration, preliminary research evaluations of the following issues were undertaken: (a) What types of students volunteer for a program of this type and in what ways are they differentiable from their non-volunteer peers? (b) What types of changes, if any, take place in volunteers as a function of participation in this program? (c) What is the general nature of the program itself, descriptively, including some estimate of range of transactions that may take place between volunteer and child in this type of setting, i.e., process analysis? (d) What relationships may be found between types of volunteer-child interactions and any one of several outcome measures available for the child? (e)

What changes in behavior and evaluation of the children who are exposed to the program take place following such participation?

## METHOD

### Recruitment of Volunteers

The prospective program was viewed as one specific, feasible model for early secondary prevention in the school setting. Its purpose was to provide a meaningful relationship and beneficial experience for emotionally disturbed children by pairing them with active, enthusiastic, ego-involved college student volunteers. The possibility that the projected program might also contribute to primary prevention through its effects on the attitudes of the volunteers was also considered. To maximize the possibility, attempts were made to recruit volunteers from among elementary education majors. If these students, who were themselves about to become teachers, could get to know, work with, and learn about children experiencing psychological difficulties, perhaps they could acquire an increment in "gut" understanding, which would have beneficial effects throughout their subsequent teaching careers.

With cooperation from the staff of the School of Education, 8 elementary education majors were recruited as volunteers for the program; there were 15 additional volunteers from an abnormal psychology class. Each of these 23 candidates was interviewed by one of three advanced clinical psychology graduate students who were to be affiliated with the program. No attempt was made to select volunteers on the basis of a set of preconceived positive personality attributes; rather the simple goal was to weed out the several students who seemed either flagrantly maladjusted or grossly unsuited for the purposes of the program. All 8 education student volunteers were accepted for the program. Of the 15 psychology students interviewed, 3 were dropped for personal reasons and another 3 because their schedule of free hours did not match those required for the program; thus there remained a total of 17 acceptable volunteers—8 from education and 9 from psychology.

## Evaluation of Volunteers

A group-testing session was set up before the program got under way. It was made clear to the volunteers that the data to be collected were not, in any way, to be used for selection purposes (which they were not) but rather were part of a research appraisal of the overall program.

The instrument used to evaluate volunteer attitudes and change in such attitudes following participation in the program was an adaptation of the semantic differential (SD) (Osgood, Suci, & Tannenbaum, 1957) designed for this purpose. For our use, the instrument included nine critical concepts, related to schools and mental health, each of which was rated in terms of 17 polar scales, mostly of the evaluative type.

This instrument was administered about one week before the program started and again about one week after it ended, thus providing some basis for a pre-post comparison of attitudes. A control group of eight education and nine psychology students comparable to the volunteers, except for the fact that they did not actually volunteer for the program, was also evaluated with this measure. It was only possible to test this latter group once; hence they are controls only for the "pre"-point in our sequence.

## Instruction and Training for Volunteers

A brief effort at orientation of volunteers was carried out before the program got under way. A fairly lengthy meeting was held at the university to discuss such issues as mental health problems in modern society, professional manpower shortages, the need for work in early detection and prevention of emotional problems, the philosophy of the present program, its objectives, and the place of the volunteers in it. At that time some possible ways in which the program might operate were considered. However,

this remained relatively unstructured, and it was stressed that the volunteer would have considerable freedom and latitude. Indeed, the project was described as an exploratory one, and volunteers were encouraged to follow their natural reflexes and to feel free to try out new ideas and to follow up hunches, viewing themselves neither as therapists nor as intellectualized analyzers of personality. Rather, we attempted to foster a spontaneous, warm, "friend" relationship with the child.

In still another preprogram meeting, the volunteer group was taken to the school where the principal, as well as the social worker and psychologist attached to the basic early detection and prevention project being conducted there (Zax & Cowen, 1967), met and spoke with them. The volunteers were given the opportunity to go through the building, to become acquainted with the equipment and facilities that would be at their disposal and to meet and talk with other key school personnel.

## Selection and Evaluation of Children

The program was housed in a single elementary school in Rochester, New York, in which was located the broader program for early detection and prevention of emotional disorders (Zax & Cowen, 1967). The school, although a relatively small one, covered a fairly large geographic area and included children ranging socioeconomically from lower-lower class to upper-middle class. The contemplated afterschool activities program was described to the teaching staff of the primary grades, and teachers and project personnel were asked to refer those youngsters who they considered might profit from it. Thirty-four primary grade children were referred, and for each, the classroom teacher submitted three types of referral materials. The first of these was a teachers' behavior rating scale, adapted from our earlier work (Cowen, Izzo, Miles, Telschow, Trost, & Zax, 1963), including 25 negative behavioral characteristics (e.g., "is dependent on others," "is upset by criticism," "is disobedient," "is critical of others," etc.). The teacher was asked to check those items which described the behavior of the child being rated and to provide an intensity ratng along a three-point scale for each characteristic so designated. In addition the teacher made a single overall adjustment rating for the child based on a five-point scale. The second measure used was a 34-item Adjective Check-List (ACL), divided equally into positive and negative items (trait-descriptive adjectives). The teacher was asked to check all relevant descriptive terms, using S and V, respectively, to designate "somewhat" and "very." The final teacher-submitted item was a prose referral statement indicating the specific nature of the child's principal problem(s) as she perceived them.

Although the majority of the 34 referrals were initiated by the teachers, a certain number were also referred by project personnel. The latter included several youngsters who had not yet manifested overt problems, but who were judged by the mental health clinical services (MHCS) team, on the basis of social work interview, psychological evaluation, and/or actual observation of behavior (Cowen, et al., 1963), to have a high probability for showing such behavior in the near future. The total pool of 34 youngsters reflected, in the main, three major classes of problems: acting-out; shyness, timidity, and withdrawal behavior; and problems of failure in educational achievement.

To establish some crude basis for preliminary evaluation, half of the youngsters were included in the afterschool activities program and became an experimental (E) group. The other half, matched roughly in terms of age, sex, grade, and judged overall severity of problem, became a control (C) group.

Parents of the experimental children were contacted via form letter over the signatures of the school principal and the MHCS team. In this letter the program was described as a recreational one, which would be made available to certain primary graders who might be expected to profit from and to enjoy such an experience. All parents so contacted agreed to have their youngsters participate, and our final E group included 11 boys and 6 girls.

The several teachers' forms were submitted for all E and C youngsters about one week before the program got under way.

The same forms were done a second time and resubmitted for all 34 children about one month after the program ended, shortly before the end of the school year. In each case the relevant observation period was defined as the two-week time block immediately preceding the ratings.

Since it was evident that the postproject ratings by the teachers might well have been contaminated by their awareness of the child's assignment to the E or C group, an attempt was made to obtain independent observation and evaluation of these youngsters by naive judges.

To this end, an 18-item behavior rating scale was developed for use in the actual classroom situations. Twelve of these items consisted of full seven-point scales ranging from a theoretically positive extreme, $+3$ (e.g., "responds pleasantly when approached") to a theoretically negative extreme, $-3$ (e.g., "rebuffs others when approached"). The remaining six items were "half-items," reflecting only the negative extreme of the continuum (from 0 to $-3$), e.g., "disrupts class" $(-3)$ or "seeks attention from teacher" $(-3)$. There was a clear-cut preference for items to reflect actual, ongoing, observable behavior rather than inferences about the child.

In a prior reliability study two naive observers, one an advanced undergraduate psychology major and the other a second-year social psychology graduate student, observed the behavior of a sample of 15 primary grade youngsters in another school. An obtained inter-judge $r = .79$, based on total scale scores, suggested that this instrument was sufficiently reliable for use in the evaluation of the afterschool activities program.

Accordingly, the judges then observed all E and C youngsters in the actual classroom setting over two 45-minute observation periods. Eight presumably healthy, well-adjusted, symptom-free children were intermixed in the observational groups, thereby providing an opportunity for a small validity assessment of the instrument. The mean behavioral rating for the combined E and C groups was 7.7, while the comparable figure for the eight normal "extras" was 16.0 $(t = 2.10, p > .05)$, indicating that seemingly well-adjusted youngsters can indeed be differentiated from children with problems on this behavioral index.

## Course of the School Program

Volunteers were assigned to the children on a one-to-one basis, although in practice, during the course of the program, they often formed small and, usually, loosely structured groups. As it turned out there were 3 male volunteers and 14 female, which did not match very closely the referral pattern of 11 boys and 6 girls. The 3 male volunteers were assigned to 3 boys for whom a male identification model was considered to be strongly indicated. All other assignments were made on a random basis. Three groups of from 5 to 7 volunteers were set up, each under the direct supervision of an advanced clinical psychology graduate student. The latter were themselves under the supervision of the clinical psychologist directing the program. Each volunteer group went to the school twice a week. The volunteers arrived at the end of the school day, at 3:30 p.m., met their children, and engaged in whatever the day's activities were to be for about 70 minutes.

Virtually the entire resources of the school were placed at the disposal of the group. This included the gymnasium, auditorium, playground, music room, arts and craft shop, home economics room, game room, several kindergartens, etc. Our belief was that a variety of activities and settings within the school building, emphasizing expression, recreation, and cathartic activity could provide potentially suitable vehicles through which the undergraduate volunteer and child might interact.

In order to arrive at some clearer picture of the nature of the modal volunteer-child transaction, a form was developed to assess the amount of time devoted to varying activities. This form included a series of descriptive categories that appeared to encompass the full range of possible activities by the child. The categories used, each defined in several sentences for the volunteer, included: *running, semi-organized physical play, organized play, exploring, competitive table games, co-operative and constructive table activities, artistic activities,* and *talk-*

*ing.* A generalized *other* category was also provided. This encompassed *reading, school-type activities, food-making,* and several others with negligible frequencies. The volunteer also provided an estimate of the percentage of total time spent by the child with others, either children or volunteers (i.e., contacts other than the specific one-to-one volunteer-child interaction).

Each volunteer submitted "process" data three times during the course of the program: at the conclusion of each third of the total program period. At these same intervals, the volunteer also submitted S-D ratings for the following two concepts: *the child that you are working with* and *the type of relationship you have had with your child.* For each set of ratings a single summed evaluative score, reflecting perceived goodness of the child and perceived adequacy of the relationship, was derived, and for convenience of data analysis, these measures were considered together with the basic process indices.

The afterschool program got under way the first week in March and lasted, on a prearranged basis, until the second week in May. It was broken twice by one week, non-overlapping vacations—once for the school children and once for the volunteers; hence, a maximum of about 14 to 15 meetings in the school setting was possible during the planned program period.

The volunteers brought considerable enthusiasm to the program and, indeed, embellished it in ways not anticipated beforehand. They would often provide certain "extras" that they felt might be helpful or interesting to their child. Illustratively, they might bring special toys or games "borrowed" from a younger sibling, relative, or friend or even purchased on their own. Several of the girls brought construction materials to fabricate toys or objects and, on quite a few occasions, brought along food to be prepared (e.g., eggs to be boiled and made into egg salad sandwiches, or brownie and other cake mixes to be baked and consumed during the activity period). Many volunteers soon began to feel the need to "do more" for the child than could be accomplished during the limited meeting periods. Several correspondences between volunteers and children sprang up during vacation periods, and a rash of special outside activities, both on individual-pair and small-group bases, sprang up. In the final weeks of the program, for example, many volunteers brought their youngsters up to the university to see the campus and to have dinner with them. Some were taken to see a baseball game or other type of athletic event. Trips were arranged to the downtown area, to an animal shelter, to the local zoo, and for picnicking. Though none of the foregoing activities were preplanned as part of the program, they reflect well the interest and dedication of the volunteers.

## Volunteer Discussion Groups

One of the fundamental aims of the program was to provide the volunteer an opportunity to think about, talk about, and integrate his actual contact experiences, primarily with the child but perhaps also with the parents or teachers with whom he might be in touch. We wished also to provide the opportunity for advanced graduate students in clinical psychology to acquire experience in a supervisory, consultative, and resource role vis-à-vis less well-trained subprofessional manpower, acting in mental health-related roles in a community setting. To further these objectives, at the very end of each afternoon's activity in the school, the volunteer group and the graduate student leader returned to the campus, as a unit, for a post-mortem discussion session, generally lasting about an hour, from 5 to 6 p.m. At these meetings, volunteers discussed specific children and the problems they presented, critical incidents that they had experienced, issues of understanding children's behavior, some of their own anxieties and concerns, and specific problems of technique, handling, and intervention. These sessions appeared to provide the volunteer a useful opportunity to learn around the vehicle of the very recent, quite vivid, concrete, and emotionally impactful experiences they had had. The experience suggests that the close temporal contiguity between activity and discussion period and maintenance of continuous group contact furthered these objectives.

Most of these sessions were recorded and were discussed weekly by the graduate student group with the clinical psychologist in charge of the program. The focus of these latter meetings was on the handling of the student discussion sessions rather than on the children themselves. Over a period of time, it became increasingly clear that the optimal role of the leader was not the "spinal cord" therapist's role, an easy and logical one for clinicians to slip into. Rather, it was one of being an issue-centered, discussion-oriented, contributing member of the group. The model was that of a teacher–discussion leader, always striving to bring relevant issues closer to the surface, paced so as to allow for the considerable perceptivity and diagnostic acumen of the volunteer. In many instances, with careful leads and transitional observations, the leader could create a situation that allowed the volunteer group, following some struggling, groping, and pursuit of blind alleys, to come to some meaningful and acceptable understandings of children's behavior, their own attitudes and behavior, and the interaction of the two. More concrete illustrations of this process in action have been presented elsewhere (Zax & Cowen, 1967).

## RESULTS

### Attributes of Volunteers

In order to determine the pattern, if any, of differentiating attributes of volunteers, direct comparisons of the volunteer and control groups, based on $t$ ratios, were undertaken for the S-D responses. A substantial number of significant differences were observed. These are summarized in Table 1. With 9 concepts and 17 scales included in the present form, a total of 153 comparisons were made between E and C group members. The 32 significant differences at $p = .05$ or beyond exceed chance expectancy and manifest an internal consistency suggestive of genuine differences between the two groups.

TABLE 1. Semantic Differential Comparisons of Volunteers (V) and Controls (C)

| Concepts and Scales | Mean V | Mean C | t |
|---|---|---|---|
| Elementary Schools cooperative-uncooperative | 2.24 | 3.35 | 2.88** |
| interesting-boring | 2.18 | 3.35 | 2.46* |
| active-passive | 1.88 | 3.47 | 3.63** |
| tense-relaxed | 5.11 | 4.00 | 2.47* |
| good-bad | 1.82 | 2.65 | 2.14* |
| strong-weak | 2.88 | 3.94 | 2.56* |
| Emotionally Disturbed Children helpful-harmful | 3.41 | 4.53 | 2.90** |
| worthless-valuable | 5.71 | 4.41 | 2.39* |
| Mental Health unfriendly-friendly | 5.59 | 4.71 | 2.44* |
| cooperative-uncooperative | 2.53 | 3.47 | 2.72* |
| good-bad | 1.59 | 2.59 | 2.16* |
| active-passive | 2.35 | 3.35 | 2.39* |
| unpredictable-predictable | 5.06 | 3.94 | 2.56* |
| Mental Health Workers cooperative-uncooperative | 1.53 | 2.12 | 2.07* |
| pleasant-unpleasant | 1.53 | 2.12 | 2.07* |
| cold-warm | 6.06 | 5.35 | 2.25* |
| Myself pleasant-unpleasant | 1.88 | 2.47 | 2.07* |
| Profession of Teaching strong-weak | 2.41 | 3.24 | 2.36* |
| School Principal effective-ineffective | 2.12 | 3.24 | 2.25* |
| fair-unfair | 1.88 | 2.88 | 2.85** |
| cooperative-uncooperative | 2.00 | 3.00 | 3.23** |
| unfriendly-friendly | 5.82 | 4.94 | 2.68* |
| cold-warm | 5.24 | 4.18 | 3.11** |
| helpful-harmful | 1.94 | 2.94 | 3.12** |
| excitable-calm | 5.71 | 4.71 | 2.96** |
| pleasant-unpleasant | 2.18 | 3.41 | 3.46** |
| good-bad | 1.88 | 3.00 | 3.78** |
| interesting-boring | 1.82 | 3.24 | 2.97** |
| Teachers cooperative-uncooperative | 1.94 | 2.59 | 2.75** |
| strong-weak | 2.24 | 2.94 | 2.13* |
| effective-ineffective | 1.82 | 2.65 | 2.25* |
| fair-unfair | 1.76 | 2.71 | 3.27** |

Note.—Each scale in the table is listed so that the adjective to the left corresponds to 1 and the adjective to the right corresponds to 7 on the actual rating forms used by Ss.
* Denotes significance at the .05 level.
** Denotes significance at the .01 level.

## Changes in Volunteers Following Participation

In order to identify the nature of attitude changes in volunteers, if any, following participation in the after-school program, comparisons of pre- and post-experience responses to the S-D were carried out. In this case, since two testings of the same group of 17 S's were being compared, a matched-pair t test was used for the analysis.

Once again, a substantial number of significant attitude changes were found when comparing pre- vs. post-experience attitudes of the volunteers. These significant differences are summarized in Table 2. With the total number of comparisons again coming to 153, the 22 observed significant differences exceed expectancy, and their patterning is an interpretable and internally consistent one.

*The nature of the volunteer-student interaction.* The process forms submitted by the volunteers after each third of the total experience were used as the basis for arriving at a descriptive summary of the children's activities during the total program. Table 3 presents means and sigmas for the several activity categories, based on the three individual summaries submitted and their total. It may be noted that there is considerable variability across volunteer-child pairs for all categories and that there appear to be generalized changes in category frequencies, over time.

## Interrelationships Among Process and Outcome Measures

*Outcome measures.* Three indices were derived for use as outcome mea-

TABLE 2. Pre- and Postprogram Comparisons in Semantic Differential Responses of Volunteers

| Concepts and Scales | Mean Pre | Mean Post | t |
|---|---|---|---|
| Children | | | |
| active-passive | 1.29 | 1.17 | 3.11** |
| tense-relaxed | 5.41 | 4.41 | 2.38** |
| Elementary Schools | | | |
| interesting-boring | 2.18 | 2.71 | 3.50** |
| active-passive | 1.88 | 2.71 | 4.20** |
| tense-relaxed | 5.12 | 4.35 | 2.62* |
| unfriendly-friendly | 5.71 | 5.29 | 3.35** |
| pleasant-unpleasant | 2.35 | 2.82 | 3.11** |
| Emotionally Disturbed Children | | | |
| effective-ineffective | 5.00 | 4.12 | 2.99** |
| active-passive | 3.71 | 2.41 | 3.39** |
| cold-warm | 4.06 | 5.18 | 3.08** |
| cooperative-uncooperative | 4.94 | 4.06 | 2.37* |
| unfriendly-friendly | 4.12 | 5.41 | 4.07** |
| Mental Health | | | |
| cold-warm | 4.94 | 5.47 | 2.73* |
| Mental Health Workers | | | |
| pleasant-unpleasant | 1.53 | 2.00 | 2.43* |
| unfriendly-friendly | 6.41 | 6.12 | 2.58* |
| Myself | | | |
| pleasant-unpleasant | 1.88 | 2.41 | 3.50** |
| good-bad | 2.06 | 2.29 | 2.22* |
| Profession of Teaching | | | |
| unfriendly-friendly | 6.24 | 5.76 | 3.77** |
| interesting-boring | 1.29 | 1.65 | 2.40* |
| School Principal | | | |
| interesting-boring | 1.82 | 2.59 | 2.34* |
| Teachers | | | |
| unfriendly-friendly | 6.18 | 5.88 | 2.58* |
| excitable-calm | 5.24 | 4.53 | 2.22* |

Note.—Each scale in the table is listed so that the adjective to the left corresponds to 1 and the adjective to the right corresponds to 7 on the actual rating forms used by Ss to evaluate concepts.

\* Denotes significance at the .05 level.
\*\* Denotes significance at the .01 level.

sures, each of which was based on some comparison of a preprogram and postprogram evaluation of youngsters in both E and C groups. The first of these, Teachers Behavior Discrepancy Score, was based on the difference between the summed preprogram behavioral ratings of the child by the teacher and her summed postprogram behavioral ratings. The second, a Teachers ACL Discrepancy Score, reflected differences in the pre- and postprogram ACL forms submitted by the teacher. The third measure, Teachers Pre-Behavior vs. Observers Post-Behavior Index, was designed to introduce some independence of observations and was somewhat more complicated than the first two. In this instance, based on the combined E + C groups, the teachers' summed behavior score, pretest, was converted to a standard score. Similarly the postexperience judges' behavior observation scores of all 34 youngsters were converted to standard scores, and a difference score between the two sets of standard scores was derived. The intercorrelations among these three criterion measures were all moderately positive, ranging from +.35 to +.50, and significant. Comparison of E and C groups on the three criterion change score measures indicated that there were no significant differences between them on any measure.

*Process measures.* For purposes of the analysis, various of the single process categories were pooled, both on logical grounds as well as to yield more stable frequencies. *Running* was a sufficiently high-frequency category so as to stand alone. *Semi-organized play,* *organized play,* and *exploring* were combined and the amalgam was labeled *physical games and exploring.* Similarly, *competitive table games, cooperative and constructive table activities,* and *artistic activities* were lumped together, the new fused category being

TABLE 3. Summary of Process Measures, by Percentage of Time Spent in
Various Activities

| Activity | First Third | | Second Third | | Third Third | | Total | |
|---|---|---|---|---|---|---|---|---|
| | Mean | SD | Mean | SD | Mean | SD | Mean | SD |
| Running | 17.1 | 15.6 | 15.3 | 13.8 | 11.5 | 12.2 | 14.6 | 9.4 |
| Semi-organized physical play | 15.3 | 8.7 | 11.9 | 9.4 | 13.8 | 8.2 | 13.9 | 13.9 |
| Organized physical games | 8.5 | 9.5 | 6.8 | 12.1 | 9.7 | 16.4 | 8.3 | 11.3 |
| Exploring | 7.9 | 6.4 | 3.5 | 6.6 | 8.9 | 12.0 | 6.8 | 9.4 |
| Competitive table games | 14.6 | 11.6 | 6.5 | 6.0 | 5.2 | 8.9 | 8.7 | 9.7 |
| Constructive table activities | 10.6 | 12.1 | 15.9 | 13.7 | 17.9 | 18.8 | 14.6 | 16.2 |
| Artistic activities | 9.7 | 11.3 | 10.3 | 14.1 | 7.5 | 9.8 | 9.2 | 12.2 |
| Talking | 6.9 | 7.0 | 13.5 | 14.4 | 14.1 | 10.8 | 11.5 | 9.2 |
| Other: includes food-making, reading, music, and other school-type activities | 9.4 | 7.8 | 16.3 | 12.7 | 11.4 | 9.7 | 12.0 | 13.9 |

labeled *table games* and *artistic activities*. *Talking*, which represented a totally different type of interaction from any of the others, was allowed to remain intact. This, in effect, yielded four substantive process categories. Percentage of time spent with others was a fifth measure used, and the sixth and seventh were the summed semantic differential evaluative ratings of the child and of the relationship. An intercorrelation matrix for these seven basic process and process-related indices was computed, based on sum score in each category for the total period. The principal substantive relations emerging from this analysis were the strong positive relation between frequency for the category *talking* and *conversation* and goodness of estimate of the relationship ($r = .58$) and the strong negative relation between actual percentage of time spent with others and both talking ($r = -.55$) and goodness of estimate of the relation ($r = -.55$).

*Process vs. outcome measures.* In order to determine whether any relationships existed between process and outcome measures, the seven process measures were each separately correlated with the three outcome measures. Although these interrelations were not strong, measures of positive-rated change related positively to frequency of *talking* and *conversation* ($r = .57$) and generally negatively with the process measure of *running*.

## DISCUSSION

Discussion deals both with specific issues raised at the outset of this investigation as well as with a general evaluation of the program and with both empirical data and clinical impressions and appraisals accreted during the conduct of the program itself.

*Who volunteers?* The findings suggest that our volunteers were indeed differentiable, attitude-wise, from nonvolunteer controls. It should be borne in mind that the volunteer group was essentially an unscreened one, only 3 of 23 interviewed students having been dropped because they seemed, to the interviewers, to be clearly unsuited for the job to be done. Comparisons of the volunteer and the control groups on the semantic differential index reveal a clear-cut and internally consistent pattern of differences. Thus, the volunteers rated a whole series of concepts, particularly "institutional" ones such as *elementary school, mental health, mental workers,* the *school principal,* and *teachers,* as significantly more favorable than did the controls. In the main, the volunteers' scale responses gravitated to the extreme positive end of the evaluative continuum on these concepts, whereas the controls gave much more reserved and neutral evaluations. One gets the impression here that the volunteers represented, initially, an enthusiastic, overidealistic, "see-no-evil" group and that they viewed institutional concepts in a stereotypically positive way.

Results of studies by Holzberg and his associates on a similar college student volunteer program can be interpreted as showing a similar pattern. Compared to controls, their volunteers are more extreme in their moral judgments (Holzberg, *et al.,* 1964), more interested in religion and social values as measured by the Allport-Vernon-Lindzey Scale of Values, and more nuturant and introceptive as measured by the Edwards Personality Pattern Inventory (Knapp & Holzberg, 1964), all of which can be seen as stereotypically positive responses. They also found no differences between volunteers and controls in attitudes toward mental illness (Holzberg & Gewirtz, 1963), a finding paralleled here in the essential absence of initial differences between volunteers and controls on the concept *emotionally disturbed child.*

*Changes in volunteers.* A second basic area of concern to us pertains to changes in volunteers following participation in the program. The semantic differential change scores for the volunteers were not only internally consistent but also fell into line nicely with the pre-experience semantic differential analyses reported above. In the main, two types of changes were observed. The first of these, a generalized one, involved a diminution of the idealized image of institutional con-

cepts held by this group before their contact experience. For example, following participation, *elementary schools* were seen as less interesting, less active, less relaxed, less friendly, and less pleasant. This is not to say that they were seen as passive, tense, unfriendly, etc.; rather the change was from an extreme positive response to a moderately positive one. It might thus be said that the postexperience ratings of institutional concepts by the volunteers were more healthily realistic. At first blush, one might argue that such a change could be viewed as a simple down-shift in response style, implicating an avoidance of extreme scores on the posttest. Data based on still another, very critical, concept, *emotionally disturbed children,* would refute that argument. For this concept, the pattern of significant scale changes was from an initially neutral position to a final positive one wherein such youngsters were seen as less ineffective, more active, warmer, more cooperative, and more friendly. Here, apparently, exposure to, and interaction with, youngsters experiencing emotional difficulties constituted a basis for more positive and accepting attitudes toward them. The general pattern of postexperience change for the volunteers, then, appears to have been a salutary one. Similar changes, to more positive attitudes toward mental illness, have been found to result from participation in Holzberg's program (Holzberg & Gewirtz, 1963) as well as movement toward more realistic moral judgments and greater self-acceptance (Holzberg, *et al.,* 1964).

## The Nature of the Process

A reasonably clear modal picture of how volunteers and children actually spent their time, granting the very considerable variability across pairs, may be gleaned from the process summary data presented in Table 3. Although this table reflects a fairly accurate normative picture of how volunteers and children actually spent their time together, certain aspects of the data remain hidden. For one thing, the group profile ill fits any single relationship, and substantial variability of volunteer-child patterns of interaction appear to have been the order of the day.

Formal statistical analyses of these data have not been undertaken, primarily because of the very small Ns and highly variable categories being dealt with. The aim here was simply to provide a rough profile of activities. Perhaps the most salient substantive inferences that can be made pertain to the initial relatively high frequency and systematic drop over time in the largely disjunctive, disharmonious, cathartive categories of *running, semiorganized physical play* (including fighting and wrestling), and *competitive table games* and to the parallel initial low frequency and increase over time in the cooperative, relational functions of *constructive table games* and *talking* and *conversation*. Perhaps this configuration hints at the operation of a type of challenge and testing of limits at the beginning of the relationship between volunteer and child, which slowly gave way to more congenial, "together" types of activities. It might be hoped that for the child the provision of a warm, interested, adult friend is facilitative in this shifting process.

*Process-outcome relationships.* Intercorrelations among the three change-score outcome measures for children are all low to moderately positive and significant, suggesting that although they are indeed measuring something in common, there remain substantial areas of nonoverlap of measurement.

The failure of these outcome measures to discriminate between E and C groups is no doubt attributable to a variety of factors. In the first place, the group Ns of 17 each were extremely small and were governed by practical expedience rather than by ideal research conditions. Second, the program itself was set up as a short-range model and "de-bugging operation." It was in effect for just over two months, broken on two separate occasions by one-week school vacations, first for the volunteers and then for the children. One of the persistent observations (indeed concerns) of the volunteers throughout the course of the program was that the total number of contacts with the child was much too few. One might expect that benefits and satisfactions to the volunteers would derive largely from *initial* exposure to, and participation in, the program and would reach an asymptote in time. For the children, however, a longer-range, more continuous process in which beneficial effects assume an additive quality over time, seems more realistic, even in the ideal. Finally, it should be noted that our control group was a particularly harsh one, in the sense that its members were simultaneously exposed to the everyday experience of another program also aimed at early secondary prevention. The latter, involving housewives working as teacher aides with emotionally disturbed children in the actual classroom situation (Zax & Cowen, 1967), though it was manifested in a very different form, shared a common set of aims and objectives with the afterschool volunteer program.

Interrelationships among the several process-type measures are limited. Apparently, in the volunteer's eyes, time spent talking with the child was seen as perhaps the most desirable form of interaction that spoke a good relationship between the two. Where the child was occupied to a considerable extent by others, the relationship tended to be viewed unfavorably.

With respect to process-outcome relationships, the major significant finding was the strong positive relationship between talking and improvement as measured by the D score between teachers' prebehavior rating and observers' postbehavior rating. In general, the process-outcome correlation matrix was hampered by the limited N, which required substantial correlation for statistical significance. It is therefore of some interest to note that the process measure of *talking*, previously described as a cooperative, harmonious type of activity, showed a directionally positive correlation with all three outcome measures, whereas the dysjunctive process category of *running* showed a directionally negative relationship to the same three criterion indices. Obviously, our Ns were not sufficiently ample here to allow for strong speculation. However, the present analysis offers one or two interesting leads and constitutes a model that may ultimately help us to achieve a better understanding of helpful, as opposed to inert, interactions and interventions.

## Implications

The volunteer program described in the present report is one that seems, in principle, to combine many potential virtues, including: furthering of the development of community-based field programs in early secondary prevention; recruitment, training, and supervision of new sources of subprofessional manpower, and modification of graduate training in the helping professions. At a clinical and experiential level, the program appears to have gone a long way toward furthering those objectives. It was certainly well received by those

who were touched by it, including parents of participating youngsters, teachers and other school personnel, the volunteers, the graduate student supervisors, and finally the youngsters themselves. On more than one occasion, for example, children who took sick in school on a program day were unwilling to be sent home, because they did not wish to miss out on this highly valued experience.

Efforts at formal research evaluation, admittedly crude and restricted because of the very limited size and duration of the program, at least provided some preliminary information and hunches with respect to several issues of primary concern. For example, we know of the original idealistic attitudes of volunteers, how these tone down as a result of participation in the program, paralleled by a significantly more favorable set of attitudes toward the target clinical group—in this case, emotionally disturbed children. We have arrived at a fair understanding of the nature of volunteer-child process interactions—preferred ones, limited-frequency ones, and those that change over time—with some preliminary estimates as to the whys behind these facts. Indeed, there are even several suggestions as to which may be helpful as opposed to inert or negative types of interactions.

The assumptions underlying the present project, hopefully, have fairly widespread implications. Certainly the school is one very important and very logical institution for fostering work in the early detection and prevention of emotional disorders. Moreover, it seems desirable to study further the effectiveness of the basic model, concretely modified as indicated, with other groups and in other settings.

# REFERENCES

Cowen, E. L., Izzo, L. D., Miles, H., Telshow, E. F., Trost, M. A., & Zax, M. A mental health program in the school setting: description and evaluation. *J. Psychol.*, 1963, 56 (part 2), 307–356.

Holzberg, J. D., & Knapp, R. H. The social interaction of college students and chronically ill mental patients. *Amer. J. Orthopsychiat.*, 1965, 35, 487–492.

Holzberg, J. D., & Gewirtz, H. A method of altering attitudes toward mental illness. *Psychiat. Q. Suppl.*, 1963, 37, 56–61.

Holzberg, J. D., Gewirtz, H., & Ebner, E. Changes in moral judgment and self acceptance as a function of companionship with hospitalized mental patients. *J. consult. Psychol.*, 1964, 28, 299–303.

Kantor, D. Impact of college students on chronic mental patients and on the organization of the mental hospital. *Proceedings of the College Student Companion Program Conference.* Stratford, Conn.: Conn. State Dept. of Mental Health, 1962.

Knapp, R. H., & Holzberg, J. D. Characteristics of college students volunteering for service to mental patients. *J. consult. Psychol.*, 1964, 28, 82–85.

Osgood, C. E., Suci, G. J., & Tannenbaum, P. H. *The measurement of meaning.* Urbana, Ill.: University of Illinois Press, 1957.

Project Re-Ed. *A demonstration project for the re-education of emotionally disturbed children.* Nashville, Tenn.: Peabody College, 1964. (mimeo)

Sanders, R. New manpower for mental hospital service. In E. L. Cowen, E. A. Gardner, & M. Zax (Eds.), *Emergent approaches to mental health problems.* New York: Appleton-Century-Crofts, 1967.

Umbarger, C. C., Dalsimer, J. S., Morrison, A. P., & Breggin, P. R. *College students in a mental hospital.* New York: Grune and Stratton, 1962.

Zax, M., & Cowen, E. L. Early identification and prevention of emotional disturbance in a public school. In E. L. Cowen, E. A. Gardner, & M. Zax (Eds.), *Emergent approaches to mental health problems.* New York: Appleton-Century-Crofts, 1967.

Jules D. Holzberg,
Harry S. Whiting,
and David G. Lowy

# Chronic Patients and a College Companion Program

The program described by Holzberg, Whiting, and Lowy is an example of a type that has emerged in recent years in an effort to enhance the therapeutic effectiveness of the mental hospital. The key feature of such a program is to bring large numbers of nonprofessionals, often college students in these cases, into direct contact with mental patients. Usually such contacts are structured merely as social or recreational interactions, but it is expected that the relationship between the college student and the mental patient will have a significant impact

Reprinted from Mental Hospital, 15(1964), 152–158 with the permission of the American Psychiatric Association and Dr. Holzberg.

on both. For the patient who generally feels, for example, isolated, forgotten, and unsure of himself, there is the chance for contact with an attractive person from "outside" who is usually brimming over with the qualities the patient lacks most. Where the patient feels dejected and defeated by life, the student, on the threshold of a career, is often enthusiastic and involved; where the patient is passive and reluctant to try, the student has great energy to invest in even the most challenging tasks. It is felt that, in the optimal case, the patient may begin to identify with and adopt some important attitudes and qualities through the relationship with a college student. At the very least, his life is brightened and hospital adjustment thereby improved by regular contact with an interested outsider.

For the nonprofessional himself there is the opportunity for first-hand contact with people suffering serious mental illness. Besides providing an opportunity to learn that such people resemble any others in so many significant ways, there is the challenge of developing a relationship and understanding just what kinds of demands are placed on one in such circumstances. Often one begins to learn about his own needs and limitations as they are tested by such a relationship. The reality that one is exposed to in these companion programs is thought to be valuable in shaping both attitudes toward mental illness and present methods of dealing with it, and career goals, which may shift toward or away from the mental health field.

Connecticut Valley Hospital's student-patient Companion Program was undertaken experimentally in the fall of 1958 as a field-work project for an undergraduate course in abnormal psychology at nearby Wesleyan University. The two institutions, both located at Middletown, Connecticut, boast a long history of close association and provide a natural milieu for programs similar to those begun earlier at Harvard and state hospitals in the Boston area. Wesleyan students, through the years, have served the hospital in a variety of volunteer activities, and have used it as an experimental laboratory for research in psychology, biochemistry, and psychopathology. The director of psychological laboratories at the hospital doubles as visiting professor of psychology at Wesleyan, and staff and students have free access to both professional libraries.

For the purpose of our experiment, we gave the psychology students a choice of writing a term paper or working with patients at the state hospital for a minimum of two hours a week—one hour with an individual patient and a second hour in supervised group activity. About forty of our fifty students elected the field work. They were organized into five groups, each with a leader from one of the mental health professions of psychiatry, psychology, social work, chaplaincy, occupational therapy, or nursing.

Our experience quickly proved that this type of volunteer work can indeed be significant for both patients and students, and can contribute substantially to the hospital's total treatment. We decided to continue and expand the program. Accordingly, during the spring semester of 1959, the hospital superintendent set up a planning committee composed of the director of volunteer programs, a continued treatment services staff psychologist, the director of psychological laboratories, and an interested Wesleyan faculty member from the department of psychology. Wesleyan students selected for positions of leadership in the program were also asked to serve on the committee.

The Companion Program that evolved from this committee's frequent meetings was further amplified and refined when the professional group leaders were selected and met with the original committee members, and the program was finally articulated in terms of actual student-patient experience when it got under way.

The committee set three major objectives:

1. To give patients the extent and kind of personal attention that is recognized as a vital factor in comprehensive treatment of chronic mental illness. We saw the Companion Program as one facet of a total rehabilitation program, designed to make social relationships less fearsome, more gratifying experiences.

2. To provide a rewarding experience, both emotionally and educationally, for the students, many of whom would become community leaders in later life. We agreed that students in the program must not be regarded as a source of unpaid manpower. We wanted them to receive a personal, maturing experience that would equip them to deal with their own adjustments to life, and, conceivably, lead some to seek careers in mental health professions.

3. To boost the morale of increasingly overburdened, often apathetic hospital personnel by bringing into the wards young, intelligent scholars, full of the social idealism, hope, and vigor of youth.

The program was conceived as one that would require the utmost cooperation between and integration of hospital and university activities. In practice, the hospital has accepted the role of a willing host for the students, welcoming them as real participants in its treatment and rehabilitation program. It accepts responsibility for the students' orientation and educational experiences, and maintains professional responsibility for all patients involved in the program. This responsibility is carried through the chiefs of the services on which the students operate and through the professional group leaders who supervise the students.

The university's responsibility is to recruit and organize student-participants, a function that the administration has delegated to the student body, which works through a student organization on the campus.

The director of psychological laboratories was designated as the professional coordinator of the Companion Program, and the administrative responsibility was given to the hospital director of volunteers.

Professional group leaders from the hospital staff are charged with maintaining a common philosophy and working out common problems. They meet together frequently and also meet with ward personnel in order to keep abreast of student performance and progress and patient reaction. Their interest also serves to win the support of ward personnel for the program. A university faculty member serves as advisor to the students and plays a key role in recruitment and organization.

Recruiting begins during the first days of the fall semester with the distribution of brochures and Companion Program publicity reprints, which the hospital provides. Interested students are invited to attend a meeting at the university during the first week of school to hear a discussion of the program and its benefits for patients, students, and hospital. Student "graduates" of the program, a professional group leader from the hospital, and the faculty advisor also attend.

## STUDENT'S ROLE DEFINED

The role and obligations of a student-participant are made clear both at the university recruitment meeting and at the first session at the hospital. His role is defined as that of being a friend to a patient, and the importance to the patient of reliability and consistency is stressed. Once committed to the program he is obligated to spend at least two hours a week at the hospital during the academic year, except for Christmas and spring vacations.

The hospital tries to be as flexible as possible in adapting itself to the time that students have available. Most groups find afternoon visits most convenient, but occasionally we have had an evening group. The actual assignment of students to specific groups, designation of the precise hours at the hospital, arrangements for transportation, and so on, are left to the faculty advisor.

All interested students are allowed to sign up for the program, because a study comparing student companions with a control student group showed that the former differ only in terms of their higher altruistic motives, not in terms of psychopathology. However, students screen themselves informally and effectively: they do not commit themselves to the program until they have made three visits to the hospital. During this period, a student can, and occasionally does, withdraw gracefully from the program. While the primary purpose of the recruiting activities is to select students for the Companion Program, a number who are unable to devote time to this program usually volunteer for other activities at the hospital.

## GROUP LEADER'S FUNCTIONS

Companions are divided into small groups, usually no more than ten, with a student leader and a professional group leader assigned to each. The first

visit to the hospital is devoted to getting acquainted with its administrative procedures through a talk given by the director of volunteers and with its physical features. The Companion Program revolves around the professional group leaders. Each one has a threefold function:

1. *Supervision.* He supervises the students to make sure that the relationship is one suitable to a "companion." He helps students to keep the relationship objective and to handle problems.

2. *Support.* Typically, students require considerable support and help in dealing with their anxieties and frustrations. Their anxieties are likely to occur on their first visits to the hospital. Their frustrations occur when their ambitions for their patients stumble upon the reality of the nature of chronic illness.

3. *Education.* During the group meetings, there is usually considerable discussion of general issues pertaining to mental illness and hospitalization. This is likely to occur most intensively during the second half of the year, when the students' anxieties are sufficiently reduced.

An attempt is made to keep discussions general rather than to concentrate on the dynamics, problems, and history of specific patients. Companions do not have access to their patients' charts, but at the end of the year the group leader may discuss selected data. This is an event eagerly awaited by the companions because it permits them to test the reality of their own conclusions about their patients.

The group leader assumes considerable responsibility both in protecting the patient and in making the companion's experience a positive one. The essential qualifications for a group leader seem to be experience with patients, a dynamic approach to their problems, and a sincere interest in working with students.

At first we felt that the success of our program would depend, at least partially, on letting the students themselves choose patients with whom they thought they could become friendly. Accordingly, the chief of the service involved, the nursing supervisor, and the professional group leader selected a group of patients for the program, and for three weeks following the initial orientation period, the professional leader, the students, and the patients met at a weekly social hour held on a ward or in a special room of the service. Often the chief of the service and members of the nursing staff also attended. Students and patients mixed freely in the presence of the professional hospital staff. Coffee was served to encourage an informal, social atmosphere.

During these three weeks, the first hour was devoted to getting acquainted with patients in this group situation; then, during the second hour, the professional group leader guided a discussion of both general issues and the students' interest in specific patients. We believed that these sessions would allay the natural anxiety of students venturing for the first time into a mental hospital. At the end of the 3-week orientation period, each student selected the patient who would be his companion for the entire year.

We have since discovered that students often prefer to have patients assigned to them, because frequently they feel guilty when they select one patient over another. Therefore, we now may assign a patient to each student, with the understanding that the assignment can be changed at any time within the first three weeks.

While most student-patient activities take place at the hospital, we also allow companions to take patients into town or on a visit to the university, if the chief of the service approves.

## CHRONIC PATIENTS SELECTED

Considerable thought has been given to the question of the types of patients to be selected for this program. While the criteria developed must remain tentative, we generally agree that patients should be chronically ill but present no symptoms or behavior that would be especially disturbing to the students, nor should they be so regressed that they would be more appropriate for a remotivation program, or so socially developed and capable of tolerating an intense interpersonal relationship that they are ready for formal individual or group therapy by a professional person. We believe that the patient best suited to the companion experience is one who has responded to remotivation and is now ready for a social relationship with an individual. We are particularly interested in the "forgotten" patient who has minimal or no contact with non-hospital individuals.

The goals of the Companion Program for the patient are improvement in his level of social communication, social skill, and social responsibility that would help effect his social recovery and hopefully lead to his discharge. Patients for group therapy are often recruited from those who have been in the Companion Program.

The problem of handling separation and termination is a continuing one. The students are concerned about the effects of these on their patients, but at times more than is justified by the nature of their relationships. We have thought about this problem, but have collectively agreed that patients cannot and should not be protected from the realities of living, one of which is the movement of people into and out of their lives. The group leader's task is to help the students carry through separation and termination so that it is not traumatic, either for the patients or for the students. Separation looms as a significant problem twice a year, at the long Christmas vacation and at the end of the school year. We have found that holding a party for patients and their companions just prior to the Christmas vacation, and a picnic just prior to the end of the year serve to allay separation anxiety for both.

## RESPONSE IS GRATIFYING

From its modest beginnings at one university, the program has now expanded to students at seven colleges— Wesleyan University, Trinity College, Yale University, Central Connecticut State College, University of Hartford, Hartford College, and University of Connecticut. During the past year over 150 students participated, including several who have been in the program for two and three years. They were organized into 15 groups, each with its own professional leader, and almost every service of the hospital had at least one group serving some of its patients. The groups were distributed over every afternoon of the week.

Attempts to evaluate the program in terms of its impact on patients have thus far rested on non-controlled investigations and on the observations of the professional leaders. One questionnaire study carried out on the first year's companions offers some basis for considering the experience a significant one for patients. Of the students who responded to the questionnaire at the end of the year, 84 per cent reported that their patients desired the companionship relationship and sought to maintain it. A typical student comment was "She seems to appreciate my visits and attention." Seventy-one per cent

reported that students and the patients conversed more freely. Sixty-five per cent reported that the patients showed positive changes in self-confidence. Sixty-four per cent reported greater interest on the part of the patient in his surroundings. A comment of one of the students in this regard was: "She's more interested in activities at the hospital. She began helping with aged patients in the infirmary. She is generally more aware of herself and her surroundings. She began corresponding again with friends outside the hospital." Another student reported: "It has brought him out from his withdrawn state. He is first starting to show significant improvement." Fifty-five per cent of the students reported positive changes in the patient's personal appearance, and 48 per cent reported that the patient's social behavior had improved during the year.

The students also reported changes in the basic psychopathology of their patients. Forty-two per cent of the students reported that their patients showed improvement in terms of realistic thinking, and 46 per cent showed improvement in their mood state, reflected in reduction of depressive indications. Over all, the students considered that 71 per cent of the patients had shown improvement during the companionship year. Twenty-nine per cent were unchanged. We considered these data quite startling considering the fact that all of the patients were chronically ill and had been in hospital for a substantial number of years.

Plans are currently underway to evaluate the patients more systematically. A comprehensive check list of ward behavior will be filled out by psychiatric aides at the beginning and end of a companion year. A comparable control group of patients not in the Companion Program will be similarly evaluated. This should yield information on whether the hospital behavior of patients is significantly altered by the companionship experience. We have also evaluated the impact of the program on the students. A questionnaire administered to them in the first year of the Companion Program revealed that all felt that they had grown in their knowledge of mental hospitals and of the effects of hospitalization. Ninety-one per cent said that during the course of the year they had become less anxious in working with patients. Ninety per cent felt that they had grown in their understanding of mental illness—both its causes and treatments. Eighty-one per cent said their feelings about patients had changed: they had acquired the ability to see patients as sick people worthy of support and aid rather than derision. Eighty-four per cent reported that their feelings about mental hospital personnel had also changed and they understood better the nature of the problems experienced by these people.

## BETTER UNDERSTANDING

A number of the students volunteered testimonials to the multiple values of the experience. Some of these are quoted below:

"This program is a good and effective method of letting others know the problems faced by mental hospitals today. I sincerely hope that it reaps a reward in the future generation."

"I feel that the companionship I had this year was more or less one-sided. I gained terrific insights into the mental hospital, its patients, and its problems, while my patient didn't seem to get too much out of our relationship."

"I feel quite strongly that all graduate students in psychology, and maybe even all majors in psychology, should take part in the program. It is a very valuable experience."

"The program has caused me to take a more objective view of my own emotional problems."

"Keep up the program. For me, and I think for most everyone, the experience has been most rewarding."

All told, 97 per cent of the students considered that their experience had contributed to their personal growth. It is evident that it has been a truly remarkable educational experience.

We completed one study that evaluated the changes in attitudes toward and understanding of mental illness and hospitalization in a more controlled fashion. The companions and a group of control students not in the Companion Program but engaged in other service activities were compared on a questionnaire about attitudes and understanding of mental illness, which was administered at the very beginning and at the close of the academic year. The results clearly indicated that the companions show a significant positive shift in their attitudes and understanding, while no such shift occurred in our control group.

Emanuel Hallowitz
and Frank Riessman

# The Role of the Indigenous Nonprofessional in a Community Mental Health Neighborhood Service Center Program

A major problem in developing programs that have a preventive impact on a community is developing a "handle" or entrée that permits the professional to bring his skills to bear on those who could benefit by them. Children can be readily engaged through schools, nurseries, recreational facilities, and the like, but adults are more difficult to contact. In the following paper, Hallowitz and Riessman describe a program that they have designed for bringing mental health-type service to relatively deprived neighborhoods. In this program, as in many others, considerable use is made of nonprofessionals, in this case people indigenous to the neighborhoods in which they work. The storefront service center offers its services in connection with a wide variety of problems, many of which can hardly be classified even broadly as being mental health problems. Nevertheless, although the role of the center in connection with many such problems is not vastly different from that of the old-time ward politician, efforts are made to render such services in a way that provides a model that the recipient of help can himself emulate. It is intended that this feature of the program will build skills that will contribute to the overall adequacy of functioning.

The Lincoln Hospital Mental Health Services represents an attempt to develop a comprehensive network of community mental health services in a highly disadvantaged urban area of New York City (4).

The Hospital district served is located in the Southeast Bronx. It is a congested, old section of the city suffering physically and socially from the classic ills of such areas: deteriorated housing; high mobility; high rates of juvenile delinquency, school dropouts, narcotic addiction, infant mortality, etc.[1] Most of its 350,000 inhabitants are Puerto Rican (55 per cent) or Negro (25 per cent).

In planning a strategy of interven-

Reprinted from the American Journal of Orthopsychiatry, 37(1967) 766–778. Copyright, the American Orthopsychiatric Association, Inc. Reproduced by permission.

[1] Compared to the Bronx, as a whole, most of the Lincoln area falls into the lowest quartile of median family income ($3,700–$5,400) and educational attainment 7.6–8.8 years) and the highest rate of male unemployment in this area is approximately twice that of the Bronx average. Similarly, the amount of overcrowded housing and school facilities are about twice that of the Bronx as a whole.

In addition, compared to the Bronx, as a whole: (1) Rates for juvenile delinquency offenses are 25 per cent higher. (2) Rates of venereal disease among youth under 21 are three times greater in some neighborhoods of the Lincoln area and 1¼ times as high as in other areas. (3) The rate of public assistance cases is approximately twice as high. (4) Admission rates to state mental hospitals are 40 per cent higher from this area. (5) Although reliable figures are not available, estimates of the percentage of deliveries of the Lincoln Hospital Obstetrical Service, in which there is no legal father, run as high as 70 per cent. (Comparable figures for the Bronx, as a whole, are not available.)

tion, it was important to keep in mind that throughout the city, services to low-income persons, particularly newcomers to urban centers, either have been inadequate or so organized and operated as to limit their full use by the poor. Because the public service agencies are fragmented, complex and bureaucratic, they constitute a frustrating, powerful and seemingly insurmountable network of barriers (2, 3). Also, the voluntary family and children's agencies have only one office each to serve the entire Bronx (former neighborhood offices and outposts have been consolidated in the interest of economy). Each is located (as are many of the public agencies) in middle-class neighborhoods at considerable distance from those who need the service most. Moreover, the traditional ways of operating waiting lists, weekly appointments, long-term service and emphasis on "talking through" are not consonant with the needs, the experience, or the life-style of low-income people (5, 8).

It was this view of our district—the people, their needs and the pattern of existing services—that impelled us to develop a network of Neighborhood Service Centers,[2] staffed by indigenous nonprofessionals under professional supervision.

## THE NEIGHBORHOOD SERVICE CENTER

In 1965 the Lincoln Hospital Mental Health Services established three Neighborhood Service Centers. The first opened on February 22, the second on June 29, the third on December 22. Two of these centers are located in a storefront at street level; the third is one flight up. Each Center serves a radius of five blocks (approximately 50,000 people) and each is staffed by five to ten nonprofessional mental health aides from the neighborhood and one or two professional mental health specialists who serve as Neighborhood Service Center director and assistant director.

The core of the NSC program is its role as a "psychosocial first-aid station"; the Center is a place where people can bring any type of problem. This formula allows residents the possibility of receiving immediate help and comfort without having to define their problem in a way appropriate for the help-giving system (1). Moreover, the fact that the Center is located in the midst of the neighborhood it is to serve provides visibility and relatedness to the community that often is lacking in the more established agencies. In addition, the employment of indigenous nonprofessionals, their naturalness and the informal atmosphere of the setting confirm the "open door" policy and enable freer contact and communication on the part of "clients" from the area.

The Neighborhood Service Center may be viewed as the first port of entry into the service system. The Center worker assumes the responsibility for helping the resident to define his problem and to determine the specific service that he and his family may require. He serves as a bridge between the resident and the service agency. The aide interprets to the resident the program and services of the agency. What might he realistically expect to receive? What are his rights and privileges? What can the agency expect of him? Similarly before making a referral, where indicated, the worker will contact the agency to interpret the specific needs

[2] The Neighborhood Service Center Program is supported by a grant from the United States Office of Economic Opportunity.